ARTS EDUCATION IN SECONDARY SCHOOLS:
EFFECTS AND EFFECTIVENESS

John Harland, Kay Kinder, Pippa Lord,
Alison Stott, Ian Schagen, Jo Haynes
with
Linda Cusworth, Richard White
and Riana Paola

D1347953

THE **ARTS COUNCIL**
OF ENGLAND

RSA
The Royal Society for the encouragement of
Arts, Manufactures & Commerce

Local Government Association

INVESTOR IN PEOPLE

006667860X

Published in October 2000
by the National Foundation for Educational Research,
The Mere, Upton Park, Slough, Berkshire SL1 2DQ

CONTENTS

ACKNOWLEDGEMENTS   i

FOREWORD   ii

STEERING GROUP   iv

PART ONE   **INTRODUCTION**   1

    1.   THE STUDY AND ITS CONTEXT   1

PART TWO   **WHAT ARE THE EFFECTS OF ARTS EDUCATION?**   **22**

    2.   A MODEL OF ARTS EDUCATION OUTCOMES   22

    3.   INTRINSIC AND IMMEDIATE EFFECTS: FORMS OF ENJOYMENT AND THERAPY   26

    4.   ARTFORM KNOWLEDGE AND SKILLS   39

    5.   KNOWLEDGE IN THE SOCIAL AND CULTURAL DOMAINS   85

    6.   CREATIVITY AND THINKING SKILLS   98

    7.   COMMUNICATION AND EXPRESSIVE SKILLS   113

    8.   PERSONAL AND SOCIAL DEVELOPMENT   141

    9.   EXTRINSIC TRANSFER EFFECTS   179

    10.   OTHER EFFECTS: ON THE SCHOOL, THE COMMUNITY AND THE ARTS   236

    11.   ARTS EFFECTS: OVERALL PERSPECTIVES   258

PART THREE   **WHAT ARE EFFECTIVE PRACTICES IN ARTS EDUCATION?**   **298**

    12.   PERCEPTIONS OF EFFECTIVE PRACTICES IN ARTS EDUCATION   298

    13.   EFFECTIVE PRACTICES IN CONTEXT   438

    14.   EFFECTIVENESS: A WIDER PICTURE   513

    15.   ARTS EFFECTIVENESS: OVERALL PERSPECTIVES   554

PART FOUR   **CONCLUSION**   **564**

    16.   SUMMARY AND CONCLUSION   564

REFERENCES   573

APPENDICES   578

INDEX   589

ACKNOWLEDGEMENTS

We would like to thank all the pupils, teachers, employers and others who have contributed to the project, for their time, thoughts, comments and kind accommodation of our research requirements. We are particularly indebted to the staff and pupils in the five case study schools who so willingly gave up their time to be interviewed, and are most grateful for their continued contribution and support throughout the three years of the study.

We would also like to express our most grateful thanks to the members of the project's Steering Group, chaired by Professor Eric Bolton, for their advice and guidance throughout the study. Special thanks are due to Sue Harries, who played crucial roles in setting up the project, in facilitating communications between the Steering Group and the researchers, and in coordinating the dissemination phase.

We are indebted to the RSA for launching the study and to the sponsors who provided the funding to make the research possible. These comprised the Arts Council of England, the Association for Business Sponsorship of the Arts, BT, the Calouste Gulbenkian Foundation, the Comino Foundation, Crayola Ltd., the Local Government Association, the National Foundation for Educational Research (NFER), and Powys and Wigan LEAs.

Thanks are also extended to Mary Ashworth, Jay Day and Nick Whybrow, who undertook some of the fieldwork in the five case study schools; to David Hewitt for his help and advice on the statistics; to David Upton for his editorial input; to Mary Hargreaves for laying out the pages; and to Enver Carim for overseeing production and publication.

FOREWORD

In 1996, the RSA (Royal Society for the encouragement of Arts, Manufactures & Commerce) launched *The Arts Matter* programme and lecture series. Its ruling hypothesis was that the arts matter because they are about serious business, central to civilised living, and not merely entertaining distractions to be bolted on to the margins of our main concerns and actions.

Furthermore, they matter, individually and collectively, because of what they are and what they do, which is to carry out a sustained, detailed and varied exploration of human motivation and behaviour every bit as important as the different, but complementary, examination of the natural world carried out through, and by, the sciences.

The lively and challenging debates set off by *The Arts Matter* programme highlighted the urgent need to complement its advocacy of the arts with a concerted, objective, and authoritative enquiry into the effects of arts education in schools, and particularly secondary schools.

As a result, in 1997, the RSA, through *The Arts Matter* programme's Steering Group, brought together a diverse group of organisations which would be willing to co-fund this research study commissioned from the National Foundation for Educational Research (NFER). The sponsors were the Arts Council of England and the Local Government Association, together with Arts & Business (formerly ABSA), BT, the Calouste Gulbenkian Foundation, the Comino Foundation, Crayola Ltd, NFER, and Powys and Wigan LEAs.

The work was guided by *The Arts Matter* Steering Group, all of whom acted as individual experts in their respective fields rather than as representatives of the organisations for which they worked. The sponsors and the members of the Steering Group should be warmly thanked for supporting this most important study.

The overarching messages from this extensive examination of the effects of arts education are that the arts, well taught by enthusiastic, specialist teachers, do generate a range of desirable learning outcomes for pupils, for the school, employment and the local community. In the case study schools used in the research, pupils refer to some carry-over of learning from arts to other subjects.

However, in the research study's larger, more generally representative sample of schools, there is no evidence of learning in the arts boosting general academic performance, nor of dance, drama and music in particular having anything more than a very limited impact on the generality of pupils. Yet, as with the case study schools, where the arts are well taught and strong, their impact on pupils is more marked, though different, across the arts.

One finding raises especial concern. In many of the schools, music seems particularly problematic, regarded by pupils as increasingly exclusive and less engaging as they progress towards key stage 4 and the GCSE.

The study's findings are an important contribution to the debate about the arts in education. They are detailed in the body of this report, and, quite properly, they, and the research methodology by which they were obtained, will be examined and discussed by researchers, and play some part in shaping future enquiries.

But this is not, primarily, a report for researchers. It has important messages for education and arts policy makers, and practitioners in both fields. It is an authoritatively objective voice, in a sphere of interest and activity frequently driven by conviction and passion, and ruled by anecdote, and that is to be welcomed and celebrated. It is also, and excitingly, a report through which we hear the voices and views of pupils, and not, as is so often the case, the opinions of those who claim to speak for them. For that reason, and much more, the full report deserves and demands to be read by all interested in the arts and in education.

There are no easy solutions to the questions and problems highlighted in this research report. However, it provides an objective identification of what the issues are; an analysis of the key factors shaping those issues; and some examples of ways in which some teachers and schools are dealing with them effectively. This report therefore offers a sound basis on which to continue the debate about why, and how, we should set out to ensure a stimulating and worthwhile engagement with the arts for all children during, and throughout, their statutory schooling.

Professor Eric Bolton CB
Chairman of *The Arts Matter* Steering Group

THE ARTS MATTER STEERING GROUP

[Members attend as individuals and not as representatives of the organisation for which they work]

Professor Eric Bolton
(*chairman*)
former senior chief inspector

Sally Bassett
education development manager, Binney & Smith (Europe) Ltd

Norinne Betjemann
senior education adviser, Arts Council of England (ACE)

Michaela Crimmin
head of arts, RSA

Peter Downes
former president, Secondary Heads Association (SHA)

Dick Downing
Creative Arts Partnerships in Education (CAPE)

Penny Egan
director, RSA

Sue Harries
arts education consultant

Mathilda Joubert
arts education coordinator, RSA

Tony Knight
principal subject officer for music, the arts and culture, Qualifications & Curriculum Authority (QCA)

Richard Martineau
vice-president, RSA

Rick Rogers
arts education specialist

Mike Smith
managing director, Binney & Smith (Europe) Ltd

Pauline Tambling
executive director for research and development, Arts Council of England (ACE)

Ivor Widdison
Local Government Association (LGA)

PART ONE: INTRODUCTION

1. THE STUDY AND ITS CONTEXT

CHAPTER OVERVIEW

This opening chapter:

* sets the study in its background policy context (1.1)
* presents the aims of the study (1.2)
* describes the research methods used in each of the four main programmes of data collection (1.3)
* defines some of the key terms used in the report, namely 'the arts' (1.4.1), 'effects' (1.4.2) and 'effectiveness' (1.4.3)
* offers an outline of the report structure (1.5).

1.1 BACKGROUND TO THE STUDY

A stock market analyst looking at the current state of arts education in England and Wales would almost certainly conclude that bullish and bearish forces are simultaneously affecting the sector. While there are recent signs of upward factors that are helping create some buoyancy in the broad area of young people's engagement in the arts, there are also downward factors that appear to be depressing the opportunities for growth in the level, status and quality of provision in arts education.

On the upside, the Department for Culture, Media and Sport (DCMS) and its predecessor, the Department of National Heritage (DNH), have sought to encourage young people's involvement in the arts (GB. DNH, 1996). More recently, the DCMS has highlighted the potential contribution the arts could make towards combating social exclusion (GB. DCMS, 1999). Various bodies supported by the DCMS have also been active in promoting young people's participation and education in the arts. These include the Arts Council of England (ACE) – most notably in its capacity as a lottery distributor and its New Audiences programme, which, with £5 million annual funding from DCMS, aims to create new audiences for the arts amongst young people in particular (ACE, 1998 and 1999).[1] As recently outlined in a joint letter from the

---

[1]   See also Harland and Kinder (1999) for a review of initiatives by arts organisations aimed at extending young people's access to the arts and cultural venues.

Secretaries of State at the DCMS and the Department for Education and Employment (DfEE) to Professor Ken Robinson (Chair of the National Advisory Committee on Creative and Cultural Education (NACCCE)), the ACE is also active in developing the educational work of arts organisations and fostering partnerships between them and schools:

> All the cultural organisations funded by DCMS have educational aims which they are required to deliver in return for subsidy. The arts organisations that are funded through the Arts Council and the Regional Arts Boards (RABs) are all required to develop educational aims, in making use of the extra £125 million that we have provided for the arts over the next three years. As a minimum, we are ensuring that they will deliver an additional 200,000 education sessions ... In addition to funding, the Arts Council is pursuing a wide range of measures to support arts education and develop better links between schools and arts organisations (GB. DCMS, 2000).

In addition, recent collaboration between ACE and the Qualifications and Curriculum Authority (QCA) has provided a publication to 'help schools consolidate and build on their existing arts teaching and learning' and to 'establish partnerships' (QCA and ACE, 2000). Initiatives such as artists-in-school residencies and projects continue to flourish (e.g. Creative Arts Partnerships in Education in Leeds and Manchester, London Education Arts Partnerships, Devon Artists into Schools) and as a reflection of this, the amount of research into the educational activities of artists and arts organisations is relatively plentiful (e.g. Harland, 1990; Downing, 1996; Hogarth et al., 1997; Sharp and Dust, 1997; Oddie and Allen, 1998; Tambling and Harland, 1998; Turner, 1999).[2]

The DCMS has also been the major player in the establishment of the National Foundation for Youth Music – a lottery-funded organisation set up to address the lack of opportunity for young people to participate in music outside school hours. In addition, the Department for Education and Employment (DfEE) has launched the Music Standards Fund to help protect local education authority (LEA) music services and has started promoting educational partnerships between schools and arts organisations (e.g. study support projects (GB. DfEE, 1998c)). Ostensibly at least, the level of arts provision in a small number of schools has been boosted through the opportunities to apply for specialist arts status (e.g. GB. DfEE, 1999)[3] and some Education Action Zones contain additional courses in the arts (e.g. North East Sheffield includes 'the development of motivational arts programmes using leading edge IT in music and the visual arts' (GB. DfEE, 1998a)).

---

[2]   Though many of these studies focus on processes rather than outcomes.
[3]   In January 2000 (GB. DCMS, 2000) there were 49 schools with specialist status in the arts.

The salient characteristics in these factors tend to be the leading role purportedly played by the DCMS (see Rogers, 1999), a focus on agencies external to provision within schools, an emphasis on out-of-school or extra-curricular developments, a reliance on launching short-term projects and initiatives, and a strong tendency towards policies that extend selectivity and diversity between schools. The new Artsmark Award (GB. DCMS, 2000) may be seen as a further illustration of this latter tendency.

Many of the crucial downside factors are well documented in Rogers (1995): diminishing LEA advisory services in the arts, concerns about the employment of experienced and specialist arts teachers in schools, and continuing problems in providing appropriate resources and accommodation for the arts in school. In addition, the decline in the arts content of initial training courses for primary teachers has caused concern (Rogers, 1998). Existing fears about the limited time allocated to the arts in the primary phase were increased in 1998, when the Secretary of State for Education and Employment announced a relaxation in the requirements for the primary school curriculum in order to allow more time for primary schools to concentrate on literacy and numeracy. Although primary schools were still required to teach music, art and physical education (including dance), it was no longer mandatory upon them to teach the existing detailed programmes of study in these subjects. For some observers, the DfEE's preoccupation with meeting national targets for English and mathematics in 2002 risks undermining the implementation of a broad and balanced curriculum. Moreover, while the requirements to teach the programmes of study for art, music and dance at key stages 1 and 2 have been reinstated from August 2000, there is, on the face of it, little in the recent revisions to the National Curriculum to enhance the status of the arts in the curriculum. Similarly, although task groups on both creativity and the arts have been set up within QCA, it remains to be seen whether the Government's response (GB. DCMS, 2000) to the NACCCE report (Robinson Report, 1999)[4] will lead to the implementation of policies that match the wide-ranging vision and recommendations set out in the report. Finally, in comparison to the level of research and evaluation surrounding artists-in-schools projects or out-of-school arts provision, there have been very few significant and recent studies of arts education provision in primary and secondary schools – Ross and Kamba (1997) being the only major exception.

Understandably, in the recent past, such factors have given rise to concerns about the future place of the arts in the school curriculum. Such anxieties are provoked still further by suspicions that these upside and downside pressures, as we have described them here, are not

---

[4] It should be emphasised that the remit of the NACCCE report is much wider than our present concern with arts education.

entirely unrelated and coincidental. Fears about a kind of hydraulic theory, whereby out-of-school activities are being pumped up in order to push down within-school provision are fuelled by a succession of hints from Government ministers (going back to Kenneth Baker) that much of the arts curriculum could be met in extra-curricular time or out of school altogether – implying a negative view of arts education as hobby or leisure-time activity.

In response to such perceived threats to the arts in the curriculum, various groups and organisations have been active in making the case for the arts (Rogers, 1995; SHA 1995; RSA, 1997; Music Education Council, 1998). Very often, their publications set out the benefits and outcomes that the arts can achieve and attempt to marshal evidence to support their claims. In the absence of much research from the UK, these advocacy publications often draw on studies from abroad, especially in connection with the so-called 'Mozart effect' – the claim that studying the arts (and music in particular) can have a beneficial impact on the development of spatial and temporal reasoning – this area being extended to impacts on general intelligence and general academic attainment by popular press, and being referred to more broadly as the 'transfer effects' of arts education. However, the methodological designs and data for many of these studies have been shown to warrant cautious interpretation (Sharp *et al.*, 1998; Winner and Hetland, forthcoming, 2000). Furthermore, while there is a growing body of literature on the 'transfer effects' or 'Mozart effects' of arts education,[5] these have not been examined in the UK as part of a wide-ranging analysis of the whole gamut of possible outcomes, or in the context of a related inquiry into the structures and practices that may produce such effects. Consequently, in view of the paucity of research conducted in this country, the contentious nature of some overseas studies, along with questions about their cross-cultural relevance, there is a critical shortage of rigorous and independent empirical data with which to interrogate the claims made about the effects of arts education. As a result of this, the absence in the literature of comprehensive and empirically based frameworks for conceptualising both the effects and the factors associated with effective provision in the arts is particularly noticeable.

In order to help redress the shortage of such studies and thereby offer the current debate about arts education in schools some much-needed empirical evidence, the RSA (Royal Society for the encouragement of Arts, Manufactures and Commerce) launched an independent research project as part of its programme called '*The Arts Matter*'. The main sponsors of the research were the Arts Council of England and the Local Government Association, with additional funding provided by

---

[5] Useful reviews of this literature can be found in Sharp *et al.* (1998) and Winner and Hetland (forthcoming, 2000).

the Association for Business Sponsorship of the Arts, BT, the Calouste Gulbenkian Foundation, the Comino Foundation, Crayola Ltd., the National Foundation for Educational Research (NFER), and Powys and Wigan LEAs. NFER was commissioned to conduct the research, which was carried out between the spring of 1997 and the spring of 2000.

The project offered a unique opportunity to investigate both the effects and effectiveness of arts education in secondary schools within the same inquiry. This report presents and discusses its results.

1.2   AIMS OF THE STUDY

The project was designed to address four aims:

(i)   to document and evidence the range of effects and outcomes attributable to school-based arts education;

(ii) to examine the relationship between these effects and the key factors and processes associated with arts provision in schools;

(iii) to illuminate good practice in schools' provision of high-quality educational experiences in the arts; and

(iv) to study the extent to which high levels of institutional involvement in the arts correlate with the qualities known to be associated with successful school improvement and school effectiveness.

1.3   RESEARCH METHODS

The evidence for the project was collected through four main programmes of data collection:

- in-depth case studies of arts education in five secondary schools (section 1.3.1);

- secondary data analysis of information compiled through NFER's 'Quantitative Analysis for Self-Evaluation' (QUASE) project (section 1.3.2);

- a Year 11 survey of pupils and schools, with related data (section 1.3.3); and

- interviews with employers and employees (section 1.3.4).

Details of the evidence collected through each of these channels are set out below. Although the information provided is important in so far as it sets out the empirical basis of the study, the reader who is less interested in methodological details may wish to skim the following pages and proceed to section 1.4.

1.3.1 The case studies

This part of the research involved case study fieldwork in five secondary schools with reputations for good practices in the provision of arts education. Following an initial period of gathering information on possible schools, including consultations with advisers, inspectors and others with local knowledge of the quality of their arts provision, five schools in different LEAs agreed to participate in this longitudinal element of the study. These five schools consisted of:

- an all-girls London inner-city school, with high proportions of ethnic minorities and with high levels of socio-economic deprivation;

- a small rural and bilingual school in Wales with strong involvement in the local community;

- a grant-maintained school with city technology college status in a fairly affluent shire catchment area in the south west of England; and

- two urban schools – one in the north east of England and another in the north west – serving mixed industrial communities on the outskirts of large conurbations.

The sample provided a variety of institutions and settings (e.g. urban and rural schools, schools of different sizes, a range of contrasting socio-economic contexts, and schools in LEAs renowned for their strong support for the arts). Equally, within each institution, a range of organisational structures for arts teaching (e.g. faculty versus departments)[6] emerged, as well as some interesting variations in the perceived strengths and public reputations of different artforms.

In the first year of the project (Phase 1, 1997), the research team spent the equivalent of eight fieldwork days in each of the case study schools. These days were used to:

- conduct interviews and have informal meetings with headteachers, heads of department/faculty, arts teachers, and, in some schools, LEA arts advisory staff and community arts workers;

- interview eight Year 7 and eight Year 9 pupils in each school (79 pupils in all);

- informally observe arts subjects being taught, followed by short post-observation interviews with teachers and pupils;

- conduct short interviews with teachers of subjects other than the arts; and

---

[6] A departmental structure is based on individual artforms, while a faculty structure groups some or all of the arts subjects. '12.5 Arts faculty or department factors' in Chapter 12 provides further detail for the reader on this.

- pilot a Year 11 questionnaire with samples of Year 11 pupils for use later in the project.

The Years 7 and 9 pupil samples were selected by asking teachers of art, dance, drama and music to nominate pupils who were making good progress in at least one of the artforms. This sampling strategy was considered consistent with the emphasis in the case study element of the project on investigating practices that were deemed to be effective. In practice, however, it should be noted that pupils who were enthusiastic and positive about one artform did not necessarily feel the same about the others.

The staff sample was chosen in consultation with the headteacher or a member of the senior management team. They defined what the 'arts' encompassed within their schools and recommended teacher representatives of each of the included artforms, as well as appropriate members of senior management (e.g. deputy heads with responsibility for the curriculum or pastoral support). In all five schools, at least one teacher or head of department for art, drama and music was interviewed – very often two teachers of these subjects were interviewed. In three schools, dance was included in the 'arts' domain and, hence, an interview was held with the dance teacher. In the fourth school, dance was not considered to be taught as part of the arts, though one of the drama teachers interviewed taught some 'dance-drama' within drama; the teacher who taught dance as a component of PE was interviewed as one of the sample of teachers of non-arts subjects. In the fifth school, dance was not taught to any significant degree, though one of the drama teachers reported teaching '*some basic dance skills*' as part of mime in drama. The heads of English were interviewed in the three schools where the headteachers believed that the school's implementation of this subject shared affinities with arts-oriented subjects.

In all, 52 full and recorded Phase 1 interviews were conducted with 48 staff interviewees including arts teachers, heads of department, school senior managers and LEA personnel. Broken down, this sample comprised two LEA arts advisers, five headteachers, nine deputies, three members of staff in other senior positions, 17 heads of department and 12 teachers of arts subjects. It can be seen that 17 of this sample held senior management posts in schools, though seven of these had a background in the teaching of the arts (including English).

During Phase 2 (1998), each of the five case study schools was visited for a further five days. These days were used:

- to interview the pupils in the two longitudinal cohorts (from 1997) as they approached the end of Years 8 and 10 (68 pupils in all);

- to observe and video lessons in different arts subjects;

- to interview the teachers and a small group of pupils involved in the observed lessons; and

- to interview a member of the senior management team about school provision in the arts.

In Phase 3 (1999), the final fieldwork visits of four days to each of the five case study schools were conducted.[7] These four days were used:

- to interview the pupils in the two longitudinal cohorts as they approached the end of Years 9 and 11 (72 pupils in all);

- to observe and video lessons in different arts subjects;

- to interview the teachers and a small group of pupils involved in the observed lessons; and

- to interview senior personnel to draw together perceptions central to the aims of the research, especially their views on a possible correlation between institutional involvement in the arts, and school improvement and effectiveness.

Across the three phases, a total of 219 interviews (up to three per pupil) were conducted with the two cohorts of pupils, half with the lower cohort (Year 7 to Year 9) and half with the upper cohort (Year 9 to Year 11)[8]. Ranging from 47 in one school to 42 in two other schools, approximately the same numbers of cohort pupils were interviewed in each school. The sample was heavily skewed in terms of gender: interviews with boys (66) amounted to only 30 per cent of the sample. This was partly due to the inclusion of an all-girls school as one of the five case study schools, but also due to the fact that all the other schools nominated more girls than boys as making good progress in at least one artform, sometimes by as much as two to one. In addition to these one-to-one interviews with the cohort pupils, a total of 53 pupils were interviewed as part of the small group interviews conducted after the observed lessons.

Supplementing the 52 interviews with staff carried out in the initial visits, 12 additional staff interviews were completed in the final fieldwork visits. A further 23 interviews were conducted as post-observation interviews with the teachers concerned. In all, 28 lessons were observed through video recording (art seven, music six, drama six, dance five and English four).

---

[7] One of the case study schools could not accommodate the final two days of fieldwork in this Phase, so only the pupil interviews were completed at this school.

[8] It should be noted therefore that two groups of Year 9 pupils were interviewed.

1.3.2 Secondary data analysis through QUASE

The NFER's 'Quantitative Analysis for Self-Evaluation' (QUASE) service provides information to schools about their own performance, relative to what might be expected in the light of their pupils' prior attainment and their social context. The rich database of information collected about the schools and their GCSE pupils enables investigators to determine the relationships between GCSE results, other outcomes, and a range of background variables at the levels of both pupils and schools. For the purposes of this particular study, the investigation focused on the possible effects of taking key stage 4 arts-related courses on general performance in GCSE examinations.[9]

The three arts-related subject areas whose impact was studied were art, drama and music. QUASE data from a total of 152 schools with up to three cohorts of Year 11 pupils taking GCSEs between 1994 and 1996 was analysed; the total number of pupils in the sample involved in the analysis was 27,607. The sample of schools included cases of all the main types (e.g. coeducational, single-sex, inner city, rural, selective, independent), and analyses of the QUASE schools showed that they were broadly similar to the national distribution in terms of type of school, type of LEA, region and GCSE performance (Schagen, 1995).

1.3.3 The Year 11 Survey

Aims of the survey

The prime purpose of this survey was to extend the analysis of the proposition that studying or engaging in the arts has a positive effect on general academic achievement in GCSEs, a particular example of what has often been called the 'Mozart effect'. In the first phase of the study, this claim was investigated through analysis of the QUASE data described above.[10] Although that analysis had the advantages of a very large sample of pupils and the opportunity to control for pupils' prior attainment, it lacked some important data, most notably pupils' degree of involvement in the arts outside of GCSE courses and the social class classification of individual pupils. This and similar information could only be collected through a specifically designed survey of Year 11 pupils, supplemented by data from schools on the pupils' prior attainment and GCSE results. Consequently, a survey of a sample of Year 11 students in the 1998 school-leaving cohort was designed to take place in the second phase of the project.

The interim report on the QUASE analysis (Harland *et al.*, 1998) suggested that the results might be telling us more about the kind of pupils who take different GCSE arts subjects than indicating any

---

[9] Further information can be found on NFER's QUASE service in Chapter 9 (section 9.2.1).

[10] The results of the analysis of the QUASE data were first reported in an interim report (see Harland *et al.*, 1998).

impact of studying arts-related subjects on general GCSE attainment. This alternative interpretation raised important issues about the place of the arts in the key stage 4 curriculum and schools' option systems, as well as the influences on students' choices at the end of key stage 3, including their perceptions of the relevance and status of arts subjects. The Year 11 Survey offered an opportunity to explore these issues further. To this end, the student questionnaire included items on the reasons for choosing or not choosing arts courses at key stage 4 and on parental support for, and/or interest in, the arts. Additionally, in order to explore the possible causes for significant variations in the initial results according to which schools the pupils attended, a school questionnaire was added to the research design.

As well as researching the indirect or spin-off effects associated with experiences in the arts, another key aim of the survey was to collect evidence on pupils' perceptions of the direct outcomes associated with arts education at secondary school. The early qualitative inquiries in the five case study schools had led to the identification and illustration of several main types of perceived effect (Harland *et al.*, 1998). The Year 11 survey presented the opportunity to examine the extent to which pupils in a random, larger and more representative sample of schools would endorse the views on direct effects expressed by pupils in the case study schools.

The questionnaires and data collection

Ideally, the Year 11 Survey sought to integrate five types of data:
- Year 11 student questionnaires (see Appendix I);
- school questionnaires (see Appendix II);
- prior attainment from secondary school entry (Year 7);
- key stage 3 national test results; and
- GCSE results.

The Year 11 student questionnaire asked pupils to indicate which GCSE subjects they were taking, which were their favourite subjects, their reasons for choosing or not choosing any arts subjects, the extent to which they enjoyed any arts lessons, whether they would have liked to have taken (other) arts subjects, their perceptions of the effects of their arts education experiences in the secondary phase, their level of extra-curricular involvement in the arts, and the extent of their parents' support for the arts.

The school questionnaire included items on the organisation of the arts within the school, the availability of specialist facilities, the time and provision for the arts in key stage 4, and the availability of extra-curricular activities and instrumental tuition in music.

The participating schools were also asked to provide key stage 3 and GCSE results, and, wherever possible, prior attainment test scores completed at the point of transfer from primary to secondary school. Researchers visited 18 of the 22 schools to administer the questionnaire. All (attending) Year 11 students completed the questionnaire, with the researcher providing students with verbal instructions and answering any questions that arose during the period of questionnaire administration. In the remaining four schools, logistical difficulties meant that the questionnaires had to be administered by post to the full cohort in each school.

Selecting the sample

An initial sample of 40 schools was drawn through the NFER Field Research Services. Included in the sampling frame were all comprehensive and grammar schools in England and Wales, including grant-maintained (GM) schools and city technology colleges (CTCs). The sample was run to ensure a range of GCSE results, as well as a geographical spread (with some clustering to aid in fieldwork practicalities). Schools involved in current or recently completed NFER Northern Office projects (including the five case study schools) were excluded from the sampling frame.

This initial sample of 40 schools was contacted via a letter to the headteacher, but as responses were slow, a second sample of 18 (drawn with the same criteria) was also contacted. In addition, follow-up phone calls were made to schools who had not responded to the initial letter. Schools agreeing to participate were offered 'value-added' feedback on current Year 11 students, and copies of any reports discussing the results of the research. Headteachers were asked to complete a pro forma indicating their interest in participating, and were also asked for details of prior attainment data available for the Year 11 cohort. Participating schools were then contacted and arrangements made for a researcher to visit the school to administer the questionnaire.

The outcome of this process was that 18 schools agreed to participate in the project; many others were interested in the research, but were unable to participate due to time or other commitments. Questionnaires were completed by pupils present at the time of the administration, though (some occasionally high) rates of absence meant that the sample size was smaller than expected. At this stage, therefore, it was considered that the involvement of additional schools was necessary to increase the size of the pupil sample. Four further schools were contacted, and as pupils were about to stand down for GCSE, it was agreed that pupils would complete the questionnaire in their own time, and questionnaires would be posted to us. Unfortunately, low response rates from these schools were experienced (between one-fifth and one-

third of the pupil cohort). However, in total, 2,269 questionnaires were completed from the 22 schools. All schools also completed the school questionnaire.

Following the questionnaire administration phase, schools were contacted and asked to provide GCSE results, key stage 3 test results and any prior attainment data from intake. A number of difficulties arose in collecting and processing data from schools; in particular, data was slow to be returned, and fewer schools than anticipated were able to provide us with prior attainment data in a form able to be used in analyses. Thus, the quantity and quality of information that the schools were able to provide was less than we were led to believe at the outset. Intake data (from Year 7 or 8) was available from ten schools. Thus, just over half the schools were unable to provide us with test data that was able to be included in the multilevel modelling analyses. Key stage 3 data was available from 21 schools, with GCSE results available from all 22 schools.

The characteristics and contexts of the 22 schools are described below. Given the self-selected element of the questionnaire administration, it would seem likely that the sample would contain more arts-oriented schools than schools without strengths in the arts. However, the sample demonstrated some key indicators of representativeness, with a range of school types and contexts, and similar rates of pupils taking arts subjects to national figures.

The school sample

All but two of the schools were comprehensive (20 out of 22). The sample contained four schools with grant-maintained status, one of which was a grammar school. It also included three all-girls schools and one all-boys school. As indicated by the number of pupils on roll, the size of the schools varied from 320 in one to 1,938 in another. The percentage of pupils eligible for free school meals ranged from 1.4 per cent in one school to 79.4 per cent in another.

Of the 22 schools, 18 per cent were in rural areas; 27 per cent were located in small/medium towns; only nine per cent (two schools) were suburban; 23 per cent were in urban areas and the same percentage were inner city schools.

Regarding the institutional organisation of arts subjects, about two-thirds (64 per cent) of the schools had a purely departmental structure, while approximately one-third (36 per cent) adopted a faculty structure. Further analysis revealed that in half of the full sample of schools, all the arts subjects constituted individual departments. Of those schools with a faculty structure, half grouped all the arts subjects in one faculty, and half had arts subjects in more than one faculty.

Only one of the 22 schools did not mention any specialist arts facilities when asked to do so. Whilst 96 per cent of schools mentioned having specialist music rooms (with 59 per cent having music practice rooms, two out of 22 having a recording studio, and three out of 22 having IT facilities), only four (18 per cent) of the 22 schools mentioned having specialist drama rooms (though 41 per cent said that they had drama space as in studio or performing space). In addition, three of the 22 schools listed a dance studio; two cited darkrooms and three mentioned pottery rooms.

Table 1.1 shows the percentages of schools offering the Year 11 sample different arts subjects at key stages 3 and 4. At key stage 4, fewer than a quarter of the schools provided dance and a third did not offer drama as a separate subject. In at least one school, music at key stage 4 was taught as part of an expressive arts option rather than as a separate subject. 'Other arts' included references to dance as part of PE, drama as part of English, textiles and media studies.

Table 1.1   **Percentages of schools offering the Year 11 cohort different arts subjects at key stages 3 and 4**

	Key stage 3		Key stage 4	
	%	N	%	N
Art	91	20	100	22
Music	100	22	91	20
Drama	64	14	68	15
Dance	32	7	23	5
Expressive arts	5	1	9	2
Other arts	14	3	14	3

N = 22 schools
Source: NFER 'The Effects and Effectiveness of Arts Education' Year 11 Survey school questionnaire

Most importantly, 86 per cent of the schools (n=19) reported that it was not compulsory for pupils to take at least one arts subject at key stage 4; hence, only three of the 22 schools required pupils to study an arts subject at this stage.

Approximately two-thirds of the schools (64 per cent) described option systems for key stage 4 that gave pupils access to a maximum of two arts subjects. However, five of the 22 schools limited their pupils' access to one art subject. Two schools offered pupils the opportunity to take more than two arts subjects.

Schools were asked to indicate how much teaching time per week was allocated to arts subjects. It appeared that within schools the same

amount of teaching time was devoted to the different arts subjects. Similarly, there were few significant changes in teaching time for the arts from Year 10 to Year 11. However, there were appreciable variations in the amount of teaching time for the arts from school to school. For example, in Year 10 at four schools, pupils experienced two hours or less per arts subject per week, whilst at three schools, pupils received two hours 45 minutes to three hours. Most typically, pupils received two hours 20–25 minutes (seven schools). As mentioned above, a similar range existed for Year 11.

The item exploring the occurrence of extra-curricular provision in the arts showed that at key stage 3 most of the schools had a choir or other singing group (86 per cent) and likewise, an instrumental group (82 per cent). Drama clubs were nearly as common, provided by 77 per cent of this sample. In addition, nearly all schools (91 per cent) put on productions in the form of plays or musicals. Extra-curricular activities appeared less often for art and dance, with 64 per cent of the schools providing a dance club or group and 59 per cent an art club or group. Only three out of the 22 schools provided creative writing groups, though eight schools did provide some other form of extra-curricular arts activity (e.g. worship band, textile groups, one-off projects and residencies). Provision at key stage 4 was very similar, though two schools no longer provided choir and singing groups and likewise two schools no longer had instrumental groups.

Finally, virtually all the schools provided instrumental tuition in music, predominantly through peripatetic services (cited by two-thirds of the schools). In two schools, pupils had to pay for their lessons.

The pupil sample

From across the 22 schools, the Year 11 student questionnaire was completed by 2,269 pupils. Of these, 2,022 pupils had both GCSE data and completed questionnaires available.

Reflecting the inclusion of three all-girls schools compared to one all-boys school, the sample of 2,269 pupils was slightly biased towards girls. Over half of the sample were female (56 per cent), with 44 per cent male.

With regard to ethnic origin, 86 per cent of the sample were white, with the remaining 14 per cent of non-whites including pupils of Black-African ethnicity (two per cent of the whole sample), Pakistani (two per cent), Black-Caribbean (two per cent), Indian (one per cent), Bangladeshi (one per cent), mixed race (one per cent), Chinese (one per cent), Black-other (one per cent), and a further two per cent of other ethnic origins.

Using the higher of fathers' or mothers' social class ranking (based on pupils' descriptions of their parents' occupations), 51 per cent of the sample were from Social Class groups I and II (i.e. managerial or professional backgrounds); 18 per cent were from Social Class III NM (i.e. skilled non-manual backgrounds); 19 per cent were from Social Class III M (i.e. skilled manual backgrounds); eight per cent were from Social Class IV and V (i.e. semi- and unskilled backgrounds); and three per cent were unclassifiable.

Thus, allowing for the slight bias towards girls and the tendency for the use of the higher of parents' occupational rankings to inflate social class gradings, the sample was broadly representative in terms of gender, ethnicity and social class. Furthermore, it was drawn from a random sample of schools, which contained a valuable mixture of schools of different types, sizes and socio-economic contexts, as well as different approaches to the organisation and teaching of the arts. These points should be borne in mind when considering the results presented later.

1.3.4 Interviews with employers and employees

The final data collection element of the study involved interviewing employers and employees on the relationship between arts education and the world of work. In all, 20 companies throughout England were visited. They comprised three banks/building societies, two advertising agencies, a city council, a large firm of accountants and management consultants, an insurance firm, a recruitment agency, computer software developers, a supermarket chain, a large confectionery manufacturer, a precision engineering manufacturer, a high street clothes retail chain, a biotech company, a local newspaper, a firm of surveyors, a theatre, a museum and an arts centre. Typically, each visit included an interview with a director or human resources/personnel manager and interviews with employees under the age of 25. In total, 65 interviews were carried out.

1.4 SOME KEY TERMS

Before moving on, it may be helpful to define how we have interpreted and used certain key terms in the study.

1.4.1 'The arts'

Wherever possible, we have encouraged the participants in the research, particularly in the case study schools, to offer us their interpretations of 'the arts'. When, for example, initial contacts were made with advisers and other informed observers in order to seek their nominations of schools with good-quality provision in 'the arts', their views on what this term embraced in practice influenced the selection of the schools. From this perspective, the dominant view was that the arts as practised in secondary schools included art, music, drama and occasionally dance. The expressive and creative dimensions to English were not cited at this stage, neither were video or media education.

In a similar way, senior managers in the schools were also asked to describe what subjects were incorporated under the umbrella term 'the arts' in their school. Again, whereas art, music and drama were mentioned in all the schools, three also included dance within the arts and three suggested elements of English – though the teaching of the latter was seldom organised in connection with, or as part of, an 'arts' programme.

In the light of these interpretations, all of the study's data collection methods have embraced art, music, drama and dance, and wherever possible, the creative and expressive aspects of English (e.g. *literature, novels and plays* in the questionnaire for the Year 11 Survey) within 'the arts'. However, the longitudinal interviews with pupils on the perceived effects of their arts courses did not focus on English. This was partly due to time constraints, but also to the difficulties experienced in disentangling the creative and expressive elements of English from its more transactional aspects. It was also difficult to collect many accounts of dance from pupils since few of them experienced this artform on a regular and sustained basis.

1.4.2 'Effects'

When analysing teachers' perceptions of 'effects', the research team identified all their references to the effects, desirable outcomes and achievable aims associated with arts subjects. For the sake of brevity throughout the report, these terms are denoted through the interchangeable use of 'effects' and 'outcomes'. Given that teachers, as providers of arts education, could be said to have a natural and vested interest in accentuating the positive benefits to be gained through involvement in the arts, their perceptions of the outcomes of arts education have been treated as 'claims' that require empirical verification. Given this, it made sense to include statements about achievable aims alongside references to actual outcomes. Although this approach – namely, turning teachers' perceptions of effects into hypotheses – has the disadvantage of underestimating the significance of a majority of teachers independently citing similar arts-related outcomes, it offers the crucial advantage of encouraging the search for valid and rigorous evidence to corroborate or refute teachers' accounts. In short, the approach provides the research with a response to the sceptical reaction of 'Well, teachers would say that, wouldn't they?'.

Pupils' perceptions of 'effects' were elicited through more direct and focused questioning about outcomes. Examples of the questions put to them included: *What have you got out of studying...?* (Year 11 questionnaire), *What do you think you have learnt in...?, What have been the effects on you of doing...?, What do you think might be some of the effects in the future?* The last three examples are taken from the schedules used in the longitudinal cohort interviews.

The effects of arts education, then, given in this report, are the outcomes of arts lessons that pupils and teachers have identified as being associated with any effect on themselves, or others.

1.4.3 'Effectiveness'

The Oxford dictionary of current English defines 'effective' as an adjective meaning: *'producing the intended result'*. While the research certainly incorporates analyses of intended effects, it is clear that this definition does not give a broad enough understanding of effectiveness for these circumstances. For example, many of the effects of arts education identified in the following chapters were not necessarily intended as a primary outcome, but were a secondary by-product of the educational practices at work in the classroom. Consequently, for our purposes, 'effective' practice is taken to mean provision that results in the unintended, as well as intended, outcomes described in Part Two.

In order to appreciate the approach taken by the research, it is crucial to draw a conceptual and key methodological distinction between 'effective' practice and such terms as 'good' or 'best' practice. For us, terms like 'good' or 'best' practice take the definition one stage further by implying relative values assigned to the various observed outcomes and effects. According to this perspective, statements about 'good practice', for example, would not only include assertions about the efficacy of certain teaching methods, but would also offer implicit or explicit valuations of the relative desirability of outcomes. In recognition of the enormous, if not insurmountable, epistemological complexity of providing empirical justifications to the valuing of outcomes, this research does not seek to make judgements about the relative desirability of different effects or outcomes of arts education. Instead, it attempts to examine effective practice without attributing value judgements to the merits of the observed outcomes.

By way of an illustration, take two contrasting ways of teaching drama: one emphasises stagecraft skills; the other focuses on social and moral issues. In adopting our approach to 'effectiveness', the research would consider the different intended and unintended outcomes achieved by the two different views of drama. Emphatically, it would not attempt to judge whether the outcomes of one, say the stagecraft model, were

more valuable or important than those of the other, in this case, the social issues version of drama. To make such a judgement, a view of 'good practice' in drama would need to be assumed.

However, it should be recognised that, while less ambitious than researching 'good practice', empirical studies of effective practice are still bedevilled by several serious methodological problems. The difficulties associated with establishing causality and the challenges inherent in moving beyond perceptual data are but two such problems.

Another difficulty encountered in this study has been caused by the lack of suitable instruments to assess baseline achievements in the learning outcomes associated with arts education. For the most part, this has rendered it impossible to consider effective practice from a 'value-added' standpoint. Such an interpretation of effective practice, for example, is preferred by Wyatt (1996), who cites the definition used by the Organisation for Economic Cooperation and Development in an international study of the quality of education: '*An effective school is one that promotes the progress of its students in a broad range of intellectual, social and emotional outcomes, taking into account the socio-economic status, family background and prior learning.*'

This definition not only considers the effects and outcomes of education in determining its effectiveness, it also makes allowances for the starting points of the pupils. Measuring the 'distance travelled' by the pupils between the initial starting point and the end of educational intervention is one way in which attempts have been made to quantify effectiveness in education. This method aims to determine what the educational provision has developed in terms of pupil achievement, over and above what the pupils were expected to achieve without the intervention. This measure has been termed the 'value-added' dimension of education, and allows comparison of the achievements of pupils starting from different initial levels of prior attainment.

However, owing to the absence of developed instruments for measuring outcomes in arts education, this research has not sought to gauge additionality nor to quantify effectiveness. Rather, its aim is to identify the range of factors which interviewees perceived to be important and which appeared through the observational data to be related to accounts of outcomes. As a consequence of this approach, it is readily acknowledged that this form of analysis cannot take account of the extent to which the efficacy of different teachers' practices is influenced by pupils' specific prior attainment in the arts.

Nevertheless, and as we shall see in the chapters within Part Three, interviewees did comment on the general significance of pupils' prior attainment as part of their perceptions of what constituted the key factors and processes that engender effects and outcomes considered to be beneficial or desirable.

The effectiveness of arts education, then, is reported in terms of the range of factors, perceived and observed, to be important to achieving the outcomes and effects of arts education.

1.5   STRUCTURE OF THE REPORT

The report is divided into four parts. An overview of the structure and the main content of the chapters within these four parts is set out below.

PART ONE: INTRODUCTION	
Chapter	Outline of contents
1	**The Study and its Context**: sets the study in its background context, outlines its aims, describes the research methods, defines some key terms and offers an overview of the report structure.

PART TWO: WHAT ARE THE EFFECTS OF ARTS EDUCATION?	
Chapter	Outline of contents
2	**A Model of Arts Education Outcomes**: presents an overall model of the outcomes associated with arts education in secondary schools. This chapter introduces each of the main types of outcome that are described in more detail in the chapters that make up the rest of Part Two. The various effects on pupils are depicted in Chapters 3–9, while the effects on schools, communities and the arts are portrayed in Chapter 10. The concluding chapter in this Part (Chapter 11) offers an overarching and comparative discussion of the different effects set out in the model.
3	**Intrinsic and Immediate Effects: Forms of Enjoyment and Therapy**: explores what are for many pupils the most immediate effects of engaging in the arts, namely, a sense of enjoyment, excitement, fulfilment, stress reduction and therapeutic value.
4	**Artform Knowledge and Skills**: examines the direct effects on the artistic development of the learner in terms of enhanced knowledge, understanding, appreciation and skills in different artforms, and, perhaps, in the arts as a whole.

INTRODUCTION

5   **Knowledge in the Social and Cultural Domains**: discusses the outcomes relating to the broadening of pupil perspectives on cultural traditions and diversity, environmental contexts and surroundings, and social and moral issues.

6   **Creativity and Thinking Skills**: portrays the effects on the development of cognitive processes such as creativity, the imagination, thinking skills and problem-solving strategies.

7   **Communication and Expressive Skills**: explores outcomes associated with the enrichments of interactive communication skills, language competency, interpretative and active listening skills, and the capacity to use expressive skills to make statements about themselves and their worlds.

8   **Personal and Social Development**: documents the accounts of outcomes relating to the growth in intra- and interpersonal awareness and skills, including the sense of self and identity, self-esteem, self-confidence, teamwork skills, awareness of others, and rounded and balanced personalities.

9   **Extrinsic Transfer Effects**: examines the evidence on the claims that the effects of arts-related courses transfer to different contexts, in particular that they have a beneficial impact on learning and attainment in other areas of the curriculum, but also that they transfer to the world of work and influence young people's engagement in cultural activities in their leisure time.

10   **Other Effects: on the School, the Community and the Arts**: describes the perceptions that, in addition to the effects on pupils, arts education in secondary schools also impacts upon parents and the community, the arts themselves, and the ethos and culture of the school – with regard to the latter, it also explores the view that a school that has high levels and quality of provision in the arts is more likely to have a strong track record in school improvement and effectiveness.

11   **Arts Effects: Overall Perspectives**: presents the findings on effects from the Year 11 Survey and draws together the results presented in the earlier chapters by comparing the weight of evidence attached to the main outcomes and by considering how the different effects may relate to each other (e.g. how advances in technical skills – depicted in Chapter 4 – interface with developments in creativity and expressive skills – Chapters 6 and 7 respectively).

PART THREE:	WHAT ARE EFFECTIVE PRACTICES IN ARTS EDUCATION?
Chapter	Outline of contents
12	**Perceptions of Effective Practices in Arts Education**: analyses pupils', teachers' and employers' general perceptions of the factors and processes associated with effective provision of arts education in secondary schools, including factors at the levels of beyond school, whole school, departments, teachers, curriculum and pupils.
13	**Effective Practices in Context**: extends the analysis offered in the previous chapter by portraying some vignettes of specific provision and examining the outcomes associated with examples, thereby illustrating how different approaches to the same arts subject lead to different patterns of effects.
14	**Effectiveness: a Wider Picture**: uses the responses from the 22 schools involved in the Year 11 Survey to broaden the discussion beyond the five case study schools and explores the factors that appear to influence the take-up of arts courses at key stage 4.
15	**Arts Effectiveness: Overall Perspectives**: offers a synthesis of the findings relating to the factors and processes characteristic of effective arts provision by collating the evidence from the previous three chapters.

PART FOUR:	CONCLUSION
Chapter	Outline of contents
16	**Summary and Conclusion**: highlights the main results for both the effects and effectiveness dimensions to the study and considers their implications for developing practices and policies.

7

PART TWO: WHAT ARE THE EFFECTS OF ARTS EDUCATION?

2. A MODEL OF ARTS EDUCATION OUTCOMES

CHAPTER OVERVIEW

This short chapter presents an overall model of the outcomes associated with arts education in secondary schools. It introduces each of the main types of outcome that are described in more detail in the chapters that make up the rest of Part Two.

2.1 INTRODUCTION

This part of the report addresses the first, and probably most important, aim of the study, namely to document and evidence the range of effects and outcomes attributable to school-based arts education. It also considers the fourth aim on the extent to which high levels of institutional involvement in the arts correlate with the qualities known to be associated with successful school improvement and school effectiveness (see Chapter 10).

The main source of evidence for this exploration of arts-related effects has been drawn from the case study schools, in particular from the longitudinal interviews with the cohort pupils and from their teachers and school managers. The interviews with employers and employees also provided material for these chapters. Additionally, Chapter 11 draws on the findings from the Year 11 Survey and Chapter 9 presents some results of the analyses of the QUASE data, the Year 11 Survey and the employer/employee interviews.

In the interim report (Harland *et al.*, 1998), we offered a provisional and tentative typology of the possible effects of school-based arts education, as seen by teachers and heads of department of arts-oriented subjects, and members of senior management. The typology was constructed by carefully trawling through the 52 staff interviews in the five case study schools and recording all references to claims about the effects, desirable outcomes and achievable aims associated with arts subjects. For the final report, the provisional typology has been developed and revised in the light of pupils' accounts of the learning outcomes to accrue from their experiences of arts-related provision. Streamlined to better convey its fundamental features, this new model is described and illustrated in the following chapters.

As in the interim report, it is important to stress that all the categories in the model were created on the basis of what was found in the interview transcripts – that is to say, a bottom-up or empirically grounded approach to the framing of the categories was used. Most certainly, they were not constructed in any *a priori* manner whereby the constructs are established in advance by the researchers and laid on the data like a template, either at the interview stage or in the analysis. It was the case, however, that many of the categories used to construct the earlier typology of effects as perceived by teachers (see the interim report) were then used with some modifications to classify the pupils' accounts of effects – through such a process, the model presented here represents an amalgamation of teacher and pupil perspectives.

When considering the model, it is also important to bear in mind that each of the presented categories represents an ideal type that has been somewhat artificially singled out as a discrete entity. This has been done in order to assist analyses and inform discussions about policies and practices in the teaching of the arts. These advantages, however, are only achieved through a process of fragmentation that inevitably sacrifices a sense of the holistic nature of an individual's experiences in the arts. Consequently, in later analyses, it will be necessary to inquire how these categories relate to one another, when looked at from the perspective of individual experiences and biographies. For example, it will be interesting to explore whether arts experiences in their entirety are greater than the sum of the individual parts or categories described in the model below. For present purposes, suffice it to acknowledge that, in reality, several of the categories often overlapped with each other and that many of the references identified in the interview material contained allusions to more than one category.

2.2   AN OVERVIEW OF THE MODEL

Two broad types of outcome were identified: effects on pupils and effects on others. The former accounted for the vast majority of outcomes nominated and described by all interviewees.

The effects on pupils comprised seven main sets of outcomes: (i) intrinsic and immediate effects; (ii) arts knowledge and skills; (iii) knowledge in the social and cultural domains; (iv) creativity and thinking skills; (v) communication and expressive skills; (vi) personal

2.
WHAT ARE
THE EFFECTS
OF
ARTS
EDUCATION?

and social development and (vii) extrinsic transfer effects. Each of these seven sets of outcome contained further subcategories and these are described in Chapters 3–9.

The effects on others broad type of outcome included three main sets of outcome: (i) on the school (ii) on the community and (iii) art itself as an outcome. These are discussed in Chapter 10. Thus, in total, ten main sets of outcomes are discussed in this report.

A diagrammatic outline of the model is set out in Figure 2.1 opposite. The arrows in the diagram indicate the main directions or flows of influence. The arrow from 'Effects on Pupils' to 'Effects on Others' is intended to indicate that the majority of the latter effects were mediated through pupil involvement in the arts. Thus, for the most part, they constitute interpersonal second-order or knock-on effects of pupil's engagement in arts education rather than any direct non-pupil-related effects of arts provision.

As illustrated in the diagram, the effects on pupils are presented in such a way as to signify a progression from the most immediate and direct outcome categories (i.e. 'intrinsic enjoyment' and 'arts knowledge and skills') through categories that entail a slight degree of transferability (i.e. 'knowledge of the social and cultural domains', 'creativity and thinking skills' and 'communication and expressive skills') to categories that represent a significant element of transferability (i.e. 'personal and social development' and 'extrinsic transfer effects', e.g. to other areas of the curriculum, leisure activities and employment). In many respects, the latter two categories may be considered as intrapersonal second-order or knock-on effects of the top five, with 'personal and social development' outcomes feeding into the 'extrinsic transfer' effects.

In suggesting a notion of progression from intrinsic to extrinsic outcomes – or from direct to indirect outcomes – it should be emphasised that there is no suggestion here that pupils advance in some mechanistic or linear manner through these levels over the course of their secondary schooling and beyond. In reality, the evidence suggests that learning proceeds as a result of a complex series of cyclical interactions between the various categories depending on the type of provision experienced. In diagrammatic terms, these interactions could be drawn to show influences 'working back up' the model as well as those progressing 'down' it. However, before any further discussion of the model as a whole, each of the seven sets of outcomes associated with effects on pupils are described in the following chapters (Chapters 3–9).

Figure 2.1   A model of arts education outcomes

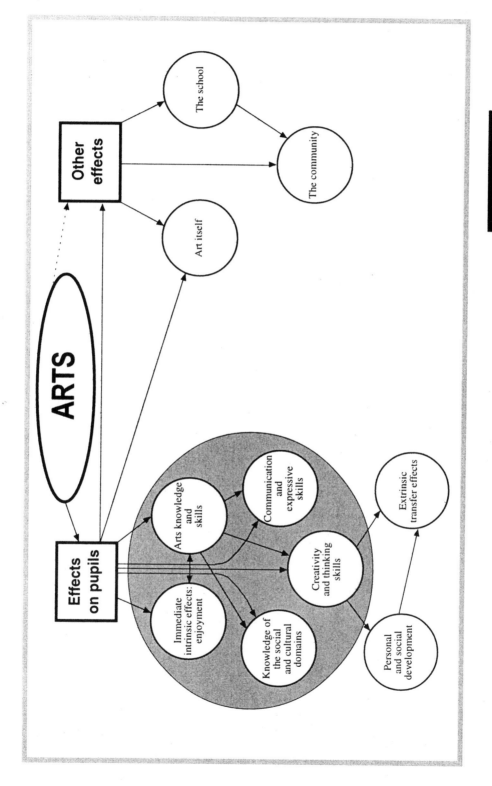

3. INTRINSIC AND IMMEDIATE EFFECTS: FORMS OF ENJOYMENT AND THERAPY

**2.
WHAT ARE
THE EFFECTS
OF
ARTS
EDUCATION?**

CHAPTER OVERVIEW
This chapter considers the first of the broad categories of effect, namely enjoyment and therapeutic outcomes. It documents the accounts of different forms of enjoyment as an outcome of engagement in the arts (3.2), and then describes various therapeutic outcomes (3.3). In both these subcategories, teacher perspectives and pupil perspectives are discussed in turn.

3.1 INTRODUCTION

This chapter explores what to many are the most immediate or obvious effects of engaging in the arts: personal enjoyment, fulfilment or an increased sense of well-being. Crucial to pupils' future motivation in the arts, these intrinsic effects can be subdivided into personal enjoyment outcomes and therapeutic outcomes.

The first subcategory of this chapter considers the enjoyment outcome, including the sense of excitement, fulfilment, fun and the adrenaline rush or 'buzz' which can come from involvement in the arts (Harland and Kinder, 1995). The second subcategory covers perceived outcomes connected with the arts offering a therapeutic effect, release of tension, a form of escapism or having a calming influence on pupils' personality.

Accounts by teachers and pupils are considered for each subcategory, and, where appropriate, the comments of employers and employees.

3.2 THE ENJOYMENT OUTCOME

This subcategory deals with testimonies made about enjoyment as an outcome of participation in the arts. This was a prevalent theme for both teachers and pupils, with a great number of comments about the arts giving rise to enjoyment, happiness, a sense of satisfaction and fun. Some of their more general comments are presented in section 3.2.1 below. Pupils however, made many more comments about their enjoyment of their arts education experience, and these are detailed by artform in section 3.2.2, and according to different stances on enjoyment, such as fun and happiness, in sections 3.2.3–3.2.6.

3.2.1 Enjoyment from the arts in general

Teacher Perspectives

Numerous responses from teachers across the arts focused on '*enjoyment*', '*fun*' and the adrenaline rush or '*buzz*' that can come from involvement in the arts. Some teachers talked about a deeper sense of enrichment here, describing how pupils gain an extra dimension through their involvement in the arts, often providing a deep sense of satisfaction and fulfilment:

> *... another dimension to their lives, which isn't just a factual, mechanical dimension. It is something that is a life inside their head; it's an imaginative life, a creative life that it gives them* (drama teacher).
>
> ———
>
> *So that at the end of a production, they are crying, a 17-year-old lad is crying, because something he knows is wonderful in his life, a major part in a school production, has ended on the Saturday night. Now, that sort of effect on someone has got to be life-changing and that is an outcome that I would want* (headteacher).

There was also a recognition by teachers of their own enjoyment and love for the arts that manifests itself in their teaching. One music teacher used the pronoun 'we' when describing the enjoyment that comes from creating music: '*We have a wonderful time; it is ever such fun making ... creating this music ...*'

One head of music cited enjoyment as an important part of the school's inclusive attitude to the arts: '*... as I said, it's an arts for all policy; it's just basically "Get involved and enjoy it" and get out what you can get out of it.*'

This category links closely to section three of Chapter 8 on personal development (8.3 'Enhanced self-worth and self-esteem'), in the sense that teachers suggested that it was often the fact that pupils could be more successful in the arts than they were in other subjects that precipitated the experience of enjoyment, that is, a sense of achievement is part of the enjoyment factor. Enjoyment was also identified as the common element for children of different abilities in the arts:

> *A child who is Grade 8 Distinction violin in Year 8, he's going to get so many more different things out of the classroom lesson than somebody who may be level 5 statement, but at the end of the day they should be both enjoying it* (head of music).

Pupil Perspectives

The sheer enjoyment of the arts was an outcome regularly cited by pupils. Indeed, this was the most frequently mentioned effect of arts education by the whole sample of pupils. In total, 285 responses referred to this effect, made by 80 pupils (some pupils made more than one comment in a particular interview and/or reiterated their view in more than one year). Several pupils specifically mentioned the element of fun and the adrenaline rush or '*buzz*' that can come from involvement in the arts.

When asked what they thought learning in the arts was for, many pupils, particularly those in Years 7 and 8, stated enjoyment, but offered no real explanation of their answer: '*they're always enjoyable*', '*I don't know, I just enjoy it*'. Some older pupils were able to clarify their enjoyment of the arts in school, in a few cases perceiving the basis for enjoyment of arts subjects as different to the experiences offered by other school subjects:

> *We always look forward to doing art, music and drama because we like it better than doing English and maths and science. We look forward to doing something else to writing* (Year 9).

Hinting that for some pupils the arts were not construed as '*work*', one pupil said: '*It gives you more enjoyment* [because in] *all the other lessons, it's just solid work*' (Year 9).

The perceived absence of a categorically right or wrong answer in the arts subjects appeared to add to enjoyment:

> *To me there's loads of different points of art, like there's the performing arts, the creative arts ... and all of it's a lot of fun. And I think a lot of people enjoy the arts because there's no right or wrong answer. Because in the sciences everything's going to be the same, but in the arts it's all different because of what you see and not what others see. You'd hardly ever get two pictures that are exactly the same, because people have different views* (Year 7).

One pupil made the comment that it was the diversity of artforms that gave him a sense of achievement, and it was this which contributed to his enjoyment of the arts in school:

> *Enjoyment and really to get something out of it. You get a lot of achievement. There are so many different forms that you can get achievement in many different ways. I think everybody enjoys the arts, because there's something in there for everybody* (Year 7).

That this also refers to accessibility to the arts reflects a similarity with the teachers' comments.

3.2.2   Enjoyment by artform

Pupil Perspectives

Comments relating to personal enjoyment varied for the different artforms, but each received general comments about enjoyment. Most comments related to art (72), with slightly fewer to music and drama (51 and 40 respectively). Dance received the least remarks (15), but it must be remembered here that fewer pupils took this subject. Indeed as a percentage of those taking dance, 46 per cent (12 out of 26 pupils) referred to enjoyment from dance, whereas 18 per cent referred to enjoyment from drama (32 out of 175 pupils). The percentages for art and music were 21 and 19 respectively. This seems to indicate a far higher enjoyment outcome for dance than the other artforms (though the small numbers involved warrant caution) and that the scores for art, music and drama are in fact similar. The frequency of comments for each arts subject also seemed to vary slightly for the different schools, and different year groups.

2
WHAT ARE
THE EFFECTS
OF
ARTS
EDUCATION

Enjoyment from art

For art, pupils from virtually all year-groups at all five schools made reference to enjoyment as an outcome. One school elicited noticeably fewer nominations than the others.

For some pupils, art was their favourite subject, being *'the most enjoyable part of the week'*. For others, it was the kinds of activity like *'drawing things and making things'* that influenced their enjoyment of art. Echoing the teachers' comments on a sense of achievement, one pupil mentioned the satisfaction of finishing a piece of work:

> *I get a lot of joy out of finishing a piece of work and like being able to say that's good, the composition of the picture is good, and I've done my best and it's turned out well* (Year 9).

Enjoyment from music

For music, at one school only two pupils made comments referring to enjoyment as an outcome, whereas between eight and 15 comments were made at each of the other four schools. The majority of remarks were made by pupils in Years 7 to 9.

As in art, some pupils referred to specific activities that gave them enjoyment – *'I enjoy composing and playing'* – while others referred to enjoyment of topics or styles of music such as 'house'. The opportunity for out-of-school development enhanced enjoyment of music. Some pupils referred to the enjoyment associated with being able to play an instrument, which did not necessarily come from school lessons:

I just love playing music and being able to do something, and I can just go to my piano and play something (Year 7).

———

I enjoy music, but I don't think that I need to take an exam in it and take it further to enjoy it. I can just enjoy it at home, enjoy listening and enjoy playing my piano (Year 9).

These types of comments beg the question as to whether enjoyment was related to musical ability, despite not wishing to take performance grades, or if other factors also contributed here.

Enjoyment from drama

The nominations for enjoyment as an outcome ranged from five in one school to ten in two others. Like art, drama was also specified as a favourite subject. Some pupils mentioned specific reasons why they enjoyed drama, including the topics and methods they were studying:

In drama I like what we are doing now, friendship and peer pressure and different kinds of friendships, what are good friends and bad friends. I enjoyed doing that (Year 7).

———

I enjoy improvisation (Year 9).

Several pupils mentioned the opportunities for involvement in drama, either through participation in the school play, or going to see plays:

I also enjoy the subject a lot and I enjoy participation in things like the school plays and things like that (Year 10).

———

We go to see a lot of plays with drama, so I just find it enjoyable (Year 10).

One pupil discussed the potential for enjoyment regardless of aptitude: '[I] *enjoy it – favourite lesson. You can just be yourself. It doesn't matter if you're good at it or not, you're just having a good time really*' (Year 10).

Enjoyment from dance

Although far fewer comments were made relating to enjoyment as an outcome of dance, these accounted for almost half of those pupils actually taking dance. (Fewer pupils were involved in dance lessons than in the other arts subjects; only 26 pupils did dance, usually as part of PE lessons.) Again, several pupils just mentioned that they enjoyed the subject, although a few were able to justify their answer, one pupil linking enjoyment of dance to music and choreography/performance: '*I quite enjoy it actually. I enjoy the music and so on. I also quite like seeing large groups of people dancing all the same moves*' (Year 9).

One comment referred to an increase in enjoyment compared to primary school: '*When we did it at primary school it was really boring, but it is quite good now, I really enjoy it*' (Year 9).

3.2.3   Enjoyment as 'buzz' and 'excitement'

Pupil Perspectives

While many of the comments on enjoyment were generally to do with particular activities or having a favourite subject in the arts, discussion on performance and staging elicited a real '*buzz*' outcome from the pupils. In using the term, pupils conveyed a sense of energy and excitement, over and above the normal response of enjoyment. Altogether, 17 pupils made 27 comments relating specifically to the buzz that can come from involvement in the arts. For many of these pupils, it was the final product or performance which gave them a thrill:

> *You get a real buzz out of doing a concert or something* (Year 9, music).

> *In music, if you go out on stage and it is all dark, and the lights come up and you know that you are doing something ... And you come off and you ... are just tingling all down your back* (Year 7, music).

> *People are looking at you, sometimes they are even paying to see you, it is just amazing. You see all those eyes upon you, and you are thinking you should be nervous, but you are not because you know what you are doing and you just get on with it. It is great* (Year 7, drama).

> *With art, when you have just done the last line to your piece it just looks amazing, and you think 'I did that!'. And it makes you think, especially if they display it or something, and you think 'Wow! I can't believe that people are going to be looking at this'* (Year 7, art).

Some pupils commented that it was the sense of achievement in a subject that gave them a buzz:

> *... composing. If you get a couple of bars done that you are really pleased with, it gives you a buzz* (Year 10, music).

> *That gave me a real buzz because I got an AA* (Year 9, drama).

3.2.4   Enjoyment as 'fun'

Pupil Perspectives

Thirty-two pupils made a total of 54 comments associated with fun as an outcome of the arts. While previously art and music had received the greatest number of comments for enjoyment, drama as a subject received the most comments on fun, indicating a different sense of enjoyment for this subject. Fun in drama was followed by art and music, while dance only received a handful of references.

Again, specific topics, activities and a sense of achievement contributed to the fun outcome. One pupil talked about drama not requiring as much concentration as the more academic subjects, which made it more fun: '*It's just more a fun subject and you don't have to put loads of concentration into it. You just have to get up there and go for it*' (Year 9, drama).

Interestingly, for music, it was composing and improvising that were seen as fun, as opposed to the more performance-based comments for enjoyment in music:

> *I like working to compose pieces with my friends. That's fun, because it's really, when you've just got something and you've made it all up yourselves, that's nice when you've just finished and everything* (Year 9, music).

3.2.5   Enjoyment as 'happiness'

Pupil Perspectives

Ten pupils made a total of 12 references to an increase in happiness, or a change in mood as a result of arts education. The majority of these comments related to art and music. Some pupils simply stated that they came out of arts lessons feeling happier:

> *I go to the next lesson feeling perhaps a little more cheerful than I did when I went into the lesson ... so, I think* [it has] *quite a happy effect on me* (Year 8, art).

> *When I did 'Joseph', you could go in in a perfectly bad mood and you could come out and be really happy* (Year 7, music).

Certain pupils seemed to suggest that they could express their feelings through the arts and that this made them feel better:

> *I like to do music, because when I am angry or upset if I can sit down and play music, it makes me feel a bit better* (Year 7, music).

> *You can draw whatever is on your mind, and if the colours are bright and colourful, it might make you feel happy. If the colours are really dark and gloomy, they might make you feel sad* (Year 9, art).

Like the perceived reasons for enjoyment and fun, a sense of achievement in a finished piece also contributed to happiness for one pupil: '*If I think that the piece I have drawn is good, then I feel happy and like it*' (Year 9, art).

3.2.6　Enjoyment as 'satisfaction'

Pupil Perspectives

Five pupils made a total of ten comments referring to satisfaction as an outcome of arts education. To most of these pupils it was a sense of achievement at having completed their own piece of work and being pleased with it which gave satisfaction. Receiving a good mark also played a part:

> *It's just a good feeling. You can look at a piece of work after it's taken six or seven weeks to complete and look back and say 'I've done that'. So it's constructive and you can feel like you have done something. It's a building process and it's nice to see something develop* (Year 11, art).

> *You know it's your own work so you get a lot of satisfaction out of it when you have finished* (Year 11, art).

> *When you kind of finish, like a dance, and when you've made it all up and I'm quite pleased with it, or you've done something in music, made a song or something and it sounds good, and you get a good mark for it, then it's quite satisfying* (Year 9, music and dance).

Throughout this section (3.2), it seems that enjoyment through a sense of achievement was more prevalent in Years 10 and 11, whereas the buzz and excitement of the arts seems to be more concentrated in the lower year groups.

3.3　THE THERAPEUTIC OUTCOME

Closely related to enjoyment outcomes were the accounts which testified to various therapeutic effects emanating from arts education experiences. The therapeutic value of the arts was an effect mentioned by both pupils and teachers as having a calming effect on a pupil's temperament, or offering a release of tension and a means of escape from the real world.

Teacher Perspectives

Interestingly, responses that fitted this subcategory came predominantly from one school, and from one teacher in particular. This head of expressive arts saw the arts as having therapeutic value, and a calming effect, enabling students to go into their *'own little world'*. From the same school, a deputy head perceived the arts as offering pupils an escape, albeit a temporary one, from the trials of everyday life:

> *You know, poor housing, unemployment – all those things that these young people's families cope with – and the kids tend to leave that*

at the gate and come in and get on with learning. And it does offer, in the same sense, that all of those arts subjects are in a sense are escaping from this into whatever piece of work you are doing. It offers an opportunity to put those things behind for a while and look at things again (deputy head).

Pupil Perspectives

Therapeutic outcomes of the arts were regularly cited by pupils, often being seen as a release from the stresses of everyday life and, interestingly, from the stress of other lessons. Commonly, pupils felt that the arts had made them a calmer person, more able to deal with criticism and with their own emotions.

In total, 38 pupils made 86 comments which referred to therapeutic outcomes from the arts. Over a third of these were made by pupils in Years 10 and 11, which is interesting since most pupils in these years only took one arts subject. It was the older pupils who made more comments about the arts as a form of relief or escapism, perhaps as a result of the increasing pressure from other subjects and assessment further up the school. Similarly, it was the older pupils again who tended to make references to the arts as being more relaxing subjects. Notwithstanding this, comments about the use of arts activities as a form of relaxation seemed to come from pupils in all year groups, as did comments referring to the arts having a calming influence on pupils' behaviour and personality.

By artform, nearly half of the citations were about art (40), with a further quarter referring to music (20). The rest were split between drama (10), the arts in general (9), English (4) and dance (3). However, this division by artform seemed to vary across the five schools. At one school in particular, a large number of references were made to music having a therapeutic effect, with drama too receiving a higher number of comments here than at any other school. All three comments about dance came from pupils at one school, and it was this school which elicited the highest number of references to art and the most references to therapeutic effects overall.

Many pupils considered lessons in the arts to be relaxing in themselves – less hectic or demanding than other subjects:

> *It's a nice relaxing subject is art because the teacher will say we are doing something on this, and he will just let you get on with it, work at your own pace, which is really good, whereas in other subjects you find that they want to push you and pull you, which can get a bit pressurising and confusing* (Year 10, art).

Comments like these came mainly from older pupils, who in some cases viewed the arts as less stressful subjects when choosing their options: '*Other lessons would be stressful. I needed a lesson that would help me unwind*' (Year 10, drama).

Pupils often perceived arts lessons, mainly the visual arts, to be more relaxing than other subjects because they required less concentration or a different kind of concentration:

2.
WHAT ARE
THE EFFECTS
OF
ARTS
EDUCATION?

> *It's more enjoyable, more relaxing than some of the other subjects, like maths, because you're not always concentrating so much* (Year 9, art).

> *I think it just gives you time to kind of relax. Like in other subjects you're like always working, facts and everything; in art you have to concentrate, but in a different way* (Year 10, art).

Arts teaching having a calming influence on pupils' anger or bad temper was an effect mentioned in a few cases:

> *It just like makes you a better person. You know, if someone said something before, like a comment or a criticism, like you get really angry, but after you have danced, you are more relaxed and you just ignore them* (Year 7, dance).

> *I think art has made me calmer. I used to have a bad temper. When I used to be really angry, I used to just draw, so that's like calmed me down* (Year 9, art).

> *It's made me much more relaxed ... I am not so hot-headed ... I don't lose my temper quickly at all* (Year 11, arts in general).

This final pupil made similar remarks about the arts calming her temper in each of the three years in which she was interviewed, making a total of eight comments. Although she made references to art, music and dance, interestingly, writing poetry also seemed to play an important part in relieving her anger and frustrations:

> *When I'm angry, I just write about how I feel, and I feel much better after I've done that, because I think that I've told someone that I've written it down and out of my system* (Year 10, English).

Similarly and by way of anticipating the links this immediate effect has to the expressive outcomes (see Chapter 7), a few pupils said that the arts allowed a means in which to release their emotions or tension:

It's like a release in a way, a good way to sort of let out your emotions and things like that. I think it's a good way to unwind and stuff (Year 11, art).

———

I think it has helped me to feel calmer in some ways, not being worried about these sorts of thing, a good way of taking away some tension (Year 7, drama).

This pupil went on to talk about drama allowing him to take on a different role, rather than being himself for a while, allowing a form of escapism. This sense of release or escape was an outcome of the arts perceived by a number of pupils:

In drama you kind of forget yourself. Even if you have got troubles or something like that, you can just be somebody else (Year 7, drama).

———

It's quite relaxing. You concentrate on what you're doing when you're painting and all that, so your mind's not on your troubles and everything (Year 9, art).

Often pupils felt that participating in some kind of activity in the arts was an effective way to relieve the stresses of everyday life, and one Year 7 pupil mentioned that these skills would be useful in the future if he had a stressful job:

It's a way of relaxing. If you're stressed out [you can] *just go and have a good thump on the piano, possibly not very tunefully* (Year 11, music).

———

Well, it's relaxing for me personally because I can like draw, so like when I am just sitting down and I feel bored or I feel I want to do something because there's nothing to do, that's the best thing for me to do, just sit down and draw (Year 9, art).

———

If you listen to music, or you do music or dance, you won't get stressed out like with a busy job (Year 7, arts).

This final observation was similar to a comment made by an employee of a large insurance company, who was asked what in her view arts education was for: '*I think arts education can provide an ideal antidote to the pressures of work and the need to survive. So, it's the nicer end of life, as far as I am concerned and an essential.*'

3.4 CONCLUDING COMMENTS

Numerous responses from teachers and pupils across all of the artforms focused on the enjoyment that can come from involvement in the arts at secondary school. While teachers commented on accessibility and a concern for enjoyment for all, pupils considered how the arts gave rise to enjoyment as a '*buzz*', happiness, fun and a sense of satisfaction and achievement. Indeed, enjoyment through a sense of achievement was a prevalent theme amongst pupils' comments, particularly in the older year groups. Accessibility was also a concern of the pupils, however. Comments from both teachers and pupils for art and drama suggested that enjoyment was not linked to ability, and that art and drama were to be enjoyed by all. In contrast, enjoyment in music was more likely to be perceived as related to ability in playing an instrument. Across the artforms, it would appear that drama elicits the most fun. Many of the references were about enjoyment as an outcome of participation in particular activities.

Although not as numerous as the references to enjoyment, a sizeable proportion of pupils identified therapeutic effects of arts education. Such outcomes included a release from stress, including the pressures and routines of other subjects, relaxation, an overall becalming effect and a means of dealing with tense emotional states like anger. Art and music were especially linked with these outcomes, though, in these and other subjects, there were clear indications that the frequencies with which therapeutic outcomes were registered varied according to the teacher's approach to the subject and its mediation (e.g. art attracted only one mention of a therapeutic effect in one school, compared to 15 in another).

By way of concluding this chapter, three points deserve to be highlighted. Firstly, it was noticeable that those pupils who expressed their enjoyment of arts subjects were more likely to identify other effects. Likewise, it was apparent that arts subjects in the schools that received high scores for enjoyment outcomes were frequently the ones to have high scores for many (though not all) of the other outcomes (see Chapter 13). To this extent, enjoyment scores acted as a reasonably good barometer of overall perceived effectiveness – especially in art and music, though less so in drama. Whilst recognising that these findings say nothing about the direction of causality between enjoyment and the achievement of other outcomes, the results are consistent with the view that enjoyment – in its various guises – is a key factor in accessing the remaining outcomes described in the following chapters. In view of this, it appears to be an outcome type that arts teachers can ill afford to ignore.

Secondly, other research suggests that the enjoyment outcomes described above are important foundations on which to build future engagement in the arts. In their study of 14–24-year-olds' participation in the arts, Harland *et al.* (1995) found that '*getting a buzz*' out of the arts was one of the most common characteristics associated with those who displayed high levels of involvement in the arts after leaving school. Hence, it would seem that establishing memories of the arts as enjoyable, inspiring and fulfilling experiences while at school is one of the most effective ways of encouraging participation beyond school.

Thirdly, the evidence presented above on therapeutic outcomes, as well as some on the enjoyment effects, underline the extent to which individual arts subjects offer pupils highly significant elements of variation in the teaching and learning they experience throughout a school day. For many, the arts provide a vital relief from the dominant *modus operandi* of listening and writing. The pupils' allusions to the different shifts in physical and psychological functioning offered by arts subjects represent an important reminder of the need for breadth and balance in learning processes, as well as in curriculum content. Moreover, in this regard, it is conspicuous that the individual arts subjects are not simple surrogates for each other – each artform offers distinctive variations in learning behaviour and types of therapeutic outcomes. Looked at from the perspective of Multiple Intelligences Theory (Gardner, 1993), by facilitating engagement in musical, bodily kinaesthetic, spatial and active forms of linguistic intelligences, the individual arts subjects provide many pupils with an essential antidote to the concentrated diet of logical-mathematical and passive forms of linguistic intelligences. Certainly, the evidence presented above on both the enjoyment and therapeutic outcomes suggests that a curriculum lacking in sufficient access to the individual arts subjects would lead many pupils to experience greater tedium, disengagement and ultimately greater disaffection at school.

4. ARTFORM KNOWLEDGE AND SKILLS

CHAPTER OVERVIEW

In moving to the second of the broad categories of effect, this chapter considers the impact of arts education on pupils' knowledge and skills in specific artforms, as well as the arts in general. The chapter discusses the evidence on four main subcategories within this broad category:

- the enhancement of knowledge and understanding of artforms and their contexts (4.2)
- the development of the interpretative skills needed to decode artistic products and processes (4.3)
- growth in the appreciation of artforms and aesthetic judgement-making (4.4)
- developments in the technical skills and processes associated with each artform (4.5).

Most of these sections offer findings for the different artforms and, as in the previous chapter, both teacher and pupil perspectives are described.

**2.
WHAT ARE
THE EFFECTS
OF
ARTS
EDUCATION?**

4.1 INTRODUCTION

This chapter covers accounts pertaining to developments in pupils' knowledge, understanding and appreciation of the arts, as well as the purported development of technical skills and capabilities, in each of the individual artforms and in the arts as a collective entity. The chapter is divided into four subcategories, for ease of reading, rather than being distinct watertight subsets of the overall category. The first relates to the artistic development of the learner in terms of enhanced knowledge and understanding of the artform and its context, and those critical skills needed to discuss artistic products. The second considers those interpretative skills needed to understand the artistic process. The third subcategory deals with the increased levels of appreciation of, and motivation towards, the arts, including awareness of cross-arts. As such the first three subcategories relate to the development of critical skills – the first in discussing works of art, the second in decoding and interpreting products through artistic processes, and the third in considering the powers of aesthetic judgement and discrimination. The fourth subcategory looks at the outcomes of technical skills and capabilities – perhaps most often thought of as those outcomes and competencies that are more directly amenable to assessment and measurement.

4.2 KNOWLEDGE AND UNDERSTANDING OF THE ARTFORM AND ITS CONTEXT

**2.
WHAT ARE
THE EFFECTS
OF
ARTS
EDUCATION?**

This subcategory relates to the perceptions by teachers and pupils about the increases in knowledge and understanding of the artform and its context, as a product, and about the general critical skills needed to discuss works of art. Within each of the teacher and pupil sections below, comments by artform are given since nearly all the insights described by interviewees related to specific artforms, with only a few about the arts in general.

Teacher Perspectives

Comments from teachers related to a 'critical studies' approach in the arts, indicating an enhancement in pupils' critical faculties. It was the art teachers, more so than the teachers of other artforms, who focused on pupils' increased knowledge and understanding of the artform in context. Drama and dance teachers acknowledged pupils' increased abilities to review and evaluate work.

Teachers on increased knowledge and understanding of art

Teachers often identified the outcome of enhanced knowledge and understanding of paintings and works of visual art, together with critical study skills and the development of a language to discuss works of art, including pupils' own work. One contribution from a teacher captured much of the character of this potential outcome:

> *I am hoping that they have got a greater awareness of art heritage, history of art, plus I always try to get them to look at things and say 'Well, do you think it is good, even if you don't like it?' when we are looking at a work of art. Like 'Why has Picasso done this face like this when he can really draw like this?' I hope that by the end of it, they have a little bit more understanding of art and that it's not just painting a pretty picture and why artists work the way that they do* (art teacher).

Descriptions of the purported effects in this subcategory highlighted how the increased use of '*investigations*', '*research projects*', '*evaluations*' and classroom displays had led to extensions in pupils' '*knowledge of critical and contextual implications*' of artists' work. It was observed that the growth in outcomes associated with 'critical studies' had been nurtured by the National Curriculum for art and the pioneering work of some LEAs in this area. Some art teachers drew attention to the importance of equipping young people with a language to discuss, interpret and evaluate works of art:

> *And you're giving them a specialist arts vocabulary, just by using it all the time in the lesson and they're picking it up and they can then apply it informally ... they discuss each other's work informally. They will even assess each other's work – 'Oh, that handle doesn't look quite right' – or whatever.*

Teachers on increased knowledge and understanding of dance

Perhaps indicating an interesting difference between the teaching of dance and other artforms in the secondary school curriculum, there was only one reference that fell within this subcategory for dance. The fostering of the capacity to appraise others' work was mentioned by a dance teacher:

> *From a dance perspective, ... developing ... an appreciation of composition, performance, analysing others, the ability to evaluate, would all come within that.*

This reference was about appraising others' work, and there appeared to be a surprising lack of any references to knowledge about the artform. No doubt, this is partly indicative of the smaller range of sources and dance 'legacies' available for critical study, but, the lack of any other references here suggests that the 'critical studies' approach in dance is less evident than in other arts-oriented subjects. If so, this carries important implications for how the effectiveness of dance teaching should be judged.

Teachers on increased knowledge and understanding of drama

Drama teachers talked about their subject extending pupils' 'critical faculties' and making them *'more discerning, more discriminating'*. For some, the application of these faculties to television was an important outcome:

> *Also, there is the aesthetic side to it as well; you want them to appreciate what is good practice. I mean there is a skills side to drama as well and you try to open their eyes to things which are right, true ... one of the things that kids do all the time these days is sit in front of the television and I honestly feel that drama enhances that experience. If they are going to do that, sit in front of the television, I think they might as well do it with some sort of discernment and I think that drama can teach that sort of thing. I get feedback from pupils all the time on that; they are beginning to realise that some things are dross and some things are really quite good, for certain reasons. They are more able to articulate the reasons that things are good and so I think that it can help them make better use of their leisure time, to not be couch potatoes, but to be discriminating.*

The critical review and evaluation of work created by themselves and others was also mentioned. Other teachers cited the appreciation of theatrical form as an outcome, especially at key stage 4.

Teachers on increased knowledge and understanding of English literature

Given its traditional role and high status within the teaching of English, this effect was often taken for granted by the departmental heads interviewed in the first phase; instead, they tended to focus on the creative 'making' dimension to the subject. Some heads of English, however, did refer to it explicitly as a very significant effect:

I also think that it is very important to make them into a critical audience when it comes to literature.

[discussing the reading and commenting on each others' work] They are capable of doing it and that immediate feedback, critical response to your own work, then enables you to go on and say 'Well right, you just looked at that from your friend' or 'You have just written your own analysis and evaluation of what you did; now here is something else to look at. What do you think of that?'

It is tempting to speculate whether the tendency for English teachers to see creativity as the connecting point with arts-oriented subjects indicates that, to some extent, they (and teachers of other subjects) fail to recognise that arts teachers share a common concern with the teaching of critical skills, evaluation and review. If so, do opportunities for joint reflection, if not cross-curriculum initiatives, go begging?

Teachers on increased knowledge and understanding of music

There was only one general reference identified as belonging to this category: the development of critical skills. This is somewhat surprising, although we will see later that teachers' comments on music related more specifically to the development of critical listening skills.

In general, then, comments from teachers related to a 'critical studies' approach for each of the artforms, and in dance, what little comment there was tended to focus on critical skills for appraising one another's works rather than critical studies of the whole artform in context or as performed by professional dance companies. Despite its emphasis in the National Curriculum Orders, knowledge and understanding of the historical context of the arts was a weak component of teachers' discussion in general: apart from in art, no significant claims were made by teachers about advances in understanding of historical context and cultural milieu in any of the artforms.

Pupil Perspectives

In contrast to the 'critical studies' outcomes emphasised by the teachers' comments, pupils' comments focused much more on the perceived developments in their knowledge and understanding of the arts and artforms, primarily in terms of recognising different styles, movements and individual artists. Indeed, pupils referred to this type of increase in knowledge of the artform much more often than they did the historical and artistic context of the artform, or their development of critical skills.

Music and art were the most frequently referred to artforms regarding an increase in knowledge, understanding and critical skills, with dance and drama being mentioned very little.

Comments relating to knowledge of the artform increased in frequency from Year 7 to Year 9, perhaps as a reflection of the National Curriculum's growing emphasis on historical understanding throughout key stage 3, but declined towards Year 11 (this is not unexpected since fewer pupils took arts subjects at key stage 4). All the comments on knowledge and understanding of historical and artistic contexts of the artforms were made by the older pupils, with none from pupils in Years 7 and 8. The development of critical skills was not confined to the older age groups. Being able to discuss and evaluate artists' work or the work of classmates was mentioned across all year groups, in fairly equal numbers, again with music and art having the most comments. However, there were no mentions at all of critical skills or context for dance education. Rather, there were four comments from pupils to do with increased knowledge in dance.

Pupils on broadening their understanding of the boundaries of each artform

For each of the artforms, a number of pupils commented on their increased knowledge in terms of a realisation that there was more than one way of doing art, dance, drama or music. These comments were made mainly by the younger cohort – Years 7 to 9 – perhaps indicating a wider exposure to the arts at secondary school than had been their previous experience:

Interviewer: *What have been the effects on you of doing art/dance/ drama/music?*

Before I used to think that art was just like picking up a pen and drawing it, but you've got to know a lot of terms ... not just painting. It's like there's loads of different parts, like branches out of art, and ... you have to understand all of them if you want to be an artist (Year 8, art).

It showed me there wasn't just one type of dance like I used to think. There's many different types and they come from all over the world (Year 9, dance).

We have learnt about different forms of acting. Before I came to this school, the thought of acting was just saying some other person's words, just like standing there, but there are lots of different forms of how you can interpret it like mime, freezes; you don't always need to be speaking to be acting (Year 9, drama).

... when I first came, I thought music were just about singing, not playing and everything ... (Year 7, music).

Pupils on increased knowledge and understanding of art

In total, 79 pupil comments related to a perceived increase in knowledge and understanding of art, along with its context and criticism. The majority of these (68) were concerned with a more general increase in knowledge of art – these comments being made by 44 pupils (13 pupils reiterating comments in more than one year, and four pupils making more than one comment about art in the same interview). In all the schools, art came behind music, in terms of the number of comments, for this effect, except for one school where art was slightly ahead of music. Comments increased in number with age from Year 7 to Year 9, as would be expected, but declined in Years 10 and 11.

The importance to pupils of learning about art and artists came across in many of the pupil comments, but it was clear from their discussions that its practical relevance to creative activity was also a vital consideration for pupils:

Some lessons we learn about painters and things, and I think that's important because you learn about all the different styles, but I think it's also important that you do a lot of creative work because it really loses the effect of art if you're just doing things like learning about different artists (Year 7).

Indeed, this emphasis on 'doing' art was apparent in many of the Year 7 pupil comments across all the schools. By Year 8 and 9, however, and again across all the schools, pupils' comments on increased knowledge were more focused upon 'learning about' art and individual artists in particular: '*We have learnt more about actual artists than just drawing*' (Year 8).

One contribution from a Year 9 pupil captured much of this progression in pupils' learning, indicating a sense of the importance of exposure to a wide spectrum of art, from techniques to artists, for this pupil:

I didn't know much about art before. I mean, a lot of it is in the last year and a half or so, Year 8 and 9, but in the first year, I mean, I knew about techniques, you know, you see them on art programmes, but I didn't know how to carry them out. And it's also introduced me to [Picasso]. *Like in Year 8 we had a postcard which we could draw and colour in at our discretion and, like, of a famous picture. That was the first introduction for me to Picasso, who's one of my favourite painters now who I've studied a lot of. It's introduced me to things like that* (Year 9).

By Years 10 and 11, comments related very much more to the personal level – pupils' talking about how knowledge and understanding of art impacted on their own work: '*Looking at other artists, designers, especially Alexander McRee, I am a fan of him, he has kind of, abstract kind of designs and stuff and I try to incorporate that into my style of drawing or design*' (Year 11). Obviously, this would be related to the individual preparation of coursework for GCSE, but pupils did seem to claim a more personal understanding at this age.

In general, descriptions of the effects in this subcategory indicated how pupils' increased knowledge and understanding of art related to '*more skills*', '*changing your ideas, and developing them*', and how it helped them to think about other artists and '*where they got their ideas from*'. It was apparent that two of the schools in particular took a 'research' approach to art, with pupils' perceiving this to be useful to their understanding and execution of their artistic making processes. A few comments here were made by the younger pupils, but with the majority being made by those in Years 9 to 11:

... researching on things like portraits, painters, still-life painters, expressionists... if you research, I think you will see what they have done to achieve that, I think that helps (Year 11).

———

We are looking more in-depth at different things. Obviously because we are coming up to our GCSE, we have to do a lot more work and look at it in more depth, so we have to do a lot more research, so I have learnt a lot about different artists and more how to look at things and draw things in depth and from different angles, interpret an artist's work, or something I see into my own view, like maybe taking part of somebody else's work and adding part of mine to make a new picture and things like that (Year 11).

Comments on historical and artistic context tended to reflect an increased understanding of individual artists' paintings and what those paintings are about. However, only three comments related specifically to this effect. These were made by the older pupils, in Years 10 and 11, reflecting a deeper criticism of art by this age, as well as perhaps a greater interest in an elected subject:

> *... we've gone through Van Gogh's work and studied him, all of his like pictures and how he expresses his feelings in his work* (Year 11).

> *Learning to accept new artists ... how to understand what they are trying to portray, what their painting is about* (Year 10).

In the light of the National Curriculum requirements, it is interesting that pupils did not refer specifically to the historical and artistic context of works at an earlier age.

A small number of pupils (seven) drew attention to the development of critical skills to discuss and appraise works of visual art (from both artists and classmates). This was mentioned across all the year groups, but it was apparent that some schools appeared to develop this area more than other schools. The comments tended to suggest a progression in pupils' powers of critical study from discussion of paintings at Year 7 and 8, through to discussion of their own work at Year 9, with evaluation of own and others' work by Years 10 and 11. Again, the personal dimension was emphasised in Year 11: '*... well in art you're meant to look at what other previous artists have done, but then you're meant to develop your own style from that ...*' (Year 11).

Interestingly, only one pupil commented on the transfer of understanding from artist to artist, as opposed to most other comments, which emphasised just one artist, and, typically, the transfer from that artist to their own work:

> *It has helped me understand painters and the way they have made things, point out the way they have used different methods to get that effect, so it has helped me understand some other painters* (Year 7).

That this was made by one of the younger pupils appears to show powers of criticism apparently lacking in other pupils' experience of art.

Pupils on increased knowledge and understanding of dance

Just four comments from pupils related to this overall effect. Two were about increased knowledge of specific elements or types of dance – turning, jumping, '*the five dance elements*' and Irish dancing and '*what it means*'. Another of the comments related to the study skills of recording their own compositions in diary format. Despite the smaller number of pupils taking dance, comments on the 'critical studies' approach were less evident in dance than in the other arts.

Pupils on increased knowledge and understanding of drama

Even more significant was the small number of comments relating to drama for this effect. Considering the larger number of pupils taking drama as opposed to dance, there were very few comments relating to this effect, just 13 altogether. Comments tended to be made by the older pupils, in Years 9 to 11.

Pupils from several schools talked about the relationship of drama to English, in particular with regard to Shakespeare. 'Understanding Shakespeare' meant 'understanding the language' for these pupils, which they maintained helped them to put the plays into practice in drama. Despite the potential for drama to extend pupils' critical skills as emphasised by the teachers, pupils would appear not to perceive much about this effect at all, comments referring only to a vague sense of talking about pieces of their own drama in order to *'improve it for next time'*. One pupil did, however, demonstrate a development in critical understanding of characters and texts through drama:

> *... I think I can now look at, say, a text and look at it from an actor's point of view and think about what drives the character ... instead of just looking at it and reading it through* (Year 10).

Almost all of the few comments on increased knowledge of drama and its historical and artistic context came from pupils in two of the schools. In contrast, the other three schools were conspicuous for having no comments for an increased knowledge and understanding of the dramatic artform, with two of these schools having comments relating only to critical skills and discussion for drama. In one school, this may reflect the approach taken to drama, where social and moral issues as opposed to knowledge about drama or theatre were the focus, although even here there was still only one pupil comment on the development of critical skills to discuss drama. For another of the schools, it is less clear why pupils did not refer to any increase in knowledge and understanding, except to say that changes in staffing and the school's approach to drama may have affected pupils' perceived effects.

Pupils on increased knowledge and understanding of music

In total, 106 pupil comments related to a perceived increase in knowledge and understanding of music, together with its context and criticism. The majority of these (90) were concerned with a more general increase in knowledge of music as opposed to the contextual or critical element. These more general comments were made by 50 pupils (14 pupils reiterating comments in more than one year and ten pupils making more than one comment about music in the same interview). Comments increased in number with age in the lower cohort, seeming very frequent in Year 9, but dropped off significantly in Years 10 and 11.

Mirroring the pattern observed in pupils' accounts of the effects of art, many pupils' comments demonstrated an increase in knowledge and understanding of music through activity – composition and performance. This was clear in comments from all the age groups, with a general pattern in the types of learning becoming apparent. Pupils talked about learning notes and instruments, and styles of music such as the blues in Years 7 and 8, whereas by Year 9 pupils said they learnt through composing. Year 10 and 11 comments concentrated on increased knowledge of composers and periods of western classical music, with '*dates*', '*history*' and '*theory*' being mentioned. Whereas the lower years talked about ''*sixties and swing*', Japanese and Indian music, no references to an increased knowledge in 'other musics' were reported by pupils in the GCSE years.

Despite this general trend in pupils' comments, there were some interesting school differences in the lower years. At one school in particular, Year 7 pupils' comments stood out as being about listening to and becoming familiar with musics in a wider context:

> *They've helped me to understand music more and it's helped me outside of school. And when I've listened to songs now, I pick out things that we've done in music* (Year 7).

> ____

> *I can understand the music, like the tone of it* (Year 7).

This contrasts greatly with pupils' comments from other schools, which emphasised the learning of notes and western classical terminology at Year 7. At two schools in particular, Year 7 pupils saw music as learning '*the basics, you know, what all the notes are ...*'. One pupil at one of these schools showed a deeper insight into what learning the basics might be for:

> *It gives me a lot better understanding of what music actually is. It's not just playing an instrument. There's – you can break it down – lots of different parts: singing, composing, the learning about how you make a tune or a melody, how you make a beat ...* (Year 7).

Despite many references to pop, dance and technology in music, pupils' perceived increase in knowledge of music demonstrated an apparent division between fun and what they saw as learning or study in music. Running parallel to this was also a critical distinction between the music of 'famous' musicians and pupils' own music – as distinct and separate entities:

... we had a project where we had to make a piece of music that did not make any sense. So we would like do all the skills of the keyboard and just press whatever we want. That was, in fact, quite famous – some man did it – it did not make any sense at all, just pressing keys here and there. That was quite fun as we did not study it, we just made it up as we went along (Year 9).

Although still comparatively rare, pupils' comments on an increased knowledge of the historical and artistic context of music were more numerous than those for art (eight as opposed to three), and indeed were concentrated in one school, where pupils appreciated going '*that stage deeper into it and know a bit more about the music*', and that through '*... learning the backgrounds instead of just being taught something ... you seem to have a wider view*'. One pupil said this was important because:

2. **WHAT ARE** **THE EFFECTS** **OF** **ARTS** **EDUCATION?**

If you ... in life you see this other culture and it's got a different type of music, you might not be able to understand it. Whereas [when] you learn about it through school, it helps you to understand. So you can think about it and make a decision about whether you like it or not instead of just going 'Oh, I totally hate that' (Year 9).

Knowing about the context and background to different music helped pupils' critical and judgmental development:

Interviewer: *Do you think the arts have had an influence on that development too?*

Yes, like opinions and knowing about backgrounds before you judge people, like in music I would have just judged blues as blues, I didn't know anything about it, I just knew it was blues and I knew the style of it but I didn't know anything about the background, so that's helped me (Year 9).

Comments about increased ability in critical study skills were made by six pupils for music, all from Years 9 to 11 and relating mainly to self and class evaluation of compositions:

Pupils learn how to listen to music and pick out things, good ideas and bad ideas and what they could have done better. You can develop by listening to other people's music and evaluating it (Year 9).

Indicating a similarity with art, many pupils linked this increase in knowledge and understanding to activity and being more able then to get on with their own work and creativity:

If you get to understand all the different types of music, you can put them together and make something new or if you're composing your own piece – I am – it helps [if] *you know different styles. So if you start with blues you can go into swing or something* (Year 9).

———

... we're doing the history of music this year and taking the ideas and the techniques that they've used to make our own compositions (Year 9).

Knowledge and understanding of the artform: summary

Overall, then, one of the most frequently referred to effects of arts education by pupils was the increase in knowledge and understanding of music and art in particular. There were far fewer references to comparable outcomes from dance and drama (perhaps reflecting their position within the National Curriculum), though with regard to drama, there were signs that the ideologies underpinning this subject were more hotly contested and the specific teaching approach adopted in a school largely determined the extent to which knowledge of drama and theatre was perceived to be an outcome.

In general, the majority of comments from pupils related to an increased knowledge and understanding for music and art in terms of particular styles, movements and individual artists, as opposed to their contextual, historical and critical elements. Furthermore, in both music and art, the predominant view amongst pupils was that the main effect of, and perhaps justification for, learning about different styles and artists was the influences they imparted upon pupils' own creative activities and technical skills. Thus, in music, for example, rather than describe increased knowledge of the historical context of blues music or the development of critical skills to discriminate between different exponents of blues music, pupils were more likely to report a better understanding of blues music as a style distinct from other genres, greater understanding of its prevailing 12-bar structure and the application of this increased knowledge in their own compositions and instrumental performances. In art, cubism could be substituted for blues music to provide another example of the typical types of outcomes perceived by pupils. In all the artforms, the pupil data suggested that extending arts knowledge was very activity-based and skills-based, with less emphasis on critical skills and on historical and cultural contexts.

Finally, the comments would tend to suggest a different emphasis of perceived effects from the pupil point-of-view compared with that of their teachers. While pupils saw an increase in knowledge and understanding of the artform as a direct outcome of learning in the arts, teachers tended to talk about the critical skills element of arts education; not only that, but also a different emphasis on artform – music in particular was mentioned much more frequently by the pupils than the teachers. Again, this appears to be because of the emphasis which pupils placed on knowledge and understanding – perhaps as a measurable outcome for themselves.

4.3 INTERPRETATIVE SKILLS

This subcategory on interpretative skills relates to the claims made by teachers and pupils about the development of pupils' ability to view and understand an artistic product. While the first subcategory (4.2) was intended to denote effects associated with the development of critical study skills at a general level, comments here refer specifically to the growth in capacities to interpret or 'decode' artistic products. As such, the notion of understanding the artistic processes falls into this subcategory. Teachers' and pupils' comments are discussed across all the artforms.

2.
WHAT ARE
THE EFFECTS
OF
ARTS
EDUCATION?

Teacher Perspectives

Teachers talked about pupils' developing abilities to interpret artistic products and processes. One art teacher succinctly expressed the point about reading works of art through appreciating the artistic process:

I am trying to show them that the work of a particular artist is not solely the end-product, it is the thinking behind it and the exploration and how they have arrived at that. To do that, you have got to look deeper than just the actual superficial thing that is hanging on the wall at the end (ex-head of art).

More specifically than in section 4.2, one drama teacher described this effect in the following way:

Then it is the sense of achievement when it works and the sense of achievement, for example, when we had a theatre company come in and the Year 7s who saw it would have understood. They did quite a subtle technique at the beginning, used a subtle style, and they can understand it. And they can use subject-specific words and that's good, that's clever, you know, they understand that, so there's a real boost there ...

A headteacher argued that this capacity to understand plays, once developed, would last into adult life.

One head of English focused on the demystification element of this subcategory:

It is about breaking the myths down about literature and encouraging them to have their own personal response to literature – very, very important. Giving them the confidence to be able to say 'Well I disagree with that' or 'I don't like that' or 'I think that is badly done, badly written'. To actually feel that simply because it is written on a piece of paper doesn't mean that that is absolute, you know, perfection.

Another head of English definitely linked the development of the competence to critically analyse and understand works of literature to pupils engaging in the processes of creative composition by understanding literature *'from the inside'*:

In terms of literature, it helps them to understand what literature is about by doing it themselves and by having to hone, that they know what – one labours the terms like similes and metaphors – but you hope eventually that they get the idea that the use of analogy is one of the main creative tools, that we describe one thing by another and that one hopes that they'll start to understand literature from the inside ... and to have understood it from the inside, that by doing it yourself, you understand it better, so that one hopes that when they come in Year 7 and they write trite four-lined quatrains that make no sense, that by the end of Year 7, hopefully, they've understood that poetry isn't just producing a lot of nonsense that rhymes, but that it's about expressing with originality and insight and careful choice of language what it is that one is attempting to – what one sees in the world and what one wants to say.

In contrast to the small number of comments on knowledge, understanding and critical skills, more of the comments for music related to critical listening and interpretation of music. One headteacher emphasised the effect of valuing, listening to and appreciating the work of fellow pupils. Similarly, a head of music stressed that the achievement of the aim of encouraging the enjoyment of music was dependent on enhancing young people's capacity to listen to and understand particular pieces: *'When they know more about the type of music that they are listening to, they sort of understand it more and they tolerate it.'* Another accentuated the analytical side of listening to music. Clearly, this outcome is also closely related to the development of auditory skills and abilities (see 4.5).

The claims by teachers for the types of critical skill developed in the arts – discussion and evaluation in 4.2 and interpreting and decoding in 4.3 – revealed differences by artform. It would appear that while art and drama require exploration of the process and techniques (rather than just the immediate visual experience) in order to interpret the work, for music, exploration of the context perhaps seems more important than the process in order to listen more critically.

Pupil Perspectives

Pupils' comments about interpreting artistic products and processes were fewer in number than those for knowledge and understanding described in section 4.2. There were just ten pupil comments on interpretative skills, being made by seven pupils. Nine related to interpretation of artistic products in a general way, with one on exploration of context. There were no testimonies to the development of interpretative vocabulary (as had been claimed by the some of the teachers for art in 4.2) and no comments were specifically about the artistic process. Most comments again related to music and art, with just one for drama (surprisingly few considering that the number of pupils who took drama was similar to the number taking art and music) and were again mostly from Year 9 pupils (even taking into account that two Year 9 cohorts were interviewed). No comments were made about dance for this effect.

Pupils' accounts revealed how, in a general way, observation and listening skills could be used to begin to decode works of art. The *'visual message'* of paintings and plays was emphasised by one pupil, with other comments for art relating to the development of the ability to view works of art better:

> *I have learnt to look at shape a lot more and also in pictures, so I can kind of look at them and work out what the artist has been doing and can look at the mood of pictures a lot better now, I think* (Year 9).

For music, pupils' comments tended to be more about interpretation through thinking (*'concentration'*) and imagination (*'... we had to close our eyes and say what it made us feel ...'*) so that they could then create their own compositions.

Two particularly insightful comments were made about interpretation – one for each of art and drama. A Year 9 pupil mentioned how you have to *'read between the lines'* in order to interpret what a poem might mean for drama, while for art, a Year 7 pupil demonstrated that an interpretative 'vocabulary' need not necessarily be verbal, and may indeed involve other skills:

> *... normally I go to a lot of galleries – the Tate and places like that. When you look at the pictures that are on the walls, you can read them like a book. You can read a picture and what it is telling you* (Year 7).

Interpretative skills: summary

Pupils' comments about being able to interpret the arts, then, focused on visual critique for art and drama, and on imagination and listening with concentration for music. Unlike the teachers, pupils made little direct connection to the artistic processes underlying the finished product, except perhaps for in visual art.

4.4 APPRECIATION OF THE ARTFORM AND AESTHETIC JUDGEMENT-MAKING

This subcategory was used to collate references to the impact of arts education on artistic discernment, aesthetic judgement and the encouragement of positive attitudes towards the arts. Naturally, there were obvious links to the development of a deeper understanding of the arts. There were, however, different emphases given to it by teachers and pupils, and particular differences between art and music in the 'types' of appreciation and judgement-making.

4.4.1 Extending appreciation and encouraging positive attitudes towards the arts

Teacher Perspectives

Many teachers talked about encouraging positive attitudes in the arts and also the impact of the arts on general artistic appreciation. Such effects were variously described:

> *When you think that we have pupils who have left here now, who have seen an artist in residence; they have been out, they have worked on sculptures, out in the car park. I mean ten years ago they would have walked the other way or thrown a brick at it probably* [laughter]. *No, that is an exaggeration, but that sort of transformation of appreciation of others, of the arts* (deputy head, i/c pastoral).

> *I think what's gained is that pupils, again it's an appreciation, it's not just a mechanical thing of drawing, as it's not just a mechanical thing of composing. We teach them how to appreciate pieces of artwork, whether it be music or drama, and I think it would be quite nice to get that into the curriculum; you know, appreciation of art ... the appreciation, which really is one of the most important things* (head of music).

For an adviser, encouraging appreciation of the arts inevitably entailed giving young people access to the arts and artists, both as audience members and by creating themselves:

> *Unless we as teachers and advisory teachers can help them to understand the conventions of dance* [for example], *of how dance actually works, then they have no way of entering into it. It is literally a closed book to them; they can't read it. Consequently, I*

suspect they may be turned off it, until they can come at it in a different way. So, it is trying to create, through the understanding of the various artforms, a way in which youngsters can be receptive to those artforms, so they can actually make meaning from them, they can actually enter them ... by talking to artists, by interviewing artists, by having works mediated for them by experts. The youngsters can enter in the discourse, they can see what is going on, they can understand what the artist was trying to do. Of course, once you can begin to do that, it becomes part of you, it becomes part of your own artistic endeavour, but at the same time allows you then ... it opens up the whole world of the arts, it gives you that, it gives you an access to artforms.

2.
WHAT ARE
THE EFFECTS
OF
ARTS
EDUCATION?

Several teachers independently recounted how when teachers and pupils work together in a creative enterprise, a certain moment can sometimes occur when all the participants instinctively know that whatever it is they are producing could not be bettered. This aesthetic experiential sense was described as acquiring a form of artistic appreciation when things are right:

That there is an appreciation of what good arts practice is about, when you have that moment when you just know it couldn't be better, the kids know it and you know it, that something really good has happened (deputy head i/c curriculum).

Hence, it is the appreciation of the aesthetic, as well as the arts, which is the purported outcome. This point is taken up by a drama teacher, when describing the impact s/he is attempting to achieve:

If you like, to open up their soul and find out what is in it. That is what I am looking to do in teaching arts subjects: to get them to look deeper than the surface and find out what is really underneath and to appreciate things that are good, and to quote Keats, good and beautiful.

Other interviewees talked about the effect of developing an aesthetic awareness. An art teacher, for example, saw the fostering of a general aesthetic sense as a key outcome of an 'arts' education:

Recognising, I like to think, good design, appreciating architecture, film, anything like that and without a decent arts education you are not going to do that.

And from a head of a department for Welsh:

[The arts] give children an appreciation and an understanding of what is valuable, other than making money if you like, because very often it's difficult to – it gives people an understanding of aesthetic work, aesthetic value, or what the value of the aesthetic [is].

Taken as a whole such comments indicated very much the aesthetic nature of an arts education, and how it is that teachers try to achieve that for their pupils. As we shall see, it is interesting that the pupils hardly commented on an aesthetic education, except perhaps for the couple of comments relating aesthetics to personal development.

Pupil Perspectives

Like the teachers' comments on appreciation and aesthetic judgements in the arts, pupils' comments also covered a broad spectrum – from a straightforward 'liking' and 'appreciation' of the subject or artform without any connection to aesthetic judgement-making, to those comments that linked appreciation to understanding of the context and techniques involved and the necessary powers of criticism to make value judgements. Some of the ways in which pupils talked about appreciation varied with artform, and these are detailed in section 4.4.2.

Extending appreciation of the arts

Overall, 66 pupil comments related to the extension of appreciation of the arts. These were made by 39 pupils, just eight of whom were boys. As a percentage of the total number of boys in the sample, this constitutes a smaller percentage than that for girls' appreciation of the arts (13 per cent as opposed to 20 per cent). Most of the comments related to music and art (22 and 21 respectively), and were again surprisingly low for drama (just four comments). Overall, however, this was a fairly large subcategory, with 16 comments also about the arts in general. Comments were most numerous in Years 7 and 11, and were also high in Year 9 (although the latter was not significant as a proportion of the year groups overall). Indeed, of most significance was the frequency of comments for music at Year 11 for this category, suggesting a greater appreciation of music with age and also by those choosing to do music. This begs the question as to whether the appreciation of music is perhaps perceived by pupils to require higher levels of knowledge and understanding, or perhaps musical ability. (Why the other artforms have so few comments for appreciation at key stage 4 appears a significant anomaly requiring further consideration.) The high proportion of comments on a greater appreciation of the arts in general at Year 7 suggests an enthusiasm for the arts during the first year of secondary school. Further study would be useful here to determine whether this is a new enthusiasm, perhaps compared with pupils' primary school experience, or an extended appreciation because of pupils' Year 7 experience.

The reported extension of appreciation of the arts was spread equally across the schools, with the exception of one school where comments on appreciation were extremely few in number across all the artforms.

Although this school displayed the greatest enjoyment amongst pupils for music especially, it would appear that pupils either did not, or were unable to, articulate appreciation here. That this school took a very lively and 'popular' approach to music begins to suggest that it could be that pupils link 'appreciation of the arts' to something more distant, more historic, being able to appreciate something that is less relevant to their interests (for example, classical as opposed to popular music).

Some pupils talked about a straightforward 'liking' of one of the artforms and its components, comparing this to their own experience where they had not previously appreciated it:

2.
WHAT ARE
THE EFFECTS
OF
ARTS
EDUCATION?

> *Then in terms of music I think that it's helped me appreciate music a lot more because before school, before high school I didn't listen to that much music but now, since then, I've developed, I listen to a lot more music, I'm a lot more knowledgeable about music and I've developed my own tastes in it* (Year 11).

Others referred to a general increased interest in both music and art, as opposed to finding the arts boring. Pupils from all the year groups commented on this, and many linked this new interest to increased understanding of techniques in particular, and '*getting into it*'. Others referred to appreciation as a recognition of the effort or hard work that had gone into an artistic product, or appreciation through understanding, but there were clear artform differences here (these are discussed below).

Most comments on enhanced appreciation related to 'other artists' works', with just one of the 39 pupils mentioning other pupils' work:

> *... seeing other people's work, like the older pupils in the school, it's really good 'cos you see some of their work on the walls and around the school and you think 'Wow, that's really good, I wish I could do something like that'. And you just try really hard in art lessons. And if you do try, sometimes it just comes out ... and you're just good at it* (Year 7).

However, as to whether the displays of work helped their understanding or judgement in art elicited a fairly non-committal response: '*A little bit, but I don't really think it sort of shows me how the world works.*'

A few of the comments displayed a real personal insight into enhanced appreciation, demonstrating the way in which arts education increased a personal accessibility to the arts. One pupil thought '*they* [the arts] *were for other people's pleasure, like the famous artists, they do their art and it's there for other people to buy or to look at*' but then explained how that view had changed through doing art at school. Just one of the pupil comments corroborated the pleasure and love of the arts seemingly with as much enthusiasm as the teachers of art and literature did above:

> ... I just love every piece of art I see – it can be the most boring art, it can be the most down. I just love it, it uplifts me, it makes me so happy because someone is drawing for the enjoyment of others (Year 9, art).

Enhancing positive attitudes towards the arts

This enthusiasm towards the arts was coded as an enhanced positive attitude for seven of the pupil comments. These were made by six pupils, all girls, and all related to art except for one on drama. These are expanded below under appreciation of art. We can note that some of the comments were akin to an increased motivation or inspiration, one girl talking about being '*inspired to do art for my options again*' and relating this to her personal development and maturity. Indeed, interestingly, a few of the pupils related appreciation of the arts to their own personal development, concurring that '*it shows what kind of person you are*' and that '*it helps you to become more rounded*'.

4.4.2 Appreciation and aesthetic judgement-making by artform

Teacher Perspectives

Extending appreciation and developing aesthetic judgements in art

Comments in this subcategory were comparatively frequent and they focused on the development of aesthetic judgements through widening pupils' experience, awareness and appreciation of the visual arts. Typical contributions from three different art teachers were:

> They have fairly fixed, traditional ideas about what they think good art is and what they think bad art is, so it is breaking down the prejudices as far as they are concerned.

> Sometimes they would say 'I don't think that is as good as that' and you say 'Why not?' and they say 'Because that is messy and that is actually beautifully drawn', and then you can go into 'Well you know there are reasons why that is good and that isn't' ... I think that they absorb such a lot.

> I try to get them to have that love of looking at works of art.

Extending appreciation and developing aesthetic judgements in dance

Only one interviewee offered a comment which was vaguely relevant to this subcategory. In contrast to the corresponding contributions for art (given above), which were specifically concerned with enhancing aesthetic judgement-making, the following comment is limited to promoting awareness and appreciation only in the most general of senses:

> *The main objective was to make people more aware, make people more aware of dance in its own right ...* [The outcomes are] *... more awareness primarily, hopefully more understanding of where they sit, not literally, but where they are within the world of the arts: whether or not they feel that their own involvement is perhaps going to the theatre, opening their eyes to productions and performances out of school, or whether or not that is something that they actually feel that they want to take away and they want to improve and they want to develop within themselves* (dance and PE teacher).

However, it is important to recognise here that dance as an artform has a much more precarious status in the curriculum than the other main artforms. As this interviewee went on to argue, it can be an outcome itself to get pupils to appreciate that dance is an artform, not merely '*a PE activity*':

> *The biggest thing that I want to get through is allowing every pupil ... the ability to develop movement potential; develop an appreciation of the artform, in that way; develop dance not as a PE activity, but as an activity that develops in its own right as complementary to other artforms. So that is my main objective* (dance and PE teacher).

Extending appreciation and developing aesthetic judgements in drama

One interviewee expressed this type of outcome as an aim: '*I want them to have an appreciation and to be able to be analytical about the things that they come across in terms of drama.*' One drama teacher's reference to the claimed effect of making pupils more discerning and discriminating has already been given, especially with regard to television (see 4.2). Another drama teacher in a different school also attempted to engender an aesthetic sense through television drama:

> *I tend to start with television because that is what they know, isn't it? That is their form of theatre. When they do go to the theatre, they are constantly blown away ... and they are so impressed by everything, by the seats ... the aesthetic tends to be learnt from school productions, and the appreciation of drama like that. In key stage 4, when they go out to the theatre and see other experts, they appreciate* [the form].

In addition, a music teacher pointed to the effect of encouraging pupils to appreciate drama and theatre as an artform.

2.
WHAT ARE
THE EFFECTS
OF
ARTS
EDUCATION?

Extending appreciation and developing aesthetic judgements in literature

Over and above the earlier extract on the development of personal responses to literature, there was only one other comment relevant to this subcategory and it was made by the same head of English:

> *I hope that they will leave with a love of the arts and that they will continue to follow that through in all sorts of different ways. That they won't be afraid to go and see a play ... and that they will go away independent and inquisitive readers.*

Extending appreciation and developing aesthetic judgements in music

The appreciation of music was cited as an effect, though, interestingly, generally without the references to the development of critical and aesthetic judgement-making evident in art and drama, for example:

> *Basically to provide pupils with an understanding of what's gone before them, so to have an awareness of the culture within music, so at the end of the day, even if they don't do any playing in school at all and they don't perform in any shows, musicals, they don't do any dance, that they go away being able to appreciate music* (head of music).

In one school, where the music department had worked very hard at demonstrating to pupils that music at school could incorporate students' own musical preferences and styles, there was the recognition that in order to extend pupils' appreciation of music, teachers needed to show first that they could appreciate the music pupils brought with them to school. Consequently, a perceived effect was the dismantling of the perception that school music equated with classical or traditional music: 'We seem to have broken the barrier in school, that music is a cool thing to do, music is a cool place to hang out ...' (music teacher).

Encouraging a sense of inspiration and motivation in the artform

As an extension to the notion of knowledge, understanding and appreciation precipitating a positive attitude to the arts, some teachers alluded to a consequential effect of increased motivation and inspiration on the part of pupils. In the words of one interviewee, pupils can become 'fired up'; words like 'inspiration', 'interest' and 'involvement' as outcomes were volunteered by many teachers. For example, an art teacher in an all-girls school remarked:

> *I think that arts education means a lot to me because I can see the influence over 28 years that I have had on different girls – the commitment, motivation, enthusiasm and skill that can be brought out of people.*

Several teachers pointed to the effect of pupils being inspired to achieve higher standards rather than accept just satisfactory levels of performance. Raising aspirations was seen as a necessary outcome prior to attaining higher levels of achievement. Others described it as the promotion of a positive and ambitious *'can do'* mentality in the arts. In English, the motivation to want to write better and effectively was seen as revolving around *'a love of the creative power of language'*. Furthermore, a deputy head described the arts' impact in terms of the constant drive to improve and reach higher:

> *In art, they say 'Well yes, this is interesting, you are working well here, have you thought about ...?' So, it is not 'That's good, fine, it's finished' – it is about the working on, working to improve whatever you have got.*

As well as inspiring individuals, a deputy head underlined the importance of having an impact on peer group cultures, if young people are to be able to engage enthusiastically in the arts without the ridicule and censure of their friends:

> *They do take part in leisure activities that directly relate to the arts now; we are talking about 13-year-olds who will go away and be a member of an art club. It is not frowned upon now. That is so important for kids of this age: if anything has not got the street cred or makes you look a swat, or whatever today's word is, yes that is right. If being an artist, or having art in your bedroom when your friends come around, or having anything like that, doesn't have that, 'Oh well, I am not going to take them upstairs because that is where I have been doing this work'. If people have the confidence to be like that now at 13, that is the important thing; if it is cool, it is ... and it is. I would never have thought that transformation could have taken place in [pupil X], but it has.*

This observation echoes the earlier comment on the way in which changes have been brought about so that *'music is a cool place to hang out'*.

It seems, then, that teachers talked about appreciation of the arts, as both an appreciation of the aesthetic, and as a motivating force for pupils – to either transform their attitudes or to inspire them to become involved.

Pupil Perspectives

Extending appreciation and developing aesthetic judgements in art

As has already been noted, quite a number of pupils recognised the effort, ability and hard work that had gone into a work of art, and this was in particular relation to visual art. Some comments were, in general, a tokenistic acknowledgement of the hard work needed to produce a 'good' piece: '*I now think that painting there looks really hard to paint*' or '*I thought it was easy just because I was good at it. There is a lot more work which needs to be put into it ...*' One comment, however, illustrated the effect of a more direct sensory experience on appreciation of effort and hard work, which appeared for this pupil to be quite special:

> *Art, sometimes because you go into an art gallery and it is just quiet because people are just spellbound by the work, because some paintings take an awful long time to make, and you just think this is all worthwhile, because if you just throw something on to a piece of paper willy-nilly ... it just does not look right* (Year 7).

For one pupil, this greater appreciation of effort in art was qualified by the condition that the viewer should be able to understand the artistic product – it should be accessible. This was important as it demonstrated a more critical judgement of the effort portrayed in the painting or work of visual art:

> *But when you see pictures, like, dots on the paper, dots inside a square on a piece of paper, some people say 'That is a wonderful piece of art, you are expressing yourself', but to us children that is a load of rubbish ... because we don't see how anyone could have spent ... well maybe the artist had a different opinion or it had a very deep meaning for them, but nobody else can understand it. We like the ones that, not tell a story, but actually show a lot of effort, you can see that a lot of effort ... like the ones on the walls. We don't see how a square can represent a life* (Year 7).

This comment was made by a Year 7 pupil, and perhaps illustrated that it can be difficult for younger pupils to appreciate something they find hard to understand or that they do not like. It could be the case that with age and increased understanding, pupils come to empathise with the artist and so extend their appreciation of art, as a Year 10 comment (from a pupil at the same school as the example above) would suggest:

> [talking about art] *... as I'm doing my work and doing projects, I sort of understand how much hard work goes behind like a really brilliant painting that, say, Van Gogh has done, or the Mona Lisa. I can understand that there's a lot of preparation while they were doing that, instead of just a great artist 'doing it' and becoming famous. [I] have worked much harder, because I'm working harder; it's like I've stepped into their shoes, if you like, and I understand them a bit more* (Year 10).

This type of appreciation through empathy was mentioned by other pupils also at this school, one pupil's view of art as '*a load of rubbish and stuff'* changing when they could see how the artist *'feels and why they do it ...'* (This kind of transformation of opinion is similar to that put forward for art by one of the deputy heads earlier.) That not more pupils articulated such a viewpoint with age implies that an increased appreciation with understanding in art can only be a tentative suggestion.

Six pupil comments related more specifically to an enhanced positive attitude towards art. These were all made by girls from just two of the schools. Taken together with appreciation of art, it was clear that one school inspired appreciation amongst its pupils more so than the other schools. A few of the girls described their positive attitudes in terms of enthusiasm, one stressing the importance of the opportunity for art when *'young and you start off experiencing what they're doing ...'*, and another explaining the importance of her Year 11 experience:

> *It's made me more enthusiastic about art; I am definitely taking it up in college. I wasn't going to because I thought ... well I am good but I wouldn't do it, but I really, really want to do it now. Yes, Year 11 has shown me that I can just sit there and do art and I want to learn more; I want to do it for a longer time* (Year 11).

However, for this pupil, enthusiasm was also balanced out with the proviso that the arts (drama) *'take a lot of hard work and dedication'*.

Overall, pupils saw aesthetic judgements in art as being about discerning how much effort, ability and hard work had gone into a piece of artwork. There were no apparent patterns with age, one pupil making similar comments about aesthetic judgements in art in all three years of key stage 3. Generally, there were only a few alternatives to the view that to count as good, a work of art should be the result of considerable effort and ability: in addition to the pupil quoted above, who added the criterion that a work of art needed to be understandable, one pupil commented on understanding the value in a product in terms of qualities conveying a sense of 'beauty':

> *You can see something ... someone might say that's hideously ugly, and you can think 'it might be ugly, but it's beautiful at the same time'. It's nice in its own little way. That type of thing* (Year 10).

Extending appreciation and developing aesthetic judgements in dance

The two pupils commenting on appreciation of dance (accounting for just seven per cent of all those pupils taking dance) referred only to a very general increased interest in dance. This was because of a broader exposure to dance – both on the television and through appreciating *'more* [things] *than I did before'*. Like the teacher comments for dance, there were no pupil comments on aesthetic values or criticism in dance.

Extending appreciation and developing aesthetic judgements in drama

There were just four comments from pupils on increased appreciation of the dramatic artform – a very small number considering the total number who took drama at school. The pupils were from just two of the schools, with the appreciation of effort and ability coming across in two of the comments, again, from the same school as highlighted above for art:

> *It is a lot of hard work, especially as I have been in two productions since I have been here. It shows you – you look at other pieces of drama on the stage very differently because you know what goes on backstage and you know all the hard work which has been put into it. So you look at it in a different perspective, you know how much work has been put in to get it to that standard* (Year 9).

Appreciation of the techniques used in drama was mentioned by one pupil, but this comment does not really display the type of analytical critique claimed by one of the drama teachers above:

> *Oh, how to really portray yourself as somebody else, like it used to be just changing your voice, but now it's like trying to change your features as well, and walking like them and looking through them, like if you were them. It has made me a lot more appreciative of different actors and things, like the way they can just jump from one person to another without blinking. Although it must take them ages to practice and things* (Year 7).

Indeed, making value judgements about the dramatic artform was hardly mentioned by pupils, who referred only to a very general ability to say whether something was '*good or bad acting*'.

Extending appreciation and developing aesthetic judgements in music

In contrast to the emphasis on appreciating effort and ability in works of visual art, appreciation through understanding was mentioned with particular frequency in relation to music. One pupil articulated this understanding as being much better than just being able to listen to a piece of music:

> *I think it's really just learning to appreciate music – all of it is – you learn to pick up; I mean, it's really good just listening to a piece of music, enjoying it for what it is, but it's something different when you can just analyse it, you know what's going on. You can say 'Oh I know what key that is, I know what the composer has tried to do there'. It's good to go that stage deeper into it and know a bit more about the music* (Year 11).

At odds with the teachers' viewpoints, this comment was very much about analytical skills and appreciation through understanding, as opposed to a general aesthetic appreciation suggested by the teachers. It could be possible that the teachers would tend to illustrate appreciation and aesthetic judgements as being within the capacity of all pupils, while pupils may perhaps feel they can appreciate music only when they understand it at this deeper level.

Another individual took the notion of listening to music a stage deeper by likening it to 'experiencing the music'. This pupil talked about appreciation of the arts through increased sensitisation, discussing listening for patterns in music and looking for techniques in art. Indeed, he made quite a significant statement on the differences between art and music, saying that in art at a young age (Year 8) you can look at paintings but not yet experience them, but that in music, through sensitisation with understanding and imagination *'you begin to almost experience the music, rather than just listening to it'*.

In particular relation to music (over and above other artforms) were a fair number of comments on increased appreciation of a broader repertoire of works. Most of these comments were volunteered by pupils in Year 11, and most were about appreciation of a wider range of styles through listening. One pupil talked about this as an increased *'confidence to listen to new pieces of music and not just stick with my style'*. The emphasis on the teenage preference for pop tunes was clear, with pupils now claiming that they *'don't just listen to pop tunes; you can listen to other things and appreciate them'*.

Alongside the ability to appreciate a wider repertoire, accommodation of pupils' own tastes in music featured highly in their comments at Year 11, combining their knowledge and understanding with their own discrimination and aesthetic preferences:

> *Then in terms of music I think that it's helped me appreciate music a lot more because before school, before high school, I didn't listen to that much music but now, since then, I've developed, I listen to a lot more music, I'm a lot more knowledgeable about music and I've developed my own tastes in it* (Year 11).

In contrast to the aesthetic values in art being based on judgements of effort by pupils, comments for music were even more tenuous – just a description of what they were hearing. It was clear that both types of judgements were based on the immediate sensory experience for these pupils, what you see for art, and what you hear for music. One pupil's discussion, however, stood out as being particularly discerning about the nature of musical performance:

... I look at the music more; it sounds really weird but they always seem to have like a different meaning each time. I don't know, it's hard to explain, probably just like the emotion in a song; that's what I've learnt the most this year ... (Year 11).

This demonstrated an understanding that music can change each time it is performed, and although not directly articulated, it illustrated an insight into the nature of music as different to art – where the product stays the same each time you look at it, although the aesthetic response might change. No pupils referred directly to the nature of the arts in this way, though.

Appreciation and aesthetic judgement-making: summary

In general, then, pupils talked about appreciation of effort and ability that other artists put into their work, and acknowledged the hard work needed to make a good product. Appreciation of a broader repertoire was emphasised for both music and art, even if the artistic work was not liked. Aesthetic judgements and values were again based on effort in art, while for music, aesthetics were more a general description of sensory experience. Comparatively few pupils testified to extensions of appreciation or aesthetic judgement-making in connection with drama and dance. In all artforms, pupils rarely mentioned the point of aesthetic education as propounded by the teachers. Similarly, while the teachers emphasised appreciation and aesthetic judgement-making as being accessible to all, pupils linked appreciation of both art and music to being able to understand the product in front of them. This final point was also put forward by one of the employers interviewed. When asked what an arts education was for, he suggested that it was to do with appreciation, but that '*if you don't read, you can't read a good book. If you don't understand art, and appreciate it, then you can't enjoy that part of what life offers, if you like.*' Another employer talked about the main outcomes of arts education as being about '*appreciation and awareness of some of the finer things in life, in other words the things that you'd enjoy if you had the time*'. Thus, the second-order intrapersonal effects of enjoyment through appreciation and understanding appeared important to these employers – not necessarily that these would transfer to the work place, but rather that they could be an important part to an overall lifestyle – either whilst at school, or at work.

4.4.3   Fostering awareness of cross-arts continuities and differences

Teacher Perspectives

The effects of cross-arts work were discussed by teachers and a few pupils. For some teachers, the effects of engaging in several artforms or participating in integrated arts programmes could be greater than the sum of the individual artform parts. This is a potentially very significant point for the research and one that will need to be borne in mind when considering the effectiveness of teaching and learning in the arts. Are certain outcomes most attainable through, if not dependent on, pupils taking several different artform programmes or some type of integrated or cross-arts projects? This music teacher appeared to think so:

> *I think that we get a lot of pupils, I think, in here that are immersed, very much, in the arts; they don't just specialise. We do get a lot of ... crossing between the two or between the three and because of that I really do think that they become very individual. We do get pupils more individual and they do pick up certain subjects specifically, but I think if you talk about what the arts are doing for the pupils as people, not just knowledge-wise, actually doing for them as people, it very much crosses across all through* [the arts].

2.
WHAT ARE
THE EFFECTS
OF
ARTS
EDUCATION?

The following is an example of the kind of project that was seen as offering such effects:

> *Then the whole thing became such a synthesis of ideas. Me and* [x] *put ideas forward and then we got some of the other pupils composing some computer music. We set up a couple of computers in there that were running continuous loops. Then we actually set speakers under the audience so that it was running their music as the play was going on. It became such an absolute ... I remember sitting back and thinking 'This is such a brilliant synthesis of all the arts; if you could video this and package this, you could sell this to anybody who wants to come in and say "What does arts do in school and how does it come in from the community?"' It started off with this sort of strange play that they were reading and it became something so completely different in many ways* (music teacher).

A head of music maintained that the effect of nurturing cross-artform perceptions was better achieved through a department rather than a faculty structure:

> *It enables them to see* [links across the arts] *... in order to see the links between artforms, which we feel are important, and hence our collaborative approach at certain times. In order to see those links, kids have got to see the differences and appreciate the difference between a performing subject like drama or discussing and performing, a performing and listening subject like music, a practical hands-on subject like art or sculpting – whatever – the more physical side of dance and so on. If they are to begin to understand the commonality, the themes, the themes of approaches, perceptions within those subjects, they have got to see the differences first.*

A drama teacher in another school (with an arts faculty) also emphasised the value of perceiving the differences, as well the similarities, between different artforms: '*So I think an arts faculty has to work very, very hard for the shared experience, whilst really appreciating the differences.*'

Pupil Perspectives

There were just four comments by pupils about cross-arts awareness – interestingly one for each artform, and from a variety of schools. The use of cross-arts in productions was highlighted for drama, emphasising how all pupils' skills can be used:

> *Well, it shows all areas of the arts really, doesn't it? Because you've got the band, and you listen to them and think 'Oh, I wish I could do that!' And there's all the lighting. People who aren't all that interested in drama and stuff, they still get to do the productions 'cos they help with the lighting and the people who like art do all the scenery and set work* (Year 7).

Another comment linked the similarities of dance and acting through movement, while another pupil talked about making use of different sensory areas than you would normally use in art by combining it with music: '*listen to music and draw what you are thinking.*'

While the effects of cross-arts were identified more strongly by the teachers than the pupils, it was clear that pupils appreciated the arts in very many general and specific ways. However, this whole subcategory was open to many pupil-specific differences and deeper insights, with no obvious progression of appreciation with age. Perhaps of most significance was the stress put on appreciation with understanding by the pupils – not specifically mentioned by the teachers. Also uncorrelated and of similar impact was the teachers' claimed effect of aesthetic education, not articulated by the pupils.

4.5 DEVELOPMENTS IN TECHNICAL SKILLS AND CAPABILITIES FOR EACH ARTFORM

Having outlined the developments in knowledge, understanding and appreciation of the arts, we now turn to a subcategory that focuses on the development of technical skills, both in the arts in general and for each artform.

Teacher Perspectives

Teachers on developing technical skills and competence in the arts

Although this subcategory was created to allow for the possibility that interviewees may cite the development of technical skills which were unique to the arts as distinct from individual artforms, in practice, none materialised that could not be assigned to the latter. However, an important point made about most of the artforms is worth making here: many of the teachers interviewed were of the opinion that the development of skills was frequently a necessary precursor to the achievement of other 'second-order' outcomes such as heightened self-esteem (see section 8.3) and improved competency in expressive skills (see section 7.5). The following comment from a deputy head touches on this theme:

> *It should enable children to understand how it is they can express themselves or an idea or a feeling in a different format, in a visual format or in a musical format, and that by learning the skills of painting, of drawing, of reading music, of playing an instrument, of being able to sing or dance, you are developing yourself and developing your ability to express yourself or an idea – whatever – in that format.*

Teachers on developing technical skills and competence in art

Most teachers of art affirmed that the acquisition of skills was a crucial outcome in their subject and that technical skills were gained and improved upon. Several of the most frequently mentioned skills included manipulative skills, motor skills, awareness of form, space, shape, light, tone, texture, colour and skills of observation.

Selecting the appropriate skills to focus upon as learning outcomes appeared to be related to a set of judgements about such factors as the relevance of skills to different age groups, pupils' previous experiences in art, and differentiation according to ability:

> *In early primary, one of the very, if you like, mechanistic values of painting, drawing and three-dimensional work – it develops motor skills.*

> ___

> *I do quite a lot of tonal drawing and they do quite a lot of work in that. I start with that in the first year because I find that junior schools don't appear to have done any of that. That is something that I flog a bit in the first year. It is important.*

> ___

> *Less able pupils tend to stay at the first stage of this learning base; more able ones go off on a tangent.*

As indicated above, for several teachers, the teaching and learning of techniques and skills were about offering an empowerment to children, equipping them to achieve other outcomes. Technical skills were seen as enabling pupils by providing them with '*building blocks*':

We then provide them with a range of skills in order that they can respond in a visual sense to that sensitivity. Then we give them the opportunity to be able to use those ... facilities to operate in a creative way.

———

The technical skills [side] is also very important as well, because that gives them the ability to do that [i.e. be creative].

———

2.
WHAT ARE
THE EFFECTS
OF
ARTS
EDUCATION?

So that colour mixing and being confident about paint – it is about techniques, simple techniques that are magic when you know how to do them ... it was one of those 'Oh, Miss I know how to do this now'. Then each week it is reinforcing what you learnt the last week so you haven't forgotten ... I love the excitement that is generated by something like that happening. They are all going 'That's a really super lesson, Miss. I really learnt'. We sometimes say to them 'Do you think you have learnt anything today?' They say 'I know how to make noses now' or 'How do you make a hand look like it is? Oh, is that what you do?'. You know, 'You go home and you do it for homework, you do three of them and then usually you know how to do it'. So it is to do with empowerment, but it is to do with gaining massive amounts of confidence straightaway when they say that they can't do it and then they can. So I believe, very much, in showing people really how; I don't leave them to find out for themselves.

Teachers on developing technical skills and competence in dance

The only significant reference to the development of technical skills came from this dance/drama teacher:

By the end of key stage 3 ... they know dance terms, they know skills, they know unison, they know where they should use those in a dance, they can create a dance and then what they can do is tell you how they have done it ... it is quite technical when you think about it, to deconstruct work that you have created and say why you have done that when you are 13 years old.

This suggests a design and planning approach in dance, combining choreography with composition and contributing to the acquisition of dance skills. A small handful of responses from dance teachers also talked about the effect that dance has on developing movement, coordination, endurance and strength. One described this as developing knowledge about *'how to treat bodies'*.

Teachers on developing technical skills and competence in drama

Most of the drama teachers volunteered the acquisition of skills as an outcome of their teaching. Although there was a noticeable reticence about using the term 'theatrical skills', by far the most common reference to outcomes associated with skills was 'performance skills'. Examples included:

> *One is the performance skills, because when it comes down to it, [drama and dance] are performance subjects and to give, not just pupils but anyone, the skills in which to perform confidently [is important] ... I feel that they need to have those skills to make sure that the product is worth presenting. I think that that then feeds back and makes my job easier, in fact, because if pupils are performing in different areas and other people are watching when they come to the lessons, then there is an expectation and there is a level of commitment and a standard that they then aim at. I don't have to keep reinforcing it; it is already there.*

> *I also over the years have realised the enormous responsibility you have, as soon as you put your pupils on the stage. You're not doing them a favour if they're not performing well, and that's important to teach them those skills.*

> *In the end, what the kids can achieve is very, very meaningful performance.*

One teacher volunteered that '*we do teach theatre skills*', but qualified it by adding that this was only to a limited extent and that they were not taught in isolation, but as part of topics on substantive themes. Another teacher also pointed to both theatrical skills and dramatic techniques as important outcomes: '*how we put the words on the stage, how we structure things, the different techniques that we use to get that across*'. Another identified the ability to write a play: '*Well there are the technical skills that if they wanted to make a play at any point in the rest of their lives, they could do so.*'

Teachers on developing technical skills and competence in literature

There was only one reference to any claimed effects on technical skills that were perceived to have any relevance to the processes of creative composition in English:

> [When discussing skills in grammar and punctuation] *I think those secretarial skills are very, very central to creativity, because they help to clarify and language is not just a mish-mash of half-expressed utterances – if you haven't got the correct word and you haven't got the right punctuation, really you can't express and very often the finest, say, with a Larkin poem within the complexity of the syntax and so on is something that allows the poem to hang together ... the school inspection brought this up; she said that we are very good on the secretarial things* (head of English).

Interestingly, apart from this comment, there were no references to technical skills associated with the actual processes involved in the making and invention of text, compared, for example, with those identified for art.

Teachers on developing technical skills and competence in music

Numerous purported outcomes in technical skills were identified for music: learning to play musical instruments, notation, keyboard skills, pitch, rhythm, compositional skills and performance skills. Others included: learning to read music, musical form, percussion, coordination, dexterity and auditory skills.

As was evident in the art teachers' responses, many music teachers also seemed to adhere to the principle of building up the technical skills gradually and progressively to facilitate the achievement of other 'second-order' effects, such as self-expression and creativity:

> So what I do is to try to expose them to, like, simple things, like the concepts of pitch and rhythm – things like that. So eventually, I am leading them to self-expression, but not in the first term of Year 7.

There were, however, suggestions that not all teachers of music were comfortable with a view of curriculum progression which meant that creativity and self-expression were postponed until minimum standards of technical skills had been achieved. An alternative approach to the sequencing of learning outcomes was offered by one interviewee:

> Pupils pick up the technical skills through the activity in many respects. I tend to teach technique and knowledge, if you like, on a very much on a need-to-know basis (deputy head).

Overall, then, teachers reported the development of technical skills as important to their artform, and that such skills could lead to other developments in expression and creativity, and enhancing pupils' self-esteem. In both art and music, technical skills were seen as the main building blocks, but developments in these were not seen as a barrier or essential precursor to creativity and self-expression. The development of dramatic techniques and performance skills were emphasised in drama, but there appeared to be few significant comments about technical developments and skills for dance. As dance was often part of the PE curriculum, perhaps it was the case that such skills were not seen as significant developments for pupils; rather, that a more general development in movement and motor skills was mentioned.

Pupil Perspectives

While the development of technical skills and competence appeared to be very much specific to each artform from the teachers' point of view, it was possible from the pupils' comments to form an overall picture of skill acquisition in general, and to draw out trends by year group as to how pupils perceived the effects of arts education on their development of technical skills. Other specific types of technical skill development varied with artform and age, with some interesting school differences, and these will be discussed later.

Skill acquisition in the arts – in general ways

Pupils talked about the acquisition of skills in various ways. Overall there were 340 comments under the subcategory of general skill acquisition, making it a very large coded item. Quite a number of these comments were general references to having learnt '*more skills*', but they also included references to:

- the elements/components or *building blocks* of the artform;

- techniques;

- approaches and methods;

- using different media; and

- designing and planning.

Many of the pupils' comments on general skill acquisition referred to the elements or components that made up the building blocks of the artform, upon which techniques were built. However, most of these comments referred simply to 'learning about' rather than 'learning how to', in terms of technical skills. This was particularly the case for music, where pupils talked about learning '*notes*' and '*rhythm*'.

Some pupils talked about the techniques used in the different artforms, for example learning how to do brush painting or mix colours in art, and freeze-frames in drama. For some pupils, learning these techniques was an outcome in itself. However, in a good many cases, pupils linked such 'learning' to the need to make a good product; to make the product '*better*', to '*make a play good*', or to '*make a good dance and interesting*'. Others substantiated the acquisition of techniques further by saying that it had taught them how to make their work look '*more realistic*' (Year 9, art) or '*more real*' (Year 10, art), and that they could now put themselves into their work. This latter point was particularly so with the older year groups. Like the art teachers' comments on greater self-esteem with increased skill, pupils recognised some second-order effects too. Related again to art, the following was a seemly example of increased ability and skill acquisition with age, and how this could have second-order effects on a pupils' own work: '*I've got more skills now than I had before. I can put my feelings into it now, the actual art work*' (Year 9).

Two pupils from one of the schools talked about how the basic technical skills learnt across all of the artforms in Year 7 would stay with you *'for the rest of your life'* and *'help you so much in your later life'*. Like the art teacher previously, another pupil saw Year 7 as providing the *'basic skills'* across all the artforms, so that later *'you can develop your own ... you can experiment with it yourself'*. One or two of the younger pupils saw the acquisition of techniques as a preparation for Year 9 and GCSE, particularly in drama. One Year 11 pupil saw the need to learn techniques to *'get the actual grades in the subject'* (drama).

By Years 10 and 11, pupils appeared to value their own skill acquisition and independence in the arts, although such comments for music were more random with age:

I have learned what I think sounds right to myself ... what notes sound good together ... (Year 9, music).

———

I have learnt to be a lot more creative and to draw on a wider scale and use different techniques ... (Year 11, art).

———

What I would look back in Year 7 as a good piece of work, now I would just think well, it's not really that good ... you sort of develop your techniques as you go on ... started off with naturalistic ... in Year 9, touching on abstract drama, so in Year 10 now, whoever chose drama got to further those skills and learn more skills (Year 10, drama).

Such comments would tend to reflect the teachers' perceptions of progression in skill acquisition leading to second-order outcomes at later stages in secondary school. Interestingly, there were far fewer comments on techniques or technical matters for music than there were for art and drama, and, as we shall see later it would appear that skill acquisition in music required different descriptors from those in art, drama and dance.

Despite mostly positive comments about their learning, some pupils – although they recognised the new skills and techniques presented – found the work difficult. After having worked on shading and perspective in art, and moving on to portraits and painting, one Year 8 pupil proclaimed that *'mine didn't turn out very good. I'm not very good at art'*. However, another pupil at the same school said how she had improved in art, despite feeling *'pretty hopeless'* at it in Year 11, because of the teachers' support. This indicated that pupils might still choose an art option for GCSE – in this case art – even if their technical ability may not be very good. This would suggest that other factors must play an important part in option choice, and indeed the role of the teacher in supporting that choice seemed evident here.

Pupils also talked about general skill acquisition in terms of approaches and methods: the different 'ways of doing', such as improvisation or role play in drama, or observation in art. Again, there were very few comments on different methods of skill acquisition with regard to music.

Other general references were made to 'using' different media, particularly in art – where pupils used clay, paints, pencils and different materials. More specific comments on learning 'how to' control those media (as opposed to general use of) are presented below under the heading 'Specific skills and tools of the trade'. Pupils sometimes mentioned design and planning in a fairly broad sense – talking about starting a project from scratch, from the design stage. Again, specific design skills such as choreography and composition are presented below under the heading 'Specific skills and tools of the trade'.

From these general comments, then, it was possible to identify patterns in progression of skill acquisition with age – most pupils referring to the acquisition of techniques in Years 7 to 9 (but referred to much less in music), with use of different media and beginning to design or create their own work in Year 9. In Year 10, several pupils commented on the need to refine and improve on skills learnt earlier in secondary school, but not really learning anything new, except in music where learning new techniques was mentioned with regularity across all the schools. Year 11 comments focused on being able to use their own skills and techniques that they had developed rather than just copying other artists – this was particularly so for art. However, these are the more general tendencies, and specific subtleties in technical skill acquisition are given by artform below.

Specific skills and tools of the trade

Pupils talked about learning specific skills of the trade – including using keyboards and instruments in music, and paints and ceramics in art. Control of the medium through learning the symbols or tools of the trade was also important, for example references to tone and light, colours, notation and rhythm. Composition and improvisation were talked about as specific approaches or techniques, for music, drama and dance. They were also referred to as being activities with second-order outcomes such as '*creativity*', '*fun*' and opportunities for '*group work*'.

Besides increased creativity and application of self, other second-order outcomes of skill acquisition included motor and visual skills, and these are discussed below, in relation to each artform as appropriate.

Pupils on developing technical skills and competence in art

Most pupil comments for art for this effect referred to increased competence in techniques: how to use the equipment (including paint brushes, and also more advanced machinery such as the kiln, or 'lino' cutters, mentioned especially in Year 9); and how to control the medium. This latter point attracted references to colour, and to tone and light, with just one on texture. There were some interesting school differences here, with one school posting 26 of the 50 comments on controlling the medium through learnt techniques. Pupils from this school also referred to paints the most. The comments were spread across all the year groups, but predominantly from Year 7 and also the upper years taken as a whole. In contrast, another of the schools had just one comment on learning the tools of the trade (tone, light, colour and texture) and controlling the medium. Pupils from two of the schools talked about using clay, with Year 9 pupils from one of these schools referring in particular to using the kiln.

A few pupils talked about composition in art, making up their '*own collages and things*' and expressing a bit more freedom in Year 9. For one pupil, composition was like improvisation: '*We had to draw things like out of our head, just straight down onto the paper ...*' (Year 7). To another pupil, this freedom helped you to be '*more imaginative, think up your own ideas better*' and '*to make up your own design ...*' (Year 9).

Nine pupils made reference to visual awareness skills in art, with comments on shape, form and space, as well as a general increased visual awareness: '*I have just noticed how much you look everywhere,*' said one pupil. The comments, across the whole age range, reflected powers of critical observation and concentration not talked about previously under critical skills:

> ... *instead of just getting a pen and paper and drawing something, we would look around and look at the object ... that we had to draw and look at it for a long time and see the different tones and colours ...* (Year 9).

> *I've learnt to see, definitely. Most people will just draw it straightaway and it won't look right but you have to look and see what you're drawing. If you're drawing faces, feel the bone structure ... look deeper than what you're drawing ... I never used to do that* (Year 10).

While two pupils described simply enjoying using their hands in art, one pupil commented on increased manipulative dexterity due to art and, interestingly, on how he saw the possible effects of that on other areas of work:

> *Using your fingers to mould the clay, you use your hands and your fingers an awful lot in any job you do. I think that logically using clay work might improve your handwriting or something like that* (Year 7).

Pupils on developing technical skills and competence in dance

As well as a small number of general references to increased skill in jumping and dancing generally, pupils from one of the schools made a substantial number of comments on technical skills in terms of composition. Comments were across all the year groups, and tended to express an element of '*freedom*', suggesting an overall school ethos here as opposed to different approaches to skill acquisition with age. One pupil disclosed the skills of putting dance and music together as being more able to '*express yourself*'. A couple of the comments reflected a more improvisatory nature to dance, saying that it was '*quite fun*' to put dances together with other people without practising them first. It seemed that the process of composition for these pupils elicited a sense of enjoyment and self-satisfaction. None of these pupils referred specifically to choreography, again perhaps reflecting a freer approach. A pupil at another school implied that the finished product in dance was perhaps more satisfying, saying that '*the best part is when you perform it at the end*'.

2.
WHAT ARE
THE EFFECTS
OF
ARTS
EDUCATION?

Nineteen comments were about movement in dance, one pupil saying that it had helped improve '*balance*'. Nearly all the comments were from one school, though (and not the same one as above where the focus was on composition). Most related to specific dance movements, flexibility, extensions and stretches; and mostly from Years 7 to 9. One pupil referred to a motivation factor here, to warm up and join in with the crowd. Another talked about how dancing and acting '*coincide, because you have to* [be able to do] *movements when you talk ...*'.

Unlike the one teacher's insight into choreography and design in dance, pupils claimed effects here seemed much more to do with linking technical skills to a broader sense of enjoyment, and being able to move about with freedom.

Some pupils talked about physical fitness in dance, with one pupil making particular reference to learning about her body. Two pupils referred to the physical fitness aspect of dance as an outcome, citing this as a reason for having chosen PE as a key stage 4 option.

Pupils on developing technical skills and competence in drama

Most pupil comments for drama for this effect were about learning new techniques and approaches to drama, for example freeze-frames and role-play. Just a few were on the actual techniques or 'elements' of acting, for example how to build 'dramatic tension' or use appropriate body language and facial expression. Some of these comments reflected those stage skills that the teachers had referred to:

> *How to treat the audience, position yourself so you are not speaking away from them, always facing them* (Year 9).

Acting. How to talk in a group. We do a lot of group talking. To work with partners that you don't always get on with. To improve your speech in front of people (Year 9).

Learnt what good 'staging' is and how to be somebody else, go in role, how to be more confident, how to perform in front of people (Year 7).

2.
WHAT ARE
THE EFFECTS
OF
ARTS
EDUCATION?

Interestingly, there were only three pupil references to 'performance' skills in all of the artforms, and two of these comments related to drama and a school production.

A design or compositional outcome was important to one pupil who talked about mixing techniques in drama in several years of his schooling:

How to mix techniques better ... thinking about what combinations of techniques go together (Year 8).

Well I'm beginning to mix techniques more and I'm finding out which ones work best with which other ones, whether you want to put a freeze in with a role play, you know, just mixing around, what combinations work best (same pupil, Year 9).

Indeed, many pupils talked about composition in drama, but there were also comments on improvisation. One pupil described improvisation in drama as *'creativity towards different plays'*. Two schools in particular stood out as having a strong improvisational approach to drama, which the pupils discussed, with one of these schools having many more comments. Pupils here talked about increased confidence through improvisation:

We just make things up on the spot and show them to the class. And that helps because then you know how to do things for yourself rather than just working off scripts (Year 7).

... that helps you talk to people and not be scared. You've got to perform in front of other people and you're not allowed to laugh or say 'Oh, I've got to start it again' (Year 7).

Pupils from Years 10 and 11 at this school talked about increased motor skills through taking drama, with particular emphasis on space and movement. Pupils at other schools did not emphasise movement skills in drama, suggesting perhaps that work with free movement and space in drama combines with an improvisational approach.

One pupil enjoyed abstract work as opposed to straight role play in drama, because of some of the second-order effects that were possible to experience, such as empathy and also freedom of choice: '*It's good because people don't actually have to represent people they can represent what ever they want to, and I really like that.*'

Pupils on developing technical skills and competence in music

Skill acquisition in music appeared to need different descriptors from art, dance and drama. Rather than learning 'techniques', pupils talked about learning '*notes*', and '*how to read music on the page*' – more like learning the elements or components of music – at Year 7. Unlike art and drama, pupils rarely talked about acquiring skills in terms of 'how to ...' in music, although a few Year 7 comments did indicate such an approach, with one on how and why: '*Well, we've learnt in pieces like "Fantasia" and things, that how they used stillness and tone and why they use it, sort of thing*' (Year 7).

2.
WHAT ARE
THE EFFECTS
OF
ARTS
EDUCATION?

By Year 9, pupils still rarely talked about the techniques of putting music together, but rather a more personal notion of what they felt sounded well together, and doing work themselves: '*... so we are learning stuff differently, it's not all about music and instruments ... it's more yourself, you do it yourself*' (Year 9).

However, a deeper skill acquisition in composition seemed evident for some pupils at Year 10:

> *Have been forced to compose – a big step for most people, going from reading music into actually creating our own stuff* (Year 10).

> *... doing more sophisticated compositions* (Year 10).

More than that, there was a deeper insight into the nature of composition: '*... I can't exactly learn to compose, but we have been given hints and tips ...*' (Year 10).

But even at Year 11, music pupils still talked about having learnt the general elements: '*learn notes and everything*'. Even more surprising was the lack of comment on acquiring techniques for singing, rather, pupils just saying '*we did singing*'. Keyboard and instrumental skills were evident in all the schools, with one school using percussion instruments to a greater extent and another a wider variety of instruments.

It was clear from the pupil comments by year group that they perceived a progression in skill acquisition – possibly at odds with the teachers' viewpoints above that skills were taught on a need-to-know basis – and such progression varied with school. The effect of one school approach on pupils' own creativity and composition was apparent. At Year 7, pupils talked about learning the elements of music but also trying out different media and instruments, in particular commenting on '*tones*' in music. This was important since later on in this school, pupils mentioned knowing how to listen, and to '*pick out certain details*' in music. The techniques for using computers in music seemed important to the pupils at this school, and by Year 9 they showed enthusiasm for design and composition, again talking about how things sounded good:

> *How to perform a piece of music, compose. Notes – how even very simple ones can be a piece and sound really good. How to put a piece of music together, tempo and pitch and all those things that come together to be a piece* (Year 9).

As such, second-order effects of improved auditory skills, and increased positive attitudes, were outcomes for music. Skill acquisition appeared to go together with increased knowledge and understanding, and the development of skill over time was evident:

> *… we have been doing dance* [music] *and that's been really good because we have been building it up gradually over quite a long period of time and we have been able to put samples of different songs, using the studio equipment and they have sounded really good at the end* (Year 9).

Other second-order outcomes for music included a '*sense of rhythm*', self-expression and creativity in composition, and one pupil also mentioned '*self-discipline*' to stick to deadlines for compositions in Year 11. Surprisingly, there were no comments on coordination or dexterity for music, and also very little from pupils on performance skills. The acquisition of skill for composing and improvising provided much detailed comment from the pupils in terms of second-order outcomes – in particular, increased self-expression and creativity, but also several comments on learning to make music with other people and one which included working independently:

> *… I have learnt to work on my own better as well, especially with composing, and in this year I am better at playing with other people in groups and working with other people like that, so that's been good* (Year 11).

A sense of fun through improvising was evident, one pupil contrasting improvising in music with maths, which was seen as doing just one set thing. Composition was also linked to enjoyment by some pupils, and for one pupil the '*chance to show everyone what you can do*' was a real '*confidence booster*' because: '*everyone loves listening to other people's music*'. Another pupil (in Year 9) explained how, once you had learnt the skills, composition could be '*a lot more to do with you and less to do with skills*', which she had thought were '*boring*'. Self-expression was evident in several pupils' comments, either seeking inner inspiration as this latter pupil had said, or taking as the basis for creativity issues from the world about them. One pupil talked about putting emotion into compositions from issues she felt strongly about such as the conflict in Kosovo, or the emotions that accompany an argument: '*I can just put out anything that I feel into my music.*' Thus another second-order outcome of music was increased empathy with others – either immediately within the classroom, listening to others; or with the wider world.

That music is perhaps different to the other artforms, in terms of knowledge and skill acquisition, and in appreciation, was implied by one pupil talking about playing and composing music:

> ... *it's like a different language and you feel as though you are important and you can do something different that someone else can't do, you have got this special quality about yourself* (Year 8).

The acquisition of skill in music required different descriptors to those for art and drama, and elicited different outcomes, in particular working with other people in acquiring composition skills. Idiosyncrasies of individual pupil comment appeared to be more frequent for music than in the other artforms. Acquiring expertise on an instrument was mentioned surprisingly infrequently – even at GCSE – and, perhaps as a consequence, there were no comments on improved motor or coordination skills. As we have already noted, some teachers talked about teaching technical skills in music on an incidental and need-to-know basis, and did not see the need to reach a minimum standard, or build up skills in a progressive fashion, in order to facilitate self-expression and creativity. The pupils, however, did not express this alternative viewpoint. Pupils perceived their progress in music to be reliant upon using the building blocks of music (learnt lower down in the school) to reach some vague notion of 'standard', before being able to profess any kind of technical proficiency – whether this be in composition, creative skills, or an ability to play an instrument *per se*. This scenario seemed, in particular, to be the case for composition, which was often not talked about until Year 9, when it would seem that creative expression could be attempted because of some of the skills acquired (although we do note school differences here, where some Year 7 pupils talked about composition).

Improved ability in the artforms

Pupils also talked about improved or increased ability and competence for all the artforms. A general pattern in progression of perceived improvement was evident throughout the year groups and across all of the schools. However, perhaps the most interesting finding was the number of comments on improved ability in art, in particular at Year 8. Some of the pupils in Year 7 emphasised an improvement on primary years' experience, while Year 8 focused on the new challenges and how this made the subject more interesting. Comments also reflected a building on to the basics learnt at Year 7. An improvement of techniques through practice and homework was mentioned by a couple of pupils. Most of the Year 9 comments reflected back on key stage 3, one pupil commenting on a real sense of achievement on her improvement. Comments at Year 10 tended to emphasise perfecting and improving Year 7 to 9 experience, whereas at Year 11 a sudden change in attitude reflected the GCSE portfolio and learning new skills quickly. Increased confidence came with improved ability at key stage 4.

There were just three general comments on improved ability for dance, one from a Year 7 pupil, two from pupils in Year 9.

In drama it would appear that in general pupils did not see any improvement in techniques after Years 7 and 8, but rather that they used a wider variety of techniques, putting them together in different ways. Several pupils talked about *'getting down to serious stuff'* in drama in Year 9, and in Year 10 furthering those skills.

Like art, pupils in Year 8 also found music more of a challenge than at Year 7. However, an overall sense of improved ability was less evident for music than the other artforms. At one school, however, pupils did mention a general build-up of knowledge throughout secondary school, and that this *'makes it easier'*.

Developments in technical skills and capabilities: summary

In discussing the acquisition of technical skill, both as an outcome in itself and as a means of accessing second-order outcomes, there were some differences in the way pupils perceived art and music. In particular, variations in the way they talked about technical developments in these subjects were apparent. Pupils saw technical skills in art as the building blocks of the subject, as evidenced in the way they talked about how they used tone, colour, light and aspects of shape and form in their own work. This was the case from Year 7 through to Year 11. In contrast, it would seem that for music, pupils referred much more to learning about notes, and about instruments and the orchestra – that is learning about the actual musical elements themselves – and thus they were perceiving technical developments in what might otherwise be seen as a knowledge (rather than skill) base of music. It was, in general, not until Year 9 that pupils mentioned composition in technical terms, and this did not appear to be being developed as a technique until Years 10 and 11 – by which time the majority of pupils have effectively been differentiated by ability. In addition, there was a notable lack of any reference to developments in instrumental skills. This would suggest then that pupils perceive the building blocks for development in musical skill to be the musical elements themselves as opposed to technical skills, or techniques for how to use those elements. With the conspicuous exception of a school where pupils from Years 7 and 8 did talk about learning how to use tone and pitch and so on, and – in Year 9 – compositional techniques, such a perception would tend to accentuate the implication that technical skill development in music is heavily differentiated by ability.

There were surprising similarities, however, in the way pupils talked about skills in art and drama – with similar progression in learning techniques and in experimenting with different methods or approaches.

4.6 CONCLUDING COMMENTS

Evidence from the pupils included many testimonies to knowledge and understanding outcomes for art and music, but much fewer for drama and dance. For art and music, these accounts of increased understanding centred on particular styles, movements and individual artists, with a noticeable paucity of comments on contextual, historical and critical skills elements.

Unlike their teachers, who, for example, made the case for developing discernment in the consumption of art, including mass media artefacts and productions, pupils across the artforms did not usually identify critical skills, interpretative skills or aesthetic judgement-making as effects of their arts education, particularly at key stage 3. However, in art and music (but much less so in drama and dance), many pupils described an extension in their general appreciation of products and performances in these artforms. To this extent, pupil perceptions signalled the achievement of enriched appreciation in art and music, but without a developed language of critical or aesthetic discrimination. Moreover, while the teachers emphasised appreciation and aesthetic judgement-making as being accessible to all, pupils often linked appreciation of both art and music to ability both in production and consumption. In drama and dance, there were comparatively very few nominations of effects relating to broader appreciation of the artform, let alone critical or aesthetic judgement-making.

The pupil data was also rich in accounts of developments in technical skills and competencies. These were especially prevalent in art. In music, it was noticeable in most of the schools that the pupils tended to construct comparable references more in terms of acquiring 'knowledge about …' rather than 'knowledge how to …' as in art, where there was a greater tendency for pupils to describe skill acquisitions in terms of applications to their practices (although as we have seen, there was this link in music to some extent regarding composition). The limits within music provision to developments in instrumental skills may be an important factor here.

By way of concluding this chapter, it is interesting to compare the outcomes portrayed by pupils with those embedded in the National Curriculum, especially since most (but not all) of the areas to be covered by the Orders for arts subjects are to be found within this one outcome category, 'arts knowledge and skills'. Taking the art key stage 3 Programmes of Study, for example, it is quite clear that pupils' accounts of effects were commensurate with the majority of the curriculum requirements. However, in the light of the above analysis, the major areas that appear to be insufficiently covered would fall under:

9.   *Pupils should be taught to:*

   ... ...

   c) *relate art, craft and design to its social, historical and cultural context, e.g. identify codes and conventions used in different times and cultures;*

   d) *identify how and why styles and traditions change over time and from place to place, recognising the contribution of artists, craftspeople and designers;*

   e) *express ideas and opinions and justify preferences using knowledge and an art, craft and design vocabulary*

   (GB. DfE, 1995).

The parallel requirements for music were also lacking in pupils' perceptions of the outcomes. Similarly, there was little evidence to suggest that the requirements within dance for pupils to be taught '*to describe, analyse and interpret dances, recognising aspects of production and cultural/historical contexts*' were being met. Without its own Programme of Study, drama does not have similar requirements in either the existing Orders or in the proposals for the revised curriculum (QCA, 1999).

The reasons why such elements as the cultural/historical context, critical skills and aesthetic judgement-making should be less apparent in pupils' discourse of effects of all the artforms can only be speculated upon. They may be taught less, perhaps due to strengths and weaknesses in teachers' initial training or perhaps due to teachers' preferences for practical activity-based work. Certainly, the decision by teachers to concentrate on the latter would be justified by the evidence presented in the previous chapter concerning pupils' sense of enjoyment and relief in the diversity of learning processes facilitated by the arts subjects. This is not to say that contextual understanding need be distinct and separate from practical work. Rather it appears that, in whatever way these elements are taught or mediated, they are not being made explicit enough to warrant pupils talking about them.

5. KNOWLEDGE IN THE SOCIAL AND CULTURAL DOMAINS

CHAPTER OVERVIEW
For the third of the broad effect categories, this chapter focuses on outcomes relating to developments in pupils' knowledge within the social and cultural domains. It offers three subcategories:
- increased knowledge of the cultural domain (5.2)
- enhancements in pupils' awareness of their surroundings (5.3)
- developments in their understanding of social and moral issues (5.4).

2.
WHAT ARE
THE EFFECTS
OF
ARTS
EDUCATION?

5.1 INTRODUCTION

This chapter moves on from the accounts about increased knowledge, understanding, appreciation, and technical capabilities of and in the arts themselves to portray the extensions in knowledge and understanding about different social and cultural contexts that may be achieved through studying arts-oriented subjects. It contains three subcategories, all of which can include references to the individual artforms and the arts in general. The first subcategory discusses the outcomes relating to the broadening of pupil perspectives on cultural traditions and diversity, including the boundaries of the actual subject (for example to non-Western artforms). The second considers outcomes relating to environmental contexts and surroundings, while the third subcategory covers social and moral issues. The subcategories are set out from both teacher and pupil perspectives.

5.2 INCREASED KNOWLEDGE OF THE CULTURAL DOMAIN

This subcategory relates to the developments in awareness and understanding of the cultural domain through the arts. Increased knowledge of the cultural domain included a greater awareness of different cultural traditions, a raising or broadening of cultural horizons and diversity, and an enriched understanding of multicultural values and perspectives. The subcategory follows on from the comments made by teachers and pupils about increased knowledge of the artforms in Chapter 4, and in particular expands our picture of pupils' awareness of the artistic and historical context of works of art and the artforms in general. Interestingly, though, like the subcategory on contextual knowledge and understanding, this was also a fairly small subcategory, with just 26 pupil comments on increased awareness of the cultural domain. Compared to the 173 comments on increased arts or artform knowledge (see 4.2), this was a surprisingly limited quantity, especially as the version of the National Curriculum which schools were implementing at the time of the research aimed to develop pupils' appreciation of the arts from '*cultures across the world*' (music, key stage 3) and from a '*variety of cultures, Western and non-Western*' (art, key stage 3) (GB.DfE, 1995).

Teacher Perspectives

All of the artforms were posited as impacting positively on young people's cultural perspectives and awareness. Music, for example, was seen as enriching the lives of pupils who played in bands and travelled widely abroad; drama attempted to broaden cultural horizons through theatre trips and widen the horizons beyond television; English encouraged the capacity to see things from a different perspective; the '*use of the work of other artists* [in art] *and reference to the context in which art was produced* [develops] *an awareness of the art of cultures other than our own*'; and '*if nothing else,* [dance] *has educated them in what other people do, different styles, different lifestyles, different cultures, history, you know*'. Cultural traditions such as brass bands, and Welsh poetry were also mentioned.

In particular, the arts were considered to have an important role to perform in shaping attitudes in a multiethnic and multicultural society – both in schools with high proportions of children from the ethnic minorities and those with very low proportions:

> One of our objectives is to use the arts as a way of enhancing our youngsters' appreciation of cultural diversity. I think in a predominantly white school that is a strong objective that you find ways of doing it. We linked with a school in central Birmingham ... our India link ... we have very strongly embraced things that access us to other cultures and the arts is often the way that different cultures communicate to each other most easily (head).

In schools with a high ratio of ethnic minority children, the arts were seen as offering an opportunity for pupils to explore their own cultures and cultural identity, as well as providing a means of sharing and incorporating the different cultures that exist within a school. They also permitted the fostering of insights into 'high' and 'low' or popular cultural forms.

Pupil Perspectives

All but two of the 26 comments here were on awareness of different cultures, the two exceptions being on broader horizons or wider boundaries of the subject. Unlike the teachers' assertions, there were no pupil references to cultural traditions as such, with only one comment indicating any multicultural benefits. One pupil did, however, mention a 'cultural identity' project. (This was in one of the schools with a high ratio of ethnic minority children, and related to art.) Like the teachers, pupils saw all of the artforms as contributing to an increased awareness of different cultures, although art was nominated far more frequently than the other artforms. It was also apparent that almost half of the comments came from just one of the schools. Interestingly, pupils at this particular school appeared also to nominate increased contextual knowledge of the artform or artist slightly more than the other schools (see 4.2), indicating a possible link between historical understanding and a wider cultural awareness.

In art, then, most pupils talked about a general broader awareness of different cultures. However, for one or two pupils, studying art was specifically about culture, history and other artists, a particularly interesting finding – reflecting much of the aims of the National Curriculum at key stage 3. For one pupil, there was also a wider religious understanding as a result of studying art. While the teachers had talked about broadening cultural horizons in drama and music through possibilities for travel, or theatre trips, no such mentions were made by pupils. Rather, pupils made a small number (three) of general references only to music from India and Indonesia.

For a number of the pupils, a real sense of enjoyment and interest was involved in finding out about different cultures' art. The possibility for certain 'cultural' topics to inspire work was also evident, one pupil enjoying the opportunity to create their own 'religious shrine' in an art lesson. While some of the outcomes reflected increased knowledge of that specific artform, for example learning about Egyptian tiles, or blues and jazz scales, other pupils stated the effects such work had on their cultural awareness and understanding. For one pupil, this meant a kind of empathy with other cultures. Talking about dance in Red Indian tribes, he said:

> *We've been learning about different cultures and what* [dances] *they do ... like with Red Indians ... we found out about their beliefs, and if they were having trouble, they would do special dances ... that's important 'cos you know not to hurt their feelings* (Year 7, dance).

2.
WHAT ARE
THE EFFECTS
OF
ARTS
EDUCATION?

For another pupil, this understanding of culture was very much two-way, and indicated a sense of awareness and appreciation on a deeper level. Talking about a topic on Egyptian art, she said:

... they do the art because it's their culture and you are not offended by it and they are not offended by you, so it's really good, it's like an understanding.

Interviewer: *What effects has this had on you? What difference has it made?*

It helps you to understand other cultures and why they do things like that and I have actually found it has actually helped me to understand my culture better, because I didn't know much about it as well, so it really does help you to accept people for what they are, through their culture and their history, and just get along with anybody (Year 10, art).

Particular multicultural benefits were highlighted by one pupil as a result of studying drama – but we note that this was both the only significant comment on drama, and the only pupil with such insight:

... [in] drama you are put into groups and you get introduced to all those new people and they are people you have never spoken to before, people you are learning about their cultures, you know, the Indian culture, the Asian culture. You get together in groups and they are performing things about their culture and it teaches you a lot more and you get to know a lot more people and have a lovely friendly atmosphere (Year 11, drama).

However, rather than being about the understanding of culture through subject content, this was very much more a reflection of the possibilities for multicultural awareness through a specific teaching approach, involving the pupils in group work.

It is interesting to note that comments on increased cultural awareness covered all the year groups – although only one at Year 7 – suggesting perhaps that these insights do not materialise until slightly later at secondary school. This could be an indication that such awareness takes time to seat in pupils' understanding, but may simply be a reflection of the content of what is taught at each year group within key stages 3 and 4.

An increased awareness of the cultural domain through a broadening of educational experiences and horizons was talked about, then, by both pupils and teachers. However, while the teachers highlighted this through opportunities presented by the arts for school trips and so on, many of the pupils experienced greater awareness of culture through the content of their classroom lessons. Indeed, one pupil indicated some of the richness of this classroom experience in the arts, by suggesting that the world and different cultures could be accessed through art without having to travel:

> *You get to know about artists and the work they've done, and from the work they've painted of different places of the world, you can learn what the world is like without travelling, in a way. Because we're doing some paintings of a portrait and there were some of places in America and Africa, paintings of scenery there or something, and I was just looking at them and then it just showed really what the world was like* (Year 9, art).

This comment was corroborated with the suggestion that art perhaps helped in '*understanding how the world worked*'. Such effects were talked about by teachers and pupils under a broader outcome of increased awareness of the world and surroundings, and these comments make up the next subcategory in this chapter.

5.3   AWARENESS OF PUPILS' SURROUNDINGS AND THEIR PLACE WITHIN THEM

This subcategory of comments was collated in order to reflect the ways in which the arts were perceived to inform pupils' awareness of the world and their surroundings. It extends some of the comments in subcategory 4.5 on greater visual awareness through the arts, by considering the outcomes of pupils' response to the world and a greater awareness of their place within it. However, although emphasised by the teachers, this particular extension was little mentioned by the pupils. Instead, other emphases on the environment and on different perspectives on the world were highlighted by the pupils.

Teacher Perspectives

Pupils' increased awareness of their surroundings was a perceived effect particularly prevalent in art, such was the force and frequency of many art teachers' exhortation to 'look' at the world as it really is:

> *I suppose in essence what we are trying to do is to sensitise individuals to their environment and to their surroundings, things that they see, touch and experience* (ex-head of art).

> *This is a very obvious thing to all art teachers; you can put a whole lot of white things together on a table – white cloth and white objects – and you can say 'What colour are they?' They all say 'White'; then you say 'What colour is this white compared to that white?'*

And they will say 'Oh, that is darker, but that really isn't white anymore; it is maybe grey, maybe bluish'. And they go 'Oh yes', you know, it is like it is there all the time but they need to be shown these things. I think that we have an awareness that we can pass on to other people that makes them go like that ... I think there is a lot of that sort of thing in teaching people to really look at things (head of expressive arts).

———

We work from direct observation so it makes them study and be aware of everything that's around them ... (ceramics teacher).

———

Seventy-five/eighty per cent of all our sense skills comes through our eyes, and yet for much of the time we use our eyes as radar, just to stop us knocking into things. Yet, there is this exciting world that we live in, that even if they never looked at another painting again, you know the colours of the trees, the sky, the change of light, the effect of light on structures, pattern, texture, all those things that we talk about art and all around them. If just a kid can say 'Hey, look at the colour in that leaf Mr [X]', even though they are just doing it to please me, that is great, but I would hope that some of that holds.

This type of outcome, however, was not completely limited to art, as teachers of other artforms demonstrated. Drama was viewed as '*a means of really looking at the world and making their own decisions about it*'. English, according to one head of department, should lead to '*an awareness that in literature there are important insights about the world that they live in*'.

Additionally, there were several testimonies to the power of the arts in general to inform an awareness of the world, to help young people make sense of their world and work out where they stand within it:

The arts are the way in which children can be offered the opportunity of looking ... of responding to their world and making statements about their world – whether it is music, language, literature, fine art – and that for me is the strength for the arts (head).

———

I think that again, art involvement, I think, for teenagers is particularly important, because I think in those years you're learning quite often to make your way in the world and to do that you have to communicate with it, yes, and to understand it, interpret it; and the creative and expressive arts allow, or provide, teenagers with an opportunity, an added opportunity other than just language (head of Welsh).

Pupil Perspectives

Like the teachers, pupils (albeit a relatively small number) saw art as particularly influential for this outcome. Although some of their comments indicated a greater visual awareness, most were more general comments on awareness of the environment – giving a different emphasis here for this effect. Pupils mentioned architecture, pollution, buildings and industry, as well as noticing things more: '... *it's like you're walking around in a daze and then when you actually come to draw something, it's like 'Oh, I never realised that was there before'* (Year 9, art).

Overall, however, this was a lightweight subcategory for the pupils, with just 15 comments, nine of them for art, and one of these relating also to music. Again, it was mostly pupils from Year 8 upwards who talked about this effect. Some pupils' comments suggested a real concern for a different way of looking at the world, again putting a different emphasis on the 'world about you' to those views expressed by the teachers. The only Year 7 comment in this category happens to illustrate this point particularly well:

> *They* [the arts] *have helped me, sort of, in some of them to come to terms with the real world ... Like music and art, you can sort of look on the world and put it down in a way you would not usually see the world. You can sort of pick it up, scrumple it about, tear it up, stick it together a bit and then put it back down again, still the same thing but shown in a different way* (Year 7).

Apart from this comment, there appeared to be no references by pupils to the deeper effects of making sense of the world and where you stand in it (i.e. a response to the world), as claimed by the teachers. However, one of the pupils indicated trying to make sense of the world through different social and moral perspectives, and it is this emphasis that makes up the final subcategory in this chapter. The importance of studying an artform at school was stressed by this pupil:

> *It makes you sort of look at the world from a different perspective than if you hadn't done drama.* [We] *have been doing something on the last woman hanged – you can see the side that she should have been hanged and the side that she shouldn't – you get behind just the everyday good and bad* (Year 10, drama).

5.4 AWARENESS OF SOCIAL AND MORAL ISSUES

This subcategory relates to the fostering of awareness of, and exploration of, social and moral issues, looking at understanding of 'real life' (as the pupils put it) and of social issues and problems.

Teacher Perspectives

Drama and English were particularly associated with this perceived effect. Most of the drama teachers alluded to this type of impact, citing the exploration of social issues, such as racism, as a significant contribution to the pupils' social and moral education:

> *One of the things that you really try to do in drama is give a wider understanding of society as a whole.*

> ――――

> [talking about the effects of drama] *You're educating in the arts, you're educating towards a better understanding of what life is like and a bit more of an idea of how groups of people can organise things and change things and develop things through the simulated activity of drama. So they're learning about life.*

English too was attributed with a similar capacity to attune young people to fundamental social and moral issues:

> *We've just finished reading* To Kill a Mocking Bird – Harper Lee *– and I think that that is a very civilising work for young people to read: civilising in the sense that it's morally enlightening without being overtly didactic. I would want to open children's minds to the power of language, the civilising power of the creative mind, attempting to encompass the beauty of the world, the sadness of the world, so I see it as a humanising discipline* (head of English).

Other artforms were also deemed to have this 'humanising' potential. Endorsing the findings of other studies based on classroom observations of art lessons, one art teacher described something of the quality of discussions of social issues that can occur during sessions when a group is engaged in an absorbing practical activity:

> *Well, if it was weddings, it might be to do with arranged marriages, it might be divorce, what it is like just living with a mum, how old you should be when you get married. There is just a lot and I think that given the right atmosphere in the classroom, which of course is up to the teacher to generate, and everyone on task, in an art lesson, you can be working and having a whole group discussion at the same time. On perfect occasions, which happens sometimes, where everyone is quietly working, you can have 25 people in the room at once working and you can have conversations with the group at once. I think that is the nicest time really, when it is like that.*

Pupil Perspectives

For pupils, this was an important outcome, given much more emphasis than the two previous subcategories on cultural education and awareness of surroundings. Like the teachers, pupils saw drama as contributing to this effect: 47 out of the total 57 comments in this subcategory related to drama; five to the arts in general; one to music; one to art; two to English, and another to RE. Pupils talked about social, moral and real-life issues.

In drama pupils became more aware of society as a whole, exploring issues such as bullying and racism, and the issues surrounding drugs and alcohol. Such topics were covered across all the schools, apart from one, which did not appear to emphasise this aspect of drama. On the contrary, one school in particular stood out as particularly emphasising this aspect of drama, taking 22 of the 47 comments. However, these were made by only nine pupils, eight pupils at two of the other schools and six at another taking the rest of the drama comments – indicating a less significant school difference in the first case. Each of the schools approached such issues through role play. For example, playing the '*person in the middle*' had significant impact on pupils' explorations of the issue of bullying: '*It made me feel really small ... being right afraid and everything,*' said one Year 7 pupil. Empathy with people in other situations was highlighted by the majority of the pupil comments. Talking about racism, one pupil said: '*... acting it out in drama made me feel how that person would actually feel.*' Exploring different people's lives in drama helped another pupil to realise that '*in anyone's life, however promising, certain events can make it all go really sour, and ruin it all*' (Year 11). Another pupil explained how '*you can really get to feel what it is like* [to be another person] *... especially if you are in a long role play ...*'.

At one school, it was possible to track pupils' exploration of issues, from Year 7 to Year 10. Pupils tackled bullying and racism in Years 7 and 8, sexism, rights and beliefs in Year 9, and violence at key stage 4. At another school, pupils tackled the issue of 'conflict', while peer pressure and friendship groups were explored at another of the schools.

Particularly noticeable were the number of comments at Year 7 for this effect, compared with the previous two subcategories, suggesting perhaps more immediate access to issues in society than wider cultural issues and traditions. By Year 9, a few pupils appeared to have developed deeper constructs about how the arts helped in dealing with social and moral issues, '*coping with life*' and '*thinking*' around issues such as '*immigration*' or '*what happens in society to make you not want to be around people*', being particular examples. The power of drama as a means of portraying and analysing social and moral issues was evident from all the comments, and one in particular demonstrated the reality of role-playing real-life issues. After talking about using one's imagination to get into role, this comment was, ironically, not about acting, but about being real:

2. WHAT ARE THE EFFECTS OF ARTS EDUCATION?

In drama when you are role playing, you have to imagine yourself as that other person. We did a piece where you had to do a confession to a friend ... And we decided that I would tell her that I was HIV positive and so we had to act it out in front of the class. You are walking down the street back from the cinema or something ... So I said to her 'I am HIV positive', and she says 'Get away from me'. The power of the moment and the audience, when you can get the audience under that kind of control, it is just brilliant ... The thing of misunderstanding people with diseases and that – people were crying in the audience; this is just in class! So imagine what you can do on stage ... (Year 7).

2.
WHAT ARE
THE EFFECTS
OF
ARTS
EDUCATION?

English was also attributed with the capacity for developing these deeper skills of thinking and reflecting by one Year 10 pupil who discussed Frankenstein and *'breaking society's rules'*. The one comment on music offered an insight into how the lyrics of songs can explore social issues.

Rather than the 'humanising' potential talked about by the teachers, pupils talked about a better awareness and even preparation for adult life, again through taking drama at school:

Well, as we said earlier, I would say that I think that one of the advantages is that it gives me a bit more experience about what the wide world, the outside world, is like and so essentially, hopefully make it a bit easier to fit into it and understand how it works and the way that things happen in it (Year 11).

Pupils from one school in particular contributed to this debate, with several comments on transferring the classroom role-play to real life situations such as bereavement, or bullying:

I reckon it helps you to like be, you know, like not socialised, but ... it teaches you about how to act in a situation ...

Interviewer: *Can you give any examples of that?*

Someone calling you names ... you discuss the best way of sorting it out ... and in a way you put that into practice when it happens in like real-life situation (Year 8).

Comments from pupils at this school also referred to personal development and thinking about careers:

I think I've grown up a lot, I understand more about life and jobs and everything ... At primary school I had a very vague idea, we hardly did any work with the arts ... (Year 9).

We've done a lot about sort of actual real life, what could happen in the future. We did a bit on careers, which went along with our options which was nice, and we've basically done about the future, our lives in the future, and it's been nice because it's like you've been able to almost try life as an adult, but you're not you know, it's been like that (Year 9).

One pupil talked about the value of the arts (in particular drama) as compared with, say, maths, as being grounded in the everyday necessity to understand social issues and society.

5.5   CONCLUDING COMMENTS

Increased knowledge and awareness in the social and cultural domains, then, are seen as one of the effects of arts education, by both teachers and pupils, and indeed employers. The subcategories 5.2, 5.3 and 5.4, as effects of arts education, were summed up by one of the employers, who when asked what arts education was for, replied: '*In general terms, I think it gives a broader understanding of cultural, social aspects of world life and the richness that goes with it*' (Senior Human Resources Consultant).

All of the artforms were seen by pupils and teachers to contribute to an increased awareness of different cultures – though these were more prevalent in art and in one school. While the teachers highlighted this through opportunities presented by the arts for school trips and so on, many of the pupils experienced greater awareness of culture through the content of their classroom lessons. Multicultural benefits were emphasised more by the teachers than the pupils, while one pupil indicated a very interesting understanding of two-way cultural interchange. That not more pupils indicated multicultural insight in terms of benefit to themselves suggests that this was not as important perhaps as the more immediate social and moral issues as presented in drama. Additionally, while many of the reported outcomes relating to cultural education amounted to very significant, and at times poignant, learning for the individual pupils concerned, the small quantity of such comments relative to the large amount of references to discipline-based knowledge and skills outcomes described in the previous chapter is worth bearing in mind.

The arts were seen to foster an awareness amongst pupils of their surroundings and also the wider world. Teachers saw this very specifically as being able to look at the world and respond to it, while the pupils talked about environmental concerns and the value of experiencing different ways of looking at, or different perspectives on, the world. Again this was mostly through visual art, although different perspectives on the world were also gained through drama, and in particular perspectives on the social and moral dimension.

Indeed, being able to explore the social and moral domain through drama was an important outcome, emphasised by both pupils and teachers. Not only that, but understanding and empathising with people in situations of bullying, racism, and dealing with conflict were significant outcomes. While the teachers suggested the humanising potential of the arts, to attune pupils to reality, the pupils' comments concentrated on the more concrete question of 'how' they would be able to 'deal with' or 'cope with' those situations if they occurred in real life for themselves. This kind of transfer of awareness and skill indicates an important aspect to drama education in particular. That pupils talked about transfer also to the future was significant. Relating 5.3 with 5.4, our employer (from the previous example) explained how arts education can affect employability through '*individuals* [being] *more interesting and better switched on to the environment in which they live*' and that '*it contributes to your own ability to build and establish rapport, through travel as well as things like that; it gives you many more hooks in terms of building relationships, in terms of common interests and things like that*'. Another manager asserted the importance of arts education in terms of fostering sensitivity towards others:

> *... you gain an understanding and appreciation of ... motives of people, also different cultures; it makes you more sensitive to other people. That's why it's important* (Sponsorship Manager).

Thus, the fact that some of the pupils looked ahead to their future careers (in 5.4) *through* the arts (and not necessarily careers in the arts) seems apt in the light of these employers' comments. Pupils fostering an awareness of the world about them through the arts may be setting themselves up as interesting and, hopefully, employable people. Indeed, one employee adds testimony to this, by acknowledging the confidence he has in the workplace as a result of his own arts education:

> *I feel I have more knowledge, broad knowledge of the world, and what others may do. I think I have the confidence in, for example, literature. There's always references to things that have gone on in the past that I understand now, so I feel sort of confident in that way* (Trainee Manager).

Overall, then, it was clear that the fostering of knowledge and understanding in the social and cultural domains was an effect associated more with art and especially drama, rather than music or dance. Additionally, compared to the weight teachers attached to cultural development and awareness of surroundings, these two outcomes were not afforded a high profile in pupils' perceptions. In contrast, enrichments in their understanding of social and moral issues were more frequently identified by pupils. Furthermore, while social and moral issues appeared to be explored right from the start at secondary school, the cultural domain seemed to be realised by pupils slightly later in their secondary school careers (perhaps Year 8 upwards), with deeper comments on real-life and reality made by the older pupils in Years 9 to 11. With the strong emphasis on role play in drama, this apparent progression may be a reflection of the particular topics being taught, but it would seem that 'cultural outcomes', as opposed to awareness in the social domain, through the arts, required more insight on the part of pupils and, hence, more attention by teachers. This would seem to be particularly important if the arts are to make a contribution to the wide-ranging agenda for cultural education aspired to in the NACCCE report (Robinson Report, 1999).

2
WHAT ARE
THE EFFECTS
OF
ARTS
EDUCATION?

6. CREATIVITY AND THINKING SKILLS

2.
WHAT ARE
THE EFFECTS
OF
ARTS
EDUCATION?

CHAPTER OVERVIEW
This chapter presents the evidence on the fourth broad-effect category, which focuses on the development of creativity and thinking skills. It is divided into two subcategories:
- the acquisition of thinking and problem-solving skills (6.2)
- the development of creativity, imagination and the capacity to experiment and innovate (6.3).

6.1 INTRODUCTION

This chapter discusses accounts of the impact of arts education on higher-order cognitive skills and competencies. It contains two sub-categories, each split into teacher and pupil perspectives. The first portrays the effects of arts subjects on the development of thinking skills and problem-solving strategies, while the second focuses upon creativity and the use of the imagination, and considers these as part of the cognitive process.

6.2 DEVELOPMENT OF THINKING AND PROBLEM-SOLVING SKILLS

This subcategory collates the citations made by teachers and pupils to the development of thinking and problem-solving skills. There were similarities and differences in the way teachers and pupils talked about these outcomes, both considering thinking skills as competencies and as cognitive processes.

Teacher Perspectives

This purported outcome attracted numerous citations to different types of thinking skills, including abstract thinking, logical argument, and thinking laterally and divergently. The arts were also seen to develop the ability to look at problems and around problems – in the words of one interviewee, '*the ability to think expansively*'. Teachers claimed an improved cognitive ability: it was widely held that the arts encouraged children to grow intellectually, to think critically by fostering the challenging of ideas and perceptions, to interpret and analyse in depth, and to think '*off the top of their heads*' (which has affinities with section 6.3 on creativity). For many, the arts were seen as developing the ability to ask questions such as '*Why should it be like that?*' and '*Why are we doing this?*', echoing the reflection process discussed in the next paragraph.

Thought processes such as reflection, internalising and interpretation were cited, as was the notion of the arts providing a way for pupils to make sense of, respond to and represent the world mentally (thus expanding the discussion in section 5.3 on looking at the world and our place within it). Further to this point, a number of teacher interviewees stressed the role of the arts in facilitating a subjective internalisation process through which pupils can be helped to construct their meanings of the world:

> *It is subjective, because it is an internalising process, and the arts cannot get away from that. It is that interpretation of the world; that is its fundamental thing – in a way that other areas of the curriculum cannot be used to help children interpret and internalise* (head).

> *You are giving them the scope to look at it from a different way, and to really give a much deeper understanding of what is happening because they are internalising more, delving deeper into the concepts beneath what is happening* (head of drama).

> *I think it is in this developing youngsters' self-confidence and tolerance, the ability of youngsters to reflect and think. Also be prepared to let youngsters understand, I think, that they have internalised our ethos; and internalising things is one of the features of arts education, isn't it?* (head).

As touched on in this last extract, some interviewees, including some headteachers, noted the development of reflection as an important outcome:

> *It slows things down; it slows things down in a way that allows one to stand and take stock of what one is doing. That is a very important skill. In a lot of the technological related subjects, we are at the next stage and it is hitting us before we know it, because the technology is there that takes us that way.*

The development of problem-solving skills was cited, and some teachers saw this as an intended aim and effect associated with most of the art forms:

> *Problem-solving, be it a piece of art work, be it trying to make a piece of music from some ideas, or the drama, this is the theme we are working on; it is problem-solving, in space and shape and dance* (deputy head).

I think that the main thing that I am hoping to achieve is some sort of independence and autonomy, so that they possess their work, they have got some sort of feeling that it is their ownership. They are generating something for themselves that they want to do and through that they are exploring all sorts of creative, imaginative sides and bringing in all sorts of problem-solving skills, that sort of thing (art teacher).

Pupil Perspectives

References by pupils to thinking skills and problem-solving were not as numerous as those by teachers. In fact this was a fairly modest subcategory for the pupils' perceptions of effects, 15 comments being made by 12 pupils. All age groups contributed, but with two schools not represented by comments for this outcome. Drama and music received the most comments (five and four respectively), with four general comments covering all the art forms, and just one for each of dance and art.

Pupils talked about types of thinking skills much less divergently than the teachers, mainly citing the ability to think more clearly and to think with reflection. However, pupils gave much more artform-specific examples of types of thinking and implicitly recognised that each artform calls upon different types of cognitive processes. They were also more reluctant to extrapolate into the territory of transfer from the particular bounded confines of the arts subjects. Learning to concentrate was cited as an outcome in each of dance, drama and music – the omission of art here probably indicating a link between a certain type of concentration and the more performance-based arts. One pupil talked about thinking around the whole subject, similar to the teacher's comment on thinking expansively, with drama and music being singled out as important to this kind of thinking, and art, as not particularly requiring such thought processes:

... in drama, if you are acting out a role play and you have to think about the composition of the piece where you stand. You have got to think about whether, who should say what and so on ... in music, you cannot just bung on a load of notes and hope that it sounds good; you have got to make sure they are all in the same key and that they sound good together (Year 9).

Problem-solving as such was not mentioned by the pupils, although the above example for drama hinted at this skill.

For two of the pupils, the ability to think more clearly was facilitated by listening to music. For one, in Year 11, this was about being more able to focus the mind, in particular through listening to background music whilst doing homework. (He mentioned, however, that it would be '*a bit of a bummer in the exam*', though, because there would be '*total silence, no music*'.) For another, thinking and listening to music related to emotional development as a teenager, and to thinking about 'life':

> *Music gives ... listening to music gives me or you or anybody really more emotion, listening to it. I mean it's kind of the traditional teenage cliché really to stay in your room kind of crying or thinking about life or something, listening to music. But it really does kind of provide a focus to help you think about things more clearly* (Year 9).

Improved thinking in music was also linked with developments in motor skills and increased dexterity:

> *... it helps with all your reflexes because you have got to be quick ... I have found myself being a bit faster thinking and that* (Year 7).

> ———

> *Like I have said, with the reflexes, if someone throws the ball to you, you turn round and grab it and you know to do that because in music you are seeing the keys on paper, you read ahead a bit but not very much* (same pupil).

One pupil described increases in left and right hand coordination, linking this to developments, or at least to different ways of thinking, in the brain:

> *Good for your mind as well – playing the piano, have to train the brain to be able to think ...* [gives example of different rhythms in each hand] *... split your mind so you're not quite thinking of either but both of them at the same time* (Year 10).

In addition, knock-on effects into improved ability to remember as a result of taking music were cited by these pupils:

> *... training yourself to remember things* (Year 10).

> ———

> *... I think it stretches your memory a lot and makes you more accustomed to remembering things like numbers, letters. It probably even helps with things like spelling because you are remembering the letters of the keys on the keyboard* (Year 7).

This kind of coordinating of thinking with 'action' was also an effect of drama education for one pupil, who had learnt to '*think before speaking*'. Thinking with reflection was evident in both drama and English (poetry), but there were no further expansions on constructing meanings of the world or pupils' thinking about their place in the world beyond those already discussed in section 5.3.

Like the teachers, the ability to think spontaneously (*'off the top of their heads'*) was cited by the pupils, in particular for drama, but this was much more to do with the development of imagination and improvisation. Such comments contribute further to the next subcategory of effects, which also links creativity and imagination with technical skills such as improvisation.

6.3 DEVELOPMENT OF CREATIVITY AND IMAGINATION

This subcategory amounted to a major perceived effect for both teachers and pupils. It encompasses the outcomes of increased ability and confidence to create, freedom of experimentation and taking risks, realising that there are no right or wrongs, and also the development of the imagination. The relationship between creativity and technical skills and contexts was also explored.

Teacher Perspectives

Many teachers referred to this outcome. In one way or another, nearly all the teacher interviewees concurred that one of the main intended outcomes of arts education was to give pupils *'the confidence to create'* and the *'ability to create'*. Learning to experiment in the spirit of exploration and take risky steps into the unknown was held to be at the heart of achieving this outcome:

> ... *they learn to risk-take and not be devastated if the results are not so great; they get a huge buzz when it is great* (deputy head).

> *Art is a bit like science: there is an experimental side and there is an applied side. Graphics is very much the applied aspects of the experimental work that goes within the fine art areas. Without the experimentation, without the involvement of investigation into work of other artists, knowledge of critical and contextual implications of what is going on, then what you do becomes very sterile in an applied sense* (ex-head of art).

> *It's just asking questions – how are you going to translate something you see in front of you or whatever, an idea, a feeling, down on to a piece of paper, a canvas, material, whatever? That translation process and just working it through it and just seeing all the different ways and just exploring – and having the confidence to do different – try different things, make mistakes and experiment and get to a final conclusion* (head of art).

The mental processes which accompany the realisation that there are important areas of human endeavour which are not susceptible to uniform 'right or wrong' answers were another important outcome for many:

> *Well, I think it can develop children, pupils, to give them a sense of their surroundings – a sense of self-confidence as well – which I think is very important. I always try and get across there's no right or wrongs, there's always questions and you've got to answer them in your own way, so it's quite a venture of self-discovery sometimes doing a piece of art work and we can all draw the same objects in the centre of the room, but come out with a totally different piece of work – and that's fine* (head of art).

In a similar vein, several teachers referred to the fostering of the related capacity for making 'imaginative' responses:

> *We like to create an atmosphere where they can be creative and use their imagination* (ex-head of art).

> *It is something that is inside their head; it's an imaginative life, a creative life that* [drama] *gives them* (drama teacher).

Some added, however, that developing creativity and the capacity to initiate the processes of exploration required the acquisition of technical skills (see section 4.5) and, like the graphic art example, an understanding of artforms and their contexts (see section 4.2). One teacher attempted to explore the relationship between creative faculties, technical skills and a critical appreciation of the art form:

> *It is learning to think in lots of different ways. Creative thinking, I would say, is one of the things that they do get from us and all the usual investigating ... I don't really know how I can explain creative thinking, except that it is something that grows as you point out ways of looking, doing, making. The next time they do it, they are more creative in their own ... they don't just think of one way ... we always try and develop ideas in more than one way at the same time. So, if they are doing that big portrait, for instance, that I just said, then they would be trying out the same idea in their sketch book several ways before they make a final decision ... if you are there day in and day out doing this and you can see something happening, but it is very hard for me to tell you what is happening, but I could see at the end of two years the difference. It is very often reminding people about what we have done before and how we thought then, or what you thought about this, or did you see and take in that? ... it is to do with building up in your little computer in your head, I suppose, a whole load of information ...* (head of expressive arts).

Pupil Perspectives

For pupils, this was an important outcome, given much more emphasis than the previous effect. In total, there were 184 comments in the subcategory, spread fairly evenly between creativity, imagination and experimentation (although there were slightly fewer for the latter – 52, as opposed to 67 and 65).

Pupils' views on developments in creativity

There were a total of 67 comments made by 36 pupils on the development of creativity. Pupils from one of the five schools contributed to almost one-third of these comments, and along with another of the schools, art predominated here. Indeed, art received by far the most nominations (27), with many general comments also (17). Comments were spread across all the year groups, with the school example for art (given above) having the most even and representative spread. Creativity was talked about as an outcome in itself, as well as being strongly linked with self-expression, composition and enjoyment (although this latter point was to a lesser extent).

It was found that quite a number of responses to the question '*What is learning in the arts for?*' were about creativity, thus illustrating the weight given by the pupils to this effect. Indeed, one pupil, when interviewed in Years 9 and 11, talked about creativity and imagination as being the key to arts education. Another pupil emphasised creativity and intellectual development – '*to have a creative mind*' – while one talked about a more all-round development and the impact of the arts on the whole school: '*I think it is pretty important to the school. Well, it does deal with moral things, amongst other things, and coping with life and creativity*' (Year 9).

There were numerous responses on being *more* creative, especially in Year 9 compared with previous years. Other references to being more creative were made to the specific art forms, such as '*music makes you more creative*'. In fact, while some pupils talked about learning in the arts making you more creative, others talked about learning to be more creative in a specific art form.

As mentioned in section 4.2, pupils saw the '*creative side*' of the arts as an important balance to historical and contextual learning. One pupil saw this creative side as coming specifically from the arts, and another pupil from the same school described how art itself was a '*creative way of learning*' – '*not just sitting in the class*', but going outside and looking at the environment too.

Many pupils linked creativity with self-expression – '*in other ways than just writing*' being important to one Year 11 art pupil. An element of freedom was expressed here, pupils relating self-expression to being able to do what they wanted themselves (in drama and art especially). In addition, creativity was related to enjoyment and fun. Creativity also linked very strongly to composition in both art and music for the pupils. Again, this was very much in terms of composing using their own ideas. As two Year 7 pupils put it: not just being *'told to copy something'*, but *'by your own ideas and not what the teacher is doing'*. For one music pupil, direction of causality was clear here:

> *I think with the composition it encourages my creativity, I can, knowing how to write a piece of music, being able to, what I hear in my head, being able to put it down on paper, that's something really good and interesting to do, and that's been built up over this past year* (Year 11, music).

2.
WHAT ARE
THE EFFECTS
OF
ARTS
EDUCATION?

Like the last teacher's observation in this subcategory on exploring the relationship between creative faculties and technical skills, this example from a pupil perhaps shows an insight into the interface between creativity and technical skills of composing in music. It also begins to explore creativity in terms of representing internalised, or *'in your head'*, ideas.

For some pupils, it was the finished product that appeared to be important as a result of creativity and composition, while for others it was the creative process that was more satisfying. One pupil pointed out the excitement of having different products but from the same starting point:

> *You can be really creative in what you do ... sometimes in music you just play the notes that are there, so everyone has got the same piece of work, but recently we are doing things like make your own piece of music with different chord structures and this, and everyone comes out with things that are really different and it's a chance to show everyone what you can do ...* (Year 9, music).

Creativity and individuality, then, was also an outcome for the pupils, in particular in music and art. In English too, this outcome was noticed:

> *I think that we've learnt like I said before, everyone has their own style. Like if two people were asked to do a poem on the same thing, it wouldn't turn out the same. If they were given the same, sort of, words to use, they'd be put in a different order ... and, like, everyone has their own style, so it brings out your own creativity ...* (Year 7).

That this, like some of the other more general comments on creativity and using your own ideas, was noted by one of the younger pupils is of some interest. It would appear that while pupils' own styles of work were found to develop later in secondary school – perhaps in Year 9 –

2.
WHAT ARE
THE EFFECTS
OF
ARTS
EDUCATION?

through developing technical skill (see 4.5 on increased ability in technical skills), pupils realised the potential of everyone to have their own ideas and styles (creativity) right at the start of secondary schooling.

An association between creativity and thinking skills was apparent in a few of the pupil comments (*'it's just using your mind more ...'*), but one pupil emphatically denied such a link: *'We haven't been learning; we've been more creative'*. Possibly creativity to this pupil was associated solely with 'doing' rather than using other faculties. Transfer of creativity to jobs and life was mentioned by several of the pupils, from different ages and different schools, but mostly to do with art:

> *Hopefully, it might get me a job or I might be like more creative* [with] *more chance of getting a job because of it* (Year 7, art).

> ----

> Interviewer: *What is important about doing art?*

> *Improving creative skills. That can by used in a lot of jobs* (Year 9, art).

> ----

> *Creativity, self-confidence and just being open, I think, which all three things, both things you get helped with and you learn when you're doing arts at school, I think, come in handy.*

> Interviewer: *Do you feel that they've given you skills that will be useful in later life?*

> *Yes* (Year 11).

On such transfer of skill, one of the employers talked about the 'special element' of the arts as being *'potentially about tapping into individual creativity, tapping into individual self-worth if they do it very well, building confidence,* [and] *encouraging people to use creativity'*. One pupil emphasised the transfer of creativity from the arts to personal development, referring to it as a motivating factor: *'It has probably made me more of a creative person – not just being bored, but going out seeing something and thinking that is interesting'* (Year 9). On the other hand, it was thought by one pupil that the arts gave him the chance to be creative and use his imagination, but *'only in that lesson, nowhere else'*, implying that creativity was not transferable.

Pupils' views on increased sense of freedom and ability to experiment

Experimentation and a sense of freedom to try out things were referred to in a total of 52 comments by 35 pupils. Comments came from all the year groups, although a sense of freedom was mentioned predominantly by those in the upper year groups (9–11). Again, art generated most of the comments (26), with seven for music, six for drama and three for dance.

While pupils did not necessarily articulate the confidence to create, they appeared to assume a sense of confidence with regard to experimentation and taking risks. For some of the older pupils especially, this was expressed as feeling more able to try things out on their own, while for one of the younger pupils, it was about being '*more outrageous in the arts ... so you could maybe go for things more*'. Being as '*wacky or as conservative as you like*' was also mentioned, this time for art. Some pupils allied experimentation with the type of work they were doing, for example '*more abstract work*' in art at Year 10. For a Year 7 pupil, a sense of freedom was linked to work that did not involve the written medium. It was clear that in the older year groups, pupils experimented more as part of their work, one Year 11 pupil saying that art this year had been '*mainly me experimenting with different techniques and drawings or ideas*'; several drama pupils felt they were given a bit '*more leeway*' to do their own thing (Year 10s); and music pupils appreciated being able to do their own thing more: '*Music has been a lot better – able to do own thing – last year everything was set for us*' (Year 10). Indeed, appreciation of greater freedom was portrayed by several of the older pupils; in one case, the teacher was perceived as making art '*enjoyable because she gives us the freedom to do what we want*'. '*Feeling free*' through having choice was also conveyed, and for one pupil this extended to a '*sense of euphoria*' when standing back and realising what he had achieved in art.

2.
WHAT ARE
THE EFFECTS
OF
ARTS
EDUCATION?

A sense that there was more freedom in the arts subjects over and above other school subjects was conveyed by one of the pupils: '*In the arts you get more freedom to do what you want, your ideas.*' One of the employees, expanded this point. Specifically about drama and being in school plays, he talked about '*learning to think in a different way*' and connected this with teaching styles in drama as compared with other subject areas:

> *You work for a team and work for a common goal, certainly, a creative outlet, as opposed to learning and not being able to respond, you know, it was an equal balance. Certainly the teacher wasn't a teacher like you had in a maths class, so you had a free flow of thinking, and at the time you don't realise but now you're posing the question, yes certainly a different method of thinking to achieve different results* (Trainee manager).

In addition, a broad view of the arts was offered by one of the interviewees, in connection with experimenting:

> *Any form of making things up and experimenting with it, usually through sound and sight. But I think it is anything to tantalise your senses really, through what you can see and what someone else has given to you* (Year 7).

Pupils' views on developing the imagination

In a similar vein to those comments on creativity, many pupils referred to the development of the imagination, with 65 comments in all, made by a total of 32 pupils. There were, however, some differences in the way that pupils talked about imagination compared to creativity. Most notable was the number of comments for imagination in drama, in particular at one school, where no such comments had been made regarding creativity. The school that emphasised creativity for art had most comments again for imagination. Overall there were 18 comments for art, 16 for drama, 15 general comments, and five each for dance and music, indicating again a different emphasis on imagination as compared to creativity. Comments for art were mostly from Years 9–11, with drama comments made almost exclusively by Years 7–9.

As well as mentioning creativity in response to the question '*What is learning the arts about at this school?*', imagination was also identified. Many pupils linked the two, but some gave specific answers about imagination such as '*coming up with your own ideas, because in art, drama and music you have to put down your own ideas*'. Some sense that this was different to work in other subject areas was evident:

> *So you're not just learning things like maths. You're learning how to use your imagination* (Year 9).

> ——

> *Art lessons are more relaxing than other subjects;* [you] *have to use your imagination a lot more* (Year 10).

This would appear to reflect both the comment on a more open approach in teaching style as highlighted by an employee above in this subcategory, and what another pupil had said previously about using improvisation in music – a different approach compared with a subject like maths (see section 4.5 on technical skills in music).

Imagination was also associated with interpretation of other artists' work, particularly in art, and, like creativity, mixing that with your own ideas:

Interviewer: *What do you think you have learnt in art?*

> *How to bring a bit of yourself into the work that you're doing … If you're drawing a still life, you get to draw the way that you see it, so sometimes it's abstract but you still get to draw it the way you see it, your opinion on it* (Year 9, art).

> ——

> *I like doing impressionism because you don't have to stick to one thing, you can adapt their skills to your own sort of thing.*

Interviewer: *So is that when there's a topic and you just do whatever you want to do and you interpret it?*

Yes, you see what they have done and how they have used the stuff ... and you just bung that into what you do in your work (Year 9, art).

———

It's all about interpretation: you look at something and you do what you want to do with it (Year 11, art).

Making things strange was an outcome of being more imaginative for one art pupil:

... now I don't do anything normal, if a teacher asks me to do anything ... I don't draw it normal as it is supposed to be seen. I just put my imagination into it and then draw the kind of things I would like to see on it. A plain face with it doing nothing just looking, I think it makes it stand out it gives you a good feeling inside you that you have this imagination inside yourself which can make you do all these things, draw things. Because drawing a normal face is just too boring for me (Year 9).

A different use of imagination was suggested by one pupil's comment in art. It was about imagining a situation or scene – sort of in your mind's eye – and then interpreting this to put it on to paper. As suggested by this pupil, this '*broadens*' our picture of the imagination, in that it appears it can be accessed and used in a two-way process in the arts – either to view something and help interpret and represent it in another medium (for example, in a painting), or to imagine something in your head, and to put that into reality. Developments in other imaginative capacities were also mentioned: one pupil, for example, talked about imagining as daydreaming, music being the artistic vehicle, and felt that this helped with other tasks requiring imaginative skill, such as writing a poem.

A sense of freedom, spontaneity and running with ideas was evident in pupils' talk about developing the imagination in drama, with some conveying a feel for an emphasis on process as opposed to product:

We just sort of ... on the spot you just think of anything and just make it up as you go along ... And so it sort of makes your brain try to imagine things. It's not like you have to act out a scene in a park or something. You just think of anything and just do it from there (Year 7, drama).

———

Interviewer: *So what is it about drama and art that makes you feel you are developing your imagination?*

You have got to think a lot about what you are doing. You can't just draw anything or do anything, you have just got to think; you don't learn you just ... it's like a spur of the moment thing (Year 8, drama).

———

Your imagination can just run riot. It's just doing stuff that you'd never thought of doing before (Year 9, drama).

This connection between imagination and thinking – imagination as a cognitive skill, perhaps – as illustrated in the first two examples above, seemed important in several other comments relating to drama. Like creativity, imagination was also linked to personal development, and having a better or more rounded personality: '*If you don't imagine anything, you're just like boring.*'

Imagination was linked to composition in music in a very general way, but there were no further comments beyond those already mentioned in connection with creativity, and no significant contributions for imagination and creativity in dance.

Transfer of imagination was mentioned by several pupils, particularly from drama to English, but also from art to English:

It's helped me in English actually, because it's made me more imaginative when I am writing stories and stuff for coursework ... (Year 10, drama).

———

... [it's] helping [with] imagining characters in books as well (Year 9, drama).

———

I think that, in a way, it would benefit me in subjects such as English, which is also using your imagination, so by using my imagination in art, it's also helping me to use my imagination in subjects like English (Year 11, art).

Six pupils from different schools talked about the use of the imagination in English lessons, one pupil asserting that '*you have to use your imagination to write stories and things, and poems*'.

6.4 CONCLUDING COMMENTS

This overall category embraced numerous responses from both pupils and teachers, indicating the importance of creativity to the arts in school. Thinking skills were given slightly more emphasis by the teachers, but pupils too talked about outcomes such as thinking more clearly and being made to think and imagine. However, unlike the teachers there was little reference by the pupils to strategic or transferable thinking such as problem-solving and the ability to ask questions or to interpret and analyse in depth. Having said that, it was evident from some of the employer and employee interviews that they recognised and appreciated the broad range of types of thinking skills as demonstrated by arts graduates in particular. One employee talked about this in relation to employability:

Interviewer: *Could I ask for your views on how arts education affects employability?*

I think it gives them a little bit more grounding, a little bit more general knowledge. There was a New Zealander, quite a big accountancy firm ... who wouldn't appoint commerce graduates. They would only appoint arts graduates, because they said arts graduates could think. Arts graduates could go to six or seven or 20 books, read all of them and give you a report that pulled out just the relevant information on two or three pages, whereas commerce, they just get the right book, they look it up, that was the answer ... Arts students tend to have a wider experience ... rather than ... this is not the way the world runs and there are other things ... (employee in education management/administration).

A relationship between thinking skills and a developed general knowledge, then, was suggested here. However, it seemed that the pupils did not talk about an increased generalised intellectual development. In addition to the teacher comments, though, pupils made important contributions on the outcomes of improved concentration in the performance arts, and also alluded to a link between cognitive and coordination skills developed through playing an instrument.

Both pupils and teachers saw creativity and imagination as an intended aim of arts education. However, unlike the many teacher comments on having the confidence to create, there were no significant contributions from pupils on this point. Rather, pupils conveyed a sense of ease in their confidence to experiment, and although not articulated by the pupils, this indicated a sense of relief, if not liberation, that there was at least one area of the curriculum where success was not based on providing categorically right or wrong answers. Creativity, experimentation and imagination for pupils were about using their own ideas, and, in essence this was what made a good arts lesson – as mentioned by at least three of the pupils, for art and drama and one for dance:

The best ones are not actually when you're taught a dance but when you are allowed to make one up by yourself ... we just have the freedom to do whatever we want ... (Year 11).

That creativity was an expressed outcome of arts education by all the year groups would tend to suggest that, while pupils may describe their developments in technical skills in terms of 'this is what I can do', or 'this is what I have learnt' (thus suggesting, for example, that composition skills are not developed until Year 9 at least, in music), they do in fact realise creativity and imagination through activity in all years at secondary school.

2.
WHAT ARE
THE EFFECTS
OF
ARTS
EDUCATION?

Overall, then, creativity (but not general thinking or problem-solving skills) was a frequently recognised effect of arts education by pupils. Two features of their accounts are particularly noteworthy: firstly, pupils used a very wide and diverse range of interpretations of 'creativity' (e.g. creativity as freedom, experimentation, imagination, thinking new thoughts, self-expression, a learning strategy, as well as process and product – see Fryer, 1996; Ashworth *et al.*, 1998); and secondly, although references were made to becoming more creative, their descriptions rarely suggested any sequential and/or progressive development in 'creativity' as a competence or cognitive process. In the light of pupils' very enthusiastic, if very varied, descriptions of creativity as an effect of arts education and in the wake of the NACCCE report and the setting up of the QCA task force on creativity, it is worth asking whether the time has come for curriculum designers to offer teachers a more explicit model of development in creativity in all its various guises. Making the learning of thinking skills and creativity a much more transparent and overt part of the curriculum (and of teacher training) could offer many potential benefits for pupils – in terms of accessing other arts-related outcomes, as well as encouraging the transference of these cognitive processes to other arenas and subjects.

7. COMMUNICATION AND EXPRESSIVE SKILLS

CHAPTER OVERVIEW

This chapter sets out the evidence on the fifth of the broad categories of effect, namely communication and expressive skills. It embraces four subcategories:

- enrichments in interactive communication skills (7.2)
- language development (7.3)
- the enhancement of critical and active listening and observational skills (7.4)
- the growth in pupils' capacities and skills necessary to make statements about their world and themselves, as well as developing the confidence to express 'themselves' (7.5).

2.
WHAT ARE
THE EFFECTS
OF
ARTS
EDUCATION?

7.1 INTRODUCTION

This chapter explores the outcomes associated with the enrichments of interactive communication skills, language competency, interpretative and active listening skills, and the capacity for pupils to use expressive skills to make statements about themselves, their own lives, and the world. This type of outcome received numerous responses from teachers and pupils, with 356 pupil comments in total – half of these relating to expressive skills as empowerment. The chapter is split into four subcategories, the first and smallest of which concerns the development of interactive communication skills. The second subcategory refers to the developments in the skills of language and speech, including a debate about eloquence (an issue for the teachers), and also speaking with confidence and clarity. The third subcategory covers the development of active listening and observational skills as related to improved communication, while the fourth and largest subcategory considers developments in pupils' capacity to use expressive skills for making statements, and for self-expression, and also to use the arts themselves as a tool for expression not through oral or written language. The four subcategories in this type of outcome are divided into teacher and pupil perspectives, and cover the arts in general and each of the individual artforms as appropriate to that subcategory.

7.2 DEVELOPMENTS IN INTERACTIVE COMMUNICATION SKILLS

This subcategory collates those references to developments in interactive communication skills, including the communication of ideas and opinions and the capacity to use those skills in areas other than the arts. As a subcategory, it is as much about interaction as it is about communication – with references to body language and expressing and interacting in group and other situations. In contrast, section 7.3 considers language communication *per se*. Both teachers and pupils nominated drama far more than any other artform as effective in this outcome.

Teacher Perspectives

Although there were some references to this effect from across the artforms, drama attracted far more than any other area. It was claimed that in drama pupils learn to convey a wide range of content messages through a variety of forms of communication (e.g. verbal and non-verbal signals). One drama teacher expressed it as follows:

> When they have suddenly found they can communicate ideas, meanings, atmosphere, subtext, emotion, through just themselves as like an instrument, I suppose our body is our instrument, as they say.

The development of such skills was seen as highly relevant to the current and future needs of young people:

> I see drama as a means of people engaging with the world around them ... and in that way hopefully develop them to analyse and communicate interactively with what is around them, and to question, and to sometimes enjoy praise. To do that, you have to give the tools of drama, because the power in the drama comes when people actually feel it as well as think it and then they say 'Oh gosh, yes'... it has become more important as the world around the kids has become more complex; their ability to engage in, receive, question and communicate in an intelligible way is becoming more and more important (head of drama).

A deputy head in one school emphasised that drama is an important means of improving the communication skills of pupils for whom English is not their first language:

> I think that the importance ... for a child for whom English is not a first language, with a philosophy that our drama people have about performance and drama, and commitment, and cooperation, and working together. In terms of building confidence, so the child who cannot attack the writing on the page can communicate, can be part of, can begin to grow and develop in confidence as part of the

teamwork and collaboration of drama, [it] *has a huge impact on that child's experience on expectation and what happens.*

To support the case for the claim that drama develops communication skills, one interviewee relayed evidence given by a group of drama GCSE pupils who were involved in a course run for major employers and industrialists in the area:

> *Afterwards the industrialists then asked the kids why did they choose to do drama and the kids were talking about teamwork ... bless them, sometimes you could just kiss them. Clearly we could not prime them; they were not primed and these kids talked about the ability to communicate, to be confident and all that* (LEA adviser).

Pupil Perspectives

While art and the arts in general received a few of the comments relating to interactive communication skills, it was again drama that attracted most of the nominations for this effect, accounting for 15 of the total 20 comments. Of the total, these were made by 17 pupils, 13 of whom were girls, spread across all the year groups – although there were more comments in Years 7 and 11. The three comments relating to the arts in general referred to communication skills in group work, the possibilities for transfer of *'communication and cooperation skills'* to later life (Year 7), and a comparison with other curriculum areas:

Interviewer: *Thinking of all the arts subjects you do, how would you describe the effect they've had on you?*

> *I'd say it's quite important to me actually 'cos, I mean, you can't express yourself with science or French ... well I suppose French people would call French an art, but ... it's helped me communicate to others a lot* (Year 7).

An awareness of the arts empowering communication, by pupils even in Year 7, was therefore apparent.

Pupils from two of the schools contributed most of the comments for drama (a third each), but interesting contributions came from a variety of schools. For the most part, pupils explained how drama had helped their communication skills:

> *I think just how to express myself more clearly. It's a way of communicating with people, an alternative way. It gives you more confidence definitely. My confidence has been built up this year. I can communicate with people and get across my ideas and opinions. So that's how I think drama helps me* (Year 11).

> ———

> *I have learnt how to communicate more in situations* (Year 11).

However, one pupil pointed out that she felt it was drama itself that needed communication skills – perhaps as an input – in order to 'work':

2.
WHAT ARE
THE EFFECTS
OF
ARTS
EDUCATION?

> *There's a lot of communication involved. If you can't communicate with someone, there is no drama basically and so communication is probably the most important thing in drama – apart from having natural talent of course* (Year 11).

As such, the two scenarios go hand-in-hand: drama contributes to communication skills, and good communication contributes to the dramatic performance.

Almost all the other significant comments related to being more able to work and communicate with a variety of people, and in a variety of situations – not necessarily just in drama lessons. In addition to this, the concept of being more able to share ideas was put forward by several of the pupils:

> *I think it has made me more willing to share my opinions and ideas and stuff like that* (Year 7).

> *... as well as work with other people, it helps you to sort of communicate and things like that. I find, that it helps me too – if you're in a situation to communicate with somebody else, you become a lot more forward in working with somebody because you don't know them or you're only there with them a little bit, it doesn't happen to be your best friend and you can still work really well with them* (Year 9).

> *Drama helps you talk more with people and not be scared to express yourself* (Year 7).

> Interviewer: *Is there a connection between feeling confident in drama and in real life?*

> *Yes, because you get better at being able to talk to people and put your ideas forward. You get better at being able to express things, how to say things* (Year 9).

As an extension of these comments about being more able to communicate with people and formulate opinions, one pupil talked about how communication in drama impacted on group work, as opposed to just self-development:

> *It makes you work together, definitely makes you work together and try to make the best you can with the people you have got, the people you are working with. You have to take a bit of initiative. Like, say there is someone in your group who won't work with anyone else in the group apart from one or two people, you are going to have to*

say 'How about we do this?' And if they disagree, then say 'Well what do you want to do?' So you have to work out your communication skills a lot better than you used to; otherwise you are dead basically (Year 7).

7.3 LANGUAGE DEVELOPMENT

This subcategory represents an extension to the previous one in that it concentrates more specifically on outcomes relating to language and speech rather than the more general and interactive communication skills. Teachers talked about language development in terms of clarity of speech and sometimes elocution, and being able to articulate opinions and speak confidently. Pupils too saw these outcomes as particular types of language development, but also talked about having the language to deal with a variety of situations. Thus, transfer to other subject areas and other situations outside of the arts became an important aspect to this effect.

Teacher Perspectives

Again, this subcategory was dominated by the perceived effects of drama. There were several references to speech, speaking with clarity, eloquence and (less frequently) elocution:

Speech skills: we did a lot of direct speech on 'Fair is foul and foul is fair'; you've actually got to get your tongue round that so we can actually do a bit of elocution – almost – and they enjoy doing it (drama teacher).

Not all drama teachers, however, would want to promote the elocution aspect of speech development as an appropriate outcome for their subject:

If they say to me it is about elocution, or it is about putting on plays, or it is about facing the front, my answers are definitely no. You know, it is just not, it is never that; it is about helping kids develop and making sense of the world around them and engaging with it. That is that; they have got to have some tools to work with that makes it work. Otherwise, it is just me and it is not theirs; they can't own it if they haven't made it ... it is a bit of a sort of coming together rather than clarity and there are certain things that I know that it definitely cannot be, like elocution [laughter].

In one school, accounts from the headteacher and the drama teacher corroborated the perception that drama was having a significant impact on the capacity of the pupils to articulate their opinions and to speak confidently in public:

I think that the pupils here are very assertive, very confident, and I think that a lot of that has to do with the work that they do in drama. We get loads of visitors into the school and the pupils here will talk to anybody. At the public meeting that we had here last night, one of our little Year 7s put up her hand and said 'I want to say something' and made a really pertinent contribution. The director of education said 'I think that is probably the best contribution that we have had so far tonight'; it was just superb. There is a real level of confidence here from the pupils (headteacher).

I think that pupils are articulating themselves. I think this is one of the strengths of our school, that they articulate themselves very well. I think there is a gap between how they write and how they actually express themselves. I think that drama has contributed to that because we have put things on in a public situation, in, like, assemblies, in year meetings. They are taking drama outside of the school and I think then that other pupils see that and that feeds back into it (drama teacher).

More generally, teacher interviewees from across the artforms cited the development of languages and vocabularies to assist pupils in their discourses about works of art and the processes of creating them. Such references had much in common with the growths in knowledge, understanding and appreciation of the arts which were recorded in sections 4.2, 4.3 and 4.4. The following was one such comment:

This is the second year that drama and dance have been together, and what I am noticing is that the language that pupils are using has expanded and they are crossing over. So when they are dancing, they are talking about audience; they are talking about creating atmosphere. In drama, they are talking about body shapes and travelling, so the two are crossing over (dance and drama teacher).

Pupil Perspectives

Like the teachers in this subcategory, pupils also saw drama as particularly associated with this outcome. There were 40 comments in total, made by 23 pupils, and, like the previous subcategory on interactive communication, drama again generated three-quarters of these. As in the previous subcategory, the majority of the comments were offered by girls. Most of the comments came from pupils in Years 9 and 11, suggesting a slight age difference with the previous subcategory of effects, although the number of comments in Year 7 was still relatively high. Notably, one of the schools had just over half of the comments for drama, with another school taking most of the six more general comments across the artforms. These related to language development in terms of speaking louder and with more confidence, and one pupil associated this with 'self-conduct'.

In addition to the teacher-perceived areas of clarity, confidence, elocution and articulation, pupils talked about voice projection, pronunciation, fluency and the language skills needed for a variety of situations. Indeed, it was possible to construct a small model of pupil perceptions of language skills and development from the 40 comments offered. This split into four areas: spoken language skills, including voice production, sense of communication and language for a variety of situations within drama lessons; understanding the power of language; written skills; and transfer of language skills to situations outside the arts.

Pupils offered numerous references to improved skills in voice production as a result of taking drama. Improved clarity was mentioned by some pupils, who used to '*mumble*'. For some, this extended to elocution and pronunciation, and '*how to speak properly*' and to use appropriate speech, for example '*at a job interview, or like now, I would not talk to you and sound* [adopts street slang]. *It makes you sound better ... nicer ...*'. English was actually cited by one Year 10 pupil as better equipping her with this skill: '*how to pronounce things and phrase things and speak better*', while she saw drama as more about '*actually doing it rather than writing about it*'. Voice projection was specifically mentioned by some pupils as a skill that had been learnt in drama, and there were several references to having more confidence when speaking, and a couple on speaking louder.

There was a similar proportion of responses on a better sense of communication, as a result of taking drama at school, as there had been for voice production. The ability to express views and articulate opinions was cited by many of the pupils. Some referred to this as '*speaking out*', while a few others related it to expressing their own views, '*... how to speak out openly; stating views and "speak out more"*'. One pupil talked about fluency and ease of discussion as an addition to her language skills:

> *I suppose, like, if you wanted to stand up for yourself or something, or discussion work in English or you want a debate over something, I think it helps being fluent talking to other people* (Year 9).

Another illustrated how she felt she now had the confidence to be able to speak on the spot, and that having the language skills to do that with clarity had been influenced by her drama lessons:

> *If I was going into the media, I think that drama has helped me in that I am able to think up things on the spot, rather than stuttering and stammering because my teacher has put me in a place where she has just asked me to think of a speech and when everybody is asking and I think if I did want to get into television, then if somebody sticks the camera in front of me, I hope I wouldn't be stuttering, but I don't know* (Year 11).

Pupils experienced using their language skills in a variety of situations in their drama lessons, and this varied with age in a similar pattern across the three schools that had the highest number of comments for drama for this overall effect. At Year 7, pupils mentioned feeling more able to talk in general to people: '*It really just helps you talk to other people more,*' said one Year 7 boy. At Year 9, pupils commenting on their drama lessons spoke more about talking to people in groups: '*We do a lot of group talking. To work with partners that you don't always get on with. To improve your speech in front of people.*' In Year 11, comments focused much more on learning to speak in front of a large group, perhaps in front of an audience – '*... how to communicate in front of a big group, how to perform ...*' – and for many, this was associated with increased levels of confidence.

While almost all the pupils commenting on this effect discussed what they had been doing in drama and how this had helped their language development, one pupil referred to the power of speech itself, demonstrating an understanding of the impact of speech in controlling certain situations: '*Mainly how to silence speech. You know, if I like shut up now, you'd be thinking "What should I say next?" So we've been doing that*' (Year 9).

Besides oral communication, there was little other reference to language development. One pupil did, however, cite clarity in the written medium as important, and felt her English lessons to be effective here:

> *Writing, because nearly every single job you have, you have to sort of write and if you don't use language that is sophisticated or anything, people just think you're not very clever or anything. So, it helps if you can use better language, like words and things* (Year 7, English).

It was apparent, then, that pupils saw language development in the arts as transferable to other current situations, subject areas and also to future careers. The immediate personal benefit of speech development for one of the pupils, as a transfer from arts lessons, was obvious. Because of '*having to speak in front of your class and things like that*' both drama and English had helped improve this pupil's speech and speaking skills:

> *At the start of school I was fairly unconfident in myself and I was always stuttering all the time, finding it very hard to say things. But now as time [has] progressed and through things like drama and speaking in front of the whole class in English, I think that my speech has improved considerably and I feel a lot more confident in myself ... I've been stuttering less, trying to say things louder. Also recently, I've been putting my hand up and saying more things,*

whereas in the past I might have held back for fear of being laughed at and things like that. But now I think that's been sorted out (Year 11).

As a result of improved speaking skills, this pupil's self-confidence also increased, and as hinted at, a positive class situation might well have contributed to this outcome. Another Year 11 pupil at a different school also recognised the particular impacts that drama education could have in certain schools, saying that *'as soon as I came to this school to do drama, it opened me up'*. He also said: *'It brought me out of my shell ... I have been able to speak to people more easily.'* Notably, both these pupils were boys – it may well be that they were more willing to disclose such personal insights into shyness and overcoming a lack of confidence. In contrast, those Year 11 girls who discussed language development at some length tended to talk about its relevance to their future.

Transfer of 'public' speaking skills from drama to English was important to several of the Year 8 and 9 pupils, making *'reading in English a bit easier'* because they would be *'not embarrassed to read out in front of the class'*, or because *'drama builds up your confidence so you feel easier reading aloud'*. As suggested by the comment for English earlier, better language for job applications and interviews was also seen as an outcome and benefit of arts education. Regarding oral communication, other pupils said:

Say, if you go for an interview, you won't be so shy about it because you've learnt how to speak, project yourself. If you wanted to be an actor, it might help! (Year 7, drama).

———

Helps you communicate, and 'just a sense of well-being' – once [you] *have spoken to people in drama,* [you] *can go out and have a conversation with them.* [I'm] *not shy about meeting people for the first time – drama helped a lot with work experience interviews – speaking to people in a friendly manner, not being too frightened of questions ...* (Year 10, drama).

One Year 11 pupil talked about transfer of communication skills – such as voice projection and talking in front of a group – from drama to a specific career: that of sports coaching and teaching.

As many of the pupils had pointed out, communicating in a variety of situations was a perceived outcome of arts education, and this was picked up on by one of the employees interviewed. The emphasis was on the transfer of communication skills, rather than artistic or technical skills, to employment:

... if you have done an art course where there would be acting, art or media art, or graphic design art, I think all those courses entice you to go out and find things out and chat to people and have a look at other people's things and give your opinion and that ... I think it helps you to express yourself and deal with various people in certain ways (administrator, employee).

By way of rounding-off this subcategory, it is noted that having the language for a variety of situations and being able to converse with confidence were not expressed solely by those pupils taking drama to GCSE level. One of the Year 11 pupils not taking drama GCSE recognised the communication skills that she had learnt in drama during her first three years of secondary school as benefiting her development both in and out of school, in Years 10 and 11:

Like in drama, drama has taught me to have a lot more confidence in myself, you know, speaking in front of an audience or speaking in front of ... not necessarily an audience, but a crowd of people and it's just you speaking. I reckon drama has brought out my confidence from Year 7 to Year 9 because you know when you come to Year 7, you are all really shy, you don't even want to speak to the teachers, but I reckon that's the thing that I enjoyed in drama. It helps you to build up your confidence; don't just sit there and be shy because it's not worth it. And then, like, in Year 10, even though I didn't pick it, [I] referred back to it when I was doing my work experience because it was talking to completely different people, adults that I have never seen – I have never met them before in my life – working with customers, how to deal with problems and everything and that using drama, just thinking back to what the teacher said in drama – 'Be confident, always face someone when you are speaking to them and don't turn your back on them' – and stuff like that, so I reckon that's built up my confidence ... (Year 11).

7.4 DEVELOPMENTS IN SKILLS OF CRITICAL AND ACTIVE LISTENING AND OBSERVATION

This subcategory of effects was constructed in order to take account of those claims by teachers for active listening skills in drama. However, it was found that pupils rarely mentioned this skill in relation to drama, but instead referred to active listening in music, maintaining a sense of transfer to listening in situations other than classroom music. Observation skills in art were also deemed to relate to interactive communication by pupils.

Teacher Perspectives

Drama was at the forefront of teachers' claims about the growth in the skills of listening to others. This headteacher saw this outcome as having a moderating effect on some young people:

> ... *one of the things that I find quite interesting is how youngsters will sometimes moderate* ... [they are] *very confident to start with in drama,* [but] *will probably develop the skills of listening to others more and reflection.*

Pupil Perspectives

There were a total of 77 comments made by pupils relating to skills of active listening and observing in the arts. Overall, 52 comments, made by 34 pupils referred to the first outcome of listening. However, unlike the teachers, pupils did not identify drama as particularly influential on this effect. Instead, there were numerous comments made about active and critical listening in music – 47 in total – and these were spread fairly evenly across all the year groups and all the schools (although two of the schools posted slightly more of the comments). For most pupils, active listening was voiced as a description of what they had been listening to recently in class, while others described being more able to pick out certain instruments, notes or themes in music:

> *When I listen to things now, I can pick certain bits out and say what instrument they are and what time they're in* ... *I've actually found it helps enjoy music more. It sounds a bit clinical* ... *but it actually does bring things more into focus* ... *actually listening beyond the melody* ... (Year 10).

Some expanded this further, attributing music with their ability to '*listen in a different way*', or to '*listening more closely*'. Several pupils also associated it with a type of concentration, '*rather than just letting it go in one ear and out the other*', as one pupil put it. Being more able to listen to live music itself – playing, performances and so on – was identified by some pupils. Others described how they were more able to listen to other people as a result of their critical listening in music lessons, communication skills thus beginning to be recognised and developed. This was not restricted by any age factor. After talking about an exercise of listening carefully to how music is put together, one of the Year 7 pupils asserted that this helped in being able to listen to people and take in what they were saying.

Just like the different aspects to the development of spoken language for a variety of situations, the arts were also seen by some pupils (although a small minority) as influential in developing listening skills for various situations – groups, teams, or being in charge of a group.

2.
WHAT ARE
THE EFFECTS
OF
ARTS
EDUCATION?

Transfer of listening skills from the arts to teamwork in PE was mentioned by one pupil (and not the same pupil who had talked about speaking in front of a group for sports coaching).

It was apparent from the pupil comments that listening was seen as an essential aspect of music and that some pupils found it an *'easier'* or more accessible element than other parts of music, such as instrumental or note-reading skills. Indeed, the link between music and listening was obvious, and was still important for the older pupils, suggesting that it should in no way be assigned a lesser status than other skills in music – despite being more accessible:

> *Music is about learning how to read music, compose, how to listen, pick out certain details* (Year 9).

> *You listen, do a lot of listening, which I'm quite good at so I find it easier* (Year 11).

As a result, many pupils talked about listening to music, and on a number of occasions this was linked directly to the development of better communication skills. Transfer to 'life' was highlighted by one pupil: '*I think music comes into your career quite a lot, being able to listen to people, and it trains your ears as well. Altogether, I think it makes you more alert*' (Year 7).

As a further active and critical skill, pupils also talked about observation as communication. Of the 25 comments made by 19 pupils on observation, 22 related to art. As an extension of those visual awareness skills already discussed in section 4.5 under the heading 'Pupils on developing technical skills and competence in art', pupils discussed how they were generally more observant, looking at and seeing things differently, and that this skill transferred to other subject areas. This helped with communication of ideas particularly in English where a picture or something observed may be used as the starting material for an essay or story. One pupil described how being able to '*look at things with an artistic eye, and describe them in words in a different manner*' would help with better communication in his aim for a career as an author. Being more observant in drama was mentioned by just one pupil, who linked it to learning to assess information.

The possibilities for developing communication skills through listening and observing were evident, although not always directly articulated by the pupils. In many ways, the pupils' comments reflected a greater ability to communicate ideas and express themselves either in a different medium, or in a wider variety of contexts and situations, as a result of listening, observing and talking in the arts. As such, their comments relate directly to the final and largest subcategory of effects in this chapter, on developing expressive skills.

7.5 DEVELOPMENTS IN EXPRESSIVE SKILLS

This subcategory collates those references made to expressive skills in the arts, and how learners are helped to make statements about the world, their world and themselves, as well as comments on self-expression and having the confidence to express 'themselves'.

7.5.1 Tools for expressive skills across the artforms

Teacher Perspectives

With numerous references by teachers from across the different artforms, this perceived effect was one of the most frequently nominated of all the subcategories. Essentially, it focused on the empowerment young people were deemed to gain through being encouraged to express themselves, their opinions, their ideas, their values and their creativity. Interviewees saw the arts as occupying a crucial place in the curriculum, largely because they offered children the space and the 'freedom' to express their perspectives on themselves and their world. (Like the freedom to create, then, pupils also have the freedom to express their opinions in the arts, and as such this links with section 6.3 on a sense of freedom and the confidence to experiment, under the subheading of 'Development of creativity and imagination'.) One headteacher captured the views of many when talking about the power of the arts to enable the making and articulating of personal statements:

> *Many of the curriculum subjects are to do with children responding to, and reacting to, a world upon which they have little influence and have little that they can record in a personal, subjective way. The strength of the arts is it is something that they take in; it is their response to the world, which they must digest and put out again.*

Arts-oriented outlets and media for self-expression were especially important for groups of pupils who, for various reasons, would otherwise find the making and communicating of personal statements difficult. One example centred on the opportunity given to pupils with limited academic ability or children for whom English is not a first language to 'open up' in arts subjects that do not require writing. Other examples included:

> *My aims are to work with the young people in a way that they don't usually get to work with others, which enables them then to find a different way of expressing themselves. We are always finding that there are people who cannot express themselves in other areas and maybe they are put down because of that, but they can really flourish in drama* (head of drama).

> ——

> *For example in the performing arts, I think you can take a child who might, for example, I can think of examples where pupils are maybe*

– have a small circle of friends, have maybe a slightly eccentric personality, maybe a little bit precocious even, or maybe a little bit more mature than their years would suggest they should be, finding an opportunity maybe in acting or theatre work which allows them to express all those things which are not possible perhaps with their peers (head of Welsh).

[Talking about art] *They can express themselves in ways that does not mean that they have to stand up on a stage and perform, nor are they going to have to sort of expose themselves to other individuals, as it were, in the way that they do in drama* (ex-head of art).

You know, kids are so often not allowed to express how they feel. You know, if they are angry, they are not allowed to go and thump someone because you just don't do that, that isn't right. They are not allowed to express by crying, because it is just not cool to cry. The arts, you know, dance, they can express how they feel in it; maybe it's one way that they can actually let go of some of their emotions (dance and PE teacher).

Sometimes it does seem that the kids who are the bad kids in other subjects, because they are the disruptive ones, are the ones who do really well in our subjects because that expression, that freedom of expression, is what they relish and they are away (drama teacher).

A recurring theme through the comments recorded under this subcategory was a perception, for some a strong conviction, that the development of expression through the arts was extremely enabling for young people (e.g. through offering an alternative language, a '*voice or voices*', an internal locus of control or a release of personal tensions and inhibitions). The following are just a selection of many such observations:

[It is about] *finding a means of expressing themselves, and looking at the world around them, and coming to terms with that. You are equipping them with sophisticated tools and, as I said, for me personally* [theatre] *is not the be all and end all; it is not about them being able to act particularly well or whatever. It is being able to manipulate those tools for their own means, so being able to do that, they feel that they have more control over what they are doing* (head of drama).

They've got an outlet for expressing themselves which makes them more relaxed about life, in control of life (drama teacher).

[Music gives] *a way of expressing what you have inside, if that makes sense. It is like ... not feelings, it is just a way ... it is another language. It is another language and I have just gained so much enjoyment from it, just being able to play and sing. I think that it is a way of release as well. I think that every child should have the opportunity to experience that* (head of music).

Tools for expression

There also seemed to be general agreement about the value and, for some, the necessity, of building the capacity for self-expression on the firm foundations of the acquisition of the technical skills outlined in section 4.5. For some interviewees, these were construed as the essential 'tools' of expression and a key outcome of arts education was seen as enabling pupils to decide which set of tools best suited each individual's endeavours to be expressive:

Here I am, up in the Lake District, and I'm moved by the sunrise, over by Lake Coniston, and unless I have got the ability ... and I may not have experienced poetry, but I might be quite an accomplished musician, I cannot write a poem about that because I simply don't have the tools. I cannot work in that way, because nobody has given me the tools to respond like that. So all I have got to do is to write it in music and to express my response in music. That may not be appropriate. Why is it that Wordsworth reacted in the way that he did to his surroundings? Is it because he didn't have a decent music education? We will never know that ... so unless we can give kids a chance to know how they can respond, and think, and work out, or what their preferred mode of activity is, then those ideas may forever just stay locked inside them; there is no way of actually exploring that (LEA adviser).

———

From the dramatic point of view, they have acquired the confidence and the skill to be able to know what is a good way of, either in role play or themselves, being able to express themselves (deputy head).

———

The different [art] *forms in which you can express these ideas or explore these ideas within the classroom and the analysis of that, and how a child coming into a secondary school has very, very limited knowledge of that artform, if any, and through the five years, or even through the three years if they don't opt to do it for GCSE, they then have the tools in which to express a variety of ideas, well endless ideas really, in a form* (drama teacher).

In several respects, however, there was a lack of consensus in the implicit messages conveyed about the precise nature of this claimed effect. While some seemed to suggest that the effect was the 'opportunity' for self-expression, others appeared to believe that the outcome was a set of positive attitudes and predispositions in young people to be expressive. Still others implied that self-expression was the application of technical skills to the making of personal statements, whereas some seemed to insinuate that there may be a set of competencies labelled 'expressive skills' that exist over and above the artform technical skills. These various interpretations of expressive outcomes carry important implications for any attempts to substantiate these claimed effects.

Pupil Perspectives

Pupils too explained expressive skills in a variety of ways. Most notably, self-expression was associated with self-confidence by the pupils. This was related to personal development and is expanded as a separate area of discussion in Chapter 8, on Personal and Social Development. In this current chapter, however, we consider pupils' perceived outcomes of the arts as a tool for expression – including expression not through language; and the arts as empowering – facilitating pupils' expressive skills in general, and enabling them to express their feelings, ideas and opinions. Overall, this subcategory of effects received 223 comments, making it – as for the teachers – one of the most frequently nominated outcomes by the pupils.

Tools for expression

Using the arts as a tool for expression attracted 35 comments in total, with 13 of these specifically relating to expression not through language. For one of the schools, this did not appear to be as significant an effect as at the other schools – of which one had a significant number of comments for drama and another for art. Overall, most comments were for art – 14, with nine for drama, nine for the arts in general, two for music (significantly less than the other artforms) and one for dance. Comments were spread across all the year groups, although most comments for art came from Years 9–11, and Years 7–9 for drama, suggesting a difference with age in art and drama as tools for expression.

Of the nine comments on expression using the arts in general as tools, six were responses to the questions 'What is learning in the arts about/ for at this school?' and 'For you, what does the term "the arts" mean?' Examples of such responses are given below:

> To help you understand different things of the subject, different ways of expressing it (Year 7).

> Music, dance, drama – ways of expressing yourself (Year 7).

Expressing yourself in as many different ways as possible. Like in art it's showing what you think in drawing. It's just trying to tell people what you think and what you're trying to say in all different ways (Year 9).

One interesting comment was about the arts as a '*way of expressing … what you want to express in a way that can be understood, or misunderstood, by other people*', indicating a sense of audience and reception. Another pupil talked about the arts as a tool for expressing a '*personal understanding of life*'. Again, expression through alternatives to writing or talking were mentioned, pupils perceiving that they would use 'different' skills (although none were specifically mentioned, but are implicit in the subcategories by artform below) for expression in the arts as opposed to say in English.

Pupils on art as an expressive tool

Art was viewed as an expressive tool from several different angles. For some pupils, it was about expressing themselves through '*drawing instead of speaking*', while for others, it was to do with having more tools to be expressive with, for example colour, paper, paints and so on. One pupil related this to emotional effects:

I think I've learnt how to express myself through drawing and I've learnt how other artists have different techniques and stuff …

Interviewer: *How have you learnt to express yourself?*

One of the teachers said to us one time, like, if you're feeling depressed today, most artists use dull colours so I can kind of tell what kind of mood you're in 'cos it kind of affects the way you paint, what colours you use [and] *what mood you're in* (Year 9).

While most pupils talked here about expressing themselves, some noted art as providing the tools for expression by others, for example, to express their cultural backgrounds:

… Like in graffiti on walls, it is showing their culture, what they believe in – I am interested in that. How they show their art, it is very expressive, showing their culture, what they believe in. It really shows what they are trying to say to each other (Year 9).

However, it was the former view on expressing themselves without speaking that attracted most attention, one pupil also indicating that the arts provided a tool for expression 'without writing'. Could it be that expression without words was important for all of these pupils? Certainly non-verbal expression seemed quite important to one pupil's sense of ease of communication:

It gives me the chance to express my feelings and I don't have to do it verbally, where you might get stuck – you want to say something but you don't want to. And you get nervous (Year 9).

Another pupil recognised the issue of accessibility and equality of opportunity for self-expression, again highlighting that not all pupils communicate best verbally:

Interviewer: *But why do you draw?*

Some people can best express their thoughts in art, in drawings, if they can't speak properly. It's just another form of expressing yourself. It's just another way of trying to get your message across (Year 9).

The possibilities for self-expression in art were compared to other subject areas, one pupil considering other subjects lacking in this outcome:

... [More] self expression in my work than from other subjects where it's just you have been told what to do, whereas in art you can do what you like and express it, express it in your way in art (Year 11).

Pupils on drama as an expressive tool

Interestingly, pupils saw drama in particular as important to both language development (as we have seen in section 7.3) and as a tool for non-lingual expression (seven of the 13 comments on expression not through language). Pupils mentioned that it was useful to be able to express themselves without language – and one cited a particular exercise in respect of this:

We had to make up a mime ... our group was a child being told off at school and you weren't allowed to use English or Welsh, and it had to be your own made-up language. And the others had to understand what you were trying ... that was a good exercise of showing, of expressing yourself without using words really (Year 9).

The ability to communicate through body language, such as using '*sounds and movements instead of speaking*' was highlighted:

It's made me come closer to my feelings. Before, I wanted to use, like, hand gestures and my facial expressions and things like that. Before, I just expressed things by mouth, by talking, but I later learnt ... I know how to use my body (Year 8).

For some, this made for '*better communication*' because it used more of themselves: '*People talk with their hands as well, and that helps you in drama. And it helps you to express yourself and say what you feel.*'

Indeed, expression of emotion not through language was emphasised in the dramatic artform, perhaps more so than in the other artforms (although, as we shall see later, expression of feelings was frequently cited for art):

Interviewer: *You mentioned earlier ... showing your emotions ...?*

Yes. There isn't any other subject that teaches you to do that. Drama's about letting yourself go and doing whatever's asked of you, and you don't get that in any other subject.

Interviewer: *Does it mean that you're able to show your emotions only within the drama lesson, or does it help you to show your emotions more in general life?*

It's more to do with the drama, showing your emotion. But also in sort of social life you're willing ... you can do that kind of out-front kind of unshy attitude towards it because that's what drama's all about. So, it relates to your social life as well. You get more confidence with doing and saying things, or whatever, and the way you act, which is good (Year 10).

2.
WHAT ARE
THE EFFECTS
OF
ARTS
EDUCATION?

A few pupils linked tools for expression across the artforms – particularly drama and art – aiding one and the other in expression without speech.

Pupils on dance and music as an expressive tool

One pupil talked about dance as an expressive tool in terms of creating a picture with the body. This differed to those comments for drama, where the emphasis appeared to be on body language and emotions, rather than creating a still picture. However, just having one comment for dance in this respect makes such generalisations rather tentative. The two music comments were about using different musical styles to express either happy or sad emotions – for example soul, and different dynamics and rhythms. For one pupil, it was important to get this across – perhaps again indicating a sense of audience.

Another music comment, in a different subcategory extended this idea of audience, to entertainment. On enabling and releasing emotions and energy, one pupil said: '... *being able to, like, release your energy in a positive way, singing and entertaining people and stuff like that, and that's nice as well*' (Year 9).

Pupils on the arts as empowerment to express

Pupils talked about the arts as empowering and enabling them to express themselves, to develop expressive skills, and to express feelings, ideas and opinions. There were 187 comments in total for these perceived effects, with art receiving most nominations (70), drama (50) and music far less, just 20. Dance was mentioned just four times in this respect, English 14 times, and there were 29 comments for the arts in general – indicating a sense of the arts as a whole contributing to expressive skills.

7.5.2 Developments in the abilities to express oneself and one's feelings

Not only did pupils make comments about developments in expressive skills by using the arts as tools for self-expression, they also referred to being more able to express themselves as people. This included expression of feelings, ideas and opinions, and the abilities to express themselves in a group – to other people.

Pupil Perspectives

Pupils on expressing yourself

Being able to express yourself was the most frequently mentioned area within this subcategory – with 128 of the 187 comments, made by 54 pupils. Again art yielded most of the comments – two of the schools featuring a high number of art nominations. One of these schools had also had a significantly high proportion of the comments on creativity and imagination and a sense of freedom in the visual arts – suggesting a possible link between self-expression and creativity or freedom in art, but we note that comments from the other school did not highlight such a correlation. Comments were made across all the year groups, with Years 10 and 11 quite well represented considering the smaller number of pupils taking the arts at this stage.

An overall sense of the arts enabling expression was given by one of the pupils, and this sets a good starting point for the following discourse around a widely varying set of responses. In answer to the question of what learning in the arts is for, this pupil covered expression in several of the artforms as well as the arts in general:

> *To learn how to express yourself in different types of ways. Be more creative and to, like, broaden your, the way you look at things ... in music you can express yourself by singing ... in art you can draw and paint the way you feel, and in drama you can get to act the way other people feel and the way you feel, to get your point across* (Year 8).

Being able to express yourself 'more' was stressed by many of the pupils for both art and drama in particular. Indeed, for drama there were numerous comments on clarity of expression, pupils saying '[I could now] *express myself more clearly*', or that '[I am] *able to express myself better*'. These comments were prevalent especially at Year 11, but also mentioned across all the year groups. Expressing yourself better by highlighting the good aspects to a situation was mentioned by one of the pupils. Drama was also linked with being able to 'express another person's being', rather than just themselves:

> *Well, it's nice, kind of, to express yourself as, like, a different person because then you take on, like, their feelings and what they think and stuff. It's quite good just doing it like that, rather than in kind of art where you're just sat down and just drawing, which is satisfying but with drama it's, kind of, you can just express yourself in different ways* (Year 9).

> *... you really can express yourself, you can play a part that isn't you – that's the buzz of it. You can be someone that you are not or if you want, you can be someone who you wish to be or be someone that you hope to God that you are not going to be, so you can just play a role that you are not because that's the fun of it. You are not playing something that you see every day in everyday life. You could be a mad psychopath or you could be this sweet little child or you could just be normal or you could be an animal – you could be a giraffe, you could be anything. That's the fun of it.*

> Interviewer: *What do you get out of having the chance to take all those different roles? What do you learn from that?*

> *You learn that deep down you have got a sense of being able to perform, you can perform. Deep down you know that you can perform in any way. You can be something that you are not. That's the fun thing about it* (Year 9).

Transfer of being more able to express yourself, from drama to normal life was suggested by at least one of the pupils: '*It makes you more confident to express yourself or whatever, because that's what drama is basically all about, so that goes with you into normal life*' (Year 11).

At one school in particular, expressing yourself in drama was linked by the pupils to their inner selves – '*do what comes from within*' – or as one pupil asserted, '*That is why they call it "Expressive Arts" at this school, because we do lots of things about feelings and stuff like that.*' Another pupil from a different school referred to this outcome as '*getting things inside you out*'.

For art, self-expression was seen as more to do with putting something of yourself into your work – linking with what has already been discussed in Chapter 4 regarding skill acquisition and development. Again, comments on being more able to express oneself were more common in Year 11, for art. For one pupil, a real sense of empowerment, voiced through enjoyment, was demonstrated regarding self-expression and skill development, from which the following illustration has been created:

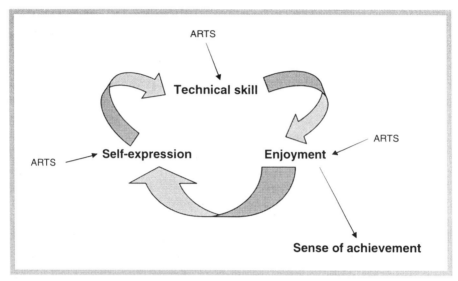

Being good at an art and being able to express yourself, I think, is one of the hardest things in life to achieve. Without an art it is hard, but being able to play a musical instrument, or act or paint or something like that, you can always achieve that. It is always hard to master, but once you have got the skill you can begin to enjoy and then you do it even more, then you get even better, so you enjoy it even more. It is just a circle (Year 7 pupil).

Further links between self-expression and increased technical skill and enjoyment are discussed in Chapter 11 of the report.

A sense of reassurance was conveyed by several of the pupils, indicating that the arts enabled or empowered them to express themselves where they might otherwise lack confidence, be shy, or be worried about what other people thought of their ideas and opinions:

That I can express myself without being worried about other people's opinions – like in drama and dance (Year 7, arts).

———

I find it easy to adapt to and I can express myself clearly and not feel embarrassed in the subjects and topics. It's more social, it's more a ... I can relate to it and I can give people ideas how I am feeling through my drama, and you can involve people and add to something and build it up so that people can see what you would feel and what you would think and stuff (Year 10, drama).

———

Yeah, because you can be more open and express yourself without worrying about what other people are saying – which is good because you don't want to be shy throughout your life (Year 9, dance).

Comparison of the arts with other subjects was also made in this respect, pupils implicating the arts as either more expressive and perhaps individual than the traditionally academic subjects, or as a necessary outlet for the expression of emotions and self:

It's more expressive because, say in history or maths, you don't really express anything in that, say, you do in dance or you do in music or anything like that. You can't really go abstract, whereas you can in the arts (Year 8, arts).

———

They [the arts] *let people express themselves, which you can't do in the sciences* (Year 8, drama).

———

With the other subjects ... you're just doing the same as everybody else. You're just writing things down or doing sums of something ... [in art] you can draw it how you want to, express yourself ... (Year 10, art).

———

Interviewer: *Do you see it as a way of expressing yourself or saying something about yourself?*

Yes, it's like yes, because a lot of people, if you are not that good at school stuff and drawing, it helps you express your feelings and yourself and that (Year 9, art).

———

... in the arts, in music, in art, it's a way of expressing emotions as well, which a lot of people need to do, without having necessarily to talk to a friend if you don't want to. It's just a way of you drawing a picture ... I don't personally, but if you look at a lot of the art work, it's faces and their worlds, like, so I think it's a way of expressing emotions (Year 11, art and music).

Indeed, not keeping your emotions pent up was one aspect of expressing yourself identified by another of the pupils, this time for drama: '*To be more expressive. Not to sort of keep things bottled up and just to sort of talk about them and then sort of use them in drama*' (Year 7, drama).

For another pupil, drama was specifically seen as a good way to express yourself, perhaps better than art in this respect:

... drama is a really good way of expressing yourself. I don't know, it might even be a bit better than art because it's like you can move

and ... how can I put it? ... you can talk and you can speak your mind and stuff and you can do all sort of things what you wanted to do in drama, even if you are not actually playing yourself, but you can get things out in different ways in drama (Year 9, drama).

Expressive skills in music were more associated with pupils expressing themselves in the music, through a style of playing that fitted their current emotional frame:

... you can express yourself with music because you can express yourself with the instruments. You can play really hard if you're angry or really soft if you are happy, whatever, like that. It is quite fun (Year 9, music).

English was cited by a number of the pupils as important to expressing themselves – one pupil seeing it as more for expressing the '*reality*' part of the arts through discussion.

Unlike the teachers, the pupils seldom referred to the arts as enabling them to choose the tools with which to work. In fact, it appeared that just one pupil referred to such an outcome, over several years of the interview process:

I can express myself and how I am feeling through colour, and I can see things and how things will work best, [and] *where, and I can express myself through art ...* (Year 10, art).

———

Interviewer: *Is it a form of self-expression for you as well? Is that an important aspect of it as well, or not so much?*

Yes, I can express myself through my art work, you know, I can choose stuff that I am interested in and promote that in my work ... (Year 11, art, same pupil).

Strangely, and despite the links between self-expression, technical skill and enjoyment suggested above by those pupils feeling more able to express themselves, particularly in Year 11 (that is when technical skill is more developed), expression was rarely linked to creativity or to expressing thoughts or 'what you are thinking'. Rather, there was a body of comment on expression of feeling, and this makes up the following discussion under the subheading of 'Pupils on expression of feelings'.

Pupils on expression of feelings
There were 48 comments specifically on expression of feelings in particular, and rather surprisingly, art attracted most of these comments (22), with drama receiving 12 and music just five. This smaller number of comments for drama seems interesting in the light of the emphasis on role play, and getting into others' shoes in drama (as highlighted in

Chapter 4), but the proportions of comments for each artform are again similar to those in the previous few subcategories of this chapter, where art has received the most attention, followed by drama.

Perhaps of most impact were the numbers of comments by pupils relating to their independence in art, being able to draw what they felt, and even being set tasks to portray their emotions on paper. '*I think it's a good way of saying how you feel; say, if you're painting by the colours you use, it brings out your personality,*' said one pupil. For some, the link between emotions and getting them down or out on paper was an association they had made for themselves:

> *Art has got quite a strong link to my emotions. If you are angry, you quite often draw something which can turn out to be quite a nasty picture ...* (Year 9).

> ———

> *How to express yourself, 'cos when you're drawing you do what you want, it's independent. You get given an outline but you can do whatever you want really* (Year 7).

As pointed out earlier in this chapter, under the subheading 'Pupils on expressing yourself', some pupils noted a link between expressive skills and increased technical skills. Similarly, with regard to the expression of feelings, one pupil described using different textures, materials and colours to express emotions – sad, happy, depression, and so on. Interestingly, the scope of art as an 'aid' to expression of feelings touched the realms of escapism for a few pupils:

> *If someone was sulking just after they had an argument, they could just go and draw and forget about everything else and you wouldn't really remember after that as much, [in] detail. And you could be friends with the person that you argued with* (Year 9).

> ———

> *Well, sometimes if I am upset or something, I will draw, as it helps me to feel better. But I don't think it helps me think* (Year 7).

This resonates with what has already been said in Chapter 3 on therapeutic outcomes, escapism and relaxation.

Comments for expression of feelings in drama were much more to do with a sense of release, than had been expressed for art. Examples of pupils' discussion include: '*in drama you can let yourself go*', '*... you can just let it all out and let it all go in drama*', '*express your feelings ... rather than keeping them all pent up*'. One of the older pupils demonstrated how feelings could be used to influence the direction of the drama work: '*You can express yourself and how you're feeling, you can shape the drama how you feel it would go, how you'd like it to go ...*'

2.
WHAT ARE
THE EFFECTS
OF
ARTS
EDUCATION?

Pupils commenting on expression of feelings in music talked mostly about expression through composing – perhaps songs – in order to express a current emotion; however, the relative paucity of such nominations for music is significant. Poetry was cited in three cases as being a *'chance to write down what you're feeling'*. Although almost every comment in this subcategory related to expression of current feelings, there was one pupil who indicated that being able to express might be important to a possible future career in social work, *'because like in drama and music you get to express your feelings, so you should be able to understand what people are going through'*.

Pupils on expression of ideas and opinions

Like the previous discussion on expression of feelings, the expression of ideas and opinions was also identified as a further type of response within this subcategory. However, it was quite small, just eight comments, and as such perhaps reflects what some of the pupils' remarks have already hinted at: that pupils do not seem to link expressive skills in the arts with thinking skills. Again, art received more comments than the other artforms – but that there were so few comments here means that art need not necessarily be more associated with this outcome than any of the other artforms. In general, pupils talked about voicing their opinions, one pupil highlighting how this outcome helped in other subjects such as English and science.

Pupils on expression in groups

By way of rounding off this chapter, it is noted that in most if not all of the subcategories relating to communication and expressive skills, pupils have talked about being more able to communicate in groups, in one form or another. Not only that, but they were more at ease in expressing themselves in groups, as the last three comments in this subcategory would indicate:

> *You get to talk and discuss and put your views across ...* (Year 9, English).

> *We have a lot of class discussions and also when you get in a group you can always contribute and let people know your ideas and what you think about things* (Year 9, drama).

> *It's easier to speak to people, like a group of people ... it's easier to talk to other people ...* (Year 9).

As in the case of the teachers, then, there was a wide variety of comment on expressive skills and expressing yourself in the arts, and it is perhaps not possible to correlate or convey the precise nature of this effect. The whole concept of expressing yourself was in fact described as 'difficult' by one of the pupils themselves. He was actually describing a day out on an art trip, and having been set the task of expressing themselves through drawing, he said:

> ... *I had never actually attempted anything like that before. It is a very difficult concept just expressing yourself and, yes, it was wonderful, and everybody got into it* ... (Year 9, art).

Little wonder then that there have been so many different attempts by pupils and teachers at conveying the outcomes related to expressive skills.

7.6 CONCLUDING COMMENTS

The development of communication and expressive skills through the arts was an important outcome perceived by both teachers and pupils, with drama contributing significantly to the first of these effects. In addition to the teachers' comments on elocution and clarity of speech, the pupils widened the discussion to include language skills for a variety of specified situations – such as language for teamwork, public speaking, interview skills, and appropriateness of language.

For the more expressive outcomes, art was nominated more frequently than drama, with music being referred to surprisingly infrequently in comparison. The teachers talked about the arts as facilitating developments in expressive skills in terms of being more able to make personal statements; and being given a vehicle for that expression. This latter point was especially implicated where communicating personal statements might be difficult – for example through shyness, through difficulties in more traditionally academic areas of the curriculum, for the disruptive child, and where an outlet for pent-up emotions might be important. Although the pupils also mentioned many of these areas, there was not such explicit mention of personal statements, or indeed statements about their place in the world, as had been indicated by the teachers. Expression in the arts was also associated by the teachers with a strong sense of enabling young people to feel more relaxed and in control of their own self-expression, and in addition was seen as enabling pupils to decide which set of artistic tools to use. This outcome was not much emphasised by the pupils, although they did talk about using the arts as tools for expression – but not particularly about being enabled to choose those tools. Indeed, it was apparent that pupils' perceptions of communication and expressive skills related very much to themselves as users of the arts – focusing on the process-base of the arts.

2.
WHAT ARE
THE EFFECTS
OF
ARTS
EDUCATION?

Some interesting differences by artform were apparent – art and drama being associated with both expression of self and others, and indicating the transfer of communication skills to other situations. In contrast, expressive skills were not often emphasised in music, and where this was the case, music was mostly regarded by pupils as facilitating expression by using their emotions or feelings of the moment, rather than indicating a transfer to other situations. Transfer of listening skills, however, from music to other classroom and learning activities was evident. The fact that pupils volunteered accounts of the carry-over to other contexts of improved speaking skills, self-confidence to express themselves, listening and observational skills is revealing. It is germane to the whole debate about transferable outcomes – this will be considered in more detail in Chapter 9.

Providing some justification for drama's location within the National Curriculum framework, the relevance and proximity of drama to English were clearly evident in pupils' accounts of language and communication effects – though, considering the whole spectrum of outcomes reported for drama, it is noticeable that the field of drama's influence is more wide-ranging and distinctive than its association with English would suggest.

Expressive skills were not very often related to thinking or cognitive skills, but were sometimes associated with technical skill and perhaps enjoyment, and specifically the therapeutic and release aspects of self-expression, thus linking with Chapters 3 and 4.

Expressive skills relating to jobs did not make up a large body of the employers' or employees' comments, but where they did contribute it was to do with clarity of communication, rather than expression of self or of feelings or opinions. One employer regarded employees with arts backgrounds as expressing themselves well, bringing *'different dimensions* [in] *that they use other parts of their brains to express themselves'*. As such, and in contrast to the pupils' views, expressive and communication skills were associated, albeit tentatively, with cognitive aspects by those in employment. The following comment by the same employer, on how arts education might affect employability, illustrates this point:

... it's a huge asset ... because they bring, you know, an enquiring mind, a broad open mind, and a great deal of confidence derived from their ability to express themselves properly (Communications Director).

8. PERSONAL AND SOCIAL DEVELOPMENT

CHAPTER OVERVIEW

Moving on to the sixth of the broad effect categories, this chapter deals with accounts of personal and social development as a result of teaching and learning in the arts. Reflecting the diverse range of outcomes identified in this area, the chapter is divided into seven subcategories:

- developing a sense of self and one's emotions (8.2)
- enhanced self-esteem and self-worth (8.3)
- increases in different forms of self-confidence (8.4)
- the development of a whole and rounded personality (8.5)
- enriched personal skills (8.6)
- growth in the awareness of others and empathy (8.7)
- enhanced social skills (8.8).

8.1 INTRODUCTION

This chapter covers perceptions of the broad area of pupils' personal and social development as an outcome of arts education. The perceived gains in self-awareness and personal and social skills correspond to Gardner's (1993) concepts of intrapersonal and interpersonal intelligences:

> ... the intrapersonal intelligence – knowledge of the internal aspects of a person; access to one's own feeling life, one's range of emotions, the capacity to effect discriminations among these emotions and eventually to label them and to draw upon them as a means of understanding and guiding one's own behaviour. A person with good intrapersonal intelligence has a viable and effective model of himself.

> ... Interpersonal intelligence builds on a core capacity to notice distinctions among others; in particular, contrasts in their moods, temperaments, motivations, and intentions. In more advanced forms, this intelligence permits a skilled adult to read the intentions and desires of others, even when these have been hidden.

> ... Interpersonal intelligence allows one to understand and work with others; intrapersonal intelligence allows one to understand and work with oneself. In the individual's sense of self, one encounters a melding of inter- and intrapersonal components (ibid., pp. 23–5).

Within the data collected, seven subcategories of personal and social development outcomes were identified:

- developing a sense of self and one's emotions (section 8.2);
- enhanced self-worth and self-esteem (section 8.3);
- increased self-confidence (section 8.4);
- developing the whole personality (section 8.5);
- improved personal skills (section 8.6);
- increased awareness of others and empathy (section 8.7); and
- improved social skills (section 8.8).

The subcategories at the top of the list deal with aspects of intrapersonal intelligence, such as one's own emotions, while the later ones consider capacities associated with interpersonal intelligence, such as social skills and awareness of others. Subcategories in the middle of the list, for example, self-confidence, straddle the two areas of personal intelligence. Each section will consider the responses of teachers and pupils, and outcomes will be discussed in terms of the arts as a whole and the individual artforms.

8.2 DEVELOPING A SENSE OF SELF AND ONE'S EMOTIONS

In the provisional typology of effects as seen by teachers (see Harland *et al.,* 1998), a category of outcome was created to cover claims that the arts develop pupils' knowledge and understanding of emotions, the world of feelings or the affective domain. Initially, this seemed to represent an advancement in what others have called 'emotional intelligence' (Goleman, 1996; Mayer *et al.,* 2000). However, when examining the full range of pupil comments, only two comments fell into this category – both were very general remarks about how emotional states or tensions like sadness or happiness had been explored in drama. Upon further scrutiny, it was apparent that pupils tended to talk about the arts as a medium for understanding their own feelings and emotions as part of a process of self-discovery and the crystallisation of one's own identity, or as part of learning about other people, and hence, for example, the need for empathy and tolerance. Very rarely did pupils construct the outcome of an increased understanding of the emotions or the affective domain as an objective reality detached from themselves or others. According to the pupils' constructions of their learning in the arts, in much the same way as creativity or thinking skills were not studied as metacognitive processes for critical reflection and examination, neither were the emotions. Moreover, when we returned to the teachers' comments in this area, it was apparent that they too tended to view explorations of emotions as integral to learning about one's self or others. Thus, the original category has been removed from the model presented here and the comments assigned more appropriately to this subcategory or to section 8.7 on 'awareness of others'. (Such comments should not be confused with those that focused on the emotional aspects associated with the response to the arts – getting a buzz, for example – which were often classified under 'immediate intrinsic effects: forms of enjoyment and therapy' in Chapter 3.) In proceeding in this manner, we are not implying that the affective domain – rather like thinking skills and creativity – should not be treated as an area of human cognitive experience worthy of explicit intellectual investigation in its own right; we are simply recognising that pupils, and in hindsight, teachers, tend to concretise learning about emotions in the context of aiding self-discovery and increased awareness of others.

Consequently, this first subcategory considers the reported effects of developing greater awareness of one's self or one's identity, often through increased understanding of one's own feelings and emotions. It also presents accounts of how the arts help to promote a pupil's individuality.

Teacher Perspectives

Developing a sense of self was a prevalent claim among teachers of most of the artforms, but especially drama. Finding out or discovering about your 'self' as a result of arts education was a common theme: phrases like *'greater awareness of themselves'*, *'feeling comfortable with themselves'* were used quite regularly. As indicated, this process of discovery frequently involved the exploration of the emotional state of the inner self. One headteacher expressed such an outcome when commenting on the process of internalisation that the arts can precipitate:

> *That internalising helps them to understand themselves, their own feelings, because I don't think we have mentioned that much, their feelings about the world and the way in which they can make statements that are aggressive statements, or sensitive statements or whatever, but they can do that through the art experience. People talk about drama being a way of directing anger and understanding relationships and tensions between two people through that drama. So, it is to do with the sense and the feelings, and the spirit.*

Other contributions included:

> [With reference to drama] *Very often, for a lot of them, they have just found out a little bit more about themselves. And they've begun to discover themselves in a way that maybe they are never given the opportunity to do* (drama teacher).

[Again with reference to drama] *The most important thing I think is that they come out and they feel they know more about themselves and about what is going on around them and they can respond to that* (head of drama).

———

The pupils also are allowed to develop individually. One of the sixth-formers, for example, I know has been doing things – sculpting out of wood, tree trunks and this sort of thing – which one doesn't find very often, but which is very appropriate for this area – totem poles and this type of thing are being looked at (deputy head).

———

It allows for individualistic ideas and views, it helps to create self-images which are important for people (head).

———

[With reference to art] *It's that gain in confidence in themselves, knowing themselves a bit more – I can't explain it, but I can see them develop and coming out of themselves, because it's a horrible age, I think, growing up, being a teenager and being confident enough to be an individual and to do things. I really do think it does help* (head of art).

One adviser extended this type of impact beyond the general effect of 'knowing your self' to the more specific outcome of 'knowing what you know', 'knowing your own intuition' and 'knowing your own values' through the channel of metacognition:

Critically, the notion of metacognition, of knowing what you know, being aware of what you're aware of, because so often our intuition is down there somewhere, we are not always in touch with it, so I think if they can be in touch with their own intuition, their own selves.

One headteacher offered a potent image of how the arts make a distinctive contribution to the development of a student's individuality:

When it is an art process, they have made those changes themselves, it is part of them that has made it and that ... and their signature is all over the piece of work in a way that it isn't over a piece of science or maths. That is an important bit, the signature bit ... this is something that only you can produce because you are you, and you are unique. Maybe that is it, the uniqueness of the individual; maybe that is why in certain societies, art is always distrusted as a dangerous thing.

Pupil Perspectives

Within this subcategory, pupils' comments focused on similar outcomes to those proposed by teachers: an increase in self-awareness and understanding (often through self-discovery and explorations of feelings, values and beliefs), promotion of self-identity, and the developing of a pupil's individuality. Overall, 43 comments were made by 29 pupils. A large number of these citations concerned the arts in general, although a similar number referred specifically to drama as a medium for this outcome, with only a handful of comments related to art.

Roughly two-thirds of the references to the arts as a means for increased self-awareness and understanding were made by Year 9 pupils (though it should be recalled that two cohorts of this year group were interviewed). Pupils of different ages seemed to discuss slightly different aspects of this outcome, which will be considered in more detail below. Interestingly, four of the five comments made by older pupils were made by boys.

'*Discovering yourself*' or finding out more about yourself was a fairly common theme amongst pupils of all ages, especially in connection with the arts in general and drama. In drama, it was recognising facets of her own personality in a character that she was acting out which enabled one pupil to know more about herself: '*If you act someone out, you tend to feel like "ah, this person is rather like me", like, she does this and that, and you begin to know more about yourself*' (Year 9, drama).

Pupils often extended this concept of self-discovery to include an increased understanding of themselves, and an increased acceptance of who they are – undoubtedly, important issues for all teenagers during the years of puberty, identity formation and personal development:

> *Sometimes it helps you to understand yourself and how you feel and how you look, see what's different about yourself* (Year 9, drama).

> ———

> *They helped me come to terms with my sexuality* (Year 10, arts).

As a continuation of this theme, several pupils cited the arts as a means to come to terms with their own problems, or deal with situations they may encounter in day-to-day life:

> *I'm colour-blind as well, so it's helped me to come to terms with that and put more in perspective for myself* (Year 9, art).

> ———

They help you to come to terms with my problems or deal with what's been going on in my life (Year 9, arts).

———

We did about this girl. Her parents were completely ignoring her. So, there was neglect, and we learnt about how people feel about neglect, being ignored completely. When we did that, it just so happened that my mum and dad had had this really big argument, and me and my brother were getting a bit neglected. So, it helped me understand how it felt at home (Year 9, drama).

An aspect of this 'self-discovery' outcome of arts education commonly nominated by younger pupils was thinking about their own views and opinions on issues, often, as in the next few extracts, rethinking their positions by taking other perspectives on board:

You get to find out what your opinions are, definitely, your views. And sometimes you might have been sure that that was your opinion, but then really you find out there's other things to consider and it might change your opinion on it (Year 9, arts).

A specific art project on identity enabled one pupil to discover more about herself and challenge her beliefs:

When we [did] identity, then I thought about myself, like, I drew myself and then I said 'That looks like me, I am good', then your background, what your religion is, if you believe in it, everything. Then you thought 'Do I believe in all this, do I do this, do I do that?' and it was cool, it was good (Year 11, art).

Three Year 9 pupils talked about the arts helping them to focus on their likes and dislikes, and what they wanted from life:

With all the different things we've done in music ... I like more sorts of music and there are some sorts of music that I like that I didn't like before. It's like discovering things that I never knew were present in me before (Year 9, arts).

———

It's also been about learning about how people work and the way that you want to live your life (Year 9, drama).

On a more practical level, several pupils discovered what they were capable of, what skills they had, sometimes totally unexpectedly:

It has made me more aware of things, like more aware of things I can do, things now I know I can do when before I did not really think I could do. ... So it has helped me understand what I am capable of (Year 9, arts).

———

*It's helped me realise that, like, who I am and what I can do or ...
like before I didn't use to do art that much, but now I've started
doing it, I've noticed I can do it quite well* (Year 9, arts).

Signalling a warning that arts education can also have adverse effects
on the formation of identities, one pupil talked about the negative
impact of her experience of the arts. Being aware of her low level of
ability in music compared to her class mates made her depressed and
self-conscious, implying that she had internalised an image or label of
her 'self' as inferior in music:

2.
WHAT ARE
THE EFFECTS
OF
ARTS
EDUCATION?

*It's just that everyone else in the class seems to be so much better
than me, and it's kind of hard to ... it's kind of depressing when
everyone seems to be doing all these brilliant compositions and you
are just playing 'Row, row, row your boat' on the piano.*

Interviewer: *So you don't feel very good about what you manage to
do?*

No, and I am quite self-conscious about what I can't do in music
(Year 9, music).

For others, the arts had been a positive influence in shaping images of
self. A couple of students from the younger year groups, for example,
thought that the arts, in particular music, gave them a sense of identity,
something by which they could be recognised:

*I suppose, if you play in a band and it gives you a commitment,
something to do, you're committed to something rather than not
doing anything, in school and out. You've got something to say, like
'I'm in a band'. People might say 'Oh, I know her. She plays the
trumpet'* (Year 9, music).

Echoing the headteacher's remarks about the importance of symbolic
signatures, another group of pupils felt the arts enabled them to develop
and express their individuality, by creating their own unique pieces of
work: '*You can experiment with different ideas and make something
your own*' (Year 8, art).

One Year 9 pupil felt that expressing his individuality was something
which had developed over time:

*I think it is true with everybody that in the start if you were given a
cabbage to draw, you draw that cabbage, and you try to make it look
exactly like a cabbage, and you have got no style, you are just
drawing that cabbage. But now I am really beginning to open up,
and I have got my own little flows and I am concentrating less on
perfection and more on myself, and on my own style. So this year
has ... it's brought me out more as an individual artist rather than
the same as everybody else* (Year 9, art).

Overall, then, the development of intrapersonal intelligence in the form of fostering self-awareness, self-identity, and a sense of individuality was a significant feature amongst both pupils' and teachers' accounts of the effects of arts education. That this outcome carries clear implications for pupils' self-esteem – either positive or negative – was illustrated and it is to this effect we turn in the next subcategory.

8.3 ENHANCED SELF-WORTH AND SELF-ESTEEM

Teacher Perspectives

This significant and frequent claim was made by teachers from across all artforms, and relates to a number of other perceived aims or outcomes, particularly enjoyment (section 3.2), the development of expressive skills (section 7.5), as well as others in the present chapter on personal and social development.

Numerous references were made to the capacity of the arts to foster positive self-images in pupils. Some responses referred generally to 'self-esteem', but interestingly, the majority of claims for this effect coupled the enhancement of self-esteem with achievement (be it personal achievements such as painting a picture or performing, or through recognised qualifications such as GCSEs). Often, the implication was that all children can achieve in the arts in some way, particularly those who are low achievers in subjects other than the arts:

> ... poor ability children ... can't quite believe what they have produced in art. They are really impressed by what they have done, because they don't achieve an awful lot in other subjects (art teacher).

> ---

> ... a boy in Year 11 who has a stutter and has really done nothing until the final exam piece, when he got really involved, and his self-esteem has just gone through the roof. He is just a changed man really ... and things like that are exciting as well (head of drama).

> ---

> ... there are so many opportunities within the arts for pupils to achieve, whether it is qualifications, certificates, in extra-curricular activities, as well as the obvious things, such as GCSEs. Also achievement is standing up there, I feel, in front of an audience of people and doing your best (deputy head).

As this last remark indicates, performance was identified as an aspect of the arts which can foster a sense of self-worth or develop self-esteem:

I think performance enhances your self-esteem quite often – if you, at the age of 14 and 15, can stand in front of a full hall and give a credible performance, whatever the length, I think that's a feather in anybody's cap. It is for an adult and, I think, given that experience of finding a way of feeling good about yourself or feeling that you've shown that you're able to do something and do it well, it's always good, it's a positively reinforcing experience (head of Welsh).

One teacher saw the enhancement of self-esteem as a result of the philosophy behind teaching in the arts, where everybody is valued:

... because of the philosophy about how they are taught, and what you bring is valued, what you are is valued and that those are positive, very positive starting points. So, I think in terms of achievement, confidence and expectation it all moves forward (deputy head).

Another member of staff, a music teacher, rather epigrammatically, stated: *'Creativity is a sense of achievement'*, whilst other teachers implied – perhaps rather idealistically in the light of earlier pupil comments – that pupils do not compare their achievements unfavourably with those of others in the arts, or feel frustrated by their lack of ability. This music teacher made a distinction between other subjects and music:

They can all start from a very equal place. I don't see that the same in other subjects, perhaps it is, but when you know you are doing simpler maths than the next person, you somehow know that you are not quite achieving the same; you know that you are eventually going to have to do their question next, but they will be on to the next question. You put a group together in music. Now they know that certain people – OK, we have got some people who have had piano lessons, and they are working in a group, but they know that their part is absolutely 100 per cent vital. They may only be playing the bass drum, but without them the keyboard means nothing. You may be playing a fabulous part, but without me you are nobody. I think that the fact that you can use arts like that, you know that there is satisfaction and you can get through to anybody who wants to try in the subject.

Pupil Perspectives

For many pupils, one significant effect of the arts, both the individual artforms and the arts as a collective entity, was to make them feel good about themselves, often linked with a sense of achievement, or pride in their work. Altogether, 38 pupils volunteered this outcome of the arts, making a total of 69 comments.

Comments were made about each artform increasing a pupil's sense of self-worth and personal achievement, although art and music were more often perceived to have this effect. (This matches accounts presented in Chapter 3 on sense of satisfaction and achievement, again pupils' comments relating mostly to art and music.) Drama too seemed to bring about this outcome for a number of pupils. The remarks made by pupils at the different schools seemed to vary in their reference to the different artforms, so at two schools the majority of the citations to this outcome referred to art and music, but at the other three schools there was a wider picture, with the number of references to each artform more balanced. The overall number of pupils who cited this as an outcome of the arts also varied from four to 11. These findings would seem to suggest that at some schools, it is the arts as a whole that have an effect on pupils' perceptions of themselves, whereas in other schools, it is the teaching of particular artforms that produces the outcome.

Pupils in the different year groups seemed to have slightly different opinions on this effect. Younger pupils were more affected by other people telling them that their work was good, whereas the older pupils were able to elicit their own sense of personal achievement and pride in their work. This would suggest that as pupils get older they develop more confidence in their own work and their capacity to judge its merit, and thereby rely less on the reassurance of others to confirm their ability. The issue of self-confidence and development of a pupil's belief in their own abilities, as an outcome of the arts, will be dealt with in more detail in section 8.4 of this chapter.

A large number of pupils mentioned that one outcome of the arts was to make them feel good about themselves. Often this was linked to a sense of discovery of their own abilities: either that they were able to do something that they had not realised they could, or they could do it better than they had thought. This type of statement was more likely to be made by younger pupils, with particular reference to art and drama:

> *When I was at primary* [school], *I used to think that I were no good at it, but when I came here I realised I were quite good at art. Because the first time we were doing art, we did these pastel drawings and I thought 'Oh no, I'm not going to be very good at this' and I got a really good mark and was really pleased with myself* (Year 7, art).

———

> *Within drama, if you do a particularly good piece of work, you feel really good about yourself. You think 'Oh yeah, that was me, I did that!'* (Year 9, drama).

For a number of pupils, particularly those in the younger year groups, it was receiving compliments about their work from others, both teachers and other pupils, which made them feel good about themselves. This theme was particularly pervasive for music, suggesting perhaps more opportunity for pupils to compare one another's work in this subject. *'If you're working in a group and the teacher comes up to you and says "Yeah, that's good", you feel good about yourself'* (Year 7, music).

It was important to one pupil, who was new at his school, that his ability in art brought him approval from other students, which gave him a feeling of self-worth:

> *I think I'm good at it and it makes me look good in front of other people in the class. Since being new here and people thinking I'm not much good, to be able to look at one subject is good. People compliment me on how good my drawing is* (Year 9, art).

2.
WHAT ARE
THE EFFECTS
OF
ARTS
EDUCATION?

This view of the arts as fostering a feeling of self-worth was reiterated by another pupil at the same school, who talked about music: *'You feel as though you are important and you can do something that someone else can't do; you have got this special quality about yourself'* (Year 8, music).

The development of self-esteem was a closely related notion inspired by the arts for a few pupils. One Year 11 pupil felt that arts lessons during her whole school career had helped to develop her self-esteem. A common theme mentioned by older pupils was that their experiences in the arts had helped engender a sense of personal pride. A high proportion of the comments nominating this effect came from pupils at two particular schools, and many referred specifically to being proud of the finished product in art:

> *Once I've finished my work I'm very proud of it* (Year 9, art).
>
> ———
>
> *I think the outcome of doing art is like ... it's a lot to do with being able to create something and I think that's a very important thing for me, like doing something constructive and like having a finished product and being, like, proud of that* (Year 9, art).

Related to this, another outcome of the arts, mentioned mainly by older pupils, was the feeling that they had achieved something: *'If your work gets chosen to go up on a display board ... you feel like you've achieved something because it's worth showing'* (Year 10, art).

For one pupil, it was looking back on her work over several years, and realising she had improved which gave her this sense of achievement:

'I mean like again, looking back on Year 7 work and looking at Year 9 work, it has improved a lot, which you know is like an achievement.'

As an extension of this, to some pupils the sense of achievement gained from the arts was something that they felt they could not get in other subjects:

Interviewer: *Do you think it has a positive effect on, like how you feel about yourself when you are doing art?*

Yes, it does, it does, because when you think 'Oh gosh, I am not good at anything', you feel a bit down and out. It shows that you can create something really beautiful, you can actually do something really good with just your hands. You don't feel small, because some of my subjects are hard, like maths, and you think 'Oh gosh, I don't know anything', and art you can just go and put your best into it (Year 11, art).

Overall, then, many teachers and pupils testified to the power of the arts to raise the self-worth, self-esteem and a sense of achievement of many pupils. However, the earlier comments from a pupil who felt low self-esteem in music due to her perceived inferiority should caution against concluding that positive self-esteem effects for all pupils are automatic in the arts. As will be illustrated in Part Three of the report, like so many other effects depicted in this Part, this outcome was highly dependent on the quality of the learning stimulated by the teacher.

2.
WHAT ARE
THE EFFECTS
OF
ARTS
EDUCATION?

8.4   INCREASED SELF-CONFIDENCE

Closely related to the raising of self-esteem was the development of self-confidence.

Teacher Perspectives

Teachers' references to this subcategory tended to fall into three groups: comments about increases in general or non-specific forms of self-confidence; comments about enhanced confidence in abilities; and comments about increased confidence to perform in front of others.

Teachers on increased self-confidence in non-specific ways

The non-specific type of comment covered many accounts by teachers of the arts *'building confidence'*, where the nature of the increased confidence was not elaborated on, for example:

Yes, I think that in this particular school, building self-confidence with quite a lot of the girls, especially maybe the Bengali girls, who are very quiet on the whole – I think for us to give them that kind of confidence is the main thing maybe that they get out of it (head of expressive arts).

In some cases, teachers illustrated this effect of the arts on particular pupils, with one teacher describing the letters received from parents after drama courses which told of their children's growth in confidence. There was a particular emphasis in this category on drama. For instance, one drama teacher was aware of the often-cited effect of *'drama builds confidence'*, and appeared keen to extend this further:

> *Well, I would place some emphasis on confidence, even though I don't mean it in quite the same glib way as I often see it kind of jotted down – 'drama gives you confidence' – but I think it's a kind of inner thing, inner confidence, which is that 'I can say what I think as long as I say it sensibly and I really mean what I say'. It's not necessarily about speaking loudly and being heard, but about 'Actually I know that my ideas are interesting and, however I share those ideas, I'm going to be appreciated and understood'; so it's a sort of confidence: I'd really like to call it a quiet confidence. But sometimes it also manifests itself in a big confidence which is 'I'll volunteer for things'.*

Again, the 'building confidence' aspect of the arts was perceived by some to be particularly important for pupils with English as a second language, and for those with lower attainment in non-arts subjects.

Teachers on pupils' increased self-confidence in their own abilities

Other teachers talked about pupils developing self-confidence through extensions of their abilities and skills in the arts. This outcome is particularly related to those described in section 8.3, since a 'sense of achievement', 'self-esteem' and increased 'self-confidence in one's own abilities' clearly feed upon each other.

One teacher, for example, valued assessment as an avenue through which pupils can realise their achievements and abilities, which were often considered to be of a higher level than pupils initially thought they were capable of. Teachers also linked this confidence with the acquisition of technical skills in the artform:

> *We sometimes say to them 'Do you think you have learnt anything today?' ... it is to do with empowerment, but it is to do with gaining massive amounts of confidence straightaway when they say that they can't do it and then they can. So I believe, very much, in showing people really how; I don't leave them to find out for themselves* (head of expressive arts).

Teachers on pupils' increased self-confidence to perform in front of others

Specific mentions of increased confidence with regard to performance were made by some teachers, particularly by teachers of music, drama and dance. One teacher stated an aim as: '... *to give, not just pupils but anyone, the skills in which to perform confidently*' (dance and drama teacher).

**2.
WHAT ARE
THE EFFECTS
OF
ARTS
EDUCATION?**

Pupil Perspectives

The same three subtypes of references to increased confidence were evident in pupils' accounts of this effect, together with one more – the self-confidence to express one's own opinions.

Pupils on increased self-confidence in non-specific ways

Pupils often talked about the arts developing their self-confidence in a rather general way. In total, 55 pupils made 141 references to this as an outcome of arts education, with roughly half of these referring specifically to drama as a medium for this effect. However, the number of pupils from each school making comments about drama evoking an increase in self-confidence varied from four in one school to 11, with this former school also generating the fewest self-confidence outcomes overall, suggesting perhaps that increasing self-confidence was not a significant aim of arts education in that school.

Rather interestingly, a disproportionately high number of nominations were made about English having a developmental effect on self-confidence. Furthermore, half of these surfaced in one school, possibly suggesting a special awareness of this as an objective of teaching in English at that school.

A large number of comments were rather vague, with pupils simply stating that the arts '*have made me more confident*'. This type of remark came from pupils in all year groups, and referred to each artform individually, and to the arts as a whole. A number of pupils reported that the arts gave them self-confidence specifically to do their work in lessons. A large proportion of these came from pupils at one school – the same school that exhibited the relatively high proportion of references in English, suggesting that the emphasis on increasing self-confidence was a deliberate priority of arts teaching at this school.

Pupils referred to increased confidence in arts lessons, and in other subjects:

> *I think it has contributed to my education because I've somehow become more confident in the lessons* (Year 9, art).

I used to be scared of what other people think of me. I mean it's helped me in other subjects, speaking up in class because I can give answers out and if it's wrong you just laugh it off and forget about it really, but before I didn't dare speak because I thought if it was wrong, people would just laugh at me (Year 11, music).

Further to this, an outcome seen mainly as an effect of drama was an increase in pupils' self-confidence in social situations, making friends, in outside activities and in dealing with people in authority:

It's given me a lot of self-confidence outside of drama and outside of school (Year 11, drama).

... when I am out of school I am more confident now, I am more outgoing, I don't know. Last year I did [drama] and I am afraid of heights for some reason. ... We went on a trip and there was an abseil and I just felt like doing it and I did it, and I don't know, it just boosted my confidence (Year 9, drama).

I think one of the effects, which didn't strike me as something which would happen when I started studying drama, was I used to be nervous of talking to people in authority, like teachers or people in shops ... but having drama ... because it's something where the teacher has to work a lot with the pupils, whereas the sciences it's teaching, with drama it's not facts, it's what you do, so it's got to be more of a relationship. So that's helped quite a lot because I can now speak to people in authority and teachers and I suppose it has made me more confident in general (Year 11, drama).

The above extracts – all volunteered and unprompted – offer clear evidence of an important kind of transfer effect. As a further illustration of the transference of this effect to other wider arenas, one boy mentioned how the confidence he had developed in dance helped him stand up for himself more:

I think it's helped me to stand up for myself a bit more, because sometimes other people think it's not for boys, if you know what I mean, and before I think I would have been pushed down to end up not doing it, but now I have been doing that, because I enjoy it so much, I have been saying 'I don't care what you think' (Year 9, dance).

Finally, a few pupils in the third year they were interviewed (Years 9 and 11) talked about how self-confidence was something which developed over time: '*As I get older, the more drama I do, I get more confident.*' A disproportionately high rate of references to increased self-confidence was apparent in the responses of the Year 11 pupil interviewees, reinforcing the link between enhanced self-confidence and achievement through the focused development of abilities.

Pupils on increased self-confidence in their own abilities

The development of pupils' confidence in their own abilities was strongly linked with the outcome of the arts nurturing feelings of self-worth and achievement (see section 8.3). Fifteen pupils offering a total of 19 comments perceived the arts to have developed their confidence in their own work and abilities. Nearly half of these came from pupils at the school identified previously as exhibiting high levels of increased self-confidence as an effect, whilst another school did not elicit any references to this as an outcome of the arts.

By artform, the highest number of citations were made to art (seven) followed by drama (three), with dance, music, English and textiles each receiving one reference. Of the latter, the low score for music is especially significant, and perhaps indicates again that, relative to art and drama, music encounters considerable difficulties in delivering a genuine sense of concrete achievement in skill acquisition to many pupils (see section 4.5).

A further five comments related to the arts as a whole. Pupils talked about an increased willingness to try things – '*I'm not so afraid of trying to draw the things that I see now*' – and an increased confidence in their work: '*Maybe, the arts have had an effect on me because I can have more confidence in my work in general. I just look at anything and think "I can draw that"*' (Year 9, arts).

One pupil talked about the arts having given him the confidence to do other things, to live out his dreams:

> *I have just started up my own band, which is at the moment not going anywhere, but we will see how it goes. I think these are all things that you want to do, you know, teenage things, want to start up a band and want to win a competition performing in front of 400 people in the National Theatre in London. I think the arts have allowed me to actually give me confidence in my own abilities to actually carry out these dreams, carry out what I want to do with my life, not just in the arts field, but also in other things* (Year 11, arts).

Pupils on increased self-confidence to perform in front of others

These comments (64 in total) relate to pupils' perceptions of the arts fostering a sense of confidence in their capacity to perform, and predictably the majority referred to drama (35) and music (19). There was considerable variation between schools and artforms. One school had roughly equal numbers of references to drama and music, two schools had significantly more references to drama, and the other two schools had more references to music – both schools that had strong traditions in mounting school music performances. This would seem to suggest that it is the approach taken to teaching specific artforms which increases pupils' performance confidence, not the arts as a general learning medium.

'It gives you confidence when you are performing' was a comment frequently made by pupils, a few of whom clarified their answers:

2.
WHAT ARE
THE EFFECTS
OF
ARTS
EDUCATION?

> *It's brought out a lot of my confidence. I didn't have much confidence at the start of the year, and I have got a lot more confident since we have performed in front of people* (Year 10, drama).

> *We play in front of the class as well and I suppose that builds up confidence as well, because, like, we make up our own little melody and then we play it out in the class on the piano or the keyboard* (Year 9, music).

Volunteering further evidence of transfer effects in the personal and social domain, some pupils recognised that this increased confidence would be useful in other areas of their lives:

> [It] *teaches you to be more confident, the performance side of things. If you can sit down and play a piece of music or sing a song in front of someone, then you're more likely to be able to go I suppose into a work place or something like that and introduce yourself and just feel at ease wherever you are* (Year 10, music).

Pupils on increased self-confidence to express opinions

With close affinities to the development of expressive skills (see section 7.5), some 15 pupils made a total of 18 claims about the arts, in particular drama, building their confidence to express their opinions. One school – the one where there was a general lack of self-confidence outcomes – did not have any nominations in this subtype, with the other four schools evoking roughly even numbers of references to this as an outcome of the arts. A large proportion of these comments were made by Year 7 pupils, although older pupils offered greater justification of their accounts:

> *Drama helps you talk more with people and not be scared to express yourself* (Year 7, drama).

> *I used to be quite quiet. Now I am dead loud and am not scared to ask teachers things and tell them what I think of things. I never used to, but now I'll tell them if it is not good, or I don't agree with something* (Year 9, drama).

Overall, then, it is clear from the above evidence that many pupils testify to a significant enhancement in various forms of self-confidence through engagement in the arts. Moreover, particularly striking in some of these accounts of this learning were the unsolicited references pupils made to the transference of these gains in self-confidence to other arenas and contexts.

8.5 DEVELOPING THE WHOLE PERSONALITY

Teacher Perspectives

Often by way of summing up the developments in the three subcategories already described in this chapter – identity formation, self-esteem and self-confidence – some teachers went a step further to describe the impact of the arts in enriching the growth and formation of the 'whole personality'. The arts were seen as an area of learning that '... *develop*[s] *them so much as people*' (music teacher). Responses were frequent across the artforms, but were often general rather than specific, for example:

> ... *learning about becoming an adult* ... (deputy head).

> *I think the personality with the imagination needed for arts; I think a personality is enriched beyond anything if they have art, music or drama* ... (head of music).

> *It's very difficult to break it down, but I think it's developing the whole person and enabling them when they leave school here to become more responsible and to put them, shall we say, ready for life after school* (deputy head).

> *I think that the arts are really quite important there in terms of spiritual development and just having examples of the arts ... in terms of developing whole pupils, I think that it really is very important. It is more than just the academic results that I think the arts contribute to* (headteacher).

More specific responses identified life-based 'issues' as an aspect of arts education contributing to pupils' personal development, and also to the creative writing process:

> ... *an artform which embraces all the birth, life and death issues that we all live* ... [it] *enables us to engage with those things, to reflect upon them and to see ourselves in relation to those things* (LEA arts adviser).

Well, I would hope that it would help their own mental and spiritual economy in the sense that creative writing should help the individual's psychology and growth and development (head of English).

The intangible nature of this effect was acknowledged by some teachers, for example: '*... I don't know – it is hard to put it into words really, what it is that is happening while they are there*' (head of expressive arts).

Another aspect of this subcategory displays continuities with section 5.2 on broadening cultural horizons and perspectives. Again, there was recognition of the part the arts can play in '*... people doing things that they wouldn't have the chance to do*' (deputy head). This same interviewee went on to say:

... there are kids here whose eyes, in spite of what I said before about them coming generally from more aware homes now, kids whose eyes and experiences are opened by the opportunities that they have been given here, even the fairly limited ones that we are able to give them.

And, referring to work done with a sculptor:

The notion of having statues on the lawn outside was 'What is this doing at [X school]?' You know this is what they do in Oxford, or somewhere like that ... the kids were quite proud to have their statues there that people noticed when they came here. Now that is just one small example of how you can lift awareness and change an outlook.

Pupil Perspectives

Pupils' comments in this subcategory covered descriptions of how the arts developed them as people, and tended to fall into three groups: comments about expanding their personality and character; comments about the arts enabling them to be more themselves; and comments about the arts offering them new opportunities and experiences. Responses were frequent, often referring to the arts as a collective entity, and in quite general terms.

One pupil declared that the arts had helped make him a more balanced or 'rounded' person:

I mean arts have always been an important aspect of my life and I feel that with arts, it helps you to become more rounded. If you have constant exposure to arts, as opposed to just facts over your school period it helps you develop into someone who is more rounded, who can appreciate things ... (Year 11, arts).

Expanding personality and character

In all, 21 pupils made a total of 40 comments about the arts having had an effect on their personality or character. This perception was fairly consistently made by pupils in all year groups from all five schools. Over half the contributions coded here (24) made specific reference to drama.

Several general comments were made about the effect of learning in the arts on a pupil's personality. '*It just helps you as a person*' and '*it helps mature people*' were fairly common themes, referring to the individual artforms and the arts as a whole. A number of pupils talked about the arts having made them more open, foreshadowing the outcome of overcoming shyness and embarrassment discussed later in this section. '*Drama brings me out of my shell*' was how one girl put it. Other pupils talked about becoming more outgoing, more outspoken and developing a '*more fun personality*' as a result of the arts.

It is interesting to note too that some employers saw involvement in the arts as making an important contribution to a more rounded or balanced education in an applicant:

> *So, for example if you did do GCSE music or whatever and you have kept it up, I think that's looked upon as quite favourable* [by employers], *probably for many reasons. It's nice to see the balance and also some creativity there … So, I definitely think it sparks an interest in the employer and to see that they have either studied or got an outside interest in the arts* (human resources consultant for a large insurance firm).

> Interviewer: *What would you say were the main effects or outcomes for students studying the arts at school?*

> *I think it's a more rounded education, it's the ability to perhaps step outside themselves … so that you can manage your stress levels, you can balance your, your life, probably have a fuller life and be able to contribute more to the whole UK PLC* (Director of Personnel in a large building society).

Enabling 'you to be more yourself'

This was a claim made by 24 pupils, again often in fairly general terms. Of the total 33 comments, 19 referred to the effect of drama, with a further nine discussing the arts as a whole. The number of comments made by pupils at the different schools varied from three in two schools to fourteen in one, suggesting that this was an issue focused on to differing extents at the five schools.

A number of pupils felt that the arts had helped them to be their own person:

> *I think it shows you how to be your own person more. I think that's what I've gained from it. You can be yourself, although I know I've changed, but this is me, how I am now* (Year 11, arts).

> ———

> *I think it's also another way of expressing yourself. It's not about being a good actor or whatever, it's about being yourself and doing what you want to do in drama, and no one should laugh at you ... Sometimes if you are a quiet, shy person and you really hate drama at first, it can help you become better and more outgoing and stuff, and you become less shy* (Year 9, drama).

2.
WHAT ARE
THE EFFECTS
OF
ARTS
EDUCATION?

As an extension of this last remark, and in connection with previous comments on self-confidence, many pupils merely stated that the arts 'helped overcome shyness', and these comments came from pupils of all ages. One Year 7 clarified this effect: *'They've made me more confident and independent, 'cos when I first started I was pretty shy, and now I join in lots of things and I've had more ideas about things to do'* (Year 7, arts).

Broader and different perspectives through new opportunities and experiences

Consistent with comments made by teachers, pupils talked about the arts broadening their perspectives and experiences, offering them the opportunity to try new things and stretching their abilities. Overall, 23 pupils made claims to these effects with a total of 31 comments. The vast majority of these were made by pupils in Years 7 to 9, indicating that these are more apparent effects for younger pupils. Roughly a third (ten) of the comments in this subcategory referred to the arts as a whole, with 13 specifically about the effects of art and six about the effects of music. Interestingly, none of the pupils mentioned this as an outcome of drama.

Many pupils perceived learning in the arts to give them a *'wider view of life'*, or a *'different perspective on life'*. This theme was also picked up by an employer:

> *I think it gives you a different perspective ... it probably puts you more in touch with more emotions than you would normally feel on a day-to-day basis* (Sponsorship Manager for a bank).

Although such observations were often related to the arts as a whole, a few pupils made specific reference to individual artforms, namely music and art:

It's probably broadened my horizons 'cos I've heard lots of different styles of music than I had before (Year 9, music).

——

Broadening your mind, so you are not just one track. It lets you look at other types, old art, different types of drama and music, rather than just pop music; it makes you look at classical as well (Year 9, arts).

The variety of styles introduced to this pupil was a theme picked up on by a number of pupils. To them, the arts gave them the opportunity to try new things, and get involved in new activities, often mentioned by younger pupils in comparison to the opportunities available at primary school. These accounts covered art, music and dance, as well as the arts as a whole:

Discovering new things and ... I'd never done sculpturing before at my old school and that was like a new experience for me (Year 7, art).

——

It has made a difference to me because at my old school we didn't really do much about it, we did some singing but that was basically it. And now I know how to play keyboards pretty well and I've had a go at a couple of different instruments (Year 7, music).

——

A chance to perform different dances, take on new heights of dance, a chance to express myself in dance as well (Year 9, dance).

A couple of pupils also mentioned that the arts gave them opportunities to '*get involved in different things*'. One particular pupil talked about the opportunity to work with an impressionist artist on an art trip. It was the fact that he had never done anything like that before which had made it so enjoyable and broadening; in other words it was the opportunity to 'try something new' in the arts which was important to him.

Overall then, while both teachers and pupils often struggled with the intractable problems of articulating this impact of engagement in the arts, there was little doubt that, in general terms, pupils' accounts of the impact of arts education on the development and broadening of the whole personality corroborated those of their teachers.

8.6 IMPROVED PERSONAL SKILLS

This section was developed to account for effects relating to personal qualities and skills, as opposed to artform technical skills (section 4.5), and communication (section 7.2) or social skills (section 8.8). However, few teachers or pupils made references specifically to the acquisition of personal skills through arts education.

Teacher Perspectives

Two interviewees in school management cited the development of responsibility as an effect of arts education. There were also two responses where teachers suggested that the arts enhance organisational skills. A third type in this subcategory was made up of the more frequently claimed effect relating to the development of independence and ownership. The arts were seen to provide opportunities for pupils to have ownership of their experiences in ways in which they may not in other curriculum areas. Some teachers related this to independence and autonomy:

> ... the main thing that I am hoping to achieve is some sort of independence and autonomy, so that they possess their work, they have got some sort of feeling that it is their ownership (art teacher).

Pupil Perspectives

Only one pupil, in Year 11, alluded to the possibility that participation in the arts had increased her sense of responsibility:

> When you are in the band and you are the older ones, you have got to be responsible for the little ones, things like that, and you have got to be more responsible (Year 11, music).

Referring to the arts as a whole and individually to music, art and drama, four pupils talked about the arts having developed their organisation skills. 'How to stage things and organise a group' and being organised enough to get art work mounted on time were specific examples of citations made to this effect of the arts.

The 11 pupil comments on the development of independence and/or autonomy made by eight pupils can be distinguished between reports that the arts enable a pupil to feel more independent as a person, and perceptions that the arts allow a greater sense of autonomy or freedom within the lessons, and, by implication, engender the capacity to deal effectively with these qualities.

Drama, art, and the arts as a whole were cited by three pupils as developing an individual's sense of independence. Little explanation was given as to how this was achieved, with comments including 'I am more confident, definitely more independent due to the arts at school'.

That pupils felt a sense of freedom within arts lessons was an outcome proposed mainly by older pupils (as seen already in section 6.3), and was often perceived to be something which developed as lessons in the arts became less structured in the later school years. Drama and art were most often the impetus of this sense of autonomy, as pupils talked about greater freedom to use their own ideas and relying less on the teacher for inspiration and guidance:

> [This year] *mainly it's been on my own, work ideas that I have, put stuff together, and it's been more independent and on your own ...* (Year 10, art).

> [This year] *we've done a lot more group plays, role plays using all of the techniques, but we've been given a lot more freedom and independence to sort of put them all together using our own ideas* (Year 9, drama).

2.
WHAT ARE
THE EFFECTS
OF
ARTS
EDUCATION?

8.7 INCREASED AWARENESS OF OTHERS AND EMPATHY

In moving on to consider outcomes associated with attitudes and behaviour towards others, this subcategory marks a definite switch from those personal and social development outcomes that tended to focus on intrapersonal intelligence to those that constitute qualities characteristic of interpersonal intelligence.

Teacher Perspectives

Drama was often depicted by teachers as an important carrier subject for increased awareness of other people, their needs, moods and problems. Recognising the outward behavioural signals of people's dispositions and emotional states was considered to be an important step towards encouraging an increased awareness of other people's inner states of mind:

> *Just a very simple introduction to mime is always, you know, 'Mould me into a teacher at the front of the class who is very angry but isn't saying anything'. You know, and they'll then become aware of 'Gosh, yes, we do know when we are giving off signals'. You know, 'Mould yourself into someone who is madly in love and is trying to hide it'. You know what I mean, looking at those subtle differences, you know, we're very fascinating animals, so, you know, we've got to live with each other, work and play with each other, so how do we understand each other?* (drama teacher)

It would be wrong, however, to give the impression that such outcomes were the sole preserve of drama; interviewees testified to other artforms producing similar effects. A deputy head, who had not taught arts-oriented subjects, spoke of the effects he had observed in pupils:

> *That greater appreciation, that greater freedom that pupils can use, greater skill as well, as I say to express their feelings, the feelings*

of others, how they have seen other people feel, either through art or through music. To actually appreciate the sadness in a piece of music means that you can transfer that feeling perhaps to someone's mood when you are talking about how people do change in terms of their mood, how they feel sadness.

Similarly, a headteacher pointed to the ways the arts generally foster insights into our shared humanity:

I think art education in some ways allows ... people to get closer as people ... it is more than individualistic, an understanding of each other's natures, calming, and understanding more of the nature of people.

A number of teachers offered observations on the arts developing empathy and the ability to see things from other perspectives. Two distinct types of responses emerged: those which focused on appreciating and valuing the work of others, for example '*I try to put across to them the importance of not destroying another person's work*', and those which concentrated on the aspect of seeing things from another perspective, for example '*I think they begin to learn that kind of consideration for the points of view of others*'; '*... to understand the other's predicament*'.

Although developing empathy and valuing others were seen as outcomes for all artforms, again they were effects particularly prevalent in responses relating to drama. The two aspects included in this subcategory (being empathetic or valuing others) provided an interesting contrast by artform. Responses for English and drama focused on pupils developing empathy through seeing things from other perspectives. For English, this was related to process factors – discussion groups and pupils working together – and to content – the themes within English which address tolerance. Drama teachers also talked in terms of process and content, and again techniques (thought tracking and going into role) were important:

Suddenly they really get inside the head of somebody else. And can understand that situation through the eyes of somebody else ...

... having to play the racist, having to play the person who doesn't have the feelings that you have. You know, that is something they don't get the chance to do. So, you know, it's a really valuable thing to be able to play those opinions, play that character without having to answer really for their, for what they said after you come out of role (drama teacher).

In contrast, for art and music, responses related to pupils respecting and appreciating the work of other pupils: '*... music necessitates listening to what others have created, patiently and politely*' (music teacher).

Pupil Perspectives

Broadly speaking, pupil responses tended to run parallel to the two aspects of this outcome exhibited by teachers: an increased understanding of other people and their different perspectives, generally and in terms of their feelings, opinions, and behaviours; and an increased appreciation of others, in terms of their work, abilities and point of view. Overall there were 80 comments relating to understanding other people and their different perspectives, made up of references to empathy (31), understanding others' feelings (28), understanding others' opinions (seven), understanding others' behaviours and actions (six), understanding others' problems (three), understanding others' beliefs and cultures (three) and seeing what others can do (two). On increased appreciation of others' work and abilities there were 18 comments overall, with six of these on appreciation of others' work by stepping into their shoes. Some of these subcategories are expanded below.

Increased awareness and understanding of others: generally

A large number of references were made to the arts enabling pupils to *'understand other people'* in general or non-specific terms. This general outcome, eliciting 31 comments, was suggested by a total of 26 pupils, the majority of whom were in Years 7 and 9, with nearly two-thirds of the comments made referring specifically to drama as a medium for this effect. Pupils often referred to the studying of specific topics, such as bullying and racism, as increasing their empathy and understanding of others.

Pupils discussed the increased understanding of other pupils as an outcome of working with them in arts lessons:

> *You do find out a lot more about people when you are working with them in a group. Like in dance, drama, music and art, if you are working in a group you do find a lot out about other people's personalities* (Year 9, arts).

> *Well, drama, that lets you sort of look into people and see what they're really like in a way that nothing else does* (Year 7, drama).

Pupils also talked about understanding other people in a wider sense: *'I suppose it helps you understand other people, like Vincent van Gogh. By his paintings you can tell that he was disturbed and sad and lonely'* (Year 7, art).

Increased awareness and understanding of others: their feelings and emotions

A further 28 comments were made by 21 pupils about the arts increasing their awareness and understanding of other people's feelings. Again, this suggestion was proffered mainly by younger pupils, predominantly with reference to drama. Acting out different roles and characters helped pupils to look at how people feel: *'By, like, putting yourself in other people's situations ... you can understand how that person might feel'* (Year 9, drama).

This view was reinforced by pupils at one school who referred to an activity called 'conscience alleyway': *'Where everybody lines up in an alley and then somebody walks down* [between the pupils, and playing a character] *and everybody says their opinion of what they think of them.'* This helped to give *'an insight into how other people think about a situation,'* said one pupil. Another pupil felt that his understanding of his fellow peers was increased by knowledge of the arts: *'You can tell a lot about people from what sort of music they play or listen to, what they draw, what kinds of things they act'* (Year 9, arts).

Two pupils also recognised that they could begin to understand how artists, within art and English, may have felt when producing their work:

> *In art, my teacher showed me a picture and it gave you a thought of what the person was feeling at the time. It was a war scene and it showed the actual war going on, but also, behind it, the friendliness of the war as well, people getting together and helping each other. I did some work on it ... I was trying to show what the person may have been feeling like at the time of painting it* (Year 9, art).
>
> ———
>
> *I mean, reading poems and things has helped me, like, feel their emotions when I read a poem, like 'Oh, he was very happy when he wrote that' ... It's just how he or she was feeling when they did it* (Year 7, English).

Increased awareness and understanding of others: their views and opinions

With seven references in total, six pupils identified that the arts increased their awareness and understanding of other people's views and opinions. These comments came mainly from the pupils in Year 9 at one particular school. Of the seven references, five related to the effect of drama, and one each to English and the arts as a whole.

We did a lot about murder and whether you think the punishment, like capital punishment, and about the way they're caught, sort things out. ... You get to look at other people's opinions, get to look at other things apart from what you've been taught (Year 9, drama).

You get to talk and discuss, and put your views across, how you feel, and 'cos it's a discussion you get a lot of different people's views. It's all different and you can see what other people think (Year 9, English).

Increased awareness and understanding of others: their behaviour

Five pupils, making six comments in total, recognised that their understanding of other people's behaviour, along with the intentions and motives behind it, had increased through their learning in the arts:

In drama, we look at why people have done things. It's like psychology – looking at why somebody, like maybe a wife who's been beaten, why she retaliated, hurt her husband. We look at why she did it, look deeper into it (Year 9, drama).

Increased appreciation of others

Turning to the second broad type of comment in this subcategory, 16 pupils made 18 comments about the arts extending their appreciation of others: their work, abilities and problems. The majority of these referred to drama as a vehicle for this effect, and younger pupils referred to this outcome more often than those in the older year groups.

Two pupils talked about learning to appreciate the work and ideas of others, in music, art and drama:

I've learnt to listen to other people playing instead, as well as just concentrating on what I'm doing. You learn to appreciate other people as well and listen to them and work with them (Year 11, music).

In art, our teacher told us to appreciate somebody else's view of art. So, like someone's view might be 'I will just do loads of real paintings of people' whilst someone else might do abstract ... In drama, if it is not your idea and you did not really like it much, they teach you even if it is not your idea think about what they did, use it as an idea to use, don't just use your own ideas and leave it at that (Year 7, art and drama).

Another two pupils found that the arts made them more aware of '*all the talents that other people have*' and enabled them to make comparisons with their own abilities:

I get to see what other people are able to do and see their personal achievements really, getting to know them really, seeing what they can do, seeing what you can do (Year 7, arts).

Associated with this, a small number of pupils (four, making five comments in total) described how learning in the arts as a whole, and in particular drama, enabled them to appreciate other people's points of view:

We did one about conflict when you're having an argument with people, and one girl who stormed out of her house and her dad was saying 'Come back here' and they started having an argument. That was quite good 'cos you can think about … 'cos most people do have arguments … you can see it from your dad's point of view as well. If you're playing the dad, you can see it from his point of view when usually you want to see it from your own (Year 9, drama).

———

It gives you a chance to like do some empathy, putting yourself in another person's shoes. And it has an effect on you that you can understand the way people feel when they do drama, and the way they express themselves and the things they say and how they feel about certain subjects (Year 8, drama).

This particular ability to '*step into somebody else's shoes and be that person*' was a specific effect of the arts raised by a small group of pupils (six, making one comment each), again mainly as a result of drama lessons. Pupils talked about '*getting into character*' as a way of discovering and understanding other people's circumstances and problems, such as bullying.

Clearly, then, the development of empathy and greater awareness and understanding of others, in a variety of facets, was endorsed as an effect of arts education by a sizeable proportion of the pupil interviewees. In particular, the contribution of drama to this type of outcome was outstanding.

8.8 IMPROVED SOCIAL SKILLS

For the final subcategory within the personal and social domain, we turn to the skills dimension of interpersonal intelligence.

Teacher Perspectives

Teachers across the artforms commented on the opportunities that the arts provide for pupils to work in groups, to nurture teamwork skills and develop group identity through playing in school bands, working on productions and undertaking shared experiences in lesson time:

And they work in groups: they've got to communicate with one another and work it out, which is quite nice for them to work in groups, rather than in isolation all the time. They have to discuss ideas and things (art teacher).

... the drama side where people work together to create a performance or to work together on a feeling or a situation and then express it (head of Welsh).

One music teacher averred that they produce a lot of people who work well together as musicians, which is not always the same as being a great player. Another teacher told of how experiences in drama had helped to unite a form group:

One kid in a Year 9 group, who are appalling at listening, cannot listen to save their lives – we have a battle every week. But they're great. When they get going, they are a good group, and she said to me 'It's brought the form together'... it brings them together as a unit, it brings them together, understanding each other, working together.

An interesting aim was put forward by one teacher: to get pupils to work together and *'pull together'* but, paralleling this, to have departments do the same, so that pupils do not see any separation between arts subjects.

Another aspect of this subcategory was the development of the skills of group work such as cooperation, negotiation within a group, getting on with people, leadership skills and listening. One teacher expressed the view that mixed-ability arts lessons provide good opportunities for all, and another described pupils *'sparking'* off each other.

As well as providing opportunities for working together, and the development of teamwork skills, claims were made by some teachers for the arts enhancing social skills and personal relationships. For some, this was on the very practical level of giving pupils the social skills to perform well in interviews or effectively engage socially in a wider circle of friends and contacts:

I am hoping it will keep them out of trouble, but will also benefit them to play each situation for what it is so when they are in the interview situation or they're, you know, at a party or whatever, they can play that situation and feel comfortable with themselves and perhaps hopefully understand other people around them (drama teacher).

One drama teacher described the learning taking place as a *'life skill'*:

I mean it's going back to the people thing again, isn't it? You can't actually do drama on your own, and you learn that through the five years that it's the fusion between my idea and your idea that makes something good, and that's probably a life skill, isn't it?

Finally, a small number of teachers, especially music teachers, referred to collaborative engagement in the arts leading to improved relationships between pupils and teachers. One head of department described shared music making as '*magical chemistry*'.

2.
WHAT ARE
THE EFFECTS
OF
ARTS
EDUCATION?

Pupil Perspectives

A large number of pupils interviewed talked about how the arts provide opportunities to work in groups and develop appropriate skills, such as cooperation and negotiation. The issue of how groups were formed (whether by enforced membership or by pupil-selection of members) and the related consequences of these arrangements, was discussed, together with the usefulness of group work in the arts for the future. A total of 136 comments by 59 pupils were made referring to the capacity for group work in the arts. Of these, 93 comments related specifically to group work skills, 17 to the effects of group membership choice and working with different people, 13 expressly about cooperation and three referring to the transfer of such skill to future use. The remaining ten comments in this subcategory overlapped with a further subdivision of effects on forming better relationships as a result of working together.

Group and teamwork skills

A total of 93 references were made to the experience of group work in the arts, and the associated effects of this. Drama was the principal stimulus of these comments at all of the five schools, with music producing a significant number of comments at two particular schools. Interestingly, six pupils, from three schools referred to dance providing opportunities to work in groups and develop these skills, which represents nearly a quarter of those taking this subject. Comments came from pupils in all year groups.

A large number of pupils talked about the opportunities that the arts gave them to partake in group activities, implying that their capacity to function effectively in groups had been extended. Similar comments were made about each artform and the arts as a whole, for example:

We had to dance in groups and keep in time with each other (Year 7, dance).

Before I came to music classes I had never really played music with other people, I had always played piano or guitar on my own. Coming into music classes, we go into groups of four or five, where we make up a composition and you all play, or you do an entire class composition. I had never done that before so it taught me how to play music with other people (Year 9, music).

———

It makes you get on with people, so, like, when you're doing scenes in drama, you work together. It makes you work as a team (Year 9, drama).

In connection with this, pupils talked about the arts developing and improving their group work skills, in their capacity to work with others: '*I've also learned to work better in a group.*'

Develops cooperation

The development of the ability to cooperate with others was an outcome of the arts mentioned by ten pupils, who made a total of 13 comments. These were made by pupils of all ages and referred predominantly to drama as a medium of this effect.

Some pupils talked about the '*importance of teamwork and cooperation*' in the arts, whilst others discussed how participation in the arts helped develop these skills. A couple of pupils considered this to be an outcome of the arts as a whole: '*'cos you work a lot in groups, you learn to cooperate with other people's feelings.*' Other comments referred specifically to this as an effect of drama, music and English:

It's good because you work cooperatively, like if you're in a band or something, and you're listening to everybody else playing so you know when to come in (Year 9, music).

———

You have to learn to be cooperative with everybody in your group and how to get on with everybody, to listen to other people's ideas and things (Year 10, drama).

Working with different people: effect of group choice and/or mixed-ability groups

Again, mainly with reference to drama, 13 pupils of all ages talked about the effect that the choice of group members had on them. Sixteen comments were made with regard to this outcome. The arts were recognised as providing opportunities to work with a variety of different people, according to one pupil '*even with people you don't like or can't stand*'. Being made to work with different people was generally seen as a positive experience:

I think it has made me work well with others, because if she did not put us with partners and groups then I would just work with the same people every time. That would not be very good (Year 7, drama).

Although two pupils stated that they *'enjoy working with friends'*, another discussed the difficulties that this might involve:

We have been put into groups and we would have to work together for about ten weeks on a production. And I have been put into groups with friends, because we were allowed to say who we wanted to work with. And it's been quite difficult to work with friends, because you are trying to accept others' ideas, but at the same time, if you are convinced yours is right, then it's not always the best thing, and sometimes I have had out-of-drama arguments with friends ... (Year 11, drama).

In addition, a few pupils described how they had learned to *'work with people of different abilities'* through engaging in the arts, although pupils tended to comment that they preferred to work with others of the same ability:

You tend to work with people that are of your own ability in music so you wouldn't ... if one person is musically minded, they wouldn't go with a person who's not very tuneful, if you know what I mean. They tend to stick together, which in some ways is bad but it helps to go with somebody the same standard as you (Year 9, music).

Use of group work skills in future

Three pupils from three different schools talked about how the group work skills that they had developed through participation in the arts would be useful to them in the future. Two referred to drama helping with teamwork in the workplace in the future, and the third talked about the effects of music and drama in a similar capacity. The importance of the arts for fostering teamwork skills was occasionally recognised by employers:

Interviewer: *Do you think that what you do now in the arts, or what you've done in the past has had any effects on you?*

I think in the sense of forcing me to work in a group they are excellent (manager in an employment agency).

Shared experience

In addition to the 136 comments on group work, pupils also referred to the shared experience of the arts in the same way that teachers did. A handful of pupils talked about the positive outcome of working together in the arts as a sense of 'togetherness', or shared experience. There were, however, just seven comments here, made by six pupils, from three of the schools. Mainly referring to music, through membership of a band, one pupil talked about how being in a band was '*like being part of a community-type thing*'. Another talked about the bond between members:

> *In a band everybody's your friend. There's nobody you don't get on with because you all have the same interest.*

> Interviewer: *But how is all that different from, say, being in a football team?*

> *I don't think the bond is as strong in a football team. You still work together but it's not like music ... I think you're just closer somehow* (Year 9, music).

An older pupil (in Year 11) cited how working with another girl on an ensemble piece for her GCSE music exam had developed her '*sense of musicianship*'.

Self-presentation skills

A number of pupils (14) talked about how working in groups in the arts had helped them '*get along with people*', made them '*more sociable*', or taught them '*how to hold yourself in different social circles*'. These improvements in social presentation skills were recognised largely to be an outcome of drama and were mainly cited by older pupils. Pupils from two of the schools in particular contributed most of the 18 comments for this outcome.

One pupil talked about the social effect of having worked with different groups in drama lessons:

> [Drama] *helps you communicate ... once you have spoken to people in drama, you can go out and have a conversation with them.* [You] *are not shy about meeting people for the first time. Drama has helped a lot with work experience interviews, speaking to people in a friendly manner, not being too frightened of questions* (Year 10, drama).

Sparking off each other

Echoing the earlier teacher comments, two older pupils from the same school talked about being able to '*bounce ideas off each other*' when working in a group in music. Some of the advantages of working in groups were suggested by one pupil:

> *I like working in a group because you can get loads of different ideas, and sometimes you work better, because if you don't understand something then you can always ask them* (Year 11, music).

Widening pupils' social networks

In all, 38 pupils made a total of 45 references to increased social opportunities as a result of the arts, in terms of talking to new people and making new friends. Comments came from pupils from each of the five schools, and referred to the arts as a whole and each individual artform, although the frequency of comments by artform varied. Seventeen remarks identified this as an outcome of the arts collectively, whilst 14 referred to drama and nine to music. Art received three comments, and dance and English one each. Half of the references to drama came from pupils at one school.

Pupils talked about the arts providing them with opportunities to '*meet new people*' and '*make new friends*', frequently as a result of working in different groups, which link in with the comments presented earlier: '*If you work with people who you would not normally work with, it normally leads to getting to know them slightly better out of lessons*' (Year 9, drama).

Often pupils talked about participation in extra-curricular arts activities, such as the orchestra, productions, or a band giving rise to new social opportunities and connections:

> *I got to know more people from going to the choir and things like that. I got more friends* (Year 9).

> ———

> *Now, I know a lot more people than I did before, through productions and through art and music* (Year 9, arts).

A few pupils talked about how they had made friends with people in different years, as a result of the arts:

> *In the productions you meet different people from the different years who you don't normally associate with* (Year 9, arts).

> ———

> *I've got friendly with more people in the older years because I was working with them in the show, and not just people in my form* (Year 7, music).

In terms of the arts developing better relationships between pupils, one boy talked about trust:

> *One of the other things, thinking how drama has helped, is with trust, because I used to have a problem with trust, but now I find it easier to trust other people, to put responsibilities concerning me in their hands, because you have to with drama, because if you were hosting something and people just don't turn up, then you are not going to get the mark for it that you deserve* (Year 11, drama).

Two pupils, one male and one female, talked about how, for them, dance and drama had helped to break down the barriers between the sexes:

> *It's really helping us to work together, boys and girls, and sort of break down the barriers that sort of separates us from working together* (Year 8, dance).

> *You used to be embarrassed to go with the boys, whereas now nobody really cares* (Year 9, drama).

Improved pupil–teacher relationships

2.
WHAT ARE
THE EFFECTS
OF
ARTS
EDUCATION?

Like a few teachers, pupils talked about the building of relationships through the arts between pupils and teachers (four pupils referred to this). A couple of pupils felt that they could form a closer relationship with their teachers in the arts, because of their personality, or because of a common enthusiasm:

> *You have a bit closer relationship because you can have a laugh with the teacher and you can just ... Basically you both have a passion for drama and you can share that passion and so you can share the ideas, and so you communicate more and I think that's ... you know the teacher more socially, so I think that's good* (Year 11, drama).

8.9 CONCLUDING COMMENTS

This chapter, then, provides great testimony to the strength and variety of outcomes of arts education relating to pupils' personal and social development. Most significant in pupils' accounts were their perceptions of effects that reflected an interaction of self with others, the greatest number of pupils' comments relating to the areas of self-confidence, as well as to the enhancement of social skills, such as group and team work. Although slightly fewer, comments on the more inner developments of a whole and rounded personality were also numerous, with a growth in awareness and empathy of others given similar standing. Again, although a little smaller in terms of numbers of comments, the subcategory of enhanced self-worth and self-esteem provides evidence for the way pupils felt good about their own work, and this naturally had an effect too on their confidence and sense of achievement and satisfaction, reported elsewhere. Although one of the smaller categories, forming a sense of self-identity and self-image detailed a range of comments from pupils, from 'likes and dislikes', to 'self-discovery' and being more able to cope in certain everyday situations. Enriched personal skills were less numerous, though a small but significant number of pupils talked about increases in a sense of independence and autonomy – thus adding to the rich tapestry of perceived effects on personal and social development.

Capturing most of the essential personal and social development outcomes reported in this chapter, this employer neatly summarises many of the intra- and interpersonal gains perceived by the pupil interviewees:

Interviewer: *What, in your view, is arts education for?*

Really to give people a wider perspective of life. I think it also puts people in tune with their feelings a little bit more as well. They have, you gain an understanding and appreciation of, you know, motives of people, also different cultures; it makes you more sensitive to other people. That's why I think it's important.

Interviewer: *What would you say were the main effects or outcomes for students studying the arts at school?*

I think it makes them more confident, and more able to articulate themselves in company. I think it enables them to understand the motives of people and why people behave in a certain way, and perhaps how to deal with those sorts of things (Personnel Support Manager in a large building society).

Before concluding, however, it is worth remembering that the evidence to support such outcomes from the arts is drawn from schools that have a reputation for high-quality provision in the arts and from pupils within them who were known to be performing well in at least one artform. Later in the report (see Chapter 11) we will describe evidence from a more representative sample of schools and pupils to show that large numbers of pupils perceive no such effects. Moreover, even in the case study schools, there were sufficient signs that not all pupils enjoyed positive developments in self-esteem to warn against any complacent belief that personal and social development through arts education can be guaranteed. Hence, we should not lose sight of the fact that the achievement of these effects is highly dependent on effective teaching and learning in the arts – as the evidence presented in Part Three will illustrate.

In this light, the testimonies of the pupils portrayed earlier assume even greater significance. Collectively, they amount to compelling and persuasive evidence of the power of the arts to facilitate the personal and social development of pupils. Evidence was garnered for all artforms, but was especially the case for art and drama.

The findings that the arts can have such positive effects on pupils' personal and social development are particularly pertinent to the Government's drive to raise inclusion and attainment levels amongst lower-achieving pupils. Given that low self-esteem has been found to be a common characteristic of disaffected pupils (Kinder *et al.*, 1995), the evident capacity of high-quality arts provision to increase pupils' sense of worth, self-esteem and self-confidence is telling. It suggests, for example, that the arts could make a major contribution to schools' implementation of the new Framework for Personal, Social and Health Education (PSHE) at key stages 3 and 4 (QCA, 2000).

The findings also provide further confirmation that the outcomes of arts education are much wider than the narrower creative and cultural remit of the NACCCE report (Robinson Report, 1999). Thus, whilst the NACCCE report incorporates all areas of the curriculum, in focusing on the creative and cultural dimensions, it embraces only a limited part of the arts agenda. The evidence offered in this part of the report demonstrates that there are whole domains of effects from arts education – such as the personal and social area documented in this chapter – that are broader and more frequent than outcomes related to creative and cultural developments. This point is particularly germane to the policy discussions that the NACCCE report may stimulate, since it draws attention to the dangers of overlooking highly important effects of arts education by assuming that 'the arts' are synonymous with 'creative and cultural education'. In their different ways, both are more wide-ranging than the other.

Finally, the chapter offered some early indications that the effects on pupils' personal and social development are not context-bound or restricted to the confines of the arts. They appear to have a wider relevance and application. Some employers testified to the importance of intra- and interpersonal intelligences to the workplace and a rounded adult life. Moreover, some pupils volunteered accounts of how they had transferred the gains in self-confidence – acquired especially through drama – to other areas of learning and the wider social arena. By way of furthering discussion of this theme, the next chapter looks in some detail at the evidence relating to such transfer effects.

9. EXTRINSIC TRANSFER EFFECTS

CHAPTER OVERVIEW

For the seventh and final broad category of effect on pupils, this chapter takes a more focused look at outcomes that were carried over or transferred from the immediate context of arts lessons to other areas of activity – so-called transfer effects. In particular, it considers the transference of effects to three wider arenas:

- to other areas of learning in the curriculum, subjects or general academic performance (9.2)
- to the world of work, employment and occupational performance (9.3)
- to leisure activities – both current and in the future (9.4).

In order to investigate the hypothesis that engagement in the arts boosts general academic performance, section 9.2 presents the results of statistical analyses.

**2.
WHAT ARE
THE EFFECTS
OF
ARTS
EDUCATION?**

9.1 INTRODUCTION

At various points in the previous chapters – especially with regard to communication skills and personal and social development – reference has been made to the manner in which some pupils volunteered accounts of how learning outcomes in certain artforms had been applied, and proved useful, in other fields and contexts. In this chapter, we examine more directly the study's evidence on claims that the effects of arts education are transferable to other arenas.

The chapter contains three subcategories that focus on the possibility of transference to:

- other areas of learning and general academic performance (section 9.2);
- the world of work and employment (section 9.3); and
- leisure activities (section 9.4).

Reflecting the high public profile given to claims that the arts, predominantly music, can enhance general intellectual development, special attention is given to the first of these subcategories: namely, whether studying the arts boosts general academic performance. Indeed, it was this issue which provided one of the main thrusts and motives for instigating this research project.

9.2 TRANSFER TO OTHER AREAS OF LEARNING AND GENERAL ACADEMIC PERFORMANCE

2.
WHAT ARE
THE EFFECTS
OF
ARTS
EDUCATION?

Searching for evidence of possible causal relationships between studying the arts and wider academic attainment has become something of a specialised genre within the research literature on arts education. Typically, research projects in this tradition examine the purported impact of taking arts courses on such outcome-related variables as general academic attainment, self-concept (including self-esteem), spatial ability, and, less frequently, locus of control, creative thinking and appreciation of the arts (e.g. Luftig, 1994). Most of this type of inquiry emanates from the USA (e.g. Du Pont, 1992; Forseth, 1980; Gardiner *et al.*, 1996; Rauscher *et al.*, 1997), though similar studies have been carried out in other countries, including, for example, Switzerland (Spychiger *et al.*, 1995) and Hungary (Kokas, 1969). Very little work of this kind has been conducted in the UK. Music is the predominant art form studied, often focusing on the Kodaly method (Fox and Gardiner, 1997; Wolff, 1978). Much of the research adopts a quasi-experimental methodology and is generally informed by a psychological, if not a psychometric paradigm. It tends to use primary or elementary school-aged pupils as its subjects. As a general rule, these studies investigate specific or additional arts-oriented teaching programmes, though data on the nature and mediation of these courses is often lacking. Recent reviews of studies in this field have been conducted by Sharp *et al.* (1998) and Winner and Hetland (forthcoming, 2000).

Empirical evidence to support a possible association of wider learning outcomes with arts education would clearly bolster the case for the arts in the curriculum. Most probably, this reason alone constitutes a key motive for much of the funding for this field of inquiry. However, couched in this way, the approach leaves itself wide open to the criticism that it implicitly assumes that the direct effects of experiences in the arts are in themselves weak grounds to claim a significant place in the school timetable. Something of these concerns, for instance, was voiced by an audience of a recent example of this line of research (Fox and Gardiner, 1997):

> *The group were very cautious about placing too much emphasis on the consequential learning which can occur from music education, and wished to stress that the raison d'être for music was its own intrinsic value* (SCAA, 1997, p. 29).

Eisner (1998) makes a similar point more stridently: in a sceptical review of the American literature on research into the alleged impact of the arts on academic achievement, he observes:

We do the arts no service when we try to make their case by touting their contributions to other fields. When such contributions become priorities, the arts become handmaidens to ends that are not distinctively artistic and in the process undermine the value of art's unique contributions to the education of the young (Eisner, 1998, p.15).

It was partly to recognise the force of such arguments that, when the RSA sought to launch a study which would include an investigation into the possible 'spin-off' or transfer effects of taking arts courses, it did so by setting this particular area of inquiry in the context of a wider-ranging analysis that would examine all the outcomes of arts education – direct and indirect alike. It is hoped that the evidence and analyses initiated in the previous chapters have demonstrated the study's commitment to this comprehensive approach.

Furthermore, it is important to stress that this initial and exploratory step into the analysis of some evidence on the possible relationship between the taking of arts courses at key stage 4 and general GCSE academic attainment should not be seen as an isolated enterprise, but as an integral and unfolding part of a much broader research agenda. For this particular aspect of the research programme, it made sense to begin by exploring the issues through an analysis of some existing data.

As a contribution to the debate about transfer effects and general academic attainment, we present and discuss (in turn) evidence from three different sources within the study:

- secondary data analysis from NFER's QUASE – 'Quantitative Analysis for Self-Evaluation' service (section 9.2.1);

- multilevel modelling from the Year 11 Survey (section 9.2.2); and

- the interviews with pupils and teachers in the case study schools (section 9.2.3).

General details of these sources have been described in Chapter 1, and where necessary, further details are provided in the relevant section.

9.2.1   Studying arts-based courses and GCSE performance: secondary data analysis from QUASE

Qualitative claims about effects which transfer from the taking of arts courses to other areas of the curriculum have included the proposition that experiences in the arts can raise general academic attainment in 16+ examinations. In view of this, and the increased availability of data for 'value-added'-type analyses of performance at 16, possible links between GCSE attainment and the taking of key stage 4 arts-oriented courses seemed an appropriate area to start an examination of the claims for a transfer effect.

Consequently, in order to study the possible relationships between studying arts-related GCSE subjects and overall performance at GCSE, secondary analysis has been carried out on data collected for the NFER's QUASE service to secondary schools. The QUASE service provides information to schools about their own performance, relative to what might be expected given their pupils' prior attainment and their social context. The rich database of information collected about the schools and their GCSE pupils enables investigators to explore the relationships between GCSE results, other outcomes, and a range of background variables at the levels of both pupils and schools. For current purposes, the investigation focused on the possible effects of taking key stage 4 arts-related courses on general performance in the GCSE examinations.

The three arts-related subject areas whose impact was to be studied were art, drama and music. Dance was excluded from the secondary QUASE analysis on the basis of the limited numbers of pupils taking GCSE dance, and therefore the limited potential sample size and associated problem of statistical significance. QUASE data from a total of 152 schools with up to three cohorts of Year 11 pupils taking GCSEs between 1994 and 1996 were analysed; the total number of pupils in the sample involved in the analysis was 27,607. The sample of schools included examples of all the main types (e.g. coeducational, single-sex, inner city, rural, selective, independent), and analyses of the QUASE schools showed that they were broadly similar to the national distribution in terms of type of school, type of LEA, region and GCSE performance (Schagen, 1995).

The possible influence of studying the above subjects was investigated using multilevel modelling, controlling for most of the school and pupil-level background variables which are known to be related to GCSE performance, including measures of prior attainment at around Year 7. Other background variables controlled for included, *inter alia*, gender, age, ethnicity, individual free school meal entitlement, ESL, SEN status, average attendance of individual pupils, type of catchment area and percentage of pupils in each school entitled to free school meals.

Multilevel modelling is a development of a common statistical technique known as 'regression analysis'. This is a technique for finding a relationship which allows us to predict the values of some measure of interest ('dependent variable'), given the values of one or more related measures. For example, we may wish to predict schools' average test performance given some background factors, such as free school meals and school size (these are sometimes called 'independent variables').

Multilevel modelling takes account of data which is grouped into similar clusters at different levels. For example, individual pupils are grouped into year groups or cohorts, and those cohorts are grouped within schools, which may themselves be grouped within LEAs. There may be more in common between pupils within the same cohort than with other cohorts, and there may be elements of similarity between different cohorts in the same school, or different schools in the same LEA. Multilevel modelling allows us to take account of this hierarchical structure of the data and produce more accurate predictions, as well as estimates of the differences between pupils, between cohorts, between schools, and between LEAs.

2.
WHAT ARE
THE EFFECTS
OF
ARTS
EDUCATION?

Setting up multilevel models

In addition to the standard QUASE variables related to sex, age, ethnicity, prior attainment, etc., some new indicators were developed for pupils who had studied the three selected arts-related subjects. These were:

ART takes the value 1 if the pupil has entered at least one GCSE in the subject area of art, 0 otherwise

DRAMA takes the value 1 if the pupil has entered at least one GCSE in the subject area of drama, 0 otherwise

MUSIC takes the value 1 if the pupil has entered at least one GCSE in the subject area of music, 0 otherwise.

Some care had to be taken, however, in including these variables as they stand in the multilevel model. There are a significant number of pupils in the model with no GCSEs at all, as well as many with just one or two. Each of the above indicators is more likely to be positive for pupils taking at least one GCSE, and therefore their effect is likely to be confounded with the overall effect of just taking one or more GCSEs. To get round this, the analysis was carried out on a subset of pupils who had attempted three or more GCSEs.

As well as examining possible direct relationships between studying each of these subjects and GCSE performance, the opportunity was taken to investigate two other aspects of these relationships: 'interactions' and 'random slopes'. An interaction between studying a subject (say art) and another background variable (say sex) would imply that the relationship between art and GCSE performance was different for males and females. As well as considering possible sex interactions, the study also looked at interactions with prior attainment, so that hypothetically pupils with lower initial attainment might do more or less well if they studied one of the arts-based subjects.

Such interaction terms were included in the multilevel analysis by defining extra 'interaction variables':

ARTSEX	Interaction between studying art and gender
DRAMSEX	Interaction between studying drama and gender
MUSSEX	Interaction between studying music and gender
ARTXINT	Interaction between studying art and prior attainment
DRAMXINT	Interaction between studying drama and prior attainment
MUSXINT	Interaction between studying music and prior attainment.

The concept of 'random slopes' is based on the idea that the relationship between studying an arts-based subject and GCSE performance may not be the same across all schools, but may vary from school to school. The size of the school-level variance gives us an indication of the extent to which any 'arts-based subject effect' is consistent from school to school.

One further variable was developed, which was intended to represent the overall tendency of pupils to take arts-related subjects:

ARTSPC	is the sum of the three subject indicators ART, DRAMA and MUSIC, as a percentage of the total number of GCSEs attempted, e.g. an ARTSPC score of 25 per cent could mean that a pupil took four GCSEs, one of which was arts-related (say, music) or eight GCSEs, two of which were arts-related (say, music and drama).

The multilevel analysis was carried out on the following measures of GCSE performance:

ENG	Average English score
MATHS	Average maths score
SCI	Total science score
AVREST	Average score on non-arts subjects.

It is considered that, in the context of the present inquiry, these variables represent the most appropriate indicators of general academic performance at GCSE. None of the other possible performance indicators which sum or average over all subjects was suitable, as they would include the arts subjects themselves.

Results of multilevel analysis

The multilevel analysis of QUASE data was carried out with three levels in the model: school, cohort and pupil. Background variables at the school and pupil levels were included, including prior attainment at or near intake to secondary school (e.g. on the basis of various verbal reasoning, non-verbal reasoning, English and maths tests). Once these basic models had been set up, the three arts-related variables and the six interaction terms were introduced. The variable ARTSPC, which measured the overall proportion of GCSEs which were arts-related, was included at a later stage.

To show the results of these analyses, the coefficients which express the estimated relationships between each of the arts-related variables (e.g. ART), the variables indicating GCSE performance (e.g. English GCSE results) and each of the background variables have been converted into 'effect sizes'. These may be regarded as equivalent to the correlation between the two variables when other variables in the model are taken into account. They represent the 'strength' of each relationship as a percentage, and allow the different variables to be compared in terms of their apparent influence on the test outcomes (e.g. SCI, AVREST), when all other variables are simultaneously taken into account.

Figures 9.1 to 9.4 show these effect sizes for each of the four outcome measures. For each variable, the estimated effect size is plotted as a diamond, with a vertical line indicating the 95 per cent confidence interval for the estimate. Any variable whose line intersects the horizontal zero axis can be regarded as not statistically significant (at the five per cent level). Positive values imply a positive relationship with the test score outcome; negative values imply that the test score tended to decrease with higher values of the given background variable.

For each of the three sex-related 'interaction variables' (e.g. DRAMSEX), positive values indicate a female bias, while negative values a male bias. Similarly, for each of the three prior attainment-related 'interaction variables' (e.g. DRAMXINT), positive values signal a stronger association for those with higher levels of prior attainment, while negative values signal a stronger association for those with lower levels of prior attainment. Interaction variables which were found to be clearly insignificant have been omitted from the figures (e.g. MUSSEX has been left out of Figure 9.1).

2.
WHAT ARE
THE EFFECTS
OF
ARTS
EDUCATION?

Figure 9.1   Effect sizes of arts-related variables on average English score

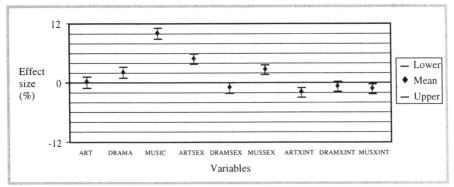

Turning first to Figure 9.1, which shows the relationships between the individual arts-related subjects and the English GCSE score, it appears that taking drama or music is significantly related to success in English. The estimated association between taking music and high attainment in English is particularly strong. Looking at interactions, art is the only subject to have a significant result for ARTSEX, and the result implies that the apparent effect of studying art is more positive for girls than for boys. Interactions with prior attainment show a stronger positive effect for art and music on those with lower levels of prior attainment.

Figure 9.2   Effect sizes of arts-related variables on average maths score

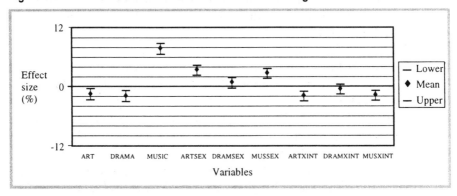

Looking at Figure 9.2, which shows the relationships between the individual arts-related subjects and the maths GCSE score, we can see that music again, as tradition would have it, is positively related to mathematics. However, the figure also indicates that there is a negative effect for art and drama: taking these subjects is associated with lower attainment in maths. Art and music are more positively associated with higher scores in maths for girls than for boys, for whom there is a corresponding negative association. Both these subjects have a stronger positive relationship with their average maths score for pupils of lower prior attainment.

Figure 9.3   Effect sizes of arts-related variables on total science score

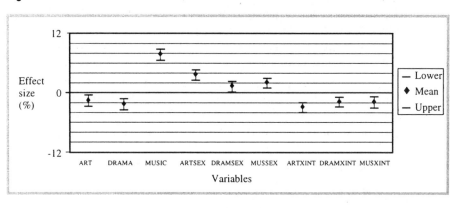

Figure 9.3, which shows the relationships between the individual arts-related subjects and the total science GCSE score, shows a similar picture to Figure 9.2. Music is positively associated with higher attainment in science, while art and drama are negatively related to science. All three arts-related subjects are more strongly positively related to doing well in science for girls and for those of lower prior attainment.

Figure 9.4   Effect sizes of arts-related variables on average score for other subjects

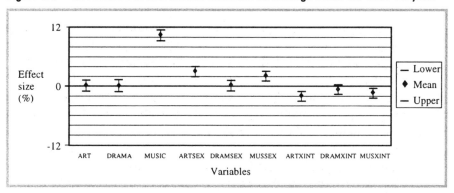

Figure 9.4 shows the relationships between the taking of arts-related subjects and the average score in non-arts subjects. A similar picture to the others is evident. Only music has a significant positive effect overall, while the other two subjects are not significant. Once again, art and music are more positively associated with higher average scores for all non-arts GCSE subjects for girls than for boys, and both have a stronger positive effect for pupils of lower prior attainment.

When we include, as a background variable, the percentage of arts-based subjects pupils took as a proportion of their total number of GCSEs, ARTSPC, there is a dramatic change. This is illustrated in Figure 9.5 for English, but it carried over into the analyses for all the outcome variables. The apparent effects of the individual subjects become much stronger and, for this analysis, art has a slightly stronger effect than music. These positive results, however, are counterbalanced by an even stronger negative effect of ARTSPC. What does this mean? One possibility is that each arts subject by itself may have some beneficial impact on performance in core subjects, but that pupils who tend to concentrate on arts subjects to the exclusion of others may have reduced academic attainment. However, it must be remembered that none of the analysis carried out here gives any indication of causality.

Figure 9.5:   Effect sizes controlling for ARTSPC on average English score

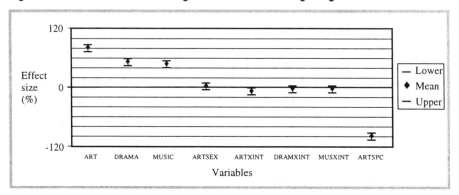

As mentioned earlier, the extent to which these relationships vary from school to school was investigated by making the coefficients for the three variables ART, DRAMA and MUSIC random at the school level. In all cases, this random effect was statistically significant, even when the overall relationship (e.g. between ART and ENG in Figure 9.1) was not apparently significant. The implication is that the impact of studying these subjects on pupils' performance is affected by one or more school-level factors. This suggests that in certain schools there are strong positive relationships between arts-based subjects and GCSE performance, while in others they may be non-existent or even negative. Table 9.1 shows the standard deviation between schools in the apparent change in GCSE performance associated with each arts-based subject.

Table 9.1   Standard deviations in slopes between different schools for GCSE results versus arts-based subjects

	Art	Drama	Music
Average English score	0.31	0.45	0.40
Average maths score	0.33	0.45	0.67
Total science score	0.88	1.08	0.95
Average score for others	0.34	0.43	0.37

For practical purposes, the results for the total science score should be halved to account for the effect of double awards for integrated science.

Discussion

When considering the meaning of these results, it is crucial not to lose sight of the fact that the analysis cannot offer any evidence of causality, or even the direction of causality. It is limited to highlighting associations between variables, which in the multilevel modelling technique deployed here are expressed as 'effect sizes', though this does not literally signify evidence of an actual 'effect'. For example, even if there is a positive association between x and y, it does not necessarily mean that x is causing y; it could also indicate that y is causing x, or that some other variable not fully controlled for is causing the association between x and y.

However, so long as these cautions about causality are respected, a number of possible and hypothetical explanations of the findings can be speculated upon, especially as a means of generating further lines of inquiry for the analysis of other sources of evidence collected during the research programme. These hypotheses may be grouped under two main types, or directions, of causality:

(i)   the impact of studying arts-based subjects on general GCSE performance; and

(ii) the 'backwash' effect of predicted general GCSE performance on the take-up of arts-based courses.

Each of these possibilities is discussed in turn:

The impact of studying arts-based subjects on general GCSE performance

In so far as they have produced some significant positive associations of the required type, the results of the analysis certainly do not rule out the possibility that taking certain arts-based subjects can have a beneficial effect on general attainment in GCSE examinations. That music in particular can have a positive transferable impact on GCSE performance in the core subjects is undoubtedly one possible and plausible interpretation of the results. Teacher accounts from the early fieldwork for the case study element of the research suggested that arts-related subjects could mediate such an effect through two main avenues: firstly, through increasing pupils' self-esteem and positive values towards school and learning and/or, secondly, through developing transferable skills and knowledge.

Proponents for the first of these avenues could argue that the findings are consistent with the view that, for some pupils, studying music is a highly positive and rewarding experience which nurtures a generalised and improved self-esteem and motivation and which in turn affects learning and performance in English, maths, science and other subjects. Thus, according to this proposition, taking music encourages a set of transferable values and attitudes that place a premium on the sense of personal fulfilment that can be achieved through learning. All the figures presented above show interaction 'effect sizes' consistent with the view that this form of effect through music may be particularly significant for pupils with lower levels of prior attainment.

Notwithstanding the above, a major difficulty for the positive values and self-esteem interpretation is that the results do not consistently display a similar effect for art and drama, contrary to teachers' and pupils' testimonies from the case study evidence. In Chapter 8, for example, teachers and pupils made more claims for generalised self-esteem and self-confidence from art and drama than music, yet this is not borne out by the QUASE results. Art and drama (see Figure 9.4), for example, were found to have no significant association with pupils' general performance at GCSE as represented by their average score in non-arts subjects (AVREST). Even more problematically, art and drama were negatively associated with performance in maths (see Figure 9.2) and science (see Figure 9.3). This may suggest that art and drama do not generate the same transferable motivation towards learning as that alleged for music or, if they do, they also encourage a demotivating effect on learning in maths and science.

Very similar interpretations of the results could be mounted for the second broad type of mediating influence referred to above, namely, the claim that arts-related subjects develop transferable knowledge and skills. From this perspective, it could be argued that the data lend support to the view that studying music leads to the acquisition of certain skills and knowledge which are relevant and helpful to pupils' performance in English, maths, science and other subjects. To some extent, this interpretation is in line with previous studies that have postulated a link between music education and the development of numeracy-related concepts (e.g. Fox and Gardiner, 1997). It is harder for this hypothesis to explain, though, why the 'effect size' for music on English (see Figure 9.1) is greater than that on maths and science (see Figures 9.2 and 9.3 respectively). Moreover, the proposition also lacks plausibility in accounting for the limited, or even negative, impact of art and drama on the test outcomes. It may be that the transferable knowledge and skills thesis is limited to music, but in the case study data, teachers and pupils saw it as much more likely to be associated with art and drama than with music (see section 9.2.3).

The finding that taking a higher proportion of arts-related subjects is associated with reduced GCSE attainment (see Figure 9.5) poses substantial problems for both the transferable skills and the transferable motivation hypotheses, in so far as they relate to arts subjects as a collective entity rather than individual subjects. If either of these was tenable for the 'arts', it could have been expected that the greater the number of arts subjects taken by a pupil, the greater the transferability effects. However, the data suggests that the reverse is the case.

Both hypotheses could account for the variation from school to school as largely due to differences in the extent to which arts subject teaching accentuates positive experiences, self-esteem and/or transferable knowledge and skills. This underlines the need to study the processes of teaching and learning in the arts in order to avoid 'black box' approaches to input-output analyses.

The 'backwash' effect of predicted general GCSE performance on the take-up of arts-based courses

Many of the results generated by the QUASE analysis could be explained (hypothetically) by reversing the direction of causality implied in the propositions mooted above. Thus, rather than seeing the findings as an indication of the impact of taking arts-related subjects on GCSE attainment, they may be signalling the effect of predicted GCSE performance on the take-up of arts subjects in the light of pupils' academic attainment and experiences during key stage 3 (i.e. after the prior attainment assessments were taken).

According to this view, the results may be interpreted as showing that those pupils who had performed well academically throughout key stage 3 (allowing for both over- and underperformers as measured by the prior attainment on intake), and were predicted to score highly in, say English (see Figure 9.1 and 9.2), were significantly more likely to take music (especially, if they were female) and slightly more likely to take drama than other pupils – though not so with art. Those doing well in maths (see Figure 9.2) were more likely to take music, but less likely to opt for art and drama; similar interpretations apply to science (see Figure 9.3) and general academic attainment, as indicated by the average score for non-arts subjects, but here there is no significant biased recruitment of high or low academic performers at key stage 3 for art and drama, though music attracts more high performers (see Figure 9.4). Why music rather than other arts-related subjects should recruit in this way may relate to the traditional perception of music carrying greater academic credibility and currency. Support for this interpretation was later found in the Year 11 Survey (see Chapter 14), which established that pupils taking music (and no other arts subject) had substantially higher mean scores in English, mathematics and science key stage 3 tests than any other group in the analysis, including those who chose not to enrol for any arts subject.

This line of argument also offers a very plausible explanation of the main feature of Figure 9.5, namely that pupils who take a relatively higher proportion of arts-related subjects have reduced attainment at GCSE. According to the reverse effect thesis, this analysis reflects the tendency in many schools for only those pupils who are predicted to perform poorly at GCSE to be advised, or allowed, to include more than one arts subject in their GCSE portfolio. Again, endorsement of this interpretation was found in the Year 11 Survey (see Chapter 14), which revealed that those taking more than one arts subject, even including music, had the lowest mean scores in English, mathematics and science key stage 3 tests compared to the other groups taking individual arts subjects.

Likewise, this set of hypotheses would probably account for the variation from school to school as being heavily influenced by the limitations and opportunities in the options structures of different schools. In this regard, the analysis may have unintentionally highlighted a set of issues that deserves further investigation. Do schools' options systems permit pupils to take more than one artform? What subjects are arts-based options usually set against? What factors, pressures and previous experiences influence pupils' choices regarding GCSE arts-based courses (e.g. whether to take a particular artform, whether to take more than one artform, or whether, as is often the case, to drop the arts altogether)? As a result of the implicit messages about the relative status of the arts contained in key stage 4 curricular structures, such questions have significant implications for both key stages in the secondary phase.

Conclusion

On balance, and with special regard to the arts as a whole, the explanation that best fits the overall thrust of the results is probably the second hypothesis, namely that the observed associations between general GCSE attainment and studying arts courses at key stage 4 reflect qualities of the pupils who take up the arts-related courses. In particular, this explanation provides for a plausible interpretation of the results for art and drama, as well as the negative effects associated with those pupils who take a high proportion of arts-related GCSE courses.

Music is a possible exception to this interpretation. Although the second hypothesis could provide a plausible account of the results for music, so could the first. Therefore, that this subject can impart a positive transferable impact on GCSE performance in the core subjects remains a possibility in the light of the analysis, although, even for music, problems with the transferable effect hypothesis surfaced in the results: anomalies were evident (e.g. the stronger association with English rather than mathematics) and in the case study research, pupils and teachers were more likely to attribute transferable effects to the other arts subjects than to music.

These interpretations are very tentative and reflect the highly complex nature of the results. It is conceivable, for example, that, given there are signs of multiple (sometimes conflicting) effects, the associations generated by the analysis could be caused by both hypothetical explanations impacting simultaneously, but in opposite directions of causality. Hence, the general drift of the results to emerge from this part of the research lends support to those who have argued the case for caution when considering the claims made for transfer effects. Clearly, there is a need for further research in this field and this initial analysis of existing data serves to highlight the case for examining the impact of school-level factors on the relationship between taking arts-related subjects and general GCSE attainment. Furthermore, the results – particularly with regard to the negative associations of those taking high proportions of arts-related GCSEs – underline the prudence of Eisner's scepticism about the search for transferable effects at the risk of devaluing the direct outcomes and benefits of arts experiences at school.

9.2.2 Involvement in the arts and GCSE performance: evidence from the Year 11 Survey

While the QUASE analysis reported above benefited from a large sample and the opportunity to control for pupils' prior attainment, it lacked any additional data that related specifically to the arts, most notably pupils' degree of extra-curricular involvement in the arts and their general attitudes towards the arts. This is an important omission because proponents of the academic performance transfer effect have suggested that pupils' extra-curricular involvement in the arts may be imparting an influence over and above any participation in key stage 4 arts-based courses. The QUASE analysis also lacked the social class classification of individual pupils and pupils' key stage 3 test scores. Again, these are significant omissions since it may be the case that social class is a key intervening variable (e.g. the correlations between high general academic GCSE performance and engagement in music merely reflect the greater probability that the children who are both high attainers and musicians are likely to be middle-class) and that key stage 3 test scores are a more accurate predictor of GCSE success and a better baseline for assessing the impact of key stage 4 courses than prior attainment at the age of 11.

Consequently, the survey of Year 11 pupils and their schools was designed to provide a wider range of variables for inclusion in a more comprehensive analysis, albeit based on a smaller sample. Most importantly, this additional multilevel modelling analysis allows us to explore the possible relationships between extra-curricular participation in the arts and general GCSE academic attainment, while controlling for such variables as key stage 3 scores, prior attainment at Year 7, social class, ethnicity and gender. The results of this new analysis are described here.

The data

For this analysis, data from the sample of Year 11 pupils and their associated schools has been combined to investigate statistical relationships between attitudes towards, and experiences in, arts education, on the one hand, and GCSE outcomes, on the other. The data came from six sources:

- pupil GCSE results, subject by subject, in 1998;

- key stage 3 scores for a subsample of these pupils;

- prior attainment scores (Year 7) for a subsample of these pupils;

- pupil questionnaires about their arts education (*Year 11 Survey student questionnaire* – see Appendix I);

- school questionnaires about their provision of arts education (*Year 11 Survey school questionnaire* – see Appendix II); and

- school information from the NFER schools database.

The derivation of a number of pupil and school variables from the questionnaires is described in Appendix III. These were used as background factors in the multilevel analysis. A total of 2,022 pupils in 22 schools had both GCSE data and questionnaire information available.

Because it was necessary to take account of prior attainment in the analysis, this reduced the number of pupils available. A subsample of 1,684 pupils had key stage 3 level information available, but only 548 had prior attainment data from starting secondary school in Year 7.

Two different types of outcome measure were incorporated into the analysis. The first type was available for all pupils, and gave indications of GCSE performance in areas not directly related to the arts (i.e. mathematics, English, science, and average non-arts grades). The second type of outcome related directly to GCSE results in arts subjects: art, drama and music. The numbers of pupils with the latter outcomes were reduced relative to the basic numbers with prior attainment.

In this section, we will describe the various multilevel models which have been run and their results, and endeavour to give a certain degree of interpretation to the findings.

2.
WHAT ARE
THE EFFECTS
OF
ARTS
EDUCATION?

Setting up the multilevel model

In this application of multilevel modelling, just two levels were assumed: schools and pupils. Table 9.2 gives a complete list of all the variables used in the multilevel modelling with a description of each (but see also Appendix III for further information on how these variables were derived).

Table 9.2   Variables used in multilevel modelling

No.	Name	Min.	Max.	Description
1	SCHOOL	1	22	School id.
2	ID	1	99999	Pupil id.
3	CONS	1	1	Constant
4	SEX	0	2	Sex (0 = male, 2 = female)
5	BLACK	0	1	Black ethnic origin
6	ASIAN	0	1	Asian ethnic origin
7	OTHER	0	1	Other ethnic origin
8	TOTSCORE	0	89	Total GCSE score
9	AVSCORE	0	7.8	Average GCSE score
10	MATHS	0	8	Maths GCSE score
11	ENG	0	8	English GCSE score (av.)
12	SCI	0	24	Science GCSE score (total)
13	AVOTHER	0	39	Average score non – arts subjects
14	ART	-1	8	Subject area E: art etc.
15	MUSIC	-1	8	Subject area L: music etc.
16	DRAMA	-1	8	Drama
17	XCOMP2	-99	25	Composite intake measure (all)
18	KS3AV	-1	8	Average KS3 level
19	DUNART	0	1	Taken subject in KS4: art
20	DUNDAN	0	1	Taken subject in KS4: dance

Table 9.2(continued

No.	Name	Min.	Max.	Description
21	DUNDRA	0	1	Taken subject in KS4: drama
22	DUNEA	0	1	Taken subject in KS4: exp. arts
23	DUNMUS	0	1	Taken subject in KS4: music
24	ARTSPC	0	50	Arts subjects as % of total
25	ARTSFAV	0	3	Index of arts subjects as favourite
26	ARTSHATE	0	3	Index of arts subjects as least favourite
27	ARTSBEST	0	3	Index of arts subjects as best at
28	WHYARTS	-3	12	Total of +/- reasons for taking arts
29	ENJOYALL	-2	8	Lesson enjoyment: all arts
30	ARTSCANT	0	5	No. of arts subjects unable to take
31	BENARTS	0	60	Total effects (benefits) of arts subjects
32	IMPARTS	0	3	Importance of arts subjects
33	ECALL	0	78	Index of extra-curricular activity: all
34	PARSUP	0	13	Parental support
35	SCLASS	10	50	Social class
36	AGEYRS	15	19	Age in years
37	Y11F1	81	174	Positive to arts in school
38	Y11F2	62	149	Arts outside school
39	Y11F3	65	188	Negative to arts in school
40	CATCH	0	4	Catchment area (0 = rural to 4 = inner city)
41	TOWNSEND	-5.36	7.16	Townsend index – 1991 census
42	PCFSM	0	18	% free school meals
43	N99	320	1941	Total students
44	HRSWK	1.23	3	Hours/week per arts subject
45	TOTFAC	0	5	Total specialist arts facilities listed
46	ARTSCOMP	0	1	Arts subject compulsory at KS4
47	ACCESS	0	5	Index of access to arts subjects at KS4
48	ACTEXTRA	1	9	Total no. of arts extracurricular activities
49	ECART	0	17	Index of extra-curricular activity: art
50	ECMUS	0	21	Index of extra-curricular activity: music
51	ECDRAM	0	17	Index of extra-curricular activity: drama
52	ECDAN	0	17	Index of extra-curricular activity: dance
53	ECLIT	0	8	Index of extra-curricular activity: literature

This table and appendix reward perusal because they demonstrate the broad array of information included in the analyses and the procedures used to calculate some of the variables (e.g. the indices of extra-curricular activity in the arts). The outcome measures used for modelling were the following (each based on converting GCSE grades to scores – A* = 8, A = 7, B = 6, etc):

Non-arts subjects

- Average mathematics score (MATHS);

- Average English score (ENG);

- Total science score – i.e. with double award counted twice (SCI); and

- Average score on non–arts subjects (AVOTHER).

2.
WHAT ARE
THE EFFECTS
OF
ARTS
EDUCATION?

Arts subjects

- Art;

- Drama; and

- Music.

For each outcome measure, the multilevel model is fitted in stages, starting with no background variables (the 'base case'). Background variables are fitted in blocks, and for each one, the model estimates a coefficient (the rate at which the outcome apparently varies with a unit change in the background variable) and its significance (whether or not the apparent relationship could occur by chance). Variables which are clearly not significantly related to the outcome measure are removed from the model until a final stage is reached in which all, or most, of the background variables included appear to be significantly related to the outcome variable.

The coefficients estimated may not be easy to interpret, since they will depend on the range of variation within each background variable, as well as the strength of the relationship with the outcome. To help with this, therefore, these coefficients have been converted into 'normalised coefficients' which represent the 'strength' of each relationship as a percentage, and which allow the different variables to be compared in terms of their apparent influence on the test outcome, when all other variables are simultaneously taken into account.

As well as the relationships between background variables and outcomes, we may be interested in the variations in outcomes between pupils at the same school, and between different schools. These are expressed in terms of 'random variances', and their values will tend to be reduced once background factors have been introduced into the model.

Results of multilevel models controlling for key stage 3 levels

Most pupils (1,684 in total) had prior attainment measures collected at the end of key stage 3, expressed as average levels over the three core subjects (English, mathematics and science). Results for this set of pupils for the four non-arts outcomes are given in Table 9.3, which expresses the apparent relationships between the background variables in the final models and each outcome measure in the form of 'normalised coefficients', as described above. Blank cells correspond to variables which were omitted from the final model due to non-significance. Values in bold represent coefficients which are statistically significant (at the five per cent level). Other values reflect variables in the final model, but whose coefficients are not quite significant at the five per cent level. Addressing the study's central concerns with the relationships between such background variables as the taking of GCSE arts courses or extra-curricular activity in the arts and general GCSE performance (in the form of four non-arts outcome measures), while controlling for key stage 3 scores, Table 9.3 is particularly important.

Table 9.3 Normalised coefficients for multilevel models relating to non-arts outcomes, controlling for key stage 3 levels

Background Variable Pupil-level variables	Maths	English	Science	Average score on non–arts arts subjects
Sex (0 = male, 2 = female)	-2.5	**13.8**	-2.1	**7.1**
Black ethnic origin	1.5	1.1	0.4	0.8
Asian ethnic origin	**3.5**	**3.3**	**4.3**	**3.6**
Other ethnic origin	1.1	0.3	0.9	-0.8
Average KS3 level	**82.8**	**73.8**	**66.9**	**74.2**
Taken subject in KS4: art		**-5.0**		**-7.8**
Taken subject in KS4: dance		0.5		
Taken subject in KS4: drama		-0.2	**-4.2**	**-8.7**
Taken subject in KS4: exp. arts		0.2		
Taken subject in KS4: music		-1.9		-3.0
Index of arts subjects as favourite				
Index of arts subjects as least favourite				
Index of arts subjects as best at				
Total of +/- reasons for taking arts		**5.2**		**4.1**
Lesson enjoyment: all arts				
No. of arts subjects unable to take				
Total effects of arts subjects		**3.8**		
Importance of arts subjects		1.7		**4.7**

Table 9.3 (continued)

Background Variable Pupil-level variables	Maths	English	Science	Average score on non–arts arts subjects
Parental support		5.5		
Social class	-3.2	-5.0	-5.3	
Age in years			-2.1	
Index of extra-curricular activity: art				
Index of extra-curricular activity: music			3.3	
Index of extra-curricular activity: drama				2.9
Index of extra-curricular activity: dance				
Index of extra-curricular activity: literature		5.1		
School-level variables				
Catchment area (0 = rural to 4 = inner city)				
Townsend index –1991 census				
% free school meals	8.9			
Total students				
Hours/week per arts subject				
Total specialist arts facilities listed	15.6			
Arts subject compulsory at KS4	12.0			10.9
Index of access to arts subjects at KS4				
Total no. of arts extracurricular activities			-21.1	

Values in **bold** are statistically significant at the five per cent level.

In a similar way, Table 9.4 shows the normalised coefficients for the multilevel analyses of the three arts subjects as outcome measures. Since these subjects are optional, the numbers of cases involved are smaller than for the core subjects above. The numbers were:

    Art: 546

    Drama: 207

    Music: 119

Because of the small numbers of cases involved in this part of the analysis, the school-level results in particular should be regarded with extreme caution, and in some cases are clearly artefacts of the particular dataset. In music, for example, most school-level variables appear to be significant; this is almost certainly a modelling problem with a very small dataset. School-level coefficients have been shown in italics in Table 9.4 to emphasise this point.

Table 9.4   Normalised coefficients for multilevel models relating to arts outcomes, controlling for key stage 3 levels

Background Variable	Art	Music	Drama
Pupil-level variables			
Sex (0 = male, 2 = female)	**19.7**	-1.0	**11.7**
Black ethnic origin	-1.3	1.7	-5.9
Asian ethnic origin	**7.2**	-1.8	**14.2**
Other ethnic origin	-0.9	-8.3	-0.5
Average KS3 level	**43.1**	**56.7**	**53.4**
Arts subjects as % of total	**-7.4**	**-14.4**	**-15.8**
Index of arts subjects as favourite			
Index of arts subjects as least favourite	**-13.6**	**-11.7**	
Index of arts subjects as best at	**12.6**	**17.7**	**27.4**
Total of +/- reasons for taking arts	**9.1**		**15.8**
Lesson enjoyment: all arts		**18.1**	
No. of arts subjects unable to take			
Total benefits of arts subjects		-9.4	
Importance of arts subjects	**8.3**		
Parental support			**16.9**
Social class	-5.2	-10.1	-6.6
Age in years			
Index of extra-curricular activity: art	**8.0**		
Index of extra-curricular activity: music		**13.7**	
Index of extra-curricular activity: drama			
Index of extra-curricular activity: dance			
Index of extra-curricular activity: literature			
School-level variables			
Catchment area (0 = rural to 4 = inner city)		*30.2*	
Townsend index –1991 census	*13.1*	*21.1*	
% free school meals		*-42.9*	
Total students	*17.4*	*19.1*	**-27.0**
Hours/week per arts subject	*15.4*		*17.5*
Total specialist arts facilities listed		*28.3*	
Arts subject compulsory at KS4		*16.1*	
Index of access to arts subjects at KS4			
Total no. of arts extracurricular activities		*-38.6*	

Values in **bold** are statistically significant at the five per cent level. School-level coefficients in *italics* should be treated with extreme caution, due to the small number of cases.

In Appendix III, the various pupil-level variables defined from the questionnaire are combined into just three main factors. The three main factors identified above may tentatively be described as follows:

(i)   Doing lots of arts subjects in school, for practical reasons, good at them, but not especially involved outside school and no particular parental support: 'positive about arts in school';

(ii) High involvement outside school and parental support, but unable to do enough in school: 'positive about arts outside school'; and

(iii) Doing arts in school, but not enjoying them: 'negative about arts in school'.

To investigate the relationships between these and GCSE outcomes, models were run which used the three factors in place of the other attitude variables. Tables 9.5 and 9.6 show the normalised coefficients for these factors for the non-arts and arts GCSE outcomes respectively. From all these results, it is clear that the relationships between attitudes to arts and GCSE performance were complex, varying according to the outcome measure considered.

Table 9.5   Normalised coefficients for derived attitude factors relating to non-arts outcomes, controlling for key stage 3 levels

Background Variable	Maths	English	Science	Average score on non–arts arts subjects
Positive about arts in school	-2.3	**3.4**	-3.5	**-3.4**
Positive about arts outside school	0.6	**8.1**	1.6	**4.7**
Negative about arts in school	0.3	-1.4	0.2	**-3.8**

Values in **bold** are statistically significant at the five per cent level.

Table 9.6   Normalised coefficients for derived attitude factors relating to arts outcomes, controlling for key stage 3 levels

Background Variable	Art	Music	Drama
Positive about arts in school	**10.8**	7.0	**17.2**
Positive about arts outside school	**10.9**	0.1	**20.7**
Negative about arts in school	**-17.9**	**-34.5**	**-19.0**

Values in **bold** are statistically significant at the five per cent level.

As well as the normalised coefficients which show relationships between background variables and outcomes, the multilevel models produced variances at the school and pupil levels. Table 9.7 shows the values of these variances, and indicates how much they were reduced by taking into account the background variables in the models. It is clear that variation between schools was massively reduced in this way (except in science), while variation between individual pupils was reduced by about half.

Table 9.7   Random variances for cases with key stage 3 levels

Outcome	Base case		Full model		% reduction in variance	
	School variance	Pupil variance	School variance	Pupil variance	School variance	Pupil variance
Non-arts						
Mathematics	0.69	2.88	0.06	1.06	91%	63%
English	0.58	2.07	0.11	0.75	81%	64%
Science	7.43	12.78	4.10	5.71	45%	55%
Average non-arts	0.67	2.44	0.10	1.08	85%	55%
Arts						
Art	0.85	2.49	0.25	1.38	70%	45%
Music	1.43	2.57	0.00	0.91	100%	65%
Drama	0.34	1.89	0.00	0.83	100%	56%

2.
WHAT ARE
THE EFFECTS
OF
ARTS
EDUCATION?

Results of multilevel models controlling for prior attainment in Year 7

A minority of pupils (548) had prior attainment data going back to Year 7 which was nationally comparable in some way and could therefore be used to look at progress over the whole secondary phase of education. However, because of the small number involved, analysis was confined to the non-arts outcomes (our main focus) and no analysis was done for the three arts subjects as outcome measures. Table 9.8 gives the normalised coefficients for this analysis, while Table 9.9 shows normalised coefficients for the three main attitude factors, and Table 9.10 shows the random variances.

Comparisons between these results and those controlling for key stage 3 levels show little difference, except that for the Year 7 dataset fewer background variables had significant coefficients. It seems that the relationship between outcome and prior attainment was somewhat stronger for key stage 3 than for Year 7, and that the former explained slightly more of the variation between pupils.

Table 9.8   Normalised coefficients for multilevel models relating to non-arts outcomes, controlling for Year 7 prior attainment

Background Variable Pupil-level variables	Maths	English	Science	Average score on non–arts subjects
Sex (0 = male, 2 = female)		**17.8**		**10.0**
Black ethnic origin				
Asian ethnic origin				
Other ethnic origin				
Composite intake measure (all)	**70.3**	**53.1**	**39.6**	**63.4**
Taken subject in KS4: art				
Taken subject in KS4: dance				
Taken subject in KS4: drama				**-11.3**
Taken subject in KS4: exp. arts			**5.7**	
Taken subject in KS4: music				
Index of arts subjects as favourite				
Index of arts subjects as least favourite	**-7.3**			-5.2
Index of arts subjects as best at				
Total of +/- reasons for taking arts				
Lesson enjoyment: all arts				
No. of arts subjects unable to take				
Total benefits of arts subjects		**10.0**		
Importance of arts subjects				
Parental support	4.8	6.0		5.6
Social class	**-8.6**	**-8.7**	**-8.8**	
Age in years				
Index of extra-curricular activity: art				
Index of extra-curricular activity: music			**6.6**	
Index of extra-curricular activity: drama				**8.1**
Index of extra-curricular activity: dance				
Index of extra-curricular activity: literature		**6.6**	**-6.7**	
School-level variables				
Catchment area (0 = rural to 4 = inner city)	11.2			
Townsend index –1991 census				
% free school meals				
Total students				
Hours/week per arts subject				
Total specialist arts facilities listed		**21.5**		
Arts subject compulsory at KS4		-5.1		
Index of access to arts subjects at KS4				
Total no. of arts extracurricular activities				

Values in **bold** are statistically significant at the five per cent level.

2.
WHAT ARE
THE EFFECTS
OF
ARTS
EDUCATION?

Table 9.9   Normalised coefficients for derived attitude factors relating to non-arts outcomes, controlling for Year 7 prior attainment

Background Variable	Maths	English	Science	Average score on non–arts arts subjects
Positive about arts in school	-2.8	2.6	-4.4	-6.3
Positive about arts outside school	2.1	**15.1**	2.2	**9.4**
Negative about arts in school	-1.3	-1.7	4.8	**-1.8**

Values in **bold** are statistically significant at the five per cent level.

Table 9.10   Random variances for cases with Year 7 prior attainment

	Base case		Full model		% reduction in variance	
Outcome	School variance	Pupil variance	School variance	Pupil variance	School variance	Pupil variance
Non-arts						
Mathematics	0.36	3.42	0.12	1.67	66%	51%
English	0.65	2.29	0.00	1.18	100%	48%
Science	9.41	11.72	8.18	8.12	13%	31%
Average non-arts	0.53	1.87	0.07	1.11	87%	41%

Summary of results

Most of the results discussed in this section will be based on the analysis controlling for key stage 3 levels, and may therefore be interpreted as referring to progress during key stage 4. Where substantially different results occurred in the analysis using Year 7 prior attainment, this will be highlighted. It should be emphasised at this stage that this kind of statistical analysis deals with apparent relationships between variables, and does not give direct information about causality. Causal links may be suggested by the results, but can only be confirmed by detailed and often longitudinal investigations of the processes involved.

General GCSE attainment (non-arts GCSE outcomes)

- Girls performed, on average, better than boys in English and on average non-arts score, but there was no significant difference for mathematics and science (see Table 9.3).

- Pupils of Asian ethnic origin had better average results than white pupils (see Table 9.3).

- There were no significant positive relationships between taking any of the arts and scores in English, mathematics, science and the average score in non-arts subjects (see Table 9.3).

- There were apparent negative relationships between (i) taking art and both English scores and the average non-arts scores; and between (ii) taking drama and both science scores and average non-arts scores (see Table 9.3).

- The index of positive reasons for studying arts subjects was positively related to both English scores and average non-arts scores (see Table 9.3).

- The number of nominated effects from studying arts, and the amount of parental support in the arts, were both positively related to the English score (see Table 9.3).

- The index of the importance of arts subjects was positively related to the average non-arts score (see Table 9.3).

- Pupils of higher social class tended to achieve better results in mathematics, English and science (see Table 9.3).

- As a general rule, extra-curricular activities in the arts were not positively related to performance in English, mathematics, science and average score in non-arts subjects. Two exceptions to this trend reached statistical significance. Extra-curricular activity in music was positively related to science scores, and extra-curricular activity in literature was positively related to English scores. There was some evidence that extra-curricular activity in drama was positively related to average non-arts scores, though this was not statistically significant (see Table 9.3).

- Looking at the three main factors derived from the pupil attitude questionnaires (see Table 9.5), it seems that the first ('positive about arts in school') was positively related to English scores, but negatively to science and average non-arts scores. The second ('positive about arts outside school') was positively related to both English and average non-arts scores. This relationship was even stronger when progress from Year 7 to GCSE was analysed (see Table 9.9). The third factor ('negative about arts in school') was negatively related to the average non-arts scores.

- Few school-level variables had significant relationships with GCSE outcomes, and because of the relatively small number of schools involved these should be treated with caution. It seemed that the total number of specialist arts facilities listed was positively related to mathematics scores, and arts subjects being compulsory at key stage 4 was positively related to mathematics and the average non-arts scores. On the other hand, the total number of arts extra-curricular activities listed was negatively related to science scores (see Table 9.3).

- Controlling for background variables (including key stage 3 levels) reduced the apparent variation between schools by up to 90 per cent (though only 45 per cent for science), and the variation between pupils by over 50 per cent (see Table 9.7).

- Looking at the three overall attitude factors, the second ('positive about arts outside school') appears to have a stronger relationship with GCSE outcomes when controlling for Year 7 prior attainment (see Table 9.9) than when controlling for key stage 3 levels (see Table 9.5).

Arts GCSE outcomes

- Girls and pupils of Asian ethnic origin performed better, on average, in art and drama than boys and white pupils, respectively (see Table 9.4).

- The number of arts subjects being studied, as a percentage of the total, was negatively related to performance in all three arts subjects (see Table 9.4).

- Putting arts subjects as least favourite was negatively related to art and music scores (see Table 9.4).

- Putting arts subjects as 'best at' was positively related to all three scores, most strongly to drama (see Table 9.4).

- The index of positive reasons for studying arts subjects was positively related to both art and drama scores (see Table 9.4).

- The index of arts lesson enjoyment was positively related to music scores (see Table 9.4).

- The index of the importance of studying arts subjects was positively related to art scores (see Table 9.4).

- The index of parental support in arts was positively related to drama scores (see Table 9.4).

- Extra-curricular activity in art was positively related to art scores, and extra-curricular activity in music was positively related to music scores (see Table 9.4).

- Looking at the three main factors derived from the pupil attitude questionnaires, it seems that the first ('positive about arts in school') was positively related to art and drama scores. The second ('positive about arts outside school') was also positively related to both art and drama scores. The third factor ('negative about arts in school') was negatively related to all three arts scores (see Table 9.6).

•   Controlling for background variables (including key stage 3 levels) reduced the apparent variation between schools by up to 100 per cent, and the variation between pupils by around 50 per cent (see Table 9.7).

Conclusion

For our present purposes, the salient finding from the above is that, once key background variables like social class and key stage 3 results are incorporated into the analysis, there is virtually no statistical evidence to support the claim that engagement in the arts boosts general academic performance at the age of 16.

Crucially, the analysis found that there were no significant positive relationships between taking any arts-based key stage 4 courses and GCSE scores in English, mathematics, science and the average score in non-arts subjects. Indeed, on the face of it, there was some evidence that could be interpreted as suggesting that taking some arts courses may have an adverse impact on GCSE performance: negative relationships were found between (i) taking art and both English scores and the average non-arts GCSE scores; and between (ii) taking drama and both science scores and average non-arts GCSE scores. However, in keeping with the most plausible interpretation of the QUASE analysis and the findings relating to the average key stage 3 scores of those taking different arts subjects, these negative associations were more likely to remain a residual reflection of the academic profile of the pupils taking art and drama.

Similarly, there was little evidence to support the proposition that out-of-school or extra-curricular involvement in the arts imparted any positive transfer effect on general academic performance in GCSE examinations. The only exception here was a positive association between extra-curricular involvement in music and science scores. Given, firstly, that out-of-school music had no similar relationship with English, mathematics or average non-arts GCSE scores, secondly, that following a course in music was not positively related to high science scores, and, thirdly, that there was a high association between science scores and pupils from middle-class backgrounds, the extra-curricular music–science anomaly is probably a residual factor reflecting the middle-class nature of both out-of-school involvement in music and high attainment in science.

Overall, then, taken together, the QUASE analysis and the findings of the Year 11 Survey failed to identify evidence on which to mount a convincing case that the arts impact positively on pupils' general academic performance. In doing so, they add weight to a growing body of literature (Eisner, 1998; Sharp *et al.*, 1998; Winner and Hetland, forthcoming, 2000) that cautions against claims that the arts in the curriculum as it stands engender a transfer or 'Mozart effect' to other areas of the curriculum or attainment. However, before leaving the subject, we need to examine whether the results of the two statistical analyses can be squared with the subjective perceptions of teachers and pupils on transfer effects to other areas of learning.

9.2.3   Evidence from the case-study schools

Teacher Perspectives

A small number of comments (9) from teachers proposed that the arts improved performance in other areas of the curriculum through general and non-specific ways:

> *The teaching and the learning styles that are used within arts will rub off in other areas* (deputy headteacher).

Most of the claims from teachers, however, were more specific than this and fell into two camps – a minor one and a major one: in the minor group, there were those (12) that suggested that general academic performance was improved through the arts encouraging positive attitudes to school in general, whereas the majority group consisted of those (71) that maintained that learning in other curricular areas benefited through the transferable knowledge and skills that the arts imparted. Each of these types is described below.

Transferable motivation and attitudes from the arts

Claims were made for the arts generally helping to engender positive attitudes to school and the classroom environment. A deputy headteacher commented that by taking an interest in the arts, '... [pupils] *tend to react and become more pro-school*'. A headteacher spoke of the arts helping a student with a '*school phobia problem*':

> *I've got him back into school now three days a week – not into classes, just got him into the school. Now, next two weeks, he's got a target of coming to school five days a week, but he's going to be an assistant tutor with the artists and the primary school children – art is motivating him* (head).

There were other references to art fostering improved school performance as a result of better motivation, behaviour and attitudes:

> *... there's a teapot made of a flower from a lad in GCSE and that is probably his finest achievement in this school and he's done that through art. But what that's given him is dignity, which has come to other areas of the school ...* (head).

Teachers commented on arts involvement having an effect on self-confidence, and thereby raising aspirations in other areas.

Transferable knowledge and skills from the arts

This type of response amounted to the most frequently claimed type of effect within this subcategory, with some teachers describing the transference of skills and knowledge as '*knock-on effects*'. It therefore links with sections of the report that discuss the original direct effect, for example, artform technical skills (see section 4.5), thinking skills (section 6.2) and teamwork (section 8.8).

Claims made for the transference of knowledge and skills from the arts to other curriculum areas tended to be artform-specific, and interesting differences by artform in both frequency of claims about transfer effects, and in the types of transfer claimed were apparent. References to drama and art were particularly dominant (26 and 20 respectively) – indeed, both artforms had more references for this effect than the other artforms put together. Music attracted only five.

2.
WHAT ARE
THE EFFECTS
OF
ARTS
EDUCATION?

Of particular note is the small number of claims for transferable knowledge and skills made for music. For example, although connections between music and mathematics have been postulated generally, there was only fleeting reference to this from the teacher interviewees – a comment about the mathematical precision required in music, and the rhythmic, numerical basis to dance. As outlined above, music has been the main focus for studies on transfer effects, and although the one reference to research by an arts teacher in the case-study schools was from a head of music, transferable skills were not the subject of claims made about their own music teaching. Hence, it is interesting that the case study data presented here do not indicate that teachers of music and other staff (notably senior management) see transfer of knowledge or skills as a key effect of music education. Indeed, in contrast to the attention given to music in previous research and recent media coverage, teachers were more likely to identify transfer effects in art and drama than in music.

For art and drama, the skills which were perceived to be transferable from the arts to other areas of the curriculum included: drawing skills, presentation, performance skills and speaking in front of a group, skills related to group work, communication skills, research skills and accuracy.

These claims for the transfer of skills were presented in two main ways: those where transfer was claimed without any reference to examples or evidence, and those where interviewees based their claims on perceived improvements in student performance. The former, in particular, assumed that because common skills are evident across curriculum areas, for example, drawing in biology and art, pupils will be able to implement this transfer and apply skills developed in arts subjects within other lessons. The following comment exemplifies the assumption that pupils will be able to '*use art*' where necessary or appropriate, in history:

2.
WHAT ARE
THE EFFECTS
OF
ARTS
EDUCATION?

If they are doing a history project, they will maybe look at cave painting and maybe in some instances where pupils really cannot communicate in terms of the written language, they have more of an understanding of being able to use art (head of art).

However, many teachers did focus on their experiences in the classroom, and provided anecdotal evidence to substantiate their claims for the transfer of skills. Interviewees from a range of subject backgrounds described noticeable differences in the work of pupils taking the arts, which they perceived were brought about because of the transfer of skills from the arts to other curriculum areas. Examples from three different curriculum areas were as follows:

... if they are good at art, then it does have knock-on effects on presentation. You know, for example, if they are doing a newspaper front page then it will look better, it will be more thought out and they will have got an idea of, sort of, special awareness of laying out a page (head of English).

_____

I notice in science ... that the spread across of artistic skills into the scientific area, literally in terms of the skill of being able to draw what they see, better ... they are now far more accurate. That is a definite improved skill and that isn't just the higher-ability pupils either (deputy head).

_____

I know that in RE ... I have had feedback from teachers saying to me, you know, 'Oh, we acted out a Christian christening ceremony' and it was fascinating to hear them say, like, 'Remember, we must face the audience' and 'No, no, no, you are not meant to be on that side. You should be on this side. Now remember, I will freeze and then we will come to life': all the things that they have learnt in drama that they are then taking out into other areas and using, which I think is very positive, when they are making these cross-curricular links (drama and dance teacher).

This last contribution, although still based on teacher perceptions, does suggest that pupils were explicitly making use of techniques developed in drama.

Although accounts of transferable skills tended to be specific to individual artforms, some interviewees spoke of the transfer of creativity or thinking skills which went across the arts. This deputy head with a non-arts background discussed the development and then transfer of critical skills (in the sense of being able to critique work) and problem-solving:

... it is learning those critical skills, and those are skills that you take across the curriculum. Problem-solving, be it a piece of art work,

be it trying to make a piece of music from some ideas, or the drama, this is the theme we are working on, it is problem-solving, in space and shape and dance ... so there are all those kind of levels of skills and experience that are transferable both across the curriculum in school, but in terms of life skills, as far as I can see.

A head of expressive arts focused on creative thinking, and the processes of investigating, making and recording as common areas of experience in the arts and other subjects:

It is learning to think in lots of different ways. Creative thinking, I would say, is one of the things that they do get from us and all the usual investigating, making, recording. Well yes, we do all those things that you do in other subjects.

Related to the transfer of creative skills and thinking were references to the transfer of creativity itself, and the transferability of an *'arts-making process'*:

I would have thought that creativity in one area of the curriculum must lead to creativity in another area of the curriculum, for example their linguistic creativity and so on; I think one does lead to the other (deputy head).

——

... the way that it's not necessarily the first idea that's the best. I mean it's not necessarily a bad thing to ditch 90 per cent of what you've just done and just keep ten per cent and go on. I mean, that kind of arts-making process is very transferable, isn't it, to other subjects, to life, to your family? ... (drama teacher).

Distinguishable from the transfer of skills, many responses also focused on the transferability of knowledge or curriculum content. Some responses (notably from drama, and indicative of the placement of drama within the English curriculum) focused on transfer related to National Curriculum requirements:

... particularly in the speaking and listening attainment target, there is a specific reference there to using drama and role play in the teaching of English and in fact all English classrooms should have some drama element (head of English).

——

[I introduced Shakespeare] *specifically through drama in Year 8 so they were used to doing Shakespeare by the time they got to Year 9 where they have to do it for SATs in English ... you would introduce it in a workshop style so that they came with the idea into Year 9 'Oh Shakespeare, goody, goody. It's fun, I like Shakespeare'* (drama teacher).

Some arts teachers talked of how their subject area was '*beneficial*' to other areas of the curriculum: for example, drama giving a deeper understanding of characters in English and history:

> *It brings it to life for them, it takes it off the page ...* (drama teacher).

———

> *For example, in English, if you were this person ... what would you do? Why? You know, when they're reading a novel in history, why did this person do what they did? Why did Henry VIII have his wives executed? I mean, hopefully they would think about that and if then you could go into role and do some drama on that, you know, they do have an amazing ability to think as other people* (drama teacher).

A further variant was to be found in the contributions of those teachers who spoke of giving pupils experiences in the arts to support the work done in other subjects. One drama teacher, for example, described work around the theme of war to back up a World War II topic in history, and another suggested that linking drama to every curriculum area was a way forward for drama, with its marginalised place within the National Curriculum:

> *I like to think of the arts going into every curriculum subject, which is what I try to do. I try to link in what I am doing, you know, to other subjects. I think that really is how drama especially has to go as we are not part of, independently part of, the National Curriculum* (drama teacher).

Teachers recognised the potential for cross-curricular themes and topics, but even within the arts themselves, constraints meant that the opportunity to work together could be lost:

> *Art makes masks; we don't do it at the same time with the same year group ... things that they do in music, I could use in drama. Do you know what I mean? Dance ... does something on the North American Indians. My mask and mime project is on a North American legend, but we don't do it at the same time with the same groups. It is a timetabling restriction and it is also our aim to get ourselves working together, you know* (drama teacher).

A final type of response centred on the use of arts-based techniques and processes in non-arts lessons. Most common was the use of 'empathy exercises' and role play, for example acting out red blood cells trying to get through a blocked artery. One drama teacher spoke of trying to encourage teachers to make use of dramatic techniques:

> *I would like to, say, do an INSET day on how they can use, other subjects can use drama techniques in their lessons. I think there is a natural, inbred fear from other departments when it comes to drama. The idea of having kids walking around talking is, is, you know, seems horrific.*

Although the wider use of teaching methods and techniques common to the arts was seen as relevant to this *'transfer effects'* category, facilitating transfer may not be the intention behind the use of role play and other techniques across the curriculum. It could be that a different rationale – such as motivating pupils, or a school-wide focus on teaching styles – underpins the borrowing of techniques from the arts by non-arts teachers.

Overall, then, with reference to teachers' accounts of transfer effects to non-arts subjects, a few suggested transfer was mediated through generally improved motivation, while a large number pointed to the importance of transferable knowledge and skills acquisitions through the arts. Comparatively few claims were made for music, and differences were evident between the claims made for art and those for drama. Broadly speaking, with regard to art, teachers made claims for the transfer of skills such as drawing, accuracy, the setting out of work and presentation to other areas of the curriculum, whilst, with regard to drama, teachers focused on knowledge and curriculum content. Teachers spoke of drama's explicit curriculum links (with health education, Personal and Social Education and National Curriculum English requirements), and of drama reinforcing work done in other areas: for example, war could be a theme for history and drama. Responses for drama also highlighted the adoption of drama-based techniques by teachers in other areas of the curriculum: for example the use of role play and thought-tracking in history.

Finally, it should be noted that in responses claiming transfer of knowledge and skills from the arts to other curriculum areas, teachers were making claims about perceived transfer. It was not evident to what extent, if any, teachers explicitly addressed and fostered these cross-curriculum connections with pupils, or whether pupils were left to accomplish the transfers themselves. By and large, the latter seemed to prevail and it appeared that pupils were not taught how to make such transfers. It is to pupils' perceptions of possible transfer effects to other areas of learning we now turn.

Pupil Perspectives

The pupils provided 107 comments on the transference of their arts learning to other areas of the curriculum or their learning behaviour in general. Following the pattern set by their teachers, drama and art registered the highest nominations (39 and 40 respectively), with music only attracting 13 comments.

Only a small minority (5) referred to transfer effects that focused on motivational or behavioural developments: two, for example, talked about *'behaving better'* and having more self-discipline as a result of their engagement in the arts. However, unlike their teachers, none of the pupils actually stated that their interest in, or motivation towards, learning in non-arts subjects had increased on the back of their experiences in the arts. Thus, neither the amount nor the nature of these comments provides any qualitative evidence to support the propositions that (a) pupils' experiences of heightened self-esteem in the arts lead to increased motivation towards learning in other subjects and (b) that such a generalised impact on motivation is sufficiently powerful to raise pupils' general academic performance. This is not to diminish the significance of the five contributions for the individual pupils involved nor is it to question the authenticity of what are genuine 'transfer' effects: according to their evidence, these pupils were '*behaving better*' and applying more self-discipline in other contexts as a result of developing these qualities in their arts subjects. It is merely to point out that their accounts fall short of evidence needed to substantiate these two propositions.

Like the teacher interviewees, the majority of pupil comments focused on transfer effects through knowledge and skills. These are described for each of the main artforms.

Art

In art, by far the largest number of remarks (25 out of 39) described the application of art-enriched drawing skills in other subjects. In addition, there were six non-specific comments, four of which referred to art's affinities with design and technology, most probably with the drawing connection in mind. The following typical extracts illustrate the transference of what were variously described as '*drawing skills*', '*presentation*' or '*pen and pencil skills*':

> *In geography recently we've had to do a project where we had to draw a poster of pollutants and write an essay to go with it. And I chose oil pollution and being able to draw helped me doing that, 'cos I drew an oil tanker crashed on a rock and I got top marks for that. And that looked good. Being able to use different media that the arts taught me, I can do good drawings* (Year 9).

> *I know it's improved my drawings, things like that, and a lot of time if you are good in drawing in certain lessons you can get quite a good mark, if you are like designing something* (Year 8).

> *... in English and history you have to draw to produce your best work. Because you have to draw something to indicate what you are writing about, you cannot just have a piece of writing. You have to decorate it, to make it stand out and look nice* (Year 9).

Well, I suppose it helps slightly in design work, just basically pen and pencil skills, more useful (Year 9).

———

All subjects involve some degree of art because like 'Can you illustrate the battle of such and such where such and such fought such and such?', and having just a little bit of art education behind you enables you to not just draw a few squiggles and say: 'That's William the Conqueror', but to have shade and tone, make it interesting and colourful (Year 7).

Although the numerous such references testify to the validity of this outcome as a genuine transfer effect, it is arguable, at least, that in themselves, drawing and visual presentation skills would not be instrumental in raising the level of achievement in many other areas of the curriculum to a significant degree. Indeed, in certain subjects, an overly meticulous concern for attractive visual representations could be counter-productive and interpreted as a diversion from the demonstration of more important assessment criteria. Accordingly, on this basis, it could be argued that the transference of skills in graphicacy alone – although, undoubtedly, important aspects of the curriculum – are unlikely to precipitate substantial gains in general academic performance. However, the remaining eight comments could have greater potential for achieving this.

These comments dealt with the transferability of more cognitive and knowledge-based outcomes from art. It was noteworthy that, in comparison to the accounts of the manual and technical drawing skills which tended to be cited by key stage 3 pupils, those that focused on the cognitive dimensions were more likely to be registered by key stage 4 pupils, indicative perhaps of the greater insight into the cerebral processes associated with creative making in art that comes with maturation and/or more sustained engagement with the artform. Examples of the latter type of comments are set out below, along with labels that depict the type of transfer identified by the pupils. The number of comments made to each 'type' is given in brackets.

Using art-based observational and imaging skills to inform expression in other media (2)

Especially with nature, it's all disappearing now, so the more you see of it the better. It's like walking round with your eyes shut: if you don't actually look, you never really experience it. Even if, though, you're just looking, you're still keeping the images in your mind. That can help you in other subjects. Like in English, if you're asked to write an essay, you can remember a picture and write an essay about the picture, what you say, or use art in stories, images that you remember you can write down (Year 9).

Using an art-based imagination and the fabrication of ideas (2)	*I think that, in a way, it would benefit me in subjects such as English, which is also using your imagination, so by using my imagination in art, it's also helping me to use my imagination in subjects like English.* Interviewer *Can you expand on that a little bit more or give me any examples of when you felt that happening?* *Well, the last piece of coursework we had to do, it was very much having to picture yourself, picture what was going on, and in art, we have to use our imaginations to try and draw what we can picture in our imagination* (Year 11).
Using an art-based capacity to interpret (1)	*It's all about interpretation. You look at something and you do what you want to do with it and I sometimes bring that in English, so I kind of read something and then interpret it. I think that I got a lot of that from art* (Year 11).
Using art-based cultural knowledge (1)	*When I was talking to, like, the French teacher at the college, they said it wasn't necessarily learning about the language, but it was learning about the culture in France as well, so maybe I would be able to … maybe that would help me be, like, 'Yes I studied that in secondary school; I studied that in art', so maybe that's the only link that I can see …* (Year 11).
Using art-based expressive skills (1)	*It also helps in drama, when you are working in groups in that, and it helps show yourself in your paintings, and that helps also in drama because you can let yourself go* (Year 8).
Using art-based concentration (1)	*Well, I think it* [art] *kind of helps you in maths as well, because you learn how to concentrate more on what you're doing, so it helps you concentrate on everything else as well* (Year 9).

While the reported transfer effects of drawing skills possessed sufficient quantity but probably lacked the quality to impact significantly on general attainment, the converse seems to be the case with the latter comments. They exhibit the kind of cognitive capacities that would seem capable of making a difference to performance in other curriculum areas, yet their limited frequency suggests that such transfers are not common currency, or that awareness of the transfer is limited. This is especially the case if due account is taken of the fact that the sample consisted of pupils who were attaining well in particular artforms in schools that were selected because of strong reputations in arts provision. In the more representative samples surveyed in QUASE and the Year 11 Survey, small proportions of pupils affecting such transfers would be expected to be found. Thus, although the pupil evidence on art-based transfer effects to other areas of learning is strong and illuminating, there are good grounds for treating these qualitative findings as consistent with the statistical results outlined earlier.

Drama

Drama attracted as many nominations of transfer effects as art, though the crucial difference was that for drama the remarks were spread more thinly across a wider range of effects. The diversity of the comments relating to transferable knowledge and skills is illustrated in the following remarks:

Using drama-based improvements in reading out loud, speaking, communicating orally in other subjects, mainly in English (12)	*English it definitely helps in that* [it is] *a lot about communication, being able to express yourself clearly and carefully, so I think that's where it helps as well. It just gives me confidence overall as well, which helps in all my subjects, answering and being in class* (Year 11). *I suppose, like, if you wanted to stand up for yourself or something, or discussion work in English or you want a debate over something, I think it helps being fluent talking to other people* (Year 8). *It also helps, I mean, if you have to present a finding, have to make a presentation in science, it helps to have the drama to give you confidence to be able – if you are not quite sure of your facts – to be able to bluff along* (Year 11).
Applying drama-based knowledge of Shakespeare and his language in English (4)	*Introduced to Shakespeare – enjoyed that – learnt about the language – doing it in English as well. That was good because we were learning the language in English and putting it into practice in drama* (Year 8). *It can teach you things, like English, because you look at and analyse things such as Shakespeare, especially in A-level courses, I read that you do nice plays and from what my friend is doing, she does the plays* (Year 11).

Using drama-based ideas and imagination in other subjects (3)	*English is the main one that it effects, because in English you are able to use things that you know in drama, to improve your English. So, when you are writing a story, because you know about so many things that have happened, like in drama, we do so many different things, it gives you ideas, so that helps* (Year 9).
	… you learn to develop ideas and that helps in other subjects as well, because it's like 'Well I have got this idea for this, this design idea in technology' – I can develop it, it just sort of rubs off. You might not say: 'Oh yes, in drama I learned to develop my ideas; I can do this in English'. It's just there, it just sort of helps. Well, I think that's what helps me (Year 11).
	Interviewer: *So do you think in geography you are learning about group work as well, or do you feel like in geography you were using the skills that you had from drama?*
Using drama-based group work skills in other subjects (3)	*I think I would say I would have been using the skills that I had gained from doing drama and things like that, but also enhancing them a little bit extra* (Year 10).
	As well as work with other people, it helps you to, sort of, communicate and things like that. I find that it helps me to, if you're in a situation to communicate with somebody else, you become a lot more forward in working with somebody, because you don't know them or you're only there with them a little bit, it doesn't happen to be your best friend and you can still work really well with them (Year 9).
Using drama-based increases in self-confidence (3)	*…like I said, my confidence. That's going to help me with law, to stand up and debate and that, and why this happened in this case and all that stuff. Yes, confidence is really going to help me in English and in computing; in law, that's definitely going to help. I am glad I chose drama because of that* (Year 11).
Using drama-based role play skills (3)	*… sometimes in history we act plays out and I think: 'I can do this, because we have done this in drama and I have learnt all the levels' and things like that* (Year 7).
Drama creates relaxed mood for next lesson (2)	*Sometimes, if we do really hard work in the lesson before, like history, and you get on with the work and sometimes you get tired and you concentrate less. I think if you are doing drama first and then we did history, then we would work harder in history because we are more relaxed* (Year 7).

Using drama-based capacity to see things from another perspective (1)

I think drama and media too. It's helped me look at things in a different light, rather than just looking at things from one point of view, getting to take it in loads of points of view. That's helped me in history when looking at sources too, so instead of looking at a source and thinking 'Well, that's wrong', I am thinking 'Well, if ...' and it helps me get into their heads more than I would have been able to (Year 11).

Other types of single responses included: *'helping with scriptwriting in English'*, *'helping generally with English'* and *'applying similar expressive skills in art'*. Clearly, there are some persuasive descriptions here of drama's capacity to stimulate effects that are, according to the pupils, transferable and pertinent to several other areas of the curriculum, but especially English. In considering the possible reasons why such carry-overs do not show up in the form of raised GCSE performance in the statistical analyses, three points may be offered. Firstly, and as with art, these drama-based transfer effects are probably making very important contributions to cross-curricular learning, but, relative to the strong influences of the key background variables, are not robust enough to appear as statistical indicators of added value over the timespan of key stage 4 courses. (A comparative analysis of pupils with minimal exposure to drama with those who have experienced a substantial amount over the full phase of secondary schooling would make for an interesting study.) Secondly, the main transferable drama-based effect, according to the pupils, emphasised various aspects of oral skills, but the role of oral assessments in GCSE examinations is limited – except in modern foreign languages, but none of the pupils mentioned a transference to this area of the curriculum. Hence, the pay-off for developments in oral skills in terms of examination performance would not be demonstrated. Thirdly, and most significantly for drama, the transfer effects identified by pupils were very diffuse. This reflects a constant finding throughout the research that, of all the artforms, drama displayed the greatest variation in interpretation and provision: different schools and teachers held contrasting views as to the nature of drama as a subject. Hence, the permutations of perceived effects varied from one school to the next. One of the implications of this lack of consensus about what should be taught in drama is that in larger samples of schools and pupils – such as those employed in the QUASE and Year 11 Survey analyses – the effects on pupils will be dissipated and any potential impact on general academic performance diluted. In line with this interpretation, findings from the Year 11 Survey show that the perceived effects from drama varied substantially from school to school (section 11.3). Moreover, and most importantly, the QUASE and Year 11 multilevel modelling analyses suggested that in certain schools there are strong positive relationships between arts-based subjects (including drama) and GCSE performance, while in others they may be non-existent or even negative.

Music

As indicated previously, music attracted a third of the number of transfer effect comments (13) received for art and drama. Owing, perhaps, to the small quantity, no particular type of perceived transfer effect from music emerged as a clear front runner, unlike in art and drama.

One pupil talked about the '*self-discipline*' developed through music and two described how their self-confidence in other lessons had been boosted through music, especially through giving musical performances:

> *I used to be scared of what other people think of me. I mean* [music] *has helped me in other subjects, speaking up in class, because I can give answers out and if it's wrong, you just laugh it off and forget about it really, but before I didn't dare speak, because I thought if it was wrong, people would just laugh at me* (Year 11).

Another Year 11 pupil highlighted the transferable skills of group-based working:

> *… working in a team, in a group, because you've obviously got to do that when you're playing in a band, listening to everybody else and getting the right balance and everything. And it helps you know when you're doing group work or practicals, say in science. It's not just in music; things that you learn in music can spread over most of the subjects.*

Three pupils touched on different cross-curricular links that had arisen in connection with learning about rhythm in music: a Year 11 boy had used his knowledge of rhythm from music to inform an art project on rhythm; a Year 7 girl referred to the relevance of music work on rhythms to her dance lessons; and a Year 11 girl drew out some interesting connections between musical rhythms and learning to speak a foreign language:

> *I'm quite good at languages, which you could say goes back to music, because of the rhythm of the language because different languages have different rhythms and sounds, so it could be related to music.*

Other pupils identified connections to history, maths and PE:

> *It just helps you in other subjects, like if you're doing the same things* [historical periods] *in history and music. It helps you in other subjects to know more* (Year 9).

> *… music and maths. It might not seem like it, but you have to time bars and things and add them up and that process helps you in other subjects* (Year 7).

... music, the skill of reading music. I think it helps you with your reflexes, probably with sports as well, with your eye–hand reactions, when you are catching a ball. When you are looking at music, you have to immediately react (Year 7).

This last pupil went on to say that playing music also helped to develop her memory, and this has already been expanded in section 6.2 on thinking and problem-solving skills.

2.
WHAT ARE
THE EFFECTS
OF
ARTS
EDUCATION?

Though interesting in themselves, both the small quantity of comments on perceived transfer effects for music and their disparate nature suggest that if studying music does enhance general academic performance, then it does so without most pupils being aware of the processes through which the impact is mediated. If that was the case, signs of the effects would need to be investigated through research based on non-perceptual data such as the two statistical analyses offered earlier, which, taken together, found no firm evidence that taking music at key stage 4 raises general academic performance.

Overall, then, the qualitative data on pupils' perceptions of transfer effects can be interpreted as broadly consistent with the findings from the two quantitative analyses summarised previously. There was little pupil endorsement for the proposition that for many pupils increased self-esteem through the arts actually translates into higher levels of motivation in other subjects, which in turn leads to higher attainment. In contrast, sizeable numbers of pupils did testify to the transference of knowledge and skills gained through drama and art to other areas of the curriculum. However, for a variety of reasons (e.g. effects that were not highly rated in assessment criteria, dissipated effects, limited frequencies), it was suggested that these perceived effects, although potentially important in contributing to effective learning in other areas of the curriculum, may not be robust enough to display a visible effect in GCSE examination performance. In addition, important variations between schools were seen to be a factor warranting further scrutiny.

9.3 TRANSFERRING EFFECTS TO EMPLOYMENT AND WORK

This section covers claims connected with the perceived transfer, in terms of skills and knowledge, from the arts in school to the world of work. Providing pupils with encouragement for further education or career-related involvement in the arts is another aspect of this outcome. The views of teachers and pupils are considered, followed by an overview of the opinions of some employers and employees. Although pupils made a fairly strong case for the transfer of specific arts skills to employment, teachers, employers and employees focused more on the work-related transfer of other skills, such as self-confidence, teamwork skills and commitment.

Teacher Perspectives

The few teachers who made comments about this outcome tended to focus on the transfer of life skills, as opposed to specific arts skills, to employment, and on encouraging pupils to enter further work-related involvement in the arts.

Drama was particularly associated with this perceived effect, and the following quote sums up this purported outcome:

> *I don't believe drama and dance to be sort of things that you put on a stage and show. I believe that the whole process of creating anything and working collaboratively, then stepping out and being solo amongst a group, are life skills* (dance and drama teacher).

An LEA arts adviser focused on the connections between skills developed in the arts and '*what businesses are saying*' they want from their employees. He emphasised the importance of encouraging children to believe that there are jobs in the arts:

> *To say to the kids 'Look, you can do anything ... you want to be an actor – what a good idea; you know we will help you', not 'Whoa – no jobs in acting'.*

Other teachers tended to focus on encouraging pupils to engage in further study in the arts, particularly at art college.

Pupil Perspectives

Pupils tended to attribute more status to the extrinsic transfer outcomes of the arts than teachers, making numerous references to these effects. In addition to the transfer of specific arts and other skills to employment, pupils made a case for the arts more generally helping them to secure a job in the future, and offering them the motivation to pursue arts-based careers.

Facilitates getting a job in general terms

Eight pupils, the majority of whom were in Year 7, made general comments about how they thought their participation in the arts would help them secure a job in the future. In many respects, pupils at this stage were vague about possible connections between an arts education and its relevance to the world of work. One pupil stated how studying the different arts '*could help me to understand which job to take in the future*', whilst three simply thought that the arts might give them '*more chance of getting a job*' or '*would come in really handy when you are older'*. Four pupils, including two from Year 9, talked about being able to get higher GCSE grades in arts subjects, something which they perceived would help them obtain a better job.

Transfer of specific arts skills to work

One outcome of studying the arts commonly cited by pupils was the enhanced possibility, in terms of the specific skills gained, to pursue a career within the field, such as becoming an actress, a musician or an artist. Altogether, 63 pupils thought that the specific arts skills that they had developed could help them if they chose to pursue a career related to the arts, and many saw this as a reason for studying these subjects.

A total of 126 comments were made by pupils from the five schools, although the numbers of comments made varied from 18 at one school to 37 at another. Comments were made about each of the artforms and the arts as a whole, but the number of comments about each artform varied, as did the balance of perceptions about the different artforms at each school. The highest number of comments were made about art (41), followed by music (32) and drama (27). One school received a particularly high number of contributions about art (17), and another attracted a large number of comments about music (15). The references to drama were made by roughly similar numbers of pupils at each school. This pattern may suggest that, when considering a career in the arts, pupils are influenced by something specific to the individual artforms, as well as to the manner in which they are mediated by the teacher(s) in particular. Four comments referring to English as a medium for learning skills of direct relevance to careers in the arts were made by pupils from two schools, whilst dance generated three comments, from pupils at two schools.

Although the transfer of arts skills to their future career was seen as a potential outcome for pupils of all ages, a higher number of comments came from pupils in the first year of each cohort (Year 7 and Year 9).

Pupils in Year 7 held fairly uninformed opinions of how learning in the arts would help them in their future jobs and careers. A great number simply stated that they personally wanted a career in the arts, for example: *'I want to be an actress'*, *'I think I'd like to become an art teacher or a dance teacher'* and *'I'd like to be a musician in a big orchestra'*. In addition to this group of pupils who were specifically aiming for a career in the arts were others who recognised that the specific arts skills developed would be useful if that was what someone decided to do, for example: *'It helps you, like, if you decided to be an actor when you grow up.'* Many of these younger pupils referred to *'becoming'* an actor, or musician, and so on, and to what they wanted to be *'when you grow up'*.

Older pupils were usually more explicit, but also more tempered, and arguably, more realistic, in their perceptions of the arts as the basis of future jobs and careers. For example, one Year 9 pupil said: '*There is no way I can predict what I am going to do, but I would like to have a music career*'. Other occupations pupils mentioned where they felt their arts skills and knowledge would be useful were, amongst others, architecture, fashion design, journalism, choreography, and interior design. Older pupils did seem to be more aware of their own talents and abilities, and saw learning in the arts at school as building on this. A few of these older pupils had obviously thought through their future career options and had specifically chosen arts subjects accordingly, for example: '*I want to be an actress, so that's why I am taking drama.*' One outcome of learning in the arts mentioned by a number of pupils was the basis for further study at college, in art, the performing arts or media studies.

Transfer of other skills developed through the arts to work

Fifteen pupils made a total of 18 comments about the arts having helped them develop other skills which would be useful in their future jobs and careers, such as communication and teamwork skills. Half of these comments cited drama as the source of this effect, and the majority were made by pupils in Year 9 or above.

Self-confidence was one quality which pupils thought could be increased through the arts and was perceived by several individuals as being invaluable for a career as a lawyer. Other skills were also mentioned as being relevant to this profession:

> *I'd like to be a solicitor or something like that and ... [drama] ...gives you more empathy and you can feel what the person you're defending is thinking about and you can project your voice well and you've got more self-esteem ...* (Year 7, drama).

In more general terms, other skills developed through the arts were discussed as being transferable to work in a broader sense, such as teamwork and communication skills:

> *I think [drama] will help me a lot with teamwork in the future. If I am going to progress into a workplace, into an environment where you have to work as a team, then it would be very helpful because I have learnt what it's like now, and I know about listening to others and I think it will help me a lot* (Year 11, drama).

> ———

> *Drama probably helped with communication and things and I still do drama out of school, and being on a stage as to do with music like singing or reciting or acting or whatever. I think that gives you more confidence and it makes you able to express yourself better in front of people, and that's probably something that you will need ... later on* (Year 11, arts).

Encouragement of involvement in arts-related careers

Six pupils mentioned a related outcome of the arts, namely that their participation in school-level arts had encouraged them to carry this on at college, or pursue an arts-based career. To a couple of pupils, it was involvement in extra-curricular activities which had offered encouragement:

> *Being in 'Bugsy' has made me think about doing it as a career, taking it at college* (Year 7, drama).

The majority of the comments in this subsection were made by pupils in Year 11 who had already made the decision to pursue arts subjects at college. Two of them felt that it was the work they had completed in Year 11 which had encouraged them:

> *It's made me more enthusiastic about art. I am definitely taking it up at college. I wasn't going to because I thought ... well, I am good, but I wouldn't do it. But I really, really want to do it now. Yes, Year 11 has shown me that I can just sit there and do art and I want to learn more. I want to do it for a longer time* (Year 11, art).

Employer and Employee Perspectives

To further illustrate the perceived relationships between arts education and the world of work, interviews were carried out with a number of employees and employers from a wide range of companies and organisations (see Chapter 1). This section aims to present some of their opinions, but does not represent a complete analysis of all the comments made. Interviewees were asked about their views on arts education, their own involvement in the arts, and for their perceptions of how arts education affects employability. In addition, employers were asked how much notice their company takes of arts experiences and qualifications during recruitment.

In the main, comments made by the employers and employees who were interviewed seem to corroborate the pupil and teacher view that the arts in school offer benefits to pupils in terms of their future employment. Notably, it was the transferable skills which the arts developed which were felt to enhance employability, rather than specific arts-based competencies.

Several interviewees gave accounts of how their personal involvement in the arts had affected their employability, either directly or indirectly. One newspaper reporter offered the following:

> *I think I've been shaped through my interest in the arts into what I am now and where I am and what I'm interested in, so therefore I suppose the kind of person I am is reflected through my interests, which are all arts-based.*

Another employee talked about the skills he had developed through participating in school-level drama, including drama competitions, and how these related directly to his field of work:

> *Teamwork, I think, was brilliant. Communication, obviously, which is really important in this job ...I suppose leadership, from a director's point of view.*

2.
WHAT ARE
THE EFFECTS
OF
ARTS
EDUCATION?

Involvement in both drama and music was seen by interviewees as having offered a balance to school work, helping to develop more rounded people which, as one employer stated: *'reflects well on any organisation'*. In more general terms, this last comment was reinforced by one human resources adviser, when asked for his views on how arts education affects employability:

> *... I definitely think that it will increase the chances of you getting an interview. I don't know about getting a job, but I think you definitely look a more rounded, well-educated person who is interested in a lot of different things, can cope with lots of different things going on in their lives. From that point of view, I think employers see it quite favourably ...*

Several employers and employees made general comments which reinforced the pupils' opinions that the arts develop transferable skills which would be useful in their future employment. One Organisation Development Manager made the broad statement that the arts subjects *'can be great skill builders'*. Skills referred to specifically included: *'initiative'* and *'determination'*. The development of teamwork skills and confidence through participation in the arts, particularly extra-curricular activities, was mentioned by several interviewees:

> *It shows that they have got an imagination. If it were a musician, it would probably give an insight into teamwork, especially if they'd played an instrument, where they were in an orchestra or a small group, or even a pop group. I mean it's still teamwork at the end of the day, just being in a band. So, again that's something you'd think was a bonus. As I say, we look for team working skills.*
>
> ———
>
> *All the people that I have met that have done theatre or drama, and there have been a few, they are very confident. That is an overriding thing: they are very confident and they work well in a group.*

Arts involvement was also seen as a way to demonstrate to employers an individual's sense of commitment and achievement:

> *... achieving Grade 8 piano ... it may be their greatest achievement, and obviously you'd recognise that there's a lot of skill and commitment involved in that.*

Exemplifying a certain viewpoint within this sample, one employer saw arts as merely performance-related, and although he was looking for some of the same skills in employees to those identified earlier, did not appreciate that arts education may help develop these:

> *I'm looking for people who are articulate, confident and their verbal and written logic is good, and they've got good interpersonal skills, and they're good with people, but the fact that they can play the piano is irrelevant.*

Another employer, when asked for his opinion on how arts education affects employability, was rather negative:

> *I suspect in truth it doesn't help, because I suspect that the general view of a lot of managers would be that it's airy-fairy ... I suspect if you were to ask any manager in any business and you had one person with a degree in music and one person with a degree in business studies, their automatic reaction would be: 'Ah, I will talk to the business studies person'.*

Despite the negativity insinuated by this final group of employers, in the main those interviewed confirmed the views of both teachers and pupils, that the arts develop skills in pupils which are transferable to future employment. However, whereas pupils projected the transfer of specific arts skills to employment, teachers, employers and employees focused more on the work-related transfer of other skills, such as self-confidence, teamwork skills, commitment and the benefits associated with a balanced and rounded personality. The uninformed, and perhaps even naïve, views of pupils in the early years of secondary schooling as to the possible relevance of the arts to the world of work may suggest that a more explicit exposition of the economic and occupational contribution of the arts within the curriculum would be a valuable addition.

9.4 TRANSFER TO LEISURE TIME

This section deals with claims connected with the transfer effect from the arts to pupils' leisure activities, whilst at school and on leaving school, largely in terms of the skills or encouragement needed to participate.

Teacher Perspectives

Although teachers did talk about encouraging pupils to continue their participation in arts activities throughout their lives, rarely did any comments centre on the transfer of skills to leisure activities, such as critical interpretative skills. Most amounted to expressions of teachers' aims for pupils to continue to make music, enjoy reading, and go to dramatic productions and art galleries, no matter what they chose as a career:

> *... it will be with them throughout their lives, because they, if they even do astrophysics, there'll still, wherever they are, there will always be an art gallery where they are, they can always go and spend an afternoon there, it's all around them and hopefully they will take that with them, it's always there. Not even just in the gallery, but all around them, wherever* (head of art).

> ――――

> *... my aims in terms of all of it is to get a sort of lifelong thirst for knowledge and enjoyment* (headteacher).

Pupil Perspectives

In a similar vein, pupils talked about an outcome of arts lessons in school as equipping them with the skills or encouragement to participate in arts activities in their leisure time, either whilst at school or in the future. It was noticeable that the majority of pupils' comments, though not all, concentrated on active participative roles in the arts rather than critical consumer spectator roles. Forms of participation included engagement in organised activities, such as amateur dramatic societies and orchestras, learning to play an instrument, and home-based activities such as drawing, sewing or playing a musical instrument for pleasure or relaxation.

Transfer of skills to current participation in leisure-time arts

Forty-six pupils commented that arts lessons had provided them with the skills to participate further in arts activities, making a total of 62 remarks. Comments came from pupils in each year group at each school, although differences in the types of involvement were evident between pupils of different ages and at different schools. Marked variations were also seen in the effect of each individual artform on pupils' participation in the arts in their leisure time.

The majority of the 13 comments which referred to participation in organised activities, such as orchestras, drama clubs and so on, came from pupils in Year 9 or above. Nearly half of the comments cited music as providing pupils with the skills to participate in extra-curricular arts activities, and a further five referred to drama. There was a distinct variation in the number of comments from pupils at each school. Whilst one school elicited six comments, pupils at another did not make a single reference to the development of skills which could be transferred to extra-curricular activities. This may be a consequence of differences in the availability and accessibility of arts-based activities in the areas surrounding the different schools.

Several pupils felt that their technical ability had improved in lessons, and that this was transferable to extra-curricular activities:

> *I am in a couple of theatre groups out of school. So when I have been doing them it helped, and for auditions at school as well* (Year 9, drama).

This next pupil felt that it was a two-way reciprocal process, and that as well as her music course in school being beneficial to her participation in the orchestra, the converse was also true:

> *Since I have been doing the orchestra out of school, it's helped me with things in my music course at school and vice versa* (Year 11, music).

For another pupil, it was his increased understanding of music which had led to a positive effect on his music-making in a band:

> *It's helped me with the band because it has made me understand music more* (Year 8, music).

Another pupil discussed how he had developed the skills to work with other people in school music lessons, a characteristic which had enabled him to form a band:

> *I think it is good that I have learnt how to play with other people really. Since the start I have formed a band, which has come out of that really, the idea of playing with other people* (Year 9, music).

The development of confidence through lessons which enabled them to pursue extra-curricular arts activities was something mentioned by a few pupils.

A total of 19 pupils referred to the transfer of skills from classroom music lessons to the learning of a musical instrument outside of school. More likely to be expressed by younger pupils, the number of pupils from each school making reference to such an outcome varied from one to six. The school which elicited only one reference to this outcome (the same school where pupils made no comments about the development of skills to transfer to extra-curricular arts activities) had a high level of socio-economic deprivation, compared with the fairly affluent catchment areas of these other two schools, perhaps suggesting that having the opportunity to learn to play a musical instrument, and therefore being able to transfer skills developed in school music lessons to this learning, is associated with socio-economic status.

Pupils talked about general effects on their instrument playing, and the transfer of technical skills, such as understanding of the notes, timing and rhythms:

The music has just helped me progress with my saxophone (Year 9).

———

It has helped me in playing the flute and everything because different music timing and everything. It helps me to read music a lot better (Year 8).

———

I can understand more notes now than I did so it's helping me with my flute, because you learnt how to play notes on the keyboard and they are really the same thing as being on the flute, so it helps me doing that (Year 8).

One pupil found that her increased understanding and appreciation of different types of music through her school music lessons helped to improve the expressive aspects of her instrument playing:

It improved the music that I do out of school, the violin and piano lessons, because you come to understand the different eras of music and you could play your piece differently and put the different feelings into your pieces (Year 9).

A total of 24 pupils, spread across all year groups, mentioned that one outcome of arts lessons in school was the development of the skills to be able to pursue unstructured arts activities in their own time. Over half (18) of the 28 comments referred to art, in terms of drawing or painting at home, whilst the others talked about music, dance and English. Interestingly, pupils from the school which generated only one reference to transfer of skills to learning to play a musical instrument, and no comments about transfer of skills to extra-curricular activities, made the highest number of comments about the transfer of skills to less structured activities or hobbies. The vast majority of this school's comments (nine out of 11) referred to art, and accounted for half of all the comments made about this artform. Other evidence pointed to the particularly strong influence of an enthusiastic art teacher. Another possible factor is that this school is in London, where pupils have greater opportunities to visit art galleries, many of which are free and which may further fuel pupils' interest in drawing. Furthermore, another consideration in areas of economic deprivation is that the resources needed for painting and drawing are less expensive than those required for instrumental tuition.

A number of pupils talked about how they used the skills which they had developed in art lessons to draw at home in their leisure time:

If I have got nothing to do and it is really boring, I like to sit down and do collages and drawing and stuff (Year 7, art).

———

I do it quite a lot at home as well, and I like doing that and it gives me techniques to use at home. I don't just do 'em in school, I use them other places as well (Year 7, art).

Sometimes, I find myself with nothing to do and you just go out with pens and pencils and draw whatever you can see. I sometimes just go out onto my balcony and I just look around and think: 'That is nice' and I'll draw it (Year 9, art).

A few pupils discussed how they used the skills that they had developed to sketch whilst on holiday:

I mean, say art, when I haven't got a camera or film or something on holiday, I've always got my sketch book so I can just take that out and basically do the outline of what I'm seeing or whatever (Year 11, art).

A couple of pupils mentioned that one of their hobbies was sewing or designing clothes, and that the art skills which they had developed at school were transferable to this pastime:

I like to go home and do some drawings of clothes and fashion design, because I am really interested in that side of things (Year 11, art).

Lessons in the other arts also developed skills which pupils felt could be usefully transferred to other activities. Four pupils indicated that their ability to dance, either at discos or whilst listening to music at home, made use of the dance skills developed in lessons, and one pupil referred to writing poetry at home using skills developed in her English lessons.

Demonstrating that not all the comments focused on active participation in the arts, four pupils described how their understanding of the music they listened to at home had increased through their learning within lessons:

They've helped me understand music more and it's helped me outside of school. And when I've listened to songs now, I pick out things that we've done in music (Year 7, music).

At home I listen to a wide range of music, classical, Bach and all that, and also Alanis Morrisette, so it ranges really widely. Listening to things at school and having to answer questions about it makes you think a lot more about rather than having it just as background music (Year 7, music).

Transfer of encouragement to current participation in leisure-time arts

Twelve pupils observed that one outcome of their arts lessons was to encourage them to participate further in the arts, either by way of extra-curricular activities, learning to play a musical instrument or in an unstructured way at home.

Seven pupils said that they had been encouraged to join organised arts activities through their school lessons in the arts. These comments came from pupils of all ages and at all schools. Two references were made to each of art, dance and drama having this effect, and one each to music and the arts as a whole.

A couple of pupils said that they had been encouraged to visit art galleries, because their enthusiasm for art had increased through their lessons:

> It's made me definitely more interested. I mean, I go to a lot more galleries and art places now, because I'm very interested in it (Year 9, art).

Interestingly one pupil, a boy, talked about how he had got involved with a dance club because he had enjoyed his lessons at school:

> Once I had got into dancing with the school, I thought that if I could get into dancing with the school, I might as well get into dancing actually in a club (Year 7, dance).

Two pupils had also got involved with drama clubs or had been encouraged to get involved in productions:

> Drama – it's made me go into 'Bugsy' and take a main part (Year 7, drama).

Being encouraged to learn to play a new musical instrument, or persevere with existing instruments, was an outcome of school music lessons for a few pupils:

> In music my teacher encourages me to play the saxophone and not give it up (Year 7, music).

> I'm going to start piano [lessons] soon (Year 7, music).

For some, studying music at school had evoked an increased general interest in music and had encouraged pupils to listen to more music at home:

> I am a lot more interested in music at home now. I listen to it loads now (Year 9, music).

Projected effect on involvement in the arts after pupils leave school

The vast majority of pupils were asked a specific question about how they thought the arts would affect them in the future. Many offered the reply that they would like to continue with the arts in some way in their hobbies, and that their study of the arts at school had provided them with the skills or motivation to do so. A total of 27 pupils made 32 comments to this effect, half of which referred to music, and a further quarter to drama.

2.
WHAT ARE
THE EFFECTS
OF
ARTS
EDUCATION?

A number of pupils simply stated that the arts would remain with them in the future by filling part of their leisure time, as hobbies. This point was made for each artform, and often referred to unstructured *ad hoc* participation at home:

> *I'll probably still carry on drawing in my spare time* (Year 9, art).

> *You could do it as a pastime* (Year 7, music).

> *I'd like to go on with music, even if it doesn't come into my career. I'd like to carry on with music for pleasure anyway* (Year 9, music).

Many pupils talked about their desire to continue playing musical instruments, mainly for pleasure, in their spare time:

> *I'll probably carry on with the electric guitar and just do it in my spare time* (Year 7, music).

> *I want to carry on playing my flute* (Year 7, music).

Other pupils thought they would probably join arts clubs or societies, mostly in drama or music:

> *I think I'd like to join a band or something and play my saxophone in that* (Year 7, music).

> *Maybe I will go on to do drama, like, in my spare time, evening activities or something like that, because I do enjoy it, but I just don't want to take it up as a proper career* (Year 11, drama).

Again reflecting the minority viewpoint on consumption rather than participation roles, two pupils mentioned how their learning in the arts at school had increased their understanding, which would have a positive effect on their future involvement in the arts:

> *If you go to a play or something and you understand why they do things, and the sets* (Year 9, drama).

Overall, then, a sizeable number of pupils felt that one of the outcomes of their school-based arts education was to increase and enhance their active participation in the arts outside of school and in their own leisure time. For these pupil interviewees, this had been, or would be, achieved either through knowledge and skills development in the arts or through the encouragement and inspiration of their arts teachers. It was noticeable, however, that there were comparatively very few references to the arts in school preparing young people for their adult cultural life as critical and discriminating 'consumers' of artistic and media products.

9.5 CONCLUDING COMMENTS

Considering that teaching and learning in schools is normally highly context-bound and compartmentalised (Hargreaves, 1991) and that pupils are not usually taught the 'bridging skills' (Feuerstein, 1980) necessary to carry over learning from one context to another (Joyce and Showers, 1982), the evidence from pupils demonstrates quite an impressive awareness of the transfer effects associated with arts education:

- The pupil interviewees volunteered a range of transferable effects from the arts to other areas of the curriculum, especially in art and drama.

- Pupils anticipated that many of the learning outcomes gained through taking the arts would transfer to the world of work – and several employers endorsed these expectations by recognising the value of such outcomes.

- Many pupils felt that their active participation in the arts outside of school had been or would be extended and enriched as a result of their school-based arts education.

However, the evidence also imposed some important limits and qualifications on each of these rather upbeat conclusions:

- Contrary to the much-vaunted claims, the statistical analyses revealed no sound evidence to suggest that the transference of effects to other areas of the curriculum extended to the point of imparting an influence on general academic performance in GCSE examinations.

- Many pupils, especially those in the early stages of secondary schooling, displayed fairly uninformed views of the relevance of the arts to the world of work and some employers were not convinced of the benefits of the arts to employment.

- The transference of critical skills and aesthetic judgement-making to beyond-school cultural behaviour was seldom recognised as an effect by pupils; neither were the mapping out of local cultural opportunities or the encouragement to access cultural venues and artefacts in consumer or spectator roles (see Harland and Kinder, 1999).

By way of concluding the chapter, questions concerning possible ameliorative measures for each of these problems are tentatively proposed for consideration.

- Could the contribution of arts-based transfer effects to learning in other areas be extended by the explicit teaching of 'bridging skills' and the development of more coordinated and coherent approaches to the teaching of cross-curricular skills and knowledge?

- Could pupils' and employers' awareness of the relevance of the outcomes of learning in the arts be raised by incorporating explorations of these issues as a formal requirement within the programmes of study for each artform?

- Could the task of preparing young people for critical audience and spectator roles, together with the provision of greater support in transferring these skills to their life beyond school, be developed by teachers of the arts and by further codification within the National Curriculum?

10. OTHER EFFECTS: ON THE SCHOOL, THE COMMUNITY AND THE ARTS

**2.
WHAT ARE
THE EFFECTS
OF
ARTS
EDUCATION?**

CHAPTER OVERVIEW

In addition to the seven broad effects on pupils, the model of outcomes described in Chapter 2 included three other indirect effects: effects on the school (10.2), the local community (10.3) and art itself as an outcome (10.4). Accounts of these three types of outcome are considered in this chapter. It also discusses perspectives on the fourth aim of the study, namely to explore whether there is a relationship between the quality of a school's provision in the arts and its propensity for school improvement and effectiveness (10.5).

10.1 INTRODUCTION

In addition to the effects of arts education on the pupils themselves, various effects on schools and communities were depicted by the interviewees, though, for the most part, it was the teachers rather than the pupils who talked about such outcomes. However, both teachers and pupils perceived the arts themselves as an important outcome, simply as a product or performance. This chapter, therefore, describes the perception that, in addition to the effects on pupils, arts education in secondary schools impacts upon parents and the community, the arts themselves, and the ethos and culture of the school. With regard to the latter, it also explores the proposition that a school that has high levels and quality of provision in the arts is more likely to have a strong track record in school improvement and effectiveness.

10.2 EFFECTS ON THE SCHOOL

The arts tended to be spoken of collectively by teachers for their contribution to a positive ethos and climate in the school, with some reference also to the effects, of drama and music especially, in the pastoral domain. The effect of the arts on the school image was also noted, particularly by interviewees involved in school management. Just one pupil referred to any such effect, and so the subcategories discussed here relate almost solely to a teacher-perceived model. We note that of the teachers interviewed, most were heads of department, or those in higher management – heads and deputy heads – and hence a slight bias towards perspectives of the whole school could naturally be expected. What is interesting is the positive bias given to the arts in this respect – even by management teams made up of non-arts specialists or from non-arts backgrounds; perhaps not only that, but also the positive view in which all subjects were held to affect the school ethos and its overall strength – and such relationships are discussed and explored in section 10.5.

We begin by considering the teachers' perspectives of the impacts of arts education on the whole school. Such effects were categorised into those focusing on school ethos, the pastoral domain and school image.

10.2.1 Effects on school ethos

Teacher Perspectives

Numerous responses addressed ways in which the arts contribute to school ethos. Although four subcategories were devised from the data, distinguishing between an 'adventurous' ethos, a 'positive and enjoyment-oriented' ethos, school pride, and school bonding, in practice it was sometimes difficult to place responses neatly into one of these. Most responses fitted more comfortably into the second subcategory, namely, claims that the arts help to create a positive and enjoyment-oriented atmosphere in the school.

Creates adventurous climate in the school

This category was created to account for responses which focused on the creation of an adventurous ethos or culture in the school, perhaps connected with the risk-taking of creativity. However, although this may be an element of the effect that the arts have on school ethos, most interviewees talked more generally about a '*positive*' school ethos. Senior management and teachers at one school did, however, talk about the widening of pupils' experiences through the arts, and the excitement of having new facilities for the arts, and the knock-on effects this had for nurturing more thinking, inventive and individual pupils.

Creates positive and enjoyment-oriented atmosphere

When dealing with school ethos, most responses focused on the arts as a whole rather than distinguishing between artforms.

One stated effect was the philosophy that all can achieve, or, as one deputy head described it, a '*can do it*' attitude which began in the arts and permeates the whole school:

> ... *these kids may live in one of the most deprived areas in the country, yes; these kids may live in tower blocks, yes; these kids' parents may not have work – that does not mean that they can't achieve. What really happened was that permeated through the rest of the school; it already existed within the arts environment.*

Another deputy head described this 'can do' attitude in the arts (that is individual pupils' success at something) as having a *'motivational effect'* on the rest of the school. One head of music at another of the schools developed the 'can do' philosophy further, seeing the arts as encouraging a supportive atmosphere by way of having no rights or wrongs. This permeated from the arts across the whole school by way of working with *'barriers down'*, and as the head of music said, '*I think that has become an ethos of the school in many ways, that the experience is far more important than whether you are always getting the right answers as such*'. In the stories told about some individual pupils, the 'can do' effect in the arts was seen as the motivating factor for their attendance at school.

A second aspect of school ethos and climate was enjoyment, illustrated by this response from a headteacher:

> *I suppose the element of our school aims is the sense of pride and enjoyment, and the arts contribute to both of those – that is our second aim. I believe, particularly with young people in their teenage years, that if they enjoy what they do and they are proud of it, then they are likely to put in more time and energy.*

Although most responses were not artform-specific, one deputy head made particular mention of the impact drama has on the school:

> *Drama has a huge input in this school, to actually the whole ethos of the school, in that you can express yourself through improvisation, you can explore ideas, you can explore emotions and all sorts of things through drama.*

This impact on positive school ethos claimed for drama was also related to drama techniques being used in assemblies by this deputy head.

In art, displays were perceived to contribute to the ethos as part of the *'value system'* where pupils appreciate and respect the work of others, and by providing a focus for interaction between pupils. Music was also mentioned in respect of this overall general outcome, but dance and English were not specified at all.

That the arts impact on the learning and teaching environment in other lessons was suggested by one teacher, in one of the schools. It was not just a one-way process, though:

> *The thing about this school is it [the arts] really does have a massive impact around the school, even though there are certain staff I don't think that would realise that they are working in a very arts way in their lesson … led by the arts, although they might say 'Oh well, it's not', and perhaps it's just become cross-transferable, and perhaps*

we have taken a bit from up there, the way in which they work, but everybody now works in a similar – I think – artistic way in many ways, far more open-ended, not just looking at the rights and wrongs ... (head of music).

At another school, the deputy head gave specific examples of how teaching could be improved in different subject areas, by transferring styles and ideas from the arts to other subjects, thus linking to improvements in school effectiveness as discussed in section 10.5. Collaboration between music and humanities staff helped teachers to think how to get *'kids' attention right at the start of the lesson'*, how to focus their thinking – for example, background music was tried – and how to keep control of lots of different activities going on at once, as is often required in drama.

Encourages pride and self-esteem in a school and its members
Another purported effect for the arts was that they encouraged pride in the school. One response captured much of the character of this outcome:

> *Pride. I have watched kids walk out of previous performances, previous plays, and seen ... and you can see a tangible sense of 'It is my school and I am proud of it'* (deputy head).

Pride was also perceived to be evident in the way that pupils respect and value works of art. This was an aspect mentioned by teachers in one school in particular:

> *The other thing that I think does come across is that it is very rarely damaged, it is very rarely touched; now, a lot of it is sugar paper and yet somehow ... we get no complaints of kids wrecking, touching, ruining in any way any of it, so that is another part of the value system, that they do learn to appreciate that the stuff is somebody's and that it is worth being there.*

Greater tolerance of all pupils' skills and abilities was deemed by one head to be influenced by the arts in the school, where pupils with skills in the arts were 'celebrated' and other pupils were proud of their peers' achievements. An example of a talent show was cited, where half of the audience was made up of supporting pupils, not taking part in the show.

Increased self-esteem not only of pupils, but also of teachers, was another perceived effect for the arts – impacting on the whole school. One deputy head talked about how *'staff motivation and morale is boosted'* when both facilities are improved, and expectations of pupils are high *'and children rise to that and meet those expectations and often exceed them'*.

Pupils wanting to be involved in school productions was another outcome cited in the case study schools, one deputy head perceiving it as '*a step forward culturally*' for the school, with arts involvement now being '*quite accepted; it's part of what you do*'. Pupils' pride in the schools' arts was evident from this. A deputy head at another of the schools expanded this further by saying that some pupils want to come to school in order to be in the school choir or school productions, and for some, that they '*enjoy coming to school for that one reason*'.

Knits or binds the school together

Another key school effect of the arts was the potential for the arts to bind the school together. Responses tended to address this at a departmental level, with a particular acknowledgement of the role of school productions to encourage involvement from departments across the school. One aspect of this was that the arts departments cooperated on projects; a second aspect was the cross-departmental/faculty involvement in school productions, where, for example, technology does the lighting, science works out special effects, and technology designs tickets and signage. Drama was mentioned specifically with regard to a claim of 'bonding', where a sense of togetherness is encouraged. However, one deputy head was more sceptical about such views: although, he recognised the potential for the arts to establish good inter-departmental relationships while a performance was on, he said that, '*once that production was over, I am not too sure how much of a knock-on effect that does have for the rest of the school*'. Indeed, a further warning about the limits to the opportunities for cross-departmental work was cited by another deputy head. Talking on a very practical level, it was pointed out that such binding can be strained at department level where monies might be seen to go into supporting the arts and not other subject areas.

Another positive aspect of this knitting effect was the way, particularly in art, that pupils from different year groups interacted with each other, thus bonding the school together on a more vertical scale, as well as the cross-departmental horizontal scale portrayed earlier. One head of art described her '*open-door policy*' in this respect, which she also saw as raising the profile of the arts within the school. Talking about the influence of individual personalities of those teaching the arts, she said:

> *Well, I think they are* [it is] *the teachers which lead down on to children's attitudes. The way I work in my room, as you came in this morning, I had different year groups all working together. I had six :.. working with Year 11, younger people come in and it's a cross-flow and they get ideas from each other and encouragement and it's quite a nice fluid way to work. I have an open-door policy, let the work be seen around the school.*

Bonding on a 'vertical' scale was also seen in music, where pupils from different year groups worked together in school orchestra and so on, at one school older pupils taking on a supporting role and creating a 'family' atmosphere:

> *We had a rehearsal last night, where two tiny little Year 7s arrived for the first time amidst all these much bigger, much uglier kids, and the older ones just kind of take them under their wing like older brother, older sisters and there's a kind of family atmosphere which you don't get any other way, and nobody can ever replicate. I don't create that; the kids create that for themselves* (head of music).

One deputy head talked about the bonding effect from micro to macro level – indicating a more complex design than just the vertical and horizontal scales suggested above (that is 'with age' and 'across departments'). The *'team spirit'* at a class level, where the *'bread and butter'* was done in the arts, was related by this deputy head to the whole-school, big event, which would, in a similar way to classroom-level enthusiasm, *'draw pupils in'*.

One deputy head talked about the knock-on motivational effects between staff and pupils as a result of non-arts teachers taking up musical instruments and joining in with school music ensembles in his school. Thus, a bonding effect at the staff–pupil interface became apparent. This was advocated by several members of staff in one of the schools with a particular emphasis on friendly staff–pupil relations – *'pupils and staff interacting, talking …'*.

On a more abstract, less tangible level, the arts were also described as providing a school with a *'soul'* and a *'heartbeat'*.

10.2.2 Effects on the pastoral domain and behaviour management

Teacher Perspectives

This claimed effect was encapsulated in two subcategories, but there were minimal mentions of the arts here. In fact, the references cited below tended to refer to individual pupils rather than suggesting that the effect operated at the level of the whole school. Drama and music were mentioned.

Supports pastoral provision and effective behaviour management
Some teachers offered comments about specific pupils who had behaviour problems in other subjects, but were not disruptive in the arts. One drama teacher perceived this to be a result of the opportunities for self-expression which exist in the arts:

... sometimes, it does seem that the kids who are the bad kids in other subjects, because they are the disruptive ones, are the ones who do really well in our subjects because that expression, that freedom of expression, is what they relish and they are away.

Although there were no specific remarks which discussed the issue of behaviour management and the arts at a school rather than at a classroom or individual level, many teachers discussed the positive effect the arts have on school ethos. Some responses included high standards and expectations of behaviour as aspects of a positive school ethos where individuals are valued and value each other.

Encourages school attendance and increased motivation

The technical side of drama was cited as an important motivation factor in school attendance for several pupils – both high and low attainers. It seemed to be discovering their own niche within drama and contributing to a greater school environment (for example, through school plays) that engaged these pupils.

10.2.3 Effects on the school's image

Teacher Perspectives

The effects of arts education on the school's image became apparent where the positive ethos of the school was seen to support displays of pupils' work and public performances. Art, drama and music were highlighted by teachers in this respect.

Promotes the profile or public image of the school

This effect was noted particularly by interviewees involved in school management. Terms such as '*public relations*', '*reputation*', and '*a showcase for the school*' were used; as one head said, '*... it's very much something we want, I want, we, as a management team are very keen to develop, just for the sake of the school rather than anything else*'.

'Parents' were a recurring theme in this type of effect, with the ultimate outcome of good publicity seeming to be that parents would send their children to the school. The arts were perceived to play an important part in this, providing good examination results, impressive displays, and high-profile dramatic productions and musical events. These responses from those involved in school management were explicit about the arts '*selling the school*':

... we have used the arts, of course, to sell the school in a big way. If you are a parent coming to look around the school, yes, you get to see around the art department; you can't avoid it.

Whenever I bring parents into this particular block, or round the school, they're amazed at the work that goes on here and they are very impressed and I think that probably in some ways makes them want to send their children here, quite honestly ... – maintain its popularity.

―――

... when they walk around the school, they see a thriving school, a school that looks good, the children are working well here. I think all that does have a positive effect on their perception of the school ...

The deputy head making this last comment on the school's public profile, recognised a link between this and the pupils' pride in their work that was displayed around the school. Teachers of art, music and drama also talked about the effect that 'success' in their subject areas can have on school image. There was an emphasis on public displays of the arts and on achievement:

At its crudest, when you are getting 93 per cent A to Cs in art and you are able to say that to parents, you are able to inspire parents to send their daughters here to get the balanced intake (deputy head).

One possibility for the absence of dance for this effect may be that it is not examinable in the same way as drama, music and art, and cannot therefore be held up as an indication of school success.

The status of the arts in terms of a public image based on examination results was perceived as a circular affair by one head. Improved public image meant improved status of the arts within the school, which in turn encouraged more pupils to choose the arts subjects. This fed back into increasing the arts' status. Not only were there increased numbers of pupils, but also increases in all levels of ability of those pupils choosing the arts. This echoes the 'all can do' attitude reported in section 10.2.1, encouraging a positive learning environment.

The high profile of the arts departments themselves in schools was seen to have an effect on pupils becoming more engaged in arts practice, mentioned in several of the schools. In one school, the head described this, again, as a *'niche within the arts faculty'* that children feel they can belong to.

Pupil Perspectives

Just one pupil made specific reference to the arts' impact on the whole school, and this was with regard to the school's public profile. It was a remark, made by a Year 7 pupil, in response to a question about how she thought the arts were viewed:

Well, it's quite important in the school actually, 'cos I think as well as getting the school lots of publicity with plays and things ...

10.3 EFFECTS ON THE COMMUNITY

Alongside the effect of the arts on school image, the arts were also seen to be encouraging the involvement of parents and the wider community in the school. Again, this effect was noted mostly by teachers rather than pupils, with all the artforms posting such comments. Effects of the arts on the community were divided into two categories: parents and the wider community.

10.3.1 Encourages involvement and support of parents

Teacher Perspectives

Teachers commented on the opportunities that arts events provide for parents to become involved in the school, either through direct involvement such as helping at productions, or through attending events as an audience member or spectator. One deputy head also described how the inclusion of a dramatic performance (involving a range of pupils) at an evening dealing with solvent abuse encouraged parents to attend:

> *It was absolutely fantastic and I just don't think that we would easily have got that mix of people without that input, because it is having an entertainment, putting on an entertainment like that, but looking at some quite serious issues.*

Pupil Perspectives

The effects on the community of the arts in school were noted by just one pupil, who talked about practical involvement of her parents in drama productions:

Interviewer: *What about your parents? Are they involved in the arts?*

> *Yes, because I go to the theatre school and I live in* [X] *and because it's in* [Y] *it takes a while to get there, maybe 25 mins, and there's no point in going then coming back again, so my mum helps with the costumes and the props and my dad helps with making the scenery and the props, so they're involved as well, so they're always there* (Year 9).

10.3.2 Encourages involvement and support of community

Teacher Perspectives

Key community effects of the arts were perceived to come from pupils performing in the community at primary schools and retirement homes, and school facilities being made available for use by community groups. One teacher described how this type of community involvement was two-way in the arts, again '*a fluid thing*' – '*parents willing to come in to school and help*' and pupils going out and joining community choirs, singing and becoming involved, in particular in the Welsh culture. One teacher at a different school also perceived that the musical horizons of the community as a whole had been broadened by the work of the school music groups:

> *The big band connection that we have had here for years and years – that has opened up horizons that* [the town] *never thought it had horizons for. Not just, as I said, in terms of the high level of skill that they have reached musically, but as I say, just to open a perspective that didn't exist.*

One head described how invitations to surrounding schools to make use of new facilities at his school had extended the 'community involvement' effect of the arts. Involvement of pupils in community-based activities was perceived as an outcome of their enthusiasm for arts in school, according to another head.

10.4 ART ITSELF AS AN OUTCOME

This final category was developed to allow for responses which focused on the making of art and art products, which were seen as outcomes of arts education in their own right. Only a few teachers talked about this as an outcome of the arts, whereas pupils also referred to their artwork having an effect on other people, which in turn was an enjoyment-type outcome for themselves – thus providing a loop back to the very first category of effect portrayed in Chapter 3.

Teacher Perspectives

Only a few responses from teachers fell into this category, and they focused on the importance of the performance or product in drama and art. The importance of art works being '*hung on walls*' was mentioned, with one art teacher linking the exhibitions with pupils feeling a sense of achievement (see section 8.3 which discusses self-esteem, self-worth and achievement). Another art teacher distinguished between the arts and other areas of the curriculum in terms of product:

> *... after all, if you sit your GCSE maths, are you going to keep your maths book sitting on the mantelpiece at home for the rest of your life? It's very unlikely, but you might keep your picture that you're proud of, or your pot that you made, for years and years and get pleasure from it and a sense of achievement. I mean there is an outcome ...*

One deputy head linked a greater awareness of the art product to a broadened artistic experience both in and out of school, so that pupils were no longer '*frightened of the idea of theatre, or exhibitions, or art or displays*'.

In drama, the longstanding debate between process and product was alluded to by some teachers. Theatrical product was identified as an outcome of drama, although this may not necessarily mean the putting on of a public performance, but more the 'showing' or 'sharing' of work within a lesson. One drama teacher saw product and process as linked, with each enhancing the other:

Now, I believe that the product is very valuable and if a child, or anybody, is proud of their product then that feeds back on their process, and then that feeds back into everybody else watching that and how they think about it.

Pupil Perspectives

In addition to considering the finished pieces of work to be an outcome of the arts in their own right, pupils also talked about the subsequent effects that these pieces had on themselves, and on other people. There were 14 responses made to this overall effect, made by ten pupils.

Art as an outcome

Five comments were made, by four pupils, about pieces of artwork themselves being an outcome of the arts. Four of these referred to the arts and one to music, and four out of the five came from pupils in Year 9.

It was the actual creating of something new which was important to some pupils:

I think the outcome of doing art is like ... it's a lot to do with being able to create something and I think that's a very important thing for me, like doing something constructive and like having a finished production and being like proud of that, so I think that's the main thing for me (Year 9, art).

Pupils seemed to get a sense of satisfaction or achievement from seeing their final piece of work, an effect which links directly to the discussion on self-esteem (section 8.3) as well as to enjoyment and fulfilment (as discussed in Chapter 3). Evaluation of their own work was also important:

Well, I get a lot of joy out of finishing a piece of work and like being able to say 'Well that's good', the composition or the picture is good, and I've done my best and it's turned out well. That's good or even a lesson where we've just been given a new piece of work to do and we've done like the initial sketches and things and you're all excited, because you know that in a couple of weeks you'll have made a new sort of additional thing (Year 9, art).

I like the finished product, I like looking at my work and thinking what I could have made better or what should stay the same and things (Year 9, art).

——

I like the finished product, once we have actually played it to the class and it's been recorded and we play it over again. I like listening to it, seeing where we could have made it better (Year 9, music).

Other people's enjoyment

Although arguably not a direct outcome anticipated by teachers, being able to have others appreciate their final piece of work or being aware of others' enjoyment were effects of the arts suggested by a number of pupils. Altogether, seven pupils from all year groups made nine such comments. Five of these comments specified music as being enjoyable to others, and there were two comments relating to drama, and two to art. Knowing that other people got something out of their work was important to pupils:

And drama if you can entertain people and make them laugh, then that's great, you know it helps them as well (Year 11, drama).

——

You can just sit and do it on your own and then afterwards other people can enjoy what you've done (Year 9, art).

——

You can entertain other people with it (Year 7, music).

Other people's enjoyment or what may be considered 'the entertainment outcome', then, was a 'pleasing' effect in its own right for these pupils. As they themselves put it: '*It pleases people. A lot of people do like our music.*' From this perspective, the finished product or piece of art was seen as an outcome in itself and did not need defining in any other way. Like the art teacher's comment on the durability of the art product itself (perhaps 'on your mantelpiece'), one of the pupils also mentioned the product of played music – and how this can amount to enjoyment for other people, as well as being a durable product in the workplace, with 'making music' being the outcome itself:

I might be able [to teach] *music to other people. And play for other people. And I can't really think of many jobs you can do playing music* (Year 7, music).

While this subcategory collated those references to art as an outcome in its own right, comments obviously resonated with those on 'public' performance, and on the achievements and sense of satisfaction of pupils, whose art and project work was displayed in classrooms, and, in higher profile, around the school corridors and entrance halls. As such, the school's public image was also implicated by these types of comments, indicating an interrelationship between all of the comments in this chapter, which so far could be summed up as portraying the 'arts as presence' in the school.

10.5 INSTITUTIONAL INVOLVEMENT IN THE ARTS AND SCHOOL IMPROVEMENT AND EFFECTIVENESS

As a way of further illustrating the interconnectedness of the effects described in this chapter, one interview with senior management and heads of department included questions on their perceptions of a possible relationship between institutional involvement in the arts and school improvement and effectiveness. This embraced the potential of the arts to influence pupils' individual development at the one level, all the way through to impacts at department and school level. Discussion did not just relate to academic achievements as a marker of school effectiveness, but the development of pupils' intra- and interpersonal skills through the arts. High levels of involvement in the arts were indicated by increases in curriculum time spent on teaching the arts, as well as higher levels of community and outside involvement in the schools. Extra-curricular activities, such as dance and drama clubs were also mentioned. Improvements in the quality of teaching and learning as a result of increased staff motivation and the resources available were also cited. Pupils' wider experiences through school art trips, going to galleries and shows and having visiting artists were of particular importance to a higher level of institutional involvement in the arts at one of the schools. At another school, staff were involved in learning musical instruments and taking part in the various school ensembles.

Such a relationship, between high levels of involvement and school effectiveness was broached with some caution in these interviews, which provided the opportunity for an open discussion on the possibilities of this suggested link, direction of causality, and exploration of whole-school issues including other subject areas. Interviewees expanded most of the outcomes already reported in this chapter to the school level, indicating their relationship with school improvement, and, more often, school effectiveness. Interviewees' comments, then, are presented below in an order corresponding with the previous sections on school ethos, school image and parents and the community. In addition, further detail on this topic is included towards the end of this chapter.

10.5.1 School ethos and school effectiveness

The contribution of the arts to a positive school ethos described in section 10.2.1 was seen as feeding directly into school improvements by some interviewees. Comments focused on the positive atmosphere which the arts can have, with confident and articulate pupils contributing to school effectiveness: that is being good at the arts was perceived to influence school effectiveness because of the increased communication skills, confidence, self-esteem, and enjoyment that the pupils were deemed to have benefited from. One head of art said:

> *The students are giving something of themselves – putting themselves in the line – gaining confidence. Why does it make a better school? I don't know. Maybe as they gain confidence it helps the school. It helps the school to have active students giving.*

Further to this point, the head at the same school commented that it was probably the arts more so than other subjects that could have an impact in this area:

> *I think the opportunity, since most of the arts education in this school is centred on the pupil ... individual development of pupils, that then has to contribute to their oral skills, their self-confidence, their self-esteem, which then builds up to make a much more effective school ... I think effective arts education probably will contribute a lot more to that than other areas of the curriculum.*

Indeed, it was the '*uniqueness of arts education*' that was seen to contribute here, even if you '*get that in history as well*' or in '*all the areas of the curriculum*', because in '*art education you seem to get all the opportunities coming under one umbrella*'.

Even those teachers who were disinclined to see the arts as any more important to school effectiveness than other subjects still argued that, at the individual level, the arts can offer something that motivates pupils to cooperate at the whole-school level. Concerned more with the whole curriculum, one deputy head was not inclined to make a specific case for the arts as relating to school effectiveness and improvement, but he was still encouraging of the status of the arts within the school, '*not sidelined in any way, but being central and having equality with the academic side ...*'

The positive, enjoyment-based ethos of the school, as purported for the arts in section 10.2.1, was reflected in a head of music's views on school effectiveness:

> *... pupils who want to learn, who want to enjoy themselves ... it has got to produce a good school, it's going to produce a school that has*

the right feeling and ethos, and when you walk around it, it will feel nice and relaxed ... and if you want to talk about adding a psychological point of view, the fact that when we are relaxed we work better ... (head of music).

2.
WHAT ARE
THE EFFECTS
OF
ARTS
EDUCATION?

The sense of enjoyment of school, and positive atmosphere, culminated, for one head, in his pupils' desire to stay on after school for extra-curricular, often arts-based, activities. This was seen as a significant *'indicator of a feel-good factor'*, leading him to espouse the view that *'when the arts are thriving in the school, it does lead to effectiveness'*. The arts were deemed to have an effect on the specific school ethos of developing pupils' self-esteem, equipping them with qualifications, and promoting a desire for lifelong learning. In several of the schools, the knock-on effects of enjoyment in the arts to other subjects were in general perceived as linked to school effectiveness.

The knitting and binding effects at departmental level as a result of the arts in schools were also perceived to be a factor in school effectiveness by one of the heads of department. Talking about general connections between strong arts and strong schools, this head of art said:

... we have got links throughout our school; even our librarian is very strong on the arts and she really does help. I know that kids will get a lot of support if they have to do research; or, if they want to order a book, she will help them. So it crosses the school, and the computers – teachers will help them get on the Internet to a gallery. It's a cross-school thing really; it extends beyond just the art room or the music room.

In addition, this art teacher also talked about the 'all can do' attitude referred to earlier, specifically in relation to art:

Well I do feel that a strong art department is a strong school, because it does cross all boundaries, we can ... not help people, but we can offer so much to everybody really, if they are willing and open to accept it.

Indeed, this 'all can do' idea was picked up on by another of the heads of department interviewed – this time a head of music – as making a specific case for the arts in school improvement and effectiveness, because, as she said, *'I think it's one subject that allows every single person to succeed; however small a part, they can get up and they can do something'*. The inclination here for teachers to support their own subject area by accentuating its outcomes and benefits was evident, but still important to the overall picture of school effectiveness.

The impact of good relationships between staff and pupils was seen by a few interviewees to have spread from the arts to the whole school, and thus reflect school effectiveness. At one school in particular, senior management and senior teachers talked about the '*relaxed*', '*comfortable*' and '*friendly*' relationships between pupils and staff, with '*mutual respect*' banded almost as a motto. 'Strong arts – strong school' was supported by the head at this school because of the '*culture of collaboration and cooperation*' and '*achievement by participation ... in artistic activity*', which were seen as the '*real contributory factor to the culture of the school*'. As a result, '*students enjoy coming to school and lessons, and so do staff...*' said the deputy head.

10.5.2 School image and school effectiveness

The 'academic' success of the arts within a school was seen by some heads and deputy heads in particular as important to school improvement and effectiveness, but several interviewees noted other subject areas here too:

> *The sustained success of the arts undoubtedly helps within the examination figures within the school ... to raise the profile of the overall results* (headteacher).

> *I feel that if you have got a good performing arts faculty, then it will help across the board, but obviously you have got to have other areas that are working with it as well; otherwise the overall school won't happen. It can't just happen in pockets, but yes, the influence of the arts, because of the range of skills that are involved, this does have an effect in all areas* (deputy head).

> Interviewer: *Does being good at the arts affect school improvement?*

> *It depends how you measure school improvement ... we are an example of continuous improvement in terms of exam results because ours have gone up steadily over five years ... I can cite examples of school improvement in terms of academic results, but I can also cite examples of school improvement in terms of the perception of students, and I think that's important* (headteacher).

Such perceptions were seen as to do with pupils' responding to the school environment and being satisfied with their work and creative achievements in the arts, not just the more measurable outcomes of examination results.

The strong image and public profile of some artforms were seen to impact on the other artforms at some schools – pulling those less 'effective' artforms up to meet high standards across all the arts.

The public profile of the school due to the arts (concerts and displays, and so on) was deemed influential to school effectiveness by one of the heads of music because it actively showed pupils and teachers participating.

10.5.3 Parents, the community and school effectiveness

The public profile of shows and concerts was also seen to impinge on the reputation of the school – and thus influence parental choice and community involvement in the schools' arts. One head of music, however, was wary that, in general, such reputations were not necessarily an indicator of the effects or effectiveness of music at classroom level. With a longstanding connection with his particular school, he was able to track the improvements within the arts, from being very much seen as having a 'reputation' for good shows (outside of the classroom situation), to parents and the community now perceiving music and the arts as subjects on equal footing with, say, English, maths and science. Even realising that *'playing an instrument is not just a bit of fun; there actually might be a career there'* was seen as an effect on the community, thus reflecting the effectiveness of arts education.

Other community effects were cited by this teacher, who reported that the community liked the school, and got involved by coming in to learn extra IT and language skills. The knock-on effects of this, back into the school, were cited: *'The pupils like working with mixed age groups ... the kids like having adults coming in and working with them ...'*

Higher levels of parental expectation in the arts, especially in terms of extra-curricular activities, were seen by one head to actually impact on the performance of the arts in the school – an effective school improving the effectiveness of the arts faculty in this respect. (As we shall see in section 10.5.4, not all teachers perceived this direction of causality in school effectiveness.)

10.5.4 Overview on the arts and school effectiveness

The possible relationship between strength in the arts and a school's capacity for improvement and effectiveness was broached with caution by the interviewees, although many gave expansive responses. Many agreed with the 'claimed' relationship, but wanted to frame their answers with examples and a concern for reflecting other subject areas too. Although he agreed with the claim, one deputy head described the link as *'too simplistic as it stands; I think it's a lot more complex than that'*. *'As an isolated subject area'*, though, he put forward some suggestions as to how the arts *'could have more effect than any other isolated subject area'*. It was because of the range of different skills developed in pupils through the arts, as opposed to, say, in maths or science, that the arts were suggested as being more effective in school improvement and effectiveness overall. Yet further circumspection was exercised in stressing that such a view of school effectiveness was caught up in a much more complex web of factors including the *'quality of the headteacher'*, *'improved GCSE results'*, *'quality of relationship between staff and students'*, *'shared values'* and a *'shared vision'* across the staff of the school. This last point caused some interesting variation across the schools. Senior management at two of the schools indicated that the arts were more likely and more able to impinge upon school vision than were other subjects. That is, arts education could have a bearing on the vision of and for the school, thus impacting on effectiveness and improvement from the department/faculty level to the school level. In contrast, senior management at other schools explained how a shared vision from senior staff could be *'imposed'* upon the school and pupils, from senior level right through to department and individual teacher/pupil level. For the deputy head at one of these schools, the arts were important in this 'model', because he felt they were more able than other subjects to take up a school vision.

Despite senior management's non-arts background at one school, the arts were still supported as contributing to school improvement and effectiveness, because of the range of skills developed in the arts, as discussed previously. Coming from a science background, the head at this school was *'conscious of the need to protect the arts and humanities'* in the ethos of *'breadth'* and *'balance'* of his school. Indeed, a broad and balanced curriculum was promoted by heads in several of the schools. Turning out well-rounded individuals was a purported effect of arts education as part of the balance of the whole curriculum, and, placing yet more support for the arts, one head asserted that *'arts education is a real contributor to the effectiveness of the school and it's something we neglect at our peril'*.

Although the argument that *'all subjects have a case for school improvement'* was advanced by many in senior management, it was their positive attitude towards the arts as encouraging greater overall impact at the individual pupil level, in terms of intra- and interpersonal skills, and, right through to staff–pupil relationships, and cross-department levels, that seemed to render the arts as having a particular (although not necessarily special) case here. (As passionately as one head felt about the arts, he could not pick them out as special to school improvement and effectiveness because he believed in a collaborative effort across all faculties.) However, a specific case for the arts impacting on school effectiveness was made by one of the interviewees in terms of the arts engendering pupil-centred learning and teaching. On the other hand, as one deputy head said, *'it's nobody's singular responsibility; school improvement is everybody's responsibility'*, perhaps warning that the arts must not be burdened with a further expected goal of improvement and effectiveness at school level.

It was interesting that one interviewee (head of music) floated the idea that a school effective in areas other than the arts might not find it easy to transfer that effectiveness to improvements in the arts. That it might be difficult for the arts to catch up would be due to lower levels of provision in the school, and a lack of group-work and working-together outcomes already cited for the arts. Other interviewees, however, indicated that an effective school, with support from the top, would impact on improving a declining arts department. A very appropriate analogy was offered by one of the interviewees on this direction of causality between arts involvement and school effectiveness. It speaks for itself:

> ... could you have successful arts in an inefficient school – that's the question presumably – you could have, but I don't imagine they are going to be as good ... can you have a good production in a badly run theatre? Yes, you could have. The actors will still come through, but if the lighting is poor, if the technical backup is not there, if the finance is not right, if the will isn't there, it's not going to be as good a production, is it? So yes, an effective school should enhance opportunities for the arts to thrive ... I am not saying they will, but they should; the two belong together, don't they? (deputy head).

As suggested in the introduction to this discussion (section 10.5.1), impacts of arts education on the whole school were related very much to transferable skills such as confidence and communication skills. One of the heads interviewed summed this up:

> Many of the skills are transferable skills to other subject areas in the curriculum and there's a large amount of critical analysis goes on within arts education – individual personal critical analysis as well as being critically analysing the outside world – and that gives strength to the students, because they begin to know themselves through the arts and their strengths and weaknesses, so I think the arts has a massive impact throughout the school ... (headteacher).

The head of music at the same school also added:

> ... and all of the extra skills that they are taking on and learning are so transferable, that that has gone on in school, and the kids have carried that round more than anyone else – more than the staff ever could – that that is dissipated through the arts, from the arts through the whole school. But the kids have got that they like working like that; they like this ethos of working with barriers down and enjoying themselves and working in groups and organising things themselves and all that, and they have taken it to other subjects and they do it everywhere now, so I think that's why it's become so successful (head of music).

The effective school was linked still further to some of the more creative outcomes of arts education, by a deputy head at another of the schools. Unprompted, he talked about risk-taking, creativity and a supportive environment as important facets of a 'healthy' school, citing arts education as particularly influential here. He concluded with:

> ... I think if a school is thriving on the arts side it would be an indicator that there's something fairly healthy going on in the school (deputy head).

10.6 CONCLUDING COMMENTS

The arts were seen by many teachers in senior management to impact on the whole school ethos, mainly by encouraging a positive atmosphere and enhancing enjoyment. Cross-department links were strengthened by such activities as school productions and shows – therefore referring to all the artforms, but especially drama. A bonding effect between pupils of different year groups was cited for music and art, and between staff and pupils for music at one particular school where staff learnt instruments too. A school's image could be enhanced by its arts involvements, through visible means – displays and concerts – and also through successful results at GCSE. Community and parents were involved to some extent in all of the case study schools. In addition, pupils were seen to become more involved in their community as a result of a positive arts education in school, although the culture of the surrounding environment had some influence here – for example the expectations of the Welsh culture that young people would join choirs and community events.

The links between arts education and the effective school tended to be related to those transferable outcomes from arts education such as communication skills, sense of responsibility, increased self-confidence, and a happier, more positive environment. Therefore, the effectiveness of the school focused very much on the micro-level affecting the whole – the personal development of individual pupils impacting on the overall school atmosphere.

While all the case study schools had good track records in the arts, for most it was not their policy to push the arts in particular – but rather to offer a broad and balanced curriculum. Offering the arts in this way seemed to resonate strongly with school effectiveness and improvement for many in senior management. However, whether it was always possible to create such a broad and balanced environment was highlighted by one head. He talked about how timetabling pressures, and pressures from the Government to enhance other areas of the curriculum, may dampen a school's capacity for change through the arts, because the arts could be squeezed out at key stage 4:

> *Well, it's very difficult with all the other elements that are being imposed upon us, it's very difficult to uphold the standard of promoting the arts. I look at the national grid for learning, the idea that ICT has come in ... technology has been a required subject ... the Government is now saying citizenship should be taught. There are all these elements that we are told 'You must do this, you must add this, you must involve this in the curriculum', and the curriculum gets more and more packed and it would be very easy to say 'Well, these* [the arts] *are not required subjects, so let's leave them out' ... and I would fight as hard as I could, but some subject areas are under pressure* (head).

However, he also went on to say:

> *... certainly at senior management level it's* [the arts] *never been something I have had to argue or defend. Even at the times when the Government were imposing more and more in terms of the National Curriculum, we have never had arguments about what is broad and balanced.*

The deputy head at this school also talked about the impact of the arts on a school's capacity for change. This capacity was deemed greater through involvement in the arts, because of its impact on changing people's *'attitudes and confidence'*: ' *... that for me is the most significant thing ... it brings about change in people ...'*. Thus, according to this perspective, the arts curriculum needs protecting and developing not only to secure outcomes at an individual level described in earlier chapters but also to facilitate collective and institutional outcomes that play a major part in fostering whole-school change and improvement.

Finally, it is worth recalling that whereas the teacher interviewees – perhaps more precisely, the senior management interviewees – postulated arts-related outcomes for the school and the wider community, the pupils did not identify such effects. While it is readily acknowledged that, because pupils' frames of reference would not normally embrace broader institutional outcomes, they could not be expected to identify effects relating to the whole school, it was conspicuous that although many of the staff's comments about benefits to the school alluded to transfer effects of the arts to other areas (e.g. increased motivation to school in general and better behaviour in general), the previous chapter could find little quantitative or qualitative evidence of transfers extending to the point that some teachers claimed in the current chapter.

In contrast, with regard to the notion of art itself as an outcome of arts education, it was the pupil voice that spoke louder than that of their teachers. Consequently, it may well be worth asking whether local and national policy makers, school governors and teachers have done enough to celebrate the art created in schools and whether there is mileage in greater investments in schools as the main arenas and resources in many communities for the production of art.

2.
WHAT ARE
THE EFFECTS
OF
ARTS
EDUCATION?

11. ARTS EFFECTS: OVERALL PERSPECTIVES

2.
WHAT ARE
THE EFFECTS
OF
ARTS
EDUCATION?

CHAPTER OVERVIEW

This chapter considers the overall perspectives of the effects of arts education as a whole. It is based on the separate accounts of broad effects given in the previous eight chapters. Using the evidence from the five case study schools, we discuss the frequencies with which the outcomes were identified and contrast the extent to which different artforms contributed to particular outcomes (11.2). We then pursue similar lines of enquiry in the evidence drawn from the wider and more representative sample of schools involved in the Year 11 Survey (11.3).

11.1 INTRODUCTION

In each of the last eight chapters, we have portrayed and discussed the different types of outcome contained within the overall model of effects that was postulated in Chapter 2. In this final chapter of Part Two, we take a more holistic and comparative look at the whole gamut of effects. This overall perspective is based on two main sources of data: firstly, the evidence from the interviews in the case study schools (section 11.2) and secondly, pupils' responses to Item 12 in the Year 11 questionnaire on the perceived effects of their arts courses (section 11.3).

When interpreting and especially comparing the results from these two sources, it is essential to bear in mind that there are major differences between them. The former source – the case study schools – were schools with strong reputations for arts provision and the pupils interviewed within them were performing well in at least one artform, whereas the schools in the Year 11 Survey were more indicative of secondary schools in general and all (attending) Year 11 pupils were asked to complete the questionnaire. Furthermore, as explained in Chapter 1, as a result of self-selection, it would seem likely that even the Year 11 Survey sample may have contained a slight bias to more arts-oriented schools. However, the main general point is that differences in the nature of these two pupil samples are considered to be highly relevant to explaining some appreciable variations in the results presented below.

The chapter concludes with an overview of the key points to emerge from this part of the research.

11.2 ARTS EFFECTS IN THE CASE STUDY SCHOOLS

As reported in Chapters 3 to 10, some of the effects and outcomes of arts education talked about by the pupils were found to be more dominant or significant than others. Overall, there was a fair degree of consistency in the emphasis placed on the seven different overall categories by both teachers and pupils, and also in the range of subcategory outcomes mentioned. However, pupils often mentioned subcategories of effects in addition to those talked about by teachers: for example in Chapter 7, pupils talked about voice projection, pronunciation, fluency, and the language skills needed for a variety of situations, in addition to the teacher-perceived areas of clarity, confidence, elocution and articulation. There appeared to be five key areas where the teachers' and pupils' views differed:

- unlike teachers, pupils seldom articulated effects on their thinking skills, and did not explicitly mention problem-solving skills (section 6.2);

- the pupil sample offered few references to the making of aesthetic judgements and, unlike the teachers, rarely spoke about the arts as 'aesthetic education' (section 4.4);

- pupils showed little awareness of the whole-school and community effects identified largely by school managers, though they did identify art as an outcome more than their teachers;

- while pupils and teachers alike volunteered accounts of transfer effects, especially from art and drama, pupils were not as expansive about the sphere of influence achieved by the perceived transfers as their teachers were; and

- while the teachers seemed to put most emphasis on personal and social skills being developed through the arts, pupils perceived most of their learning to be about artform-based technical skills and knowledge – with personal and social development coming second to knowledge and skills (see Table 11.1).

This latter finding may be a reflection of the way pupils perceive and receive the National Curriculum as being about learning artform knowledge and skills for each subject, and that, for the arts, in order to 'advance' to the next stage, acquisition of technical skill is deemed necessary (see section 4.5, where it is suggested that this is particularly the case for music). Although still significantly emphasised by the pupils, the impacts on pupils' personal and social development were seen as one of the driving forces of arts education by the teachers, and far less emphasis was placed on the acquisition of technical skill. One head of music's comment illustrates this, talking about the effects of arts education on pupils:

... it's always been highlighted up, this thing of ... teaching pupils, rather than teaching a subject and I think that is still the main thing that ... that we deal more with process than what the kids are doing in a lesson and how they are working, and how they are working with each other and how they are reacting to you, than really what's there. And it will still always be true, I think, that whatever they take away from the arts, when they are leaving GCSE it will not be, most importantly, what a crotchet is or the fact that they can organise a play. What they will take away is very much personal skills and interpersonal skills and that ability ... and I honestly think that that's the real strength of the arts is the fact that you are just developing students who can work independently, who can think for themselves ... or how they should work with other people, the way in which they should approach tasks ... (head of music).

However, this chapter is mostly concerned with the pupils' perceived effects, and it is to this that we now turn for the rest of our discussion. As well as there being more and less dominant effects perceived by the pupils, there were also differences in effects by artform – the three most focused on being art, drama and music. In order to give as fair a picture of dance as of the other artforms, variations were little emphasised since so few pupils in the sample took dance. Although the case study schools all had good track records in the arts, variations of effects for each artform by school were also found, indicating that there were different versions of drama, music and art, and this depended on how they were interpreted and taught and various other school factors. For some of the outcomes, there were signs of age-related developments in pupils' perceptions of effects. These were often related to the content of the curriculum, but clearly they also reflected pupils' own stage of personal and social development. By studying these carefully it was possible to see some links between the different types of effects, and how and where they interrelate at various stages in pupils' education. The following subsections explore each of these areas in turn, in order to provide an overview of the key findings so far.

11.2.1 Pupils' perceptions of the most dominant outcomes: overall frequencies of effects

By way of illustrating the overall frequencies of effects, this section offers two tables that show the number of references to the broad categories as set out in the chapter headings and the most common of the specific effects (or subcategories) as cited by pupils. The use of frequencies aims to provide a general or broad-brush sense of the most and least dominant outcomes in terms of amounts of citations received.

One difficulty with collating a numerical representation for each effect was that of multiple coding, which was used in order to cater for interview responses that raised more than one effect. Another difficulty with comparing frequencies in the broad categories was that some contained many more subcategories of effects than others. Hence Tables 11.1 and 11.2 must both be taken together and interpreted only as illustrative of the discussions in the respective chapters.

Table 11.1   Frequency of broad categories

Chapter	Broad categories of effects	N
4.	Arts knowledge and skills	1177
8.	Personal and social development	736
3.	Intrinsic immediate effects: enjoyment and therapy	371
9.	Extrinsic transfer effects	363
7.	Communication and expressive skills	356
6.	Creativity and thinking skills	199
5.	Knowledge in the social and cultural domains	98
10.	Effects on the school, the community and the arts	15
	NB 4. is made up of:	
	Technical skills	*871*
	Knowledge, understanding and appreciation	*306*

Table 11.2   Frequency of subcategories of effects

Section	Subcategories of effects	N
4.5	Developments in technical skills and capabilities for each artform *General developments in technical skills: 442* *Specified developments in technical skills: 429*	871
3.2	The enjoyment outcome	308
8.8	Improved social skills *Social skills for group/team work: 167* *Social opportunities/better relationships: 79*	246
8.4	Increased self-confidence	242
7.5	Developments in expressive skills *Empowering expression: 187* *The arts as tools for expression: 35* *Enabling choice of tools/expression: 1*	223
4.2	Knowledge and understanding of the artform and its context *Knowledge of the artform: 173* *Critical skills/studies: 22* *Knowledge of the artform in context: 17*	212

Table 11.2 (continued)

Section	Subcategories of effects	N
6.3	Development of creativity and imagination	184
9.3	Transferring effects to employment and work	173
9.4	Transfer to leisure time *Leisure: 79* *Extra-curricular activities: 56* *Transfer to 'life': 29*	164
8.5	Developing the whole personality	108
9.2	Transfer to other areas of learning and general academic performance	107
8.7	Increased awareness of others and empathy	106
3.3	The therapeutic outcome (relaxation, escapism, de-stressing)	86
4.4	Appreciation of the artform and aesthetic judgement making *Extending appreciation and positive attitudes: 72* *Making aesthetic judgements: 8* *Awareness of cross-arts continuities and differences: 4*	84
7.4	Developments in skills of critical and active listening and observation	77
8.3	Enhanced self-worth and self-esteem	70
5.4	Awareness of social and moral issues	57
8.2	Developing a sense of self and one's emotions	54
7.3	Language development	40
5.2	Increased knowledge of the cultural domain	26
7.2	Developments in interactive communication skills	21
8.6	Improved personal skills (independence, responsibility)	20
5.3	Awareness of pupils' surroundings and their place within them	15
6.2	Development of thinking and problem-solving skills	15
10.4	Art itself as an outcome	13
4.3	Interpretative skills	10
10.2	Effects on the school	1
10.3	Effects on the community	1

(N does not necessarily sum to N in 11.1, since Table 11.2 includes citations where multiple codings have been allowed.)

Table 11.1 clearly shows that effects relating to pupils' 'arts knowledge and skills' (Chapter 4) received substantially more references than any other broad category, and that 'personal and social development' also received a large number of citations. The note at the bottom of Table 11.1 highlights that the overall category 4 included the whole range of comments on both knowledge and skills – arguably the largest and most influential areas of the National Curriculum in music and art – and hence, it was not surprising that there were more comments in this field.

Table 11.2 shows, however, that the main reason for the top ranking of 'arts knowledge and skills' was the high frequency of the subcategory of 'developments in technical skills and capabilities'. It is clear from Chapter 4 that pupils perceived a large amount of their learning in the arts at school to be about gaining skills in the artform and learning about the tools of the trade and how to use them. They also made many general references to improvements in their capabilities (included in the 'general developments in technical skills' score in Table 11.2). As already alluded to in the introduction to section 11.2, pupils perceive first and foremost the effects of arts education to be about learning 'in and about' the arts, with the personal and social impacts on themselves as learners, as well as all other forms of outcome, perceived as secondary to this principal effect.

While Table 11.1 shows that 'personal and social development' was the second highest broad category, Table 11.2 indicates that this was largely due to increases in 'self-confidence' (section 8.4) and in developments in skills for group work and social relationships (section 8.8). Other subcategories of effects relating to this overall broad outcome received less mention – the next highest being 'developments on the whole personality' (section 8.5).

From Table 11.1, we can see that the immediate and intrinsic effects related to enjoyment and therapy (Chapter 3), transfer effects (Chapter 9) (including comments about leisure time and transfer to the future world of work and employment) and communication and expressive skills (Chapter 7) received a similar number of references. Table 11.2 shows however, that as a subcategory of the overall broad category for intrinsic effects, 'enjoyment outcomes' received more comment than the highest of the separate subcategories for personal and social development, making this a particularly important outcome for pupils. Table 11.2 indicates that a substantial amount of the citations for transfer effects are attributable to pupils' references to the future and out-of-school activities, as opposed to transfer to other subject areas – although this was still important.

Creativity and thinking skills (Chapter 6) were cited substantially less often than communication and expressive skills. Looked at from both tables, it can be seen that the high frequency associated with developments in communication and expressive skills is due to the higher number of comments about expressive skills and self-expression (as discussed in Chapter 7) and that this was more than that for creativity and thinking as a whole. Knowledge in the social and cultural domains (Chapter 5) received a smaller number of references than the whole of the knowledge, understanding and appreciation elements of Category 4 (see note at the bottom of Table 11.1). Indeed, as pointed out in Chapter 5, and as Table 11.2 indicates, increased knowledge in the cultural domain (section 5.2) was talked about far less than knowledge of the artform, and received a similar number of comments to the critical studies element of knowledge and understanding of the artforms (section 4.2) (26 comments and 22 comments respectively). Despite its emphasis in the National Curriculum, pupils rarely talked about any aspects of their arts education related to the cultural domain.

2.
WHAT ARE
THE EFFECTS
OF
ARTS
EDUCATION?

Despite the large body of overall comment on personal and social development, pupils made surprisingly little reference to any personal qualities and skills, such as organisation, sense of responsibility, and developing independence, in relation to their arts education experiences.

Finally, we can note that pupils very rarely mentioned any perceived effects on the school, the community or on the arts as outcomes in themselves – although, as was noted in Chapter 10, pupils stressed this latter point more than did the teachers.

In terms of the broad frequencies of testimonies to the effects of arts education, the pupil and teacher data are generally compatible. Notwithstanding this, different artforms produced notable variation in perceived effects; and, significantly, in each of the arts subjects, certain categories of outcome did not emerge. It is to this that we turn in the following section of this chapter.

11.2.2 Variations in effects by artform

As discussed in each chapter of Part Two, certain of the broad categories varied by artform – and this became particularly apparent at the subcategory level, in terms of perceptions of how the effect functioned, and the significance attached to it. As can be seen in the brief overview of each artform that follows, no single artform appeared to provide the full canon of effects. However, while many of the comments were about specific artforms – art, dance, drama or music, and sometimes English – a number of the pupils also made comments about the arts in general, or a general comment that was not specific enough to be counted in one of the artforms. While this cannot be taken to be a picture of the arts overall, it is interesting to compare Figure 11.1 with the overall frequencies of effects in Table 11.2 – the skills and knowledge base of the arts being noticeably less emphasised.

For each of the artforms below, the six most frequently referred to effects are given, and for art, drama and music, these all had nominations of 50 or above. (Note, though, that the last effect given for music had just under 50 nominations.) For dance, there was an overall lower frequency of nominations of effects, due to the lower number of pupils taking this subject. However, the six most frequently cited effects had frequencies of between seven and 60 (thus reflecting a similar proportion of comments to pupils taking that artform, i.e. the lower limit of seven comments to 26 dance pupils is similar to 50 comments for the 180 pupils taking art). Some of the least mentioned effects (three or under mentions in the pupil case study data) are also given at the bottom of each of Figures 11.1 to 11.5, in non-italicised print. For all artforms, effects on the whole school ethos and on parents and community were only mentioned once each – in the 'arts in general' section, but this consistency across the arts is not tabulated here, in order to make room for other effects.

Figure 11.1   Effects from the arts in general

Effects most often mentioned
Increased self-confidence (8.4)
The enjoyment outcome (3.2)
Improved social skills (8.8)
Development of creativity and imagination (6.3)
Developments in expressive skills (7.5)
Developments in technical skills and capabilities (4.5)

Effects least often mentioned
Improved personal skills (8.6)
Awareness of pupils' surroundings and their place within them (5.3)
Interpretative skills (4.3)
Art itself as an outcome (10.4)

(NB In each of Figures 11.1–11.5, the most and least often mentioned effects are given in rank order: most mentioned, first; least mentioned, last. Numbers in brackets indicate sections in the report where each effect is presented.)

The most significant effect claimed for the arts in general was that of increased self-confidence, with enjoyment outcomes also being mentioned frequently. Improved social skills, creativity, imagination and expressive skills also proved to be frequently commented on. Although still scoring highly in pupil citations, technical skills and capabilities were perhaps mentioned less often here, because such references would be more likely to be artform-specific. Indeed, it is perhaps not surprising that developments in confidence, social skills and enjoyment outcomes are all mentioned the most frequently without being artform-specific, although, as we have seen in previous chapters, different types of social and personal development, and enjoyment are also associated with different artforms.

Figure 11.2 Effects from art

2.
WHAT ARE
THE EFFECTS
OF
ARTS
EDUCATION?

Effects most often mentioned

Developments in technical skills and capabilities (4.5)

Enjoyment outcomes (3.2)

Expressive skills (7.5)

Knowledge and understanding of the artform and its context (4.2)

Development of creativity and imagination (6.3)

Transferring effects to employment and work (9.3)

Effects least often mentioned

Developments in interactive communication skills (7.2)

Development of thinking and problem-solving skills (6.2)

Awareness of social and moral issues (5.4)

Language development (7.3)

Not surprisingly, developments in skills and capabilities were referred to the most frequently in art, as indeed they were in all of the artforms. In Chapter 4, the pupils placed much emphasis on learning to use the tools of the trade in art – such as colour, and tone and light. Enjoyment outcomes were always high for art, in each of the sub-outcomes identified within section 3.2, except for the specific outcome of 'fun', where drama received more comments.

There was not a focus in pupils' accounts for art developing communication skills (sections 7.2 and 7.3), thinking skills (section 6.2), or an awareness of social and moral issues (section 5.4). Although ranked fairly low amongst overall effects, art was, however, mentioned more often than any of the other artforms with regard to developing pupils' awareness of their surroundings (section 5.3).

Interestingly, there was somewhat of a focus in pupils' comments on the transfer of skills from art to the world of work, and as discussed in Chapter 9, these were related to specific art skills, such, as the ability to draw neatly and to design things.

Figure 11.3 Effects from dance

Effects most often mentioned

Developments in technical skills and capabilities for each artform (4.5)

The enjoyment outcome (3.2)

Improved social skills (8.8)

Development of creativity and imagination (6.3)

Increased self-confidence (8.4)

Transfer to leisure time (9.4)

Effects least often mentioned

Developing a sense of self and one's emotions (8.2)

Awareness of social and moral issues (5.4)

Art itself as an outcome (10.4)

Awareness of pupils' surroundings and their place within them (5.3)

Interpretative skills (4.3)

Developments in interactive communication skills (7.2)

(NB all of these had null mentions for dance)

2.
WHAT ARE
THE EFFECTS
OF
ARTS
EDUCATION?

Pupils perceived one of the main effects of dance education to be the developments in technical skills and capabilities associated with their dance lessons – specific types of dance movement, as well as more general comments on increased movement and motor skills. Also included in this were references to the physical aspect of dance, with pupils remarking on the benefits to health and fitness, as well as being more aware of their bodies.

There was little mention, however, of any increases in knowledge about the artform (section 4.2) and very little pertaining to the social and cultural domains (Chapter 5). Neither did pupils perceive any effects of dance relating to communication skills (section 7.2), or, surprisingly, in developing a sense of one's emotions (section 8.2). Empathy and valuing others did, however, receive some mention (section 8.7), as well as pupils evaluating and critiquing others' work in general ways (section 4.2). Expressive skills in dance were not far behind the six top outcomes listed above.

The frequency of pupils' comments on transfer to extra-curricular and leisure time, is perhaps indicative of the appeal of dance to young people at this age, as well as the popularity of after/before school clubs in some of the schools.

2.
WHAT ARE
THE EFFECTS
OF
ARTS
EDUCATION?

Figure 11.4 Effects from drama

> **Effects most often mentioned**
>
> *Developments in technical skills and capabilities (4.5)*
> *Improved social skills (8.8)*
> *Increased self-confidence (8.4)*
> *Increased awareness of others and empathy (8.7)*
> *The enjoyment outcome (3.2)*
> *Developments in expressive skills (7.5)*
>
> **Effects least often mentioned**
>
> Awareness of pupils' surroundings and their place within them (5.3)
> Art itself as an outcome (10.4)
> Interpretative skills (4.3)
> Increased knowledge of the cultural domain (5.2)

Although technical skills were mentioned the most frequently of all the effects for drama, they were cited less than in either music or art. For drama, such comments related to techniques and methods such as role play and improvisation. In comparison with art, drama was associated far more with the personal and social outcomes of Category 8 (three of drama's top six most frequently mentioned effects belonging to this overall category). Increased self-confidence (section 8.4) was perhaps the most significant outcome for drama – having almost four times as many comments than in music, and even more than that compared with art. This particular subcategory of effects did not appear in the top six for either music or art.

Although still in the top six perceived outcomes for drama, enjoyment was mentioned less in this subject than in either music or art. However, drama was associated with expressive effects, more so than was music, but less so than in art. Interestingly, though, drama seemed much less related to the outcomes of creativity and imagination than had been the case in art. Hence, any link between creativity, freedom and self-expression would be difficult to deduce from the evidence garnered so far in art and drama.

Communication skills (Chapter 7) were more associated with drama than any other artform, although interestingly they came below any of the transfer effects (sections 9.2, 9.3 and 9.4) and developing the whole personality (section 8.5), as outcomes for drama. However, when added together, communication skills and language/speech development (sections 7.2 and 7.3) had similar numbers of mentions as these other subcategories, but not more.

Unlike in art and music, knowledge and understanding of the artform seemed a less accentuated effect in drama (ranking sixteenth in effects perceived for drama), and knowledge in the cultural domains had just two comments (section 5.2). Drama did, however, receive a large body of comment on social and moral issues (section 5.4), by far the most in all the artforms, and it ranked just below the expressive outcomes given in Figure 11.4. However, as we shall see in section 11.2.4, this effect varied across the schools.

Figure 11.5: Effects from music

Effects most often mentioned
Developments in technical skills and capabilities (4.5)
Knowledge and understanding of the artform and its context (4.2)
The enjoyment outcome (3.2)
Transfer to leisure time (9.4)
Improved social skills (team work elements) (8.8)
Developments in skills of active listening and observation (7.4)
Effects least often mentioned
Interpretative skills (4.3)
Awareness of social and moral issues (5.4)
Language development (7.3)
Developments in interactive communication skills (7.2)
Awareness of pupils' surroundings and their place within them (5.3)

The strong emphasis in music on knowledge and skill-based outcomes (sections 4.5 and 4.2) reflects a different type of perceived outcome in music compared with the other artforms. This was discussed in Chapter 4 as pupils perceiving their learning in music to be 'learning about' the rudiments of music – the notes, the orchestra, 12-bar blues and so on, and comparatively little on 'learning how', to compose, for example, and what techniques to employ. This linked very much with discussion in Chapter 6 on creativity, where, in general, pupils were found to talk about creativity in conjunction with composition only at a later stage in their secondary schooling, perhaps not until Year 9. There were, however, school differences here, and these are discussed further in section 11.2.4.

The emphasis on the perceived transfer of skill and enthusiasm to leisure and extra-curricular activities (section 9.4) was interesting in music (where there had not been this focus in drama, even though all the schools had good track records in drama productions and school shows). For music, this perhaps relates to the strong ethos in most, if not all, of the case study schools on school music ensembles, and in many cases, learning to play an instrument. One headteacher raised a very important point in this respect, which is perhaps pertinent to more schools than just his own:

I have a feeling that there is possibly, at times, too much emphasis upon extra-curricular music at the expense of what happens in the curriculum, and I think there's a correlation between that statement and the lower number of pupils choosing GCSE music, and that's an [important] issue ... how do you raise the numbers choosing music at key stage 4 ...? (headteacher).

Several other members of senior management across the case study schools also raised this issue, talking about how music could be seen as 'elitist':

... so music has been a less popular option and I wonder whether that's because it's seen as more of an elitist subject – unless you are very good at it, you don't do it – which certainly isn't the case in drama and isn't the case with art: a complete cross-section of pupils will choose to do those ... (deputy head).

The pupils' perceived emphasis on extra-curricular activity, then, perhaps has some bearing on the high mention of improved social skills in music (section 8.8) – since pupils were playing music in groups outside of school hours, as well as composing and working together in lessons. It is of note, though, that this particular outcome (section 8.8) was nowhere near as significant as it was in drama, but it was much more prominent than in art (both in terms of number of nominations and ranking).

Unlike in drama, the emotional development (section 8.2) and other personal and social development areas of Chapter 8 featured less in pupils' comments about music, and were more similar in terms of number of mentions to those in art.

Although communication and interpretative skills (as depicted by sections 4.3, 7.2 and 7.3) received little mention for outcomes relating to music, active listening (section 7.4) was a significant perceived effect here, perhaps indicating something of a critical aspect to music 'appreciation' that had not previously been found in the subcategory discussions in sections 4.2, 4.3 and 4.4. This often referred to listening with concentration, or being able to hear more parts in the music, but was also related by pupils to listening in other areas of life, or other subject areas (see section 7.4).

Overall, then, there was a very strong emphasis in pupils' discourse about their learning in the arts on gains in technical skills and capabilities. This was at slight odds with the teachers' comments, which tended to reflect more the social and personal development of pupils, but was way above the number of pupil nominations for other subcategories, apart from in drama, where social skills and self-confidence ranked a close second and third in terms of frequency of comments. However, to the questions on '*What is learning in the arts for or what are the arts about?*', pupils often mentioned expression and creativity (see Chapters 6 and 7), expanding in a more general way about their whole arts experience, but giving artform-specific examples. That enjoyment occurs within the top six subcategories of effects for each of the individual artforms places this outcome firmly at the centre of pupils' arts education experiences – undoubtedly, a positive and affirming outcome for all involved in arts education, though it should be remembered that the data is drawn from pupils performing well in at least one artform.

It is noticeable from Figures 11.1 to 11.5 that pupils rarely perceived outcomes of arts education in relation to their surroundings or their place in the world, and that cultural and contextual awareness was also an area given little weight. This seems to suggest a focus by pupils on skills and knowledge rather narrower than that aspired to by either their teachers or the National Curriculum Orders. In contrast, the personal and social development outcomes perceived by pupils – particularly important in drama – and the potential for art for self-expression could perhaps require further attention in curriculum design and delivery.

In summary, different artforms produced notable variation in perceived effects. Certain effects undoubtedly emerged only from examples of high-calibre teaching, but an overarching implication of the variability in outcomes between artforms clearly seems to suggest that a comprehensive arts education requires a contribution from all arts subjects. In corroboration of this, one headteacher, talking about criteria for effective arts education, said:

> *I would have thought that criteria are different subject to subject, because if the criteria are all the same, you could say that they were interchangeable, and to some extent they are, because if we believe that an arts experience is worthwhile in statutory education, which we do, then to some degree they are interchangeable, so we would be arguing that music is valid for some people, art is valid for others and drama is valid for others and you then have to give the element of choice. But I think there are some basic criteria, I suppose, for all three, but then within that context there are major differences. The student that goes on to do drama is going to get a very different experience from the student who does fine art and similarly music … (headteacher).*

11.2.3 Variations in effects by school

Obviously, perceived effects within artforms could vary by school, depending on a number of factors including the teacher's individual approach, ethos and interpretation of priorities within the subject, as well as facilities and resources. School variations were particularly noticeable in drama, but also in music where one school took a different approach to the others in many respects, and in art where there were slight variations in pupils' emphases on outcomes relating to skill, but more so in connection with effects of transfer to jobs and the future, where one school stood out in this respect. Such variations have given rise to what we have called different types of dramas, musics and arts. It was difficult to detect any such variations in dance, since so few pupils took it in comparison to the other artforms. Many of the school differences have been detailed in each of the previous chapters, but the following brief discussion gives a flavour of some of these dramas, musics and arts, as depicted by the pupils' perceptions of effects. Further detail is presented on specific examples of artforms from the case study schools in Chapter 13 in Part Three.

Drama

Of all the artforms, school differences in pupils' perceived effects were most noticeable in drama – and this is perhaps not surprising considering the greater curriculum flexibility afforded to this subject compared with music and art. It was also found that drama elicited a wider range of response from teachers on effects – the process/product paradigm of the arts being most pronounced for this artform, with comments from teachers at both extremes of the spectrum. Although most schools emphasised skills and processes in terms of pupils' perceptions, at one of the schools it was the product, productions, and stage and theatre 'acting' skills that were more prevalent in pupils' comments (section 4.5). In contrast, another of the schools emphasised the outcomes of awareness of social, moral and real-life issues to a significantly greater extent than was illustrated by pupils' perceptions in the other schools. In direct association with this, pupils at this school also talked about developments in empathy, valuing others and their work, and others' feelings (section 8.7) quite a bit more than they did in the other schools. Enjoyment was not related any more significantly to either of these 'dramas', but in fact was highest in another of the schools, where teamwork, expressive skills and communication all received slightly higher numbers of comments. However, this latter point was not significant enough to warrant making any direct or causal links between such effects.

Music

While two schools demonstrated that there were different 'dramas', with other emphases at the other schools also, one of the case study schools in particular illustrated a different 'music'. Pupils talked about enjoyment slightly more than at the other schools, and in addition they also talked about skills and knowledge, and not only the 'rudiments' of music, right from Year 7. This was reflected in their comments about 'tone' in music, with the emphasis on skills relating to creativity and composition, rather than learning the basics *per se*. The popularly perceived effect of active listening was particularly prevalent, with a critical element illustrated by some comments on evaluating others' work in music. As pointed out in Chapter 4, there was little comment on appreciation (critical skills element) of music at this school, rather the focus of pupil comment being on a straightforward enjoyment aspect – perhaps indicating a more accessible type of music here. This was indicated by the pupils' enthusiasm for using computers and technology in music – both boys and girls making comments to this effect. The links between technical skills (development and improvement), enjoyment and self-expression (as suggested in Chapter 7) are somewhat portrayed by this school's 'music', although creativity and freedom would perhaps be more appropriate in place of self-expression. Indeed, other schools' 'musics' could be likened to this model of developments in technical skills relating to enjoyment, with group work and creativity perhaps seeming a slightly more important factor in this than expressive skills. As an example, another of the school's 'musics' was more heavily skills-oriented in pupils' perceptions, with a focus on artform knowledge and contextual knowledge perhaps having a bearing on extended appreciation of music, not articulated in the first case study school cited in this discussion.

Art

In art, different types were more evident in pupils' perceptions of skill – one school having a higher number of citations on colour, tone and light than the other schools (section 4.5), as well as more comment by pupils on being creative, experimenting and using their imagination (Chapter 6) and being able to express themselves (Chapter 7). This was perhaps a reflection of their perceived technical capabilities, by Year 11 comments relating to being more individually creative, expressive and free than in previous years. Transfer of such artistic skills to jobs and leisure was particularly emphasised by pupils at this school, reflecting either or both of their location (London) with proximity to many galleries and so on, or their teacher's, and hence their own, enthusiasm for art at this school. Another of the schools also had this expressive and individual flavour to art, but the pupils gave slightly less emphasis to creativity, and more to knowledge about the artform. This is not to suggest that these are two opposing outcomes of arts education – knowledge and creativity (there is no evidence to suggest this from any of the schools, or all the schools combined) – but that in fact they are both important, and almost definitely reflect a different teacher's approach in the arts – at this school pupils talking much more about skills of observation and interpretation of works of art.

Variations in effects by school: summary

Different types of drama, music and art, then, were found in each of the case study schools – although some highlighted these more than others. School variations in drama were most prevalent in focus on the skills versus the social domains, as well as in the dichotomy of process and product in drama – which the pupils experienced to varying degrees depending on individual teacher's values in respect of this. This was portrayed in the different types of 'content' being taught – social and real-life issues at one school, Shakespeare and plays at another school. In contrast, different types of music were reflected in the pupils' perceived effects in the fields of creativity and composition, relating to technical skills and capabilities – and, importantly, at what stage they perceived such outcomes to come into effect. School variations in art were again seen in the areas of technical skills, but also in powers of self-expression.

Before moving on to the final discussion within this subcategory, other important issues to consider within school and artform differences were the teacher and pupil variations in definitions – in particular of creative and expressive skills, as highlighted in the conclusions of each of Chapters 6 and 7. In Chapter 6, a wide variety of individual and idiosyncratic comments was found on creativity and thinking skills from both teachers and pupils. Pupils, for example, talked about creativity as freedom, experimentation, imagination, thinking new thoughts, and links with self-expression, but, although references were made to becoming more creative, their descriptions rarely suggested any sequential and/or progressive development in 'creativity' as a competence or cognitive process – as had been hinted at by the teachers. In Chapter 7, comments on expressive skills also varied. For teachers, they were about the application of technical skills to personal and expressive statements, and also to a set of positive attitudes and predispositions in young people to be expressive. On the other hand, pupils talked about expressive skills in terms of being able to express in the arts things that they might not otherwise be able to, to express their feelings, but not really to make personal statements, or to make choices of tools for expression – the focus of self-expression being on empowering rather than enabling.

11.2.4 Variations in effects with age

In response to the longitudinal nature of the research, each of Chapters 3 to 10, pertaining to the broad categories of perceived effects, reported variations in effects by age, and in particular referred to any general developments in pupils' perceptions as they progressed through secondary school. In so doing, it was possible to begin to interrelate some of the effects, through their knock-on element to other effects. It was particularly in the areas of skill and knowledge, and individuality of working style, that similar comments tended to occur at similar ages in the pupil sample across all of the schools. From this, aspects of creativity and expressive skills could also be seen to interrelate with each of the other effects. Obviously there were some differences, by artform, school, and with individual pupils, but some general patterns did emerge.

It was apparent that knowledge and skill outcomes for the arts were highlighted across all year groups, but were more focused on 'learning about' in Years 7 and 8. Pupils in Year 9 began to talk more about creativity and their own compositions in art and music, with those in Years 10 and 11 emphasising their own individual work across all the artforms. In drama, learning 'how' to use techniques was mentioned right from Year 7, whereas music rarely had this 'how' effect until Year 9. (Some school differences were expanded in section 11.2.3.) For art and music, these findings seem to reflect very much an increase in individuality of work with age, perhaps not surprising as pupils concentrate on the individual preparation of work for portfolios and GSCE assessment submissions in Years 10 and 11. This is not to say, though, that the arts purport or necessitate a progression of 'learning about' before 'learning how' (although this did seem to be more the case in music at many of the schools) – it simply reflects much of the content of the National Curriculum and what is taught when. A further example of this was found in the way pupils perceived outcomes relating to social awareness at a younger age than they did cultural awareness (sections 5.2 and 5.4). As suggested in Chapter 5, this probably echoes pupils' ability to access the social domain more easily at a younger age, but may also be a reflection of what is being taught at what age.

The individual nature of many of the Year 7 pupils' comments needs further exploration here. In looking for progressions in pupils' development in arts education, we must be aware that, in this research, we are taking Year 7 as the baseline from which to track pupils' perceived effects. It must not be forgotten, however, that pupils come to secondary school with varying experiences, including their arts experiences, and hence some of the most idiosyncratic (and therefore sometimes most illuminating) comments have come from those pupils in Year 7 – for example, the suggested link between technical skills, enjoyment and self-expression being 'circular', coming from one pupil in Year 7 (see section 7.5). A further feature of Year 7 comments was the high incidence of references to extrinsic and instrumental purposes, particularly noted by younger pupils as an effect of their arts education generally. Although this study is almost exclusively concerned with arts education in the secondary phase, many of the Year 7 pupils' comments intensify concerns about the level of technical skills in the arts at the end of key stage 2 and about the poor quality of pupils' understanding of the purposes of the arts curriculum on entering key stage 3.

Notwithstanding this, developments in pupils' perceptions of effects of arts education were apparent, and helped to relate effects with one another, and also to point out where they were distinct and different. Thus, the differences between Year 7, Year 9 and Year 11 responses about art produced evidence to suggest that technical skills (section 4.5) and knowledge, understanding and appreciation of the artform (sections 4.2, 4.3 and 4.4) were very much the building blocks to achieve effects in the domain of creativity (section 6.3) and expressive skills (section 7.5) – more dominant in Year 9, and slightly more so in Year 11. Having said this, though, it was clear from discussion in Chapter 6, that pupils also perceived creativity in the arts right from the start of secondary school. This is not to view it simply as an adjunct to knowledge and skill, but developing and progressing alongside knowledge and skill. Indeed, pupils in Years 9, 10 and 11 were found to work in a much more individual way (due to the nature of GCSE assessment), and hence comments such as *'being more creative'*, *'doing my own thing'* became more prevalent by key stage 4. What was particularly noticeable in art was the way the number of comments on the relaxing and therapeutic potential of art (section 3.3) increased as pupils got older – perhaps indicating the need for different types of working and thinking, especially during the GCSE years. As pointed out in Chapter 3, the pupils' allusions to the different shifts in physical and psychological functioning offered by arts subjects, noted most in art, represent an important reminder of the need for breadth and balance in learning processes, as well as in curriculum content.

By contrast, in drama, not surprisingly, nominated effects appeared to cluster particularly around social skills (section 8.8) right from Year 7, with awareness of others (section 8.7) and developments in self-confidence (section 8.4) also cited. In connection with this, Year 7 pupils were slightly more likely to offer comments about developments in communication (sections 7.2 and 7.3) – presumably relating to increased levels of confidence – and probably as part of a two-way direction of causality. Self-expression (section 7.5) did not, however, receive much mention until Year 9, and understanding of others' emotions (part of 8.7) was much more prevalent at Year 9 than in previous years, again suggesting that arts effects are in some way linked to a maturation process. Developments in technical skills ('techniques' for drama) were mentioned in force not until Year 8, with group work being mentioned just slightly more in Year 7 than in Year 8 and the older years. This perhaps correlates with the way in which teachers work with Year 7 in drama, but may also be a reflection of pupils' growing confidence to work with new people, in groups, as compared say with their previous Year 6 experience.

**2.
WHAT ARE
THE EFFECTS
OF
ARTS
EDUCATION?**

Like art, it appeared in music that pupils perceived technical skills and learning 'about' music to be the building blocks to future creativity, although as already discussed, knowledge and skill were not expressly seen by pupils as precursors to creativity. It was clear, however, that composition and, probably in direct relation to this, teamwork and group work skills, were not mentioned as a focus of the pupils outcomes really until Year 9 – although there were school differences here.

As already intimated, the relationships between developments in technical skill, enjoyment and self-expression – or perhaps creativity, as the pupils' comments would tend more to suggest – are not that of one skill 'waiting' for another to be developed but, as the pupil in Chapter 7 said, more of a cycle of effects, feeding one into the other. The relationship, however, between levels of self-confidence and technical capabilities may be a little more directional. Certainly, while pupils perceived their levels of self-confidence to increase in drama right from Year 7 (see 8.4), they appeared to develop confidence in art and music only as they progressed through key stage 3 and into key stage 4. Their comments would suggest that, for music in particular, levels of self-confidence may be associated with perceived ability in the subject, and hence this would impinge on the often purported viewpoint of the 'arts as accessible to all', as highlighted in particular by the teachers in Chapters 4, 8 and 10. Despite the 'all can do' attitude purported for the arts in Chapter 10, it was apparent from some of the pupils' comments on knowledge and skill in Chapter 4, and also in Chapter 8 on sense of self-worth and achievement, that music in particular was not always viewed as accessible to all, but rather, slightly set apart as perhaps for the talented. However, since most, if not all of the pupils expressed the view that the arts allowed for the development of creativity and expressive skills through participation right from Year 7, the accessibility of the arts, irrespective of ability but rather in relation to participation, was upheld.

To conclude, it is appropriate to return to the purposes of creating a typology of effects – which was to create distinct and discrete 'pockets' of effects as far as possible in order only to help categorise, discuss and report a vast amount of data collected over three years. It was not to try and separate what, in many ways, are inseparable effects concerning the personal and social development of pupils at a time of change in their lives; nor was it to try and knit them back together. Rather, it is clear from the sometimes complex discussions involved in Part Two of this report that many of these effects relate and interrelate with and around each other. Further, although the pupils in the sample were very much favourably disposed towards at least one of the artforms, their perceptions were not always coloured by their capabilities in the subject, but rather, they perceived the possibilities for the arts to allow for creativity and expressive skills to develop – these two being the most popular answers to the question – *What is learning in the arts for at this school?*

11.3 ARTS EFFECTS IN A WIDER SAMPLE OF SCHOOLS

To explore how pupils in general across a sample of more representative schools perceived the effects of their arts education at secondary school, the Year 11 questionnaire included a question on this issue (see Appendix I). The impact of the arts subjects on pupils was examined by asking the Year 11 respondents to circle as many of the 12 proposed effects of studying each subject (throughout their entire time at secondary school, Year 7–11) as were applicable. They were asked, *What have **you** got out of studying these subjects during your time at secondary school?*, and were provided with a list of proposed effects, derived from interviews with teachers and pupils in the case study schools (Harland *et al.*, 1998). Table 11.3 presents the percentages of the whole sample of pupils that circled each proposed outcome for a particular arts subject, and the ranking received for each outcome within a subject area.

Table 11.3 Pupils' perceptions of the learning outcomes for each of the arts subjects studied at secondary school (Years 7–11). Percentages of whole sample

I think taking this subject at school ...	Art %	Art Rank	Dance %	Dance Rank	Drama %	Drama Rank	Music %	Music Rank	English %	English Rank
Teaches particular skills	33	[3]	11	[2]	21	[4]	22	[1]	30	[2]
Gives you confidence socially/ helps you get on with people	8	[10]	9	[4]	31	[1]	7	[8]	7	[11]
Helps you to feel good about yourself	15	[6]	7	[7]	15	[7]	9	[6]	6	[12]
Helps you learn in other subjects	5	[11]	1	[12]	6	[12]	3	[11]	25	[4]
Helps you to think and clarifies your thinking	11	[9]	2	[10]	9	[11]	6	[10]	24	[5]
Helps you to understand people's feelings and emotions	12	[8]	4	[8]	21	[4]	9	[6]	33	[1]
Helps with a future job or career	15	[6]	3	[9]	10	[10]	7	[8]	21	[6]
Gives you knowledge of the art form and appreciation of people's work in it	38	[2]	8	[6]	14	[9]	16	[4]	20	[8]
Helps you express yourself better	21	[5]	9	[4]	24	[3]	12	[5]	19	[9]
Gives you a sense of pleasure/ enjoyment/satisfaction	32	[4]	10	[3]	20	[6]	19	[2]	13	[10]
Helps you learn more about social issues and problems	2	[12]	2	[10]	15	[7]	2	[12]	21	[6]
Helps you to be more creative/ imaginative	49	[1]	12	[1]	28	[2]	19	[2]	28	[3]
No Response	39		79		60		63		46	

N = 2,269

NB *Respondents could give more than one response, so percentages will not sum to 100 per cent.*
Source: NFER 'The Effects and Effectiveness of Arts Education' Year 11 Survey, student questionnaire

A very noticeable feature is that for each arts subject there was a high percentage of pupils giving no response to this question, most especially for dance, where 79 per cent gave no response, but also music (63 per cent) and drama (60 per cent). English and art produced a response from a greater number of pupils, though the non-response rate was still high, 46 per cent and 39 per cent respectively. From the data produced, it is not clear to what extent the non-responses are attributable to pupils feeling the subject had no or negligible impact on them, or due to irregular or insufficient time being made available for the subject. It is hard to avoid the conclusion, however, that a majority of students felt that three of the artforms – dance, music and drama – generated none of the pre-selected outcomes.

2.
WHAT ARE
THE EFFECTS
OF
ARTS
EDUCATION?

Clearly, the dance and perhaps drama percentages for non-responding pupils may, to some degree, be an outcome of the limited time afforded these subjects at many schools – insufficient perhaps to generate significant levels of perceived impact. Music, however, could hardly claim the same mitigating circumstances. Its high non-response percentage, combined with it showing the lowest ratio of nominations relative to the number of pupils that responded to this question (3.5:1) suggests that, generally, music produced (comparative to other arts subjects) fewer perceived effects on pupils, both in terms of the range of effects, and of the number of pupils nominating any effects. In other words, it had a relatively narrow range of effects on a limited number of pupils. Drama had the highest ratio of nominations to respondents (5.3:1), despite a high percentage of non-respondents; hence, those pupils on whom drama had impacted could identify a fairly broad range of effects.

Given the large amount of time allocated to the subject, English still had a fairly high proportion of pupils not registering any effect, though it did exhibit a reasonably high ratio of nominations to respondents (4.6:1) – suggesting that those who could perceive effects identified a fairly broad array. With an average of four nominations per respondent, art, whilst impacting on a greater number of pupils than the other artforms, displayed a narrower range of effects. Very few pupils (11 per cent) indicated any effects produced by dance, and those that did gave on average 3.6 nominations each (on a par with music), though it may be that the effects of dance are deemed by pupils to be more specific, perhaps more obviously physical than cognitive, leading to a lower average of nominations per pupil on 'learning' outcomes.

Looking at individual subjects, it appears that, for art, half of all pupils felt that the subject helped them be more creative and imaginative. This was the most frequently nominated effect for art. The next most commonly perceived outcome was that art helped give a knowledge of the artform and appreciation of others' work within it: 38 per cent of pupils circled this. Also, about a third of the sample felt that it taught particular skills and that it gave a sense of pleasure and fulfilment. Another fairly frequently perceived outcome was that it helped self-expression, registered by 21 per cent. Few pupils indicated that art had helped them to develop social skills (eight per cent) or learn in other subjects (five per cent) and very few indeed felt that it had helped them learn more about social issues (only two per cent).

In view of the small number of pupils nominating any effects for dance, there were only small differences between the percentages of pupils nominating each of the pre-selected outcomes. Over half of the proposed outcomes were each circled by only between seven and 12 per cent of pupils. These were, in rank order, 'helps you to be more creative/imaginative', 'teaches particular skills', 'gives you a sense of pleasure/enjoyment/satisfaction', 'gives you self-confidence ...' and 'helps you express yourself better'. Least frequently perceived outcomes were 'helps you to learn in other subjects' (one per cent) and 'helps you learn more about social issues ...' (two per cent). Echoing a finding from the case study element, compared to art, there were fewer references to the enhancement of knowledge and critical studies about dance as an artform. On the other hand, dance was ranked more highly for increasing self-confidence in social settings than art.

Notably, the most frequently perceived effect of drama was 'gives you confidence socially and helps you get on with other people' (31 per cent of all pupils nominated this). This top-ranking outcome for drama stood in sharp contrast to its limited references in all other artforms. The development of social skills was closely followed by 'helps you to be more creative and imaginative' (28 per cent) and then 'helps you to express yourself better'. Approximately one-fifth of pupils circled each of the outcomes 'helps you to understand people's feelings and emotions', 'teaches particular skills' and 'gives you a sense of pleasure/ enjoyment/satisfaction'. Although technical skills in drama and knowledge/appreciation of drama as an artform both attracted less support than in art, drama was more likely to be associated with enhancing understanding of the emotions and awareness of social issues than art. The least frequent effects nominated for drama were that the subject was useful for learning in other subjects, or for a job/ career, or helped develop thinking processes.

Music was distinctive in that it was the only artform in which the acquisition of technical skills was considered to be the primary outcome. Fairly close behind were 'improved creativity and imagination' and 'a sense of pleasure/enjoyment/ satisfaction'; 'gaining a knowledge of the art form and appreciation of people's work in it' was also relatively common amongst those produced by music. Very low percentages of pupils (two to three per cent) circled 'helps you learn more about social issues and problems' and 'helps you learn in other subjects'. The latter finding is interesting since it adds further weight to the earlier evidence that pupils themselves very seldom refer to or recognise any indirect, cross-curriculum or Mozart effects of music education. Thus, approaching two-thirds of all pupils appear not to see any direct effects accruing from studying music throughout Years 7–11 and indirect effects are ranked amongst the most unlikely of outcomes.

Marking it out from all the other artforms, 'helps you understand people's feelings and emotions' was the most frequent effect produced by English (33 per cent of pupils). Additionally, 'helps you learn in other subjects' was ranked much higher in English than in any other artform, though here it may well be that pupils were alluding to the development of 'secretarial' language skills which have daily relevance to other areas of the curriculum rather than to the skills inherent in the more artistic and creative dimensions to the subject. Interestingly, 'helps you think and clarifies your thinking' was also elevated to a higher level than in other art forms, though again it is not clear from the wording of the categories presented to pupils what aspects of 'English' the respondents may have in mind. Rather surprisingly, 'helps you express yourself better' and 'a sense of pleasure/enjoyment' were both ranked in the lower orders relative to other artforms. Finally, only six and seven per cent of pupils respectively indicated that improved self-confidence socially or feeling good about yourself were outcomes of English.

In the light of the later finding (see Chapter 14) that a major reason for pupils declining to opt for the arts was that other subjects were considered more important, it is noteworthy that none of the artforms (with the possible exception of English) scored highly for an effect on relevance to jobs or careers.

11.3.1 Variations by pupil attributes

Art

For art, the percentage of middle-class pupils that nominated 'teaches particular skills', 'gives you knowledge of the art form', 'helps you to express yourself' and 'gives you a sense of pleasure/enjoyment/ satisfaction' was slightly higher than the working-class percentage. Interestingly, the only outcome that was more likely to be circled by working-class pupils was 'gives you self-confidence socially/helps you get on with other people', though again only slightly.

The self-confidence outcome was also the only one that a greater percentage of boys considered to result from their art lessons, than did girls. Girls were more likely to respond to 'gives you more knowledge of the art form and appreciation of people's work in it', 'helps you to be more creative/imaginative' 'helps you express yourself better', 'helps you to understand people's feelings and emotions' and 'gives you a sense of pleasure/enjoyment/satisfaction'. Only two outcomes varied according to a pupil's ethnicity: for both 'gives you self-confidence ...' and 'helps you to think ...' percentages were higher for non-white pupils than for white pupils.

Whilst only of low significance, it is nevertheless pertinent that art was more likely to provide outcomes of self-confidence in boys than girls, pupils from working-class backgrounds than middle-class ones, and non-whites than whites. Also the development of knowledge and appreciation of the artform and enhancement of expressive abilities were outcomes more likely for girls than boys and slightly more likely for the middle classes. A sense of pleasure and fulfilment was slightly more likely both for girls and for the middle classes.

The statistics clearly showed that pupils were more likely to associate a particular outcome with art if they felt they were good at the subject. For each outcome, the percentage of pupils that felt art was one of the two subjects they were 'best at' was at least double the percentage of pupils that did not list art as one of the subjects that they were 'best at'. This relationship was particularly strong for 'helps with a future job or career', and was also for 'helps you to feel good about yourself' and 'helps you to think and clarifies your thinking'. Furthermore, 45 per cent of those who did not nominate art as one of the subjects they were 'best at' felt that it had not impacted on them at all, whilst only six per cent of those that did list it were not able to record an effect.

2.
WHAT ARE
THE EFFECTS
OF
ARTS
EDUCATION?

Likewise, there was a clear link between pupils considering art to be one of their two favourite subjects and identifying outcomes from it. Again, for each effect, the percentage of pupils that listed art as a favourite subject was at least double the percentage of pupils that did not register it. Outcomes where this was very strong were 'helps you to feel good about yourself' and 'helps with a future job or career', and, to a lesser extent, 'gives you self-confidence ...', 'helps you to think ...' and 'gives you a sense of pleasure ...'. Similarly, 47 per cent of those who did not list art as one of their two favourite subjects felt that their lessons throughout secondary school had not impacted on them at all, whilst only five per cent of those citing art felt that it had no effect.

Dance

Social class appeared to have little bearing on the perceived outcomes from dance, with the exception of 'teaches particular skills', which was slightly more prevalent amongst the middle classes. As could be expected, there were quite marked differences for dance outcomes according to gender. Girls were more likely than boys to choose all outcomes, though sometimes insignificantly. The outcomes most appreciably more likely to be chosen by girls were 'helps you to be more creative/imaginative', 'gives you a sense of pleasure/enjoyment ...', 'teaches particular skills', 'helps you express yourself', 'gives you self-confidence ...', 'helps you to feel good about yourself' and 'gives you knowledge of the art form ...'. Of the male pupils, 89 per cent did not perceive any outcomes as a consequence of dance lessons (for whatever reason – as discussed earlier, the amount of time given to the subject must be an important factor and it may be that some boys had fewer opportunities to opt for dance than girls and therefore fewer noticed any impact from dance); in contrast, 70 per cent of girls did not perceive any outcomes.

With regard to ethnicity, though non-whites were fractionally more likely to choose most outcomes, the differences between these two ethnic groupings in the percentages of pupils circling each outcome were insufficient to warrant comment. Overall, though, whites were slightly more likely to give no response at all for dance.

Perceptions of outcome from dance were very strongly associated with whether the pupil considered dance was one of the two subjects they were 'best at'. Only one of the 35 pupils that listed dance as one of their two best subjects did not indicate that it had any impact on them, whilst 80 per cent of those that did not nominate dance suggested that no outcomes resulted from dance lessons. For each outcome, the percentage of pupils that did register dance as one of the two subjects they were 'best at' was seven to 20 times greater than the percentage of those who did not list it. A very similar trend was apparent for pupils who did and did not select dance as one of their favourite subjects.

Drama

Drama outcomes often showed a small variation in frequency according to social class (slightly more noticeable than for art). In each such case (listed as follows), middle-class pupils were more likely to have circled the outcome: 'teaches particular skills', 'gives you self-confidence ...', 'helps you to understand people's feelings and emotions', 'gives you knowledge of the art form ...', 'helps to express yourself better' and 'helps you to be more imaginative and creative'. In addition, working-class pupils were more likely to feel that drama had not impacted on them at all.

While ethnicity had no apparent effect on pupils' perceived outcomes for drama, gender did make a difference, occasionally quite considerably. For all but one of the outcomes, the percentage of girls circling it was approximately double to treble the percentage of boys nominating it – the exception being 'gives you knowledge of the art form ...', where the percentages were still 17 per cent for girls compared to ten per cent for boys. Furthermore, the percentage of girls that felt drama had not had any effect on them at all was 23 per cent lower than the percentage for boys, 49 per cent compared to 72 per cent.

As for dance (though not quite to the same degree), perceptions of outcome from drama were strongly associated with pupils feeling they were good at it. For all the outcomes, the percentage of pupils that listed drama as one of the two subjects they were best at was three to seven times higher than the percentage of those that did not register it. Sixty-four per cent of those that did not list drama as one of their best subjects indicated that the subject had not impacted on them at all, whilst only four per cent of those that did list it gave such an indication.

Again, the trend and figures were very similar when considering pupils who listed drama as one of their two favourite subjects and those who did not.

Music

The data showed little in the way of meaningful differences in response according to social class, though what is perhaps most noteworthy is that, as for art, 'gives you self-confidence …' was the only outcome not to have a higher percentage of middle-class pupils circling it than working-class. The only two outcomes that actually exhibited interesting differences between the percentage of middle-class pupils who nominated them and the percentage of working-class were 'teaches particular skills' and 'gives you knowledge of the art form …'.

For all but two outcomes, females were more likely to give a response, but often this was only marginal. The only outcomes with appreciable differences were 'teaches particular skills', 'helps you to be more imaginative/creative', 'gives you knowledge of the art form …' and 'gives you a sense of pleasure/enjoyment …'. Ethnicity produced no significant differences in perception of outcomes from music.

There was the by now familiar association between pupils considering that they are good at music and perceiving outcomes from it, not to the extent exhibited by dance but greater than by art. The percentage of pupils who listed music as one of the two subjects they were best at who circled an outcome was approximately three to 11 times greater than the percentage of pupils who did not register music. Again, similar statistics can be seen when looking at pupils who listed music as one of their two favourite subjects and those who did not.

English

Generally, perceptions of outcomes in English appeared to be more variable according to gender, social class and ethnicity than in the other arts subjects.

With the notable exceptions of 'gives you self-confidence…' and 'helps you to feel good about yourself', middle-class pupils were more likely than working-class to circle all outcomes. They were especially more likely to select 'helps you to be more imaginative/creative', 'teaches particular skills' and 'helps you to understand people's feelings and emotions', and, to a slightly lesser extent, 'helps you learn more about social issues and problems', 'helps you think and clarify your thinking' and 'gives you knowledge of the art form …'. In addition, while 51 per cent of working-class pupils indicated no effects by English lessons at all, only 40 per cent of middle-class pupils did so.

There was a marked trend for girls to be more likely to identify outcomes than boys, though this was certainly not as great as for dance and drama. Percentages were greater for girls than boys for all outcomes, and to a marked extent for all, except 'gives you confidence' and 'helps you to feel good'. Boys were also more likely to have indicated no impact at all from English, with 58 per cent giving no response, compared to 37 per cent of girls. Interestingly, English generally seems to have more impact on non-whites than whites. For all outcomes, the percentages of non-whites were greater than the percentages of whites, though only some differences were to a meaningful extent

11.3.2 Variations by school

Pupils' perceptions of the effects of their arts education at secondary school varied enormously across the 22 schools. They differed along such lines as:

- the number of respondents and non-respondents to the item – schools had contrasting percentages of non-respondents indicating no perceived impact;

- the ratio of responses to respondents – in some schools, the pupils who responded could detect more effects than in other schools;

- the proportions of pupils taking each subject for GCSE – generally speaking, GCSE pupils in a certain subject were more likely to nominate outcomes than non-GCSE pupils in that subject, so the results could vary according to how many pupils were doing the subject concerned in each school; and

- the type and profile of effects identified with varying frequencies.

In the following sections, we try to illustrate the considerable differences between some schools for each of the main artforms. In the discussion that follows, it must always be remembered that by looking at the statistics by school we are often dealing with small numbers of cases. In order to obviate the effects of different non-response rates in different schools and allow the patterns of perceived outcomes to be compared across the schools, the percentages in the tables are expressed as proportions of the pupils who circled at least one outcome.

Art

From the outset, it is worth noting that 32 per cent of the whole sample were taking art GCSE, that 39 per cent of the whole sample indicated that they could not see any effects emerging from art throughout key stages 3 and 4, and that the ratio of responses to respondents to the effects item was 4:1 (i.e. on average, pupils who responded cited four effects). As outlined above, a higher percentage of GCSE art pupils circled at least one outcome than the percentage of non-GCSE pupils (e.g. in one school, 24 per cent of those taking art GCSE indicated no effect compared to 81 per cent of those not taking GCSE art). Moreover, all outcomes were generally nominated by a higher proportion of GCSE art pupils.

Firstly, it is important to illustrate the tremendous variation that existed in the three quantifiable indicators of impact of art on pupils from school to school – the first three bullet points opposite – before looking at differences in the type and profile of effects identified. The percentages of non-respondents (i.e. those indicating no effect) in each school ranged from 23 to 66 per cent; the range of the ratios of responses: respondents ranged from 2.8:1 to 5.4:1 (almost double); and the percentages of Year 11 pupils taking GCSE art in each school ranged from 14 to 57 per cent.

2.
WHAT ARE
THE EFFECTS
OF
ARTS
EDUCATION?

Considering how these indicators occur in combination in different schools, there are many instances where high percentages of pupils doing GCSE art do not correlate with a low rate of perceived non-effect or a high ratio of responses to respondents and vice versa. For example, one school had only 15 per cent doing GCSE art, yet the rate of perceived non-effect was close to the average and the ratio of responses: respondents was high (4.5:1) – this may suggest that the teaching of art was generally impacting well, but some other factor, such as the school's options system, had resulted in a low percentage choosing art. Another school (School 5) with a slightly low percentage doing GCSE (28 per cent) had a markedly low percentage indicating no effect, but a very low ratio of responses to respondents (2.8:1) – so the impact in terms of the number of effects was slight, but they covered a wide range of pupils. Another variation was found in School 19, which had an unusually high proportion studying GCSE art (56 per cent), yet a non-response rate and a ratio of responses: respondents no higher than the average for the whole sample – it appeared that there was a factor at this school that was resulting in a high proportion taking art at GCSE, even though in general the effects of art were rather limited. Upon further investigation, it was established that this school was one of three schools that required all pupils to take at least one arts subject. One school (School 2) – an all-girls inner city school – was exceptional in that it had the highest percentage taking GCSE art, a very low non-response rate (i.e. very few pupils indicating no effect) and a high ratio of responses to respondents. Here, it seemed likely that the teaching quality and effective organisational structures were resulting in an intensive and widespread impact from art.

In order to illustrate the type and profile of effects identified for art, Table 11.4 displays the contrasting results for six schools. The highlighted cells show the highest percentage for each outcome across the schools selected for the Table – in the majority of cases, they were also the highest across all 22 schools; where they were not quite the highest across the 22, they were no more than three percentage points lower.

2.
WHAT ARE
THE EFFECTS
OF
ARTS
EDUCATION?

Table 11.4   Percentages of pupils who circled outcomes for art at six schools
Based on percentages of those who selected at least one effect

I think taking this subject at school ...	Sch. 5 %	Sch. 2 %	Sch. 11 %	Sch. 17 %	Sch. 1 %	Sch. 8 %	Overall %
Teaches particular skills	48	72	48	49	56	54	54
Gives you confidence socially/ helps you get on with people	9	13	43	9	4	12	12
Helps you to feel good about yourself	6	33	33	23	22	39	24
Helps you learn in other subjects	9	7	8	10	9	23	9
Helps you to think and clarifies your thinking	11	42	20	11	27	39	18
Helps you to understand people's feelings and emotions	9	29	13	33	33	23	20
Helps with a future job or career	22	32	23	14	25	39	24
Gives you knowledge of the art form and appreciation of people's work in it	52	85	45	54	79	66	62
Helps you express yourself better	16	47	18	38	56	31	35
Gives you a sense of pleasure/ enjoyment/satisfaction	34	79	48	43	57	65	53
Helps you learn more about social issues and problems	1	1	15	6	3	0	4
Helps you to be more creative/ imaginative	65	96	78	78	87	81	81
(N) =	(113)	(72)	(40)	(110)	(79)	(26)	(1383)

NB *Respondents could give more than one response, so percentages will not sum to 100 per cent.*
Source: NFER 'The Effects and Effectiveness of Arts Education' Year 11 Survey, student questionnaire

School 5 is an example of a limited-impact school with consistently low nominations for each outcome type (in all but one, lower than the overall percentages in the final column). It also displayed the lowest ratio of responses to respondents. By way of contrast, School 2 – a very high-impact school – normally posted percentages above those for the overall sample and it also achieved the highest ratio of responses to respondents. It displayed five of the most central outcomes for art (highlighted in the table), for which it attracted the highest percentages: technical skills, knowledge and appreciation of the artform, creativity, thinking skills, and a sense of pleasure and enjoyment in art.

The profile of School 11's effects is atypical in that it registers comparatively high scores for socially relevant outcomes: 'gives you self-confidence socially/ helps you get on with people' and 'helps you learn more about social issues and problems'. This may reflect a particular emphasis that is placed on the art curriculum in this school. Suggesting another kind of curricular emphasis, Schools 17 and 1 appear to be accentuating the expressive and emotional dimension to art education. School 8, a generally high-impact school, is unusually high in what may be considered second-order outcomes: transfer effects to other subjects, the improvement of pupils' self-esteem, and career relevance.

Drama

Again, when considering the following, these overall statistics should be borne in mind: 14 per cent of the overall sample were taking GCSE drama; 60 per cent did not respond to this question for drama, thereby signalling no effect; and the ratio of responses: respondents for this question was 5.3:1. As for art, a higher percentage of GCSE drama pupils circled at least one outcome than the percentage of non-GCSE pupils and again all outcomes were generally nominated by a much higher proportion of GCSE drama pupils.

Whilst enormous variation was evident from school to school for the three measurements of subject impact on pupils for art, it was still markedly more extreme for drama with the percentages doing drama GCSE ranging from 0–60 per cent (or, in schools where drama was an available GCSE option from 4–60 per cent). This fact in itself, given the increase in response from GCSE pupils, suggests wide ranges for the other two measures: the proportion of pupils not responding at all ranged from 36–90 per cent and the ratio of responses: respondents ranged from 3.5:1 to 7.1:1.

Again, as for art, there was not always a straightforward correlation between the percentage of pupils doing GCSE drama and the two other measures of impact, and the profiles regarding these three statistics varied according to the school, suggesting the involvement of other factors.

Table 11.5 presents the contrasting results in drama for six schools. Again, the highlighted cells show the highest percentage for each outcome across the schools selected for the table – in the majority of cases, they were also the highest across all 22 schools; where they were not quite the highest across the 22, they were no more than three percentage points lower. The low numbers of respondents in some schools should be noted as grounds for caution.

With the lowest percentages for three effects and highest for none of the outcomes, Schools 11 and 12 exemplify low-impact schools for drama. Interestingly, though, they are not consistently under-represented in all outcomes; it appears that each is associated with sporadic weak areas: School 11 in creativity, career relevance and enjoyment and School 12 in social self-confidence, self-esteem, social issues and expressive skills. In sharp contrast, School 9 was the strongest in four effects: social self-confidence, emotional development, expressive skills and enjoyment. With very few references to growth in knowledge and appreciation of the artform, this school seems to be concentrating on a personal and social development agenda rather than one that focuses on theatre studies. Symptomatic of this latter interpretation of drama, School 2 differs from the previous one by registering exceptionally high scores for technical skills and the enhancement of knowledge and appreciation of drama as an artform. Moreover, for every outcome, it attracts percentages greater than those for the overall sample. School 15 also outperforms the overall sample in every outcome and scores especially well for transfer to other areas of learning. School 4 – like School 2, an all-girls school – also displays high percentages relative to the overall sample and is particularly strong on career relevance.

Table 11.5   Percentages of pupils who circled outcomes for drama at six schools
Based on percentages of those who selected at least one effect

I think taking this subject at school ...	Sch. 11 %	Sch. 12 %	Sch. 9 %	Sch. 2 %	Sch. 4 %	Sch. 15 %	Overall %
Teaches particular skills	33	57	46	79	50	65	52
Gives you confidence socially/ helps you get on with people	58	48	91	81	86	88	78
Helps you to feel good about yourself	33	9	18	43	38	60	38
Helps you learn in other subjects	8	9	0	19	15	29	15
Helps you to think and clarifies your thinking	25	13	36	38	35	25	23
Helps you to understand people's feelings and emotions	25	44	73	72	64	57	53
Helps with a future job or career	17	13	18	33	39	37	26
Gives you knowledge of the art form and appreciation of people's work in it	33	44	9	59	33	53	35
Helps you express yourself better	42	30	82	72	73	75	61
Gives you a sense of pleasure/ enjoyment/satisfaction	25	39	91	66	59	71	50
Helps you learn more about social issues and problems	25	9	55	66	58	43	37
Helps you to be more creative/ imaginative	25	57	82	86	85	84	69
(N) =	(12)	(23)	(11)	(58)	(66)	(75)	(911)

NB Respondents could give more than one response, so percentages will not sum to 100 per cent.
Source: NFER 'The Effects and Effectiveness of Arts Education' Year 11 Survey, student questionnaire

Music

To set the context for the school-based comparisons of perceived effects for music, it should be stressed that only eight per cent of the overall sample were taking GCSE music and 63 per cent of the whole sample indicated that they could not perceive any effect from music at secondary school. Consequently, the sizes of the subsamples responding from many schools were low and caution should be taken when interpreting the results. As for art and drama, a higher percentage of GCSE music pupils circled at least one outcome than the percentage of non-GCSE pupils: while only eight per cent (of the eight per cent) taking GCSE music registered no effect, 68 per cent of those not taking it saw no effect. In one school, 86 per cent of those not taking GCSE indicated no perceived outcomes from music compared to 45 per cent of those not taking it in the school with the lowest proportion of non-respondents. In a school which did not offer GCSE music, 92 per cent signalled no effects from music through key stages 3 and 4. Again, all outcomes were generally nominated by a much higher proportion of GCSE music pupils.

Table 11.6 displays the contrasting results in music for six schools. Again, the highlighted cells show the highest percentage for each outcome across the schools selected for the Table – in the majority of cases, they were also the highest across all 22 schools; where they were not quite the highest across the 22, they were no more than three percentage points lower. There were two exceptions to this: one school recorded 36 per cent for career relevance and another posted 79 per cent for creativity.

Table 11.6   Percentages of pupils who circled outcomes for music at six schools
Based on percentages of those who selected at least one effect

I think taking this subject at school ...	Sch. 8 %	Sch. 2 %	Sch. 11 %	Sch. 17 %	Sch. 21 %	Sch. 22 %	Overall %
Teaches particular skills	26	77	59	50	71	79	59
Gives you confidence socially/ helps you get on with people	42	25	50	32	19	21	20
Helps you to feel good about yourself	21	23	18	44	43	28	25
Helps you learn in other subjects	11	21	18	11	10	3	8
Helps you to think and clarifies your thinking	5	16	32	22	19	17	17
Helps you to understand people's feelings and emotions	5	25	14	37	43	21	24
Helps with a future job or career	21	25	23	27	29	21	18
Gives you knowledge of the art form and appreciation of people's work in it	26	59	36	40	48	59	42
Helps you express yourself better	11	55	23	45	48	45	31
Gives you a sense of pleasure/ enjoyment/satisfaction	32	66	50	58	52	52	50
Helps you learn more about social issues and problems	0	7	5	8	5	3	4
Helps you to be more creative/ imaginative	37	68	46	52	62	62	52
(N) =	(19)	(44)	(22)	(102)	(21)	(29)	(841)

NB Respondents could give more than one response, so percentages will not sum to 100 per cent.
Source: NFER 'The Effects and Effectiveness of Arts Education' Year 11 Survey, student questionnaire

School 8 exemplifies a low-impact school for music. Although it was comparatively high for social self-confidence, it scored the lowest percentages across all 22 schools in three categories, notably technical skills development and expressive skills. Related to these weaknesses, it also scored relatively low for the acquisition of knowledge and appreciation of music as an artform. In stark contrast, once again, School 2 demonstrated strengths in most of the outcomes. School 11 appeared to generate a particular strength in social self-confidence outcomes, though unlike School 8, this was achieved – in the main – without putting other effects at risk. School 17 (a 13–18 school) is interesting partly because of its high response rate and therefore relatively low percentage (45 per cent) perceiving no effects. It is also distinctive in the high degree of self-esteem it seems to engender, as well as its inclusion of awareness of social issues. Relative to other schools, pupils at School 21 emphasised the growth of empathy through music, as well as expressive skills. School 22 was another school that recorded consistently high percentages in virtually all outcome types, with particular strengths in music skills and knowledge of the artform.

Considering all the results presented in this section, five key points consistently emerged from the data:

- the widespread low proportions indicating that they could not detect any of the pre-selected effects from their arts education at secondary school has got to give cause for concern;

- in many schools, the nomination of multiple effects seems to be generated by small minorities of pupils;

- there is evidence of substantial variations in both the quantity and quality of perceived outcomes of arts education across schools;

- generally, some schools exhibited a weak array of perceived outcomes in all the artforms, though some schools demonstrated strong provision in different artforms; and

- the outcomes for one school signalled strong and effective provision right across the arts subjects, indicating that in the current educational climate and prevailing curricular requirements, it is possible to offer high-quality arts education in all its forms.

The challenge would seem to be how to bring the rest up to the standards of the best.

11.4 ARTS EFFECTS: SUMMARY AND CONCLUSIONS

The main findings to emerge from across the different analyses of effects and outcomes are summarised below.

**2.
WHAT ARE
THE EFFECTS
OF
ARTS
EDUCATION?**

1. The evidence presented in Part Two clearly documents a high level of wide-ranging effects from pupils who were performing well in at least one artform in schools that enjoyed a reputation for being strong in the arts. Foremost among these effects were outcomes relating to advancements in pupils' skills in and knowledge of the specific artforms. At a time when there is much attention given to claims about indirect or 'spin-off' effects associated with arts education, the results provide a timely reminder that the predominant outcomes centred on the enhancement of direct artform skills and knowledge. In addition, however, a broad and impressive array of other outcomes was also evidenced, including enjoyment, social skills, self-confidence, expressive skills and creativity. Many of these outcomes (e.g. improved self-esteem and developments in the personal and social domain) are highly pertinent to the Government's priorities of tackling disaffection and social exclusion amongst young people. It was noticeable that the range of outcomes associated with strong arts provision was wider than that codified in the relevant Orders of the National Curriculum and broader than the current policy focus on 'creative and cultural education'.

2. Again on the evidence from arts-friendly pupils in schools strong in the arts, it was apparent that each of the main artforms generated different, and occasionally unique, effects. For example, dance offered increased awareness of the body and movement; art was strong on expressive skills; drama on the development of empathy and the valuing of others; and music extended active listening skills. Thus, providing stronger confirmation of what was tentatively suggested in the study's interim report (Harland *et al.,* 1998) to achieve the full canon of effects from the arts, pupils need access and exposure to each of the individual artforms. To this extent, the use of the term 'the arts' can be unhelpful if it promotes the erroneous view that the individual artforms embraced by the term are so interchangeable that to study more than one is unnecessary as it only duplicates the same learning gains.

3. Looking at the schools with good reputations for the arts as a whole, there appeared to be some gaps or underemphasised areas in the general outcomes achieved by the pupils. The most noteworthy of these included:

    •   development of aesthetic and discriminating judgements;

- placing critical skills in an historical context;

- the furthering of thinking skills, or perhaps more accurately, a meta-awareness of the intellectual dimensions to artistic processes;

- technical skills development in music at key stage 3; and

- preparation for cultural life as a critical active 'consumer' beyond school.

4. From a wider sample of schools, there was no sound evidence to support the claim that the arts boost general academic performance at GCSE. From the case study schools, however, staff and pupils identified some transfer effects, especially in art and drama but less so in music. It was considered, though, that these perceived effects probably lacked the quantity and quality to produce a visible effect in GCSE statistics, once background variables like prior attainment and social class had been taken into account. These findings add further weight to the emerging literature which strikes a cautionary note on the purported 'Mozart effect'. Certainly, on the basis of the evidence relating to 14–16-year-olds, this approach would not appear to be the most prudent form of arts advocacy at the moment.

5. From both the case study schools and the schools in the Year 11 survey, the contrasting patterns and permutations of effects indicated an appreciable degree of variation in the ways that schools and teachers defined and approached the teaching of, ostensibly, the same subjects. Whilst this was especially apparent with regard to drama – which has a low level of specification within the National Curriculum – both of the main sources of evidence demonstrated that art and music also exhibited considerable variations – in spite of comparatively high degrees of curriculum prescription. The extent to which this represents a problem or a virtue depends on the relative priorities placed on the value of diversity in the mediation of the curriculum or the value of offering pupils a common curriculum entitlement.

6. A more immediate and pressing problem was to be found in the substantial variation in the range, frequency and quality of arts-related outcomes achieved by different schools. The Year 11 survey revealed substantial differences between schools in each of the artforms: only a small minority of schools registered high-outcome scores in all of the main artforms and had higher than average pupils opting for GCSE courses in the arts; the majority attracted low-outcome scores in at least one artform. The evidence

suggests that a limited proportion of schools and teachers are succeeding in achieving effective provision in all the major artforms, but many are falling well short of the standards set by the best. It is difficult to avoid the conclusion that there is a need for serious and urgent measures to address this lack of consistency in the quality of outcomes achieved by secondary schools.

**2.
WHAT ARE
THE EFFECTS
OF
ARTS
EDUCATION?**

7. Also a cause for concern was the limited impact of arts education on the generality of pupils in many schools. A majority of pupils in the Year 11 survey indicated that dance, drama and music generated none of the pre-selected outcomes, and a significant proportion registered the same for art (39 per cent). Too often, effects were only registered by the committed pupils, especially in music, and there was some evidence of differential responses with biases towards music, girls and those good at the arts. To this extent, and linking with the results from the case study schools, the often aspired to view of the arts as 'accessible to all' is perhaps not that concrete. Certainly in terms of technical capabilities, music was sometimes seen by pupils in the case study schools as 'special' and for the elite. Although the arts may be accessible in terms of 'participation' as a concept, the variation in the range of outcomes by school, in both the Year 11 survey and the case study schools, indicates that the arts may not be accessible to all in the same way. That there is no level-pegging or level ground for the arts in terms of provision implicates pupils' varying perceptions of their arts experiences in spite of the National Curriculum.

8. The findings from the different artforms implicate varying messages for policy. The case study data indicated that art clearly posted the greatest variety of effects on pupils. Amongst all the artforms, art also had the highest proportion of pupils taking it for GCSE – thus lessening any weaknesses that might be suggested, such as its smaller perceived impact on social and moral issues, or in developments on thinking and communication skills. Both drama and dance registered an impressive array of outcomes for those pupils who took them, but both also appeared lacking in status – in terms of curriculum coverage and the exposure that pupils received. For drama, this was more specifically related to the possibilities for more varied approaches, afforded by its location in the National Curriculum, while dance appeared vulnerable because of the smaller number of pupils taking it and some of the 'missing' artform-based outcomes. Perhaps the most vulnerable aspect of music was the low numbers of pupils opting for it at GCSE. Evidence from the Year 11 survey indicated that music had the highest proportion of 'no impact' responses, and, from the

case study schools, a more limited range of outcomes compared with drama and art. In particular, the lack of skills *development* at Years 7 and 8, despite the focus of pupil comment on knowledge and skills, gave music a less convincing range of outcomes than the other artforms. These findings corroborate other research that has revealed that pupils at key stage 3 often see music as lacking in relevance to their current and future needs and that pupils' levels of enjoyment in music decline significantly over the duration of key stage 3 (Ross, 1995; Harland *et al.*, 1999), thus culminating in lowest levels of entry to GCSE courses for any National Curriculum subject. As Ross (1995) has argued, music is ailing largely because of its lack of appeal to pupils, many of whom, ironically, are engaged in music activities outside of school more than any other artform. If school music provision is to secure the interest of pupils in 'school music', an urgent and well-resourced programme of professional development may be needed to allow many teachers to learn from those teachers and schools that are achieving substantial outcomes and above-average GCSE enrolment rates in the subject.

9. Hitherto, research and evaluation in the arts have tended to be input- or process-based and very few previous studies have examined effects and outcomes. This study represents a modest and provisional attempt to address this shortcoming in the arts-related research. It is hoped that the approach highlights the need for more studies of outcomes in the field of arts education, and in other areas of the curriculum for comparative purposes. Perhaps, it also underlines the case for assessment in the arts to focus on a wider range of effects and outcomes than it currently does.

PART THREE: WHAT ARE EFFECTIVE PRACTICES IN ARTS EDUCATION?

12. PERCEPTIONS OF EFFECTIVE PRACTICES IN ARTS EDUCATION

CHAPTER OVERVIEW

Part Three of the report consists of four chapters that focus on identifying the various factors and processes associated with effective teaching and learning in the arts. This – the first of the four chapters – describes how members of school management, teachers, pupils, employers and employees perceived effective teaching and learning in the arts. Their perceptions have been organised into six broad groups of factors that affect the quality of arts education in secondary schools:

- beyond-school factors (12.3)
- whole-school factors (12.4)
- arts faculty or departmental factors (12.5)
- curriculum factors (12.6)
- teacher factors (12.7)
- pupil factors (12.8).

The main sources of evidence for the chapter are the case study schools and the interviews with employers and employees.

12.1 INTRODUCTION

This chapter marks a shift from Part Two, which considered the effects of arts education on young people, to Part Three, which deals with the issues surrounding the effective provision and teaching of the arts in secondary education. In doing so, it addresses the second of the study's aims, namely: '*to examine the relationship between these effects and the key factors and processes associated with arts provision in schools*'.

This chapter examines the perceptions of key members of school management staff, teachers, pupils, employers and employees. In order to do this, it makes use of five main sources of data, as described in more detail in Chapter 1:

- Phase 1 and Phase 3 interviews with key school staff;

- cohort pupil interviews at all phases;

- observed pupil interviews at all phases;

- observed teacher interviews at all phases; and

- interviews with employers and employees.

However, the classroom observations and post-observation interviews are utilised more fully in the next chapter dealing with selected classroom situations in relation to specific outcomes. Therefore, in this chapter, unless otherwise stated, '*pupil interviews*' refers to the interviews with pupils in the longitudinal cohort group.

This chapter is based on a typology of effectiveness which was developed by examining all of the interviews conducted, and noting every reference made to factors and processes which interviewees felt impacted on the quality of arts education received and its attendant learning outcomes. Although at some stages of the research, interviewees were asked direct questions about what they felt constituted '*effective*' education in the arts, these questions were not asked at all phases, and interviewees often also volunteered relevant comments at other points during the interviews, and in response to other questions. The full range of comments made by all interviewees was used in the analysis of each issue – whether made in response to a specific question, or proffered during discussion of a different topic. In this way, none of the expressed perceptions were overlooked.

During the interviews, interviewees often referred to '*effective*', '*good*', or '*best*' practice within arts education – using the terms seemingly interchangeably, but at this stage it was felt necessary to distinguish between them. This chapter considers '*effective practice*', which we have defined (see Chapter 1) as: '*practice which encourages the development of effects or outcomes perceived to be beneficial or desirable – developed intentionally, or unintentionally, via education*' – making no value judgements about the relative benefits of the different outcomes. ·

12.2 A MODEL OF PERCEIVED EFFECTIVENESS IN THE PROVISION OF ARTS EDUCATION

A model of the different factors of effectiveness perceived by the different interviewees was developed in order to map out the areas relevant to the debate. The model is divided into six main groups of factors which progress from the macro level – 'beyond school' – to the micro level – 'teachers' and 'pupils':

Figure 12.1   A typology of factors in effective arts education

Although the chapter considers each of the six categories in turn, it is recognised that, like the typology of effects, this represents an ideal-typical view and that in reality, there are many areas where the categories interrelate and overlap. Within each section of the text, references are made to other sections where details can also be found.

12.3 BEYOND-SCHOOL FACTORS

The various groups of interviewees identified four main types of 'beyond-school' factors which they felt impacted on the effectiveness of arts education:

- local community and school catchment area;

- local education authority and other external support;

- teacher networks; and

- initial teacher training.

It is clear from the interviews with pupils (both cohort pupil and post-observation pupil interviews) that they perceived little impact on their arts lessons from factors beyond the boundaries of their own school. However, as might have been expected, teachers, key members of school staff and senior management were more aware of these external factors.

12.3.1 Local community and school catchment area factors

Key members of school staff – teachers and senior managers – made various comments about how local traditions and socio-economic factors affected the teaching of the arts within their schools. The community and school catchment area factors that were raised fell into three broad categories:

- economic factors;

- cultural factors; and

- community relationships.

3.
WHAT ARE
EFFECTIVE
PRACTICES
IN
ARTS
EDUCATION?

Economic factors

The adults interviewed raised a number of issues relating to the impact of economic factors in the locality of the school on arts education. One area where economic factors were perceived to be particularly telling was pupils' arts participation outside school. The arts activities which pupils were able, and encouraged, to take part in (including homework) were thought to have discernible knock-on effects within arts lessons. A particularly obvious example given was pupils attending private music tuition. One music teacher, now head of the expressive arts faculty in one of the case study schools, summarised how influential extra-curricular music lessons could be:

> *... at the end of the day, music in particular, I feel, is quite an elitist subject because you've got to have money to pay for lessons and those pupils who have instrumental lessons succeed. I wouldn't be here today if my parents could not have afforded to give me instrumental lessons, so although we say we have an arts policy for all, which is very true, at the end of the day those kids who can receive instrumental lessons obviously have the advantage* (music teacher).

It is clearly a problem that, in some areas, parents now have to be able to pay for peripatetic music lessons which were once available free through LEA provision. One teacher expressed the view that this meant achievement in music was now more closely linked to social class than it used to be.

Economic factors were also raised by an art teacher, and a head of art, primarily concerned with the quality of homework produced by pupils from more disadvantaged social backgrounds. They suggested that many pupils from 'less well-off' families did not have access to art books, or equipment, outside school and that this adversely affected their level of achievement:

> ... *if you are setting a homework, you know hardly any children will have books at home to do with the arts. Hardly any children have been to museums, so it does have some implications* ... (head of art).

> ... *it is just that they won't even have crayons. If you asked them to do any crayoning, they haven't even got them at home. They don't come with the right equipment; they don't even come with a pencil, some of them that come from the poorer homes* (art teacher).

However, despite the concerns of art staff, this did not appear to be an issue across all of the artforms. A drama teacher did not identify with the art teachers' view, explaining the positive contribution that pupils from different social backgrounds could make:

> ... *arts can cross all the boundaries. And the kids who are from the very nice middle-class homes ... have just as much right to their opinion in drama as the kid from the working-class background. And because they come from different backgrounds, they can bring in different ideas to drama* (drama teacher).

This seems to be linked, to a certain extent, to the understanding that in drama the only equipment required is the body, and imagination or ideas – equally available to pupils of any economic means. In art, the problems for the less well-off lie with the tangible equipment – pens, pencils, paints, paper, etc. – that are essential for most activities.

Another area where staff identified differences based on affluence was the support and expectations of parents. One deputy head explained that the school catchment area generally comprised the higher end of the socio-economic spectrum, and described the effect that this had on parents:

> *Parental expectation is higher – parents would expect that their children are going to have experiences other than the classroom, that they are going to have a rich experience here. There is also, of course, the opportunity – the parents tend to be generally rather more aware of arts things themselves and they tend to be rather more supportive, perhaps. They are very keen for their youngsters to take up opportunities that are offered* (deputy head).

Pierre Bourdieu has theorised at length about the impact of social factors on the outcomes of educational intervention. His theory of '*cultural capital*' (Bourdieu, 1977) describes education as a mechanism whereby social groups are reproduced. He depicts the range of cultural abilities – aesthetic, language, etc. – as *'cultural capital'*, which similarly to economic capital can be passed from generation to generation. This theory would explain the increased parental expectation of parents whose aim is to pass on cultural and arts awareness to their children. A deputy head had also observed that some parents from lower social groups expressed negative views about the relevance of their children continuing to take arts subjects for GCSE – in keeping with Bourdieu's theory.

The full implications of parental attitudes are explored in the *'pupil factors'* section, 12.8.

Cultural factors

In addition to economic factors, staff interviewed also referred to the impact of culture and local traditions. However, because of the differing nature and locations of the case study schools, the issues, and the opinions held, varied considerably.

Several teachers expressed positive views about how the diversity of cultures within the local community affected the cultural balance of the school. A teacher commented on the range of experiences which different pupils could bring to English lessons:

> ... because there are so many different communities in the local area, then you would expect, and I think we have, a thriving sort of atmosphere in terms of the mix of cultures and what the girls bring into school. I think the interchange of those ideas is very, very positive. I have been doing some work with some of my Year 9s ... which looks at how they began reading, their very early memories of early picture books and things right the way through to now. We had one fascinating lesson when we were talking about various ways of teaching reading in secondary schools – we had someone who had been to school in Turkey, someone who had been privately tutored in Bangladesh and someone else ... in the Caribbean. They all spoke about their experience of reading and the differences. One of them had been taught to memorise poetry and she actually put down her love of poetry to that, she could date it back to that point. It made me think 'Well, I don't do very much of that', but in fact the kids do seem to like it. So you get those interesting ideas coming in (head of English).

However, another teacher recognised that care had to be taken within lessons that, whilst maximising the useful impact of cultural diversity, it did not lead to some pupils' isolation:

> ... if we think about the big religious festivals that happen – the problem is that it does not encompass everybody. If you are talking about Eid [Islamic religious festival], *even if it is 70 per cent of the*

3.
WHAT ARE
EFFECTIVE
PRACTICES
IN
ARTS
EDUCATION?

population, there is still the rest of the school that isn't involved in Eid. If we are talking about Christmas, that is the other half that isn't, so it does fragment – although there are huge obviously religious festivals so of course you use their experience, but you try not to isolate other people (drama teacher).

It is clear that whilst the positive outcomes of cultural diversity should be encouraged, care must be taken in how these are achieved. Illustrating the possible difficulties in embracing pupils' different cultural experiences of music, one music teacher said:

We have a lot of Asian children who come to this school. It makes teaching music quite hard actually because a lot of the things that I do are quite new to them. Not only the Asians, there are Africans. A lot of white children, but because there are so many foreigners it just makes what I do quite difficult, in that I have to start right at the beginning to introduce the culture of this country to them, right from the beginning.

Interviewer: *Do they bring much knowledge or experience in their own musical traditions, or do they have musical traditions that they are aware of?*

I do try to leave room for that, so that they can bring what they have learnt before to the classroom, but a lot of them ... I don't know if they are shy, or they feel that their music is so different from ours that they don't want to share it, but no, I would not say that they do use a lot of their own background in the classroom.

In the rural Welsh case study school, a similar problem was faced in bringing together the pupils with a different choice of first language. One member of staff cited the importance of Welsh family traditions and culture in terms of participation in the eisteddfod, in encouraging the development of musical ability, but also suggested that Welsh-speaking pupils gained more from their eisteddfod experience than non-Welsh speakers:

... the children from Welsh homes are, I would say, more encouraged at home to study piano. They're more inclined to be confident singers and performers as well ... Generally their experience of the eisteddfod from junior school has given them a familiarity with performing and being on stage and using instruments and what have you that maybe is not quite part of the culture of those children who are not Welsh-speaking.

In addition to the question of language, the rural isolation of the Welsh school also created some problems. In terms of location, the main obstacle faced was transport – pupils had little access to galleries and museums, and would always require to be collected by parents from after-school activities. One teacher gave an example of the effect of the pupils' limited sphere of experience:

> ... we took about 50 up to the Tate Gallery in September ... we had one of those tours and they were taken around these pictures – Rembrandt, Turner, etc. and they were asked questions about things they knew extremely well, like composition, tone, line, etc. and they were absolutely silent, and this guy in the end he got cross and said: 'Look, if you're not prepared to help, I really think you're just wasting your time', and I said: 'Hey look, these children have never been out of the local town before; this is the furthest they've ever been, some of them; they've never spoken in public and they're just incredibly shy', and he just couldn't believe it, and added to that 'Over half of them, their first language isn't English', and he said: 'I never thought, I never thought of where you'd come from. I'm so used to children just calling out, putting their hands up ...' (art teacher).

However, earlier in the interview, the teacher had described one way in which the school was trying to overcome the problem – by setting up their own gallery within the school grounds, which would become a valuable resource for all the community:

> They don't have a strong background knowledge – resources such as museums and galleries are distant. Quite often when we take them on various trips, that's perhaps their only experience of going to a gallery. Transport is difficult ... we do have local galleries and we're hoping to set up a new gallery within the school grounds for all the community.

Community relationships

The previous example – the rural Welsh school – serves to highlight the importance of the school location and context, but it can also be recognised that the community themselves have a role to play in the effectiveness of the arts in schools.

One of only two comments on *'beyond-school'* factors which were made by pupils made a direct link between community attendance at productions and the quality of drama teaching within the school: '... *drama is really high in this school because they are always doing plays and everyone always comes*' (Year 7).

The deputy head at one of the schools agreed – giving a possible reason for the relationship – that the wholehearted support of the local community was influential in providing encouragement to both pupils and arts teachers:

3.
WHAT ARE
EFFECTIVE
PRACTICES
IN
ARTS
EDUCATION?

> *... it's parental support as well that's important – confidence to go for it, and support from the institution to let them go for it, and then, when they succeed – and they do – the applause, the appreciation, the praise that comes in just shifts you up a gear, it just moves the place up and gives you the courage for the next risk and there's no doubt that there is, I think now, a greater awareness in our community here of what we do. More parents are coming to productions, for example; more kids are involved in productions, so the word is out in the community: 'Hey, this is good; if [the school] is putting something on, we go and see it' or 'Our kids are involved in it; we are going to go and see it' ... I think we are influencing the community; they are, I think, more appreciative of arts as it can be produced in school ...* (deputy head).

This deputy head had raised a similar issue in a previous interview – he described an arts week that was held at the school, and the resulting positive outcomes:

> *... adults, not just teachers, but adults coming in from outside and working with the kids, and doing things that you would not allow yourself to do and having fun, and it was great. It was a great experience and worth ... worth the headaches ... and the hassle. If we all stuck to our timetable through life, we would not really achieve a great deal, would we? ... It is those things that make a difference to the quality of what you are doing. It will be those things that most of our kids remember ...* (deputy head).

Another school encouraged the participation of teachers and adults in a school orchestra, with similar positive benefits.

A head of administration from a local theatre company, who was interviewed as an employer, explained how they were involved in supporting the arts in schools, and he described their rationale in providing specialist educational programmes:

> *... we felt that they were important. You can look at it from a very selfish level, that if we don't inculcate an interest in the arts and theatre in young people, then our future customers, putting a commercial slant on it, will not come along, they won't see any relevance in it when they're older, and to a certain extent we suffer that problem ... If people didn't do the arts at school, our source of one – customers – and two – potential employees – would dry up. But even accepting that extreme isn't likely to happen, I think it's just the notion of that breadth; that people appreciate the fact that there is a cultural life that they have an investment in, and that they see it as valuable to them, as part of their values...*(employer, theatre company).

It is clear that pupils' engagement with the arts in settings beyond school can be a positive addition to their education, but that the interaction can be mutually beneficial. Theatres who provide education programmes sustain their supply of customers for the future, and community support for the arts within schools can maintain the feasibility of extra-curricular activities and performances.

12.3.2 Local education authority and other external support

In addition to the community and school catchment area, the importance of the support that they received from beyond the school was also emphasised by the staff interviewed. The main source of support which was cited came from the local education authority, although one comment referred to input from Social Services.

LEA arts advisory support

Three teachers who were interviewed, representing two LEAs, made comments about the LEA provision of advisory support for the arts. Two of the teachers were linked to drama provision and one was an art teacher. Unfortunately, advisory support did not always appear to fulfil the needs, or expectations of teachers. One drama teacher expressed some dissatisfaction:

> ... I've met him once. But I haven't, we haven't, I haven't seen anything more from him. Again, there's only been one course for drama teachers this year run by him. That really was so wide for teachers in all schools that it wasn't, we didn't go into ...

Interviewer: *Primary and secondary?*

> Yes, so it really wasn't going to do much for us, you know, it wasn't (drama teacher).

In complete contrast, positive comments came from two other teachers – of drama and art. A section from the interview with the drama teacher shows their far more favourable opinion of the LEA:

> ... they have got an excellent team of advisers who are always on hand should we need them. They are really cooperative; they will come in and do practically anything that you ask them to do. They came in and helped with the dance on our last production. We usually use them for the movement stuff because neither [of us] is qualified to teach dance and we are aware that this is a hole really in our curriculum. So we invite them in to come and fill that gap.

Interviewer: *Would this be a dance advisory teacher?*

> He is a drama adviser actually, but his speciality is dance and he is excellent, he is very, very good at it. As I say, it is just a matter of getting on the phone and asking and he will be there. They do

3.
WHAT ARE
EFFECTIVE
PRACTICES
IN
ARTS
EDUCATION?

support us – if ever we need anything at all, they are very, very supportive. They have a really good team and they run some very good courses too. They are always amenable to suggestions for courses and we have been on quite a few of them (drama teacher).

Whilst highlighting the benefits of a helpful advisory service, this comment also shows that dance and drama can be successfully combined – at least within an advisory capacity – and that a drama adviser specialising in dance can make a valid contribution to dance in a school where the drama teachers do not feel able to teach it adequately.

It is clear that the teachers and others involved in the management of schools attach some significance to the benefits provided by a strong LEA advisory service. The importance of the advisory service as a means of sharing knowledge and connecting teachers from different schools was highlighted by a head of English: *'I think that we are losing because of the sort of weakness in some ways, the advisory service being slashed, we are losing the contact with other schools in the area, which I think is a real pity.'*

Teacher networking is considered in section 12.3.3 later as an issue in its own right.

LEA facilities and resources

In addition to school arts advisers, some LEAs also provide specific facilities or resources on which educators can draw. One art teacher gave an opinion about the provision of a local arts centre:

There are artists working there all the time and you can actually book a day in with one of your classes. It is hard to get in because it is very popular. It is a pity that there is not more than one but it is very good, it is worthwhile taking the children there.

In one area, where a negative comment was made about arts adviser provision, the headteacher explained how the LEA had helped them in bringing practising artists into the school. It seems that the type of support offered to schools by the different LEAs may vary quite substantially, perhaps reflecting variations in the levels of resources available to different LEAs:

We have had two artists in schools, one a weaver – that was great – for three weeks and then we had [an artist] *here for a whole year: he was based here and we made a studio for him and he did outreach from here into the primary schools. That was organised by the authority with authority funding, so we have done very well. Then, of course, that is because we are an arts-identified school ... Inevitably advisers go to the schools where they know they are going to get a welcome if they have got projects that they want to get off the ground.*

This remark raises another important issue – that of the *'virtuous circle'* whereby schools that have a good reputation for the arts are more commonly approached, and on the receiving end of arts funding. The result is that they can continue to improve and develop their reputation still further.

Other types of external support

It is clear that whilst the LEAs provide many of the services on which teachers draw, they are by no means the only potential source of support. However, one deputy head brought to light a difficult situation where support from Social Services, which was thought necessary, was not forthcoming. She argued that support systems had to be in place so that teachers could do their job – teaching – effectively:

> ... we are not social workers, we are a learning community, but if you are part of the community and you have got none of those structures out there working for you, you are suddenly having to look again either at your role, your job, or how you can actually get rid of those things that are impediments to learning.

Obviously, in order for teachers to be able to concentrate as fully as possible on the quality of teaching and learning experiences that they provide, other supporting services need to be in place and functioning efficiently.

12.3.3 Teacher networks

In addition to the support provided by external sources such as the LEA and Social Services Departments, several teachers and school staff referred to the importance of opportunities to meet with teachers from other schools. Discussing ideas and providing a useful support network were two of the potential benefits mentioned. One teacher who valued this said:

> We do have good connections with drama teachers across the city ... so we go to see each other's productions ... So, that is great and that is where really the input has come this year ... but that is in our own time. It would be nice if somebody ... who was being paid for this could actually ... do their job and get us together ... sharing ideas – sharing ways of tackling different drama subjects in drama. You know, we don't have a curriculum, so therefore actually what we are teaching needs to be a wide, varied diet: you don't want always to be doing bullying in Year 7 ... it is just ideas, it really is. Being creative together, that's what you need.

Unfortunately this was not always possible and the time in which to develop these networks appeared to be a major constraint – largely due to teachers' increasing regular workload. The need for LEA coordination was also apparent. This situation was described by one school curriculum coordinator:

> *... it is increasingly difficult to hold meetings* [between teachers from different schools] *because of the amount of work and pressure that staff are under and the amount of time that they have to give to meetings outside school. It is very difficult to actually get groups of staff together in their own time to ... put forward any initiatives.*

A suggestion made by several of the teachers on this issue was that coordination of support networks for subject teachers would be a valuable activity which could usefully be undertaken by the LEA advisory service. One teacher described a way in which he had achieved this whilst on secondment to the LEA as an adviser:

> *I put together a directory of practising art teachers ... If we take the authority as a massive pool of resources and expertise, the idea was that we identified what that expertise was. We found out that these were the areas that staff were claiming to have experience of teaching in schools ... So if you are saying that you are an etcher, then you must have done that with students in the classroom because what we are going to do is put together a directory so that somebody can go to ... Let us say that they are interested in introducing etching into their curriculum. They look at the appropriate section, where they will find a list of people who have said that they have been etchers ... the idea being that they could ring them up and say 'Is there any chance of me making a visit on such and such a day? I gather you have taught etching. What groups have you taught it to? What are the problems? What facilities do we need? How can we get hold of materials?', and so on.*

He believed that this initiative had created a valuable resource which arts teachers could access, despite the problem of continually updating the information. It also demonstrated the achievements of an arts teacher who was able to spend time in an advisory role, developing such initiatives, whilst released from day to day teaching responsibilities. In an earlier part of the interview, the teacher had explained that it was very difficult for teachers who did not have the luxury of secondment to the advisory service to find time, amongst their usual activities, for the development of this type of network.

12.3.4 Initial teacher training

Although many of the factors beyond the control of the school which impact on the effectiveness of arts education provision are currently occurring, one which must be taken into account is the product of past education systems. Only one teacher mentioned the direct impact of teacher training on effective education, and this was also related to the location of drama within English provision in the National Curriculum:

> *I think the biggest problem is that a lot of people are frightened of it – I think you do have to have training; I don't think you can just suddenly do a bit of drama. Mostly when people have done that – with the best of intentions – mostly they're not very good at it ... I think you've got to have someone who's trained and I think you've got to make provision for retraining and ... having time and space to themselves where they just get new ideas ...*

This is perhaps an area which would warrant further directed research in order to expose the full range of views about the interplay of teacher training with the provision of effective arts education (see Rogers, 1998).

Staff from three of the case study schools brought up this issue in a slightly different context – that of the contribution currently made to the school by trainee teachers on teaching practice:

> *Although we are training them, they also bring in a tremendous amount with them – they are bringing the ideas in. A lot of staff development goes on from that process – the trainers are learning as much as the trained. So that is one way in which we are keeping staff development going, if you like, an awareness there.*

A headteacher explained how the presence of student teachers in the school encouraged the development of a 'learning culture' – where both staff and pupils were seen to be involved in lifelong learning. Another described the contribution of specialist skills which could be made by PGCE students who already had a degree in their chosen artform.

12.3.5 Summary

By way of summarising the key points on 'beyond-school' factors, the evidence indicated that:

- there was a general consensus that the social, economic and cultural background of individual pupils was a major determinant of the efficacy of the arts education they experienced;

- the nature and vitality of the cultural life of the school's local community were also considered to be an important influence;

- LEAs' support and advisory systems demonstrated the potential to make a significant difference to the effectiveness of arts education, though this potential was generally perceived to be realised in only one of the five authorities – in the others, LEA support was considered to be patchy, of variable quality and, most importantly, in a state of decline;

- interviewees believed that networks that brought together teachers from different schools could make a valuable contribution to developing current provision;

- teachers made surprisingly few references to the significance of their own initial teacher training or professional development; and finally

- there were few explicit references to the general value of partnerships with local or national arts organisations.

12.4 WHOLE-SCHOOL FACTORS

Factors which related to the whole school were mentioned by pupils, teachers and key members of school staff alike. Issues raised included:

- senior management;

- school ethos and atmosphere; and

- timetable issues.

12.4.1 Senior management

Perhaps unsurprisingly, none of the pupils made any comment about the effect of senior management, and no relevant remarks were made by teachers during post-observation interviews. Therefore, this section is based entirely on opinions expressed at the beginning and end of the project by senior managers, key members of school staff, and arts subject teachers. There were two main themes for consideration:

- headteacher; and

- flexibility and responsiveness.

Headteacher

One in five of the staff interviewed addressed the importance of the role, and influence, of the individual school headteacher. Robinson (1982, p. 48) advanced the view that:

> There are many schools where the arts flourish. In every case the headteacher and other staff appreciate and support them. In those schools where the headteacher thinks the arts are marginal, they suffer, whatever the economic circumstances.

A drama teacher explained her own understanding of the importance of the background and personal interests of the headteacher, and how she felt these impacted on the provision for her subject in particular:

Heads rule OK, it's as simple as that. For all that there's parental involvement now and charters and National Curriculum ... at the end of the day, if a head wants something in the school, it is likely to happen and if the head doesn't, or isn't interested, it isn't likely to happen – no matter how interested anybody else on the staff is. I think it is crucial what the head's personal commitment is. That's not to say heads can't be influenced and some, if they're reasonably open, might feel that something which they hadn't considered can be considered, but I think it's a particular problem with the arts. If you get a head who isn't very arts-oriented himself, or herself, it's very difficult to get it beyond the minimum requirements of the National Curriculum – that's a particular problem for drama because it isn't in the National Curriculum; drama is part of English in the National Curriculum ...

Two out of the six headteachers interviewed had backgrounds in the arts – one was previously an LEA arts adviser, and the other (the new head at one of the case study schools) was a practising musician and a music teacher. Both felt that this was an important feature of their character, and a valuable asset to their school. However, at a different school, the headteacher explained that none of the senior management team, including himself, were involved in the arts, but that the school was successful in the area in spite of this. He felt that the most important factor was not necessarily senior management's direct participation in the arts, but their appreciation of the contribution that the arts made to the school, and their general management abilities. He said:

... I have no arts background at all. I am a scientist – in fact the whole management team are scientists ... It is mildly amusing that we are considered to be a good arts school, because they probably do it despite us, but we are managers and we see the values of the arts. I have no arts background – my involvement is supportive – finding funds, creating opportunities and then relying on the people [arts staff] to make it happen ...

The teachers of ceramics and music from another school made similar comments:

... [the headteacher] is a scientist but he's very pro the arts and I think it's largely down to his interest and his backing that it's developed the way it has.

———

I think the headmaster, by giving us this building ... believes in our abilities and I think he appreciates that arts is important. Otherwise, I don't think we'd have this lovely building. I think he believes in us.

The vision of this particular headteacher had resulted in the bringing together of the arts subjects in the new building mentioned, which included art rooms, a drama suite, music teaching rooms, and music practice rooms. Previously an attempt had been made to integrate the arts into a single faculty, replacing the departmental structure. However, this was not successful. Bringing the subjects together within the same building was seen as a very effective compromise.

It is clear that whatever the relevance of the headteacher's direct involvement in the arts, the sense of direction, and leadership which is provided seems crucial in maintaining an effective school. This was implied by many of the comments made, but particularly in one made by a deputy head:

> ... there are so many things that make for an effective school, the greatest one being the quality of the headteacher, and in this school the quality of the headteacher is outstanding and he has a huge effect on the effectiveness of the school.

Later in the interview he returned to the same issue:

> ... if you have got a very weak head who doesn't provide strong leadership and management, then it's difficult for people in the middle level to bring their departments on because they have no support, they have no direction, and people are all pulling in different directions, which is no good at all ... I think, if you have got an underperforming area, you get a strong management team, particularly a strong head, an effective head, then they will deal with that underperforming area ...

Overall, while there were many references to the influential role of the headteacher, staff in two schools corroborated the views of some headteachers and described how the arts had developed and flourished without any special support from the headteacher or senior management team. In such schools, it would be appropriate to view the development of the arts as being bottom-up and reactive on the part of senior management: for example, arts teachers had enhanced their practice to a level at which senior management had realised that these strengths could be promoted as distinctive school qualities. This model contrasts with top-down forms of development, in which the headteacher takes a more proactive role in leading the advances in arts provision, from the front, as it were. Both approaches were evident, to varying degrees, across the five case study schools. It is noteworthy, however, that in one of the possible 'bottom-up' schools, the strong support for the arts from the LEA was a significant factor. To some extent, this may have compensated for the initial lack of special support from the school's management. Suffice it to say at this point that, whilst there was a general consensus that headteacher support and encouragement for the arts was a vital factor, there were also accounts which suggested that it was not a *sine qua non*. To this extent, the evidence highlights the possibility of developing arts provision, even in schools where there is no extra or special headteacher or senior management support for it.

Flexibility and responsiveness

Comments about senior management were made by staff from all schools, and at all levels – from individual arts teachers to senior managers and headteachers. The exact nature of the comments varied. A headteacher appointed just prior to the start of the research explained that she wanted to change the way in which the senior management team interacted with the rest of the school staff. She said:

> ... *I think that there has been a gap between the work of the senior management team and the work of some of the faculties. Sometimes I think the senior management team have felt that what is in their heads is also in the heads of the faculties, and I don't think that is always the case ... So I think it is really focusing the school.*

This comment is linked to communication between senior management and teaching staff, although two teachers from other schools put forward positive opinions about the way in which senior management listened, and responded, to their ideas and requests. One said:

> *I think we're very fortunate as regards timetabling and money and I think we have a senior management that listens – to us and to the children. If the children want a facility, or time, or a subject on the timetable that doesn't fit, they* [senior management] *will try their best to find it* (art teacher).

The other teacher suggested that sometimes the senior management at her school had been quite bold in listening to arts teachers, and allowing them the flexibility to develop their own ideas:

> *I think they have been very brave because I think they do have a very set way, or some of them are quite stuck in their ways, and they really have tried to let us come in with our new ideas and to let us do things. They have been very good particularly with me – who can go in a bit like a whirlwind at times – and want to change the world in 60 days, you know. They have been very patient with me and have let me get on with it, which is great, which is what I have needed. They are very supportive ... you need to have the support from them to be creative ... If I am not able to, perhaps, do the production I want, or to explore the topics that I want to explore, then I don't feel that I can give my best as a member of staff* (drama teacher).

This teacher had identified a connection between the freedom that was allowed (and supported) by senior management, and her own creativity. This seems likely to have had an impact on the content of her lessons, and the enthusiasm with which she approached them. This link between the freedom to experiment and the development of creativity in teaching is an issue raised by the NACCCE report (Robinson Report, 1999).

A music teacher from a different school made an unusually similar remark when he said: '... *they* [senior management] *see the energy and the way we work, and the way we do it ... and I think, without a doubt, they encourage us to do it our own way, do our own thing ...*'

At another school, the deputy head felt that it was important for him to maintain some teaching responsibilities – to keep in touch with the realities of teaching, and allowing him to maintain good relationships with other members of staff. He described why he felt this was so crucial:

> *... I think that it is absolutely essential ... for lots of reasons, I think there is a credibility factor with the staff and with the students that you can still do the job. I mean, for my own part, I am a good teacher, I like teaching the arts and I mean there was a lot of thought made to the decision to actually move out of the arts into senior management. This offered me the ideal opportunity actually to continue, for 11 hours a fortnight, being an arts teacher, which is just something that I value and I think that is really important.*

This comment also shows the value that an arts teacher placed on being able to continue with the classroom practice of teaching the arts – a possible reason why so few senior management staff appear to have a background in teaching the arts.

12.4.2 School ethos and atmosphere

The atmosphere and ethos of individual schools were seen to be pertinent in the effectiveness debate by all of the different groups of pupil and adult interviewees. The role of the headteacher in developing the overall direction of the school has already been explored, but one teacher emphasised the point that it was crucial for the views of the headteacher and senior staff to be filtered down throughout all ranks of the school.

None of the pupils or teachers who were interviewed following lesson observations made any comments about the general atmosphere of the school. Therefore, this section is based on interviews with key members of school staff, and pupils in the longitudinal cohort group.

One pupil, who had recently moved schools, explained that something about the atmosphere in his current school, which he was unable to define, made him want to try harder in arts subjects than he had at his previous school. He said:

I don't know what it is – kind of an impulse, I suppose – to work. At my old school I just couldn't be bothered, but since I've come here, I don't know, it's probably the atmosphere or something. The teachers just made me want to work – so I do.

Senior management and teaching staff described the importance of positive attitudes towards the arts in schools. A headteacher from one of the schools volunteered a list of some of the factors he felt to be germane to the subject:

Open-mindedness – from teachers, from pupils, from parents and from governors. An acknowledgement that the arts contribute something unique to children's development, and that the school will be a poorer place without it ... it's actually giving ... the arts a high-profile status in the school – that we value it, it's an important part of the curriculum, we have given them a superb building, we use children to perform in assembly, drama and music, we have regular concerts ... so the arts has a high profile in the life of the school and I think children feel there is a niche within the arts faculty that they can belong to, so I think the effectiveness comes from the feelings of satisfaction that children get from being engaged in arts practice.

It would appear that these factors might contribute to the type of atmosphere which the pupil was responding to (albeit subconsciously). Fostering and developing this type of positive atmosphere might be one way of increasing the effectiveness of not only arts education, but all subject areas within a school.

Attitudes towards the status and role of the arts at key stage 4 were sometimes mentioned as a potential factor in the school's arts achievement. The five case study schools varied in the emphasis placed on arts choices at key stage 4. At two out of the five schools, pupils were required to choose at least one arts option at key stage 4. In the three other schools, this was not compulsory – but all pupils were encouraged to take an arts subject.

One headteacher explained that, in his view, requiring pupils to take an arts subject at key stage 4 would reinforce their view of them as an area of the curriculum on an equal footing, in terms of status, with other subjects:

We don't operate, for example, a carousel curriculum – they have an hour of music, an hour of drama and an hour of art a week, and that happens right the way through the school, and we expect them to carry on with [at least one] arts GCSE, so I think a lot of the children will see the arts as being [as] important as the humanities, as the languages, as the design subjects.

A pupil at this school demonstrated her agreement with the headteacher – explaining her belief in the positive effect of valuing the arts. She said: '*I think it* [the arts] *is viewed quite important at the school, because everybody takes it seriously and I think it is really good they take it seriously.*' Unfortunately, she did not explain the rationale behind this opinion.

However, these views were contrary to the opinion expressed by another headteacher who thought that by the time pupils were choosing their key stage 4 subjects, they should have already been instilled with the importance of the arts, and should therefore choose to take an arts subject for themselves:

> ... *we have quite deliberately ... at key stage 4, allowed the arts to stand on their own two feet and not make them compulsory, because we think it's important that people choose them because of their intrinsic merits and not because we tell them to ...*

This quote implied he felt it was important for pupils to make option choices themselves, rather than through compulsion – this bears similarities to a view that pupils need to take ownership of, and responsibility for, their own choices. This was illustrated when one pupil described the lack of enthusiasm which had resulted from others being forced into a subject that they did not wish to take, and the effect that this had on its outcomes:

> *You've got to have a certain amount of enthusiasm for it. I know a couple of people who wanted to do PE but they couldn't get on the course so they had to do art and they just really didn't want to so they didn't make any effort or do anything, and so enthusiasm is quite a major factor* (Year 11).

The section on 'class formation' – 12.8.3 – explores in more detail the differences between mixed classes, and classes solely made up of pupils choosing a subject.

It is apparent that very different ways of inculcating an appreciation for the arts can be employed within schools, and that each has its supporters and opponents. However, the important factor which has been identified is that, in one way or another, for arts provision to be effective, schools must find a way of demonstrating the value and contribution that the arts can make.

12.4.3 Timetable issues

The factor which the pupils in the longitudinal cohort group mentioned most frequently in terms of whole-school issues was the timetabling of arts lessons. This included: the amount of time allocated to each subject; the length of individual lessons; and the arrangement of lessons within the timetable. These factors were also widely recognised by both teaching staff and senior management.

Length of time devoted to arts subjects

During the cohort pupil interviews, 14 pupils (16 per cent) commented on the total amount of time devoted to the arts within their school. All of the comments supported a view that more time should be available for the arts; however, the reasons given were varied. Many of the pupil attitudes towards the length of time spent in arts lessons were not specifically linked to the importance of developing the effects identified in Part Two of this report, but seemed to simply suggest a preference for the processes and activities involved in the arts, over those of the more traditionally academic subjects:

> *I feel we didn't get as many drama lessons as we would have liked – I think it was one every two weeks by the end. It might have been more. I just found one lesson isn't really enough but that's me personally because I really enjoy drama. I don't know what the others felt about it.*

Interviewer: *So that was one lesson of an hour?*

> *Yes, I think 55 minutes. It might have been one lesson a week but I just didn't feel it was enough* (Year 9).

One pupil suggested a potential remedy for this situation – supplementing arts lesson with more opportunities for using arts facilities at other times. Although extra-curricular activities and opportunities are often available in music, and to a lesser extent drama, this pupil had identified the benefit of being able to practise beyond lessons:

> *... sometimes I do some art work and I would like to go back at lunchtime to finish it off ... I would like there to be a club or something where you could just finish off your art work, because even though it is good to come back to the lesson and finish off work, I would like to get the whole thing done there and then, because when you have to mix colours, you will mix colours differently the next time and it won't be exactly the same, so it would be good if we had a lunchtime club or something like that. I think if all of the art teachers were able to do that, that would be better ...*(Year 9).

This was a solution which was also favoured by a deputy head who was responsible for timetabling issues, who tried to locate arts subjects before breaks so that students could continue to work. This was seen as far from ideal, but the only way in which more time could be allocated.

**3.
WHAT ARE
EFFECTIVE
PRACTICES
IN
ARTS
EDUCATION?**

Teachers also felt that the amount of time allocated to the arts was insufficient. Looking at the actual provision for time for the arts, subtle differences were distinguished between the case study schools. At key stage 3, the amount of time per week ranged from 30 minutes (drama) at one school to 105 minutes (art) at another. However, the way in which this time was arranged within the timetable varied considerably:

Table 12.1 Average minutes per week allocated to arts subjects at KS3

	School 1	School 2	School 3	School 4	School 5	Average provision across all schools
Art	90[1]	60	100[2]	75	105[3]	86
Drama	60	60	60	60[4]	30	54
Music	60	60	100[5]	75	60	71
Average provision across all arts	70	60	87	70	65	70[6]

NB Dance was provided at four schools only as an aspect of other subjects (either drama or PE) and therefore is not included on this table.

Key:

Above-average provision for the subject

Below-average provision for the subject

[1]   Provided as 120 minutes in Y7, 60 minutes in Y8 and 90 minutes in Y9

[2]   Provided as 120 minutes in Y7, and 60 minutes in Y8 and Y9

[3]   Provided as 150 minutes in Y7, 120 minutes in Y8 and 60 minutes in Y9

[4]   Provided as 50 minutes in Y7, and 75 minutes in Y8 and Y9

[5]   Provided as 60 minutes in Y7, 120 minutes in Y8 and 60 minutes in Y9

[6]   This figure represents the average provision across all three artforms, across all five case study schools

At key stage 4 the amount of time allocated to arts subjects was very similar across all five schools. For three of the schools, this was 150 minutes per week; the remaining two provided 160 minutes and 120 minutes per week.

Two teachers (of art and music) described the necessity for an adequate amount of time on the timetable in which to teach their subjects effectively:

You have got to have the time because certainly in music it's all about the time you put in to train them to end up with high levels of performance and academic success. I mean, for example, the A-level and GCSE results we have just had have been more or less the best ever and I am absolutely certain that that was due to the time that was put into them, way and above the time in class for GCSE, two-and-a-half hours a week, for A-level, four hours a week – there was a great deal more time went into it than that ... now somebody has to provide that time and provide that space and that's the problem ... actually finding a way of doing that ... (music teacher).

———

... they don't get enough time at key stage 4. I was here until half past seven, I never go home before five, because they are just desperately trying to finish off their coursework. So they don't get anywhere near the time ... They get two periods a week. If those two periods were just put together, the same as the first years have, then you wouldn't have the explanation time, the clearing up time, which does take a long time when they have got plaster, clay, paint and all sorts of things like that. So just putting those two periods together would make a huge difference and really, I think, another period, a separate period (art teacher).

Increasing the amount of time available for the arts in the timetable might be seen as one way of increasing the effectiveness of the teaching. However, it was suggested that this should not be achieved at the expense of other subjects.

Length of lessons

Similar to the issue of the total length of time devoted to arts lessons, the actual length of individual subject lessons was also an important issue for both teachers and pupils.

Fourteen pupils (16 per cent) within the cohort group expressed an opinion about the length of arts lessons. In general these comments were requesting longer lessons. However, one comment came from a pupil who currently had very long art lessons who actually felt that sometimes lessons could be too long:

I think one- to one-and-a-half-hour periods are good but sometimes it would be nice to get on with it all morning – like this week I had a three-hour morning period which is all right because we had a two-hour block and then after that we had a break and then we came back and the last hour was a bit of a slog really because it was waiting for things to dry and starting again and tidying up, and things are piling up and you've got tired eyes by then and you're not paying attention ... I think one to two hours is a good length of time – one-and-a-half hours' practical work and quarter of an hour either end setting up and clearing up and discussion (Year 11).

On this issue, the opinions of teachers and pupils were broadly in agreement. Almost one in four of the staff interviewed mentioned lesson length as an important factor in the effectiveness of the subject. Contrasting remarks were made by a drama and an art teacher from different schools:

Drama

I actually think two hours, for the kind of commitment we ask, and discipline that we ask for the kids in the lesson, is a long time – it is a long time for them and they can get very tired ... I personally think that the single periods work most effectively.

Art

I find 55 minutes [a single lesson] *a bit short – we used to have one hour and ten minutes and I thought that was perfect. I used to find that I had time at the end of the session when we had cleared up to discuss the work that they had been doing, whereas at the moment I find that I don't often get that in, by the time they have cleared up. It is a very short time is 55 minutes because it is not 55 minutes by the time they have arrived to your lesson and you have taken the register ... plus for the exam groups they are single periods, which is not good at all. We used to have them for all morning or all afternoon, which was much better. I don't teach exam art now but when I did they would say 'Oh, it is not worth getting that out now', when they were setting something up, perhaps screen-printing or whatever. They didn't feel that it was worth getting it out because it was a single period.*

These extracts demonstrate the two ways in which the length of lessons is determined. The second teacher describes the reduction of single lessons from 70 to 55 minutes, and the effect this has had on her lesson planning. The other way in which longer lessons can be affected is by blocking multiple lessons together. As has already been described, sometimes this produced lessons which were an equally ineffective use of time due to pupils' limited attention span.

The comments also highlight the different needs of the arts subjects. Art teachers clearly favoured longer lessons, in order to maximise the amount of useful work that could be achieved, whereas the drama teacher felt shorter lessons were more effective. This provides one rationale for consideration of the separate subject areas that make up 'the arts' as independent entities.

The main reasons pupils gave for their request for longer arts lessons included the desire to be able to complete work within the lesson and the length of time required for the teacher to give individual help to each pupil in the class. This second factor was also linked to the size of the class – the effects of which are considered in section 12.8.2 dealing with 'class formation'. The length of time needed for developing ideas (in all arts) and showing work to the class (in drama) was also highlighted.

In relation to art, the length of time taken in getting equipment out and clearing up at the end was an important reason for having longer lessons:

> *All three subjects that we are talking about ... have five per cent of the curriculum time at key stage 3. We run a two-week timetable, 60 periods ... they actually have three periods each a fortnight, which means that it is split – that is the thing that they don't like – as a double and a single. Now art thinks that it should have two doubles, basically, they would argue that they need ... a double a week is what they would argue. The single, they would argue, also, and I would sympathise with this, especially with art – it is a 50-minute single, but by the time you have got all the paint out and by the time that you have got all the paint cleared up at the end, you have lost quite a bit of time. It is much better to run those in double; it is just the way that the curriculum is panned out to do everything that we want to do* (deputy head).

Clearing classrooms for drama, where no dedicated drama suite was available, and pupils getting changed for dance, were also cited as taking up valuable lesson time.

Frequency and arrangement of arts lessons

The cohort pupils made ten comments about the problems or benefits they associated with the frequency of individual arts lessons.

The main comments from pupils about the arrangement of lessons fell into one of two camps – four comments centred on the problems of remembering the topic when lessons were only once a week, or once a fortnight, and two comments were made about the problem of missing lessons due to illness and bank holidays, and it then being several weeks before the next lesson. On a positive note, three comments suggested that the pupils chose to work harder in lessons that were less frequent, because they felt they should maximise the opportunities provided. The large majority of these comments about the infrequency of lessons were made regarding drama and music.

One of the teachers interviewed highlighted a particular problem which was faced by one class within the timetable. At key stage 3, drama was allocated a double lesson, but unfortunately the only way in which this could be timetabled was as two single lessons, one on either side of lunchtime – this was far from satisfactory, especially for drama lessons which were given over to dance:

> *... they have to change – if they are doing dance, they change four times – they change at the beginning, they change at the end, then they come back after lunch and change and change again. So we have tried absolutely everything to stop it but there was just no way that we could fix that.*

It is clear that a considerable amount of time is wasted by this arrangement of the timetable, and this situation was deemed to be severely detrimental to the subject.

Good and bad times for arts lessons

Interestingly, pupils passed frequent remarks about the times of day, or days of the week, that were both good or bad times for arts lessons, but this issue was raised only infrequently by teachers or by school management.

Twenty-three cohort pupils (27 per cent) ventured an opinion about the arrangement of their lessons within the school timetable. Most of the comments related to the subject areas of art and drama. None of the pupils referred to the location of dance within the timetable. Table 12.2 summarises the times and days which cohort pupils felt were good or bad times to have arts lessons.

Table 12.2   Pupil perceptions of good and bad times for arts lessons

	Number of pupils mentioning	
	Good times	Bad times
Times of day		
First lesson/early morning	4	6
Late morning	5	-
Early afternoon	3	-
Last lesson/late afternoon	3	12
Days of week		
Monday	1	2
Midweek	1	-
Friday	4	6

Looking at the comments made about bad times of day for arts lessons, the pupils who made comments were all in agreement – stating that the first or last lesson would be bad. This view was supported by a pupil whose last lesson of the day – art – was observed as part of the research. She said: '*Sometimes we have art lessons last lesson of the day, and everyone wants to go home, so at the end of the lesson they are really noisy*', but also commented that this particular lesson was distinctive as pupils were paying more attention that day than they usually did – presumably responding to the presence of the camera.

No pupils suggested that the middle of the day would be a bad time for an arts lesson. However, when suggesting good times for arts lessons, the opinions varied – just slightly more pupils favouring mornings than afternoons.

Another pupil who was interviewed, following an art lesson observation, concurred with the cohort pupil interviews that the last lesson of the day was usually a bad time because the class wanted to go home and were noisy. A music teacher whose lesson was observed suggested that the first lesson after lunch could also be difficult, although no specific reason was given.

In terms of the days of the week, Friday was most commonly cited as being both a good and a bad time for a lesson. Five pupils specifically mentioned Friday afternoon, or Friday last lesson, as being a particularly bad time.

In addition to specific times or days, two pupils felt that it was generally bad to have an arts lesson after a difficult lesson, or during a difficult day, and another observed that lessons which came after exciting or practical lessons in the timetable were often difficult – commenting that the class could be '*giddy*'. However, one pupil referred to how the warm-up done at the beginning of drama lessons helped them to recover from whatever difficult lessons they had had earlier. This might suggest that such a warm-up activity may be a valuable prelude to a lesson in any subject, rather than simply a precursor to drama.

The pupils interviewed made quite clear references to the times of the day and the days of the week which would be the best, and the worst, times for arts lessons. However, it is purely a matter of speculation whether this pattern might not be repeated for any subject within the curriculum. Although the question was phrased in terms of arts lessons, only four out of 26 responses were related specifically to the arts, or an individual artform – the others were general. From this it might be concluded that the pupils would respond favourably to a revolving timetable – where lessons occur at different times each week. This would appear to be especially true for subjects with a limited number of lessons each week, such as drama, where being located regularly at a bad time of day, or on a bad day of the week (such as first lesson Monday, or last lesson Friday), could have serious negative implications.

12.4.4 Summary

By way of summarising the key points on 'whole-school' factors, the evidence indicated that:

- generating a positive school ethos in which work and achievement in the arts are valued and celebrated was widely held to be a major contributor to the effectiveness of arts education;

- providing sufficient time for the arts, with scheduling and periods of lessons appropriate to the different artforms, was also seen to be a crucial factor;

- a senior management team that was responsive and encouraging to teachers' ideas for fostering creativity was considered to be another pertinent feature of effective provision; and finally

- it was generally noted that the support of the headteacher was extremely beneficial (e.g. in facilitating the above three bullet points), though cases were found where the arts had flourished without this.

12.5 ARTS FACULTY OR DEPARTMENT FACTORS

Two main issues were identified which were perceived to affect the provision of arts education within the case study schools:

- the organisation of faculties and departments; and

- the resources available to faculties and departments.

These issues were raised frequently by both staff and pupils.

12.5.1 Faculty or department organisation

Nineteen teachers and school senior managers (43 per cent) made comments about the advantages and disadvantages of the different ways in which the teaching of the arts in secondary schools could be organised. However, the opinions – and the structural arrangements within the schools – varied widely. The following table summarises the different ways in which the arts were provided by the case study schools.

Table 12.3   Structures for teaching the arts in case study schools

School 1	School 2	School 3	School 4	School 5
Departments of art, drama and music.	Music and drama in the **Faculty of Expressive Arts**.	Art, dance, drama and music all in the **Faculty of Arts**.	Art, music and drama all within the **Faculty of Expressive Arts**.	**Departments** of creative arts, drama and music.
Dance within PE.	Art in the **Faculty of Art and Design.** Dance now within PE, moved from Faculty of Expressive Arts.		Dance now within PE rather than its original location of drama.	Dance not provided.

Perhaps the most positive comment in favour of arts faculties came from an LEA arts adviser who was interviewed. He explained why he was such a strong believer in this type of organisation:

> *... first of all it delivers at least one very experienced teacher – because you can aspire to be a senior teacher in a school and still stay within the arts, you don't have to give it up and go off to be a pastoral teacher, or a deputy head or something ... they stay as arts specialists – they don't have to give that up, so that is important. It also provides a structure whereby the arts can come together on a regular basis to discuss issues of common concern ... One of the things that I think does also deliver a coherent arts curriculum is that debate ... that interaction between the arts. Unless there is a forum for that debate to have happened, then it is very difficult for the arts to spark off each other and to be coherent. I think the other thing that it looks at is common ways of assessing, of valuing, what is going on in the arts as well, and planning for arts activities.*

Teachers and staff at the three schools currently employing a faculty structure were divided on the issue of whether they felt this structure was beneficial.

At one particular school, there was disagreement on the advantages (or otherwise) of being organised around a faculty structure. The headteacher was very much in favour of the Faculty of Expressive Arts (including art, music and drama), whilst recognising the independence and strengths of the individual departments it contained:

> *There is a faculty, but then there are these very distinct departments that co-exist within that faculty ... I think there were quite separate, and probably quite disparate, departments once upon a time. I actually like the faculty structure. I think that there are many benefits from it in that it does bring those disparate departments together to discuss educational issues. So you do get some sort of cross-fertilisation and you do get them discussing, for instance, how would you differentiate in an art lesson and how do you do it in a music lesson? So that there is some sharing of good practice and sharing of ideas, which I always think is really very beneficial ... Faculties have a lot of power and a lot of strength and sometimes you find that they are actually working against each other because they have got quite different aims and quite different philosophies. So I think to actually have an arts faculty, which has a clear, agreed philosophy of what the purpose of arts education is and what its role within the school is, is very good. I think that it has actually brought those areas together in that there is now quite a lot of cooperation between them.*

**3.
WHAT ARE
EFFECTIVE
PRACTICES
IN
ARTS
EDUCATION?**

Other staff in the school were unconvinced that this was entirely the case. Criticisms of the faculty structure were made by the head of music, and by a drama teacher. She said:

> *I have never been in a faculty yet that has worked ... as a group of people we do work together, but the subjects are very, very different. I have talked about transferable skills and they are transferable skills in art, music, drama, PE, they are all the same, but the assessment criteria is very different and the way that you work is very different. To say a child is good at music ... then obviously they are going to be good at the other arts subjects is a nonsense.*

It was implied by one interviewee that one of the reasons why staff from these subject areas expressed dissatisfaction was the favouritism conferred by the faculty head on his own artform – art. It would appear that a faculty arrangement may face problems where such accusations are made, and subject areas do not feel equally supported by management. Moreover, it may well be the case that faculty structures encourage liaison between arts subjects at the expense of individual artform subjects' links with other areas of the curriculum, which may suffer as a result (e.g. drama with English, art and design with technology, dance with PE).

The alternative to a faculty structure for the arts was adopted by the other two schools – where the arts were provided by separate departments. Again, opinions were divided over the efficacy of the system. Perhaps surprisingly, the teachers who worked in departments were equally critical of current arrangements as those working within a faculty structure. Comments were made particularly by representatives of drama. One said: '*People don't talk to each other very much ... unless they have to, and that's not because they won't; it's just that physically we're all very separate and tend to ... I mean we're all beavering away at lunchtime in our own little places on our own subjects.*'

Another drama teacher from the same school described her vision for a performing arts faculty, and explained what she perceived to be the advantages of such an arrangement:

> *I'd like to see a performing arts faculty: one with somebody coming in for dance, somebody for drama, somebody for music and maybe media as well, to make the term 'performing arts' rather than a drama faculty ... I think that a lot of the aims and objectives are the same, and reporting would be easier, assessing, and it would be useful not to work in isolation but to be able to discuss your own ideas and thoughts and see what other ideas other people have got ...*

**3.
WHAT ARE
EFFECTIVE
PRACTICES
IN
ARTS
EDUCATION?**

An art teacher from the other school with separate arts departments agreed that encouraging staff communication would be a valuable activity, but that this did not rely simply on reorganisation into a faculty: *'I like the way that the arts department is set up at the moment. What I would like to see is more communication between the arts departments and maybe a little more ... cross-curricular things going on. I don't think I would like to be merged into a faculty.'*

It seems that both systems of organisation had their merits and drawbacks, supporters and opponents. The staff in schools with no overarching faculty structure often felt that this would be valuable in providing coordination and increasing staff communication. However, where faculties had been implemented, this was sometimes found not to be the case in practice – members of arts faculties often identified with the strength provided by individual departments. It is clear that this is a difficult decision and that no consensus regarding it was found amongst the interviewees.

12.5.2 Faculty or departmental resources

A more significant issue than the organisation of faculties or departments was the funding and resources which were available to the arts within the schools. This was raised frequently as a crucial factor by both staff and pupils. The types of resources which were cited included:

- accommodation – buildings and rooms;
- facilities and equipment; and
- artefacts and visual stimuli.

Accommodation – buildings and rooms

A third of the pupils interviewed talked about the location of their arts lessons. Only two comments made suggested that the accommodation for arts subjects was irrelevant to the question of effective education.

A common theme was the need for adequate provision of space for the arts. Eighteen pupils made a relevant remark – ranging from the lone individual who thought that the size of the room available was of no consequence, to those who felt strongly that they needed considerably more space than currently provided. Some comments related to all of the different artforms, but most were in discussion of drama provision:

... there's two drama rooms and when we're in the bigger room we have more space, and in the little room it's all a bit cramped and you're kind of fighting over chairs and whatever, so it's better when you're in the big room (Year 9).

... the drama studio is really good because it's a big space and you have got lots of room to rehearse and when you are performing, everyone can sit down and watch really well. Sometimes, you have to do it in the gym – well most of the time you do it in the gym – and it's OK there but I prefer the drama studio because it's more of a good atmosphere for drama. Gym reminds you more of PE so it doesn't really work (Year 9).

A drama teacher, at a school where a new drama suite had recently been provided, agreed with the pupils – that the most important factor was space:

If you get as far as getting a drama studio, people seem to think that: 'Oh well, we'll get a drama studio', so you get an architect in and they build you this thing called a drama studio – they don't think about all the other things you need for drama. I would far rather not have a studio if it meant that I was going to lose classroom space because you also want them to be able to sit down, you want them to be able to make things, you want them to draw costumes, you need a decent-sized space, with tables. You need a large physical space, far bigger than they've actually catered for here – you can't get in ... You don't need an expensive dance floor; you need a bigger hall. OK it's nice to have lights and all those nice things to play with, but a huge space is the most important thing ...

Art lessons were also faced with similar problems – with pupils needing space in which to spread out their artwork.

However, one headteacher made a forceful comment when he insisted that the teachers within the arts were more important in influencing the quality of education than either the rooms or buildings. He said: '... *I think the people in the arts are probably as important as the building, but it is nice to be in a nice facility.*'

Music faced its own particular problems in terms of location. Pupils often referred to not being able to hear themselves think whilst the whole class were composing on keyboards:

... it's hard because when you are practising your music piece you are in the same class and everyone else is practising it, so it's really hard to hear and you get a surprise when you hear it by yourself when you are performing it (Year 9).

One solution to the problem, which was adopted by two of the schools, was the use of smaller music practice rooms (known as '*the cells*' in one school). These smaller rooms allowed pupils to develop their music independently, and, as one pupil identified, it often helped her to be less self-conscious, and therefore more creative:

... we can all spread out to different rooms, and it's really nice because you have your own space to do it and you're not thinking about 'Oh, other people can hear what we're doing'. You're not thinking 'Oh, this sounds really bad'. You can actually just get on with it and think 'Well, no one else can hear; let's just give it a go'. I think that's really nice (Year 9).

Accommodation for lessons was one of a number of difficulties faced by the music department of one of the case study schools – seen by the head of arts as reflecting poorly on the reputation of the subject within the school:

... we have two classrooms downstairs. They were built when you had 15 in a class and now they have to have 30, which is appalling. You just can't even get them in the room ... it is very poor accommodation ... these offices are right above it, and it must drive them mad in here having meetings with that going on all the time, repeating the same thing over. Really it is not properly sound-proofed and there is no space (head of arts faculty).

3.
WHAT ARE
EFFECTIVE
PRACTICES
IN
ARTS
EDUCATION?

It is clear from all of these comments that in order for the arts to develop, adequate attention must be paid to the accommodation with which they are furnished. Pupils and staff alike have recognised that without sympathetic accommodation provision – in terms of volume of space and suitability for purpose – the arts simply cannot flourish.

Facilities and equipment

In addition to adequate space within buildings, pupils and teachers also recognised the need for good facilities and equipment within the rooms.

Thirty-nine per cent of the cohort pupils made some comment about how materials, facilities or equipment affected their learning in the arts, or their attitudes towards it – with little difference in numbers observed between art, drama and music. Only one remark was made about dance – referring to the enjoyment gained from being able to use gym equipment in lessons.

Art

In art, the main theme of the pupil attitudes was related to consumable materials (paper, paint, etc.) and equipment such as brushes. A Year 9 pupil stated that art lessons were most effective '*when you have good paints to use, good pencils to use, you know, when the materials in general are good – because it means you're more likely to produce a better piece of work*'. An older pupil at the same school said:

The materials which the school provides are pretty good – they don't provide things like specialist ... I mean, I know art's a specialist subject, but things like wire – if you want to use wire you've really got to find that and bring it in yourself, or if you want to use large amounts of oil paints for your final piece you really ought to go and buy ... and some good quality glue for mounting up – you've got to go and buy that as well, but I think that's fair enough (Year 11).

This comment, whilst praising the quality of the materials the school does provide, also suggests that pupils must expect to purchase some specialist arts materials for themselves. This provides a practical illustration of one way in which pupils from less affluent backgrounds might find themselves disadvantaged in the subject (see section 12.3.1 – '*Local community and school catchment area factors*'). In another instance, the remarks made by a pupil showed some sense of dissatisfaction: '... *in pottery recently there was a limited number of colours available for glazing dishes, and this was further restricted due to misbehaviour in the class, so resources are limited* [or] *confiscated.*'

She associated this situation – where practical resources were limited, and then further reduced as a punishment for the poor behaviour of the class – with '*a bad lesson*'. There is little evidence that this action constituted an effective form of discipline – in this instance, the effect was to turn the pupil off the subject.

Music

In music, the issue of facilities and equipment was framed slightly differently. There were few occasions where consumable materials were used (as in art), but more dependence on musical instruments, and latterly also recording equipment and computers. Almost three-quarters of the music-related remarks specifically mentioned the value of the provision of a range of musical instruments:

> ... *the keyboard might sound better for what you're doing than a xylophone and we ... have lots of things, like we have guitars to play, and xylophones, and keyboards, and drums – a whole variety so you can make different music* (Year 9).

The quantity and quality of the instruments available were also concerns:

Quantity
> ... *there are loads of keyboards in the music room, so even if the teacher is helping someone else you can just turn round and carry on with your own work, so there's never any time wasted in music. There's always something you can be doing, so yes, their facilities help us learn because they are always there for us, they are available for us* (Year 11).

Quality

> *... sometimes the keyboards aren't that great. You know, they don't work and are a bit dodgy. When you have a good keyboard to work, it's got lots of different things you can add in, lots of different background sounds, you can use beats on them and things ... (Year 9).*

Showing some empathy for the teacher's needs, one pupil suggested that good equipment to work with provided encouragement for the teacher. When asked about the factors he felt encouraged learning in music, he replied:

> *... I think for the first time I'm going to say equipment because I think it is important and it does improve the capability. It's sort of a booster for the teacher.*

Interviewer: *So you mean instruments you use and things like that?*

Yes (Year 9).

Teachers also outlined the benefits of adequate provision of equipment. One described her perception of the advantage generated by good music facilities:

> *Basically, it enables you to do your job properly – at the end of the day, you can't teach music on two keyboards and two tiny glockenspiels. We cannot do singing for every single lesson, which some schools have to resort to. Kids shouldn't be copying out of books and just listening to pieces of music – there's more to music than that, and it does provide every child with the opportunity ... to make music, to perform music, to appreciate music ...*

Not all of the case study schools were equally well equipped. At one of the case study schools, the facilities available to music were heavily criticised by both pupils and staff. One Year 9 pupil said:

> *... we need more instruments and that, because a lot of the time there's about five people crammed on to one keyboard. I think it would make it better if we had more variety of instruments to play with, because usually we have a keyboard, piano and a drum or something, people doing the beats, and that's good because everyone loves working with keyboards, but if we learnt other things as well, not complicated things but just learnt to play other instruments, I think that would be good as well.*

This view was echoed by the head of music, who was quoted previously talking about the lack of space for the subject. She defined her list of key factors in effective music teaching as:

Enough resources for every child, proper electrical equipment, a decent room – just resources.

Interviewer: *Keyboards and things like that?*

Keyboards, percussion instruments – enough for one each. Just enough for everybody so that they can use them on their own, they don't have to share.

It is clear that this school faces a difficult task if it is to improve the situation for music. The provision of new accommodation and the number of musical instruments thought necessary would be a major financial investment, but one of which pupils and teachers from other schools have described the potential benefits.

Drama

Whilst drama attracted similar numbers of comments about the facilities and equipment available for the subject, issues were not voiced as powerfully, and they seemed to be of less concern than in art or music. One pupil made the point clearly:

The atmosphere [in drama] *is created mainly by the pupils that are working in it – the room is not important, you can do drama anywhere; the props – again you don't need them or you can make do with something else, like if you need a chair you can use a block or if you need some lighting you can do without. The props aren't important: they can help, but they're not important* (Year 11).

Other pupils were not so sure that this was the case, and described how they felt props and technical theatre equipment could help them in drama lessons:

Lighting helps, when they use the lighting and you can create a really nice atmosphere and it just makes it a whole lot better (Year 9).

… we have got a very sophisticated stage and everything and that's a very good incentive for working on it, and when it's actually shown on the stage it's going to look very good. The place we are in at the moment, that's particularly designed for what we need to do, so yes, it's perfect, and all the lighting and equipment and sound and everything, it complements it very well. Everything we need really (Year 11).

One pupil explained that he had '*gone off drama a bit*' recently because lessons had been located in different classrooms – with few specialised drama facilities. He described how this had affected his enjoyment of the lessons: '*We have been in temporary rooms so they have not had any of the lighting or anything, so it's not been as fun, it's not been as realistic or anything*' (Year 8).

3.
WHAT ARE
EFFECTIVE
PRACTICES
IN
ARTS
EDUCATION?

Teachers, however, did not isolate their perceptions of facilities or equipment for drama from their views on accommodation. Accommodation was thought to be very important – especially space – but no comments were made specifically on this issue.

Artefacts and visual stimuli

In addition to the arts accommodation, and the facilities or equipment with which pupils interacted directly, mention was often made about other resources available in rooms dedicated to arts teaching. Often noted were the positive benefits of visual stimuli – in the form of other pupils' work, images, or collections of artefacts and objects. Not surprisingly, most of the remarks related to art. The head of the faculty of arts from one school was particularly positive on this theme:

> *... when they walk into a room, they absorb things that they don't even know that they are absorbing.*

Interviewer: *So you stimulate them with this visual art?*

> *Yes, yes I do. I have always tried very hard to make my room as exciting as possible with a lot of different things in it and changing around six weeks is probably enough, because you don't look any more after six weeks ... I sometimes change the room completely as well. It is not in squares, the whole room is changed and we are sitting in different places.*

The pupils also seemed to respond positively to the idea of classrooms containing objects and images related to the subject. Nine pupils (11 per cent) remarked on it and they described a variety of ways in which they felt it could be of benefit:

Developing ideas

Interviewer: *Anything else you can think of that helps you to learn?*

Having other paintings around the room as well, looking at other people's work, getting some ideas and things (Year 9).

Learning different ways of working

... the class that I work in – that also helps a lot because it's a nice big room where you can have your work everywhere and there's also lots of work stuck on the walls and things, which helps you to learn different ways of working (Year 11).

Motivation to develop

... because you have got, like, plants and sculptures everywhere, so it's ... you look around and sometimes you see a really good piece of art that, like, got A*, and you look at it and say 'Well, why has that got an A*?' Then you think to yourself 'Well, she got an A* because she did this, this and this, and maybe I will try and apply that to what I am doing so then maybe I can get my grades'. It's good – it gives you inspiration ... (Year 11).

One teacher described an LEA resource on which local schools could draw to provide this type of visual material:

> ... *we have a resource centre up the road which the school pays about £500 a year to belong to and we can borrow anything, and so can any other subject, borrow anything from there. That resource we have used in art more probably than anything else because we can have a theme and we can go up there and it is stuffed with costumes and artefacts from all around the world. It is just brilliant. We could not afford, or have the space, to use those things, things like canal boat art. I did a project last year linking to the canal in the area, and history. We had these boxes of canal boat art. I would not even have been able to find them, let alone buy them myself. So that has been a really invaluable resource and I think that is the sort of thing ... that art departments know how to use these artefacts; it is not just putting it on a table and drawing it, at all. There is so much ... Primary schools probably do a lot of that sort of thing, but I think a lot of secondary school subjects don't. If I am covering other lessons sometimes, I often think that if I had got that here, I would have been using a lot more visual stimulus in whatever subject it was* (head of arts faculty).

3.
WHAT ARE
EFFECTIVE
PRACTICES
IN
ARTS
EDUCATION?

This contribution also touched on how visual stimuli could be utilised by other subject areas – an idea with which one pupil agreed. He suggested how being surrounded by images and objects in music helped him to concentrate on that particular subject:

> ... *if* [the music lesson] *is in the music room, it's quite good because it's big and there's lot of, like, posters and pictures around to remind us about music.*

Interviewer: *How is that helpful, having the posters around?*

> *Because it gets you in the mood for doing music, rather than doing other lessons or other subjects* (Year 9).

It seems possible that all curriculum areas might benefit from this type of resource – a means of directing pupils' thoughts towards the subject which they are learning via visual stimulation rather than simply aural methods.

12.5.3 Summary

By way of summarising the key points on 'faculty and departmental' factors, the evidence indicated that:

- access to buildings, rooms, facilities and resources designed to meet the particular requirements of each artform was widely considered to have an important bearing on the quality of teaching and learning in the arts; but

- there was no agreement among the interviewees as to whether faculties or separate departments were the most beneficial.

12.6 CURRICULUM FACTORS

Issues surrounding the arts curriculum were not restricted simply to what happened within the classroom – pupils and teachers were concerned with a wide range of issues which related to the curriculum in its broadest sense. The main issues for teachers were the planning and mediation of the arts curriculum in school, and fulfilling the requirements of the National Curriculum. Pupils, on the other hand, were keen to describe their experience of the curriculum – the outcome of the teachers' concerns. Five main themes were identified:

- the National Curriculum;
- curriculum content and planning;
- processes and activities during arts lessons;
- differentiation; and
- assessment.

3.
WHAT ARE
EFFECTIVE
PRACTICES
IN
ARTS
EDUCATION?

The location of '*curriculum factors*' within their own category recognises the importance attached to this set of perceptions, but also separates it from association with either '*whole-school*' or '*faculty and departmental*' factors. It is recognised that with the introduction of the National Curriculum, the Government have held considerable power over the content and structure of the curriculum, but it is also known that within the National Curriculum for the arts there exists considerable flexibility for teachers to develop their own ideas – Part Two of this report offered further evidence of this in terms of the wide variety of noted effects. Considering the curriculum as a separate entity allows flexible analysis of all the factors which have a role to play, at whatever stage of curriculum planning, development or mediation they occur.

12.6.1 The National Curriculum

The introduction of the National Curriculum has clearly had major implications for the development of school curricula across all subject areas – the arts included.

Thirty per cent of the school staff interviewed during the initial phase of the research made some comment about the relevance and impact of the National Curriculum. Comments were made by staff from all levels of school management and teaching, and from all case study schools. However, the opinions expressed varied widely – highlighting both advantages and disadvantages of the National Curriculum in arts lesson effectiveness.

There were also illustrations of the specific problems faced by drama and dance – artforms not represented as individual subjects within the National Curriculum, but components of English and PE respectively. Teachers of these subjects often described both the advantages and disadvantages of their subject's particular position.

All the remarks about the advantages of the National Curriculum were made by teachers and school staff. Only two pupils made any mention of the National Curriculum – both negative, and both with regard to music. It appears that pupils have little to say regarding the influence which the Government exerts on the curriculum – seeming to believe more in the influence of the school, the teacher of a class and their own contribution.

Advantages of National Curriculum

The advantages of the National Curriculum were seen to fall mainly into one of two broad categories:

- increasing pupil entitlement to the arts, and subject credibility; and

- helping teachers focus ideas, and introducing new elements.

Increasing pupil entitlement to the arts, and subject credibility

These two closely related factors were both seen as positive outcomes of the introduction of the National Curriculum which included requirements for the provision of arts education.

Two arts faculty heads, a head of drama, and two arts subject teachers (drama and ceramics) (ten per cent of the total number of staff interviewed) made reference to the improvement of the status of arts subjects within the school curriculum. One teacher commented on how the introduction of the National Curriculum had provided an entitlement to arts education for all children. When asked about its impact on art, she said:

> *I think probably on the whole it's been a good thing. I think it has raised the entitlement of all pupils to an art education. We've always provided it, but I am sure there were schools that didn't … so it's probably improved the availability of an arts-based education to a wider number of students* (art teacher).

This increasing entitlement was mirrored in an increase in status for the arts subjects:

> *In a sense, perhaps, it has had a good impact. I mean, there are always pluses and minuses for these things. It has possibly had a good impact in the sense that it has made art seem more worthwhile in the timetable because there has always been the issue that art is not a serious subject. So, in a sense, it has kind of built up the credibility.*

There was a general consensus that this was the case, although comments were made to the effect that drama was sometimes excluded from this increase in status because of its omission from the National Curriculum as a separate subject – it being included as part of English. Despite its similar circumstances, there were no such comments for dance (which is part of the National Curriculum only through PE prevision) – but this may simply be a reflection of a general lack of comments of any type relating to the subject. Dance as an artform area has been poorly represented throughout the research, and therefore it is difficult to draw any conclusions from its omission in this context.

Despite the National Curriculum Orders for drama, in all the case study schools it was still preserved as a separate subject, and this may prove to be a factor in its success. The head of drama at one of the schools said: '... it [the National Curriculum] *impacted on drama's aims here ... because I kept it ... as a separate subject ... So we are delivering English Orders, but that is not our ... you know, I don't sit down with the head of English and say "Yeah, I am going to do this and this, this week" or whatever.'*

Despite this positive step, she continued to explain the balance between positive and negative outcomes, and her continuing concern for the subject – a view echoed by another drama teacher, who said:

> *I am still sort of a little dismayed that drama ... generally that it is the poor relation in the arts subjects since it is not a National Curriculum subject ... I would like to see* [drama] *achieve parity with them* [music and art] *again. It is out of my hands, isn't it? That is just one thing that dismays me a little bit about it.*

The head of the arts faculty at the school described how he felt that he may be accused of paying more attention to the other artforms – thus propagating its second-class status:

> *... the two drama teachers do feel that I place more emphasis on art and music as head of the faculty. I may do, but I don't feel as if I do, but simply because a lot of the legislation involves music and art. A lot of it has to be enforced through law, whereas a lot of the drama stuff has not got that part behind it.*

It is apparent that the introduction of the National Curriculum has been a very valuable step in increasing all pupils' entitlement to the arts and requiring its provision within secondary education. However, there is still a danger, because of the way in which subjects were grouped, that dance and drama could become second class artforms – marginalised within the curriculum in favour of the independent artforms – art and music. It will be important that this situation is monitored for future consideration of its impact.

Helping teachers focus ideas, and introducing new elements

The other group of related, positive, influences of the National Curriculum comprised comments from teachers and school staff about how its requirements had helped them to clarify the content of the curriculum, and introduce new processes and activities – thereby extending the effectiveness of the arts education they provided. Six school staff (12 per cent of those interviewed), representing all schools, and all levels of seniority, made comments on this issue. One head of an arts faculty said:

I think it has been for the better.

Interviewer: *In what way?*

A lot of staff had an awful lot of trouble with National Curriculum when it came in because a lot of the arts staff worked intuitively. I think it would be fair to say that many of the arts staff would walk down the corridor on the way to their lesson and say 'What shall we do?', and be thinking what they were going to do on their way down to the lesson. Now we have specific modules of work which are designed to last between six and eight weeks, we have to get to the end of those modules and we have to complete at least four modules per year ... I am a great advocate now of using modular work because we can assess it and because it gives children a target – particularly if you can explain to the children at the beginning of the module what you are going to do and you work together towards the end-product ... It is a target and I think that children work towards targets much better.

This was also an issue for the teachers concerned, who identified attainment target 2 for art – knowing and understanding – as a valuable addition within the curriculum – countering the traditional focus on making and doing. This was raised by an art teacher who said: '... *it means that everyone has to go out and look at the work of other artists and relate it to their own work and obviously looking at the work of other artists firsthand ...*' The addition of this element of the arts curriculum clearly goes some way towards redressing the balance between 'doing' and 'appreciating' the arts – particularly beneficial to those pupils who become disenchanted with the arts due to their lack of practical ability.

One headteacher also recognised the importance of a knowledge and understanding of cultural traditions across a range of different artforms. He said, of the National Curriculum:

I think that the thing that it highlighted, and I actually supported, was that an awareness of the traditions, particularly of music and art were made more explicit in the knowledge and understanding objective. Although some resented it, I have no problem with that and I actually think that it should be a part of arts education. It is interesting that drama does not have such an explicit objective, although the English teacher picks up part of that obligation on their behalf, I suppose.

It does appear that the introduction of the National Curriculum has impacted on the content, processes and activities within the arts. The content, processes and activities practised within the arts are subjects for further discussion later in this section of the report.

Disadvantages of National Curriculum

Not all of the comments made about the National Curriculum were positive. Two members of school staff interviewed at different schools mentioned disadvantages of the National Curriculum – their comments were directed toward its restrictive nature, and the lack of freedom and choice available to both teachers and pupils.

The head of the art and design faculty at one of the schools described how the writing of full schemes of work, in order to satisfy the requirements of the National Curriculum, meant reducing the amount of time spent on developing creative ideas. She said:

> *To write a full-scale scheme of work and to actually put all the aims and objectives, to write down the homeworks and to actually know exactly how many homeworks have got to be done in the term etc., takes a long time. Whilst you are doing that, you are not thinking, you are not sparking and coming up with brand-new ideas. The flexibility, I think, has gone. When I first came into teaching you would certainly have a project idea, you would have it written down, but if suddenly something took a particular direction, you were much more able to go with it, whereas now I feel that you are not because you are very conscious of the fact that over the key stage they have got to have covered particular things and they must not miss out on something else. You have got to be sure all the time that all pupils have covered all the same materials and they have had all the same experiences. I suppose in the past that wasn't quite so targeted.*

She continued to explain that she felt this left pupils with a curriculum which appeared far more rigid than it was, but that the introduction of academic rigour had increased the level of status and respect attributed to the subject within the school. However, a headteacher highlighted the need to maintain some freedom for pupils within the limits of the prescribed curriculum when he said:

> *... what I am more concerned with about the National Curriculum is allowing children to develop their individual freedoms. You see, if the National Curriculum does not allow children to access their*

skills and abilities, it is no good to me, it is no good to them. So, the professionalism is to allow children to run in such a way that they meet any preordained criteria but in a way that the pupils are happy with ...

As mentioned earlier, cohort pupils only made two comments about the National Curriculum, both negative, and both related to music. One pupil was in agreement with the headteacher above – suggesting that in his experience of music, studying purely the contents of the National Curriculum had restricted the time available for creative experimentation:

I think at the moment we are doing very basic sort of National Curriculum ... you have got to do such and such and such and such – I think we are just doing that. We are not going off and being really creative and exploring different methods; we are just going rather by the book at the moment. There's so much in music to explore and so much we don't know, and I think we should be concentrating some of our time in doing these different things (Year 9).

Another pupil, from a different school, thought that the National Curriculum for music should include more music technology, and that this would be particularly beneficial for those pupils who were not proficient in playing musical instruments:

... you don't really learn much about that or about recording skills, because if we did that then it would be easier to get better marks on our compositions ... because I can't read music, I can't write down music for someone else to play to accompany me or something – if I'd learnt how to use a four-track, I could have, sort of, composed different instruments ... but because we don't get taught music technology, I didn't get chance to do that. So I think that could, a bit of basic recording studio, sort of, skills would make it a lot better ...(Year 11).

This may be one practical way in which the inequalities between experienced musicians and less experienced musicians could be decreased. Also, considering the increasing use of technology within the music industry, it would seem to be a logical step in increasing perceptions of the value of a music qualification to the world of work. The issue of the specific contents of the curriculum is discussed in more detail in the following section.

A drama teacher explained that some of the problems described here were not experienced within drama because of the absence of a prescribed National Curriculum. She said:

... the brilliant thing about not being on the National Curriculum – you can do what you need to do. You can tailor-make things for classes, you can go off on a tangent, and you can do a cross-

curricular with art if you decided – you have that flexibility with it. I believe in that flexibility – say if you have a class that has an interest in something or has a problem with something, you can write a scheme of work that ... hopefully will take them through that.

According to the perceptions of teachers, it would appear that whilst dance and drama as artforms continue to suffer a loss of status as a result of their location within other subjects in the National Curriculum, they have also maintained some advantages because they are not restricted in the same ways as other artforms. It would therefore be of interest to examine, in more detail, what impact this has had on the individual subjects.

It seems that the message for effective provision from this section is again the importance of a sense of balance between Government prescription and individual teacher and pupil flexibility and freedom. Although the legislation makes it obligatory to teach the arts to all pupils, it is clearly of limited benefit if the arts curriculum does not allow pupils and teachers to explore the subject in a creative manner.

12.6.2 Curriculum content and planning

A range of different factors was seen to be relevant to the effectiveness of arts lessons, in terms of their content and planning. Teachers and pupils both had relevant remarks to make, although the extent to which their views overlapped was surprising. The issues relating to the curriculum which were most frequently commented on by pupils were:

- pupil enjoyment of the curriculum;
- provision of an up-to-date and relevant curriculum;
- the challenges posed within the curriculum; and
- the length and variety of topics.

The issues which were commented on most frequently by staff included all of the points made by pupils, plus:

- teacher enjoyment of the curriculum;
- schemes of work; and
- the balance of topics.

Enjoyment

As has already been described, both teachers and pupils identified a significant need to enjoy the curriculum that they were teaching or experiencing. However, the importance of pupils' enjoyment of the curriculum was mentioned far more times than teachers' enjoyment, by both groups of interviewees.

Enjoyment for pupils

Sixty-two per cent of the cohort pupils interviewed identified their own enjoyment of the subject matter of arts lessons as a vital factor in shaping their perceptions of the provision's effectiveness. The pupils invariably described '*good lessons*' as those where they found the lesson content, in terms of both topic and activities, to be enjoyable.

Comments were spread across all the artforms, but art and drama were the most frequently mentioned. Music was cited fewer times than either art or drama, and dance attracted a very small minority of comments. Typical comments included:

Art

Sometimes when we just write things out of books, copying things, it is a bit boring and you don't concentrate too much on it. And you don't learn as much as when you are enjoying it (Year 9).

____

I think a good [art lesson] *is when everyone is concentrating and you are doing something that you enjoy. In still life, when we were doing that, that was really boring and everyone just started messing around and then the teacher goes mental and puts you on detention, so that's not very good* (Year 9).

Drama

Interviewer: *You talked about how last year you think you liked drama more than you did now, so do you think there were different effects that drama was having on you last year?*

Last year I enjoyed the topics on what we did in drama, like, we did more enjoyable things … this year we are doing just boring things which I don't enjoy, which I think it's partly that – the things I am I doing – I don't enjoy the themes … (Year 8).

____

Drama, a good lesson would be when you have got [something] *really fun to do, when you have got like maybe a funny piece of acting, something like that, and everybody is really enjoying themselves* (Year 8).

Music

I have a personal opinion about music – I don't really like it because of the teacher. 'Cos I just don't think he's a good teacher. That's because he just doesn't do interesting things. Sometimes we do practicals but we only get a few weeks to do them. Then other times we're just writing and it's boring (Year 7).

Dance

I think with dance a lot of it is if people are enjoying the lesson ... there's a good piece of music which people like, you're going to have people trying a bit harder to get a nice dance to it or whatever ... A bad lesson of dance would be if no one liked the music so therefore no one wanted to make a dance to it and everyone just messed around and didn't do much (Year 9).

From these examples it appears that the substantive topics and activities which provide the vehicle for development in the arts are a key factor in the pupils' enjoyment of the lessons. This in turn is seen to be significant in influencing the effectiveness of the learning which takes place as a result.

Six of the key staff interviewees also mentioned the importance of pupils enjoying the content of the curriculum. This was sometimes equated with the relevance which pupils associated with the topics. A deputy head at one of the schools described what, in his view, made a good arts teacher:

> ... *a very good rapport with the kids, a real empathy, they really care about the kids and can get on with the kids at the right level, they don't lose the children, they are not over the head, they work with children all the time, using the appropriate language, they know ... what the kids' motivation is, so for example, if they do music they are not using tambourines and doing some weird music that the kids can't latch into, they are doing things like rap music, like blues music ... They know what the kids will be interested in and they go for it and get their interest and then bring them along, and then introduce other sorts of music as well once they have got their interest, so they have got that as well, and the same is true for drama and for art and then for dance.*

3.
WHAT ARE
EFFECTIVE
PRACTICES
IN
ARTS
EDUCATION?

The head of expressive arts agreed with the headteacher – describing how the music department provided enjoyment for the pupils through the topics studied, and the resulting increase in motivation. He said:

> *Some of the stuff that we do excites them beyond belief. In Year 9 we do a house music project using Cubase and we use the sequencers on the keyboards and they are so into that. IT creates its own motivation anyway in music. A lot of the stuff that we do is very poppy, very jazz-oriented and they tend to react to that very favourably. Otherwise they use the media stuff that we do. Everything that we do is relative to their life here and they do feel that it is relevant. They become very, very captivated by it, very interested in it.*

This again highlights the link between enjoyment of the curriculum and pupils' perception of its relevance to their own lives. The importance of a curriculum which is up to date and relevant to the lives of pupils in contemporary society is discussed later in this section.

An art teacher in a different school, whose lesson was observed, explained, however, that correlating learning with pupil enjoyment was not always possible – and that there were some topics which had to be studied, but which pupils often found difficult:

> *I think there are some fairly vital things that they are learning, so I feel quite happy with the content. Even though they get very bored with doing still life, they have got to do it. They would rather not do observational work, but it is vital for everything else they do, so I do feel it's worthwhile and they are getting something out of it. All of them will have improved their observational skills if nothing else by the end of it.*

This posed a challenging situation for teachers – where the requirement for learning specific processes or skills could necessitate lessons that were difficult to make enjoyable for pupils. One pupil made a practical suggestion that, in the case of still life work, the pupils could be engaged by the specific objects which were chosen for the pupils to observe. The pupil described her own enjoyment of still life work on this basis:

> *I like it when they do still life and they bring in interesting things for us to draw like things they have borrowed from museums or something, because that's very different. You might not have seen it before, like new fruits that we might not have seen. I like things like that when they just try and be different* (Year 9).

In summary, it seems that in order to achieve effectiveness in arts lessons, the curriculum and teachers' schemes of work must be designed to maximise the enjoyment which pupils can glean from it. Pupils and teachers alike have recognised the benefits of pupils' enjoyment of the topics to be studied and the processes and activities to be used. Both of these elements are discussed further in the remainder of this section of the report.

Enjoyment for teachers

In addition to pupils' enjoyment of the curriculum, one pupil made an insightful remark that the teacher enjoying the lesson could also be a contributing factor to the effectiveness of lessons. When asked what would characterise a '*good lesson*', she replied: '*We get a lot of work done faster, we get more people cooperating and more people feeling happy;* [if] *the teacher enjoys it, we just do a lot more work*' (Year 7).

This was something which was more commonly recognised by the teachers themselves. Three teachers made specific remarks about how their own enjoyment of the curriculum impacted on their teaching, and therefore the overall outcomes of the lesson. One head of art said:

> In terms of my ethos of getting the subject across, I think if you are genuinely interested and enthusiastic about what you are teaching then that is the best way of encouraging them, you know, getting the children's attention.

The head of music at a different school agreed – suggesting that the mechanism by which this happened was the subconscious messages which were transmitted by the teacher to the pupils:

> You've got to enjoy doing it ... because you're really sending out these little messages to the children that 'Yes, you can enjoy doing this', and I think education is all about enjoying learning more than being forced to learn.

One teacher whose drama lesson was observed made this point particularly clearly:

> ... it has to be something that you are passionate about. I mean, I am passionate about drama and about teaching, but also about the things that I am doing, the topics that I am raising. The topics are a vehicle for the drama. You are disguising learning about techniques etc., or the aims that you have for a drama lesson. You are disguising them behind a topic or a scheme of work.

This extract picks up on the importance of the teacher's enjoyment of the subject, but also relates to the earlier issue of how subject matter and topics can be utilised in the learning of potentially difficult techniques or skills.

From all of this evidence it would seem as though the teacher's enjoyment of the topic was a factor in pupil motivation and that enthusiastic teachers could encourage pupils to recognise that they too could enjoy the subject. This contributory influence is also considered in section 12.7 on 'teacher factors'.

An up-to-date and relevant curriculum

Providing an up-to-date and relevant curriculum was one way in which teachers and pupils believed that pupils could be enabled to get a '*buzz*' or sense of enjoyment out of arts subjects.

Only nine of the cohort pupils interviewed (11 per cent) remarked on the significance of a curriculum with a contemporary theme, or which they found relevant to their own circumstances. However, this was

3.
WHAT ARE
EFFECTIVE
PRACTICES
IN
ARTS
EDUCATION?

also implied by many of the pupil comments relating to their enjoyment of the curriculum. Exactly half of all the comments made by pupils on this topic were related to music. Two examples from pupils highlighted different ways in which relevance could be achieved:

Up-to-date processes and activities	*... they should bring in more up-to-date things* [types of music] *... use more computerised stuff, more keyboards, more different ways of making music ...* (Year 8).
Up-to-date and relevant topics, popular culture	*... we have done about reggae music and blues music. We have made up our own tunes and at the moment we are doing scenes from West Side Story, and I think that's really good ... You can make up things and you can experiment with different types of music and do music that you want to hear and stuff, so that's really good* (Year 9).

It must, however, be borne in mind that a relevant curriculum was not always a curriculum which solely covered contemporary works – as one example from drama illustrated:

> *... we've been doing about, like, 14-year-olds, which is, like, how old I am ... some of it we did about Romeo and Juliet and about running away and all that, and some of it I found interesting and could sort of relate to me* (Year 9).

This teacher had succeeded in making Shakespeare relevant to pupils by relating it to their own experiences and attitudes. A drama teacher at the pupil's school suggested that this was deliberate, on the part of the teaching staff, when he said: '*Any lesson or any subject you touch, you need to engage them in what you are doing. So whatever you are doing has to be relevant to them and make sense to them.*' This is one way in which it was recognised that teachers could get over some of the obstacles and preconceptions that may hinder pupils' enjoyment of certain more traditional artforms, topics or genres.

The implication of this finding is that those planning the curriculum must take into account the interests of the pupils and teachers, thus allowing both groups to engage fully with the subject matter. Several of the remarks made about the importance of enjoying the curriculum, and finding it relevant, have shown the positive outcomes that this can produce.

A challenging curriculum

Eleven different pupils from the cohort group made a total of 17 references to the importance of the challenges posed by arts curriculum content. Only one of the comments centred on negative outcomes linked to the excessive difficulty of the work being set. Over half of all comments were divided between music and drama. Unusually, only one comment was made about art, and two were made about dance.

The types of challenges which pupils felt were valuable in arts lessons included:

Interviewer: *Is there anything else that might make a lesson not so good that you can think of?*

Having a broad topic to work within

When we are asked to do a topic that isn't very interesting or it doesn't give you a chance ... like do a play about drugs or bullying, and there's only so many things that you can do, so if you are given something else like do a piece of abstract drama about a zoo, I mean that is a lot easier to do because there's lot more things that you can do (Year 11).

Dealing with complex or serious issues

... [it's good] when we've got something pretty complicated to do that can keep us occupied and no one's ... everybody takes it seriously (Year 10).

Interviewer: *OK, is there anything that your art or drama teachers could do that would make lessons better for you?*

Exploring a specific issue in depth

... sometimes I would like to take things further, or go deeper into things rather than just touching on the surface, but obviously with people of different abilities at GCSE level it's not as easy to do, but that is something I would quite fancy (Year 11).

Learning something new

You need to be doing something that you haven't done before, something that you want to do, something that's interesting and not just sketching what you did last week and the week before, and you want a very challenging homework at the end of it as well (Year 7).

This was not an issue which the school staff interviewed raised directly. However, there was evidence from a drama teacher, whose lesson was observed, that providing pupils with challenging subject matter was a conscious intention:

... what I was trying to do was a challenge. What they had to think about was a challenge. The beauty of small-group work is that you can pose questions to them as you are going round, so: 'OK, you have touched the surface there ... superficial, but why are you saying that? What are you doing there? What's the movement there?' and deepening it that way and they respond to that – making them think about it rather than coasting – and that is the

challenge. If you didn't push them, that exercise could have just been pointless. You have to set up your aims. They know what I wanted them to look at.

A former head of art, now in charge of coordinating the curriculum, described the importance he attributed to constantly challenging the pupils through the development and progression within the curriculum – stating that one of the factors he would expect to observe in an effective art department was:

... evidence of a clear developmental structure within the department which would enable students to build upon areas of expertise and skills that they acquire over the course of each key stage.

It is clear that because all pupils are different – and present with different levels of initial ability – the difficulty for teachers is in providing appropriate levels of challenge for all pupils in a class. The issue of achievement, which is raised later within '*pupil factors*', shows that pupils are at risk of becoming disaffected with subjects which do not challenge them to develop. Yet again, it seems that differentiation is a key issue – in this case, the differentiation of the level of challenge with which pupils are presented during arts lessons.

Schemes of work

In order for a school to successfully mediate an arts curriculum, time must be spent in developing practical programmes of work for pupils. As teachers indicated in section 12.6.1, there was deemed to be space and flexibility, within the National Curriculum, for them to choose some of the topics or themes to be covered. There was also the opportunity to devise teaching methods which were most appropriate for the pupils to be taught.

Only one cohort pupil made any comment about the school's planning of the curriculum – specifically related to music. She described the logical planning and progression of the scheme of work, and how she felt this maximised her opportunities for success in her music exams:

... you do most of the composing in the fourth year ... when you get into the fifth you will do a bit more composing but you can focus mainly on your coursework that had to be in, and then on listening – because your listening paper is in about four weeks so I have to start really listening ... so I can understand it better. I think if we learnt it in the fourth year we would have forgot it, so there wasn't really much point in doing it, so he is saving it all till now so that it sticks in our head so we can remember it for our exam (Year 11).

Developing schemes of work in order to meet the requirements of the National Curriculum was clearly an issue further to the fore in the minds of teachers and school management. It was commented on by

13 interviewees (30 per cent) during the initial round of key staff interviews. Very little distinction was drawn on this issue between the different artforms – many of the interviewees referring to '*the arts*' as an umbrella term.

One headteacher talked at length about his attitude towards the balancing of the whole curriculum across all subjects within the school:

> *... there are no faculties in this school; each department is free-standing. For a long time we had the idea of curriculum directors responsible for areas of what was jokingly called, and not so joking, 'the* [headteacher's name] *curriculum' spectrum. So that you had a range of experiences, and my theory was that you had experiences for children which were very hard-edged and objective ... and maths is one. So two and two makes four whether a kid is involved in the process or not. If you take the other extreme, painting a picture depends on all the experiences that a child has before he gets to the piece of paper, the brush and the paint to create that experience. So one is highly objective and one is highly subjective. Now so what we were trying to do was to say 'Right, all children have a right to all these different sorts of ways of looking at the world' ... a curriculum spectrum to give experiences that are best delivered through certain vehicles. In other words, if you are looking for a hard-edged objective experience, art and design is not exactly the ideal vehicle for that, but maths is. If you are wanting to look at the way in which the world works, the humanities through history and geography is a way of doing that.*

However, the issues which seemed to be of most concern involved the flexibility of schemes of work, and the scope for individual teacher creativity. These were also identified as key themes within teachers' responses to the National Curriculum. One curriculum coordinator suggested that he aimed for:

> *A structure which is dynamic enough to accommodate change, because I think art teachers are very good at innovation by the very nature of the subject. I think that the worst thing in the world is for an art curriculum to be imposed and remain static over a number of years. I think it is something that you, sort of, need to look at constantly with a view to improving upon it.*

An unusual case was highlighted by a drama teacher who had been involved in the writing of a drama scheme of work. She described how this scheme of work had helped define the requirements of drama and provide a framework for teaching the subject. This was particularly important for a subject where some of the teachers were non-specialists – i.e. English teachers rather than specialist drama teachers. When asked whether the scheme offered enough scope for individual teacher creativity, she said:

... we made sure there was, because what we didn't want to do ... we have some non-specialists teaching drama, not so much this year. We have only got two periods taught by non-specialists, but the year before we had this horrendous situation where we had nine non-specialists teaching drama. We wanted people to be free to do what they felt most confident with and most enthusiastic about, whilst delivering certain elements that we felt were crucial. So, there were certain skills that we felt had to be taught at certain stages, but how they taught them was very much a matter for them. We would give them suggested schemes, in case they were lost as something to do, but encouraged them really to do something that they felt enthusiastic about because that is what we feel is the most important thing. You know, if you can communicate that and you can get people fired up about something, it is when you begin to get results.

According to teachers' perceptions, this would seem to be a valuable attitude for all teachers involved in the preparation of schemes of work – whether designed for specialist or non-specialist teaching staff. In this instance, the scheme of work defines the outcomes which are to be sought, and suggests practical ways in which they may be achieved, whilst allowing teachers to contribute their own interests and enthusiasm to the lessons. A similar situation was faced by a dance teacher who had written a scheme of work to be mediated partly by PE teachers, in order to steer them away from teaching '*a sports dance, or a running dance, or a jumping dance or something*'.

A headteacher agreed with the importance of allowing teachers to express their individuality when he declared:

Arts is dead if there is no scope for individual creativity. You might as well not bother in my opinion ... we can't encourage creativity amongst kids and expect it to thrive, if we are in a curricular straitjacket.

In summary, whilst the benefits of defined schemes of work were identified as consistency across classes and years, and support for less experienced teachers, a lack of opportunity for teacher creativity was recognised as a potential drawback.

Variety and length of topics within the curriculum

The arrangement of topics – in terms of their length and variety – were issues on which just over a third of pupils remarked. These are closely associated with the way in which schemes of work were arranged by arts teachers – discussed previously, although pupils did not explicitly make this connection.

Variety of topics was particularly an issue within the drama subject area. One pupil described how different topics allowed the use and development of different techniques:

> *... sometimes we'll have a really, really serious topic where only a few techniques can be used, whereas in a more light-hearted sort of comedy thing you'd be able to use totally different techniques entirely. So it's good to have a variety of different topics; otherwise we'd only be using one or two techniques* (Year 9).

A curriculum coordinator agreed that variety was important – he said he wanted to be able to observe *'evidence of range and variety in terms of the type of work that was being produced'*. He felt that this was an essential feature of an effective arts curriculum.

However, pupils made more references to the importance of the length of the topics which they studied within arts lessons – with little difference observed between the artforms. Despite the number of comments, there was some division between pupils who preferred longer topics, and those who preferred a greater variety of shorter topics. One pupil held opposing views for different artforms:

**3.
WHAT ARE
EFFECTIVE
PRACTICES
IN
ARTS
EDUCATION?**

> *... it would sometimes be nice to have a little more time to do drama and stuff ... sometimes you don't get to finish things off properly ...* [in contrast] *... in music, it would be nice to do it a bit quicker – get too long to do things ...* (Year 8).

Arguments were made in support of both longer, and shorter topics, although slightly more pupils opted for longer topics. Some of the examples given included:

Preference for longer topics

> *A good drama lesson is when we're set a task to do a role play and we're set the whole lesson to do the task and then at the end we show the rest of the class what our group has done ... I don't like it when she does, like, freezes, like, little bits of sections and just, like, build on it. I prefer it when we can just have the whole lesson to do one thing instead of lots of little things* (Year 9).

> *... sometimes if it's, like, a short topic then we will spend only, like, half the lesson working out a routine or something and then we will show it at the end, but I like to do it, like, over the space of a few weeks and then you're really proud of what you have done ...* (Year 9).

Preference for shorter topics

It was a good art lesson because we did a lot of different things, not just drawing every lesson, and we had our little projects that we worked on over a time, and it was just a matter of making it interesting with a variety of different things (Year 9).

Again it seems, in terms of topic length, that the key word is '*balance*' – pupils' preferences were for a variety of different topics, but enough time to be able to complete each topic to their satisfaction. This presents a difficult management task for teachers, and a challenge to those planning schemes of work within the arts.

12.6.3 Processes and activities

Throughout the interviews with pupils and teachers, many of the processes and activities involved in the provision of arts education were discussed. All but two of the pupils interviewed mentioned at least one process or activity in relation to the effectiveness of their arts lessons. However, only half of the key staff interviewed made such comments. The issues raised by both teachers and pupils fell broadly into three main categories:

- arts practice;

- arts theory and appreciation; and

- other, general, learning processes and activities.

Arts practice

The practical demonstration of the arts is one activity on which considerable emphasis has traditionally been placed, and it is clear that it still fulfils a vital role in the provision of effective arts education in schools. Despite the introduction of the National Curriculum, and the inclusion of arts theory, knowledge and appreciation, considerable store is still placed on the ability to perform within drama, dance and music, and produce accomplished works of art.

The importance of pupils' participation in the practice of the arts, along with the development of the necessary artistic skills, were seen to be a substantial component of effective arts education provision, by both pupils and teachers. It is clear that there are a number of related issues to be considered – each of which will be raised in turn. These are:

- practical activities, performing, and learning through doing;

- creativity, developing ideas, and self-expression; and

- pupils' freedom to do their own thing.

Practical activities, performing, and learning through doing

Of all the effectiveness factors identified in this report, this was the factor most frequently commented upon by the pupils interviewed. All but two of the cohort pupils interviewed (98 per cent) referred, in some context, to the involvement of practical activities within lessons. However, very few of the comments which pupils made could actually be seen to suggest how practical activities affected their learning or development within the lesson – most were simply stating a preference for practical activities over writing or theory. Forty-one pupils (48 per cent) made such comments.

The remarks which pupils made which did explicitly link practical activities with learning were spread across all the artforms, although a cluster was identified within music – the focus of exactly half of all '*effectiveness*' comments made. The contents of the pupil interviews suggested one reason for this distribution – the range of abilities within music classes, and the differentiation which could be applied. As one Year 9 pupil described, it was far easier to provide work for all pupils, at their own level, during practical work, than if theory was being taught:

> *We've been working more on the keyboards and making up our own pieces of music, which I find I'm quite good at, with me having the advantage of me being able to read music and know rhythm timing, and, well, you know, just more basic stuff than what everyone else knows.*

Interviewer: *So are other people being taught those things?*

> *... yes, other people are being taught it, but, like, ... on parents' evening, my music teacher said I'm already at GCSE level for composition so I already really know ... so really I have to go a bit further in my class work from this, you know, so my piece really stands out from the rest.*

Later in the interview, she continued:

> *A good lesson is where you get in there and you know you're doing practical work, and you know, like, a bad lesson is when you have to listen and write things down, you know, and for me it does get a bit boring because I already know the stuff and I'm wanting to play on the keyboard or compose my own song or something ...*

The head of music also recognised the challenge of teaching music theory to mixed-ability classes, but the ease with which different methods of differentiation could be applied to practical lessons. She said: '... *theory is just theory and you can't really water it down. Do you understand? ... A fact is a fact and they either learn it or they don't, but for the practical you can always give a less able child something easier to play, something easier to read. It is the theory that is hard.*'

Teachers made few comments on the importance of practical activities in the arts, but at many stages of the interviews it was subtly implied. It may be that this was such an obvious point that it was often overlooked, or simply not articulated. One head of art made the point clearly when he said: '*I think all that cycle of making and responding, presenting and evaluating are fundamental.*'

Similarly, over half of the pupils interviewed mentioned the involvement of performing – in drama, and music, and, to a considerably lesser extent, dance. However, in this instance, a third of the pupils made a direct link between performing and the effective production of outcomes – mainly the development of increased confidence. Typical comments supporting the view that performance increased pupil confidence, both generally and specifically in arts performance, were put forward for both drama and music:

3.
WHAT ARE
EFFECTIVE
PRACTICES
IN
ARTS
EDUCATION?

Drama

It's brought out a lot of my confidence. I didn't have much confidence at the start of the year and I have got a lot more confidence since we have performed in front of people, and we have learnt to make, like, a poem or something come to life through drama, through movement, and we have done a lot of movement which we have enjoyed (Year 10).

Music

... when I first came here I was quite shy and now from drama and music and performing in front of the rest of the class I'm a lot more confident.

Interviewer: *So you think that performing in those subjects has helped your confidence?*

Yes (Year 9).

————

Interviewer: *What is it about a music lesson that helps to develop that confidence?*

A gradual build up – at first we just performed in lessons; have also had concerts for parents. It builds you up slowly (Year 10).

A small number of similar comments were made relating to dance performances.

Confidence was an outcome of drama identified by the deputy head at one of the schools in the project. He listed a range of practices in drama which he felt contributed to the outcome he had observed:

We have very confident pupils here, and I think one of the things that contributes to that is drama in particular, in allowing pupils the scope to work with individuals they wouldn't normally work with, in making them speak out loud in front of other people and perform in front of other people, which they now do fairly naturally, and losing the inhibitions to do that, and I think the effect of that on confidence has been quite major.

One pupil described how the attitude of pupils in her class towards drama had changed when the teacher started selecting groups to perform, rather than giving all groups the opportunity:

> *... the new teacher that we have got at the moment is like ... our old teacher and our teacher before that – they all watch every single ... she will watch all six, whether she has got time or not, whether it's in front of the class or not – she will watch your performance, but the teacher we have got now it's, like, you put so much effort into your work and she just picks, like, two groups to show, and, like, say, you have worked so hard and you really want to show the class it's, like, she doesn't really pick you, so everybody is starting to slow down in drama and starting not to like it ...* (Year 9).

It is clear from further discussions with this particular pupil that the long-term effect of this strategy has had a negative impact on the motivation and work ethic of the pupils. The pupil described how the outcomes of drama had '*gone downhill*' as a result.

Part of the significance attributed to arts practice and performance appeared to be generated from its association with assessment and evaluation. Clearly, in the arts in schools, the product – be it a piece of art, or a performance, often forms the basis for assessment. The value that pupils placed on the frequency and style of assessment of their work is described later in this section.

The other way in which arts practice and performance were valued was in their dependence on '*learning through doing*'. This was an issue which was described by teachers in relation to several of the lessons which were observed. One art teacher said:

> *... they were learning by doing, which certainly, I find, is much more effective than just learning by being shown or learning by being told. It's always more effective if you are learning by doing, and they were learning by looking at each other's work as well.*

This was certainly seen as one of the strengths of lessons across all the arts, as one pupil suggested:

> *... I find with more academic subjects it's all on paper and art subjects can give you more hands-on, more physical, more ... you can learn more sometimes, not just textbooks, if you're actually physically doing it, going out and experiencing it. It's better sometimes to have experience than knowledge. Doing it in theory is not as good as doing it in practice and I think all art subjects really do that* (Year 11).

**3.
WHAT ARE
EFFECTIVE
PRACTICES
IN
ARTS
EDUCATION?**

The conclusions which could be drawn suggest that there is still a considerable reliance, within the arts, on active pupil participation in artistic activities, including performing, although it is clear that sometimes pupils fail to recognise what they are learning through the activity. However, for an insightful few, it would appear that the old saying: '*hear and I forget, see and I remember, do and I understand*' still holds true.

Creativity

In addition to the practical demonstration of skills and techniques, a facet of participation in artistic activities which was often thought to be an effective vehicle for learning was the application of creativity and the use of imagination. Pupils, however, made considerably more references to the significance of this aspect of arts practice than teachers or school staff.

Only two of the staff interviewed made mention of using imagination, self-expression, creativity or the development of ideas within the arts. However, this unexpectedly low number of remarks may not be an accurate reflection of the status of these factors, rather a result of their being overlooked as an innate feature of education in the arts. The deputy head at one of the schools recognised that the arts were an area which allowed pupils to utilise skills which were complementary to the rest of the curriculum:

> *I also think that allowing pupils to develop and use their skills has been quite a big thing within arts education – we have a high number of pupils who see music and drama and art as somewhere they get a chance to really excel and express themselves and use skills that they don't necessarily use elsewhere and there's a significant proportion of pupils who almost attach themselves to the expressive art faculty, as somewhere where they really feel that that's their home. I mean, the amount of pupils who are still there at half past five, having practised and gone through things and produced things themselves, so I think it's been a major confidence builder and a major area where pupils can really feel that there's something that they can excel at and use.*

This was something which was clearly a part of the ethos of the school – an important aspect raised previously within this chapter. The arts appear to provide an outlet for pupils where they can develop an alternative, creative means of communication and self-expression – in this case providing pupils with increased confidence, and a sense of belonging where otherwise they might not.

The benefits and enjoyment which pupils felt they gained from creative activities and developing their own ideas were transparent during the interviews. Almost one in five mentioned creativity specifically – with one example explaining what made art different, and more enjoyable, than other school subjects:

> ... *the other ones are all fact-type subjects ... it's a bit boring really 'cos you're not doing anything new. Everyone's been doing it for ages and ages. When you're actually creating something, it's, like, yours. When it's facts, it's, like, all these other people have been doing it* (Year 8).

Similar comments were made for all the artforms, with little distinction drawn between them. It is clear that pupils often gained a considerable sense of satisfaction, and personal ownership of work that they produced in the arts, which often seemed more personal and more important to them than learning the facts associated with traditionally academic subjects. Many of the pupils referred to the enjoyment and '*buzz*' that they gained from being able to '*work by ourselves and create something out of our own minds*' (Year 9).

Pupils' freedom to do their own thing

This was one of the factors which pupils often identified as one of the strengths of all the artforms – the ability, whilst following the National Curriculum and learning specific skills and techniques, to develop their own ideas, and follow up areas of their own interest within the subject. It was closely linked to the idea of using imagination, creativity, developing ideas and self-expression.

Freedom of topic and activity were not issues raised often by the school staff interviewed, although one of the music teachers whose lesson was observed commented on the pupils being given a free choice of subject matter, allowing them to choose a subject relevant to their own lives and circumstances:

> *The pupils knew what was expected – a journey ... they had a free choice of what journeys they were doing, and the boys were going to space ... they were free to choose whatever journeys they were happy with.*

The teacher seems to imply, in this instance, that being able to choose their own journeys to portray through their music would provide the pupils with increasing motivation, and allow each to develop their own interest. This is clearly one way in which the teacher can provide a relevant and up-to-date curriculum for all pupils, which was identified earlier as a key factor of effective arts lessons.

Fifty pupils (58 per cent) made some reference to the benefits of being able to choose their own topics or activities within arts lessons. As with

**3.
WHAT ARE
EFFECTIVE
PRACTICES
IN
ARTS
EDUCATION?**

other issues, many of these comments were simply stating a preferences for this freedom, without giving any rationale or suggesting how this was of benefit to their learning. However, in this instance, two clear explanations for this preference did emerge – being able to choose areas of interest (thus increasing motivation of pupils) and being able to express their own individuality. Pupils recognised that classes where all the pupils were allowed to produce something different made for a more interesting atmosphere. One pupil said:

> ... you've got your individuality from how you choose to do work because you get set a project and then you do it how you want – you get to design your own things to make ... if everybody was doing the same thing, it would just be boring and pointless (Year 9).

Another agreed, illustrating the point with an example:

> ... I think art is completely based on what you think and not what anybody else thinks. Like, artists, have become, like, famous because they've chosen their own designs and things, not basing it on anybody else's, like, changing the course of history just by themselves, if you like (Year 9).

Despite these comments, there was again a sense that there had to be some kind of balance. One pupil said, of drama:

> I think a good drama lesson has a certain amount of respect or sort of discipline in it, but also interest, and I think giving a certain essence of freedom and sort of allowing a sort of an open subject that you could use various techniques with, or on, sort of do differently every time (Year 9).

This pupil identified the fact that whilst allowing pupils the freedom to develop their own ideas, there has to be some discipline and control. It appears that 'balance' is a key word in determining effectiveness – too much freedom and pupils run the risk of becoming bored or disruptive, and too little freedom allows too little scope for imagination and self-expression – already identified as important facets of any arts education.

Arts theory and appreciation

The introduction of the National Curriculum, and attainment target 2 – knowing and understanding – has increased the requirement, and occurrence, of the theoretical aspects of arts subjects. Pupils and teachers both made reference to the inclusion of this theory, and the way in which it was experienced within the curriculum. The key themes raised were:

- music theory; and
- historical and contextual studies

Music theory

The teaching of the theory of music was one area which was often identified as problematic for a variety of reasons. A high proportion of the pupils described how they disliked music theory, or writing in music lessons – many because they already played an instrument and had already learnt the theory – resulting in boredom. This highlights the main problem with music theory – that of differentiation to take into account the vastly different previous experiences and abilities of the pupils in the class.

However, one pupil explained that whilst she disliked the theory element, she could also appreciate its value and importance:

> *Well, when we do notes, like I said before, like, we learn how to do the notes, it can get boring but if you do it then it helps you ... like with my flute and things like that – if you learn them and it can get boring but if you do it then it will help you, so that helps me in school and out of school* (Year 9).

Another pupil explained that he understood why there was a requirement to cover music history and theory within the curriculum – but thought that it would have been more useful, and less intense, balanced throughout the course, rather than condensed into one section in the run-up to the exams:

> *I think we should have learnt it in a different order. In years before we should have learnt more about the history of music – I think that should have been done earlier because it seems to me it's been sort of left a bit till last minute. I mean, I'm not saying we're not going to learn it on time because it's obvious that we are, but I think we should learn that from the start more about music history, types of music and then it would be easier if you just kept a happy medium all the way, like, say have alternate lessons – like, have one where you learn music history, theory, things like that, and then another lesson where you're doing composition. I think that would work a lot better than the way it's been* (Year 11).

The history of music and musical styles was often distinguished from the theory of music (i.e. the theory underpinning the playing and production of music) and is considered in more detail in the next factor – historical and contextual studies.

The challenge, in equipping pupils with a sound knowledge of music theory, is to help them recognise its importance for the creative and practical work that they produce. However, it must also be recognised that there are many pupils who will have learnt the basics of music theory through previously learning to play a musical instrument. Some

3.
WHAT ARE
EFFECTIVE
PRACTICES
IN
ARTS
EDUCATION?

way of engaging these pupils, and encouraging them to further develop their knowledge and ability, must also be sought, in order to protect them from the risk of disengagement and boredom.

Historical and contextual studies

The introduction of the National Curriculum, and specifically attainment target 2 – knowing and understanding – has generally increased the content of historical and contextual reference within the arts curriculum.

Surprisingly, only one of the staff interviewed made any mention of teaching the historical background to the arts – but he emphasised that this was a crucial part of effective provision of arts education. This curriculum coordinator described how, within his view of effective arts education provision, he would wish to see *'significant evidence of the use of the work of other artists and reference to the context in which art was produced'*.

Fourteen pupils described their involvement in learning about artists, styles of art and composers – only a small minority of remarks related to drama or dance. The pupil remarks which were made were divided equally between those who enjoyed learning about the background, and felt it was valuable, and those who did not enjoy learning about the history of artforms, and preferred to be involved in more practical activities. Arguments on both sides included:

For

I didn't really know the background of jazz or blues. I just knew it as music. I didn't know why it had come about and now I know that it was, like, the slaves who brought it over and things like that ... learning the backgrounds instead of just being taught something and not knowing anything about the backgrounds, you seem to have a wider view (Year 9).

In art I like to know the history of the artist. Most of the time he tells us, but if he doesn't, then I will make sure that I know or I will research it myself. Then I know what I am drawing and that makes it more interesting. You can even find out different tips on how to draw properly (Year 8).

Against

It's a bit boring [contextual and historical studies]. *Even though I learn a lot from it, I think it's really boring* (Year 7).

I took music more for the performing side rather than the information side, learning about different composers and stuff, more history. I don't like history (Year 11).

Within this area of the curriculum, there were two ways in which pupils referred to the importance of looking at the artistic works of others – the evaluation and appreciation of the works of professional practitioners as an arts consumer, and the application of techniques and ideas gleaned from looking at the work of others to their own artistic endeavour. Both of these factors contributed to the rationale for the inclusion of critical studies and arts appreciation strands within arts education curriculum.

Many of the pupils seemed to hold fast to the traditional view – emphasising performance or participation in practical arts activities over critical and appreciative engagement with the arts. However, approximately half of the pupils made some positive remark about how background work could inform their practical work, or expressed their enjoyment of it as valuable learning experience in its own right.

One pupil also felt that actually practising an artform was an important factor in appreciation of the works of others. He said:

> ... *every time I look at a picture or painting, I think 'That is really hard, you know, to paint that'. Before I would just think 'Oh, there is another painting, another painting'. I now think 'That painting there looks really hard to paint'.*

Interviewer: *How come you have managed to start realising this, then?*

> *Because when you actually draw it is really hard to get a picture, it is really hard to paint and it is really hard to get it really neat and things like that* (Year 7).

The head of English at one of the schools agreed:

> *Being a practitioner enables you to also understand the processes, and reflect on, and criticise, the work of others. I know that, particularly in art, that they do that: there is a great emphasis on actually the work that they produce and evaluating that. Within drama again, it is quite stunning ... I don't know if I could manage it, but they are able to set up small groups to perform and then get the rest of the class to actually, not in a horrible way, not in a destructive way but in a very constructive way, to sit and to say 'Well, you could have done this; that was very good, but ...'. We would do exactly the same thing with a piece of writing. Quite often we would do a first draft and then you literally pass it to the person sitting to your left or right and they go through, look at the work, read the work and then they will actually write a comment at the bottom. We set up all sorts of rules for that in terms of saying you can make a helpful suggestion and you should try to say at least one positive thing. You are not allowed to say 'This is rubbish' or whatever, but they do it. They are capable of doing it and that immediate feedback, critical response to your own work, then enables you to go on and say 'Well, right. You just looked at that from your friend, or you have just written your own analysis and*

evaluation of what you did. Now here is something else to look at. What do you think of that?'

It would seem, on balance, that the pupils' arguments in favour of including historical and contextual studies are far more persuasive than those against. It could also be suggested that those pupils who declared a dislike of this aspect of the arts curriculum might be more inclined to be able to see past their dislike if they were more able to recognise its value. Again, the challenge for teachers is to make this part of the curriculum enjoyable and relevant for pupils – highlighting its importance in a way which allows pupils to recognise its value to their own creative arts practice.

Other, general, learning processes and activities

Despite the differences identifiable between the arts and other school curriculum subject areas, some of the processes and activities involved are common to all teaching and learning situations. This section deals with those issues – examining some of the general, non-arts-specific processes and activities, and the extent to which, it was perceived, arts teachers could effectively utilise them within arts lessons. These included:

- group work;

- listening to the teacher; and

- practical demonstrations.

Group work

Group working was one strategy which was employed to varying extents within the different artforms, and was raised as an issue in the efficacy of lessons by both pupils and teachers.

There was a clear division between the artforms in terms of pupils' preferences for working in groups or independently. Of the 35 different comments made by the cohort pupils relating to working in groups, 12 were specifically about drama and 11 were directed at music. For example:

Drama

In terms of what the teacher could do for a good lesson, I think that I enjoy ... although I enjoy working in the groups with the people that I know, because I think that makes it seem a lot easier ... but I generally think that it would be a good idea for us to do more work where, for instance, everybody was just put in their random groups so they could try and communicate ideas with people they don't actually get on with too well (Year 10).

Drama

I prefer working with other people because when I am with more people there's more contributions and you are not just relying on yourself all the time or anything. Other people might be more helpful to getting it together and everything. When you are by yourself, you don't quite get the comments and suggestions from anyone else and you just do your own thing, which sometimes isn't as good as a group discussion and what they put into it, so I prefer group (Year 11).

Music

You can bounce ideas off each other [in groups] *... if you don't do something, it's both your fault rather than just yours (Year 10).*

In contrast, of the 18 comments where pupils stated that they preferred to work independently, nine were about art.

I prefer [working] *on my own more because sometimes I disagree with people, and you can get on with what you want to do, working on your own (Year 10).*

Art

I usually sit by myself so I can concentrate and I can get a lot done, so I am really pleased with myself, especially if I get the whole thing done ... I like to carry on by myself.

Interviewer: *So a good lesson is where you can just work away and get things done?*

Yes, no distractions (Year 11).

Only one pupil mentioned a preference for working independently in drama, and only five preferred to work alone in music.

In general, working in groups was a situation favoured by 22 pupils. Of those pupils, 14 were in the lower cohort group, and eight were in the upper. Two pupils specifically mentioned the whole class working together in drama. However, working independently was mentioned by 15 pupils, nine of whom were in the upper cohort group.

This would seem to give an indication of the grouping strategies which may work with different ages of pupils and in different subjects. Working in groups in drama and music seems to appeal to younger pupils, and older pupils seem to prefer to work independently in art. Unfortunately, however, from this information it cannot be deduced that younger pupils would not also prefer to work independently in art, or that older pupils would not prefer to continue to work in groups for music and drama.

Listening to the teacher

Listening to the teacher was one activity which pupils identified as important in determining their learning. Thirty-three pupils remarked, at some point during an interview, on the activity of listening to the teacher. However, of the 42 individual comments made in total, 16 were general in nature, rather than specifically related to the arts. Of those 16 general comments, 81 per cent suggested that listening to the teacher was a positive and effective method of teaching and learning. However, of the 26 comments made relating specifically to the teaching of the arts, only 23 per cent were positive. Considerably more support was identified, within the arts, for 'learning through doing' or 'practical experimentation' – active forms of learning, rather than the more passive activity of listening to the teacher. It would seem therefore that whilst 'listening to the teacher' is generally perceived to be an effective method of teaching, it is not well received by pupils in the teaching of the arts. Typical comments included:

> *I don't like the teachers when they just stand up and give a big lecture and you have just got to listen. I like it when she goes round and helps us individually* (Year 8).

> *... in art you don't really learn anything, like facts or anything, it's just, like, skills – how to hold your brush and how to do different types of paint and things like that. So the teacher comes round and individually, she goes round and says 'Do this and do it like that' so she doesn't, like, stand in front of the class and say, as a whole of the class, and say 'Do this and do that'. She goes round individually and says 'Hold it like this and look there' and things. So she tells you by yourself so I think that helps you learn* (Year 9).

> *You're not really there for talking are you. You just want to get on in doing art really. That's all you're there for – you might as well get it done* (Year 11).

Only one teacher made a comment on the issue – recognising the important balance between practical activities and passive learning from listening to teachers:

> *... one thing I think some people fear is that they fear spending too much time talking about it, which I think is absolutely vital to reflect on. Again, I am so pushed for time that it is so desperately, you know, yes you must work practically, and in that respect I think it is difficult. The proportion of time would be, I suppose if we grouped all that time together, it would maybe be sort of four-and-a-half hours of performance out of practical involvement and an hour to an hour-and-a-half bits and pieces here and there of discussion time* (dance teacher).

Whilst listening to the teacher was a method of learning described by some of the pupils, most of the evidence suggests that teacher communication with the whole class group is deemed (by the pupils) to be an inefficient way of teaching the arts. The traditional model of arts teaching also supported this assertion – many arts departments have held tight to the workshop model of individual teaching which developed from the earlier *'apprenticeship'* system – whereby pupils learnt through working alongside a qualified arts practitioner. The reliance on individual, rather than group or class, teaching is an obvious remnant of this system.

However, it was also recognised that within the interview data very few mentions were made of the ways in which theory and contextual information were transmitted. It is therefore possible that the most effective way of getting this information across would be precisely the type of whole-class teaching which pupils did not seem to respond to in this instance, although this issue is masked by their infrequent comments about the theoretical aspects of the arts. This is perhaps an area which would warrant further consideration.

Practical demonstrations

The previous section emphasised the pupils' dislike for purely listening to the teacher within the arts, and pupils often suggested practical demonstrations were an effective alternative. Learning through the observation of a qualified arts practitioner was the traditional way in which the arts were propagated from master to apprentice, and it is clear that both pupils and teachers find it to be an effective form of communication.

Two art teachers made the point very clearly, but in many of the other teacher interviews, instances were described where teachers would show pupils how something was to be done, rather than simply telling them. The two art teacher comments were both particularly revealing. One said:

> ... *I believe, very much, in showing people really how – I don't leave them to find out for themselves ... I show them a trick, a way of doing something, and then make them mess around with different ways of doing it after I have shown them how. I wouldn't want people to spend hours being frustrated, working things out themselves really.*

The other identified that the process of giving a demonstration also had the effect of motivating pupils – through showing them what they were going to produce and providing an opportunity for the teacher to identify the areas where pupils may face practical difficulties:

> *I think that it is important that whatever I am doing ... I think that it is important if I ask them to do something that I show them how*

to do it first. I suppose it is a bit like Blue Peter – this is the finished product, this is how you make it, because not only can they see the finished product that you have made, if you have had any difficulties at all in making it, you know what those difficulties are so that you can then foresee the problems with the students. I feel that is important, so I always like to demonstrate whatever I am expecting them to do, first of all.

This theme was also linked quite closely with the pupils' attitudes towards the teacher of a particular arts lesson – an issue addressed in more detail later in this chapter when we report on how pupils described their gain in respect for teachers who were able to demonstrate their practical ability in the subject. The converse of this was that if the teacher did not give such practical demonstrations, the pupils felt it more difficult to appreciate their teachers' knowledge and skill.

Although 36 pupils made reference to the importance of demonstrations within the arts, almost half of all the comments made related to art, with small numbers being general in nature, or related to music or drama, and only one relating to dance. Invariably, pupils identified the benefits that they felt they gained from watching how to do something. Typical comments made included:

… at the beginning of the lesson we spend about five minutes just covering what we're going to be doing. We all sit round a table and the teacher shows us something that will help us or shows us something and then we're told to get on with [our] work and we've got ideas from what we've just been told so we carry on.

Interviewer: *Is it important that the teacher is quite knowledgeable and skilful in art themselves?*

Art

Yes, because if you get stuck they can show you how to do it and then you can do it for yourself, so it does help a lot. I mean if you have got a supply teacher for one lesson, it's not very good. I don't like that (Year 9).

… with the mixing of the colours, I didn't know that, when I first came to this school and she showed us … ever since I don't have to ask her any more, so it's like her skills have rubbed off on all of us, so we know what colours to mix and what to use, what paint to use, everything. All her skills have like gone on to us now. We know exactly what we have to do. As long as she tells us what the topic is and what exactly we have to draw, then after that there's no problem because everyone knows what to do (Year 9).

Drama	*When I first started doing drama, nobody in the form really liked doing things but now they all just do it ... the teacher will do it first so you know they're doing it and other people ... say, there's one good actor in the form, she'll get him to do it first and then everyone will feel confident, saying 'Well, he's done it. No one's laughing at him'. So everyone else will do it then* (Year 9).* ... in drama, sometimes, like, teachers might act something out – that's nice because you get a chance to see an experienced person doing something, not just telling you to do it. They will give you an example – that's nice, that's good as well* (Year 9).
Music	*I think demonstration on their part* [teacher] *is really important – it helps it to sink in a bit more clearly if you see someone else doing it, someone who knows what they're doing. So if they've tried to explain something, you're sat there, scratching your head; you don't know what's going on. If they just get up and show you, maybe, and just go through it with you step by step, that makes it easier, especially in music* (Year 11).* When they're doing demonstrations and stuff* [it's good] *and it makes a big difference when we've got a supply teacher because they can't do demonstrations and we're usually doing written work and stuff so really you need, like, a music teacher to help us with it* (Year 9).

3.
WHAT ARE EFFECTIVE PRACTICES IN ARTS EDUCATION?

It would appear, then, that the traditional apprentice model of arts education may still have considerable relevance for the pupils of today in terms of learning the skills and abilities involved in active participation in the different artforms. However, it is also clear that exploring theory and contextual information could be done through demonstration – perhaps more practical methodologies may be sought in order to appeal to pupils' preferences for active, rather than passive, learning.

12.6.4 Differentiation

Differentiation within the curriculum is a critical factor which has featured in many of the comments made by teachers and pupils. Many of the other factors which were raised as significant clearly suggest, or subtly imply, that differentiating work for pupils of different abilities is a key to effective arts provision and practice.

Thirteen members of school staff who were interviewed (27 per cent) identified the importance of some form of differentiation within arts lessons. Literature on the subject often distinguishes two broad types of differentiation, and both were referred to by interviewees:

- differentiation by *task* – where pupils of different abilities are set different tasks, or where extension work is provided for the most able; and

- differentiation by *outcome* – where pupils are initially set the same task, but the levels of achievement expected are different depending on the pupils' differing abilities.

However, it was seen that the arts tended to rely to a greater extent on the latter of these two types of differentiation. The arts was seen as an area of the curriculum which was equally open to pupils of all abilities and backgrounds – where pupils could take a set task and respond to it at their own personal level. This was seen as a very valuable aspect of the subject area. The deputy head at one of the schools made the point specifically:

> ... all the arts groups are mixed-ability ... and I know that staff are very good at differentiating the work, not always by task at the start, but the way they interact with the students while they are going through the work. The work is very project-based anyway in the arts, ongoing, and the staff are very good at interacting with the students and questioning, leading, helping to the right amount with the right-ability students ... that's a very important factor in the learning.

The comments from teachers relating to differentiation were spread broadly across art, drama and music – a pattern which was quite different from that shown by the pupils' remarks. Twenty-three pupils (27 per cent) commented specifically on issues relating to differentiation, all but two of the 32 individual comments being in reference to music. The LEA arts adviser associated with one of the schools explained the specific differentiation problems which were faced by the music subject area, and which the pupils were clearly identifying:

> ... in the music classroom you get, very often, somebody who is a grade 6 flautist say at Year 7 or Year 8, against kids that can hardly bash a glockenspiel. So you can't teach them differentiation there, you can't look for differentiation, so you are looking for other ways in which you are going to challenge those youngsters. Is the flautist going to bring ... her flute in and use it in composition when she is working with others and she is going to help others along? Particularly when it comes to homework, sort of homework tasks, I mean for heaven's sake, they should not be the same for those two youngsters and I have to say that the teacher is getting much better

at that now. So we are looking for extension work; we are looking for challenging that child much more ... It is a great challenge for arts teachers, I think, and I think that is one of the areas where it does vary in the artforms. I think that there are different ways in which differentiation is approached and made explicit.

The section dealing with the spread of abilities within classes, and previous extra-curricular participation in music, also provides clues as to why differentiation in music is such an issue for pupils. The comment above also indicates an awareness of the differences in ability of pupils which can be observed in music lessons. This was thought to be far wider than the range of abilities within other artform lessons.

The conclusions of many other sections of this report refer, in passing, to the significance of differentiation within the arts curriculum. Thus, differentiation is an underlying issue which needs to be addressed within many areas of arts education. Overlaps from other areas of this report are illustrated in Figure 12.2:

Figure 12.2   Links between differentiation and other effectiveness factors

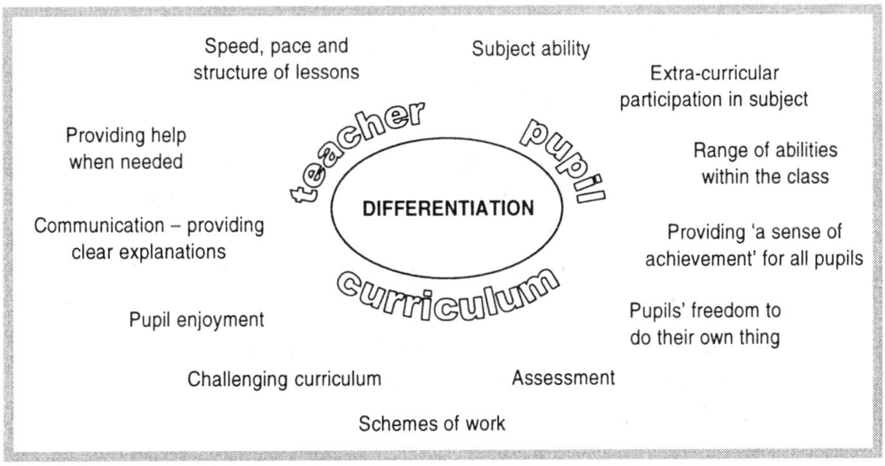

It is clear, therefore, that all teachers, those in the arts included, face the challenge of responding to their pupils as individuals, to ensure that each gains the maximum potential from the lesson.

12.6.5 Assessment

Assessment, in a variety of different forms, was recognised to play a significant role in determining the effectiveness of arts lessons, despite its sometimes problematic nature. It was widely appreciated that assessment in the arts was often a subjective matter rather than a purely objective judgement. Both pupils and teachers made comments on a range of assessment-related issues, including:

- marks and grades;
- teacher comments;
- peer review;
- self-assessment and evaluation; and
- frequency of assessment.

Marks and grades

Twenty-five pupils (29 per cent) referred to the marks and grades that they received in arts subjects; however, the opinions expressed were mixed in their emphasis. It was clear that, particularly in art and music, formal grades were seen as a valuable way in which pupils could monitor their long-term progress. This was mentioned on 11 individual occasions, and exemplified by one pupil who said that he could tell how well he was doing in art by *'looking at grades – flick back through sketch book and think "I've definitely come on there"'* (Year 8).

Surprisingly, marks and grades which were awarded to pupils for their work in the arts appear to have been a double-edged sword – pupils referred to good marks, and their desire to maintain good standards, but they also referred to poor marks, and the increase in motivation which resulted from wanting to improve.

Few teachers or school staff made comments about the provision of formal marks or grades, but those who did appeared to understand the pupils' position. One said, of the provision of marks in drama: '*I think the pupils would like it ... they are very black and white really. It gives them an idea of where they are.*' An art teacher agreed, when she said:

> *... they expect it – if the children do a piece of homework, they want you to give it a mark, they want you to say how good it is, they are really keen on having some kind of mark.*

Despite these comments, there was a common recognition of the subjectivity of such marks and grades. One pupil was particularly critical, saying:

> *Grades are only a reflection ... on how the teacher views it. If you had a different teacher, she could give you a completely different grade, so, although it's nice to get an A, if I get a B+ from another teacher, I really don't care, because it's how I view the art rather than how the teacher views the art. If I get satisfaction from something I've drawn or made, composed, I really don't care how other people view it. It's what gives me pleasure rather than what gives teachers pleasure I think* (Year 8).

3.
WHAT ARE EFFECTIVE PRACTICES IN ARTS EDUCATION?

The remaining pupil remarks were generally directed towards the problems associated with over-reliance simply on marks and grades within the arts. Pupils often referred to their need for comment and explanation of the marks awarded, in order to inform their future work, and help them improve. A typical reference came from one pupil who said: '*I don't think she really informs us enough on what our grades actually mean*' (Year 8).

Discussion of this theme raised an important distinction to be drawn between the different purposes of assessment. Two distinct purposes were identified:

- evaluation and monitoring of progress; and
- defining areas for consideration and improvement.

The comments which pupils made highlighted their belief that marks and grades fulfilled the former of these two purposes, but were inadequate in terms of the latter. It was suggested that only comments and additional information from the teacher could enable pupils to direct their attention towards the areas of work where they needed to improve in order to increase their levels of attainment. As one pupil explained, in music:

You just get a grade. They don't say anything. Well, our teacher doesn't ... I think the other ones do, but ours doesn't.

Interviewer: *And the grade doesn't help?*

No, because you don't know what you're targeting. They don't say 'Well, you were bad on that point' so you could try harder next time.

Interviewer: *How does that compare with what you said about grades in art?*

In art they say at the end that it's pleasing, but in music they just say 'There's your mark'. So you don't get any comment until report days. And you might already have finished your second piece of work by then, so you wouldn't have known what to target because you wouldn't have got your report yet. You should really have a report for every piece of work you do, so you know what to target and how well you've done (Year 7).

This was a situation which one art teacher was specifically keen to avoid, by making appropriate, and helpful comments, in addition to giving a mark, for every piece of homework which pupils completed. It would appear that this would be one way of providing pupils with a means of tracking their own progress and development, whilst directing them towards the areas where more work was required. In general terms, then, this would provide for both purposes of assessment which were identified as important.

One particular music teacher took the idea of development and improvement through assessment particularly seriously, evidenced by his marking pupils' work twice – once after the initial attempt, and then again after the pupil had had a chance to improve on it. One of the pupils felt that this was a good system, saying: '... *you have a go at your work, and then you get to try again and then he will regrade it*' (Year 9).

Teacher comments

The previous factor indicated the pupils' belief in the value of comments from the teacher on their work and progress. Pupils proceeded to describe this in specific terms, referring to teacher comments delivered both orally and in writing.

Almost half of the pupils interviewed talked, at some point, about the teacher discussing their work with them, and providing feedback. In general, the remarks were positive – indicating that pupils felt oral comments from the teacher to be beneficial to their learning and development in the arts. Comments made included:

Art

He [the teacher] *grades our work as if it was GCSE so we know what level we are at now. He sees us one-by-one and he says 'You can improve on this' or 'You can improve on that', which is a great help ... every other week we get to see him with our homework, and while we are working in class, he comes round and sees as many people as possible, so it's nearly every lesson* (Year 10).

... the teacher usually, sort of, tells you how well you're doing and tells you that you're getting better, and ... like, she kept telling me that I was getting better, and when I said I wasn't doing art, she was saying 'Why aren't you doing art, because you're really good at art?'. And it's just things like that make you realise how good you are (Year 9).

Drama

If we do an improvisation and she [the teacher] *thinks something's wrong, then she'll just tell us. She won't write it down – keep it from us. She will just say it to our face, like, 'I don't think you were very good then. You could have done this or that' – which really helps for the next time you do it* (Year 7).

... at the end of every lesson, and quite a bit of the time, we get good reports like 'It has been better this week. I hope you can keep this up. Some of you might be a bit dodgy, but we can work on that'. You will get feedback and if it is bad the teacher might say 'There is some dodgy old stage in

there', and just make you aware of what you are doing … you come out of the lesson and you think 'Oh she is not happy with us' and you can't wait for next lesson when you go in there and think 'I have got to do some good work or she will not be happy with us again' (Year 7).

Both art and drama attracted a large number of such references. However, it was noted that an oral commentary from music teachers was far less commonly mentioned, and only a minority of the comments came from pupils who felt they received enough oral communication from their teacher. It appears that, according to pupils, music teachers could be more forthcoming in their suggestions and feedback to pupils, and that pupils feel this would be of benefit. This was mentioned in one of the pupil comments, in relation to the marks and grades given by music teachers, as the only form of assessment (see previous section on *'marks and grades'*).

A small number of teachers also made positive suggestions about the benefits of providing pupils with oral feedback. One head of an arts faculty talked about discussing progress with pupils. She advocated the wide-ranging benefits of this approach:

Assessment is not just grades and reporting grades to parents. Assessment is actually being with the child at that particular moment in time … and actually sitting down and talking to that child to show where they are, to show ways of progression, or to give ideas. I think that is far more important than giving them a grade, even at the end of a performance.

One pupil also felt that oral communication with the teacher was more effective than the teacher simply providing a written report. She said:

… whatever we perform, [the teacher] *tells us how we've done and what we need to improve on. And at parents' evening she tells our parents … I find that a lot more useful than people writing it down because when they write it down you never know whether they're writing 'Oh well, it looks as though she's tried hard but it's not that good, so I'll write "very good" anyway'. But when she's saying it to you, you know what she's really thinking. You understand it more 'cos they always use long words when they write it down* (Year 7).

This was an interesting point – perhaps referring more to the style of written reports, rather than the message they were trying to convey. It is clear that pupils rely on the comments of teachers in supplementing any marks and grades, but that the way in which this additional information is communicated plays a significant role in its value.

Sixteen pupils (19 per cent) made some comment about the teacher's provision of written comments on their work. All but two of their remarks referred to the positive benefits of written comments (although not all pupils received them), and over half were directed specifically towards the art subject area. Typical responses included:

> *We get a mark out of ten and a comment ... The comment I can compare with my other comments and see how well I've improved and also I compare it with my friends as well and see how I'm doing* (Year 7).

> *With the grades you can really see how you're getting on with it and you can see which parts you have to improve on and maybe which parts you've got to actually work a lot harder on if you're ... because they put a comment like 'Must improve your colouring' or whatever, and then you can practise doing that* (Year 7).

As was mentioned, a few of the pupils who referred to the importance of written comments did not feel that they were given enough of this type of feedback. One said:

> *She grades us, does our art teacher, on what we do ... she grades us on our homework, and, like, if we get, sometimes we get B2s and A1s ... She sometimes puts, like, if we get a good grade, she'll put, like 'Excellent drawing', but she doesn't put, like, if you get a B2, what's wrong with it* (Year 7).

Another said:

> *The teacher gives us, like, an effort grade and an attainment grade and it's either like a 1–5 or an A–G, so if you get like a G1 that's very, very good, a good effort and, like, a G3 is OK and a G5 is very, very* [bad] *... The only problem is that she doesn't tell you what you have done wrong, so if you draw a picture, she might give you, like, a 3C or something and you want to know why you have got that – what you are doing wrong – and you might improve next time ... it would be more useful if you know what you did wrong* (Year 8).

The provision of written comments in the form of assessment and evaluation was not an issue which was mentioned by teachers or school staff, although it is clear, from the pupils' comments, that many teachers were utilising this method. The pupil references also suggest that they would respond favourably to this method, and that it would supplement the marks and grades given – allowing pupils to have a written record on which to reflect, and through which to observe their own progress over time.

Peer review

In addition to the assessment and evaluation which pupils received from the teachers of arts lessons, pupils and teachers both referred to the importance of the evaluation of work taking place within groups of pupils. This type of peer review was raised as being positive for both the pupil whose work was being discussed, and the pupils who were providing the feedback. As has already been identified, evaluation and looking at the work of others were listed as important processes and activities within effective arts lessons.

Almost half of all the pupils interviewed raised the issue of having their work evaluated by their peers, or taking part in evaluating the work of others within lessons. Despite the evidence from pupils of their participation in this type of activity within arts lessons, none of the teachers interviewed raised peer reviews as an important factor in the assessment process. There was no clear reason why this should be the case.

As with the pupils' perceptions of the value of teacher comments and evaluation, the pupils' comments about the evaluation of work by their peers were also generally related to the art and drama subject areas. Examples included:

Drama

... sometimes [the teacher] *gives us comments. When we've done our play, she says 'Is there anything that they could've changed?' and the rest of the group puts their hands up and says 'Well, they could have changed this or that'. If nobody says how, it was a good lesson, but if loads of people say how, it doesn't make you feel that good* (Year 7).

... now [in Year 9] *you're more relaxed – you can just say what you have to say and other people are a lot more understanding and will just sit and listen to you and then they'll just give constructive criticism and you'll become a lot better through that.*

Art

... other people in the class, they usually compliment your work sometimes, which gives you ... encouragement. If you didn't have any encouragement, you wouldn't really try and create a better piece of work. And so that's how you get better really (Year 9)

I like sort of sitting with my friends because I feel, like, I can learn there because I can talk to them more about it, and not feel so shy around them so I actually sort of learn more when I'm talking to my friends about it (Year 9).

These comments highlight two different ways in which pupils perceived the positive outcomes of evaluation of their work by their peers. They suggest that pupils could gain personal satisfaction from the support and affirmation of their peers, but also that the suggestions made could help them to improve in the future.

Drama attracted 46 per cent of the total number of comments made, and art 32 per cent. This may suggest that in the five schools explored in depth, the culture of assessment within art and drama was far more discursive – involving dialogue between pupils and teachers – than in music, which was seen to rely far more heavily on marks and grades.

Constructive criticism

Throughout the references made to assessment and evaluation – whether carried out by teachers, or other pupils within a class – a key factor in its effectiveness was identified as its constructive nature. There was widespread recognition, amongst pupils and teachers, that the products of the arts could be very personal, and that harsh criticism could therefore be very destructive and hurtful for the individuals involved. This was not thought to be of benefit to anyone, in any circumstances.

Five of the school staff interviewed recognised the importance of the ways in which criticism and advice were framed – in order to ensure its welcome reception by the pupils. However, one teacher recognised that this was not always easy. She said:

> ... in Years 10 and 11 especially it can be, I don't mean this in a negative way, some of my lessons can be quite stressful ... I demand a lot from them and I demand high standards ... it is forever looking at how you can improve your work and looking at how you can develop your work. Never do they come to me and I go 'That is very nice. Well done. Goodbye'. We are always discussing work. I think you will find this throughout the art department. We are always giving them opportunities to explore it even deeper (head of art).

A similar issue was described by a pupil referring to the comments made by other pupils when evaluating work in drama. He said:

> ... you don't want people criticising you. Well, you can take criticism if it's [constructive]... We have a talk afterwards about the actual piece that a certain group has done, and criticise it or say how good it was or anything, but if they're constantly criticising ... you need to find good points and bad points – you can't just go with the bad points ... that's it really, I think (Year 9).

It was clearly important to this particular pupil that comments made were constructive, and not just negative or critical. Such comments were made by approximately two-thirds of the pupils interviewed, and indicate the widespread significance attached to this factor in general. It is clear that some of this concern could be founded on the fact that the arts elicit very personal responses from pupils, and few of them wish to have their work devalued in this way.

Self-assessment and evaluation

Self-assessment was recognised as being an integral part of all participation in, and assessment of, the arts, by both teachers and pupils. One in four pupils made some comment about evaluating their own work, although only three teachers or school staff referred to it at any point. One art teacher who highlighted the value of self-evaluation within the arts said:

> *I think right the way through the processes a lot of self-evaluation has to go on, because they are aware of what they are doing and when they have got to modify something, when they have got to change what they are doing. So I think they are more aware when they get to the end of the sort of results that they are expected to have. It is easier for them to say 'Yes, well OK this bit didn't work as well; I can see that I didn't bring that artist's work back into that' ...*

Another described how the use of stone carving within art had encouraged pupils to apply a constant process of self-evaluation and consideration, which was observed to have an extremely beneficial effect on the work produced:

> *... traditionally we have always used clay as a means of sort of opening up opportunities for working in three dimensions. That has been the sort of standard that we have used, on the basis that carving is more difficult to do because it is purely a productive process. Carving, if you make a mistake, you are really sunk; whereas with clay, if you take a bit off and it doesn't look right, you put a bit back on again. The interesting thing that we found with this, and I have always thought that it would be quite an interesting area of research to look at in terms of education [of] students at school, is that students who had limited success three-dimensionally working with clay had much greater success when they were working on stone carving. The reason that they gave was that because stone carving takes longer to do, it forces them to think about what they are doing, whereas clay is instant, so it is just purely an exercise of playing with the material. They don't really think about the forms that they are creating, whereas if they are stood outside with a hammer and chisel and they are knocking bits of stone off, they are looking at it and they are concentrating. The results that the students achieved were significantly better* (sixth-form curriculum coordinator).

This provides a clear indication of the importance of the arts practitioners' self-evaluation – not only in terms of appraising the final product of the artistic endeavour, but throughout the entire process. This type of evaluation, and the process of making, evaluation and modifying, have been identified in previous research as essential components of successful arts activities.

Pupils also recognised that self-evaluation was an integral part of their work in the arts. Over one in four made a reference to self-evaluation at some point during an interview. There was little distinction between the artforms (excluding dance, for which very few comments of any type were recorded).

3.
WHAT ARE
EFFECTIVE
PRACTICES
IN
ARTS
EDUCATION?

Art

... I think if you look back, you can see an improvement and you realise something in your head ... you realise what you're trying to do and how ... you've got the picture, you know what you're doing ... (Year 9).

Generally, it's measuring yourself up against yourself or your expectations, is normally how I do it. I mean, marks count but ... I measure myself up more on personal ... what I can achieve (Year 9).

Drama

I suppose when you feel more confident to be able to, then you know you can act better (Year 9).

Music

When you listen to it again, what you've produced, you can tell your mistakes, and you do it again and make it better (Year 9).

One pupil, whilst recognising the long-term benefit of self-evaluation, found the process to be tedious and boring:

... we have to do a diary about what we have done in each of our music lessons – that is really boring, but when you refer to it, because you put down in it things that you have learnt in the lesson, that will help you learning them (Year 7).

Others felt that too much time was spent on this type of evaluation, and that overuse of the activity could lead to a loss of effectiveness, in a similar fashion to the overuse of antibiotics in curing disease. One pupil said:

It is quite useful [self-assessment] *but we spend too long on it, because people want to get straight into the thing, people get restless when we have to write 'We did this; we did that'. So in a way* [it's good], *but if we spend a couple of lessons on it, then it is not good (Year 7).*

Another presented a similar argument:

> ... we do self-assessments and then the teacher will talk to you about your self-assessment ... but you just get to do so many self-assessments, in all our subjects, you just get so bored writing the same thing you wrote last term (Year 7).

This would suggest that formal types of self-assessment may need to be limited to an acceptable level, but that pupils should be encouraged to participate in more informal types of self-assessment throughout their work. Clearly, this is an issue which could be addressed through activities such as that involving stone work – where continual self-assessment and appraisal were a crucial element in success.

Frequency of assessment

This was a minor issue relating to assessment which was commented on by 15 per cent of the pupils interviewed. The vast majority of remarks were made regarding music, and the consensus of opinion was that too little feedback was provided. Common attitudes included:

> It's a bit difficult because we don't get told individually how well we're doing that often. We get the record of achievement once a year for general. In music, it's kind of the whole group thing – they'll say 'This group's doing well, or that pair'. You don't find they talk to you individually, only in your pairs (Year 9).

Another said:

> They do grade you, but they don't really let you know about the marks that you get ... It does [help], but you don't really get it often enough. There's records of achievements and my teacher's got a mark book, but we don't really get to see them (Year 9).

Only two of the school staff interviewed made any comment about the frequency of assessment within the arts – they were both in agreement that providing regular, almost constant, feedback was vital in encouraging pupils to improve their work. One deputy head, who had observed changes in the frequency of assessment in the arts, said:

> ... staff now, generally, are very good at giving feedback and praise to the students and fairly quick feedback. That was an issue in art ... feedback wasn't very regular and it wasn't very constructive. In fact, it was often destructive, so as well as expectations being low, when those low expectations weren't met, there was a very negative feedback about that and not very constructive in the way things were taken forward and reward was not very common. We don't want that with the arts department, and that again has been part of the reason for the increase in performance, as well as expectations being higher. Reward became more commonplace, more frequent and more appropriate.

This was seen as a very positive step, which had improved performance across the arts subject areas. It would appear that those who have considered this issue rate it as an important aspect of improving pupil performance, and an important indicator of progress made.

12.6.6 Summary

This section has highlighted a number of significant differences between the artforms, and some key messages have been identified. By way of summary, the evidence suggested:

- pupil engagement with, and enjoyment of, the curriculum – in terms of topics, activities and style of mediation – were identified as crucial in determining their success, by both pupils and teachers;

- this was closely linked to the provision of an up-to-date and relevant curriculum which provided an appropriate level of challenge for all pupils;

- individual teaching and teacher support through differentiation between pupils, mainly by outcome, were seen as a major benefit to all artforms;

- the dependence on practical activities was seen as a vital (and effective) characteristic of the arts;

- pupils expressed significant preferences for participation in practical, active learning activities within the arts, rather then more traditionally academic, passive, learning methodologies;

- pupils and teachers also identified the freedom to develop their own interests, within a broad educational framework, as a strength of creative arts practice;

- practical demonstrations were seen as a valuable teaching strategy – leading to increased understanding on the part of pupils, and their increased respect for teachers' own abilities; and

- although formal assessment of the arts has traditionally been labelled as highly subjective, pupils and teachers identified the value of regular and constructive feedback – from teachers, and pupils. Pupils' self-assessment and the evaluation of the work of others were also identified as contributory activities.

12.7 TEACHER FACTORS

Teachers of arts subjects, in the same way as teachers of any subject, are unquestionably an important factor in determining the quality of the outcomes of their lessons. Not only do teachers have their own opinions of what should be included in lessons, but clearly they also have the power to influence how pupils experience the curriculum. To explore this important area, factors relating to teachers have been divided into four subcategories:

- teachers' methods and pedagogy;

- teachers' specialist knowledge and skills;

- teachers' personal qualities; and

- absence of usual teacher.

12.7.1 Teachers' methods and pedagogy

It is recognised that teachers are a very important interface between the National Curriculum, the schemes of work developed within the school, and the pupils. How this mediation is approached, and the teaching methods which are employed, are therefore prime factors for consideration in the discussion of the impact of teachers on effective arts provision. The factors which were cited include:

- providing help when needed;

- teacher communication;

- speed/pace of lessons;

- structure of lessons;

- classroom ambience;

- teacher–pupil relationships; and

- behaviour management.

Providing help when needed

This was cited the most frequently, by both teachers and pupils, as a significant teacher-related factor influencing the quality and effectiveness of arts education. Seventy-three pupils (86 per cent) alluded, at some point, to the issue of teacher help and support. However, only nine of the key staff interviewed mentioned the help provided by the teacher during lessons – although there was a sense of consensus between them.

The means by which teachers provided help during lessons was one area which pupils were keen to comment on. Providing help to individuals or small groups, or '*going round the classroom*', was a teacher activity frequently cited as being a valuable mechanism for pupil learning and development. Teachers mentioned their deployment of this technique, and provided a variety of reasons for its use:

Once they have started, I find that I never have a minute – you are just going around and helping all the time where you can. Always wanting help, you usually find that there is somebody who wants help ... In the arts you are always busy (art teacher).

The main reasons which teachers gave for providing help to pupils – especially relating to the use of one-to-one help – were: treating the pupils as individuals and responding to their individual work in the arts; and being able to differentiate their help according to the ability of each pupil. Differentiation has been a recurring theme throughout the report, especially in the previous discussion of 'curriculum factors' within section 12.6.

3.
WHAT ARE
EFFECTIVE
PRACTICES
IN
ARTS
EDUCATION?

One pupil comment suggested that it was important for the teacher to:

... spend individual time with everybody, because that's what you will need ... a lot of us book the workshop after school and he [the teacher] sometimes comes in and helps us then ... he nearly always does ... (Year 10).

The pupil draws attention to the benefits of having such a committed teacher, prepared to spend time helping the pupils with their work beyond the confines of timetabled lessons. The following year, the same pupil described exactly the same situation, but with increased recognition of the outcome of the additional effort:

... he [the teacher] does play a big part. I mean, he doesn't go and sit in an office and let us get on with it. He will help us and help us along. I mean, he's the one that puts aside most of his time for going in the workshop ... he'll stay with you after school and you'll do some work, then he'll come and see what he thinks of it and suggest things. Although it is your own work, he'll, like, take you through ideas and show you how to develop them, which is obviously part of the learning process. Someone needs to show you how to develop your ideas (Year 11).

However, not all pupils felt that they were so lucky. One pupil described her attitude towards an art teacher, and made suggestions about how her lessons could be improved:

... her room is, like, quite big, so she is always trying to keep it tidy ... so I think if she paid ... a little more attention to when people need help, I think everybody would move a lot faster and, like, she is not always around – she just, like, gives us our work and then she is off doing something, so, like, when you need help you either have to ask somebody who is really good at drawing or, like, just sit down and try and draw it for yourself (Year 9).

Again, the dependence on help and advice – either from the teacher or from other pupils who are thought to be good at the subject – is mentioned as an important factor in development.

One potential problem caused by a teacher providing individual help to pupils within the class was identified by a Year 8 pupil. He said that a bad lesson was caused by the teacher spending too much time with one person, which led to the others in the class becoming attention-seeking and acting stupidly. Of the other pupils, he said: '*If they're not controlled properly, it can be awful.*' Teachers, therefore, need to be careful that the help which they provide to individual pupils does not cause other pupils to feel neglected. Later on in the same interview, he continued the theme with a more specific focus, saying:

> *You need a teacher who's willing to help out the not so able kids in the lesson, and still encourage the people, the pupils that he knows will do a good piece of work* (Year 8).

Another pupil described how the absence of the teacher – along, therefore, with the help that the teacher could provide – had had a negative impact on what he felt he had learnt in art lessons:

> *I don't want to run the teacher down or anything ... but the teacher is not there all the time and you are usually left to get on on your own. It's not very focused teaching, so we are left to ourselves really and we have had to develop our own skills and if we make a mistake or rush it ... or it goes wrong, the teacher will come in afterwards and will look at it and then he will give you advice, but I wouldn't say I have learnt anything really new. I have learnt, like, practical skills, but nothing that's given me different ideas ...* (Year 10).

This situation – where the teacher gives advice after pupils have made an effort – does not always seem to be the most appropriate, from the pupil perspective. The pupil illustrates a need for help and advice during the process of working, as well as in evaluation of the outcome.

However, another positive theme to emerge from the pupils' attitudes towards teacher help and attention was suggested by a small minority of generally able pupils. These pupils sometimes felt that the teacher providing individual attention to those who were less able allowed them the freedom to continue their own work – a freedom which they relished. One pupil gave an example of her belief in getting on with the work without the constant assistance of the teacher:

> *... I think the teacher ... leaving you alone to get on with how you want to do it ... I think it makes a difference when people are left alone to do their own thing in drama because I think drama's very much your own – what you want to make it. I just think that's the main thing really – being allowed to do what you want to do. I don't think that there's many other ways that drama can be changed ...* (Year 9).

She later described a similar attitude to music:

> *... when the teacher comes round to help, the teacher normally says 'Do you need help?' and if you say 'Yes', then she'll help, and if you say 'No', then she'll leave you to it. I think that's really good, and she also tends to come round and listen to what you've done so far to make sure you're actually getting on with it and doing it as well. I think that's good because then she can say 'Ooh, you're doing this wrong'. I think constant checking up, in a way, is good because it really does help* (Year 9).

Some pupils equally preferred not to ask for help for a different reason. One Year 10 pupil in particular described a good lesson, saying: '*I don't know why, but if the teacher doesn't help me, I'm really proud of myself.*' Not requiring the assistance of the teacher during a lesson is clearly one way in which this pupil recognises her achievement, although some pupils implied that teachers must be alert to the proud nature of some pupils, who would prefer not to ask despite needing help.

Teacher communication

The pupils interviewed were extremely forthcoming in providing their opinions about the benefits of clear communication from the teacher of a class in aiding its effectiveness. Fifty-one pupils (60 per cent) made some comment. The remarks made fell mainly into one of two categories – providing concise instructions of the tasks to be completed, or providing clear explanations of concepts or techniques. Six pupils referred directly to the communication skills possessed by their teachers as being a factor in their learning.

Providing good explanations of techniques and concepts seemed to be a particularly important factor, in the opinion of pupils – 43 of the comments encompassed this issue. One pupil summarised the teacher's role:

> *I think the teacher is important ... she helps you understand. If she just says it once, then you don't really understand. But she goes over it again and she tells you, like, what a word means ... She makes it clear and then it's easier to learn* (Year 9).

One Year 11 pupil was slightly dissatisfied with the communication skills of a music teacher – and suggested that the lessons could be improved by more careful explanation: '*... it's such a hard subject, a lot of people get lost sometimes. I think if he just went over things, explained things more carefully* [it would be better] ...'

This attitude was not raised particularly frequently, but where it was suggested it was often in relation to music. It seems that pupils found music to be a subject requiring more explanation of concepts and techniques than other arts subjects – but that this was sometimes lacking. It may also have been a reflection of the fact that pupil abilities in music lessons were seen to vary widely – it may be that the differentiation of explanations is what was actually being referred to. One pupil made the point specifically:

Maybe the explaining could improve so that everyone could understand, not just the people who've ... I've probably got an advantage over other people because I know a lot of stuff already, and if it was explained better, it would probably help the other people.

Interviewer: *So you think there are people who don't really understand what to do?*

Yeah and then it holds everyone else up, so if it was explained perfectly clearly to begin with, it would probably be better.

Another pupil described how, in the arts, whilst explanation and information were important, it was also essential that the teacher did not overwhelm the pupils and provide them with too much assistance. Being able to develop their own ideas and learn techniques by themselves was also a factor in how pupils believed effective learning took place. As one pupil remarked:

... they [teachers] *give you some tips so they don't overpower you ... they don't actually do any of it for you – they point out your mistakes and stuff so you can learn from them* (Year 9).

The other main issue relating to teacher communication which was raised frequently by pupils was the need for clear and concise instructions about the tasks to be undertaken. Section 12.8 on *'pupil factors'* – which examines how they functioned within lessons – explores pupils' need to understand what they are meant to be doing. The link was clearly made by 30 pupils between this and the way in which the teacher describes what is to be done.

A good dance lesson is when I know exactly what I should be doing – she has explained it really clearly ... she can come round and help us ... (Year 9).

Sometimes he gets us round one table and he talks about what we are going to do and he explains it in detail. Then he just lets us get on with it, which is a good lesson because at least we know what we are doing and then we can work at our own pace (Year 10).

One Year 9 pupil went a stage further by suggesting that instructions for drama could be written up on a blackboard for further reference during the lesson. She said: '*When she writes things on the board like how long she would like it to be, how many scenes and things. Clear instructions, that helps.*'

3. WHAT ARE EFFECTIVE PRACTICES IN ARTS EDUCATION?

Examples and demonstrations were another valuable way in which pupils felt teachers could communicate what was to be done during the lesson. One said:

> *I like them* [teachers] *to give an example first so that we can see exactly what we have to do instead of just starting straightaway, because we can do it wrong sometimes* (Year 8).

Perhaps it is significant that teachers themselves did not seem to pay as much attention to this aspect of pedagogy as their pupils. The only teacher or member of school staff to comment on this issue, an art teacher, agreed with the above pupil:

> *I think that it is important that whatever I am doing, if I am expecting the children to do something ... that I show them how to do it first. I suppose it is a bit like Blue Peter – this is the finished product, this is how you make it. Not only can they see the finished product that you have done, if you have had any difficulties at all in making it, you know what those difficulties are so that you can then foresee the problems with the students. I feel that is important, so I always like to demonstrate whatever I am expecting them to do, first of all.*

This teacher also suggests a link between providing a good explanation and the perceived benefit of actually giving a demonstration of what was meant. This would appear to be particularly valuable in practical subjects such as the arts. The teacher also explains that this helps her to predict where the difficulties are going to arise with a project – which helps in the preparation for assisting the pupils with their own work.

The subject of demonstrations was discussed more fully in section 12.6.3 on 'processes and activities'.

Again, as with the explanation of concepts and techniques, some pupils felt that in the arts it was important that the tasks were not over-defined, and that pupils were still given scope and opportunity to be creative. One Year 11 pupil expressed this opinion particularly concisely, whilst recognising the need for some teacher direction:

> *You need to know what you are doing.*

Interviewer: *... that would be clear instructions, then?*

> *Not instructions, but guidelines of what you can do and what you can't do, and then you can do what you want within the guidelines ... You can be more, like, creative and do your own thing – if it's just instructions you all end up with the same thing.*

Interviewer: *So it's having room to experiment a bit?*

> *Yes.*

It is clear that providing pupils with confidence that they understand what is to be done, and the room to experiment and be creative, is a difficult balancing act, which would also need to be differentiated for pupils of different ability. However, the pupils seem to have identified this as important to them, and therefore it would seem a worthy endeavour.

Speed/pace of lessons

Seventeen pupils (20 per cent) made some remark about the speed or pace of their arts lessons, and how this affected their learning. Most of the comments were directed towards the art and drama subject areas, although music was also referred to occasionally.

The pace of lessons was felt to be important for a variety of reasons, the most obvious cited by one pupil who said:

I suppose you learn more if you get more done in the lesson really, so if the lesson is not slowed down by anything then I suppose you would learn more then, wouldn't you? (Year 9).

However, another Year 9 pupil recognised that there was an important balance to be struck:

I think if we are going more slowly you do learn it more, but if you get bored with it you just end up completely blocking out to it ... Sometimes you just go over the same things again and again and again and it gets really dull, so I think if you take it a bit slower you do learn more, but not too slow because you just get bored.

Yet another indicated the negative effect of a teacher taking too much time, but never appearing to complete a project. She found this disheartening – and thus preferred other arts areas. She said:

In pottery ... the teacher is, like, a bit slow ... we will start loads of projects but I don't ever see them get finished and things – so I prefer the painting part and stuff. It's a lot better (Year 9).

In terms of completing their own creative work, most pupils felt that they would prefer to have more, rather than less, time. Similar comments relating to both music and drama were made:

Drama

... if you get given enough time so that you can feel confident when you walk up in front of people on to the stage, and you get given enough time to sort everything out, make sure it's all crisp, and then you have got ... if you can go up there with confidence then it will never look bad, because even if you get something wrong you will still be able to carry on, you won't burst out laughing or something (Year 9).

Music

... if you have got to rush your work, that does have an effect, because you might be spoiling it ... you should take it in your own stride – don't let other people rush it. Like the teacher – if the teachers do rush you, you can give it in and then when it's all rubbish and they say 'Look, it's not good enough', you will say 'Well you shouldn't have rushed me'. So it's really good that you don't get rushed by teachers ... it's good to take it in your own stride (Year 9).

The head of art at one of the schools expressed her opinion that keeping the lesson moving, and stimulating the pupils, helped in managing the class and maintaining discipline. This was the only comment made during any of the general teacher interviews. However, 14 of the teachers interviewed following lesson observations raised the speed of the lesson as being a factor in its effectiveness – for a similar range of reasons to those proffered by pupils.

It would appear, from the information provided, that although many pupils and teachers felt that pace was an important factor when considering effectiveness, there was no one preference for the speed or pace of a lesson. Therefore, it might seem that the most effective teaching methods would encompass a variety of different speeds of lesson. It would also be possible and desirable, with the individual teaching which often takes place within arts subject lessons, to differentiate the speed of teaching to correspond with the motivation and ability of the individual pupils.

Structure of lessons

This is another issue which was often linked with the speed or pace of lessons. It was mentioned by a small number of pupils, and by fewer teachers.

There was considerable disagreement between the pupils on the most effective type of overall structure for arts lessons. Both positive and negative viewpoints on the splitting up of work into smaller pieces were put forward during pupil interviews. Some pupils suggested that if teachers split up the work into manageable pieces it was easier, but others thought they would rather have a teacher explanation at the beginning and then be free to continue with their own work:

Negative effect

... If you have to do one little piece then act it, then do another little piece – quite annoying really – you don't have very long to think about what you have to do.

Positive effect	*I think it's unusually good when we're doing lots of role plays and when we do lots of still pictures, just like one after the other, and then sometimes when we work as a whole group we get to decide what happens next.*

In complete contrast to their opinions about teachers providing thorough explanations, and setting the tasks to be done clearly, the pupils interviewed also raised the issue of the proportion of lesson time which was devoted to listening to the teacher. Nineteen pupils commented on this issue – and all were in agreement that lessons were better when they had more time to complete their own work in the arts, and spent less time listening to the teacher talking, or explaining what was to be done.

It is apparent that pupils feel more able to remember what they were working on in the previous lesson than they believe the teachers give them credit for. Many of the pupils made comments similar to the examples below, which expound this theory specifically:

> *When the teacher goes on at the beginning of the lesson – repeating what to do after giving instructions at a previous lesson – [it's] a waste of time* (Year 10).

> *Sometimes they do over-explain things, 'cos you already know what you are doing* (Year 9).

These and similar remarks show the attitudes of pupils towards the length of time which teachers spent recapping what was to be done, or providing explanations. However, pupils also approached this issue from another angle – they recognised that the arts were essentially practical subjects, and therefore they associated good lessons with actually doing, or producing, the work, rather than listening to the teacher. This seemed to apply equally across all the artforms:

Art	*You're not really there for talking, are you? You just want to get on in doing art really. That's all you're there for. You might as well get it done* (Year 11).

Dance	*... we didn't have that much time because the first few lessons they spent talking quite a lot about what we would be doing, explaining to us ... At the beginning of every lesson they sort of said over and over again what we were doing and we know what we were doing so they just need to step back, you know, and then help us when we need it because in a lesson like that when you're supposed to make things up yourself you don't really need their help* (Year 11).

This is clearly a problem for teachers, who, if pupils are to be believed, need to find ways of providing explanations which include practical work, rather than simply speaking to the class. A 'good lesson' was described by one of the interviewees:

> *When you can really get stuck into and the teacher does not explain for ages ... I don't think that is good. I think we should explore, find out* [for ourselves] *what colours can make a different colour* (Year 7).

The pupil recounted how the teacher had spent a whole lesson going through all of the different colours. This pupil would clearly have preferred to explore colour mixing, and find out how it worked for herself. Teachers themselves were not forthcoming in discussing this issue.

Active learning and experimentation were issues considered in section 12.6.3 on 'processes and activities'.

Classroom ambience

It was recognised, by both teachers and pupils, that the teacher of a class had a considerable role to play in generating the ambience or style of the lesson. Pupils and teachers both made comments which suggested ways in which the different atmospheres within lessons could impact on the outcomes observed. Two main factors were suggested which pupils and teachers felt were worthy of consideration:

- the provision of a relaxed classroom context; and
- letting pupils talk in class.

During interviews with members of staff at the case study schools, four teachers mentioned the benefit of creating the right classroom ambience. These teachers were from four different schools, and represented art, drama, and music subject areas:

> *... we like to create an atmosphere where they can be creative and use their imagination. The technical skills is also very important as well, because that gives them the ability to do that ... We encourage them as individuals, we try to be positive. I think they enjoy all the different sorts of opportunities within the art department ... I think that they enjoy the whole atmosphere of the department* (head of art).

Having said that, the drama teacher at one of the schools explained her belief that giving pupils too much freedom could be counterproductive. She suggested that a positive atmosphere must also be accompanied by a structure in which the pupils could feel safe and supported – where they were able to take risks, confident in the knowledge that they would

**3.
WHAT ARE
EFFECTIVE
PRACTICES
IN
ARTS
EDUCATION?**

not be ridiculed if something should go wrong. Her way of encouraging this was through discipline, lesson structure, and routine:

> *... it's very tightly structured, it's very disciplined, but within the discipline and the structure you can do anything you want and that's a real key. It goes wrong if you give too much freedom, and it goes wrong if the child doesn't feel safe with the teacher and the rest of the class so you are working quite a lot to create the right atmosphere because if you feel somebody's going to laugh at you, you're not going to do it ... so the conditions and the routines are very, very important ...*(drama teacher).

The view from a head of music was very similar:

> *... essentially you have got to start getting the kids to really work in a very relaxed way ... you have got to set up an environment that's very easy to learn in, an environment that's very relaxed, but still have got all the rules there, they know what's going on ...*

Pupils were equally supportive of the relaxed atmosphere which arts teachers encouraged in their lessons. Almost half of all pupils (41) made a remark on this subject at some point during the interviews, the vast majority relating to art and music. Unexpectedly, smaller numbers of comments were reported for drama. Some pupils recognised that the class as a whole had a significant role to play in creating an atmosphere conducive to creative work:

**3.
WHAT ARE
EFFECTIVE
PRACTICES
IN
ARTS
EDUCATION?**

> *Well, in the class* [art] *there are a couple of people that I would describe as troublemakers and sometimes they don't stop talking and then the teacher says to everybody 'Just shut up' and we're given five minutes of silence, and if somebody starts talking in the middle of it, then it starts again, and so that puts me in a negative frame of mind* (Year 9).

> *If everybody's enjoying themselves you can pick it up in the atmosphere. They think they're doing well and that rubs off on everybody else and they'll start doing well* (Year 9).

A pupil described how music lessons were relaxed – based on the teachers' recognition that what was important was the pupils' desire to learn:

> *All music lessons, I think, are good because there is a very relaxed atmosphere;* [the teacher] *realises that she can't force us to learn if we want to learn, we will; if you don't want to learn, you're not going to. There's nothing she can really do to change that. So there is always a relaxed atmosphere and there is* [a] *very friendly relationship between the teacher and the students – it's not very formal* (Year 11).

A considerable number of pupils explained that the mood and personality of the teacher were a major factor in the atmosphere created within the lesson, and that this in turn impacted on the outcomes and effectiveness of the provision.

One pupil offered a very telling observation on how a positive atmosphere in lessons could affect both pupils and teachers. The benefits of having a teacher in a good mood is highlighted in section 12.7.3, which examines teachers' personal qualities, and this pupil believed that the atmosphere of the lesson could help encourage teachers to be in a good mood, saying:

> ... if people are just messing around, the teacher gets angry and then he doesn't really want to teach and it spoils the enjoyment for us and for him as well (Year 9).

3.
WHAT ARE
EFFECTIVE
PRACTICES
IN
ARTS
EDUCATION?

However, having identified the benefits of a positive classroom ambience, 26 pupils went on to suggest that this was linked to the amount which the teacher would allow them to talk in the class. They generally felt that allowing pupils to talk quietly in arts lessons was of considerable benefit – one pupil described the relaxed atmosphere that ensued from teacher and pupil communication, and the positive benefits:

> ... when we're allowed to, like, talk and stuff and it's just 'right relaxed' and when it's, like, really tense you can't get down to it, but when you're, like, relaxed, you can do it more and you're asking people how it's looking and stuff, and the teacher's just, like, talking with you and having a laugh with you and getting on with it that way (Year 11).

This requirement for communication was particularly the case in arts lessons which relied heavily on group work. One pupil failed to understand how group work could be effective unless effective communication between members of the group was encouraged:

> ... sometimes they don't let us talk and if you are working in groups it doesn't help because you have to, like, choose which colour to use on that certain part, or where you are going to put that, so it doesn't help when we have to keep silent (Year 8).

This factor encompasses all the issues relating to the atmosphere of the class – which both pupils and teachers have identified as being particularly relevant to the effectiveness of the lessons. It is apparent that teachers must pay attention to the atmosphere that they create – and recognise that their own mood and personality have an impact on the ambience of the lesson. Teacher mood and personality are discussed in section 12.7.3.

Teacher–pupil relationships

Many interviews with pupils and teachers identified the relationships between pupils and teachers as a significant factor in the effectiveness of arts lessons. Only four teachers commented during interviews with key members of school staff. However, the issue was raised more frequently by teachers following lesson observations – who described the specific implications of their relationships with the classes being taught.

References by pupils to the relevance of their relationship with the teacher of a specific class in determining its outcomes were common. Statements that were often made included references to the amount of work pupils would do in lessons where they liked the teacher, the advantage of good communications between teacher and pupil, and the benefits of a teacher's knowledge of individuals – especially in tailoring teaching and advice to the needs of individual pupils.

Liking the teacher appeared to be a major factor in the pupils' perceptions of enjoyment and achievement in arts lessons. Seven pupils made direct references to this – most from the same school, and split broadly between art and drama. Pupil references included:

Art

... if there's a teacher I don't really like I don't tend to try very much and so if I have a good relationship with a teacher it makes me want to please them more than if I don't care what they think ... (Year 11).

... if you had a horrible teacher then you wouldn't be able to maybe concentrate or she wouldn't be as relaxed, so it wouldn't make the work as fun (Year 11).

Drama

... if you don't really like the teacher you don't really work as hard and you don't concentrate as much but if you like the teacher then you want to work harder (Year 9).

One young employee reiterated the significance of this factor when he explained some of his reasons for choosing to take art GCSE:

I was quite good at it really ... but also the teacher, I liked her a lot, and she encouraged me to do it because towards the end of the first part I was producing some quite decent things, so she encouraged me to do it.

It is interesting to note here that although ability in the subject seems to have been the first consideration, the second factor in choosing the subject was liking the teacher, and her encouragement. This shows just how influential the relationship with a teacher could be – the pupil liking the teacher, and the teacher being able to encourage and advise the pupil were factors in the choice of an arts subject option.

Pupils from two of the schools made far more comments on this range of factors than pupils at the other schools – 69 per cent of pupils interviewed at one school, and 41 per cent of interviewees from another. This was thought to be linked to the importance placed on such relationships by pupils, teachers and senior staff at the schools concerned. Interestingly, however, it was the deputy head from a different school who suggested that this was the case:

The ethos is one of a mutually caring environment, whereby there is a lot of respect for teachers shown by students, and for students shown by teachers. I think that the relationships there are so strong, but it comes over as a very, very caring ethos based on mutual respect. That, I would say, is one of our major strengths because without that I don't see how anything else can really follow. If you have got a fear environment where 'You will do what you are told because I say so', you are not going to develop a child any further than doing just what you are saying. If you want a child to be an independent learner and to take things further, learning further and get involved in extra-curricular activities and so on, work hard at home, develop ideas, then I think you have got to have that tension-free relationship between teachers and students that will enable that to happen.

Teachers often intimated that the relationships which could be developed between pupils and teachers were related to the quality of communication between them – particularly reliant on the communication skills of the teacher. A deputy head at one of the schools thought this was a particularly valuable teacher skill:

... I think that it is about a skill of teaching really. Yes, all artists are charismatic, but they obviously have ... they have got the subject itself to stimulate the student, but it needs much, much, much more than that if you are going to get performance. Maybe science will stimulate someone. You take the teacher away and it doesn't matter. I don't think that you can with the arts. I think that communicator, that person who can do the interpretation, that is vital, and their character ... The relationship that they can build up is vital, and if they are not a relationship-type person, I don't think ... it just doesn't work.

This teaching skill is undoubtedly important in helping pupils to obtain the maximum benefit from their arts lessons. Teachers' communication skills are considered in the later section 12.7.2 on 'Teachers' specialist knowledge and skills'.

**3.
WHAT ARE
EFFECTIVE
PRACTICES
IN
ARTS
EDUCATION?**

A music teacher described the mechanism by which the arrangement of school lessons impacted on the quality of relationships he was able to build up with the pupils. This particular problem was faced because each class had few music lessons, which meant that the teacher taught a large number of individual pupils across the whole school. A subject for which pupils had more lessons per week would mean that an individual teacher would teach a lower total number of pupils – allowing better relationships to be formed:

Interviewer: *Can we talk about organisation in key stages 3 and 4? I noticed in the handbook that Year 7 do one period of music and then Year 8 do two and Year 9 do one ...*

It was only brought in this year. It has helped a lot ... I felt a big change this year – I actually feel that I know the pupils better ... because I have not got quite as many, because I have got a Year 8 that is doubling across.

Interviewer: *What do you mean by doubling across?*

The fact that I have got my Year 8 twice means that I obviously can't teach another class at that point. Now in my first year here, every lesson that I had was one lesson, so I think I saw about 580 kids every week. Now that has gone down, I think, to less than 400 I see in a week, which has made a big, big change to the way I feel that I can build relationships with the kids, in the classroom, with their work, actually knowing more of the background of the work and just knowing more about them. It is easy to look in your mark book and see marks. It is very easy to do, but you don't see the pupils there, you don't really see where they are coming from, their background, what they are dealing with when they are working towards that.

In summary, it would appear that building appropriate relationships between pupils and teachers – thus encouraging pupils to like their teachers, and fostering effective communication between them – is a key factor in the outcome of arts education. It has also been suggested that, to a certain extent, this is a factor which is reliant on teachers' pupil management skills.

Behaviour management

This final factor relating to different aspects of pedagogy deals with the way in which teachers managed the classroom situation in terms of discipline and control. Despite what may be imagined, pupils were relatively keen to comment on this topic and its relevance to effective teaching and learning in the arts. Twenty-nine pupils (34 per cent) made comments about the way in which the teacher controlled the class. Teachers also made very occasional related comments.

Several pupils explained that they felt arts lessons were more effective when the teacher maintained a level of discipline and control. As this pupil said, a good art lesson required:

> ... *a good teacher who can control the pupils. It's the discipline – because if everybody is concentrating, you find it a lot easier to work and your work's better. Whether you like doing what you're doing or not, you can still make it good if you're concentrating* (Year 9).

This was not as unusual as might have been expected – despite pupils' earlier expressed preferences for a relaxed classroom ambience. Clearly, the conclusion which must be drawn is that there needs to be a balance between freedom to be creative and discipline that prevents pupils from being distracted by others.

**3.
WHAT ARE
EFFECTIVE
PRACTICES
IN
ARTS
EDUCATION?**

The way in which the teacher managed pupils who were misbehaving was, however, sometimes seen as a mixed blessing. One pupil referred to the proportion of lesson time which was taken up by the teacher trying to maintain control over other disruptive members of the class:

> ... *in our class, everyone's always talking and then half the class gets sent out because they just can't stop talking, but that way we'd have more time to do the work because she's always telling somebody to shut up and five minutes go there and then five minutes go there so you end up with only half the lesson, like half an hour* (Year 9).

Supply teachers, and student teachers came in for some criticism of their ability to control classes. As one Year 9 pupil noted: '*Sometimes people go a bit silly 'cos we've got a student at the moment and he's not very good at controlling them.*'

Pupil and class behaviour is discussed further in the later sections 12.8.1 on 'Pupils as individuals' and 12.8.3 on 'Class formation'.

12.7.2 Teachers' specialist knowledge and skills

Almost half of the cohort pupils interviewed (46 per cent) referred, at some point, to the importance of the teacher's knowledge or personal skill in their subject. One pupil spoke against popular opinion, suggesting that art may rely less on the personal skills, or knowledge, of the teacher than other subjects:

Interviewer: *Do you think it's important that they have got a good knowledge of art themselves, the teacher?*

> *Yes, because otherwise ... they might be teaching you the wrong thing, sort of thing. I don't suppose it's that bad in art, but in different subjects, if the teacher hasn't got a clue what they are doing ...*

Interviewer: *So it doesn't tend to be such a problem in art, you think?*

No, because it's just your own work really. You can't sort of get it off someone else; it comes from your own background or whatever (Year 9).

However, all of the other pupil views disagreed with this remark, for a variety of different reasons, one of which related to the subject curriculum:

... it's not much use having a teacher teaching something to children if they don't know the subject well themselves. I think teachers do need to be experienced, especially in art, because in other subjects, non-arts subjects, there's quite a clear definite sort of ... set out of work you have to learn and stuff, a sort of order in which you've got to learn, which I don't think is quite so true in art. So you need the teachers' experience more to sort of carry it (Year 11).

The arts adviser from one LEA, who was interviewed at the suggestion of the case study school in the area, endorsed this pupil's view – that effective provision for the arts was reliant on the subject knowledge of the teacher:

... unless you have got a good teacher, who is skilled in teaching in the arts, then all the understanding and all the reading in all the world comes to nothing ... I think that we must not underestimate subject knowledge. I think that one of my concerns is that we make sure that the teachers that we employ are very sound in their subject areas – hopefully in more than one ... Unless you have got that and that love for whatever it is that you are doing ... then it becomes very arid and can become quite formalistic.

Other suggestions were made about the importance of teachers' knowledge and skills in their specialist areas, and one pupil's view highlighted a clear preference for teachers who were able to demonstrate their own practical skill:

... one of the other music teachers, he's left, and we were kind of the guinea pigs, so to speak, for the new teachers who were going to come in and we had to choose which one we thought was best, and there was one of them who couldn't really play the piano very well, and if you can play the piano then you can do most things in music, because you'd be able to show people what to do, you'd be able to read music. But he wasn't actually very good at playing the piano. I don't know why but it just didn't seem right having a music teacher that couldn't really play the piano very well. I don't know if that's stereotyping or what, but it just didn't seem right. So I think yes, teachers with musical knowledge and stuff is much better (Year 11).

**3.
WHAT ARE
EFFECTIVE
PRACTICES
IN
ARTS
EDUCATION?**

A similar comment from another pupil developed the idea slightly further by suggesting that the teacher's own enjoyment of the subject was an important influence on lessons:

Interviewer: *Do you think that it helps you to learn when you have a teacher who does art themselves and has knowledge and skills about art?*

Yes, because that means that she enjoys the subject herself and that comes through in the way that she teaches us, and I think that's better.

Interviewer: *So you think that's better than just having someone who doesn't know as much or isn't an artist themselves?*

Yes (Year 11).

3.
WHAT ARE
EFFECTIVE
PRACTICES
IN
ARTS
EDUCATION?

An English teacher who was interviewed agreed that this was the case, saying:

... in my subject you would need to have staff who are preferably genuinely interested in the subject ... and I think you need specialist staff who are committed to the subject and have a genuine interest in it (head of English).

Unusually, two pupils made references here to dance lessons – both supporting the concept of having specialist dance teachers in secondary schools. When asked whether it was important for dance teachers to be specifically experienced in the subject, one pupil replied enthusiastically:

Yes it is. One of the teachers we had, he used to be a dance teacher and he was much more helpful than the PE teacher because being a dance teacher he did, like, all dance and the PE teacher did sort of a bit of everything, so she wasn't as experienced in dance as he was. So it was actually really helpful having him. She could only, sort of, give her opinion on something. He could actually teach us how to do it and he was the one who taught us how to write everything down and that. It was, yes, much more helpful having an actual dance teacher (Year 11).

It is clear that the abilities of the teacher within their own specialist area are a considerable influence on their teaching, and the effectiveness of their lessons. For this reason, teachers must be encouraged to maintain their own interest and participation in their artform. This also has implications for the recruitment of teachers – suggesting that the most effective teachers would be those who have a broad background knowledge of their specialist subject, and a continuing enthusiasm for it.

12.7.3 Teachers' personal qualities

Pupils were keen, during interviews, to express how they felt the personal qualities of the teacher of a specific lesson impacted on their enjoyment and perceived learning in that lesson. Despite the number of comments made, they related, almost without exception, to one of two different teacher characteristics:

- personality; or
- mood during lessons.

It should be noted, however, that these factors are more difficult to control through outside intervention. Teachers can be encouraged to develop their own, personal knowledge and skills in their subject, but would find it far harder to change their own, in-built personality. This again has implications for the training and recruitment of teachers.

Personality

A third of the cohort pupils interviewed made some mention of the personality traits of their teacher as being an important factor in the effectiveness of the lesson. Almost all of the examples which pupils cited were times when their teacher had displayed a positive personality factor. Descriptions which the pupils most commonly used were 'nice', and 'friendly'. Other (slightly less frequent) descriptions included: 'funny/humorous', 'fun', 'happy', 'supportive', 'helpful', and 'a good laugh'. One of the pupils suggested that having friendly teachers made it easier to learn:

> *I think art lessons as a whole aren't as strict as other lessons. Teachers are a lot more friendly and stuff and that makes it a lot easier to work. I don't know whether it's done on purpose. That's just what art teachers are usually like, and it does help* (Year 11).

However, one pupil described how the personality and mood of a teacher could completely change the atmosphere of a lesson (see earlier section within 12.7.1 on 'Classroom ambience'):

> *Our art teacher is actually a very stressed person ... not a lot of people get on with her ... they won't try ... I find her completely patronising sometimes ... I get my worst marks in art. It doesn't necessarily mean I'm really bad at it.* [It] *starts off bad if people haven't brought in homework – teacher gets angry with you. If she's angry at the start of the lesson, then it will carry through ... and then if she's angry, everyone else will just be really annoyed at her and just play up on purpose* (Year 8).

There was very little variation in the number of comments relating teacher personality to effective lessons between the different artforms.

Only one comment relating to dance was made, but art, drama and music each received between six and ten individual statements.

Only one teacher (head of music) made a comment on this subject – supporting the views of the pupils – that the personality of the teacher *'counts for a lot'*. He went on to say that *'a good day or a bad day is also very important'*.

Mood during lessons

3.
WHAT ARE
EFFECTIVE
PRACTICES
IN
ARTS
EDUCATION?

Apart from the teacher quoted just previously, no other member of school staff made any remark about how a teacher's mood during a lesson could impact on the effectiveness of the provision. However, in a similar fashion to their comments about the teacher's personality, pupils were particularly willing to comment on the effect of different teachers' moods during specific lessons. In all cases, pupils were in agreement that teachers in good moods contributed to good lessons, and vice versa. In terms of subject distribution, art attracted over half of the comments, whilst drama and music shared the remainder. As one pupil suggested:

> I don't think you can have a miserable art teacher. It's hard, art is really demanding, that's the only ... I have seen Miss, like, fly around – she has always got things to do but she has always got a smile on top of it. That really helps because when you see her smile you think well let's just all smile and we will all do what we have got to do (Year 11).

Other pupil interviews suggested that, whilst the underlying personality of a teacher could affect their performance in lessons, their mood during a specific lesson could be a more influential factor. This pupil described her belief that the level of relaxation of the teacher – affected by mood and previous lessons – was important in providing the atmosphere for an art lesson:

> I think if she relaxed more, and if it was more relaxed ... it's probably not her fault, you know, she might have had a bad class before ... This applies to any teacher really. If the teacher is more relaxed, then the lesson can be slightly more relaxed. I think in art you need a relaxing atmosphere to actually produce something really nice because otherwise I think you'll rush into something and it will just be ruined. I think it should be a lot more relaxed (Year 9).

This issue would also seem to be related to the development of an effective class ambience or atmosphere which was raised earlier in the chapter in section 12.7.1. It seems that pupils are more aware than might have been expected of teacher moods. However, one member of staff put forward the suggestion that an effective teacher needed to be able to 'perform' during a lesson, and then switch off after it:

I often say to the students that we get in that teaching is about the performance that you give in a classroom and you have got to be able to turn the performance on and then turn it off again. If you don't, you will take your work home with you. It will eat into you and you will end up being a worse teacher at the end of the day. You have got to be able to have this sort of switching on, switching off. The best staff that I have seen have been able to gather themselves together. They can walk into a classroom and the performance goes on for the hour and then they walk out and then switch it off (sixth-form curriculum coordinator).

His view was that this was of value particularly for the teachers. However, the evidence here would seem to suggest that this would also carry considerable benefits for pupils in that it would help prevent pupils from experiencing the negative effect of teachers in bad moods, or having bad days.

12.7.4 Absence of usual teacher

The absence of a teacher for a specific lesson, or a series of lessons, poses particular problems for schools, which are often dealt with in a variety of ways. For short-term absence, it is usual for other teachers within the school to cover a class, using work set by the absent teacher, if this is possible, or by other teachers within the department. For longer-term absence, the appointment of a temporary supply teacher may be considered.

In discussion of this issue, pupils often failed to recognise the difference between supply teachers and school cover teachers, but they were quick to demonstrate their attitudes to any type of substitute for their usual teacher. Twenty-one pupils (25 per cent of those interviewed) referred at some point to the absence of their usual teacher from their lessons and 17 (20 per cent) talked specifically about the impact of having cover or supply teachers. The negative effects which were described fell mainly into four categories:

- the general lack of continuity caused by changing teachers;

- the effect of having to do work set by another teacher, often copying theory from books, or writing, rather than practical;

- the effect of having a non-specialist teacher, not qualified to teach the subject; and

- the effect of having an independent supply teacher.

The lack of teacher continuity which pupils mentioned generally related to the problems faced by the school when a teacher was unable to take a timetabled lesson. Some of the pupils who were interviewed as part of the cohort group had experienced disruption of their lessons due to teacher absence, and one Year 9 pupil described the problems of continuously changing teachers: '... *recently our teacher has been quite ill, so we have been having lots of other teachers, so it's been a bit messy really.*' Another spoke from a similar viewpoint about her experiences of drama supply teachers:

> ...*some of them are* [qualified] *drama teachers, but it doesn't really help when you have loads and loads of different teachers. We have had about five different teachers this term for it ... we have been juggled about and things* (Year 9).

The headteacher at a school which had faced the particular problem of teacher absence commented that it had not caused a particularly negative effect, although it was implied that some impact was noted in the results obtained by the GCSE pupils. He said:

> ... *we have had a period, in the last six months, of interruption because of an absence of a colleague, but even allowing for that fact, the GCSE results were still good and the quality of work produced by the kids was good.*

This was the only comment made by school staff on this issue – despite the fact that several of the case study schools have faced problems of teacher absence during the period of the research.

3.
WHAT ARE
EFFECTIVE
PRACTICES
IN
ARTS
EDUCATION?

Having boring work to do when their teacher was absent was an issue for around a third of the pupils who commented on teacher absence. This was also compounded by the fact that a cover teacher would often be a teacher with little experience in the arts, and this would restrict the practical work that could be undertaken. One pupil commented:

> *Sometimes when* [the teacher] *isn't in we'll just have a substitute teacher and they'll give us something to copy out. It'll be something about music and you have to copy it out and answer the questions, and that's not much fun* (Year 9).

Another pupil from the same year-group at the same school made a very similar remark when asked what they felt characterised a bad music lesson:

> *When we have to sit down and write a sheet about hip-hop or rap. That's really boring. You don't learn anything. When people write out of books, they're not learning nothing. But that's only when the teacher's off* (Year 9).

The final resort for schools in covering long-term teacher absence is to provide a supply teacher to cover all of the absent teacher's lessons. However, the pupils made various negative remarks about this solution.

One pupil explained her understanding of some of the problems:

> *... they don't really know what they're talking about and they're only really following instructions so you don't really get as much information as you would from an actual teacher.*

Interviewer: *Are they not a music teacher themselves?*

No I don't think so

Interviewer: *So do you think it's important that you have a music teacher who is into music themselves?*

> *Yes, because then they can kind of demonstrate what they want you to do and things. It's a lot better than just being told what to do and kind of expected to get on with it really* (Year 9).

Unexpectedly, none of the school staff interviewed mentioned this issue in any way. However, it is clear, from the weight of pupil opinion, that they feel this to be a very significant factor in their learning – and one which often has a detrimental effect. It is unfortunate that teacher absence is one factor which does not have an obvious remedy. However, it suggests that attempts should be made to acknowledge the occurrence of teacher absence, to minimise its frequency and to make provision whereby the maximum assistance can be given, and the quality of provision provided can be maintained throughout the period of the absence.

12.7.5 Summary

By way of summarising the key points on '*teacher*' factors, the evidence indicated that:

- providing differentiated help and support to individuals or small groups was a teacher activity cited by a large majority of pupils and some teachers as being a valuable mechanism for facilitating pupil learning in the arts, particularly if this could be achieved without leaving other members of a class feeling neglected;

- a majority of pupils emphasised the benefits of clear communication from the teacher, especially when explaining techniques and concepts, or in the setting of tasks – while, at the same time, avoiding over-prescription which may narrow down experimentation and creativity;

- about half of the pupils attached considerable importance to the teachers' capacity to evoke a positive, relaxed but attentive classroom ambience that was conducive to creative practical work;

3.
WHAT ARE
EFFECTIVE
PRACTICES
IN
ARTS
EDUCATION?

- good relationships between teachers and pupils were identified as having a significant influence on both communication between parties and the atmosphere of the classroom;

- notwithstanding the last two points, effective behaviour management and class control were considered to be an essential ingredient of effective provision;

- again, about half of the pupils and some staff stressed the importance of teachers' knowledge and skills in their specialist areas, occasionally highlighting preferences for teachers who were able to demonstrate their own practical skill;

- approximately one in three pupils made some mention of the positive personality traits of their teachers as being influential factors in effectiveness (e.g. *friendly, humorous, happy*) and many added that the mood of the teacher was another major contributor to the efficacy of lessons;

- the pupils also registered some forceful and quite salutary messages about the disruptive effects of teacher absences; and finally

- pupils' comments underlined the delicate balance teachers have to strike in judging the most appropriate pace and structure of the lesson (e.g. between teacher exposition and time for pupils to make and create), often signalling again the need for differentiation according to individual aptitude.

12.8 PUPIL FACTORS

Educationalists and teachers have long recognised that pupils are first and foremost individuals and do not all react in the same ways. This section considers the significance of those differences in assessing the effectiveness of arts education. However, it is also recognised that pupils do not act entirely independently – interacting within the classroom setting. Therefore three different types of pupil factors are addressed:

- pupils as individuals;
- class formation; and
- class action.

12.8.1 Pupils as individuals

As expected, the interviews with teachers revealed many factors relating to individual pupils which they felt had an impact on the effectiveness of arts lessons. However, perhaps more surprisingly, the interviews with pupils themselves were also a revealing source of data. The degree to which pupils recognised their own contribution to the effectiveness of arts education was wholly unexpected. Several main themes relating to individual pupils were identified:

- family background;
- subject ability and extra-curricular participation;
- attitude to subject/desire to learn/enthusiasm;
- subject enjoyment;
- working hard (effort);
- achievement; and
- pupil mood in lessons.

Family background

The views of the teachers which referred to the background of pupils were mostly expressed in general terms – e.g. the influences of catchment area, local community and culture (as discussed in section 12.3 – 'Beyond-school factors'). However, one drama teacher commented specifically on the range of socio-economic backgrounds of pupils within an observed lesson, and how this had directly affected their individual drama improvisations:

> ... the ones who do come from the better backgrounds tended to do an improvisation about an underprivileged family and the way that they see it ... so those who did the underprivileged family, and did it well, were the better ones – the more academic ones from the better backgrounds. Similarly the other ones wanted to try out what it was like to live in the other type of family, and they perhaps didn't succeed as well because they haven't got the background, the capabilities and so on, to express themselves as the other ones had – it's very easy to take a step down, but it's not so easy to take the steps up, if you haven't got the vocabulary and you haven't got the experience of being in that sort of family ...

The teacher recognised that the different backgrounds of the pupils had impacted on the performances they had given in the lesson. When asked to reflect on her teaching of the lesson, and how she might have improved the educational experience for all the pupils in the class, she replied:

> I think perhaps that I realised [during the lesson] that we hadn't done enough talking about the language aspect of things. It is a very difficult thing to talk about because the intake tends to be from lower-class backgrounds ... and they are not really familiar with sophisticated language, and I think if I did it again, before we did that [the improvisation] we would talk more about the type of language that is used by ... professional people and by more ordinary people ... I think examples would have been a good idea ... I think you have got to feed in more ideas about the difference in language and study it a little more closely, because they just don't come up with it of their own accord.

None of the cohort pupils made any general comments about the effect of the local community or catchment area on the outcomes of arts lessons, but they were far more able to suggest how their own, personal, family background or culture affected their learning. One pupil explained how the attitudes held (and openly expressed) by his father had influenced his decision to opt out of taking arts subjects for GCSE:

> *I actually wanted to be an architect at one point, and I thought of going to arts college, except it was a big no-no for my dad* [who said] *'You go to art college. You become a hippie, smoking pot. You won't become an architect. You will become some interior designer who puts ... hippie stars on the wall, and all that kind of stuff' and I said 'Alright, then', and changed my mind* (Year 11).

Two other pupils referred directly to the way in which they felt their family background and upbringing affected their participation in the arts. One said:

> *... it's all to do* [with] *when you are very small. They really encouraged me to get a piece of paper and scribble on a piece of paper and gradually that scribble grew better and better and better and better. You can be born with the genes of Einstein, but if you are just stuck in front of the telly all the first seven years of your life, you are going to turn out as thick as two short planks, and that's just how it is. It's very important, your home environment, and it all stems from your early childhood, and at about 15 or 16 it's more difficult to learn* (Year 9).

The other pupil agreed:

> *I think it's basically the background that you've got. If you've got a musical background, I'm not saying it will come easy to you, but you understand things better.*

Interviewer: *Is that like parents and things you mean?*

> *Yes, I mean, like, my mum's a music teacher so I've got her influences on me. I'm not saying they've been pushed on to me because they haven't. I've taken them on because I wanted to, but that obviously helps when your parents and your family are interested in what you do and they will come and support you when you have concerts and such like. So I think it's the background and another thing is, I'm going to sound really big-headed, but I've been told that, you know, like, when you play, you either sort of have that musical feeling in you or you don't, and people say 'Well, you know, you can't develop that, you can't learn to have that feeling inside you'. But people have told me that I have and that obviously helps a great deal. I'm not saying I would be rubbish without it. I would still be able to play, but it's just like putting emotion into what you play and what you do and your composing and your emotions come into that* (Year 11).

The last remark, particularly, describes an issue which has long been debated across all areas of education – whether ability is predetermined by nature – implying that parents with arts abilities have children predisposed to achievement in the arts, or developed, through nurture – e.g. encouragement, support, education, and training. It is accepted that both factors have a valuable contribution to make, but their relative importance remains a topic for heated discussion. The pupil quoted previously exhibits belief in both the nature and nurture arguments, whilst another relied more heavily on the nurture element:

Interviewer: *Are there any ways your parents are involved in the arts?*

Not really – they encourage me to play the flute and want me to play different instruments as well – saxophone or something like that.

Interviewer: *What do they think about the arts?*

They enjoy it a lot, just listening to it [music], *and they come to some concerts at school. They're not the kind of parents who say 'Oh, you don't do this and that, do you?' or say 'Oh, don't be stupid and join drama' or something like that. They enjoy what I do and they take interest in what I do* (Year 7).

An LEA arts adviser identified the nurture effects of both teachers and parents:

There are ways in which you can almost bully kids into being quite good at the arts, particularly music, I think – where there is a long history of kids being bullied into being quite reasonable musicians ... one department ... in particular, where we don't have a particularly good music teacher, but despite all of that the kids actually, somehow, come through. We are forgetting the home life. We are forgetting the support of the parents, the way that parents are viewing arts education, and so on ... When you have the two coming together, of course, you have got a wonderful cocktail there that really can move things on quite significantly.

It is clear that effective arts education must find a way of maximising the potential of any natural talent for the arts which pupils possess – whether an inheritance from parents, or more simply a matter of chance. However, in order to overcome what earlier research has identified as a significant obstacle to participation in the arts, a *'talent barrier'* (Harland *et al.,* 1995), some teachers stressed that schools must also seek to nurture arts ability in all pupils, and encourage the parents and guardians of young people to make their own contribution to this venture. Put simply by one head of music:

... the most important ... people involved in the school are the kids and their parents. And I think a lot of us involved in education forget about the parents ... we know what we would like out of parents,

*ideally, and we often say privately amongst ourselves we have got
to educate the parents as well.*

Perhaps this aspiration deserves more consideration as a policy objective
than it has hitherto received. If parents could be provided with support
from a very early stage in their children's development, perhaps they
would be more equipped to provide the encouraging, nurturing
background which so many pupils and teachers have identified as
critical in determining their later achievement in the arts.

Subject ability and extra-curricular participation

A factor which pupils often referred to when discussing what, for them,
made a good arts lesson was their own ability in the subject. Twenty-
nine pupils made some comment about the relationship between their
own ability in arts subjects, and the outcomes they experienced. One
way in which abilities in arts subjects were developed was through
extra-curricular participation – a factor mentioned by a similar
proportion of the pupils as being related to their level of achievement
in arts lessons.

The vast majority of the pupils' perceptions were positive – suggesting
that natural ability, or previous participation in a subject, helped them
to enjoy the lessons (although conversely, if they felt that they had little
natural, or previous ability in the subject, that they disliked them).
However, it must be noted that some pupils tended to describe 'good
lessons' as those which they had enjoyed, rather than those in which
they felt the most effective learning had occurred. The following
sections from pupil interviews illustrate the two sides of the effect of
natural talent:

> *... I think a lot of people are just naturally, have got* [a] *naturally
> good sort of artistic eye. They're naturally good at sort of drawing
> things or whatever ... I think a basic or a not so basic natural skill
> certainly helps* (Year 9).

The reverse of this was described by a pupil who felt weak in music:

> *I am not very good at music. It's been harder for me to learn much.
> It's kind of ... music is all right, but it hasn't really affected me
> much, just made me sure I am not going to take it for GCSE ... I don't
> think I would be any good at that subject at GCSE, and it probably
> wouldn't be any use to me later on.*

> Interviewer: *So you don't really think it has had much of an effect
> really?*

> *Not much of a positive effect.*

Interviewer: *So you think there's been a bit of a **negative effect** then?*

Yes, kind of ... It's just that everyone else in the class seems to be so much better than me and it's kind of hard to ... it's kind of depressing when everyone seems to be doing all these brilliant compositions and you are just playing 'Row, row, row your boat' on the piano ... (Year 9).

The comment above shows the potentially negative impact of a perceived lack of prior ability on the outcomes of arts lessons. This was echoed by an employee – recollecting his own experiences in music several years previously:

... when I was at school, I was forced to take music and I can see, sitting in that music room ... it was a real penance to me, and I hated it, and this awful woman would say 'Write down what notes I played'. Well, I hadn't got a clue what notes she had played, and as a consequence, that had a very detrimental effect on my appreciation of music, at that time anyway.

Furthermore, the two sides of the effect of previous participation in a subject, or extra-curricular activities, were also identified by pupils. Seventy-six per cent of all pupil remarks about extra-curricular participation expressed the perception that it enhanced (or would enhance) their experience of that subject within lessons:

... I suppose at home is the only real place where you're going to learn large amounts – just by picking them up [musical instruments] and playing or composing ... something at home and then developing it ... I think that's how you develop proper skills for music (Year 9).

I play an instrument, I play the flute ... I have got quite a big advantage ... over other people who don't, so I think I'll do well ...(Year 9).

... I think it would be better if I had ... I used to have music lessons outside of school – if I had stuck with that and actually learnt how to read music, I think that would make it a lot easier to get by because all my friends can read music and I am like a step behind ... I think that would be the only thing that could really help me (Year 9).

Similarly, a few pupils suggested that their extra-curricular activity was improved by the experience of school arts lessons. For example, one pupil explained the benefits he had found of playing in a group in music lessons.

**3.
WHAT ARE
EFFECTIVE
PRACTICES
IN
ARTS
EDUCATION?**

... because I never played to other people before and I played drums and percussion. I am not doing that officially, like, having lessons. But as a result of being able to play with the music group, it's enhanced that a lot, because especially with ... drums in percussion, it doesn't work as a solo instrument. So you need to play it in a group, which has helped a lot with music and my own playing. I play a lot out of school as well, mainly on my own (Year 11).

Teachers also recognised the advantage to be gained by pupils having participated in the arts prior to secondary education and GCSE option choices. One teacher's perception of the importance of extra-curricular participation in the arts centred on her belief that pupils should only be encouraged to take music at key stage 4 if they were already able to play a musical instrument. This opinion was based on the realisation that achievement in GCSE music was heavily dependent on musical performance skills, which were difficult (though not impossible) to develop within two years of school music lessons:

... you need to be able to perform. Thirty per cent of the [music] *exam is performance. I can do* [teach] *all the rest, but the performance part – after saying that, I had one last, well he's just done GCSE this year and he started his instrument in Year 10 when he chose to do music and he's just passed grade 5 with distinction now in his guitar playing and he did that in two years. So if I know that that pupil really wants to do it ...*

The negative views of the arts, associated with a perceived lack of natural ability, or a lack of previous experience, were not the only negative influences on lesson outcomes which pupils mentioned. One pupil cited another potentially detrimental factor – that of too much ability in the subject:

... abilities range, in music especially, ... a bad lesson for me is, well, I've been playing instruments for a long time, and if the teacher gives us something incredibly simple to do, something which isn't challenging at all ... I feel very restrained and controlled by that ... I hate being held back like that.

Many of the remarks made about the affect of prior knowledge in the arts were made specifically in reference to music. It appears, from the statements made by both pupils and teachers, that pupil abilities within a music class have the potential to spread over a far greater range than most other subjects would expect, based on the traditional culture of extra-curricular music provision.

A small minority of pupils appeared disillusioned, or at risk of becoming disillusioned, with music lessons. They described feelings of not learning very much, not being challenged, or not having to try very hard to remain at the top of the class:

... what we've been doing in the class I already knew. It's just the basics that we do in class (Year 7).

———

It gets a bit dull sometimes because we are going over really simple things and if you actually can play an instrument, it gets really boring ...(Year 9).

———

Music is so easy if you know an instrument – you don't really have to try that hard (Year 8).

Teachers' comments on pupil ability were generally made in reference to whole classes, or the range of abilities within a class, rather than directed towards individual pupils. They are therefore described in section 12.8.2 on 'Class formation'.

It seems, therefore, that it is inadequate simply to relate the outcomes of arts education to the natural ability or previous attainment of the pupil. The evidence does not suggest that, in all cases, the pupils who display the greatest number or level of outcomes of arts education are those who were initially the most able. If anything, it would appear that those pupils who perceived the most positive benefit of arts lessons were those who were neither top, nor bottom, of the class, in terms of prior attainment.

There are clearly very important issues to be considered with relation to how all pupils can be challenged, and stretched, within arts lessons, in order that they reach their maximum potential, rather than simply the average level of achievement of the class. Lesson differentiation again appears to be a key concept, as discussed in 12.6.4 – 'Differentiation' within the 'curriculum factors' section.

Attitude to subject, enthusiasm, and the desire to learn

These three related issues were each occasionally remarked upon within the cohort pupil interviews, but together show a general view that positive, enthusiastic attitudes towards a subject are valuable factors in the development of arts education outcomes.

Fourteen pupils (16 per cent) expressed opinions which were considered to relate to the combined issues of attitude to the subject, desire to learn and enthusiasm. Almost half of the comments were general, showing mostly that the pupils felt that a positive attitude, desire to learn, or being enthusiastic in any lesson would improve its effectiveness. A very definite example of this type of comment came from one Year 8 pupil who said: '*You can make anything good if you want it to be good ... it's all about attitude.*' One of the headteachers agreed, saying:

I don't believe that people learn effectively if learning is imposed upon them all the time. They learn effectively when they want to be

> *in a place, when they are happy to come, and they feel secure in a framework of achievement and support ...*

Smaller numbers of comments were directed specifically towards each of the individual artforms, excluding dance – for which very few comments of any type were recorded. Examples of this type of comment included '*There needs to be, inside you, the feel for drawing. You need to like it*' (Year 9) and '*... if you don't enjoy your music, you're not going to be able to do that well in it*' (Year 11). A male dance teacher at one of the schools described teaching boys with ingrained negative attitudes towards the subject:

> *... if you have got boys who are completely against the idea of doing dance because they are, like, 'Hey, dance is for girls. I don't want to do this' ... then it is a battle ... they have such terrible stereotypical views of it. I think that is one of the reasons why they employed me – because my specialisms are dance and rugby, which is, like, trying to break that stereotypical role ...*

Finding ways of breaking down the stereotypes (for example, employing a male dance teacher) may be one way in which pupil enthusiasm for participation, and therefore achievement, in the arts could be increased. Pupil attitudes towards the specific topics, processes and activities included in the arts curriculum were discussed in section 12.6 dealing with 'curriculum' issues, and pupils' like or dislike for their teacher was raised in section 12.7.1 – on 'teacher–pupil relationships'.

Subject enjoyment

The extent to which pupils and teachers related to the contents, processes and activities included within the arts curriculum has already been discussed. However, pupils' enjoyment of individual lessons was also an important issue – linked to their desire to learn and their enthusiasm for the subject. How much pupils felt they enjoyed arts lessons was germane in terms of whether they deemed the lesson to be 'good' or 'bad'. Thirty-six pupils (42 per cent) made some comment about their enjoyment of lessons, and its impact on effectiveness. A typical pupil statement made direct links between achievement, working hard, and enjoyment of the subject:

> *If you're enjoying yourself, then it must mean that you're enjoying doing your work, and if you enjoy it, then you do better than if you find it boring and you're not working as hard* (Year 7).

One headteacher also identified enjoyment as a key factor, saying:

> *I believe, particularly with young people in their teenage years, that if they enjoy what they do and they are proud of it, then they are likely to put more time and energy.*

**3.
WHAT ARE
EFFECTIVE
PRACTICES
IN
ARTS
EDUCATION?**

The converse of this – pupils not enjoying lessons – was also described. One Year 9 pupil was asked what he had learnt in music. He replied: '... *not an awful lot really. I was never really keen on music, and if you're not really keen on a subject, you don't really tend to learn as much.*'

The opposing extremes of the comments show how much significance was attached to the enjoyment of the learning experience by both pupils and school staff. The implications of this are clear – subject matter, processes and lesson activities must be chosen with care, to provide enjoyment for all pupils. If this is not achieved – if pupils do not enjoy the subject, or the way in which it is mediated by the teacher – then it is recognised that they do not put as much effort into learning. This in turn is perceived to have a detrimental affect on the outcomes.

Working hard

As described previously, pupils' enjoyment of lessons tended to lead to their perception of an increase in attention paid to the subject, and effort expended. Eleven pupils (nine per cent) referred directly to the impact of working hard in lessons. A high proportion made a link between the amount of effort they, themselves, put into lessons, and the outcomes produced. As was stated earlier, they also linked working hard with their enjoyment of lessons. Typical responses included:

> *We all learn exactly the same things, unless you don't pay any attention in class. It just depends how much effort you put into your work at the end of it all* (Year 8).

> *... you've got to work at it ... you won't get a good mark without working for something* (Year 9).

However, one pupil defined a bad drama lesson – where the amount of effort put into the work made little difference, or where the lack of effort on the part of other pupils prevented her own achievement:

> *The bad drama lessons would be either where you're trying really, really, hard but you just can't think of anything, or you're trying really hard and everyone else is just talking and not working and things* (Year 11).

The issue of the attitude of the whole class towards working hard in arts lessons is considered later in section 12.8.3 – 'class action' issues.

Teachers and school staff, on the other hand, did not mention the effort which pupils put into the subject as a factor, although it is possible that this was simply taken for granted. It is hard to believe that, if asked directly, teachers would not link increased lesson outcomes with the effort put into the work by pupils.

Achievement

A large percentage of the pupils said that they felt lessons were '*good*' where they were competent at the subject, or the specific topic being studied. However, on closer inspection, this did not seem to provide a complete picture. The other facet of this theme appeared to be that of a sense of achievement, as distinct from the development of absolute abilities.

Almost half of the pupils interviewed thought that their own sense of achievement was notable in defining a good lesson. Various different types of achievement were cited, including: general academic success; reaching the targets set (both by themselves as a pupil, and by the teacher); completing a piece of work; learning something new; or just a general sense of satisfaction at having made progress.

Interestingly, by far the greatest number of remarks were related to art. Forty-eight different statements were made, by a total of 31 pupils. For example:

> *A good lesson in art is where I've got an idea of what I want to do, where I want to go by the end of the lesson, and it's getting on with that ... getting all the things I've set out done, it's like achieving something. If there's something that's been lingering for a while and you finally achieve it, that's a good lesson ... a bad lesson is where you've got so many things to do and it's like stopping and starting, because if you're painting you've got to wait for it to dry and then you've got to wash up your paints and then you can start again ... it doesn't flow from one thing to another* (Year 11).

It has already been shown that pupils' enjoyment of a lesson is not always directly proportional to their ability in the subject. The highest- and lowest-ability pupils often reported considerable dissatisfaction with lessons. However, the concept of 'achievement' may go some way to explaining the phenomenon – pupils of higher abilities finding little challenge, or scope for achievement, within lessons, and lower-ability pupils feeling unable to achieve any of the targets set. Again, this reiterates the need for appropriate differentiation within lessons – providing adequate challenges for those of the highest potential, and opportunities for achievement for the lower-ability pupils.

Pupil mood

Pupils frequently expressed their perceptions of the implications of having arts lessons at different times of day, or days of the week (considered previously in section 12.4 – 'Whole-school factors'). However, 13 pupils similarly suggested that the effectiveness of a lesson was influenced by their own mood at the time. Over half of the remarks suggested that good art lessons were related to pupils' good moods, and four pupils had similar opinions about drama. Only two pupils commented on the effect of their mood on the outcomes of music, and no pupils made any dance-related remarks. One pupil summarised the type of mood she felt would make a positive contribution to the outcomes of an art lesson:

> *I reckon, when you are really focused and you are really in the mood, I reckon ... this morning I just came in and I knew I had art this morning so, like, that's good* (Year 11).

Another described the same factor in music:

> *If you have a headache or you're just not feeling very well or you're just thinking about something else, or something bad has happened, and then the rest of the class are just banging on the drums or doing their own piece or something where they're on the piano and it's just, like, 'No, OK, look, I'm really having a bad day, I do not need this' and there's nothing you can do about it. If you're having a good day and you're feeling really happy and confident and you're pleased with the world and everything, then it's normally a good lesson, and you can cope with everything* (Year 11).

3. WHAT ARE EFFECTIVE PRACTICES IN ARTS EDUCATION?

Individual pupils' moods in lessons were not an issue which any of the school staff interviewed commented on as being a particular factor in the effectiveness of lessons. However, a small minority of the teachers who were interviewed following lesson observations did refer to the mood of the class. One comment related to music particularly illustrated the point:

> *... they're a difficult class ... sometimes they're a very difficult class because there are those four or five who demand a lot of attention and when they don't get it you know they'll shout out or whatever and particularly if it's a listening activity and you really want them to ... listen hard and they're not in the mood, you've got to work hard at getting them into the mood to actually be receptive.*

As a result of this difficulty, the teacher mentions working hard to change the atmosphere and mood of the lesson, for the benefit of the whole class. This is clearly a strategy which would need to be employed in order to encourage the good moods which pupils felt were so significant in determining their achievement.

Some teachers were also quite forthcoming in talking about the impact of their own mood whilst teaching. This was discussed in more detail in section 12.7.3 – 'Teachers' personal qualities'.

12.8.2 Class formation

Having examined the way in which individual pupil differences influenced the effectiveness of arts lessons, it is also important to consider the individuals as members of a larger body – the class. Pupils do not act in isolation, and the interaction between members of the class was raised as an important part in shaping the outcomes of lessons.

How individual classes were formed was undoubtedly significant – affecting the way in which they functioned, and the likely outcomes of lessons. Several key issues were identified for further consideration:

- class size;
- range of pupil abilities within the class;
- criteria for membership of the class; and
- social relationships within the class group.

Class size

The size of class groups which are taught in both primary and secondary schools has been a contentious issue for both teachers and pupils, and an issue on which the current Government has focused considerable attention. It was raised a number of times during this research, by both pupils and teachers. This was a factor mentioned by almost a quarter of the pupils interviewed – mostly in connection with art and music.

By far the most common reason for the discussion of class size was the amount of individual help and attention that pupils could receive from the teacher. Twelve of the pupils suggested that this was the reason for their preference for smaller classes. It was described how small classes meant more individual attention, whilst big classes sometimes left pupils waiting more than one lesson for the teacher's help:

I think that actually the groups in art should be a bit smaller, because sometimes she [the teacher] *starts at one end of the room and works her way down, but if you are at the far end of the room then you have not got much of a chance of being seen during that lesson* (Year 9).

One particularly talented pupil suggested that sometimes, in art, the teacher being occupied in giving help to others was an advantage:

... when you need help that's fine but if they're [the teachers] *always interfering, really I just want to get on and do it, and work out my pieces – which isn't really a problem because my teachers just really let you get on ... with me having a big class the teacher has to come round everyone. It's not a problem for me because I just get on and do it so the teacher doesn't really come over and interfere ...* (Year 9).

The benefits of smaller class groups were most frequently recounted by the upper cohort interviewees – Year 10 and Year 11 pupils. They often contrasted their current class sizes with those further down the school, which were invariably larger. The pupils were wholeheartedly in favour of their current situation. However, individual attention was not the only factor which pupils experiencing smaller class sizes thought was relevant to the debate. Four pupils specifically referred to other benefits of smaller classes – class cohesion and respect, better group work, better class discussions, and the availability of adequate facilities and equipment:

Class cohesion	.. it's not a huge class, which is good because drama in a big class can get a bit anti-personal, but we have got a moderate-sized class so it's easy to get to work with everybody and get to know everybody *(Year 11)*.
Lesson enjoyment	Enjoyed Welsh and music classes more – more of them, and classes are smaller *(Year 10)*.
Class atmosphere and teaching methods	… it's a good lesson because there's only 13 of us in our class so it's like one big conversation between the class – it's not like all little group conversations … *(Year 11)*.
Individual help, facilities and equipment	Only ten people in the group so get more chance to talk to the teacher if stuck, and don't have to race to a keyboard *(Year 10)*.

The only other factor which pupils thought was related to class size was the importance of each pupil having enough space within the classroom. This has been considered previously in section 12.5.2 – 'Faculty and departmental resources'.

It is important to recognise that class size is an issue felt to be important to pupils for a variety of different reasons – from the physical space to work in, to the amount of individual attention that can be received. The suitability of rooms, class sizes, and teaching methods employed must therefore be carefully taken into account when planning the curriculum and timetable, for the benefit of all the pupils to be taught. Surprisingly, this was not an issue which was often raised during interviews with key members of school staff, or teachers. Only four adults made any relevant comment. The most telling opinion was put forward by a music teacher who recognised the value of individual attention and feedback to pupils, but realised that class size could be a constraint:

This individual approach and the individual feedback at exam time and things like that is fine for the numbers that I've had. Anything bigger than this would be almost impossible to do. It demands a lot of time to really keep your finger on the pulse of where they're at with their work and, as we said right at the start, this kind of lesson doesn't work unless you know each composition quite closely that they're working on and that's hard; that's something that's come over the years. So yes, the feedback thing's fine. It works at the moment but with more kids I'd be pushed, really pushed.

It is hard to imagine that, if asked directly, more teachers would not recognise the constraints of class size as an issue in the effectiveness of the teaching and learning in the lesson. Given the Government's interest in the subject, it would, perhaps, be an issue which warranted further research.

Criteria for class membership

This factor covers all the ways in which pupils might find themselves allocated to classes within the school. It was a factor which both teachers and pupils felt was important in determining the effectiveness of lessons. Two main issues contributed to the understanding of this theme:

- setting and streaming – controlling the range of abilities of pupils in a class; and

- option choices – classes made up of pupils choosing the subject.

Setting and streaming – controlling the ability range of pupils in classes

The influence of the range of pupil abilities within a class has already been considered. However, this section also recognises that, in some situations, schools hold some control over the ranges of abilities within classes – through the way in which classes are arranged. Eleven pupils (13 per cent) commented on the abilities of the pupils within their classes, and the comments were divided almost equally between art, drama and music. There was a little disagreement about the advantage gained by homogenous ability groups. Typical comments included:

Against mixed-ability groups

... well when we were learning the graphics score I got it straightaway – everyone else didn't, so I was just sat there while they went over it and over it and over it and it was really, really boring (Year 11).

If somebody's not very good at art, and somebody else is very good at art, and they sit next to each other, there can often be a lot of jealousy (Year 8).

For ability grouping

Now we've been put into sets for Year 8 ... we encourage each other more and we work better together, now people who are similar to each other are put together. I think that really helps (Year 8).

3.
WHAT ARE
EFFECTIVE
PRACTICES
IN
ARTS
EDUCATION?

For ability grouping

... normally they all are good lessons [art] *because we've been put into groups this year, for once, rather than just us just staying in us forms, and it's just getting used to everybody else, how they do their other work* (Year 9).

For mixed-ability groups

... the different abilities do different kinds of dances – the simpler dance for the people who aren't as good at dance, or kind of don't really know dance. Then there's the sorts of people that have lessons of whatever and are really gymnastic and maybe better so they're obviously going to get better marks. Maybe they should mix them up a bit so the people who kind of aren't as good go with the people who are good ... that helps having the groups mixed up (Year 9).

I think in art it's very important to be sat near someone that actually is good at art because if you can look at their work and think 'Ooh, I should be doing that', you know, and I think that really helps as well.

Interviewer: Learning from other people in the class as well?

Yes, so if you're sat in mixed-ability groups, it's a lot easier (Year 9).

One particular pupil even expressed different opinions for the different subject areas – suggesting initially that all her lessons had been improved by setting, but later in the interview, that she now enjoyed art and music less than previously because she was no longer at the top of the class.

Pupil opinion generally pointed towards a preference for groups arranged broadly according to ability. This would appear to make differentiation of the work – a vitally important issue – considerably easier for teachers to achieve.

However, the views of teachers were not directly in agreement with the pupils – only two of the teachers cited any problems with teaching mixed-ability groups, and many were positively in favour of mixed abilities. On the negative side, one comment made was related to the teaching of music theory – perhaps the most traditionally 'academic' aspect of the arts curriculum. The head of music said:

... theory is just theory and you can't really water it down ... A fact is a fact and they either learn it or they don't, but for the practical you can always give a less able child something easier to play, something easier to read. It is the theory that is hard.

3.
WHAT ARE
EFFECTIVE
PRACTICES
IN
ARTS
EDUCATION?

The other negative point about mixed-ability groups was made with reference to those with special educational needs. The interviewee said:

> ... there are occasions when we get students with profound learning difficulties and it is very difficult to manage them in mixed-ability groups. I suspect that sometimes if you get students with particularly low ability it might be fairer for them to actually group them together because there are things that you can do with them that you can't do when you have got a totally mixed group (sixth-form curriculum coordinator).

However, a number of teachers believed that this was an inappropriate way to deal with these pupils – suggesting that the mix of abilities within a class would allow teachers to spend more time with pupils requiring a little more help, without jeopardising the achievement of the more able pupils. An art teacher described the way the school had changed its attitude to the arrangement of arts classes, and the impact that had had:

> ... we used to get them in bands of ability. At one time we used to be linked with the humanities, so the humanities set them in these bands and I am not sure how it worked but they would go to humanities for a day and then on the next day they would come to us within this banding of groups. I think it is better now because you would get a whole class – good, if they were top-level – but some of the bottom-level classes were quite difficult to take. Whereas now because they are mixed-ability, if you have got children that are struggling, you have got others that will help them. It was hard work if you had a whole class that were demanding help and attention all at once.

This situation also presupposed that ability in the arts would be correlated with ability in the humanities – clearly not in line with the views of many teachers who believed in the arts as a specific range of skills and abilities which could not be linked with other academic attainment. It is also seen that within this sample, the ability of individual pupils varied from artform to artform – for example pupils who were highly able in art were not necessarily equally proficient in music. Clearly, then, it is important that any ability groups are determined on the basis of the individual artforms concerned, rather than by setting or streaming across the arts as a homogenous group.

All of the other adult interviewees described their belief in the teaching of the arts through mixed-ability groups. A typical example came from the head of expressive arts at one of the schools, who said:

> It is mixed-ability. They are taught in forms and each form contains a mixture of socio-economic groups of children. So we have bright

students, we have middle students and we have special needs students. We are aware of the needs of the special needs students in our classes and we try, as much as possible, to differentiate the work accordingly. I think that it works very well. What I do particularly like about teaching in forms is the continuity – because, to me, teaching students that I have a relationship with and that I know is far better than teaching students that are banded together and called bright. That, to me, does not help me at all. It makes life easier for me, but that is all and I am not here to make my life easy. I am here to get the most out of the students who are in my care. I think the arts has a lot to teach other teachers about differentiating work, about mixed-ability work and about attitudes to teaching as well.

This highlights the strength of belief of teachers in this method of teaching – working with the individual, differentiating work, and allowing relationships to develop between the members of the class and the teacher.

The arts advisory teacher who was interviewed also made a very important observation – that pupils could sometimes be limited, in their achievement, according to the labels placed on them by the education system. He said:

Increasingly what we do find is that when my team work with youngsters in the schools, and teachers observing their classes, the youngsters that they perceive to be lower achievers are doing far better than their expectations. So I think this labelling ... the way that staff label youngsters, actually limits their responses sometimes ... the arts if they are taught well, as it should be, are accessible to all ability ranges ... I am constantly amazed at what youngsters can achieve and the limit on that is what we put on them as teachers ...

It is clear that, again, there is a balance to be struck between the views of the pupils and those of the teachers. The teachers recognised the value of mixed-ability teaching in the arts, but many of the pupils preferred occasions where they were taught with pupils of their own ability.

Again, perhaps, the issue is not the way in which classes are arranged, but the way in which teachers differentiate the work, so that all pupils can develop – even if they are taught in particularly mixed-ability classes. This was suggested by one interviewee:

... all the arts groups are mixed-ability now. I have watched ... because we review all faculties – I have watched drama, art, music lessons and some dance, and I know that staff are very good at differentiating the work, not always by task at the start, but the way they interact with the students, while they are going through the

work. The work is very project-based anyway in the arts, ongoing, and the staff are very good at interacting with the students and questioning, leading, helping to the right amount with the right-ability students. So differentiation really ends up by outcome, but it's the way that staff are interacting with them. Rather than setting different tasks, they tend to get the same task at the start, but then the staff interact appropriately to take them through that task and they end up with different outcomes at the end. But the staff have interacted very well to differentiate. So that's a very important factor in the learning (deputy head).

Option choices – classes made up of pupils choosing to take a subject

This issue was raised by both teachers and pupils, and was often linked with the previous point. In terms of pupil attitudes, what tended to happen was that pupils who had chosen to take a subject at key stage 4 were often the more able pupils, and the result was that groups of pupils who were taking a subject had less of an ability range within them.

However, the other factor to be taken into account was the motivation levels of the pupils. This was another aspect of the effect of pupil choices that was described.

None of the key school staff interviews touched on this subject. However, two of the post-observation interviews with teachers did consider the effects of option choices. A music teacher who was observed teaching a Year 9 class identified the particular problem that, in the class, some of the pupils had already decided that they were not going to continue to take music, and were therefore nor particularly motivated in the lessons. He said:

... you have got to get a different way of motivating them, because they don't ... it gets to a point where it's no point pushing these people any longer to learn to read music, because it's not going to be a skill that they are going to use after next year. If I get them to work well in a group and work well with other people and use those musical skills as more of a people and more of an individual, personal skills, that's far more useful to them, because after this year, in some ways I am going to lose them. It becomes a slight shift of emphasis, the use of the subject ... to teach people to be different people and different things, rather than just music, whereas for other ones it takes on the opposite perspective – because they start realising that this is something I really do want to do and they become far more interested in the really nitty-gritty of the subject ...

Pupils picked up on the same theme. One said:

> *In Year 9, there were people in the group who didn't care about drama. Miss had to pick subjects that were things that everyone could do, where this year because people have chosen it because they actually want to do drama, it's a lot more, it involves a lot more skill to do it rather than just mucking about. You can, it's a lot ... harder than it was before but it's also more interesting ... go into things in depth. Some of the subjects that we've covered aren't anything like we did last year 'cos last year we did Romeo and Juliet and this year we were doing mental illness and things like that* (Year 10).

In summary, it seems that pupils felt groups made up of like minded and similar-ability pupils were a valuable asset to an arts lesson. However, the teacher's response above indicates that it may simply be more of a case of identifying the factors that will motivate pupils, even if they have decided that they do not wish to pursue the subject. Option choices within the arts are an issue considered in Chapter 14 of this report.

12.8.3 Class action

Having considered the ways in which classes and pupils were arranged by schools, we now turn to the ways in which classes function. Interactions between class members, and the ways in which they work as a group, appear to be vital factors in the overall effectiveness of arts lessons. Three main issues were recognised:

- social relationships within the class;
- class cooperation and support; and
- class behaviour and discipline.

Social relationships within the class

Seven pupils described their attitudes towards the people in their class, and in general, it appears that they prefer to be arranged in classes with their friends. Getting on with people in the class was seen to influence the atmosphere of the lesson and the pupils' willingness to take risks. Two pupils gave key examples of these effects in drama and art:

Art

> *I have a good conversation and that helps relax and you get to absorb things much more better with your friends around and you help each other. It's like a little bit of community spirit-type thing in the class, so yes, that helps, having good people around you who are willing to learn ...*(Year 11).

Drama

Drama has been a lot better [this year] – got more into it – was shy before and didn't get very good marks. Now [I] don't mind getting up in front of the class and speaking.

Interviewer: What's made that easier to do?

Have got to know more people, more friends (Year 8).

**3.
WHAT ARE
EFFECTIVE
PRACTICES
IN
ARTS
EDUCATION?**

One pupil from the upper cohort (Year 11) recognised that whilst her preference was to work in a class made up of all her friends, her learning would be more effective in a class made up of a range of different pupils. She said:

I think if I was in a group just with all my friends, that would be perfect for me, but you can't have it like that. It's probably helping me learn more to be with different groups of people ...

The impact of friendship groups was raised more commonly, by pupils, in relation to group work within the class, rather than in a whole-class context. This has already been discussed more fully under the group work heading in section 12.6.3 – 'Processes and activities'.

Teachers made very few mentions of the effect of relationships within the class on the effectiveness of lessons. Again, more of the comments were directed towards the impact of friendships on group work, and were discussed previously. However, one music teacher commented, following a lesson observation, that this was sometimes an influential factor. He described how peer evaluation sessions could sometimes be used by pupils to *'have a go'* at each other – but that this was not the case with the class who were observed. He said:

... they are a quite good form in general. When you [they] listen to each other's music they are quite positive towards each other – they weren't very willing to be negative about each other's music – they never are. In general, you do get some forms where you will get people who constantly needle people, and it's any chance to 'have a go', but that form is not like that ...

This teacher clearly believes that this particular class benefit from their positive relationships and attitudes towards each other. It would seem that this is something which could usefully be encouraged – relying to a certain extent on the pastoral care provided by form teachers and the school, as well as by individual subject teachers. This is also linked to the ethos and atmosphere of the whole school.

Class cooperation and support

This section is closely related to the previous one, and considers the way in which a class supported each other, and worked together –

providing mutual encouragement. Twenty-seven pupils suggested that, in some form, cooperation between members of the class, mutual support and respect were important factors. Over half of the remarks were made about drama, and this, again, seems to reflect the dependence on group working within the subject. One pupil described the benefit of these positive relationships:

My form tutor at the moment is a drama teacher and ... my form is really good because we all sit and listen to each other and we discuss it afterwards and people just take the points. They don't, like, go off in a strop if they don't like what somebody else has said.

Interviewer: *So it's quite a nice supportive group?*

Yes (Year 8).

Another described how a drama group made up of pupils who had chosen different languages at key stage 4 had had an obvious divide between friendship groups. He continued to explain that this had been broken down over time, and that this was a positive contribution to the outcomes of the lessons:

With our drama group there was quite a heavy divide to start off with between the French half and the German half of the class, because the German half are a bit more rough and ready than the French half and there was quite a bit of ... segregation. I think it's good when now we've moved along and the divide has completely gone – we all integrate and we can all get on well ... I think it's a bad lesson when somebody starts to stir up issues like that or if somebody is being blatantly disruptive and not paying attention to people's work ... when you show a piece of work to the rest of the group and somebody is sat there not paying attention – it's not a good feeling. I think it's a good lesson when everybody is working together ... (Year 11).

In art, the comments that pupils made about cooperation and support were less frequently directed towards how pupils worked together, but more towards how pupils could support each other in completing their own individual work. Two comments made by pupils from different schools exemplified the point:

I like the atmosphere in the art room. It's very friendly because nobody is told to do anything. Everybody is happy and they just do whatever they want to do, so we all help each other. We all give each other ideas (Year 11).

———

People are helping each other. They explain to each other what it's meaning and basically we all get on well (Year 7).

This highlights an important difference between the artforms with relation to their reliance on pupils working in groups. Whilst drama relied heavily on group work – requiring pupils to cooperate directly in terms of working together – art involved more individual work, but pupils felt that supporting each other in that was also important.

Similarly to the teachers' consideration of social relationships within classes, pupils tended not to raise the issue of cooperation and support within lessons. It seems that cooperation and support were considered to be important 'effects' of arts education, but were only described in terms of their impact on effectiveness in the context of group work – rather than whole-class issues. One teacher of art did raise a similar theme to the pupils – that of mutual support and encouragement – suggesting that '*they all feed off each other in the group*'.

Cooperation and support within groups was discussed more fully in the section dealing specifically with the issue of group work, within section 12.6.3 – 'Processes and activities'.

Class behaviour and discipline

The behaviour of the class within lessons obviously impacts on the quality of learning within all lessons – not simply those in the arts – and both pupils and teachers made comments to this effect.

Very few of the pupils had considered their own behaviour during lessons to be a significant factor in their perception of the effectiveness of the lesson. However, they were far more forthcoming in making suggestions about the behaviour of the whole class – implicating the other pupils in the class rather than themselves. Over half of the cohort pupils interviewed mentioned the behaviour of the whole class, or other members within the class, as being a factor in the outcomes of the lesson which they experienced. In contrast to the impact of social relationships and class cooperation, behaviour seemed to be more of an issue in art than any of the other artforms. Almost half of all comments made referred to art, whereas drama attracted 29 per cent, and music 21 per cent. Only two remarks referred to dance.

Examples of typical comments made for each of the artforms are shown below:

Art
> *... some people start shouting and talking really loud and stuff like that and nobody is getting on with their work. Then the teacher, like, shouts at you, tells us to be quiet and tells us to be silent and then we all have to get on with [our] work, and you just can't be bothered if you get told you are not allowed to do something. You just don't feel as enthusiastic about it* (Year 8).

Drama	*When people start being silly, sometimes fights get included in the acting and when they start taking it too seriously, actually people start getting hurt and stuff like that and the teacher starts shouting and we all get made to, like, write something out, it would be a bad lesson* (Year 8).
Music	*We weren't settled in Year 7, so we got shouted at a lot ... we got in trouble a lot and sometimes we got the instruments taken away from us and we had to do written work or something ... I think we missed out a lot, because now in Year 8, our teacher's saying 'Didn't you know that?' ... we've missed out a lot, we should have been taught more* (Year 8).
	I think when we are doing practical music lessons it's better because we have a lot more fun. When we are just sitting there just listening to tapes, everyone gets really bored and start having paper fights and that type of thing and then the teacher goes mad (Year 9).

These comments distinctly recognise the importance of the behaviour of the class, although very few of the pupils actually included their own behaviour in the same category. One of the comments about music underlines the point that the long-term implications of teachers' behaviour management strategies can be counterproductive. The pupil remark about the lack of practical music tuition, resulting from the removal of instruments as a punishment for poor behaviour, shows that, in imposing discipline, teachers need to be careful not to create more problems.

The only comment made by a member of the teaching staff related how the ability of the group sometimes caused behaviour problems which had to be remedied by the teacher:

> *... for the low-ability group it is really difficult to sort of, because really it is their concentration which is lacking and their discipline which is lacking and their behaviour and to try and keep them on task all the way through a drama lesson* (drama teacher).

Teachers whose lessons were observed sometimes made comments about the specific behaviour of a class, and the impact that their behaviour had had on the outcomes of the lesson. However, it again appears that this may be an issue which teachers find too obvious to comment on – it is hard to believe that so few teachers thought the behaviour of a class was a factor in the effectiveness of the lesson.

The amount of effort which pupils were prepared to put into lessons, and their paying attention to the teacher, have not been considered as separate factors here, because they were recognised as being inversely related to the behaviour of the class. Both teachers and pupils associated working hard and paying attention with good behaviour, and conversely, not working hard and not paying attention with poor behaviour.

It is clear that pupils feel structure and discipline are important, but often resent the ways in which teachers endeavour to impose them. The evidence points to the importance of the teacher in managing the behaviour and discipline within the class, whilst recognising the wider implications of the imposition of punishments and controls.

12.8.4 Summary

By way of summarising the key points on 'pupil' factors, the evidence indicated that:

- echoing the earlier discussion of a school's social, economic and cultural context (see section 12.3 – 'Beyond-school factors'), what pupils bring with them to arts learning in schools – in terms of their family background, ability, out-of-school experiences, attitudes, motivation and their propensity to enjoy the arts – was deemed to be a salient factor in shaping the effectiveness of arts education in schools;

- a number of pupils also referred to their own mood as exerting an influence on the effectiveness of specific lessons;

- over half of the cohort pupils interviewed mentioned the behaviour of the whole class, or other members within the class, as being a key factor in shaping the quality of the outcomes from a lesson which they experienced – this was particularly prevalent in connection with art;

- closely related to this point, about a third of the pupils drew attention to the benefits that accrue from working in a class which is mutually supportive, cooperative and appreciative of one another's work and ideas;

- approximately one in four pupils and several teachers mentioned the contribution that smaller class sizes can make to increasing effectiveness; and finally,

- a not insignificant minority of pupils considered that the formation of classes according to similar rather than mixed abilities in the arts helped enrich the quality of learning outcomes, although several teachers supported the concept of mixed-ability arts teaching.

12.9 CONCLUSION

This chapter has outlined all the factors which school senior management, teaching staff, and pupils perceived to be involved in determining the effectiveness of the arts within secondary schools. The factors were described according to a typology ranging from factors 'beyond school', to 'whole-school', 'faculty and department', 'teachers', and finally 'pupils'.

As expected, the issues that were raised by the different groups of people interviewed varied considerably. Pupils made few references to factors beyond school, such as the LEA, community or catchment area, although they were keen to talk about their likes and dislikes in terms of curriculum processes and activities, and how arts classes were arranged. Teachers, on the other hand, commented on issues broadly ranging across the whole typology.

12.9.1 Key issues for effectiveness perceived by teachers

The teachers and school staff interviewed described many different factors which they perceived to affect the quality of the arts education provision in their school, across the whole typology described within this chapter. However, the themes where this group of interviewees were the most vocal – were:

- teacher factors – including the need for arts specialisation, enthusiasm and the provision of help and encouragement to pupils;

- school arts organisation and resources;

- curriculum issues – including the importance of practical activity, group work and evaluation; and

- the length of arts lessons.

Teacher factors

It is clear from the remarks made that the teachers and school staff who were interviewed felt that the individual teacher responsible for mediating arts lessons was the most significant factor in determining their effectiveness.

Teachers and school staff demonstrated a firm belief that effective arts provision relied heavily on specialist teachers for the individual artforms. This has particular ramifications for dance and drama – subjects often taught by PE and English teachers respectively. However, within art there are also distinctly identifiable areas of specialisation such as ceramics and textiles, and in music there are different instruments and styles of music production. Ideally, these should also be taken into account.

The main reason given for the need for specialist teachers was the enthusiasm that they brought to their subject. Teacher enthusiasm for their artform, and for teaching, were also issues raised in their own right as being crucial for effective teaching and learning in the arts.

The provision of help and encouragement to pupils were activities which the teachers and school staff interviewed felt were vital in ensuring pupils had a positive experience of arts education, and gained maximum benefit from it. Many teachers described classroom situations where pupils worked individually or in small groups whilst they '*went round the class*' providing help and encouragement.

All of the factors which teachers perceived to be important in the provision of an effective arts education can be seen to relate to a belief in the importance of a teacher's devotion to their artform. This would clearly explain teacher enthusiasm, and also the vigour and zeal with which arts teachers were perceived to communicate this to their pupils – providing constant help and encouragement within arts lessons. Perhaps this would also go some way towards explaining the paucity of comments indicating teacher training as an important issue – suggesting that, in the perception of teachers, specialist knowledge and skill and love of the artform far outweighed the impact of a formal teacher training qualification.

**3.
WHAT ARE
EFFECTIVE
PRACTICES
IN
ARTS
EDUCATION?**

School arts organisation and resources

The interviews with teachers and school staff highlighted two important themes relating to the specific provision for the arts within schools. The organisation of the arts into individual departments or an overarching arts faculty was perceived to be a factor that influenced the quality of arts provision, although there was little consensus about the structure which would be most beneficial. There was a clear sense of the '*grass being greener on the other side*' from many interviewees in both departments and faculties.

However, despite the lack of agreement on a faculty or departmental structure, a more significant issue was thought to be the support which the arts received in terms of their physical location within the school, and the facilities and resources available to them. Staff were clear in their perception that without adequate, and appropriate space for the arts, and the provision of the specialist equipment and materials required, the arts would be severely hampered in what they could achieve. Some interviewees did note that the arts were flourishing in their school despite the poor quality of the facilities, although this was clearly recognised as far from ideal, and the additional advances which could be made with increased financial support were often emphasised.

Arts curriculum issues

The dependence of the arts on practical activity within lessons was recognised by virtually all of the staff interviewed. This included creativity, developing ideas and self-expression, and also often resulted in performance or displays. To a certain extent this was identified as the traditional component of the arts curriculum – highly dependent on 'doing' rather than (passive) 'appreciation of the artform'. Despite the introduction of attainment target 2 (knowledge and understanding) within the National Curriculum, it was still noted that the majority of arts lessons focused on practical arts activity as a vehicle for learning.

Group work was perceived by many of the interviewees to be an important activity, although it was infrequently referred to in relation to art. It is clear that drama, dance and music contained far more of this type of work, which the interviewees felt was a feature of their effectiveness. However, its absence from art was not specifically described as having a negative impact, simply emphasising that interviewees' perception of art as an activity centred on the individual.

The evaluation and assessment of work produced was perceived to be a crucial element of the cycle of pupil development within the arts. However, this was not often described merely in terms of formal assessment, but more generally in relation to the provision of informal feedback, encouragement and constructive criticism. Frequent teacher and peer evaluation exercises were seen as playing a vital role in fostering improvement, and encouraging pupils to appreciate and value the work of others.

Length of arts lessons

Providing sufficient time for the arts within the timetable was very important to the arts teachers interviewed, although other school staff – particularly those with responsibility for curriculum planning – recognised how difficult this was amongst all the other pressures of the National Curriculum.

However, a factor that was mentioned more frequently than the overall amount of time available to the arts was the length of individual lessons, and their arrangement. Art teachers clearly favoured longer art lessons, thus allowing for the time spent in getting equipment out and tidying away, and maximising the available practical time. There was also the need for art teachers to be able to give individual help to each pupil in the class. On the other hand, drama teachers referred to the problem of pupils' short attention span, and their inability to remember work from lesson to lesson where they were infrequent. They, therefore, expressed a preference for shorter, but more frequent lessons.

These perceptible differences in the preferences for the arrangement of lessons expressed by teachers of different artforms serve to highlight the need to consider each artform according to its needs, and provide sympathetic timetabling arrangements wherever possible.

12.9.2 Key issues for effectiveness perceived by pupils

The pupils who were interviewed as part of the longitudinal cohort group made many references to the factors that they felt impacted on the quality of the arts education that they experienced. However, these comments tended to be directed towards specific aspects of the developed typology – focusing mainly on the curriculum as mediated and experienced, teacher factors, and issues relating to themselves as learners and class members. Those that received the most references during interviews were:

- **arts lesson activities** – including practical versus writing, working in groups, freedom to do their own thing, developing ideas, and performance;

- **teacher factors** – including generation of a relaxed classroom ambience, providing help when needed and giving clear explanations of both tasks and concepts; and

- **pupil and class issues** – including their enjoyment of the subject and the specific curriculum content, the behaviour of the class, and their level of achievement.

Arts lesson activities

As may have been expected, the pupils who were interviewed firmly believed that the nature of the activities that they experienced as part of arts lessons exerted the most influence on the outcomes they developed. One aspect of arts lesson activities on which virtually every pupil interviewed made some comment was the dependence of the arts on practical activities, rather than writing. However, pupils generally described their preferences for this type of activity, rather than articulating its advantages in terms of learning.

In line with the perceptions of teachers and school staff interviewed, many pupils referred to their belief in the importance of group work within the arts, but especially within drama and music. Again, art was seen to be almost devoid of group working activities, but this was not identified in a negative manner. In drama and music, group work was viewed as a very valuable part of the subject – allowing pupils to learn from each other in addition to from the teacher.

Another theme which pupils felt to be important was the freedom they were allowed within the arts to 'do their own thing', and develop their own ideas. This was a feature of arts lessons to which many pupils responded positively, and which they felt set the arts apart from other school subjects. This freedom also allowed them to take the work set by the teacher and develop it with relation to their own personality and interests – thus exerting their own influence on their experience of the curriculum.

In addition to the arts' dependence on practical activities, the pupils interviewed also recognised performing, or displaying work, as a vital aspect of teaching and learning. Performance was seen as an important activity in itself, but was also recognised as crucial in providing opportunities for critical review, evaluation and assessment, which pupils thought crucial to improvement. Pupils described their need for frequent opportunities for feedback on their work – from both the teacher and their peers, with a dependence on constructive criticism. There was also a sense of celebration of the work and achievements of others in the arts.

**3.
WHAT ARE
EFFECTIVE
PRACTICES
IN
ARTS
EDUCATION?**

Teacher factors

Not surprisingly, the next most important factor in the development of outcomes from arts lessons was felt to be the individual teacher. Pupils recognised that the teacher was the central figure in terms of generating the ambience and atmosphere within the classroom, and they felt a relaxed classroom was a key characteristic of effective arts education provision.

Communication on the part of the teacher was another issue which pupils felt was critical in determining the efficacy of their arts lessons. They described how important it was that the teacher was able to give clear instructions and definitions of concepts, although they felt that too many instructions could restrict their creativity. They also felt that communication between teacher and pupils was improved if there were good working relationships between the parties.

The other main issue which pupils related to their teacher was their need for individual help and attention within arts lessons. Providing help to individuals, or small groups, within lessons was a teacher activity that teachers and school staff recognised as an important feature of arts lessons, and it seems that this was widely appreciated by the pupils interviewed. Finding a balance between helping individuals and monitoring the situation of the whole class was an issue that pupils felt to be a key to successful teaching and learning in the arts.

Pupil factors

The third most important group of factors which pupils identified as influencing their learning in the arts related to themselves, both as individuals and members of groups or classes. Pupils volunteered, quite insightfully at times, that their own background and predisposition for the arts affected the outcomes that they could develop through arts lessons.

Pupils widely recognised that their enjoyment of the arts, and the specific content and activities within arts lessons, directly contributed to the outcomes which they observed. However, they also described a balance between work which challenged them, and work through which they could feel a sense of achievement. It appears that for pupils:

Challenge + Achievement = Enjoyment

In this sense, during interviews, pupils often appeared to equate enjoyment directly with their perception of the effectiveness of the lesson.

In addition, pupils identified the behaviour of the class, or other individuals within the class, as having a bearing on their own achievement. In many cases, pupils described others within their arts classes who did not take the subject seriously, and who caused disruption for everyone else. This was particularly seen to be an issue within art. Clearly, they felt that class discipline was important, but this trend may also suggest one negative implication of mandatory arts participation at key stage 4 for those pupils who do not wish it.

12.9.3 General conclusions

Having explored the issues pertinent to each of the groups of interviewees, some general conclusions can be drawn about the factors which are most frequently perceived to be significant in determining the effectiveness of arts education provision in secondary schools. These factors are:

- teacher factors;

- curriculum factors;

- pupil factors; and

- school context and arts management.

Both staff and pupils felt that the teacher of individual arts lessons, and the curriculum experienced through arts lessons, were the most influential factors on the effectiveness of those lessons. However, the two groups differed in their emphasis – the staff interviewed ranking arts teachers as the most influential factor on the effectiveness of arts lessons, and the pupils identifying the curriculum as the most significant influence. Clearly, these two items are closely related – the teacher having some impact on the content and pupil experience of the curriculum, and the curriculum exerting some influence on the way in which teachers conducted arts lessons.

Factors which pupils identified as having a particularly strong influence on the outcomes of arts lessons were their own personal predisposition and aptitude, their enjoyment of the artform, and their willingness to learn. These factors were infrequently cited by teachers or school staff, although this was perhaps an oversight of the widely accepted and obvious, rather than a deliberate omission. Certainly, the arts awareness and predisposition that pupils bring into the school with them has a bearing on the outcomes that they can develop throughout their education.

There was also a clear sense that the context and organisation of the school could, to some extent, impact on the quality and effectiveness of the arts provision which pupils experienced. The case study schools represented a wide variety of different school types and locations, and this was seen to have some consequence for their arts provision. There were also different forms of organisation – in terms of faculties or departments, different emphases within the timetables, and different levels of resources. All of these factors were thought to have an appreciable, if subtle, effect on the provision for the arts.

Clearly the four main themes identified here – the teacher, the curriculum, the pupils, and the school context – were perceived (by teachers, school staff and pupils) to form the backbone of the effective provision of arts education in secondary schools. However, the results presented within this chapter must be treated with some caution – based as they are on the perceptions of pupils and school staff, rather than quantifiable evidence. The next chapter within this part of the report aims to illuminate effective practice within arts education provision, by closer analysis of specific lesson observation data.

13. EFFECTIVE PRACTICES IN CONTEXT

CHAPTER OVERVIEW

Whereas the previous chapter described interviewees' perceptions of factors that make for effective teaching and learning in the arts, this chapter – the second in Part Three – takes a more analytical perspective. It examines classroom observations of arts lessons in schools that were particularly successful in achieving high levels of outcomes identified in Part Two. In this way, effective practices in each of the four main artforms are portrayed in turn:

- **dance (13.2)**
- **art (13.3)**
- **music (13.4)**
- **drama (13.5).**

**3.
WHAT ARE
EFFECTIVE
PRACTICES
IN
ARTS
EDUCATION?**

13.1 INTRODUCTION

The purpose of this chapter is to present detailed portrayals of the ways in which dance, art, music and drama are actually experienced in the classroom, thus further identifying the effects of – and effective practice in – arts education. In this way, the chapter addresses the third of the study's main aims: *'to illuminate good practice in schools' provision of high-quality educational experiences in the arts'*.

Of the numerous lessons captured on video during the research at each of the five case study schools, two were selected for each artform, and are presented – illustrating each artform in turn. It must be borne in mind, throughout this chapter, that each of the video observations analysed here represents just one individual lesson, and that the presence of the video camera may be an influential factor. However, both pupils and teacher were given an opportunity during post-observation interviews to reflect on the possible differences between the observed lesson and usual lessons, and few were reported (mainly concerning moderately improved pupil behaviour). The observed lessons for analysis were selected on the basis of the distinctive array of effects and outcomes of the artform nominated by all the pupils interviewed from that school throughout the length of the research.

There is a saying that goes *'writing about music is like dancing about architecture'*, and, in some ways, the same incongruity of trying to fully convey one creative discipline by the use of another medium might also apply here. Attempting to capture the full meaning and import of an arts teacher in action proved a challenge: observing arts lessons (and discussing them afterwards) was, without doubt, to be witness to a unique – and collective – creative performance by teacher and pupils. Each observed lesson provided examples of spontaneous and responsive learning interactions underpinned by the long-term script that is national and school curriculum imperatives. In addition, these learning occasions were totally influenced and bounded by a specific historical context that included the histories of the main players (teacher and pupils) as well as the institution itself. To appreciate these arts lessons thus also requires an understanding of this wider context.

Hence, to address these issues, the present chapter includes depictions of arts teaching in three different sections for each of the selected schools:

(i) The effects and outcomes of arts education within the school as a whole and as perceived by pupils are reported. This section is based on the data derived from pupil interviews, and focuses on the number and range of nominations that particular effect received during those interviews.

(ii) The second section is based on interview data covering the teaching approaches (and the underpinning 'philosophies') of the arts teachers themselves, supported by relevant contextual data, such as the school's ethos and relevant local socio-economic and cultural implications.

(iii) The third section attempts to apply and expand the information derived from the previous sections through the reporting of a detailed classroom observation session. Narrative, interpretative accounts of arts lessons are presented, supported by graphical representations of their different phases and focuses. In addition, pupil and teacher retrospective views on the lesson are relayed.

In addition, looking across all disciplines, four major common 'movements' or activities involved in an arts lesson were detectable:

Lesson logistics/housekeeping is the category within which classroom activities such as room organisation, equipment distribution/collection, handing out books are located. This accounts for the time spent by the teacher in 'sorting out' and managing the classroom/learning space, the pupils and the medium they are to work with. *Lesson logistics* featured highly in those artforms where equipment and materials are central to learning, such as art and music, while dance (taking place in non-specialist facilities in both schools observed) had virtually no investment in this element.

Task setting/instruction (whole class) includes the time spent by the teacher in addressing the whole class, including reviewing previous lessons, detailing the present lesson's task-content and aims and also reviewing work/concluding the lesson. This is the part of the lesson which is 'teacher-led'.

Practical/independent activities defines the component of the lesson in which the pupils are actively engaged and participating in the particular artform, individually or in a group context. The teacher's role within this is essentially supportive, assisting and commenting on the arts activity being undertaken. It is in this stage of the lesson that teachers' interactions are carefully calibrated to the youngsters' needs: the interchange might simply affirm, encourage and praise work under way, or offer advice and input to ensure a better quality outcome. This advice might be proffered in the form of negotiation, be quite directive or even be modelled by the teacher to guide the pupil(s) towards improvements in their output.

Performance and product evaluation refers to the proportion of the lesson when the whole class's attention is focused on observing a performance/piece of work and then commenting and evaluating. This stage of a lesson appears to serve many purposes: celebratory, ensuring a sense of completion and achievement, encouraging reflective insight and discourse on the artform.

In the following narratives, diagrammatic representations of these four elements of a lesson structure accompany the text. In addition, each narrative attempts to capture some of the discourse between teacher and pupils. Another common factor across all these artforms is how positive encouragement and acclaim dominate such interchanges: above all, the arts teaching exemplified here operates a 'Praise Culture'. Pupil achievement is constantly identified and celebrated; youngsters work in a learning ambience utterly permeated by positive feedback on their output. Is this the distinguishing feature of effective arts teaching?

Following the presentation of each of the three sections outlined above, a discussion and review of such issues for each individual artform is presented.

DANCE

'The body never lies.'

Martha Graham

3.
WHAT ARE
EFFECTIVE
PRACTICES
IN
ARTS
EDUCATION?

13.2 DANCE

School 1

13.2.1 *School 1: the effects of dance education*

Pupils from School 1 recorded the highest number of responses about dance, and equally significantly these responses (along with School 2 following) included a greater range of different effect types than the other case study schools. In each year group where dance was discussed, pupils nominated intrinsic 'enjoyment' effects. Similarly, 'personal and social development outcomes', in terms of confidence and a sense of achievement (*'feeling good about myself'*) and also social collaboration, featured in the pupil accounts in each year group. The school also claimed the highest number of nominations for 'knowledge and skills' of dance. Uniquely, pupils noted 'expressive outcomes' in each year of key stage 3. 'Creativity' was mentioned more than once in Year 8 and Year 11. Extrinsic transfer effects were also noted: youngsters identified links with drama, music and maths,

3.
WHAT ARE
EFFECTIVE
PRACTICES
IN
ARTS
EDUCATION?

as well as possibilities of links with leisure and extra-curricular activities. Put together, the outstanding range and quantity of effects suggest the value of closer investigation of School 1's dance teaching.

13.2.2   School 1: teaching approaches and context

The school, servicing a town and its rural village catchment area, was defined as: '*a real comprehensive*' with the full range of academic ability. A wide range of socio-economic status was also present, but the school population was defined as: '*more affluent*' by a number of staff. This may be relevant to the fact that a number of the female pupils could take up the opportunity to have private dance lessons. Teachers also spoke of the general amenability of pupils: '*They are lovely to work with, very friendly.*'

Senior management were seen to be supportive of the arts and also aware of the need to develop dance within the school: hence the appointment of a male newly qualified teacher (NQT) with specialism in dance as well as PE.

Despite the local opportunities for private tuition, dance within education apparently had fewer amenities to call on. However, the school was said to have links with the LEA's dance project and it was reported that the LEA adviser had run a dance festival, provided valuable INSET on dance and given three days of workshops for Year 9 pupils in the previous year. The local regional arts board had offered advice on developing a dance studio in the school, but, at the time of the research, no specialist facilities were available.

Staff within the PE department taught dance, although in Year 9 it was timetabled as part of expressive arts, where pupils received 16 hours of dance tuition (two hours a week for an eight-week block). This involved the PE teacher with a dance specialism in planning with the expressive arts faculty. In Year 7 and Year 8, pupils had dance in the winter term for seven to eight lessons (each of one hour) and this was planned exclusively with the head of PE.

Restricted timetabling and the ramifications of dance being sited within the PE syllabus and that department's staffing structures emerged as an issue, with the view that the majority of PE teachers '... *don't want to teach dance because they are not confident with it*' being stressed: '*They will teach a sports dance or a football dance ... pretend we are dribbling ... they end up not teaching dance, just running around to a bit of music.*'

Extra-curricular opportunities were offered as dance clubs for key stage 3 and key stage 4 separately and there was also reference to a dance production undertaken in Year 9, (which was something senior managers were keen to promote).

The observed dance teacher (who specialised in rugby) had become involved in – and indeed inspired by – dance during his four year BEd in Physical Education, and had continued to attend jazz dance lessons after qualifying. He said: *'It helps me to learn new things ... rather than just stopping I am actually still developing.'*

In terms of personal values in dance education, the teacher saw *'enjoyment and the opportunity to take part and get involved'* as a main aim, citing his own conversion as an example: *'... I would never have seen myself* [doing dance], *you know. If someone had said to me "Do you want to dance?", I'd have said "No, that's not for me ... it's a girls' thing". Then I had the opportunity. I did it, and I absolutely loved it.'*

Other aims for dance included *'educating pupils about different lifestyles and cultures'* as well as *'the physical side'*. In addition, the teacher highlighted how the expressive and emotional side of dance, which he considered important, was given no priority or mention in the National Curriculum.

Approaches to teaching included modelling (*'teacher-led dance to get them going'*) and task setting (*'We will brainstorm different ideas and say "Right, you pick an idea and say how you would express that in movement"'*). Other characteristic components of dance lessons included: *'learning to work with others ... touching and supporting others ... having to be aware of where someone else is in the room ... developing good social skills'*.

Thus, a teacher who was highly committed and skilled in the artform was observed in action.

3. WHAT ARE EFFECTIVE PRACTICES IN ARTS EDUCATION?

13.2.3   School 1: the observed lesson

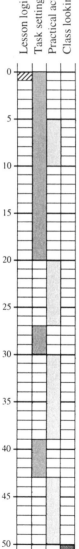

The class whose lesson was observed were having their second lesson in a dance module. It took place in a gym – noted as a far from ideal venue by the teacher. The class had been learning the 'action components' of dance (travel, turn, jump, gesture and stillness) and during the lesson incorporated four 'movement skills': copy, mirror, contrast and interdependence. (This '*dance discourse*' was repeated by the teacher throughout the lesson.)

The first five minutes involved the class seated on the gym floor listening as the teacher revisited the theme of last week by questioning: '*Last week we did five different things to do with dance ... what were they?*' Then, in a self-chosen space, as a prelude to the '*warm up*', the class received more precise details of the previously learnt routine: '*four beats of travelling, four beats of turn, four beats of travel, four beats of gesture ...*'. Reminders and suggestions of '*finding a space*' were made several times.

With each child working alone, the teacher then talked them through, modelled and orchestrated the routine. There were two run-throughs and praise ('*Excellent*') after each performance. References to '*performing*' were made, as the teacher advised on stillness at the completion of the routine.

The teacher then introduced the music, again supportive, saying '*I'll count you through it*' and indicating the speed of the rhythm. The music was in the contemporary '*house*' tradition. Still working on their own, two run-throughs were undertaken: once with the teacher instructing the moves, and a second time '*without me telling you ... I'll guide you*', where the teacher modelled/accompanied the routine. Praise ('*Fantastic, brilliant, well done*') completed this revision section of the lesson.

The children were then seated around the teacher who, noting '*We are going to make it more complicated*', introduced the concept of the four movement skills described above. He demonstrated these with one class member and suggested that in pairs they should '*apply those four skills*' to their routine. One pair member was instructed to remember the five action components and the other the four skills. He acknowledged: '*That's a lot of information. I'll be coming round to help you.*'

The class, in pairs, then embarked on devising their routines, with the music left playing. The teacher moved round the pairs, spending no more than 90 seconds with each. His approach was to ask the pair to '*show me one skill … show me one thing*' and then encourage them to identify '*What skill was that?*' Praise featured in each interchange, with the teacher also suggesting improvements, and pinpointing inaccuracies in their timing or movements, for example: '*Excellent, but is this travelling?* [teacher models the pair's action] *You can change it by going forward … excellent.*' Each pair was visited at least once. On two occasions, the teacher stopped the class and reminded the group of common errors and ways of improving the routine. The first of these was more focused on generally encouraging the class to stay on task, i.e. recognise that '*it will get easier*' and '*Take two to three minutes to plan it and then just get on with it*'. In the second whole-class input, he modelled and encouraged the class to '*be expressive, express yourself*' and also to recognise that many were '*going past the time*', suggesting they realise that '*travelling is thinking time*'. He reminded the class that professional dancers practise one second of dancing for one hour. His final message to the group was: '*Don't worry if it's not perfect … convince yourself, be positive, larger than life, get the timing right and ENJOY it!*'

In the final five minutes, half of the class presented their routines to the other half and vice versa. The teacher encouraged clapping and whooping to demonstrate the achievement of each of these performances. One final run-through was then undertaken for a teacher who happened to be passing through the gym ('*[Teacher], you've just missed the most superb dancing … we'll have to have everybody showing you*'). This teacher also lavished praise on the group.

The children were then instructed to get changed.

Activity	Time (mins)	Time as % of lesson time
Lesson logistics/organisation/housekeeping	2	3
Whole-class task setting/direct instruction	27	49
Pupils engaged in practical activities	28	51
Class looking at the work of others/evaluation	5	9

NB Percentages in this table do not sum to 100% due to multiple activities occurring at the same time within the lesson.

In discussion following this lesson, the teacher indicated that a number of intentions had underpinned the activity, all basically revolving around a positive initiation into the dance medium. Hence, introducing and reinforcing '*the basic skills of dance*', '*the skills of working with other people*', '*a few ideas about performance … like standing still at the beginning and being quiet at the end*' were noted. Above all, it was stressed that '*the emphasis is really that they will want to dance next year, to encourage them'*. Each of these aims was clearly being realised throughout the lesson: the discourse of dance, the praise, the explicit references to enjoyment and being expressive, and so on were all interwoven into the activity. Notwithstanding this culture of acclaim, the teacher interventions were also focused on improvement and ensuring quality:

> *... the most important thing is to encourage them in what they are doing so they don't feel they've failed. So, yes 'What you've done is brilliant' but deep in the back of their mind is still 'I've got to achieve this standard of getting to the end of* [the dance] *and getting it all in', so you're trying to keep the quality but you're still allowing for them not to achieve it.*

Equally, during the interchanges with the working pairs, the teacher was fully aware that he was '*gaining knowledge*' of each child and their abilities. By these teacher interactions, the pupils also '*got an idea of where they are at*' and '*they actually changed and improved* [their dance]'. Thus, a careful calibration of supportive praise and suggestion for development was occurring in each of the brief interchanges. The teacher was aware of engaging with each child, however briefly, and saw this as a significant feature and teaching goal given the early stages of their dance experience and their learning relationship with him.

Further, the occasion of performance at the end of the lesson had a *de rigueur* significance: despite acknowledged time constraints, the teacher stated that: '*Whatever happens, you need to give them chance to perform it because otherwise they go out and feel they've wasted an hour and they forget what they've done next lesson.*' Indeed, the lesson conveyed a sense of evolution, progression and completion. Perhaps equally striking was how the teacher constructed a lesson which constantly balanced a long-term goal of pupil engagement and confidence in the dance medium with short-term improvement and success. The sense of a teacher learning about his pupils while they acquired his intended learning goals was also particularly noteworthy.

And what of the pupils' perspective? Both post-observation interviewees selected '*the performance at the end*' as something that had gone particularly well in the lesson, perhaps corroborating its symbolic celebration of achievement. They said '*I didn't do anything wrong ... I was pleased with my own performance*' and '*When we performed at the end it was good because it went well*'. In addition, one boy focused on the lesson's structure and the sense of progress and completion noted above: '*It was a really good speed ... because we had a good length of time for practising, and performing at the end was just right, so it was good timing.*'

Equally, both interviewees recognised the pedagogical contribution to their achievement, again corroborating the teaching approach:

> *It's just the way he teaches. Like, he's not commenting on the bad bits; he's seeing how you can build on things and gives you more confidence.*

> *... he came round and told us what we were doing wrong and what we were doing great. He always said* [our dance] *was fine but you could do this to make it better ...* [that was helpful] *otherwise we wouldn't have got it in time or anything.*

They variously referred to learning about *'basic steps', 'how to work with partners', 'how to be more bold and express yourself'*, again confirming teacher-intended outcomes. It is noteworthy that the pupils had absorbed and repeated actual phrases used by the teacher in the lesson. Finally, the teacher's overarching aim of encouragement and inducement to further involvement was perfectly echoed by one boy:

> *I think because I haven't really done dance before, I quite enjoy it. I like doing it* [at this school]. *Yes, it's really good.*

School 2

13.2.4   School 2: the effects of dance education

School 2 also figured highly in the sheer range of outcomes nominated by its pupils. Uniquely, it featured responses suggesting 'knowledge of social and cultural domain' as an effect accruing from dance, while 'enjoyment', 'knowledge and skills', 'creativity' and 'personal and social development' were also cited. Again, it was noteworthy that one youngster felt they had learnt: *'how another feels'* from the dance experience. This (along with the 'knowledge of cultural domain' effect) was no doubt related to the explicit use of cultural references in the dance syllabus: native American Indian and 'street dance' were used as the lesson contexts, involving whole-class discussion of these cultures and their values.

For these reasons, School 2 was selected for an in-depth observation analysis.

13.2.5　School 2: teaching approaches and context

The school served a catchment area that was perceived to offer a genuine comprehensive intake in both socio-economic and achievement terms. As one teacher stated: '*The school is pretty good for general, across-the-curriculum achievement for all pupils.*' Its academic reputation (for '*better exam results*') meant a number of pupils with '*strong dance backgrounds*' attended the school, despite the nearby presence of a school with arts college status.

The nearby city was said to offer '*a very active opportunity for anybody wishing to advance*' dance, with two modern dance centres providing classes and courses which the observed teacher had attended in a private, as well as professional, capacity. The LEA's PE adviser was also described as having: '*an active interest*' in the subject, and examples of collaboration between a network of dance teachers and the PE adviser to institute courses in dance were described. Indeed, this network were said to '*challenge the boundaries*' in terms of the current status of dance within education.

Senior management were also said to be '*very interested in advancing dance as an artform within the school*', and cross-curricular collaboration between arts teachers was noted: '*We always had a tight-knit arts community in the school ... we do look for time to bring the groups together ... we discuss what we are doing and see if we can tie it in.*'

Despite this positive ambience and support, the opportunity to teach dance was again felt to be severely restricted by '*National Curriculum timetabling constraints*' and by its position within the PE curriculum. A six-week block (i.e. six hours per year) was the total amount apportioned to dance in each year of key stage 3, and in Year 9, this six-hour opportunity was actually just an option.

The marginal position of dance generally was felt to arise largely from its presence within the PE guidelines and hence staffing structures in school. A generally held view among the local network of dance educators was that dance as an artform received '*neither time nor credit*' because of this PE association. However, extra-curricular dance activities were offered by the observed dance teacher, including lunchtime and after school clubs and having dance as one option in an 'arts circuit week' held in Year 8.

Despite an interest in artists-in-residence schemes for dance, these proved prohibitively expensive, and '*no money*' was available to finance such additions to the dance curriculum.

The observed teacher held a BEd in Physical Education, choosing to specialise in dance during the four-year training, and described a personal '*passion*' for the subject (which included, as noted above, continuing to attend dance classes). In terms of personal influences, the teacher also noted that she came from '*a cultural background where social dance is very much part of culture ... it is a way of celebration*'. This enthusiasm is noteworthy when compared to descriptions of many PE specialists who were ill at ease with their dance responsibilities, and had a concomitant '*lack of knowledge and interest in the arts*'.

The teacher saw '*nurturing and giving pupils the ability to develop natural movement potential*' as a primary aim, as well as '*communication, building composition work, understanding cultural traditions*' and '*developing an appreciation of the artform*'. Outcomes, given the limited opportunity to experience dance, were defined as '*an appreciation of composition, performance, analysing others, the ability to evaluate*'. This teacher saw '*talking to pupils about what they have learnt*' as an important component of a dance lesson: '[it] *is absolutely vital they reflect on it.*' This was set against the backdrop of time constraints: within the six hours of dance teaching per year, this teacher suggested that one-and-a-half hours were spent in discussion and context-setting. Indeed, the teacher believed that the association of dance with cultural and social beliefs and interests should be made explicit, and it was ensured that the content in Year 7 and Year 8 covered '*two very different dance forms*'. Observed lessons saw this teacher undertaking a dance of native American Indians with Year 7 and rap dance with a Year 8 group. The teacher noted: '*We talked about the history of where rap had originated, who was involved, why ... what are they singing about how do they move and why?*' The contemporary nature of this dance context was thus clearly apparent.

3.
WHAT ARE
EFFECTIVE
PRACTICES
IN
ARTS
EDUCATION?

13.2.6　School 2: the observed lesson

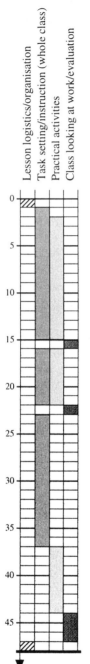

A Year 8 class were observed during the third and final session of a dance module, which took place in a gym. The pupils had already learnt a sequence of moves, using the Jason Nivens/Run DMC dance track 'It's like that', the video of which had also been looked at.

The teacher took the register, and then described how they were going to: *'finish off'* their *'last session of dance ... it's been very, very, short'*. She noted that the lesson would incorporate *'32 beats for you to put in ... work out a small sequence of your own'*.

The session started with a routine of *'warm-ups'*: arm stretches, side steps, marching, and bending knees – all directed and modelled by the teacher.

The sequence already learnt was then incorporated into the warm-up, the teacher first talking them through it – modelling, and pupils accompanying her. This included revisiting certain steps and moves, with 'technical' terms like *'anti-clockwise, swivel, scoop, strong punches, starting-positions'* being introduced. The group practised this several times in smaller sequences, the teacher pointing out where they were going wrong and suggesting *'Let's try it again'* on each occasion. The music featured in some of these revisions of the mini-sequences, until the whole sequence was thus eventually completely revisited. The group then practised the whole dance sequence first without, and then with, the music: the teacher accompanied and modelled, and gave verbal directions. Throughout this revision and final 'performance', there were examples of teacher praise and encouragement.

New moves were then introduced by the teacher (*'We've one bit to add on'*) using demonstration and modelling with accompanying spoken explanation. This section of the lesson was completed by another run-through: *'Let's try the whole thing.'* The sequence was then repeated from the beginning with the new moves added on.

The class were then asked to *'sit in the middle for a second or two'* and the teacher instituted a discussion. First, she encouraged them to consider ways that they could continue to participate if they *'went wrong'* in the sequence rather than *'abandoning it'* and then turned to the topic of the song, the

The chart labels (vertical axis): Lesson logistics/organisation; Task setting/instruction (whole class); Practical activities; Class looking at work/evaluation. Scale: 0, 5, 10, 15, 20, 25, 30, 35, 40, 45.

3.
WHAT ARE EFFECTIVE PRACTICES IN ARTS EDUCATION?

meaning of the lyrics, and also how to describe the movements and the *'message we're trying to get over ... "What sort of messages are in the dance so far?"'*. She elicited that their dance conveyed the participants as *'lively'*, *'confident'*, *'energetic'*, *'strong ... not someone to be messed with'* and concluded the discussion with reference to appreciating people who have *'different lives, life-experiences, different views on life'*. She noted to the class that their dance symbolised that *'we're all working together to achieve something worthwhile'* but was also going to allow individual approaches. Thus, the next practical activity was introduced: there was to be pair work and the pairs had 16 beats in the music to devise: *'canon style'* and *'question-and-answer style'* moves. This was demonstrated by two pupils.

The pair work commenced and the teacher moved round the pairs in turn. She encouraged their ideas, suggested improvements, and so on.

The teacher then told the class they had *'run out of time'*. She let two pairs demonstrate their work, and offered praise and then suggested: *'Shall we try it right from the beginning?'* She apologised to those pairs who were not visited during this section of the lesson.

The group then performed the dance *'from the beginning'*. Much praise was given by the teacher, who concluded the lesson by inviting them to do dance as part of the art circuit week during the summer term, saying: *'You're very, very welcome to come along.'*

The lesson ended with the class being told to hurry to their next lesson.

Activity	Time (mins)	Time as % of lesson time
Lesson logistics/organisation/housekeeping	2	4
Whole-class task setting/direct instruction	34	68
Pupils engaged in practical activities	26	52
Class looking at the work of others/evaluation	5	10

NB Percentages in this table do not sum to 100% due to multiple activities occurring at the same time within the lesson.

For the teacher, the cultural context of this lesson had particular significance. There was an important 'match' of using contemporary music to be of interest and relevance for a Year 8 class and, in addition, the teacher confirmed: *'... it's looking a little bit more into the music, thinking about the culture and also interpreting the music a bit more, looking at the lyrics and considering what's being said.'* Other intentions for the lesson were mentioned in the post-observation interview: again a focus on ensuring pupil engagement in these early encounters with the dance medium – *'In Year 8, as well, it's about fun, it's about enjoying it'* – and also engendering *'a feeling of togetherness, of working as a group, and working as a whole and achieving it'*. As well as that, the teacher saw technical aims in terms of dance composition – *'... focusing on the composition of dynamics'* – and then *'an input of creativity from themselves, the ability to personalise something, put their own stamp on it'*.

Notwithstanding this, this teacher was well aware of the constraints of time. By featuring class discussion to ensure context and cultural understanding, the lesson had considerably less time for pair work and hence pupils' own input into the dance was limited. She noted this but also acknowledged that: *'In Year 8, they can work very, very well in small groups.'*

3.
WHAT ARE
EFFECTIVE
PRACTICES
IN
ARTS
EDUCATION?

The pupils interviewed noted outcomes which clearly reflected the teacher's intentions of 'togetherness'. One youngster said she had learnt that:

> *... we've got to work as a group. You can't just work individually when you're doing it, 'cos you've got to help everyone else ...* [the teacher] *wants us to learn how we should come together as a group.*

Another stated: *'The big dance went really well ... I like it when we're all doing it in time, all together in one.'* Both referred to the quality of teaching – *'She* [the teacher] *teaches you well and I've learnt lots'* – and noted teacher feedback as a part of the learning process:

> *... she* [the teacher] *let us know how we were doing. She came up and watched us, see how we were going on.*

> *... if you do well as a class, then she'll say 'Oh you've done well'.*

Equally, both pupils were able to convey the outcome of enjoyment and engagement with dance and, in addition, both noted the severe shortage of time available for dance opportunities.

> *I'd like to have a bit longer to do everything. It's a bit short, what we do ... an hour is a bit short to do it and three weeks is not very long, I don't think, to do it.*

13.2.7 Concluding remarks

This section offers some comparative comment upon the two observed lessons, although, as the tables opposite demonstrate, some remarkable parallels are apparent in the way both sessions apportioned time to the four arts lesson 'activity-components'.

Activity	Time spent (in mins and as % of lesson length)	
	School 1	School 2
Lesson logistics/organisation/housekeeping	2 (3%)	2 (4%)
Whole-class task setting/direct instruction	27 (49%)	34 (68%)
Pupils engaged in practical activities	28 (51%)	26 (52%)
Class looking at the work of others/evaluation	5 (9%)	5 (10%)

NB Percentages in this table do not sum to 100% due to multiple activities occurring at the same time within the lesson.

Thus, though operating in different time spans, both lessons used about one-tenth of the time on actual performance. If pupil activity included the occasions that the teacher directly accompanied/ modelled the dance moves, both lessons involved action for half the lesson: the major difference being that School 1 pupils had small-group activity for about 40 per cent of the lesson (23 minutes), whereas in School 2, this type of learning approach occurred for only about one-fifth (seven minutes) of the lesson time. Here is reflected a major difference between the two lessons: one group was predominantly learning a specific dance routine, choreographed almost entirely by the teacher; the other session's major focus was for pupils to experiment and choreograph their own. Nevertheless, both sessions had a component where pupils were in 'repose' mode, and both teachers apportioned just over one-quarter of the available length of time of the entire lesson for this. School 2 pupils discussed the cultural context of their dance routine at this point, while in School 1, the pupils received technical information about their impending performance task. This difference is corroborated in the effects identified overall: School 1 did have the highest nominations for artform knowledge, while School 2 received the highest ratings for 'cultural domain' effects.

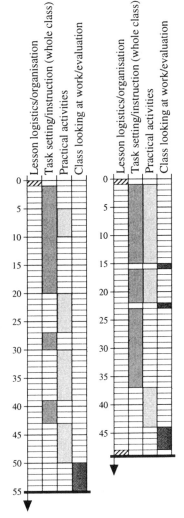

In addition, despite both lessons showing minimal housekeeping roles for the teacher, there was still some sense of constraint within the available time to give to performance.

Both teachers ensured its presence, and thus its symbolic celebratory and completion function was evident for the pupils.

Notwithstanding this, the limitations on time for dance, at both the micro-level of a lesson and on the macro-level of overall timetable availability, do suggest that this artform remains the 'Cinderella' of school arts. This lowly status is perhaps further exemplified by the fact that both schools highlighted a lack of specialist facilities, and the degree to which it is non-dance specialist teachers who influence the delivery and planning of dance at school level. Of all the artforms observed, dance proved to be the one where the teacher 'modelled' and accompanied pupil activity most: this again may be ironic given the general issue of non-specialists often teaching dance. The fact that two enthusiastic specialists were the focus of this chapter may signal a key factor underpinning the notably high number of nominated effects outlined by pupils in School 1 and School 2. Effective practice seems inextricably linked to subject expertise and commitment.

3.
WHAT ARE
EFFECTIVE
PRACTICES
IN
ARTS
EDUCATION?

ART

'Art does not reproduce the visible; it makes it visible.'

Paul Klee

13.3 ART

School 1

13.3.1   *School 1: the effects of art education*

Among the five case studies, pupils from this school made the greatest total number of references to the effects and outcomes of art education (on average, each pupil made 13 individual remarks relating to effects and outcomes). Three types of outcomes predominated: 'arts knowledge and skills', 'extrinsic transfer effects' and 'enjoyment and therapy'.

Many of the knowledge and skills outcomes that the pupils described were related to their development of practical art skills and abilities, and art-specific knowledge and understanding. Acquiring technical art skills such as using tone, light and colour was often described in detail. The development of creativity and the use of imagination was also recognised by pupils. Critical skills, appreciation, and knowledge of art (of both artists and techniques) were another related group of outcomes which pupils cited often as being developed through their art lessons.

In addition to the technical skills, some of the most commonly cited outcomes were transfer to employment and leisure activities, and also to other subjects within the school curriculum. Pupils described how their art skills were applicable to other areas of the school curriculum – helping them to draw pictures, posters or diagrams in a diverse range of school subjects including English, French, history and geography. Unusually, the single effect which pupils from this school nominated most frequently was the transfer of skills to a job or career – in stark contrast to all the other case study schools where pupils mentioned this infrequently. Similar numbers of comments were made by pupils of all age-groups at the school, although the nature of the comments changed with pupil age and maturity. Older pupils could cite quite defined intentions of applying art skills to particular forms of employment.

The next most frequently cited outcome for art related to enjoyment and relaxation, and School 1 was outstanding in the number of references made here. Gaining enjoyment and relaxation from art activities was also often the reason given for pupils' participation in art as a leisure activity beyond the confines of the school curriculum.

Thus, given the sheer number and range of outcomes from art education identified by pupils at this school, it was selected for more in-depth analysis.

13.3.2 School 1: teaching approaches and context

This case study was an all-girls school of 900 pupils aged 11–16, with high numbers of pupils from ethnic minority groups. It is in an area facing considerable social deprivation but despite these factors, the school has a very high reputation for art education provision and has recently been nominated as a Beacon School in the field of the art. The general ethos of the school was described by senior management as:

> *Focused very much on learning, and the students know that is what they are here for ... if you talk to them, they will always refer back to their learning ... it is a very positive, work-oriented ethos, but at the same time it is also a very supportive, caring ethos ... There is a way of doing things which is very focused on high achievements, high expectations and also on valuing everybody.*

Linked to the belief in valuing everyone within the school, senior managers identified the importance of supporting arts entitlement for all:

> *... one of the important things about the arts side of it is that we all learn in different ways and we all have different strengths and weaknesses. Therefore, I think that it is vital that arts education is an entitlement for everybody in the school.*

Art was a highly regarded subject within the school (as well as the wider LEA community) for its good results. However, senior managers noted that other outcomes were also seen as important:

> ... in terms of pupils' personal, social and moral development ... it is the creativity, it is the imagination, it is the freedom to try things and make mistakes. It is the freedom to be able to express yourself.

The art teacher whose lesson was observed as part of the research was the head of art, and also the head of the expressive arts faculty. She had taught at the school for over ten years. The visual art department comprised two other members of staff. Classes within the department were rotated as a matter of course, so that all pupils were able to gain maximum benefit from the different skills and abilities of all the staff in the department. In this regard, the teachers worked very much as a team.

The art teacher maintained the philosophy that, whilst the therapeutic effects of art lessons were secondary to the main outcomes observed, the art department provided a place of calmness within an otherwise busy school environment. Her art room was arranged so that most of the pupils sat at desks that faced inwards, towards an extensive central display of artefacts. However, there were also some desks that were placed at the sides, in the corners of the room, and some overlooking the school grounds. These were specifically positioned in order to provide pupils with a place that they could '*retreat to*', should they feel the need. One senior manager corroborated this ambience, recognising that the art department provided '*a quiet space to reflect, to explore an idea, to explore how ideas can grow ... The quiet and calm of that in the chaos around us is also very important*'.

Considerable emphasis was placed on the evaluation and celebration of pupils' work, and the visual displays within the art room provided a focus for this. The art teacher expressed her belief that being surrounded by artwork encouraged pupils in a process of critical consumption, reflection and evaluation without them ever being aware of it.

The display of artwork was said to exert an influence on the whole school. According to one of the deputy heads:

> ... you will often see the kids just standing there, just looking at someone else's painting, observing and wondering at it, and it raises their own standards ... it is the first thing that hits you when you walk into the school – the artwork on the walls.

3. WHAT ARE EFFECTIVE PRACTICES IN ARTS EDUCATION?

The art teacher interviewed also commented on the culture of displaying work around the school when she said:

> *I have never been in a school where it has been safe to leave GCSE displays in a corridor that is used by hundreds of girls daily, and not have anybody write on it, or deface it in any way.*

Within art, the practical project work was generally organised into themes – ranging from four weeks in duration in Year 7, up to half, or a full term at GCSE level. The themes were often chosen to be controversial or contentious, and the teacher believed strongly in art as a vehicle for the discussion of a wide range of issues – not always directly related to art practice. An example of this type of theme was '*weddings*' – of which the teacher remarked:

> *... it might be to do with arranged marriages, it might be divorce ... what it is like just living with a mum ... how old you should be when you get married ... I think that given the right atmosphere in the classroom, which of course is up to the teacher to generate ... in an art lesson you can be working and having a whole group discussion at the same time.*

Again, this linked closely with the teacher's philosophy of art providing a physical space, and time within the curriculum where pupils could deal with personal issues.

As already noted, the school is located in an extremely culturally diverse area, with many different ethnic minority groups. A total of 34 different first languages were spoken by pupils in the school. In some schools, art (and also drama) have faced challenges in relation to different religious beliefs – especially in terms of representation of other people in drama, and drawing portraits in art. However, staff did not think that this was an issue at the school: the careful and sympathetic choice of themes in art allowed the cultural and ethnic diversity to be encompassed and positively celebrated – to the enrichment of the school and all the pupils.

During the pupils' early years at the school, the emphasis within art was very much directed towards the teaching and learning of specific, art-orientated skills, although pupils from all age-groups made reference to art skills as an outcome of art lessons. The teacher referred to her emphasis on 'showing how' and providing practical demonstrations within art. She said:

> *... it is to do with empowerment, but it also to do with gaining massive amounts of confidence straightaway when they say they can't do it, and then they can. I believe very much in showing people really 'how' ... I don't leave them to find out for themselves ... don't*

let us waste an hour and a half to try to find out how to do it – I do it in five minutes. I show them a trick, a way of doing something, and then I make them mess around with different ways of doing it after I have shown them how. I wouldn't want people to spend hours being frustrated, working things out for themselves ...

Differentiation is provided mainly by outcome; as the art teacher said:

A girl with special educational needs can produce interesting work in her own way, in the same project, at the same time, without necessarily showing up as being particularly different.

Group assessment, evaluation, and sharing were identified as crucial elements in the teaching of art at the school. The art teacher said:

... you can go into your own little world when you are working, and then you can share it ... sometimes at the end of the lesson, if I think people are getting a bit bored, I pack up early and we just look at the work and talk about it ... it is sharing ... it is being able to think about things.

3.
WHAT ARE
EFFECTIVE
PRACTICES
IN
ARTS
EDUCATION?

This clearly followed on from the ethos of displaying pupils' art work, and the culture of supporting and valuing all groups and individuals within the school.

13.3.3 School 1: the observed lesson

The lesson which was selected for analysis was a single (45-minute) Year 9 lesson. It was the final lesson of a series of three focusing on composition involving five- to ten-minute sketches of people in various positions. The art room was a generously proportioned room, which contained considerable visual material in the form of artefacts and pupil work. This was a defined part of the teacher's philosophy of art education – surrounding the pupils with visual stimuli, and encouraging critical discourse and analysis.

During the initial phase of the lesson, the teacher recapped the work done in previous lessons on the topic and explained the tasks for this session. One piece of work – deemed exemplary – was shown to the class for comment (which was enthusiastically positive and celebratory). Whilst the pupils organised themselves to begin the practical work, the teacher ensured that they all had the correct equipment, and arranged the position of the first pupil who was to pose.

Once the pupil was in position for sketching, the class started their own practical work. They were well behaved, and concentrated hard on the tasks set. Between the five different pupil poses which the class were asked to draw, the teacher arranged the next pose, and the pupils in the class were given a short breathing space. They used this pause in directed activities to complete the previous sketch, and prepare for the next. During the practical, the teacher walked around the class and monitored the work that the pupils were producing.

In 65 instances where the teacher addressed the class, or individual pupils, she provided reassurance and positive affirmation of their work. Examples of this type of praise and encouragement included: '... *that's nice ... well done ...*', '*Well done, I'm really pleased*', and: '... *you've improved loads since the first lesson when we did this ... good ...*'.

There were other instances (noted 31 times) where the teacher advised pupils on the ways in which they could improve their sketches. In a quarter of these cases, the teacher framed her advice as a suggestion for negotiation between pupil and teacher, but in the remaining three-quarters, she simply told the pupils what they needed to do. Examples of such advice included: '... *how are her legs ... look ... if you stand up and see the position her legs are in, because they're not straight out ...*'. In other instances (24), the advice became a direct instruction: '*That's nice ... I like it with all those lines ... that's good. Don't rub all those lines out ...*'

One of the pupils who was interviewed after the lesson had received help from the teacher and she said:

> ... *she* [the teacher] *was giving me more confidence, and making me add some bits – telling me I should do more shading or do more tones or do a little bit of smudging, and all kinds of things, and I just followed that a bit.*

This was clearly help which the pupil had found valuable and encouraging.

In seven cases, the teacher actually helped the pupils in practical ways – drawing something on their paper to help get them started with a sketch, or altering pupils' lines. This was seen to be directed generally towards the weaker pupils, and was one way in which the tasks were differentiated for those of differing abilities.

3.
WHAT ARE
EFFECTIVE
PRACTICES
IN
ARTS
EDUCATION?

The culture of praise and support, evident during the practical phase of the lesson, was commented on by one of the pupils. She related this very much to the beliefs of the teacher when she said:

> [the teacher] *really enjoys art, you can tell. She really wants us all to enjoy it as much as she does, and she's, you know, running around the classroom making sure we've all got pencils ... she makes us look at everything in art, you know, she makes us get all the details. She tells us the right things to do ... she really enjoys teaching it, I think ....*

One of the pupils in the lesson explained that the topic of sketching people had provided all the pupils with a challenge, which they had found difficult at the beginning, but at which they improved through the series of lessons. Clearly the encouragement and support of the teacher were vital in reassuring pupils that they would improve. The pupil also described how the breaking of the practical into small, fast sketches left them with little time for worrying about their work, and that it resulted in them getting a lot done and learning a lot. Another pupil described that what she had learnt from the lesson was that: '... *if I put my effort into it I could do it ... I thought it was going to be really hard, but it's alright after a while.*'

Following the practical section of the lesson, there was a transitional phase during which the pupils tidied up, and the homework from the last lesson was collected. After this, the teacher proceeded to mark the homework books at her desk whilst most of the pupils gathered round to watch, and listen to any comments made. However, not all of the pupils were drawn into this activity – some choosing to remain at their own desks and talk. This was a situation that the teacher was clearly aware of, allowing pupils the freedom to choose whether to be involved.

The evaluation of the homework involved another round of positive affirmation and constructive comments, similar to those which the teacher provided during the practical activities. Examples of this effusive praise and support included: '*Oh, that is just … another A* I think … excellent …*' and '*Brilliant! … wow! … that is definitely A * … that is unbelievable! … I think I should photocopy some of these to put downstairs on the wall … that is so good …*'. There was also a place for constructive criticism such as:

> … *that's quite good … it would be nice if they were a bit bigger … can you make them a bit bigger like these ones, because your positions are good, but they're too tiny really … so I'm going to give you a B++ for that because I think they could be A if they were done bigger …*

In addition to the teacher evaluation of the work that was being marked, the pupils also made comments to their peers: there was a clear sense of the pupils encouraging and supporting each other, and celebrating each other's achievements. For example, some of the comments that pupils made were: '*I think that is so good … how do you draw so good?*' and '*That's great … how do you get those pencil marks?*'. One pupil also remarked to the teacher: '*These are really good*', when looking at the homework. The teacher replied: '*Yes, I know … I'm going to photocopy them and put them downstairs …*' Thus again, the teacher affirmed her pupils' evaluation.

Marking their homework was an activity which most of the pupils appeared to enjoy. One of the pupils said: '*… we're all excited to see what she's going to give us … I think everyone in the class enjoys that.*'

Following the homework marking, the natural progression of the lesson was to the setting of homework to be completed before the next lesson. This was also accompanied by a discussion of the new work which was to be started in the next lesson – which influenced the teacher's decision to give the pupils a free choice of subject matter for homework. The lesson finally concluded with the teacher thanking the class for their good behaviour and performance during the lesson.

In summary, the lengths of time involved in the different main lesson activities were as follows:

Activity	Time (mins)	Time as % of lesson time
Lesson logistics/organisation/housekeeping	23	54
Whole-class task setting/direct instruction	8	18
Pupils engaged in practical activities	20	48
Class looking at the work of others/evaluation	5	11

NB Percentages in this table do not sum to 100% due to multiple activities occurring at the same time within the lesson.

462

3.
WHAT ARE
EFFECTIVE
PRACTICES
IN
ARTS
EDUCATION?

School 2

13.3.4   School 2: the effects of art education

School 2 emerged as another case study where the number and range of pupil-nominated outcomes was notably high. Art knowledge was the outcome most frequently referred to by pupils from this school, with little apparent difference between the views of older and younger pupils. Examples of the comments citing this type of outcome included:

> ... you've got to know a lot of terms ... not just painting. It's like there's loads of different parts ... branches out of art ... you have to understand all of them if you want to be an artist ... you get more knowledge

> I have learnt a lot about different artists ... to interpret an artist's work or something I see into my own view, like maybe taking part of somebody else's work and adding part of mine to make a new picture ...

The outcomes which were next most frequently remarked upon by the pupils were intrinsic immediate effects, particularly enjoyment and relaxation. Expressive skills also featured among this discourse. Pupil comments included: 'I've learnt how to enjoy art a lot more from being here ... we can enjoy our art – have it displayed in the school' and '... it's quite relaxing and I suppose you can express yourself in some ways'.

The third most frequently cited group of effects and outcomes generally comprised the art skills and abilities that pupils felt they developed, and then their transfer to future employment and other areas of the school curriculum. Pupils described a general increase in practical competence and ability, but also specifically mentioned advances in their use of colour, tone and light. It is clear that whilst pupils made more comments which recognised knowledge of art as an outcome than practical skills, considerable importance was still attached to practical art activities. Practical activities, in which the development of art skills was inherent, were a focus of art lessons which pupils appeared to relate closely to the personal outcomes described previously.

Two main themes thus emerged from the pupils' descriptions of the effects and outcomes of art lessons at their school and constituted a distinctive contrast with School 1. The predominance of pupils' belief in the development of knowledge and understanding of art over practical art skills and abilities was particularly notable. However, practical art activities and development of art skills were very evident, providing a vehicle for pupil self-expression, and leading to pupil enjoyment and relaxation.

13.3.5 School 2: teaching approaches and context

School 2, in contrast to the previous one described, is a rural Welsh school of 700 pupils aged 11–18. The school is designated bilingual – providing education through both the English and Welsh languages. The catchment area is very wide, covering 240 square miles, and the local community relies heavily on agriculture for its economic support. The arts are well provided for within the school, and the results achieved by pupils reflect this support. Throughout the life of the research project, this school has been involved in a considerable amount of development and expansion of its arts provision. This development has also involved establishing close links between the school and the local community – for which the arts have provided a focus.

The headteacher explained that the school had good relations with a local arts group, and because of a European Rural Renewal Grant, given on the basis of the area's economic deprivation, a practising artist had been appointed as a community enterprise worker. Both of these links provided considerable opportunities for interaction between the art in the school and the wider community. The school was also involved in bids for National Lottery funding to develop workshop space and a gallery out of an old stable block on the school grounds, which would provide space for local artists to work alongside pupils from this school and the surrounding primary schools. The arts have also been equipped with a new building which brings together art, ceramics, music and a new drama studio, and thus highlights the status of the arts within the whole school curriculum.

There was a clear rationale within the school for the entitlement of all pupils to a broad and balanced education that included the arts. One art teacher explained that there were two distinct aims for art education at the school:

> First of all to provide a pathway for any pupil who wants to pursue any kind of arts career, to give them the skills and the qualifications that they need, and [secondly], for the children who don't want an arts career, to offer a broad range of exciting opportunities for them to express themselves.

It was felt that the main, influencing factors which produced the positive outcomes of art education observed at the school were:

> ... commitment by the teaching staff ... obviously the facilities are going to help, but we were here before the facilities and maybe it's because of our commitment under really quite grim circumstances that got us this building.

The headteacher supported this view, saying:

> ... *it's about the quality of the person who's teaching ... my greatest asset in this school is the member of staff in front of the class, because that's where the interaction is. I have as many systems as I want, I can have as many structures as I want, but at the end of the day the most valuable person that I've got is the member of staff ...*

Within the art department, the teaching staff worked very closely together, and there was considerable communication between them. It was felt that the informal atmosphere of the department was a very positive factor:

> ... *it's enjoyable and it's essential because there's a constant interchange of ideas and stimulus and the children do the same – they like to come in and see what other age groups are doing and since there's so little exemplar of work, in* [local] *galleries, it's good that they see what other children do.*

Another element of the whole school ethos which was heavily subscribed to by the art teaching staff was that of allowing pupils to take responsibility for their own learning and conduct. The head of art, whose lesson was observed said:

> *I think lots of lessons in school they have to queue up outside, sit down, shut up, be quiet ... but I try and encourage them to just be themselves a bit more and take responsibility for their equipment and their work.*

She also said:

> ... *my philosophy is that they come into the room and get out their equipment, get their work out and get working before I start talking to them. I don't like them just sitting there with nothing to do, looking at me, waiting to be filled.*

The class whose lesson was observed were a mixed-ability class – in line with the art department belief that pupils of all abilities had a valuable contribution to make, and that all pupils could learn from each other. This was seen to work particularly well in the light of the individual pupil-centred teaching methods that were employed. As one of the art teachers said:

> *I would like to think that everyone can work as an individual, so while the project might be set, the outcome should be very personal, so I tend to get everybody going and then I go round* [providing help to individuals], *so I'm not stood at the front, I'm on the move.*

In general, and as a result of the focus on the individual, differentiation within art occurred by outcome, although it was also suggested that it was important to push each pupil to develop to their maximum potential. However, differentiation was also occasionally approached by task, and the head of art felt that the key to appropriate differentiation was the flexibility to treat each pupil as an individual. During the observed lesson, one pupil had already completed the collage task which had been set, and was working on a very small-scale watercolour. The teacher had specifically set her this piece of work in order to encourage her to slow down, and take more care with her work, rather than rushing to complete something quickly.

Evaluation was a very important process within the art department, for both teachers and pupils:

> ... [evaluation] *should be positive, should be useful, should enable the pupil to improve their work, and it should also show up anything that we've* [teachers] *done wrong, either in not explaining something or assuming a knowledge perhaps that wasn't there ...*

Peer review was a routine activity at the end of projects, although this was absent from the observed lesson as the project was ongoing. Clearly the division of time between practical activities and the evaluation of work would have been different during lessons at other stages within the project. The teacher said:

> ... *we look at them all together afterwards. They are all pretty mature in saying what they thought worked well and what didn't work well ... what they like about other people's work, and maybe what they might try next time. We will have a discussion at the end about how we can develop it further, or what would happen ...*

The teachers stressed the importance of relationships with their pupils, as evidenced by the availability of the art room and art facilities outside lessons: '*A lot of them come in at dinner time to do extra work, so you get to know them on a personal level, which I think, for art, it's good to get to know the children personally.*'

In addition to the relationship between the teacher and the pupils, there was an emphasis on the way in which the class worked together. They were encouraged to sit around one group of tables within the art room, and this allowed them to help and support each other during the lesson. Again, the informality of the environment supported these nurturing and supportive relationships. The teacher thought the positive interaction between the pupils was of enormous benefit.

13.3.6   School 2: the observed lesson

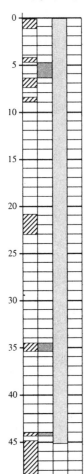

The class who were observed at this school were in Year 10, in the first term of their art GCSE course. The lesson took place in a large classroom which contained many displays of pupil work. There were various arrangements of desks within the room, but the pupils in this class all sat round one large block of tables, with the teacher at the head of the block.

The theme of the project that the pupils were working on was fruit and vegetables, and the lesson observed was part of a series involving observational drawings. The theme had been ongoing for some time – involving a number of different pieces of artwork, which were to be gathered together at the end of term as a whole unit towards the art GCSE. The specific piece that the pupils were working on during the observed lesson had also occupied several previous lessons, and was due to continue for at least one more. This length of time spent on one topic and individual pieces of work was commented on by pupil interviewees after the lesson:

> [the teacher] *says '... it's best to do one piece of work really, really well, than doing lots of pieces that are OK but you've not really finished them'. So we tend to work on things* [quite] *a bit.*

In subsequent discussion, the teacher explained that fruit and vegetables had been chosen as a theme because they were readily available and provided a wealth of opportunities for exploring colour and texture through different art media. The teacher's rationale for this was that the experimentation would give the pupils confidence to understand their own strengths and weaknesses, and stand them in good stead for planning their Year 11 project work. The pupils also recognised this aim of encouraging exploration of mixed media within the lesson.

When the pupils came into the art room, they immediately started getting their previous work out, and continued with their observations of chillies and pomegranates. Once they had stopped moving around the room, and were all seated and drawing, the teacher addressed them as a class – recapping what they had done during the last lesson, and reminding them of some of the things they should bear in mind whilst producing their artwork. For example, she said:

> *... we've been looking at backgrounds ... background is just as important as the actual object ... getting you to think about how to divide the picture plan up ... the composition can be done a thousand different ways ...*

3.
WHAT ARE
EFFECTIVE
PRACTICES
IN
ARTS
EDUCATION?

This section of the lesson was in line with the teacher's philosophy of pupils taking responsibility for continuing with their own practical activity and learning, with little teacher direction.

Post-observation interviews with pupils indicated they responded positively to this philosophy. One commented:

> *I think it's nice that* [the teacher] *talks to us while we're doing our work, rather than have to sit around for ten minutes at the beginning of the lesson while she tells us what to do. That's nice that we get straight into it.*

During the remainder of the time that the pupils were engaged with their practical, the teacher monitored what they were doing, and provided many examples of different kinds of supportive intervention. Positive affirmation occurred in at least 34 instances, a typical example being: *'Well done. Good ... well done ... that's a nice piece there. Well done, very good.'* Constructive advice was evident in 59 instances. For example, the teacher said to one pupil:

> *... it's quite dark at the back there, isn't it, behind those pips?* [indicating the area on the chilli] *There are some areas – you'll have to do some darker areas and you'll get that illusion of depth, won't you?*

In addition to the reassuring comments, the teacher provided verbal assistance directly related to the work in progress, sometimes 'negotiating' the advice (42 instances):

> *... you've just got to think about doing something totally different ... contrasting colour, or stripes, or echo the shape ... think about it ... you can see how other people have tackled it, can't you? ... do something totally different that no one else has done yet ...*

Less often, there were examples of giving direct instruction (16 instances): *'... do a bit of collage work first, and then do some pastels on top ... Do something different from everybody else ...'*

It can be seen clearly that on balance this teacher provided only 34 remarks of a purely reassuring or encouraging nature – preferring instead to provide active advice or constructive remarks related to the art work. However, there was only one instance where the teacher gave actual hands-on assistance with the art work – actually mixing paint colours for a pupil. One pupil noted how typical this teaching style was: *'She gives us advice on what we are doing, and gives us ideas and stuff. That's just like a normal lesson.'*

**3.
WHAT ARE
EFFECTIVE
PRACTICES
IN
ARTS
EDUCATION?**

During the lesson, the teacher's attention was focused away from the pupils in the class for eleven-and-a-half minutes (almost a quarter of the length of the lesson). During this time, she painted props for the upcoming theatrical production, moved other work within the art room, and arranged work for another class. Nevertheless, throughout these activities, the teacher was always on hand to address any issues arising, or help pupils if they requested it. The teacher showed considerable faith in the pupils that they would continue with their own work and ask for help if they needed it. The pupils appeared to respond positively to this freedom, continuing with their work responsibly, and never abusing the trust that the teacher placed in them.

Ten minutes before the end of the lesson, the teacher stopped the pupils from working on their practical, and instructed them that it was time to clear away the different art media and equipment – paint, glue, tissue paper and magazines, etc. – that they had been using. Getting art materials out and putting them away again took up a considerable percentage of the lesson time.

Throughout the clearing up, the pupils placed their artwork on another central table in the classroom, and as they did so the teacher made individual comments to them about their progress. Occasionally, other pupils would also make comments. It was noticeable that this lesson involved no whole-class evaluation of work. However, as already noted, this lesson was one in the middle of a series, and the main evaluation phase of the project had yet to be reached. The teacher had provided individual evaluation throughout the practical activity, and the seating of pupils around one central table allowed them to look at each other's work, and make supportive and yet evaluative remarks. The teacher explained that evaluation and reflection activities were an important aspect of teaching and learning within art, but that they would take place in a formal sense at the end of the unit.

The lesson concluded with the teacher reminding the pupils about the homework that was due to be handed in later in the week, and telling them that they had all worked well during the lesson.

Activity	Time (mins)	Time as % of lesson time
Lesson logistics/organisation/housekeeping	12	24
Whole-class task setting/direct instruction	3	7
Pupils engaged in practical activities	45	88
Class looking at the work of others/evaluation	0	0

NB Percentages in this table do not sum to 100% due to multiple activities occurring at the same time within the lesson.

13.3.7 Concluding remarks

Having examined art education provision within two vastly different school settings, it is clear that there are some distinct contrasts and similarities. Simply comparing the two art lessons which were observed at the schools immediately highlighted some important issues:

Activity	Time spent (in mins and as % of lesson length)	
	School 1	School 2
Lesson logistics/organisation/housekeeping	23 (54%)	12 24%)
Whole-class task setting/direct instruction	8 (18%)	3 (7%)
Pupils engaged in practical activities	20 (48%)	45 (88%)
Class looking at the work of others/evaluation	5 (11%)	0 (0%)

NB Percentages in this table do not sum to 100% due to multiple activities occurring at the same time within the lesson.

In School 1, lesson logistics accounted for over half of the available lesson time – being taken up with arrangements for the practical activities, arrangement between individual pupil poses, collecting in the homework, and arrangements for future lessons. In School 2, less time was spent on this type of activity, although preparing for the practical and clearing away afterwards still took 12 minutes out of the 50-minute lesson – almost 25 per cent.

It is clear that the impact of getting practical work started and clearing away afterwards could be lessened by sympathetic timetabling for art lessons. In this case, both of the lessons observed were single-period lessons, but adjusting the available time into double lessons would maximise the available practical time by minimising the preparation and tidying-up time.

It is noticeable that within the observed lesson at School 2, the teacher spent less time in directing and setting tasks for this class. This no doubt related to the pupils' maturity and independence, and their continuation of a piece of work from a previous lesson. The teacher explained that in Year 10, the pupils were

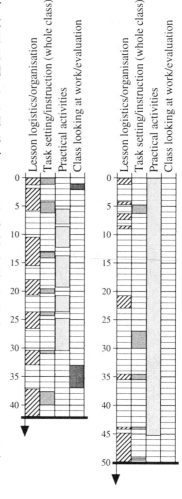

3.
WHAT ARE
EFFECTIVE
PRACTICES
IN
ARTS
EDUCATION?

expected to get on with their work with the minimum of instruction. However, in School 1, double the amount of time was spent by the teacher in explaining to the class what they were to do. Although the lesson did follow on from the previous one, it was more of an independent entity, and therefore the teacher needed to provide the pupils with instructions for this individual lesson.

For similar reasons, the amount of time which the pupils spent engaged in practical activities also varied considerably between the two observed lessons. At School 2, the pupils immediately started their practical work on entering the classroom, and the teacher addressed the whole class once they were all involved in their own artwork. However, in School 1, the practical activity was split into five small sections, with organisation occurring and instruction being given at the beginning and between each.

The other main reason for the difference in practical time was the inclusion of homework marking and evaluation at School 1 as part of the lesson. This was a regular activity within art lessons at the school, which the pupils enjoyed and the teacher thought was valuable. Evaluation and assessment were also an important part of art education at School 2. However, it was not apparent during the observed lesson because of its occurrence during the practical phase of a longer project cycle. At School 1, the lesson structure described a whole cycle – previous lesson recap and evaluation, instruction, practical and then evaluation – whilst at School 2 a similar cycle was described by the teacher but existed over a period of several lessons.

Throughout both observed lessons, there was a clearly apparent culture of encouragement and reassurance provided by the teacher. This manifested itself in several distinct ways. In both schools, the teachers made comments which were intended to increase the pupils' self-confidence – these were generally simple positive statements such as 'Good', 'Well done', which were lavished on pupils frequently. The culture of the art classroom was one very much based on encouragement and appreciation of each individual's talents and abilities. The art teachers were always seen to identify something positive in a pupil's work. However, in addition to the positive encouragement and reassurance that the teachers provided, they also made constructive criticisms and provided art-related advice on how pupils could improve their work. This was often on an individual basis, but very occasionally, where appropriate, the teacher would explain an issue to the whole class.

In both schools, art lessons were seen to be highly dependent on individual work, although the atmosphere within the classes was seen to be friendly and informal. In both observed lessons, the pupils talked and helped each other, and good relationships were developed between pupils, and between pupil and teacher. This informality and the close working relationships which resulted could be one factor in the number of pupil references to enjoyment and relaxation as an outcome of art lessons.

Evaluation and celebration of work produced were an important part of art provision within both of the schools, although the specific lesson observed at one of the schools did not contain this activity because of its location within a longer project. At both of the schools, displaying pupil work within art rooms and around the whole school was an important part of this evaluation and celebration process.

**3.
WHAT ARE
EFFECTIVE
PRACTICES
IN
ARTS
EDUCATION?**

MUSIC

'Music is an explosive expression of humanity; it's something we are all touched by'.

Billy Joel

13.4 MUSIC

School 1

13.4.1 *School 1: the effects of music education*

School 1 was chosen for closer investigation as a result of the overall high numbers of effects mentioned by pupils and particularly its high nominations for 'artform knowledge and skills' and 'personal and social development'. This school received the highest number of nominations for 'arts knowledge and skills' but pupils mentioned actual 'technical skills and competence' less often than in two other case studies, perhaps suggesting a wider approach to music education.

The school also had the (joint) second highest number of nominations for 'immediate intrinsic effects' in music education, based largely on references to 'enjoyment' outcomes (e.g. *'I like playing the keyboard altogether really; it's fun'*) with a few further nominations for the 'therapeutic' outcomes.

The second highest number of nominations for 'communication and expressive skills' was also evident in School 1: these outcomes chiefly related to the acquisition of 'listening and interpretation skills' whilst the development of 'expressive skills' was more rarely mentioned. It also received the second highest number of nominations for 'personal and social development'. Within this category, it was the top-ranking school for outcomes relating to self-development, such as confidence and self-worth, but with fewer references for 'group work' than in some other case studies of music teaching. However, one pupil stressed that as a result of the observed music lesson, '*I learned how to play along with, like, a group of people*' and, in a similar way, another stated: '*Our keyboard kept going a bit funny but we sorted it out and we were just helping each other play.*'

This school received only the third-highest number of nominations for extrinsic transfer effects, only half that of the top-ranking school. Although having the most references to 'transfer to other subjects', it received amongst the fewest for both transfer to career, and to extra-curricular or leisure activities. Hence, links and transfers within the school setting were nominated as outcomes of music education at this school to a greater extent than transfers beyond the school.

'Knowledge of the social and cultural domains' received just two nominations, one for the 'awareness of different cultures' and one for the 'understanding of social issues and problems'. This school received the fewest nominations for 'creativity and thinking skills'.

Thus, given its high incidence of comment of arts knowledge and skills, enjoyment and confidence, School 1 was selected for further consideration of its approach to music education.

13.4.2   School 1: teaching approaches and context

This school was located in a changing socio-economic context, where a traditional 'working-class' area was witnessing new housing developments and new populations. A member of the school's senior management team noted that, although still very comprehensive, the school's intake was generally increasing in its abilities. Despite recent changes, it was asserted that the locale remained, to some extent, a '*cultural desert*'.

The teacher of the observed lesson stressed the importance of arts and music at the school, noting that '*as a school, we pride ourselves on our arts*'. This view was reflected in his personal views of, and aims for, music within the school, illustrated by his intention to write a musical event that would include all pupils and as many parents as possible. This clearly demonstrated the belief that music was about participation and was also seen as a vitally important tool in the relationships between pupils, parents and the school.

Extra-curricular activities, including music, were seen by the teacher of the observed lesson as essential and powerful components of school life: '*It is the extra-curricular that knits the place together.*' It was through participation that pupils were seen to gain self-esteem, confidence and identity. Such notions were exemplified with reference to the presence of many pupils of all ages congregating in the music block before the start of the school day in order to engage in musical activities: '*Those little Year 7s who come in, you can almost see them bursting with pride because they can stand with the musicians.*'

The teacher's personal orientations towards music – its teaching and its effects – coincided with such sentiments when he spoke of the '*magical chemistry*' which occurred when accompanying pupils on the piano. In addition to the enjoyment derived from seeing '*so many different examples of the way in which kids have grown emotionally, intellectually, their self-esteem, their abilities ...*', this teacher was also confident that he had '*got something to give the kids*'. Hence, the teaching process was very much a two-way relationship.

Within the classroom, the teacher aimed for a relaxed ambience and an informal teaching approach:

> ... the idea is '*This is fun – let's do it because it's fun*'. *If I was to say that it was a laugh, it would give the wrong impression, but we have fun and we learn on the way, and that's what we're after.*

This was, however, also a disciplined environment in which much control over the class was maintained by '*keeping them busy – keep them occupied, keep them on task*'. The individual teaching style was described as being '*democratic ... until I am pushed into being an authoritarian*'. Similarly, classroom management was deemed to be structured and directed – '*We've got to lay the law down to allow kids to get the best out of the resources*' – as was clearly illustrated in the observed lesson. For example, after entering the room, pupils stood by their chairs until told to sit down by the teacher. This, however, was not '*because I'm an old-fashioned authoritarian. They come in and they stand ... because that's actually the least risky way of managing the room*'. Hence, the teacher applied and enforced fairly strict behaviour rules as a means of effectively 'protecting' the resources – namely the electronic keyboards on the desk-tops. In a similar way, the lesson was brought to a halt before the expiry of its allocated time as a means of settling the pupils and allowing an ordered, controlled exit '*so you don't have keyboards being pulled off the desk because they're in a rush to get out*'.

**3.
WHAT ARE
EFFECTIVE
PRACTICES
IN
ARTS
EDUCATION?**

This was presented as being a negotiated situation between the pupils and the teacher in which there was a common ethos and understanding. The pupils were seen to accept and respect the rationale behind the '*golden rule of bums on seats at all times*' as well as other issues such as '*not to fiddle about with the plugs*' on the grounds of practicality and good sense. There was leeway within this framework as pupils were allowed to sit where they wanted, usually in friendship groups, although it was preferred that they used the same type of keyboard each week.

Finally, in terms of organisation and behaviour management, the teacher stated that the nature of lessons involving the acquisition of keyboard skills meant that:

> *The keyboards, to some extent, create their own classroom management because the headphones are on and they are encased in their own little world. We have a rule that you don't play, unless told to, without headphones.*

3.
WHAT ARE
EFFECTIVE
PRACTICES
IN
ARTS
EDUCATION?

In terms of learning content, he stated that, as a general rule, '*we differentiate by outcome rather than by task*' and described an 'inclusive' approach to music education, ensuring that '*the high-fliers*' with strong musical skills and abilities were not the only pupils to enjoy and succeed in the subject. Hence, he promoted and operated a flexible approach to suit all ability ranges in the class so that it was possible to vary or adjust the programme or lesson content to meet the particular needs of individual pupils. For example, the observed lesson was part of an ongoing series based around the acquisition of basic keyboard skills. Consequently, a pupil with advanced piano skills was allowed to go into another room during some parts of music lessons and practise on his own before returning for '*the bit of the lesson that matters*'.

Lessons were thus designed and delivered to ensure a sense of success amongst all pupils.

> *They all manage something, even those two who said they hadn't done it. They had. It's just they hadn't done it fluently and that's the biggest struggle; they tend to knock themselves.*

As part of the lesson structure, this 'success' or achievement was concretised when the teacher instructed the pupils to write in their planners the number of songs/tunes they had learned to play that day: in effect, a formal record-keeping of success. A lack of self-esteem and confidence was regarded as being a major problem shared by many pupils, and the teacher endeavoured to address this by giving instantaneous feedback and positive affirmation of pupils' work- and non-work related behaviour. For example, in the early stages of the observed lesson, when giving the books out, the teacher halted the class and raised the question in an imposing voice: '*Who put the books away last week?*' After a short gap, a somewhat reluctant admission was offered by a pupil. The teacher replied: '*Congratulations, young man. They are all in order of desks. That's excellent!*'

Notwithstanding the all-inclusive ethos of his approach to music education, the teacher of the observed lesson advocated perfectionism as he wanted pupils to reach their full potential: '*It is trying to teach them about going for higher standards and not accepting something that is just OK.*' Such notions can be seen to reflect his wider musical orientations: '*There is no room for the performer who isn't really bothered about the high standard ... there is plenty of room ... for people with lots of enthusiasm.*'

Contingent with the development of musical knowledge and keyboard skills, the teacher was keen for pupils to learn about group working and cooperation, whether it was '*working in a small group of two on a keyboard or working in a large group and making way for other people*'. This was illustrated by an episode in the observed lesson when two pupils playing flute and violin performed out loud, and the rest of the class:

> ... slipped into the habit of 'We'll sit back and listen to them without making a noise and disrupting them or even being rude' and that was very nice, that there wasn't a lot of jealousy or envy ... I think they just accepted that these are kids who have lessons, and it's music, so why shouldn't they?

In a similar way, the teacher was keen to actively encourage group-working and cooperation, and this was especially apparent in relation to the more able pupils. During another episode in the observed lesson, pupils who played the piano, flute and violin were encouraged to work collaboratively. This was intended to provide a basis for subsequent lessons in which the class members were to work on their own compositions so that these particular pupils could work together in order to '*spark off each other*'.

Hence, the approach pursued was one of order and direction, in which the pupils were encouraged to develop their musical, as well as social, knowledge and skills. These issues can be seen to permeate the observed lesson in the following section.

13.4.3 School 1: the observed lesson

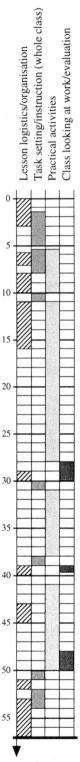

This observed lesson was a 60-minute Year 7 music lesson, taking place in a music room equipped with electronic keyboards on tables facing the front of the room. There was a piano at the back of the room, and the walls were adorned with posters depicting musical notation and songs. The lesson was led by the music teacher, and a student teacher was also present.

Pupils entered the room chatting, and proceeded to stand by their chairs whilst the teacher informally urged the class to be quiet: '*Right, you miserable shower, are you going to shut up?*' As the class was settling, the teacher noticed and rectified the unsatisfactory appearance of one particular pupil, in a light-hearted, jovial manner. After being directed to sit down, the pupils were informed that they would need their planners and a pencil. The teacher was mobile throughout the classroom, distributing worksheets while he explained the lesson. This was interspersed with a conversation with a pupil who informed him that he had just sat a grade 4 piano exam that morning, to which the teacher responded:

> *... very good. We will wait for the result, hopefully before Christmas, and if it's a pass, it's a pass; if it's a merit, we'll all cheer; and if it's a distinction, you can throw the party. How's that?*

Once the task of distributing worksheets was completed, the teacher instructed the pupils to study them whilst he explained in detail what was expected. Questions on the sheet were read out by the teacher, walking round the room, and pupils were then asked to answer: '*I have no objection to you sneaking a quick look at the poster on the notice board to remember the names of the notes.*'

At this stage, the teacher asked direct questions, such as '*Right, what's the first note?*', as well issuing specific instructions to the whole class:

> *Remember the first lesson? Index finger pointing at the ceiling, now find 'D' and play 'D'* [to a specific pupil] *Right hand. Now, where's 'E'? I don't want an answer, I want you to think. How many 'E's do you play? Look at the sheet.*

Hence, this section of the lesson was very structured and directed and also illustrated the first instance of differentiation. Direct instructions were given to the class on how to play a sequence of notes on the keyboard – '*Put your middle finger on the "E". Get your little finger ready to play "G", right hand; your thumb ready to play "C"*' – whereas one particular pupil

with advanced keyboard skills was told: '*When you play it ...
you've got to play it* [with] *both hands and put the chords in.*'

The session continued along the same lines with the pupils being
guided through the first stages of the worksheets enabling them to play
certain Christmas songs on the keyboard. The names of these tunes
were then requested, assisted with games of 'hangman', with various
class members, on the board, to elicit the missing or unknown words.
Technical questions were also posed, although not to the pupils in the
class with more advanced musical knowledge: '*I know these people
who play another instrument know. This is revision for everybody else.
OK? I'm not ignoring you.*'

Once the initial stages of the worksheet had been completed under
direct supervision, the class was told '*Now you're on your own*' and
instructed to complete the sheet in exactly the same manner as before.
Pupils worked in pairs at their keyboards, each wearing a set of
headphones. Many instances of organisation and troubleshooting then
occurred, such as leading a pupil to the storeroom to issue a pencil and
picking up a book from the floor: '*Who's been throwing their planner
around? Vandal!*' The lesson was also characterised by numerous
technical hitches and problems with the keyboards and headphones.
These were dealt with efficiently with good humour from both pupils
and the teacher, as illustrated by an incident in which a pupil's
headphones kept falling off:

> *What's up* [pupil]*? You've got a funny-shaped head, that's what it
> is. Don't blame my equipment if your head's funny-shaped* [puts
> headphones back on her head after adjusting them, and laughs].
> *There's not a lot we can do about that, love. It seems it wants to
> collapse every time* [proceeds to find an alternative set of
> headphones].

One of the pupils interviewed following the lesson also referred to the
technical problems encountered, saying: '*Our keyboard was going a
bit funny, but we sorted it out and we were just helping each other play.*'

This lesson format continued for a further ten minutes, during which
time several more instances of 'hangman' occurred, more instructions
and reminders were issued to the class as a whole, and individual pupils
were given specific help and encouragement in their tasks. Throughout
the session, the teacher engaged in different levels of communication
with different pupils according to their levels of ability. In addition to
the pupil with piano skills, two pupils who played the violin and flute
were encouraged to complete the exercises using those instruments
instead of the keyboards. Soon after suggesting this to these pupils, and
locating the relevant instruments, the teacher provided piano
accompaniment for them to play the exercises. Although this was not
a formal/structured whole-class evaluation or performance, most of

the class interrupted their own work to watch and listen, encouraged by the teacher: '*Christmas music with giggles. I think she just needs a couple of moments to compose herself.*' The brief performance was met with a '*Well done*' from the teacher and applause from the class. This episode was repeated for the second tune, after which the teacher questioned the whole class to ascertain which members had completed the first keyboard tune to a standard at which they could play it out loud. Following a show of hands, these pupils were instructed to remove their headphone splitters and proceeded to play 'Jingle Bells', with the teacher's piano accompaniment. The class was then informed that in five minutes, the same procedure for the second tune would take place.

**3.
WHAT ARE
EFFECTIVE
PRACTICES
IN
ARTS
EDUCATION?**

The teacher then continued to give advice to individual pupils, as well as dealing with numerous technical problems with the keyboards. Following the class performance of the second tune, which involved pupils playing keyboards as well as the flute and violin, the teacher showed the pupil with piano skills how to play a third tune on the piano in preparation for the next performance. Although the demonstrated piece was beyond the pupil's capacity, the teacher urged him to: '*Have a go. Trial and error. Use your ears. Doesn't matter if you can't find it. Have a go. Just try.*' After about five minutes, the teacher called the class together to perform this tune, again involving pupils playing the violin, flute and keyboards as well as '*our own expert accompanist*'. This was said to have been '*Excellent*'. This clearly demonstrated the flexibility of the approach and the efforts of the teacher in tailoring aspects of the lesson to the needs and interests of pupils with advanced musical skills and integrating their potential/contribution within the whole-class and whole-lesson contexts.

Following this final performance, the teacher halted the lesson – '*Shut up. Shut up or else it's chaos*' – and asked the pupils to identify how many songs they had learned to play. One pupil responded to the question: '*How many people have not managed one?*' and was instantly told: '*You have! Because I've seen you do it.*' Whilst the teacher spent a few minutes with the pupil demonstrating a tune on the keyboard and closely assisting him, the rest of the class returned to playing their tunes. Once the pupil had mastered playing his tune, the teacher then instructed the class to start packing away, and requested a volunteer to collect the books in. When this was completed, the pupils were instructed to get their planners out, turn to the back, write the date at the top of the page and enter the number of Christmas songs they had learned to play during that lesson. This was then rounded off with some encouraging comments from the teacher: '*Now that was a very good lesson. Most people worked and worked hard, so let's get on* [our] *feet and go out the usual fashion please.*' After packing their belongings away, the pupils stood in silence by their chairs, facing the door at the back of the room, waiting to be selected to leave by the teacher.

Activity	Time (mins)	Time as % of lesson time
Lesson logistics/organisation/housekeeping	19	34
Whole-class task setting/direct instruction	12	21
Pupils engaged in practical activities	36	64
Class looking at the work of others/evaluation	4	7

It is evident in the above table that the percentages do not sum to 100. This demonstrates that several activities were taking place simultaneously throughout the lesson. It is clear, however, that for the majority of the lesson, pupils were engaged in practical activities, with only a very small amount of time devoted to whole-class evaluation and review. It is also apparent that the teacher spent much time 'housekeeping', especially dealing with technical problems on the keyboards.

3.
WHAT ARE
EFFECTIVE
PRACTICES
IN
ARTS
EDUCATION?

School 2

13.4.4   School 2: the effects of music education

School 2's distinctive array of effects included a particularly notable number of pupil nominations for 'arts knowledge and skills', 'personal and social development' – especially 'group working' – and 'extrinsic transfer effects'. The school also received the highest number of references to immediate intrinsic effects of music education based on 'enjoyment factors'. Typical pupil comments here included:

> I like music ... it's really interesting and everything, and you learn a lot [more] new things than you would if you just went to a normal music lesson and we have got lots more facilities at school

> ___

> No one really hates music lessons ... they prefer them because it's different.

Nominations for 'arts knowledge and skills', were the second highest ranking among the five case studies, and within that, the school received the most nominations for 'technical skills and competence'. 'Knowledge of the artform and critical skills' were not so highly featured (two other schools had more nominations) and this may indicate School 2's very practical orientation of music education.

'Creativity and thinking skills' was a category of effects/outcomes in music which received the fewest mentions across the whole sample of five schools, although this school received most. These focused on 'developing creativity', but evidence of thinking skills did emerge from pupil comments following the observed lesson:

3.
WHAT ARE
EFFECTIVE
PRACTICES
IN
ARTS
EDUCATION?

... it's also just thinking for yourself really ... if he did [talk for the whole lesson], *which he doesn't do, it would be a bit boring; it would be, like, his piece of music and not ours ... I prefer it when he lets us do our own thinking.*

School 2 again received marginally more nominations for 'communication and expressive skills' than the other schools, these outcomes chiefly relating to the acquisition of 'listening and interpretation skills' with considerably fewer mentions of 'expressive skills'. (This same pattern was evident for the other schools.) The school also received the most nominations for 'personal and social development', and the largest proportion of these were derived from 'group work': almost double the number of nominations from the school ranked second. Pupil comments included:

... he likes us to work in either small groups or large groups ... so we have either loads of people's ideas or you just have yourself and somebody else.

... we were supposed to learn just to work in groups, to fit in together, not just have your own piece and perform it and then let someone else do theirs. You were supposed to be involved with everybody's.

Finally, the school received by far the highest number of nominations for 'extrinsic transfer effects' of arts education and this may be related to the value placed on 'technical skills and competence' and to the importance and high profile of extra-curricular activities at the school. Similarly, School 2 received twice as many nominations for 'encouragement of involvement' than the next highest scoring school. This again points towards the active and participatory aspects of education within the school and wider community.

13.4.5   School 2: teaching approaches and context

The local socio-economic setting of School 2 was described as being a declining industrial area in which coal mining had been especially prevalent: however, population and labour market changes were increasingly evident. The school's catchment was described as being '*truly comprehensive*' as a result of the presence of social deprivation and unemployment alongside the influx of a more affluent population.

Interviewees stressed the importance of continuing the traditional values and role of music in the local community and stated that the school was a fundamental component of this. Many school–community links were presented, including the regard with which the school's performances were held in the locality, as well as direct links, such as older musicians assisting and participating in the school's brass bands. Similarly, talented pupils were encouraged to join local authority bands in the area, reflecting the quality of music education at the school and the support for musical participation in the local setting. The school's senior management, although not of music, or even arts, backgrounds, was highly supportive of music education in the school. The music department itself was seen as highly resourced, with dedicated, purpose-built rooms, a 24-track recording studio and considerable investment in a wide variety of equipment, including electronic and acoustic instruments, as well as PCs and related software.

The school's ethos was characterised as being vibrant and friendly; it was a '*high-energy school*' with mutual respect, good discipline and good relations between staff and pupils. The pastoral system was said to be a strong component of this ethos.

Music education was a component of a wider arts faculty that was deemed to provide not only a highly effective organisational structure, but also to present a consolidated approach to arts education. It was asserted that cooperation between staff members from the various arts departments, such as resource sharing and participation in each other's events and performances, encouraged a sense of group working amongst the pupils. The pupils '*don't see the barriers or crossovers ... they see it all as just working together quite happily*'. This ethos was also regarded as permeating the whole-school context, with the arts acting as an involving and integrating factor. A member of the senior management team, for example, highlighted the range of other inputs into an expressive arts open evening. The technology department provided lighting for the event and incorporated this into a stage-lighting project, and the IT department became involved in the ticketing operation and programme production. This type of event was said to be: '*where arts really have an influence in school, where they begin to pervade the whole ethos and working atmosphere*'.

These issues were reflected in the observed lesson in which the pupils were active – encouraged to think for themselves and experiment musically. A relaxed, non-threatening atmosphere was thus seen as a prerequisite for pupils to become excited by the tasks in which they were engaged. It was asserted that the ethos of music education and the music department itself had changed so that '*not many pupils would say that music is irrelevant*'. This statement was exemplified with reference to the popularity of the Year 9 IT-based 'house music' project, with which the pupils were said to have been captivated: '*Everything we do is relative to their life here and they feel that it is relevant.*'

Classroom ambience was described as being a '*relaxed environment, but one with all the rules in*', complemented by teaching styles and approaches. A member of the senior management team noted that: '*I don't believe that people learn effectively if learning is imposed on them all the time.'* Similarly, the faculty head stated that his personal teaching approach had been modified and refined as his career progressed, so that rather than following a heavily didactic approach, he now acted more as facilitator. Although it was necessary for pupils to be taught the basic skills of creating music, he stated that the enjoyment of music and the emotional effect it had were the central focus.

Music education at this school, as clearly demonstrated in the observed lesson, had a heavy emphasis on practical activities, which was deemed to develop and facilitate the pupils' learning in several ways. According to the teacher:

> *... the piece of rap music they have written is there. It's on tape and they can listen to it and enjoy it. But that's all that really is, and in the end it goes in a drawer and it gets saved up or assessed ... what they have had to think about and the way they have had to work is way more important.*

Hence, communication, cooperation and the importance of teamwork in working through a task underpinned the nature and structure of lesson delivery, in which group work was considered to be the preferred way of working. Much of this was attributed to the need to *'teach them to be people and to work together'* and the teacher of the observed lesson related this to his experiences as an ensemble musician where everyone had an essential role to play. Music lessons were, therefore, delivered in a context which allowed guided or monitored exploration in which the pupils were given *'a real framework to work within, so you define the parameters, but then you allow the students to be creative within those parameters'*. The teacher of the observed lesson elaborated on the notion of music being a *'fantastic educational tool'* by asserting that he used the subject as a vehicle to:

> *... guide them and let them explore whilst you're watching them – [a] journey – think about where they're going, how to get there. Is that the right decision or direction?*

In addition to the acquisition of musical 'skills', such as increasing competence in the use of musical instruments and the correct use of appropriate terminology, it was hoped that pupils would increase their thinking and cognitive development. Music education was *'not about rights and wrongs'*, as experience was regarded as being of greater value to the pupils than always getting a right answer. Consequently, the notion that the learning process is based on *'getting things wrong, working things out for yourself, realising your own ideas'* was clearly demonstrated in the observed lesson. Pupils were constantly engaged in discourse with the teacher, offering answers and ideas as the lesson progressed. It was asserted that as a consequence of not being told things, or given information directly:

**3.
WHAT ARE
EFFECTIVE
PRACTICES
IN
ARTS
EDUCATION?**

... in some ways I don't think they realise what they are picking up from the subject ... they get it in the end, understand why they weren't told so directly at the time, but at the time it can seem frustrating.

The approach to teaching music at this school was regarded by teachers as an excellent mechanism by which achievement barriers and hierarchies could be broken down. The classes were mixed-ability and music was seen as a vehicle through which every pupil could achieve and succeed. The teacher of the observed lesson stated that:

... you really can get through to every single pupil. We can forget a lot of these barriers that pupils do naturally have [bad handwriting, literacy and numeracy], *... you can break every single barrier down. They can all start from a very equal place.*

3.
WHAT ARE
EFFECTIVE
PRACTICES
IN
ARTS
EDUCATION?

The teacher noted that work was differentiated not necessarily by task at the start of the lesson, but by interacting with students throughout. Different levels and types of assistance were given to different pupils so that everyone was able to have a feeling of *'pride, self-belief, self-worth'*. This was argued to contribute to the feeling that: *'they have worked together to produce something that has been worthwhile ... they are proud of their own skills'*.

This teaching approach was seen as an effective means of producing people who were skilled players of instruments – *'they work extremely hard to perfect skills'* – as well as developing more rounded and contextualised skills, abilities and understandings. According to the teacher of the observed lesson: *'We do produce a lot of good performers – not always great players, but good performers, people that can work well together.'* Much of this 'maturity' was attributed to the approach and content of lessons that emphasised cognitive, creative and cooperative development. The structure of idea development, rehearsal, performance, review and refinement was said to force pupils to *'deal with their own insecurities in front of someone else'*. Hence, peer review was seen as an important component of the learning process as it helped pupils not to be frightened of expressing their opinions and comment on their own work and that of others. It was also asserted that: *'They really take that* [personal development] *on to everything else they do.'* Hence, this approach, based on teaching the pupils as well as the subject, was intended to deliver more than specific music education. The real strength of music education was deemed to be *'developing students who can work independently'*, inspired by the teacher's qualities:

I honestly think we send a little bit of us away with the kids, our way of thinking ... the way in which we think we should go and work in the workplace ... how they should work with other people ... the way in which they should approach tasks.

13.4.6 School 2: the observed lesson

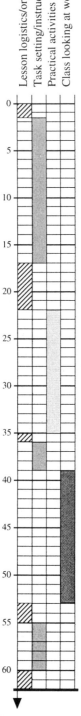

This observed lesson was a 60-minute Year 9 music lesson which took place in a music room that the pupils had never been in before. The lesson was led by the music teacher assisted by a student teacher who had taken the previous week's lesson. The room was organised with chairs and tables facing the front of the room – orientated towards a blackboard and a piano. Cupboards, shelving and benches on the remaining walls contained various acoustic musical instruments and electronic keyboards.

Pupils entered the room during the first three minutes or so of the lesson, chatting whilst they proceeded to sit at tables, generally in groups of four. The teacher was already present at the front of room and talked informally with pupils as they arrived. As well as some light-hearted encouragement from him for pupils to hurry up and prepare for the lesson, they were asked to write the word 'variations' – the lesson topic – in their planners and then to put planners and pens away as no homework was to be set. Whilst the class was settling, the teacher was scanning the room and informally asked where particular pupils were and why some were absent.

Once the class had settled (by about the fourth minute), the teacher explained that he was not in last week's lesson so asked pupils what they had done and required an explanation of 'variation'. This process began with a particular pupil being selected to answer, although the rest of the class was informed that others would also be asked:

> *I wasn't here last week. You were working with* [student teacher] *so you can all tell me …* [pupil], *you start – what's a variation? Doesn't necessarily mean a musical one, what is a variation? I'm going to go round* [gestures to the whole class], [pupil], *you start us off.*

There then followed a sustained but fast-moving series of dynamic exchanges between teacher and pupils on an individual, multiple or class basis. This involved recapping and expanding on previous work on variations, focusing on developing and applying the appropriate musical terminology to the ideas raised. The highly interactive style involved the teacher asking or posing questions and waiting for replies – either from pupils with their hand up, or by singling out particular pupils. Hence, active involvement and pupil participation were key elements of the lesson delivery. Much encouragement and support was given to pupils to answer questions or contribute to the discourse throughout this time:

Teacher: *Come on, lads – I've got about eight girls ...*
[lots of girls with their hands up]

Male pupil: *Dynamics.*

Teacher: *Good – what's the tune's dynamics? What's the dynamics mean, I've forgotten?* [writing on board] *You tell me, I don't know.*

Male pupil: *High and low sound.*
[Teacher demonstrates high and low on piano]

Teacher: *I don't think it means quite that, but I can't remember ...* [plays loud and quiet on piano] *... something to do with ...?*

Pupil: *Louder.*

Teacher: *Yes, softer and louder, which is slightly different to high and low.*

Pupil: *Tempo.*

Teacher: *Good, tempo. What does that mean?*
[Pupils answer and continue to suggest words which are then written on board]

Pupil: *Instruments.*

Teacher: *Instruments, good ... dead easy one. Play the tune on different instruments. Good, the list is coming on. This is very good.*

Hence, the teacher's narrative and explanations were frequently characterised by truncated sentences or deliberate pauses alongside encouraging gestures to solicit and motivate replies from the class. Pupil responses were then incorporated into the continuing discussion and musical terms were written on the board and also acted upon, with the teacher demonstrating particular answers on the piano and electronic keyboard. This occasionally involved the deliberate exaggeration and misinterpretation of some responses as a means of focusing and refining the pupils' thoughts and contributions. These instances were then explained and jovial apologies offered to the pupils concerned. Questions frequently referred to issues raised in previous lessons, topics and projects:

[After playing a random selection of notes on the piano] *Why was that not a variation? I'm not really having a go at* [pupil], *'cos she said change some of the notes and I changed all of the notes. Why was that not a variation* [pupil]?

The teacher became mobile around the room, from the piano, to the keyboards, then to the other end of the room, indicating where the different types of instruments could be found. Pupils were asked the names of particular instruments in an entertaining, enthusiastic manner:

> *What are these things called* [laughing]? *Come on – beat you all at this – we should play this game more often. What's it called? ... Begins with a 'G'. Find out for next week. I'll give somebody a merit who can tell me. What's the proper name for these? ... Sticks? Banging things?*
>
> [pupils shout out answers, including 'claves']
>
> *Claves, correct ... Have a merit and go to the top of the class.*

Then, having completed the discussion of 'variations' and the particular tune from the previous lesson, the teacher described the present lesson's practical component, aims and structure. The class was divided into groups through cooperative negotiation between the teacher and the pupils. Before the final dispersal into an adjoining room, the task was again described and the class asked if everything was understood.

3.
WHAT ARE
EFFECTIVE
PRACTICES
IN
ARTS
EDUCATION?

Pupils formed into groups and collected the instruments of their choice, including electronic keyboards and percussion instruments, and one group elected to use the piano. Three groups of pupils remained in the observed room and the teacher proceeded to visit groups in each room, applying the same style of involving the pupils in dynamic exchanges as he had done in the earlier whole-class context. In some cases, the teacher actually demonstrated how to play a particular tune on a particular instrument; in others, he offered suggestions, whilst in others, he asked questions as a means of generating ideas within the group. Following the lesson observation, one of the pupils remarked:

> *... he* [the teacher] *kept on coming to see us every so often, to show us what we could do to improve it and things like that.*

Interviewer: *Do you find that useful?*

> *Yes, a lot.*

After some time (13 minutes), the groups from the adjoining room returned and sat down whilst the teacher again engaged the class in discourse concerning the aims and benefits of collectively listening to, and evaluating, the impending performances. As before, certain information was given, or questions asked, in order to solicit and inspire/ encourage comments from the pupils. This pattern continued after three groups had performed their pieces. The entire class left the observed room for four to five minutes to repeat the exercise in the adjoining room. On their return, pupils proceeded to return the instruments in a cooperative and orderly way, assisted by the teacher, who moved some of the larger items and gave advice on the correct location for some of the instruments.

The class was encouraged to settle and the teacher began to offer a positive review of the pupils' achievements, relating what they had done to the list of potential musical variations they had constructed in the early stages of the lesson. The many questions posed by the teacher in this section of the lesson served to encourage the pupils to reflect and think, rather than stimulate direct teacher–pupil exchanges, although these did still occur. (By this time, the end-of-lesson bell had sounded.) Finally, the teacher reminded the pupils that all the things they had spoken about and that had been demonstrated and played would have to be remembered for the next lesson. At this stage, the student teacher was asked to briefly outline the plan for that lesson, and the pupils were allowed to leave the room. The teacher talked informally with the pupils as they were leaving.

13.4.7   Concluding remarks

The following discussion draws together some of the issues raised in previous sections as a means of consolidating understandings of effective music education. Although certain differences and similarities will be highlighted, it is not intended to show that any particular lesson or teacher style/approach was superior or inferior to any other. Similarly, the contexts of each lesson should be seen to underpin such an exploration and factors such as the age of the pupils, for example, must be taken into account when considering the style and approach of a teacher.

Both the observed lessons contained strong practical components in which the pupils were active in making music, a feature identified as a significant outcome of music education by the pupils at these schools. Within this, however, it is evident that the lessons varied in structure, content and character.

Observations of the lesson at School 1 showed that following an organisational stage of a couple of minutes, the pupils were quickly 'on task'. After a four-minute introductory and explanatory phase in which the aims and expectations of the lesson were articulated, the pupils became engaged in the practical pursuit of keyboard skills by the sixth minute of the lesson. In a very different way, the observed lesson at School 2 began with a two-minute period of organisation and $14^1/_2$ minutes of task setting and whole-class explanation led by the teacher, although there was a high level of pupil involvement. The actual practical component of this lesson began about one-third of the way through (22 minutes).

3.
WHAT ARE
EFFECTIVE
PRACTICES
IN
ARTS
EDUCATION?

Activity	Time spent (in mins and as % of lesson length)	
	School 1	School 2
Lesson logistics/organisation/housekeeping	19 (34%)	12.5 (20%)
Whole-class task setting/direct instruction	12 (21%)	22.5 (36%)
Pupils engaged in practical activities	36 (64%)	13 (21%)
Class looking at the work of others/evaluation	4 (7%)	14 (23%)

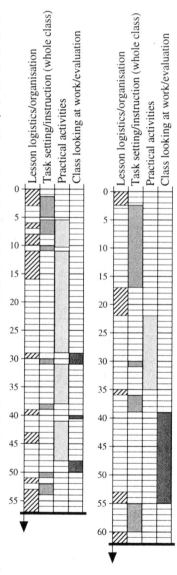

Of the total 36 minutes of practical activity in the lesson at School 1, the first six minutes were directly controlled by the teacher whilst the remaining time was allocated for the pupils to work independently with assistance from the teacher as required. At School 2, the practical component of the lesson lasted for about 13 minutes, during which time the pupils worked autonomously in groups, with occasional interaction with the teacher. This practical session was a precursor to the section of lesson allocated for whole-class evaluation and review of the work of different groups. This lasted for 14 minutes, roughly the same duration as the practical component. This was very different from the situation at School 1 in which whole-class review or performance accounted for only four minutes of the total lesson and was not announced as an important part of the lesson in the early/preparatory stages as it was in School 2.

Following the evaluation/performance phase, the lesson at School 2 concluded with two minutes of equipment return and a five-minute discussion and lesson review, which, although teacher-led, still contained considerable pupil input. The review of the lesson at School 1 was much shorter and most of this time (about two minutes) was spent with the pupils completing a log of their achievements.

Hence, the lesson at School 1 was predominantly based on pupils working independently in a structured framework with only a very short time for performance and review. The lesson at School 2 demonstrated a more cyclical approach based on phases of task-setting/explanation, practical participation, performance and evaluation and rounded off with a comprehensive review.

Within these different structures, the teachers can also be seen to have fulfilled different roles and carried out different functions. In the lesson at School 1, the teacher acted as a figure of authority, directing and controlling the lesson content and the pupils' learning. This involved seeking answers to direct questions as well as posing questions for the pupils to think about whilst working alone. The pupils were also encouraged to think through the solutions to particular problems or queries for themselves, although the teacher sometimes aided this process through the instigation of games of 'hangman'. Hence, the pupils always succeeded. Praise was given to individual pupils and the class as a whole on several occasions throughout the lesson, although this was generally couched within the calm, controlled and subtle expressionistic style of the teacher. A considerable amount of this teacher's time and attention in the lesson was spent in a caretaking role, especially in relation to sorting out problems with the keyboards and headphones, as well as supplying several pupils with pencils and books.

The teacher of the observed lesson at School 2 can be seen to have applied a highly dynamic approach. Within the well-defined structure of the lesson, pupils were encouraged to participate to a great extent, and a strong, interactive dialogue was encouraged by the teacher, who tried to include as many pupils as possible in the discussion. Hence, during the early stages of the observed lesson when the previous week's work was being reviewed and the present lesson explained, pupils were fed with sentences to complete and develop. The teacher of this lesson acted very much as a facilitator – allowing, motivating and encouraging the pupils to learn and develop their musical abilities. Praise, celebration and encouragement were highly significant components of this lesson, the whole-class evaluation sessions reflecting this. Pupils were encouraged to assess their own work and that of others, identifying strengths, weaknesses and possibilities for improvement.

In addition to the acquisition of musical skills, much of the observed lesson at School 2 involved the development and application of social skills, illustrated by the emphasis on group working. Even the formation of the groups prior to the practical component of the lesson was a cooperatively negotiated process between all the pupils and the teacher.

It is possible to argue that music at School 2 comes across as being regarded by the pupils and the teacher alike as more than just a 'school subject' and much of this may be derived from the importance of music in the area and local context of this school. It could be that music education completes the circle, as much of what the pupils learn and achieve then feeds back into extra-curricular activities and community-based broader contexts. Music education at this school can be seen as an intrinsic part of the continuation of participation in musical activities. Hence, the nature of the specific observed lesson and its wider role can be considered to be an organic experience, which, although structured, was flexible, responsive and linked in to wider areas of school, leisure and even work life.

Consequently, the importance of contexts and backgrounds should not be overlooked in the understanding of effective music education. Without wishing to make any explicit links or assumptions, it could be possible to argue that the differences in the nature of approach to music education may be, in part at least, related to the different musical experiences of these two teachers. One teacher, for example, was heavily involved in performing in a wide variety of musical forms, whilst the other had a background of musical composition and direction. Hence, it may not be an unrelated fact that one style was orientated around expression and experimentation, whilst the other was more directive.

Effective music education can thus be argued to stem from a structured, practical – hands-on – experience for pupils in a supportive, relaxed atmosphere. Pupils respond well to being involved in the lesson and its content fostering a sense of ownership. Both teachers were keen to encourage their pupils to 'have a go' and push themselves regardless of the consequences – that is, it was deemed better to experiment and not get the right answer, than not to try at all. This was a key element in the ethos of music education. In addition, genuine demonstrations of musical commitment and enthusiasm from teachers are required to inspire and motivate the pupils.

Although pursuing slightly different lines of approach, both the teachers of the observed lessons appeared to be motivating and encouraging the pupils to learn and develop their musical and social skills, reflecting the issues and outcomes raised by the pupils.

DRAMA

'In everyday life, "if" is an evasion; in [drama] "if" is the truth.'

Peter Brook

13.5 DRAMA

School 1

13.5.1   *School 1: the effects of drama education*

This school registered the highest number of nominations for 'knowledge of the social and cultural domain' effects, particularly awareness of social issues. In addition, it ranked highest in 'personal and social development' outcomes, in terms of both 'increased self confidence' and 'understanding of how another feels', i.e. both inter- and intrapersonal skills accruing from drama were identified by pupils. As well as that, there were most references to 'transfer effects' relating to the world of work and leisure. Hence, a strong sense of the medium of drama activating and enhancing life skills was evident.

In contrast, the school ranked lowest in relation to 'knowledge of the artform' (although references here were rare in all the case studies). The pupil sample from this school made the second highest number of references to 'general skill enhancement', but again, in marked contrast to two other schools, very rarely suggested 'technical skills' such as improvisation.

References to 'creativity' (albeit rare in all five case studies) were uniquely evident in both key stage 3 and key stage 4 at School 1, while 'expressive skills' received more nominations than any other school.

This school ranked second in terms of pupil responses indicating 'intrinsic' effects, with 'enjoyment' particularly noted by youngsters in Years 9 and Year 10. Sustaining interest and enthusiasm at these crucial stages of possible pupil disaffection is noteworthy indeed.

Thus, an array of effects indicating a particular emphasis on both pupil relevance and engagement make School 1 a case study to explore further.

13.5.2   School 1: teaching approaches and context

School 1 is in an area where, in the past, '*the arts were somewhere in the background and getting a job was top of the shop*'. That situation has, however, been '*reversed*' in some respects: the socio-economic status of the catchment area has become more varied so that the school now has '*a fairly realistic comprehensive intake*'. One of the implications of this for arts education in the school was said to be that 'parental expectation' had become higher – '*parents would expect that their children are going to have a rich experience here*' – and within that, therefore, tended to be more supportive of the arts.

The school management described the school as being caring and supportive of its pupils and having strong links with the community: '*All the kids know that they are being supported ... because the school's reputation is very positive in the community now they have a standard to achieve and reach.*'

The school management promote the arts as an important part of the whole school experience, but not at the expense of other subjects: as the headteacher put it:

> *I was keen not to promote the arts to the disadvantage of the others. On the other hand, I was determined that the arts would have equal say and maybe that is the reason that we are as we are.*

Several arts teachers maintained that the headmaster's sympathy with the arts made it easier for them to implement new initiatives.

The drama department in the school functions as a separate department. According to the head of drama, the departmental resources were far from ideal, as they had no specialist facilities, but they made do with what they had. All Year 7–9 pupils do drama for one hour a week. Pupils can then choose to continue with drama to A-level standard.

The specialist-trained PGCE drama education teachers at the school were also involved in city-wide drama initiatives. They enjoyed the '*freedom*' derived from drama not being a National Curriculum subject, but did follow the '*basic guidelines set for drama within the English curriculum*'.

The drama teachers, as well as the school management, recognised the benefits of using group work in class, perceiving it as having a contribution to make to pupils' social development – particularly their ability to work with other people. Drama teaching was approached as an interactive process, characterised by high levels of communication and participation:

> *I always start off the lesson in a circle ... Very much a sharing idea. I will sometimes dictate the lesson; sometimes I leave it very open to them what I want them to do – quite a bit of small group work, techniques that I get them involved in such as forum theatre – not so many drama games and things. I do those as a warm-up or a warm-down but I don't make it a part of every lesson. I just get on with the story that we are doing, or the ideas we are working on. So, it is quite structured, but then I will let them have their freedom within that structure, if you know what I mean.*

The teacher in the observed lesson described her teaching 'style' as very '*active*' – participating in role plays, demonstrating things, and having a '*presence*' in the classroom. She chose topics that stretched over several lessons that she felt passionate about as '*a vehicle for learning the drama techniques*'. She expressed her opinion that there was more value in the process of developing the performance than in the performance itself, and that the lesson should pose a challenge to pupils, but not be too difficult either. She saw her role as a guide – asking questions to lead pupils in the right direction rather than providing all the right answers. Exploration of active themes and content was often done by means of question-and-answer sessions, rather than just through pupils listening to the teacher talking.

The drama teachers maintained and enjoyed a friendly and relaxed relationship with the pupils. Though the observed teacher saw having a relaxed class atmosphere as essential, she also recognised the importance of having adequate discipline:

> *I suppose I'm quite natural but then ... I think I've got a discipline there as well, as in I can relax with the kids but when I have to turn on the stern voice I can do. And I guess it is playing a role very often. But, you can be honest with them, you can relax with them. You know, I never went in for the 'never smile before Christmas thing'. I can never be like that; I am me with them.*

The teachers' perceived outcomes for drama teaching made great reference to pupils' personal and social development: '*I think we are here to help support the fully rounded human being.*' The skills learnt in drama were seen as a means to an end rather than an end in themselves:

495

3.
WHAT ARE
EFFECTIVE
PRACTICES
IN
ARTS
EDUCATION?

... it's about finding a means of expressing themselves, and looking at the world around them, and coming to terms with that. You are equipping them with sophisticated tools and, as I said, for me personally that is not the be all and end all. It is not about them being able to act particularly well or whatever. It is being able to manipulate those tools for their own means. So being able to do that, they felt that they have more control over what they are doing.

Acquisition of technical drama skills was identified as having social, personal, cognitive and performance-related spin-offs. Asked what pupils gained from learning those technical skills, one of the drama teachers noted:

... socially, I guess, it's working in the group to structure that piece of work and to then impart their knowledge ... Then it is the sense of achievement when it works ... And they can use subject-specific words and that's good, that's clever, you know. They understand that so there's a real boost there. And then actually dramatically to show that it does enhance their work and that very often the techniques for the kids who are going to find it really hard to play that role with true emotion and true feeling, they can then still do something.

The teachers also described the enjoyment or 'buzz' pupils gained from self-expression and discovering things in drama that they thought were relevant to them.

The school's drama and musical productions were a source of enjoyment for both pupils and the community.

Differentiation by task was noted: according to their drama ability, different expectations and outcomes were set. One teacher described splitting groups to include pupils of mixed ability, prescribing more to lower-ability pupils (so that they had to make fewer choices) while posing more questions to those of greater ability. Above all, the culture of encouragement and affirmation was evident in all of the observed drama lessons from this school: teachers attempted to recognise even the achievement of pupils who had not met the required criteria:

... there are always different outcomes for different kids ... you have got to make it clear that you think they have done very well, even though ... they are not at the level you might expect ... at that time. For them, they are doing excellently – you know, they have tried really hard.

In addition, the high status and importance given to feedback within a drama lesson were noted:

I will always work to that. That's something we always do, feedback on everything, whether it be a whole-group exercise or small groups or individual, even if it's 'What did you feel then?', 'How difficult was it for you?'. Stopping and reflecting, it's one-fifth of the GCSE, interaction, so it's important right the way through the lower school drama as well.

13.5.3 *School 1: the observed lesson*

The lesson which was observed at this school was a Year 9 drama lesson of 55 minutes, which took place in a medium-sized, basic classroom, equipped simply with chairs for the pupils to sit on.

The lesson began with the pupils sitting in a circle, and the teacher taking the register. She then recapped the work of the previous lesson, which was to form the starting point for the activities to come. The previous lesson had comprised a whole-class drama which considered the history of racial equality in America. The teacher explained:

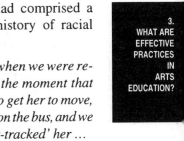

> *... we did a whole-group drama last week when we were re-enacting the bus scene, and we looked at the moment that Rosa says 'No' to the white man who tries to get her to move, and then we looked at everybody's thoughts on the bus, and we looked at Rosa's thoughts, and we 'thought-tracked' her ...*

The teacher also used questions to help pupils in their recollection of the previous lesson. For example, she said: '*We started, last week, talking about two people ... Edgar Daniel Nixon and Fred Grey ... Who were these two people?*' and: '*... Edgar Daniel Nixon, from the NAACP ... Can anyone remember what that stands for? ... it's hard ... it's a mouthful ... Can anyone remember what they do?*' The pupils put their hands up, and the teacher chose those to answer the questions. She then provided praise and reassurance in response to the answers given, sometimes choosing to develop pupils' answers further by way of explanation.

The recapping activity then moved seamlessly into explanation of the activities for this lesson, which were to start with a demonstration role play, for which the teacher sought four volunteers. Pupils were keen to volunteer, and four were chosen. Two of the pupils were seated on chairs facing each other, and each of the other pupils stood next to one of those seated. She said to the standing pupils: '*You're his thoughts* [to one of the standing pupils, and indicating one seated pupil]*, and you're her thoughts* [to the other standing pupil, and indicating the other seated pupil].' The teacher then proceeded to question the remainder of the class about the specific content of the role play. She said:

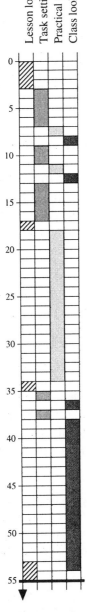

What I would like is first of all a situation where [one of the seated pupils] *has got to persuade her* [the other seated pupil] *to do something, or agree to something ... What do you think that situation could be? ... and it's not to go out with him ... we don't want that.*

The class found this final remark particularly amusing. The teacher continued to ask the class questions until all the factors relating to the role play had been decided. Just before the volunteers were to start, the teacher said:

I don't want to spend too long on this, but, as with forum theatre, if anyone's got any suggestions for either of these two [the main characters], *or for either of the thoughts ... if you think, for example, that there should be a silence there, or this thought should have said something like this ... then go along with it ...*

Once the role play had started, the pupils put their hands up to make comments, and the teacher stopped the action in order to discuss what had been said, and make further suggestions about how the scene could develop, or how it could be improved. At the end of the sketch, the class gave an appreciative round of applause, and the teacher moved the class into the next activity by saying:

Alright ... that's exactly what we're going to do, but we're going to relate it to Rosa ... so we're going to show the conversation between Edgar Daniel Nixon and Fred Grey. Edgar Daniel Nixon walks into the lawyer's office to try to persuade him to take up Rosa Parkes' case ... she refused to stand up for a white man on the bus, she was thrown into jail for it, she's on her own ... she needs a good lawyer...

In preparation for the group work, the teacher drew the pupils' attention to some statements written on the board which described some of the main characters' motivations. These had been developed during the previous lesson, and were discussed again before the group work began. Pupils also made suggestions which were added to the list during the lesson, the teacher saying in response to one: '*Yes, good idea ... I'll put that on the board.*' The teacher then told the class to organise themselves into groups of four for the practical work. One group was left with only three members, so the teacher took on a role. She stayed with this group for the first part of the practical work, but then moved around the groups – watching their role play development, talking to them, and giving ideas and suggestions.

When helping each group with their role play, the teacher listened to them, asked questions to elicit their ideas, provided input, and occasionally demonstrated a role or suggested ways of portraying characters' motivations through 'thought-tracking'. To one group she said:

If he [one of the characters] *says 'Look, I'm frightened', then maybe, that's a moment for silence, and for you to really look him in the eyes and say 'Look, you've got no need to be frightened ... you're going to win this' ... you know?*

In many cases, her advice was framed in terms of questions, which were clearly intended to prompt the group into thinking of the answer for themselves. For example, she asked one individual: *'What do you think Fred's "thought" would be thinking? ... he's being given this really hard sell, isn't he? ...'* However, despite this constant questioning, she was careful to find something positive to say about each group.

Following the practical development, the pupils were instructed to make their way back to the original circle, and the remainder of the lesson was spent in watching and evaluating the role plays which had been developed. The teacher performed with the group with whom she had prepared a role play, making humorous remarks about her own participation. After each group had completed their performance, the class gave them a generous round of applause, and then the teacher asked questions which prompted pupils to evaluate what they had seen. For example, of one role play, she said:

What persuasion techniques were being used there [between the characters]*? ... I mean ... how many ... hands up who was thinking, just screaming inside their heads 'Just say yes!', I mean. I was ... it was getting me so wound up ... but what persuasion techniques were being used?*

In this case, the pupils gave lots of different answers, each of which was validated by the teacher, who also made her own suggestions, and developed some of those made by the pupils. Again, something positive was found within each of the performances.

Unfortunately, the lesson ended before one of the groups had had a chance to perform their role play, although the teacher expressed her own opinion that the group concerned were not too keen to perform anyway. The teacher concluded the class by describing what they would be doing during the next drama lesson. Pupils then tidied up the classroom and proceeded to their next lesson.

Activity	Time (mins)	Time as % of lesson time
Lesson logistics/organisation/housekeeping	6	11
Whole-class task setting/direct instruction	13	24
Pupils engaged in practical activities	18	33
Class looking at the work of others/evaluation	18	33

The observed lesson was characterised by clear task-setting and abundant opportunities for pupils to communicate and explore ideas relating to various aspects of the topic in the class and in groups. Apart from initial task-setting, the teacher performed a facilitating and monitoring function throughout, giving directive input. She supervised the lesson organisation, monitored group progress while pupils were engaged in practical activities, gave advice and input as required, sometimes through modelling and demonstration, and continuously affirmed and praised pupils' efforts. She monitored and organised their performances and guided their analysis, evaluation and celebration of their work. Equally, feedback and evaluation were much in evidence and showed the teacher pushing for these to be a considered component of the lesson:

> *When they are excited about something, they are raring to go and they want to just see everybody's and they don't want to talk about it and you are making them talk about it and making them analyse, but they like praise and also constructive criticism.*

During the post-observation interview, the teacher noted that her intended outcomes were personal and social development issues such as empathising with characters through playing them and their thoughts. She also focused on reinforcing the skills of 'thought tracking'. In the area of communication and expressive skills, she wanted pupils to analyse and explore the use of persuasion techniques used by the characters. She perceived the lesson as challenging, because the pupils had to consider characters' motivations while playing them.

When asked what they had learnt in the observed lesson, one pupil focused on the technical drama skills practised during the lesson, for example 'thought tracking'. This pupil said that he always enjoyed drama lessons and that it was his favourite subject. The other pupil focused on personal and social development issues – such as valuing others and having empathy, as well as on acquiring knowledge about social issues, in this case human rights and racism. They perceived the pace and level of the lesson as suitable. In addition, the post-observation interviews showed pupils recognising that the constant feedback, constructive criticism, acknowledgement and encouragement formed an integral and valuable part of their lessons:

> *Well, when we were doing something, and she thought something was good, she would actually say so. She would actually say whether it was good: 'I like that idea' etc.*

———

> *She does give us feedback and she lets us know and sometimes say if we are not [exploring] ideas properly. She will, like, help us out or give us ideas to play around with ... and if she has time we can show her ours ... and then she can, like, say comments about it, so we can make it better, or say if it's all right or not.*

School 2

13.5.4   School 2: the effects of drama education

School 2 received the highest nominations in several areas of the outcomes model. First, pupils made most mention of certain aspects of social development effects, in particular that of drama enhancing social opportunities ('*making new friends*' and '*talking to different people*'). Perhaps distinctive ways of grouping youngsters in drama lessons were significant here? There were examples of pupils from both key stage 3 and key stage 4 seeing drama as resulting in '*helping us know how another feels*': School 2 was the second highest ranking school (after School 1) to note this outcome.

In addition, the school had the most references to 'intrinsic' outcomes: enjoyment and particularly therapeutic effects (drama being associated with relaxation and becoming calm) were noted.

That drama resulted in being able to '*express yourself*' was another outcome particularly stated by pupils in School 2.

Specific knowledge and skills in drama were not greatly noted and neither were 'creative' outcomes. However, uniquely, two youngsters in Year 8 saw drama as: '*helping you to think*'.

Given the distinctive cluster of nominated outcomes, particularly around therapeutic effects and social development, School 2 became a case study selected for further investigation.

13.5.5   School 2: teaching approaches and context

This school has a wide catchment area, with the full spectrum of socio-economic status coming from the local town and its rural environs. It is perceived as a school where pupils can have a '*broad and interesting arts experience*'.

The focus of drama teaching is on the pupils' experience within the school rather than on extra-curricular productions. Still, the school production is seen as important also '*to display a bit of work that we do*' and '*to involve many pupils in those productions*'. The school has outreach projects with local primary schools as well as links with the local college, but it does not see community links as its priority. The drama teachers are involved with some local and national teacher networks; however, currently there is no involvement in drama productions outside the school context.

Both the head of drama and the observed teacher were specialist drama education graduates, with ongoing links with community arts and theatre in education. There were also two part-time arts teachers who teach some classes.

The school has '*state of the art*' facilities for the arts. Drama is grouped in a faculty structure with music. Pupils spend about an hour a week on drama and can take it up to GCSE level. The teachers again seemed to welcome the fact that drama was not a National Curriculum subject, as that freed pupils to do drama primarily to enjoy it and learn from it, without external pressures:

> *I think it's possibly got a positive effect. They have no SATs; they've got no pressure to kind of conform to a national norm. They just do this drama and they do it for themselves, they do it for the class and they do it for the school, and it's good.*

Still, the school has an arts policy document and drama lessons are planned to fulfil GCSE assessment criteria. Apart from that, the drama teachers prepare their own schemes of work which they share with each other and with other faculty colleagues.

3.
WHAT ARE
EFFECTIVE
PRACTICES
IN
ARTS
EDUCATION?

The school is supportive of the arts and there is a focus on quality:

> *... the school's very happy to be led – as long as it can be assured of quality – but it does trust you to get on with it and do it and I think that fosters good arts practice really because you need the kind of wide open opportunity, but you need the support as well.*

The observed drama teacher commented that because drama was seen to be successful, it contributed to the school management's support of the subject: '*The school bends over backwards really to accommodate us as the same status as everything else, partly because we're successful.*'

Teachers described the school as having a '*can do*' ethos for both pupils and teachers: '*a very positive feeling that people can do things, children can do things and staff can do things as well*'. School management was described as being appreciative and trusting:

> *They have provided the facilities and one of the things that I do very much value about the management is that they actually trust us to get on with it and they are not looking over our shoulders every five minutes. There is a trust that we are doing the job. That is not saying that they are not interested, and they don't take an interest in what we do ... but they think that we are professionals and we are doing the job.*

Drama was described as a means through which pupils could engage with the world around them, encouraging their questioning and analysis of that world. Importantly, pupils could also learn to '*enjoy praise*' through drama. The observed teacher saw the main outcomes of drama education as pupils' personal and social development and the acquisition of communication and expressive skills. Knowledge of the artform or technical skills were the vehicle through which pupils reach those outcomes:

> *I think you're doing a lot of things when you're educating in the arts. You're educating towards a better understanding of what life is like and a bit more of an idea of how groups of people can organise things and change things and develop things through the simulated activity of drama. So they're learning about life, but they're also learning it in quite a rigorously structured way and the artform element of that, I personally, find very exciting – the different forms in which you can express these ideas or explore these ideas within the classroom and the analysis of that...*

Drama was described as giving pupils a '*quiet*', '*inner*' confidence which was '*not necessarily about speaking loudly and being heard*', but about knowing that their ideas were seen as interesting and that, however they might share those ideas, they would be '*appreciated and understood*'. This confidence might manifest itself in a social context outside the classroom too, such as in pupils' increased participation and volunteering for things. Drama teaching, then, produced effects in the domains of personal and social development and the acquisition of communication and expressive skills, which could be transferred to pupils' lives outside school:

> *I would hope that they feel better about themselves in relation to other people and that they feel they can work with other people and that they've got an outlet for expressing themselves which makes them more relaxed about life, in control of life, and that they've got the artform in which they can be proud of, proud of what they've achieved. Because they've achieved it through a process of elimination and trial and error and time and working with other people, you'd hope those* [would] *transfer outside school.*

The drama teachers at School 2 acknowledged the importance of learning drama techniques to challenge pupils intellectually, but also to equip them with crucial communicative skills. One commented: '*Effective drama teaching has to be engaging and challenging, and stretching for pupils, if it is to have any meaning.*' Pupils should be '*fairly conversant with some dramatic technique and terminology*' and see the subject as one that '*involves thinking*' and that would require them to work, interact and be challenged. The learning of drama techniques gave pupils '*some ownership of the form*' that was necessary for them to engage with the teacher and other pupils in a creative way.

The observed teacher also embraced these views, seeing a connection between structured drama activity and a relaxed and trusting atmosphere in the classroom. Effective drama teaching was:

… very tightly structured, it's very disciplined, but within the discipline and the structure you can do anything you want and that's a real key. And it goes wrong if you give too much freedom, and it goes wrong if the child doesn't feel safe with the teacher and the rest of the class. So you are working quite a lot to create the right atmosphere because if you feel somebody's going to laugh at you, you're not going to do it or you're only going to do it to a certain tiny level. So, the conditions and the routines are very, very important.

A greater amount of structure might also be appropriate for Year 7 pupils who were not skilled in drama. One of the teaching aims in Year 7 was to break down some of the negative preconceived ideas pupils might have about drama: they:

… tend to come in quite nervous about drama and anxious that they won't be able to do it, particularly boys and shy girls who haven't been particularly good performers in the primary school and they tend to think that it's going to be about performance and they won't be able to do it. A lot of the boys think it's going to be boring because some of their experiences have been about repeating activities many times or following very precise scene structures from a radio programme or from a book of ideas about drama … So there's quite a lot of preconceived ideas which I do quite a bit of work to knock out really quite quickly.

To do this, the teaching focus in Year 7 was on how the pupils experienced drama and on making them feel comfortable, creating a 'can do' culture in the classroom. The observed teacher described an attitude change in 'sceptical' pupils quite soon after the first lesson, with pupils realising '*I can do this, I know, this is all right*'.

An emphasis on group work, preferably in groups of mixed gender, was noted. The observed teacher stated that she did not always allow friends to work together, which no doubt coincides with the pupil perception of 'meeting of new friends' as a significant outcome of drama in School 2. Similarly, the observed teacher noted how she planned activities in the lesson to maximise the benefits of using individual, group and whole class work: '*My initial tasks are usually designed to split people up and calm them down and be an individual before they get into the group.*' Perhaps this approach, very evident in the observed lesson, also accounts for the high number of references to 'therapeutic' effects made by School 2 pupils.

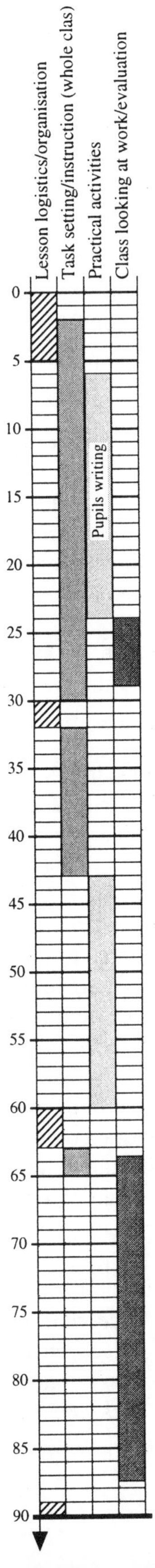

Chart axis labels (vertical timeline, 0–90 minutes):
- Lesson logistics/organisation
- Task setting/instruction (whole class)
- Practical activities
- Class looking at work/evaluation
- Pupils writing

13.5.6   School 2: the observed lesson

The lesson which was observed was a 90-minute session with Year 7 pupils. It took place in a specialist drama studio equipped with lighting. Some blocks and other props were around the edges of the room, but there were no chairs or tables.

The lesson started with pupils taking their shoes off and sitting in a circle on the floor. The teacher began by asking pupils to recap the previous lesson, which had considered the story of two World War Two evacuees. One of the pupils gave his synopsis, to which the teacher replied: '*Good ... Excellent.*' She continued to explain: '*We had the train journey and people being upset because they didn't want to leave their mums, but can we try and fill in a bit more detail now? ...*' The pupils continued to make suggestions, and the teacher asked questions in order to prompt them. This introduction led into the first task for the class, who were asked to move into a space in the class, individually.

The teacher provided a detailed description of the first task which the class were to undertake, explaining that she wanted them to imagine they were an evacuee who had just arrived at their new home, and to write a letter to their mother about their experiences of the first day there. She provided some ideas, and some explanation of the types of things that they might want to include. For example, she said:

> *Maybe you're in the same place as your brother or sister. Maybe you've been split up from your brother or sister. Maybe you're on your own ... maybe you're with another child – someone you've never known before – and you're going to have to share a room with them for goodness knows how long ...*

There was also discussion of issues which clearly related to history – why the letter would probably only be addressed to their mum, and how the blackout would probably mean the letter being written by candlelight. All the pupils were then given a piece of paper, and started to write, whilst the teacher continued to provide ideas and explanations of what they might want to write about. She also changed the lighting in the room, and lit a candle, to provide a more atmospheric situation.

At the end of the writing process, several of the pupils were chosen to read out what they had written, and the teacher gave positive feedback. The reading of the letters prompted discussion which progressed into description of the main drama task – in which the letters were going to be used. The teacher started by asking the pupils to organise themselves into

3.
WHAT ARE
EFFECTIVE
PRACTICES
IN
ARTS
EDUCATION?

groups of three, saying '*We're going to have two girls and a boy, or two boys and a girl in our threes*', and she provided direction where it was needed.

The teacher spent some time setting the scenario for their role play – where the adult whom the child evacuees were staying with came into their room at the end of the first day, and saw them writing their letters. She said:

> *... they are a bit concerned because you're still up, you've got the candle on and it's supposed to be sleep time, and they might read the letter – they might be angry with what they read, they might be upset with what they read ...*

The teacher added to this description by giving a brief demonstration of an adult's possible reaction to one of the pupils' letters. She said: '*When the man hears "the lady's nice, but her cooking's not very good", what do you think he would say, if he was just listening at the door ... what would he do?*' The pupils made their comments, and the teacher incorporated some of them into her demonstration. She then let the pupil groups get on with preparing their role play, telling them that they would be asked to perform them in about 15 minutes. One of the three pupils was to play the adult, and two were to play the roles of the evacuees.

Whilst the pupils started developing their ideas for their drama, the teacher moved around the classroom, observing what the pupils were doing, and occasionally talking to pupils, giving them ideas, or even demonstrating some alternative ways that a pupil could play a role. To one group she said: '*are you alright? ... have you got an idea?*'. To another she suggested: '*perhaps you could say ...*'. On two occasions during the practical the teacher stopped the class, and talked to them about issues arising – how they might be likely to act if they were meant to be asleep but were secretly writing letters, or how they could use props effectively.

After 17 minutes, the teacher instructed pupils to stop the group work, and the performances began. These were undertaken one at a time, in the central space. Each group performed around the lit candle in the darkened room. Blowing out the candle signified the end of their performance. The candle was then re-lit for each group.

After each of the role plays, the teacher provided a simple positive comment such as '*Good, well done*' or '*Excellent ... nice ending*'. However, after some performances, the teacher also asked general prompting questions such as '*What was good about that one?*' or more specific questions like '*What might Carrie have said to Nick when Mr*

Evans had gone out of the room ... what might she have said?' The pupils made their suggestions, and the teacher offered positive feedback and encouragement.

When all the groups had performed their role plays, the teacher requested that the lights be turned back up in the room. There was a brief discussion about the effect of using a candle – pupils suggesting how it had impacted on the atmosphere and their own performance. Then the teacher explained a quick exercise that would conclude the class:

> *... can we go round the class ... think about what you wrote in your own letter* [at the beginning of the lesson], *and imagine that you are the mother who reads the letter ... I'm just going to spotlight everybody ... what do you think when you read that letter from your son or daughter?*

The teacher moved round the circle of pupils, and as she passed each they provided a brief statement (in role) about how they would feel at the receipt of the letter. When the teacher reached her original starting point, she said: '*Excellent ... good. OK, now we need to tidy up ...*' Finally, the pupils tidied away all the blocks, and props, put their shoes back on, and left the class.

Activity	Time (mins)	Time as % of lesson time
Lesson logistics/organisation/housekeeping	11	12
Whole-class task setting/direct instruction	33	37
Pupils engaged in practical activities	17	19
Class looking at the work of others/evaluation	29	32

As noted earlier, the drama teachers at School 2 indicated that they saw drama as a means to help pupils '*engage with the world around them*', thereby '*hopefully developing them to analyse and communicate interactively with what is around them, and to question, and sometimes enjoy praise*'. These social and personal development effects could be seen being engineered in the observed lesson.

The lesson involved a carefully planned and structured series of activities that formed a unit in terms of topic, activity and pupils' thought processes. The teacher had used this lesson – indeed, this series of lessons – in previous years and adapted and refined it to suit Year 7 pupils. She felt that this lesson was relevant to the emotional needs of Year 7 pupils, as it touched '*on all sorts of anxieties that they*

3. WHAT ARE EFFECTIVE PRACTICES IN ARTS EDUCATION?

have, like what it's like to be picked and what it's like to stay with people you don't know, so I think it's a good one for them'. As such, the lesson fitted perfectly into the teacher's philosophy that structured drama activity contributed to enjoyment and a relaxed and trusting atmosphere in the classroom.

Like the previous observed lesson, this lesson was characterised by clear task-setting and ample opportunity for pupils to communicate and explore ideas relating to different aspects of the task, in groups as well as individually. The writing activity that the teacher had built into the lesson helped ensure that there would be a variety of activities to engage pupils and also no doubt cater for pupils' different levels of confidence.

3.
WHAT ARE
EFFECTIVE
PRACTICES
IN
ARTS
EDUCATION?

Apart from setting the three tasks during the various stages of the lesson, the teacher acted as a facilitator and adviser throughout, asking directive questions and/or offering input. She supervised every stage of the lesson without placing unnecessary constraints on pupils and monitored individual and group progress while pupils were engaged in practical activities – giving advice and input as required. She sometimes modelled and demonstrated a character's actions while moving between groups as pupils worked. Like the teacher at School 1, she continuously affirmed and praised pupils' efforts. She monitored and supervised pupils' performances and guided their analysis and evaluation of their work. The lesson was carefully paced so that pupils would have sufficient time to explore ideas in a variety of activities. The teacher gave frequent indications of the amount of time pupils had to complete certain activities. In the post-observation interviews, a pupil reported finding these 'timing landmarks' reassuring.

There were five brief instances during the lesson when the teacher had to address the behaviour of individual pupils or the class as a whole; however, this behaviour modification did not detract from the relaxed atmosphere in the classroom. The teacher ensured, for example, that the pupil she had to discipline was engaged in the class again soon by involving him in reading out the letter he had written and by giving him encouraging feedback:

> *I was very happy with the behaviour and I was happy with the way the boy who was being silly to the camera desperately didn't want to be alienated from whatever was going to happen, because I said 'Perhaps you'd be better if you sat out for a bit', and he said 'Oh no, no. I'll be fine'. Then I tried to give him quite a bit of positive feedback then, for the rest of the lesson, to show that he wasn't a naughty boy, because I think sometimes in drama if you, if they think they're naughty boys, then they behave like them. I was trying to show that, and he is quite good. He's just a bit exuberant, I suppose.*

The intended outcomes for the lesson, as stated by the observed teacher, concerned pupils' personal and social development, the development of their communication and expressive skills and the acquisition of performance skills and knowledge of stagecraft. These outcomes were addressed in the lesson. Personal and social development issues, such as empathising with characters and thinking about the effects of utterances on others, were explored:

> *Then the learning about life, that people don't always say what they feel, that it's not always appropriate to say what you feel. That something that you say and express can affect others in different ways.*

The lesson focused on communication and expressive skills such as the use of tone of voice to create atmosphere and to enhance performance. The simple use of a candle in a variety of ways guided pupils in the use of lighting in theatre performance.

For the teacher, the main focus of the lesson was not, however, stagecraft or even the pupils' performances, but the understanding of emotions, which was why she introduced a follow-up activity:

> *I thought 'We've spent so long performing these', I didn't want to leave it just on the learning about performance or that the goal of the lesson was just to perform your piece as opposed to understanding the issues and the feelings and I wanted to get back to that so that's why I did the quick once round.*

Pupils at this school reported that they derived great enjoyment from drama teaching, and it is probable that the 'structured freedom' they had, the constant engagement with tasks and the amount of affirmation, praise and encouragement they received in the drama classroom contributed to that sense of enjoyment. Pupils mentioned that they found feedback helpful: '*After we did our role plays she told us what was good about them and how we could improve it.*'

When asked what they learnt in, or got from, the observed lesson, pupils again focused on personal and social development issues, mentioning especially how much they learnt from working in groups in which they do not usually work: '*Well, I've never acted with just boys before because usually I'm, like, nervous to work with boys but now I'm more confident about it.*' They also mentioned learning how to create atmosphere by using the voice in different ways and by manipulating lighting.

13.5.7   *Concluding remarks*

Activity	Time spent (in mins and as % of lesson length)	
	School 1	School 2
Lesson logistics/organisation/housekeeping	6 (11%)	11 (12%)
Whole-class task setting/direct instruction	13 (24%)	33 (37%)
Pupils engaged in practical activities	18 (33%)	17 (19%)
Class looking at the work of others/evaluation	18 (33%)	29 (10%)

The methods of drama teaching at these schools have much in common. One of the most striking similarities was the constant pupil engagement in drama classrooms. Both of the observed lessons were characterised by high levels of pupil activity throughout. This activity was tightly structured, but allowed pupils much freedom to express their own ideas in a way that they found suitable. Another commonality was the focus of teachers on pupils' personal and social development as well as on pupils' acquisition of expressive and communication skills. The learning and use of stagecraft skills were seen as a means towards an end, the end being more effective and confident personal expression.

The classroom ambience in both these cases could be described as relaxed, though there was a detectable 'buzz' in the classroom with pupils obviously engaged in an activity and deriving enjoyment from it. The use of group work, and also individual and class work, provided variety and an opportunity for pupils with different degrees of self confidence to be successful. In both lessons, activities were structured to form a unit that gave the lesson a feeling of closure and satisfaction towards the end.

Another noticeable similar feature was the constant feedback which pupils received during activities. This was sometimes in the form of peer analysis and evaluation under the guidance of the teacher. At other times, the teacher

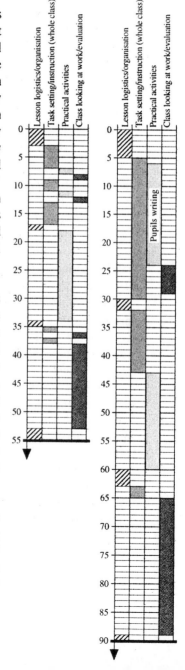

herself gave the feedback. In both lessons, this was always positive and constructive, affirming and praising pupils' efforts, but still giving guidance as to how their work could be improved. These features appear to be common to the 'praise culture' and 'engagement' theme that runs through effective teaching of the arts.

13.6 CONCLUSION

This chapter has attempted to show the rich variation and also distinctive similarities between the learning activities that are offered to pupils by four artforms. Looking across the eight illustrated and contextualised lessons, the following emerge as common features.

First, all of the arts teachers were, as individuals, given support and recognition by their senior management team. Individual prowess was well known and acknowledged. Notwithstanding this, there did seem considerable contrast in the degree of investment in specialist facilities. Resources sometimes available in art, music and drama were not matched in dance, although, in both of the case study schools selected, the act of appointing PE staff with a dance specialism was seen as a distinct statement of senior management commitment to developing that artform.

3.
WHAT ARE
EFFECTIVE
PRACTICES
IN
ARTS
EDUCATION?

The second common feature of these observed case study teachers was their intense commitment to teaching their artform. That commitment invariably included a personal interest and enthusiasm for their subject, but even more, the sheer enjoyment of teaching young people seemed particularly evident. It is perhaps this synergy of artistic and pedagogical skill that suffuses the observed lessons. In all instances, the pupils seemed jointly and inseparably engaged in the process of learning *with* their teacher: cooperation and commonality were apparent. Lessons seemed organic, with all participants fulfilling individual roles that made a greater whole. Teachers modelled and engaged directly with the art form and pupils seamlessly.

Moreover, as previously noted, a further common aspect of these lessons was the constant discourse of praise and encouragement, which was also well recognised by the pupils. This 'praise culture' nevertheless still provided support and direction for improved attainment: it was, in counselling terms, a 'high-challenge/high-support' model of interaction. 'Unconditional positive regard' might be another counselling term to borrow in order to define the distinctive ambience of these arts lessons. Implicit within that ambience is the notion of 'respect', and it might be that one of the essential factors in arts teaching relates to this esteem which teachers convey about their pupils' products and performances.

A final common component of these arts lessons relates to their construction and overall execution. The four 'movements' of an arts lesson – logistics, teacher instruction, practical activities and performance – were in evidence in each, but the different art forms produced differing calibrations of these lesson components.

Both drama lessons spent about a third of their allotted time in performance and evaluation; both dance sessions used about ten per cent of the lesson on this component. In all observations, art and music had considerably more 'logistics' (between a fifth and a half of a session). These differences perhaps exemplify the need for sympathetic timetabling for the arts as individual artforms, rather than as a homogenous group, an issue which was highlighted by arts teachers in Chapter 12.

Time allocated to 'task-setting' was very much lower in both art sessions than other artforms.

Independent practical activity might vary in time allocation (indeed from one-fifth to over four-fifths of a lesson) but the presence of the teacher, demonstrating and developing the discourse of their art form, was always in evidence.

The observations show young people are learning an arts language as well as its skills as they work with their teachers in that special relationship and ambience which appears to be a characteristic of arts lessons.

14. EFFECTIVENESS: A WIDER PICTURE

CHAPTER OVERVIEW

**By drawing on evidence from the 22 schools involved in the Year
11 Survey, this chapter widens the discussion of factors that affect
the quality of arts provision in secondary schools. It discusses
issues in the following areas:**

- **variations in the rates at which pupils enrol for GCSE arts
  courses (14.2)**

- **factors which affect pupils' choices of arts subjects at key
  stage 4 (14.3)**

- **pupil attitudes to arts subjects (14.4)**

- **pupils' views on their parents' interest in the arts (14.5)**

- **pupils' views on their parents' participation in the arts (14.6)**

- **parental support for the arts (14.7)**

- **pupils' extra-curricular involvement in the arts (14.8).**

3.
WHAT ARE
EFFECTIVE
PRACTICES
IN
ARTS
EDUCATION?

14.1 INTRODUCTION

The previous two chapters within this report dealing with the
effectiveness of teaching and learning in the arts have presented data
extracted from the five case study schools. In Chapter 12 this was
presented as a typology of interviewees' perceptions of the factors
involved, and in Chapter 13 specific examples from observed lessons
in each of the artforms were described. This chapter seeks to broaden
the debate by considering data from the questionnaire completed by
2,269 Year 11 pupils from 22 schools. It also widens the discussion by
addressing a number of issues which have not been focused upon in the
previous two chapters and yet which are germane to any consideration
of effective arts practices in secondary schools.

Although some of the results from the Year 11 survey concerning
effects were presented in Part Two of this report, some questions on the
questionnaire were clearly pertinent to the discussion of effectiveness
within secondary arts education provision. Therefore, the issues which
are described in the remainder of this chapter are:

- enrolment on to GCSE arts courses;

- factors affecting pupils' choice of arts subjects at key stage 4;

- pupil attitudes towards arts subjects;

- pupils' views on their parents' interest and support for the arts; and

- extra-curricular involvement in the arts.

14.2 ENROLMENT ON TO GCSE ARTS COURSES

Firstly, on the questionnaire, pupils were asked to circle the subjects that they were taking for GCSE. It is suggested here that a school's success in recruiting pupils on to GCSE arts courses may be one measure of the pupils' perceptions of the value of an arts education, or the effectiveness of arts teaching at their school.

Art was the arts subject most frequently taken, circled by nearly a third of the sample (32 per cent). Drama was taken by 14 per cent (under half the number that took art), and even fewer enrolled for music (eight per cent). Very few pupils took dance (three per cent) and expressive arts (one per cent). These figures are considerably lower than the numbers taking other non-core subjects such as technology (71 per cent), French (61 per cent), history (40 per cent), geography (39 per cent), and also, for the most part, lower than business studies (25 per cent), PE (23 per cent), German (22 per cent) and RE (19 per cent). This picture of the percentages studying the arts at key stage 4 was not improved by considering the numbers following non-GCSE arts courses, since none of the arts subjects had more than 0.5 per cent of the sample taking it for a qualification other than GCSE, and likewise for no qualification at all.

The sample's rates of enrolment on the main GCSE arts courses corresponded quite closely to national trends for the full population of key stage 4 students. For example, as a proportion of the total number of 15-year-olds in English educational establishments at the start of the 1996/97 academic year (N = 586,766), 34 per cent were entered (at the end of the 1996/97 academic year) for art (compared to 32 per cent for our 1997/98 sample), 14 per cent were entered for drama (the same as our sample) and seven per cent were entered for music (compared to eight per cent for our sample) (GB. DfEE, 1998). The similarity between these results gives grounds for confidence that the sample is broadly representative of the Year 11 student population as a whole.

3.
WHAT ARE
EFFECTIVE
PRACTICES
IN
ARTS
EDUCATION?

Table 14.1   Percentages of Year 11 pupils taking GCSE art courses, by gender

	Art		Dance		Drama		Expressive arts		Music		Total sample	
	%	N	%	N	%	N	%	N	%	N	%	N
Female	53	374	90	67	71	216	54	12	62	108	56	1231
Male	47	327	10	7	29	89	46	10	38	67	44	982
(N=)	100	701	100	74	100	305	100	22	100	175	100	2213

Source: NFER 'The Effects and Effectiveness of Arts Education' Year 11 Survey student questionnaire

Table 14.1 shows that, taking account of the percentages of male and female pupils in the whole sample, proportionately more females than males were taking music, drama and dance at GCSE, particularly drama and dance. A similar breakdown of the results by social class revealed that, in relation to their numbers within the whole sample, middle-class students were more frequently enrolled on drama courses than their counterparts from other social classes.

Moving on to look at the ethnicity of those that chose art subjects at GCSE, it can be seen from Table 14.2 that, compared to the overall percentage of non-whites (14 per cent), dance and especially expressive arts attracted a high proportion of non-white students (with percentages of 19 and 29 per cent respectively) – although the low numbers taking these subjects mean that the results must be interpreted with great caution. Music had the lowest percentage of non-white students.

3.
WHAT ARE
EFFECTIVE
PRACTICES
IN
ARTS
EDUCATION?

Table 14.2   Percentages of Year 11 pupils taking GCSE arts courses, by ethnicity

	Art		Dance		Drama		Expressive arts		Music		Total sample	
	%	N	%	N	%	N	%	N	%	N	%	N
Non-white	14	96	19	13	16	49	29	6	12	22	14	301
White	86	597	81	56	84	254	71	15	88	154	86	1916
(N=)	100	693	100	69	100	303	100	21	100	176	100	2217

Source: NFER 'The Effects and Effectiveness of Arts Education' Year 11 Survey student questionnaire

Having set the scene with some basic frequencies, it is important to stress that the percentages of pupils doing drama, dance and expressive arts appear artificially low as they are percentages of the whole sample of pupils, many of whom had no opportunity to take the subject at GCSE level because it was not offered by the school they attended. For these subjects, it is therefore more valid to look at the percentages of pupils that selected the option as a proportion of the numbers who were offered it. Examined in this way, the percentages for art and music, which, like many of the non-arts subjects, are normally offered to all pupils, can be more appropriately compared with figures of 18 per cent for drama, 18 per cent for expressive arts and 14 per cent for dance. Thus, once the availability of a subject is taken into account, expressive arts, dance and drama, whilst considerably less popular than art, were more frequently chosen at GCSE than the raw frequencies imply. However, the comparative popularity of art is still clearly apparent and the lack of enthusiasm for GCSE music is even more pronounced. (Two schools actually did not offer music: however, taking this into account, the percentage of those offered music that were taking it remained rounded off at eight per cent.)

For the same reasons, analyses were carried out to compare the social class, ethnicity and gender of pupils taking the different arts as a proportion of the social class, ethnicity and gender of those offered the subject rather than of the whole sample. For all three variables, however, the results were similar to the trends displayed above.

14.2.1 Variation by attainment

It has been suggested that the rate of take-up of GCSE arts courses may be related to different levels of general academic attainment. In addition, reactions to the multilevel modelling analysis outlined in the present study's interim report (Harland *et al.*, 1998) included anecdotal evidence from some teachers and advisers which pointed to a close association between the taking of more than one arts subject and lower academic attainment. Both of these propositions received firm empirical support from the survey data.

The average (mean) key stage 3 scores for pupils taking different arts subjects were calculated and the results are displayed in Table 14.3.

Table 14.3   The average key stage 3 results of pupils taking different arts subjects

	Art + no other arts		Drama + + no other arts		Music + + no other arts		Music + one or more arts		No arts	
	Mean	*N*	Mean	*N*	Mean	*N*	Mean	*N*	Mean	*N*
KS3 English	4.89	*454*	4.91	*175*	5.40	*90*	4.55	*29*	4.93	*785*
KS3 Maths	4.96	*437*	5.09	*170*	5.33	*93*	4.54	*28*	5.01	*789*
KS3 Science	4.88	*460*	4.94	*172*	5.22	*92*	4.52	*33*	4.81	*789*

Source: NFER 'The Effects and Effectiveness of Arts Education' Year 11 Survey: key stage 3 results provided by participating schools

Clearly, pupils taking music (and no other arts subject) had substantially higher mean scores in English, mathematics and science than any other group in the analysis, including those who chose not to enrol for any arts subject. Those taking more than one arts subject, even including music, had the lowest mean scores in all three subjects compared to the other groups. Both these findings give further credence to the view that the associations apparent in the initial multilevel modelling analysis reflect variations in the type of students selecting different options rather than any purported impact of arts-related courses on general GCSE performance. As in Chapter 12, this data supports the pupils' perception that their own background and predisposition impacted on the effectiveness of the arts education they experienced. Contrary to expectations, the table also shows that the group opting for drama did not have higher than average scores in English. Those doing art had mean scores very close to the scores of those taking no arts subjects at all.

14.2.2 Variation between schools

Perhaps the most striking findings in this section were the substantial differences in the proportions of pupils taking arts subjects at different schools. Table 14.4 attempts to illustrate this by showing the range of percentage take-up for art, drama and music.

Table 14.4 The range of percentages taking arts subjects in different schools

	Art		Drama		Music	
	%	N	%	N	%	N
Lowest	14		4		3	
Highest	57		61		21	
Overall	32	716	14	307	8	179

Source: NFER 'The Effects and Effectiveness of Arts Education' Year 11 Survey: key stage 3 results provided by participating schools

3.
WHAT ARE
EFFECTIVE
PRACTICES
IN
ARTS
EDUCATION?

The rate of take-up in art, for example, varied by a factor of four. However, since four schools posted percentages over 50, the 57 per cent registered by the school with the highest share taking art cannot be dismissed as a freak result. Interestingly, in only one of these four schools was there a compulsory requirement to opt for at least one arts subject. In contrast, three schools had less than 20 per cent taking art.

A school with 61 per cent studying drama was an exceptional result and perhaps it is significant that this school had a compulsory arts policy at key stage 4. The next highest were three schools that had percentages of between 29 and 33 per cent taking drama and one of these also required students to select an arts subject.

The rate of enrolment for music varied by a factor of seven. Six schools, including two in which at least one arts subject was obligatory, had percentages of 13 per cent or over. On the other hand, seven had percentages of five or less.

Too many schools did not offer dance to permit a meaningful analysis, but of those that did, one school had 15 per cent of its pupils studying the subject and four schools had ten per cent or over. Again this included two of the three schools with a compulsory arts policy.

Of the 22 schools, five schools had consistently high rates of take-up across most of the arts, as well as the highest percentages taking at least one arts subject at key stage 4. These five schools included the three where at least one arts subject was required of all pupils; in two others there was no such requirement. Hence, it appears that whilst compulsory requirements can increase enrolment across the board, high involvement in the arts can still be achieved without it. For example, a school without any such requirement was the only one to appear in the top three places for rates of pupils taking up art, dance, drama and music. This was an inner city, multiethnic all-girls school with a fairly high free school meal ratio (33 per cent) and a faculty structure for the performing arts and art.

14.2.3 Opting out of the arts at GCSE

It was found that half (49 per cent) of the pupil sample were not taking any arts subject at GCSE; conversely, 51 per cent of the pupils were studying at least one arts subject. The characteristics of these two groups were analysed in order to identify the type of pupils most likely to fall into either category.

It was apparent, for example, that those pupils who went to urban schools stood out as being most likely to have opted out of taking any arts subjects – 63 per cent chose this option. This can be compared to 37 per cent of pupils from suburban schools, 40 per cent from inner city schools, 43 per cent of rural schools, and 50 per cent of pupils from small/medium sized towns. Similar comparisons for social class and attainment in key stage 3 tests produced no significant differences between the two groups.

Males were very slightly more likely not to be doing any arts than females – 48 per cent of those doing no arts were males, compared to 44 per cent in the sample as a whole.

Not surprisingly, pupils in the non-arts group were more likely to see the arts as relatively unimportant. As will be described more fully in section 14.4.4, pupils were asked to indicate how important the arts were to them by circling one of the following – 'very important', 'quite important', 'not very important' or 'not important at all'. Of those not doing any arts at GCSE, 60 per cent considered that the arts were either not very important or not important at all, whereas 19 per cent of those that were doing one or more arts subjects responded negatively. Of equal significance, however, is the fact that 40 per cent of those not taking an arts subject considered them quite or very important. This prompts the crucial question as to why, if the arts were deemed to be relevant and meaningful to them, they were not studying an arts subject at key stage 4. To explore this and similar issues, we consider next the various factors that appear to have influenced pupils' arts-related option choices at the end of key stage 3.

14.3 FACTORS AFFECTING PUPILS' CHOICE OF ARTS SUBJECTS AT KEY STAGE 4

This section considers pupils' reasons for actively choosing to study the arts at key stage 4. However, it also examines whether there is an unmet pupil demand for arts subjects which could be addressed, and the broader reasons pupils gave for opting out of the arts.

14.3.1 Reasons for choosing arts subjects

One item in the student questionnaire explored the reasons behind pupils' choice of arts subjects for GCSE. Derived from the pilot interviews, 11 possible reasons (including an 'other reason') were proposed and pupils were asked to circle as many as were applicable. The results for art, dance, drama and music are presented in Table 14.5.

Without doubt, the most common reason for studying each of the artforms was 'for personal interest and enjoyment'. Approximately four-fifths of the pupils taking each of the artforms nominated it as a reason. It is a matter of speculation as to whether such intrinsic motives would be so prominent in other areas of the curriculum. It also seems pertinent to enquire about the implications of such perceptions and expectations of the arts for the ways in which they may be taught in secondary schools. In support of this factor, Chapter 12 described the weight which pupils attached to their own enjoyment of an arts lesson in determining its effectiveness.

The second most common reason for choosing each of the arts subjects was 'because I'm good at it' – the talent factor – which was circled by approximately three-fifths of each of the four subsamples. Again, pupils identified their own arts talent as a factor in the effectiveness of arts lessons (see 12.8.1) – also clearly supporting their belief that some natural talent in the artform was a prerequisite for choosing it at key stage 4.

Less common, but still proving the third most important motive for choosing each of the four artforms was 'because it may lead to a career'. Around a third (32–36 per cent) of pupils taking art, dance or music circled this reason. It was particularly important for those opting for drama, with 42 per cent of drama GCSE students nominating this reason.

Table 14.5   Percentages of pupils taking each art subject at GCSE, who circled a particular reason for opting for it

	Art %	Dance %	Drama %	Music %
Advice from parents	16	14	15	27
Advice from school	19	26	18	27
For personal interest and enjoyment	81	77	85	84
Because it may lead to a career	34	32	42	36
Because of the teacher teaching it	5	11	14	7
Because I'm good at it	62	54	59	59
Because there wasn't much choice/ limited options	15	5	14	12
Because there was no choice/ school required me to take it	1	1	1	1
Because it's an easy option	16	4	12	9
Because friends chose it	8	10	11	6
Other	1	1	1	3
No response	7	11	5	5
(N) =	(716)	(74)	(307)	(179)

Source: NFER 'The Effects and Effectiveness of Arts Education' Year 11 Survey student questionnaire
NB Respondents could give more than one response, so percentages will not sum to 100 per cent.

3.
WHAT ARE
EFFECTIVE
PRACTICES
IN
ARTS
EDUCATION?

Of the other reasons, 'advice from school' proved a fairly influential factor, affecting 18–27 per cent of pupils' decisions to take a particular art subject, with music and dance being the highest in this range of percentages. 'Advice from parents' also played a part in a significant proportion of pupils' choices, with 14–16 per cent of those taking art, drama or dance giving this as a reason for selecting the subject. Moreover, for music, parental advice appears especially influential – with 27 per cent of pupils mentioning it as a factor. With reference to music, the comparatively high percentages for both school and parental advice are particularly interesting, given the limited numbers who enrol for the subject and the bias it displays towards higher academic performance. Does this suggest that both schools and parents appear to be more likely to encourage pupils (particularly those of higher academic ability) to opt for music above any other artform?

The fact that a particular teacher was taking the subject at GCSE influenced only a small proportion of pupils in their choice of a particular arts subject, with 4–14 per cent of pupils circling this reason. Although the low frequencies warrant caution, it is interesting to note that the influence of a particular teacher on subject choice proved most positive in drama and dance, and least significant in art.

'Because there was no choice/school required me to take it' was an insignificant factor, though 'because there wasn't much choice/limited options' did affect 12–15 per cent of pupils' decisions for art, drama or music. 'Because it was an easy option' was least common for dance (four per cent) and music (nine per cent), but most common for art (16 per cent). Additionally, friends choosing the arts subject affected between 6 and 11 per cent of pupils' decisions to take it (music being the subject with the lowest percentage in the range). 'Other' reasons included *'helps you relax'*, *'a break from normal lessons'*, *'helps communication'* and *'it's practical'*.

14.3.2 The unmet demand for arts at key stage 4

For each of the artforms, pupils were asked *'If you are not currently taking any of the subjects listed below, would you like to be taking any of them?'* It appears that 45 per cent of these Year 11 pupils either did not respond to the question or did not wish to be taking arts subjects other than those they were taking. Notably, however, 55 per cent of the sample would have liked to have been taking at least one, or an additional arts subject. This means that over half of the full sample of pupils had unfulfilled wishes in terms of arts education provision at their school, or in the key stage 4 curriculum.

3.
WHAT ARE
EFFECTIVE
PRACTICES
IN
ARTS
EDUCATION?

Drama was the subject that the greatest number of pupils (22 per cent of the whole sample) would like to have been doing, but weren't; 17 per cent would like to have been taking dance; 17 per cent would like to have been taking art; 14 per cent music, and seven per cent expressive arts. Expressed as percentages of those not taking the subject who would like to be doing it, it was revealed that one in four of those not taking drama would like to have done so; the same ratio was evident for art; one in six for dance; and one in seven for music.

Girls were slightly more likely to express a desire to be taking additional arts subjects than boys. Of those wanting to do more arts, 64 per cent were female and 36 per cent were male, which can be compared to the 56:44 per cent female:male ratio of the sample. Most of the male requests for more arts were for art, drama or music, whilst most of the female responses were for drama and dance. Artforms exhibiting large gender differences with respect to this question proved to be drama, dance and expressive arts: amongst those pupils who would like to have been doing dance, drama or expressive arts, girls were much more common, especially with regard to dance – 94 per cent were girls, only six per cent were boys.

The overall level of unmet demand for the arts at key stage 4 begs the question why, when so many pupils would like to study more arts courses, such small proportions are actually taking them. The next section offers some possible answers to this question from the pupils' perspective.

14.3.3 Reasons for not taking the arts

Pupils who indicated that they were not taking an arts subject yet would have liked to have done so, were then asked to answer '*What stopped you from being able to take it this year?*' by circling as many reasons as were applicable from a list of seven (including 'other'). The results are set out in Table 14.6.

Table 14.6   Percentages of pupils not taking each art subject at GCSE who circled a particular reason for not opting for it

3.
WHAT ARE
EFFECTIVE
PRACTICES
IN
ARTS
EDUCATION?

	Art	Dance	Drama	Expressive arts	Music
	%	%	%	%	%
Subject not available at my school	1	64	35	74	8
Advice from parents	11	5	8	4	10
I feel other subjects are more important	48	33	42	18	47
Advice from the school	3	2	3	1	4
Clashes with other subjects on the timetable/options	37	16	23	14	36
I'm not very good at it	31	12	15	7	25
Other	1	2	2	2	4
No response	8	5	8	5	8
(N) =	(374)	(378)	(506)	(169)	(310)

Source: NFER 'The Effects and Effectiveness of Arts Education' Year 11 Survey student questionnaire
NB Respondents could give more than one response, so percentages will not sum to 100 per cent.

There appeared to be three major deterrents for taking art. In rank order, these were: 'I feel other subjects are more important', 'clashes with other subjects on the timetable' and 'I'm not very good at it'. This suggests that pupils face at least three kinds of potential barriers when considering whether or not to act upon their desire to take art: the perceived lack of relevance and status of the subject, unsympathetic timetable and option structures, and a talent or skills barrier. In addition, 'advice from parents' (selected by 11 per cent) was a relatively high factor for art.

Almost exactly the same could be said for music, though here, somewhat contrary to expectations, the talent or skills barrier was slightly less evident than in art. There was some evidence to suggest that non-white pupils were more likely to point to the skills barrier as a reason for not opting for music than their white counterparts. The only additional significant factor was the unavailability of the subject, primarily due to two schools not offering music at key stage 4.

For dance, the key obstacle was undoubtedly the lack of provision: almost two-thirds (64 per cent) of those not taking dance indicated that this option was not available at their school. As a consequence of this, the percentages citing 'I feel other subjects are more important' and 'clashes with other subjects on the timetable' naturally fell, but relative to the limited availability of dance, they still represent significant barriers. It is difficult to establish whether the lower percentage circling 'I'm not very good at it' implies that a skills barrier is less of a problem for dance than other artforms, although it is clear that many pupils would have had insufficient experience of dance education to determine their own level of ability.

Expressive arts followed the same pattern as dance, but with more extremes. Nominations for unavailability were higher, with corresponding falls in 'I feel other subjects are more important' and 'clashes with other subjects on the timetable'.

So, whilst art and music produced a very similar profile of reasons for not taking them, dance and expressive arts together exhibited another profile (though expressive arts was more extreme). Drama displayed a pattern of reasons which resembled a mixture of the two types of profile. It clearly had an availability problem, as well as slightly reduced versions of the three barriers identified for art and music (namely, unsympathetic option structures, a perceived lack of relevance and status for the subject, and a talent or skills barrier). To this extent, of all the artforms studied, drama faced elements of all the apparent major problems.

14.4 PUPIL ATTITUDES TO ARTS SUBJECTS

As was clearly evidenced in Chapter 12, pupil attitudes towards arts subjects were considered, by pupils in particular, to be an important factor in the effectiveness of arts education provision in secondary schools. Their attitudes also partially account for their choice of subjects at key stage 4. For this reason, pupils attitudes towards the arts were examined as part of the Year 11 pupil questionnaire.

14.4.1 Favourite and least liked subjects

Pupils were asked to select from their current Year 11 curriculum their two favourite subjects and the two they least liked. As most liked across all subjects (arts and non-arts), English (23 per cent) and science (21 per cent) topped the rankings, but art was the third most popular, with nearly a fifth (19 per cent) of the total sample nominating it as one of their two favourite subjects. Mathematics and PE were not far behind. Drama was mentioned by nine per cent, though music, with only four per cent nominating it, was the lowest of all the National Curriculum foundation subjects.

The arts in general were rarely put forward as least liked subjects: music and art were both cited by two per cent and drama by one per cent. The most frequently least liked subjects were French (registered by 34 per cent of the sample and with only a comparatively small percentage nominating it as one of their favourites), mathematics and science (both mentioned by 32 per cent of pupils).

The responses to these questions are obviously more informative as percentages of those taking the subject, rather than as percentages of the whole sample. Looked at in this way, the arts are amongst the most appreciated areas of the key stage 4 curriculum. The popularity of art, for instance, was apparent from the fact that 62 per cent of those taking the subject proposed it as one of their two favourite subjects and only six per cent of those taking it mentioned it as one of their two least liked subjects. Drama did slightly better: 69 per cent of those taking it gave it as one of their favourites and six per cent as one of their least liked. Dance also scored well, with corresponding figures of 57 per cent and three per cent. Music, though still popular with those taking the subject when compared to mathematics and science, for example, was markedly less well liked when compared to the other arts with 45 per cent of those taking it proposing it as one of their favourite subjects and 13 per cent as one of their least.

14.4.2 Perceptions of relative performance and ability

The pupils of the Year 11 sample were also asked to identify the two subjects which they felt they were 'best at'. For art, dance and drama, about half of those taking the subject (49–55 per cent) felt it was one of the two subjects they were best at. The corresponding results for music and expressive arts were lower (40 per cent and 35 per cent respectively).

Interestingly, the percentages of pupils selecting an arts subject as one of the two subjects they felt most able in were generally higher than those for non-arts subjects. Of the latter, the ones with the highest percentages of pupils who felt it was one of the two subjects they were 'best at' (as a percentage of those taking the subject) were IT (42 per cent), business studies (36 per cent), English (27 per cent) and geography (26 per cent). French was noticeably low at 11 per cent. With 57 per cent of pupils nominating it, PE was the only non-arts subject to exceed the percentages for art, drama, and dance.

The reason for the high percentages of pupils nominating the arts as the subjects in which they feel most able may relate to their motives and perceptions underlying their option choices at the end of key stage 3. Given that the arts were widely perceived by pupils to be relatively unimportant subjects, there could be a greater likelihood that more pupils who have a particular flare or talent in an artform decide to opt for it than is the case with other subjects. It has also been identified that the primary reason given by pupils for choosing a subject was their own enjoyment of it, followed closely by their own talent or ability in the artform. In contrast, other subjects may recruit pupils not necessarily because they feel especially competent in them, but because they are compelled to or feel obliged to because the subjects carry currency for academic and career advancement. In other words, comparatively more pupils take the arts because of the skills and talent factor than a relevance factor. Therefore, two potential methods for encouraging more pupils to continue their arts education into key stage 4 seem clear: providing more confidence in the development of knowledge and skills throughout earlier key stages and encouraging greater awareness of the practical, creative and intellectual relevance of the arts.

Generally for all arts subjects, there was a close correlation between pupils listing the subject as one of their two favourites and nominating it as one of the two they were 'best at'. Without exception, for all arts subjects, 78–89 per cent of those who felt the subject was one of the two they were 'best at' also felt it was one of their favourite subjects. This equates well with the description of pupil perceptions in Chapter 12 – where pupils identified effective arts lessons as those which they enjoyed, and related their enjoyment of a lesson to their ability and achievement in the subject.

14.4.3 Enjoyment of arts subjects at key stage 4

Pupils were asked to circle whether, for each of the arts subjects they took, they enjoyed their lessons 'always', 'most of the time', 'sometimes', 'hardly ever' or 'never'. The overall results are set out in Table 14.7, where for ease of presentation the first and second, and the fourth and fifth categories have been merged.

Table 14.7   Pupils' enjoyment of arts lessons at key stage 4: percentages of pupils taking a GCSE arts subject

	Art	Dance	Drama	Music
	%	%	%	%
Always/most of the time	76	73	84	65
Sometimes	16	12	10	21
Hardly ever/never	2	0	2	9
No response	6	15	4	5
(N) =	(716)	(74)	(307)	(179)

Source: NFER 'The Effects and Effectiveness of Arts Education' Year 11 Survey student questionnaire

Overall, drama appeared to be the arts subject most frequently enjoyed, followed by art and dance. In line with the findings on pupils' favourite subjects, music had the lowest percentage enjoying it 'always or most of the time' and the highest indicating enjoyment 'hardly ever or never'.

In all arts subjects, females were more likely than males to indicate that they enjoyed lessons 'always or most of the time' and males were more likely than females to indicate that they enjoyed the lessons only 'sometimes' or 'hardly ever or never'. This gender difference, however, was particularly marked for drama, less apparent for dance than art, and slightly less for music.

The level of enjoyment varied substantially across the 22 schools. Art lessons in one school, for example, were considered enjoyable 'always or most of the time' by 96 per cent of the subsample taking art, whereas the corresponding figure in another school was 57 per cent. It is interesting to note that, of the five schools mentioned earlier for posting high percentages taking most artforms, only one (the all-girls inner city school) was placed in the top five rankings for enjoyment in art – it was actually ranked second with 92 per cent indicating that lessons were enjoyable 'always or most of the time'. The remaining four – including the three schools where there was a compulsory requirement to take at least one arts subject – had only average to below average scores for enjoyment in art. At least as far as art was concerned, there seemed to be a risk of a trade-off between the achievement of high or universal involvement in arts courses and the level of enjoyment experienced by all pupils. In achieving both goals, only one school appeared to have avoided sacrificing one for the other.

Music also displayed great variation across schools, though here the much lower numbers taking music in many schools made it easier for some to register high percentage scores. It was still conspicuous, however, that none of the five schools with high involvement in the arts across the board figured in the top eight places for high level of pupil enjoyment. Furthermore, the seven highest schools had groups of ten or less taking music. Clearly, the challenge of recruiting sizeable numbers, while simultaneously offering a sustained enjoyable learning experience for pupils, seemed especially acute for music teachers. It may also suggest that while 84 per cent of pupils doing music had apparently chosen to take it because of their personal interest or enjoyment of the artform, they found that the actual experience of music lessons at key stage 4 did not meet their original expectations.

**3.
WHAT ARE
EFFECTIVE
PRACTICES
IN
ARTS
EDUCATION?**

Although again exhibiting wide variations across the schools, dance and drama differed from art and music in so far as the top two rankings on the enjoyment scale for both subjects went to three schools from the five with high arts involvement. Of all the artforms, drama seemed capable of attracting significant numbers, while registering very high enjoyment scores, frequently in schools with a large-scale investment in the arts generally. Only drama, for example, had equivalent percentages nominating enjoyment levels of 'always or most of the time' from schools with and without a compulsory requirement for at least one arts subject at key stage 4. For art, dance and music, the corresponding percentages were lower from schools with such a requirement.

Endorsing a finding from the early phase of the qualitative research (Harland *et al.*, 1998), it appears that schools find it extremely difficult to provide top-quality enjoyable provision across all of the arts at the same time. None of the 22 schools managed to emerge in the top five places for three, let alone, four artforms. This may suggest that variations in the quality of teaching are a crucial issue for arts education in secondary schools which impinges on the level of pupils' enjoyment more than whole-school-related factors.

3. WHAT ARE EFFECTIVE PRACTICES IN ARTS EDUCATION?

14.4.4 The importance of the arts to pupils

A further question provided data on the importance of the arts to pupils. Pupils were asked to rate the importance of the arts on a four-point scale, but for ease of analysis and presentation of the data, these have been collapsed into two: those who defined the arts as '*very*' or '*quite*' important, and those who defined them as '*not very*' or '*not at all*' important.

Of those who responded to this question (there was a seven per cent non-response rate), 62 per cent responded positively that the arts were either '*very*' or '*quite*' important to them, compared with 38 per cent who described them as '*not very*' or '*not at all*' important. In line with the patterns emerging in analyses of other questions, when the question '*How important would you say the arts (or any particular artform) are to you?*' was broken down by gender and ethnicity, more girls and non-white pupils responded positively. These results are set out in Table 14.8.

Table 14.8   The importance attached to the arts, by ethnicity

	Total sample		Female		Male		White		Non-white	
	%	N	%	N	%	N	%	N	%	N
Very/quite important	62	1296	68	804	52	465	60	1089	69	185
Not very/Not at all important	38	809	32	371	48	426	40	714	31	82
(N=)	100	2105	100	1175	100	891	100	1803	100	267

Source: NFER 'The Effects and Effectiveness of Arts Education' Year 11 Survey student questionnaire
NB Approximately seven per cent of the sample constituted missing cases for this analysis.

A slight difference was also evident in the rating of the importance of the arts by pupils from different social class backgrounds (see Table 14.9). Pupils from social class categories I and II were most likely to rate the arts as 'very' or 'quite' important to them (66 per cent compared with 59 per cent of those in other social classes).

Table 14.9   The importance attached to the arts, by social class

	Total sample		I & II		III (N & M)		IV & V	
	%	N	%	N	%	N	%	N
Not very/quite important	62	1296	66	622	59	400	59	85
Not very/not at all important	38	809	34	302	41	281	41	60
(N=)	100	2105	100	942	100	681	100	145

Source: NFER 'The Effects and Effectiveness of Arts Education' Year 11 Survey student questionnaire
NB Approximately seven per cent of the sample constituted missing cases for this analysis.

Data on the importance of the arts to pupils was also analysed against the question on the school questionnaire which asked whether it was compulsory for Year 11 students to take at least one arts subject for qualification at key stage 4. Although only a small proportion (13 per cent) of the pupil sample attended schools where taking an arts subject at key stage 4 was compulsory, a trend was evident. Pupils in schools with compulsory key stage 4 arts were more likely to rate the arts as being important to them: nearly three-quarters (74 per cent) of these pupils rated the arts as 'very' or 'quite' important, compared with 60 per cent of those in schools where there was no compulsion to include an arts subject in key stage 4 option choices.

Thus, it would be plausible to interpret these results as indicating that compulsion at key stage 4 can bolster the perceived status and importance of the arts, but at the price of increasing the challenge to achieve high levels of pupils' enjoyment.

14.5 PUPILS' VIEWS ON THEIR PARENTS' INTEREST IN THE ARTS

Pupils were asked to indicate the artforms their parents were interested in (by circling as many artforms as applied). Just under half (48 per cent) perceived that their parents were interested in music, followed by literature 33 per cent, art 27 per cent, drama 19 per cent and dance 12 per cent. Over a quarter (29 per cent) gave no response – this could either mean they did not perceive their parents to be interested in any of the artforms, or that they did not know.

Breaking this down further, a relationship was evident between perceived parental interest and social class background, but there appeared to be only a marginal relationship between parental interest and ethnicity. Relationships also emerged between perceived parental interest in each artform and whether a pupil was taking the corresponding subject for GCSE, and with the importance of the arts to the pupil.

14.5.1 Variation by social class

Most noticeably, professional parents (social classes I and II) were much more likely to be perceived by their son/daughter to have an interest in the arts, across all artforms. Thus, for example, over a third (34 per cent) of parents in social classes I and II were perceived to be interested in art, compared with under a quarter (22 per cent) of those in social class III, and less than a fifth (18 per cent) in social classes IV and V. The pattern was repeated for music, drama and literature. Interestingly, perceived parental interest in dance did not appear to relate to social class.

The same pattern was also evident in 'no response' rates. Although a fifth of pupils from social classes I and II gave no response, this rose to over a third (36 per cent) of pupils in social classes IV and V. As outlined above, one interpretation of these 'no response' rates is that pupils did not perceive their parents to be interested in any of the artforms.

Table 14.10 Parental interest in the arts (as perceived by pupils) as a percentage of total sample, and by social class

	Total sample		I & II		III (N & M)		IV & V	
	%	N	%	N	%	N	%	N
Art	27	604	34	334	22	156	18	27
Music	48	1085	58	571	45	323	43	66
Drama	19	428	26	252	15	111	15	23
Dance	12	278	14	139	13	92	11	17
Literature	33	741	44	437	28	200	22	34
No response	29	655	20	195	30	215	36	54
(N=)	100	2269	100	986	100	723	100	152

Source: NFER 'The Effects and Effectiveness of Arts Education' Year 11 Survey student questionnaire

3.
WHAT ARE
EFFECTIVE
PRACTICES
IN
ARTS
EDUCATION?

14.5.2 Variation by ethnicity

No strong relationship was evident between perceived parental interest in the arts and ethnic background of the pupil; that is, similar proportions of white and non-white pupils perceived their parents to be interested in each artform. However, white pupils were slightly more likely to perceive their parents to be interested in art (27 per cent of white pupils perceived their parents to be interested, compared with 22 per cent of non-white pupils), whereas non-white pupils were slightly more likely to perceive a parental interest in music, drama and dance. This was most noticeable for dance, with 17 per cent of non-white pupils perceiving their parents to be interested in dance, compared with 12 per cent of white pupils. There was no difference evident for parental interest in literature.

14.5.3 Importance of the arts to the pupil

3.
WHAT ARE
EFFECTIVE
PRACTICES
IN
ARTS
EDUCATION?

A relationship was evident between parental involvement in the arts, and the importance of the arts to the pupil: of the pupils who perceived their parents to be interested in one or more artform, 68 per cent responded positively when asked about the importance of the arts; in comparison, less than half (46 per cent) of the pupils who did not respond that their parents were interested in any artform rated the arts as important.

This relationship was even stronger when looking at parental active involvement in the arts. Pupils who responded that their parents had actively taken part in the arts were very likely to rate the arts as either 'very important' or 'quite important': 70 per cent of those whose parents had taken part 'to some extent' were positive about the importance of the arts, and this rose to 77 per cent of those who responded that their parents had actively taken part 'a great deal'. Of those who responded that their parents had not taken part at all, just over half (56 per cent) rated the arts as 'very' or 'quite' important. This may be a manifestation of Bourdieu's theory of cultural capital – with interest and importance attributed to the arts by pupils being related to the involvement and interest of the parents (Bourdieu and Passeron, 1977).

14.5.4 GCSE option choice

Based on the sample of pupils who responded that their parents were interested in one or more artform (N = 1,614) – and thus omitting those who did not perceive parental interest in any artform – those pupils taking a subject for GCSE were more likely to perceive their parents to have an interest in that artform. For example, 59 per cent of those taking art for GCSE perceived their parents to be interested in art (compared with 37 per cent of the whole sample of pupils who responded to this question). Although evident for all artforms, this relationship was particularly strong for dance, with nearly half (47 per cent) of those taking dance for GCSE perceiving their parents to be interested in dance (compared with just 17 per cent of the total sample responding to this question).

14.6 PUPILS' VIEWS ON THEIR PARENTS' PARTICIPATION IN THE ARTS

The next question on the pupil questionnaire asked pupils *'To what extent, if any, have either of your parents actively taken part in any of these artforms during the last two years?'*. On a three-point response scale, 48 per cent of pupils who responded to this question (there was an 11 per cent non-response rate) believed that their parents had actively taken part in an artform during the last two years (most of these were in the *'to some extent'* category rather than *'a great deal'*). Slightly more than this (52 per cent) responded *'not at all'*. Breaking this down by ethnicity, the same proportions of white and non-white pupils believed that their parents had taken part in an artform during the last two years. However, Table 14.11 outlines some interesting variations by social class.

Table 14.11 Parents actively taking part in the arts (as perceived by pupils), by social class

	Total sample		I & II		III (N & M)		IV & V	
	%	N	%	N	%	N	%	N
Not at all	52	1057	43	392	59	381	64	87
To some extent	39	786	44	400	37	239	30	41
A great deal	9	178	14	125	4	28	5	7
(N=)	100	2021	100	917	100	648	100	135

Source: NFER 'The Effects and Effectiveness of Arts Education' Year 11 Survey student questionnaire
NB Approximately 11 per cent of the sample constituted missing cases for this analysis.

Table 14.11 shows that pupils from a professional or managerial background (social classes I and II) were much more likely to perceive that their parents had been actively involved in the arts over the last two years (combining *'to some extent'* and *'a great deal'*, 58 per cent were perceived to be involved to some degree), and to have been involved *'a great deal'*. For the other social class categories, perceived participation rates were around 40 per cent, with most of these falling in the *'to some extent'* group. Pupils from backgrounds where parents work in semi- or unskilled occupations (social classes IV and V) were most likely to perceive that their parents were not involved at all (64 per cent).

Consistent with previous data on the relationship between pupils taking an arts subject for GCSE and perceived parental interest in that subject, a similar pattern emerged for parents actively taking part in the arts. The relationship appeared strongest for music and drama:

- 61 per cent of those taking music perceived their parents to have actively taken part in the arts (compared with 48 per cent of the total sample); and

- 59 per cent of those taking drama perceived their parents to be have actively taken part in the arts (compared with 48 per cent of the total sample).

14.7 PARENTAL SUPPORT FOR THE ARTS

3.
WHAT ARE
EFFECTIVE
PRACTICES
IN
ARTS
EDUCATION?

Finally, provided with a list of potential forms of parental support, pupils were asked *'Do your parents support your involvement in the arts in any of the following ways?'*. Table 14.12 outlines responses for the total sample, as well as a breakdown by social class.

Most forms of support were circled by just less than half of the pupil sample. Eight per cent of the sample stated that their parents did not provide any support for their involvement in the arts, and a fifth of pupils did not respond to this question at all – one reason could be that the pupil was not involved in the arts. The lowest response was received for support labelled *'pay for lessons, membership of a club'*.

It is evident from Table 14.12 that for all forms of support, the percentage of pupils who deemed their parents to be supportive of their arts participation decreases from social class I to social class V. It would appear, however, that class background makes more of a difference in the provision of material forms of support, that is, paying for lessons, providing equipment and providing transport. For example, over half (53 per cent) of parents from a professional background were reported to be providing equipment, compared with 40 per cent of parents from skilled occupations, and just 28 per cent of those in the semi- and unskilled categories. Although there was still a difference by social class evident in the non-material forms of support (asking questions and encouraging involvement), the difference between social class categories was noticeably less.

Table 14.12 Parental support of involvement in the arts, percentage of total sample, and by social class

	Total sample		I & II		III (N & M)		IV & V	
	%	N	%	N	%	N	%	N
Encourage you to be involved	48	196	56	555	47	341	40	61
Ask questions about what you do in the arts	46	1047	52	510	47	343	38	58
Attend concerts, plays, exhibitions you are involved in	41	934	52	509	39	279	36	55
Pay for lessons, membership of a club	33	737	44	432	28	202	25	38
Provide equipment, e.g. instruments, costumes	42	953	53	525	40	292	28	43
Provide transport	47	1056	59	582	45	324	28	43
Don't provide any support	8	178	6	62	8	55	11	17
No response	21	469	14	142	20	143	23	35

Source: NFER 'The Effects and Effectiveness of Arts Education' Year 11 Survey student questionnaire
NB Respondents could give more than one response, so percentages will not sum to 100 per cent.

Small differences emerged in the level of support by ethnic background (differences of under five per cent), but in every case, non-white pupils were less likely to respond that their parents were providing support for their involvement in the arts, than white pupils were. Eleven per cent of non-white pupils responded that their parents did not provide any support, compared with seven per cent of white pupils. Although these differences are marginal, they are interesting in the light of findings that non-white pupils are more likely than white pupils to participate in extra-curricular arts activities, and to have actively participated in the arts in the last two years.

Further analyses also revealed that parents perceived to be either interested in an artform, or actively involved in the arts themselves (either 'to some extent' or 'a great deal'), were much more likely to provide all forms of support. Nearly three-quarters (74 per cent) of parents involved 'a great deal' were reported to be encouraging their son/daughter to be involved, compared with 40 per cent of those who were not actively involved themselves, and 55 per cent of parents actively involved (to any extent) in attending concerts, plays or exhibitions, compared with 35 per cent of parents not active in the arts themselves.

**3.
WHAT ARE
EFFECTIVE
PRACTICES
IN
ARTS
EDUCATION?**

14.8 EXTRA-CURRICULAR INVOLVEMENT IN THE ARTS

Although pupil perceptions of the importance of extra-curricular participation in the arts were discussed in Chapter 12, this section examines actual levels of previous and current extra-curricular activity as reported by Year 11 pupils from the 22 schools involved in the survey. It also considers extra-curricular activities specifically at primary and secondary school ages. This clearly contributes to the perceptual information on the impact of extra-curricular arts participation on the effectiveness of arts education provision in secondary schools.

14.8.1 Extra-curricular involvement at primary and secondary ages

Question 13 of the Year 11 pupil survey asked them to indicate their extra-curricular involvement in each artform, (defined as involvement *'both at school but not in your main lessons OR in your own leisure time'*) at primary and secondary ages. More specific questions then asked about participation (both 'active' and 'audience'- or 'consumer'-oriented) over the last two years. It must be emphasised that responses to Question 13 were low (levels of non-response were between 12 and 34 per cent). Where applicable, therefore, non-response rates have been included in tables.

Table 14.13 and Table 14.14 show the basic frequency results (in percentage terms) when the sample was asked about their extra-curricular arts involvement at primary and secondary ages. For each artform, pupils were asked to circle *'not at all'*, *'a little'*, *'some'* or *'a great deal'*. Respondents applied their own interpretation of this rating scale, and the degree of participation is therefore subjective. Table 14.13 presents the data from primary age.

Table 14.13   Primary age extra-curricular involvement in the arts, percentages of the whole sample

	'not at all'		'a little'		'some'		'a great deal'		No response		Total	
	%	N	%	N	%	N	%	N	%	N	%	N
Art	20	458	27	601	27	618	11	245	15	347	100	2269
Music	19	428	21	481	24	536	19	425	18	399	100	2269
Drama	22	502	24	539	23	520	13	304	18	404	100	2269
Dance	34	760	21	470	13	305	13	285	20	449	100	2269

Source: NFER 'The Effects and Effectiveness of Arts Education' Year 11 Survey student questionnaire
NB Due to rounding, percentages may not sum to 100.

Although differences between artforms were not great for involvement in primary extra-curricular activities, the following points are worth noting:

- 65 per cent of pupils had some extra-curricular involvement in art, compared with 64 per cent in music, 60 per cent in drama, and 47 per cent in dance;

- over a third (34 per cent) of pupils had no extra-curricular dance involvement, compared with about a fifth of pupils for other artforms; and

- art had the highest proportions of pupils involved in extra-curricular activities *'a little'* (27 per cent) and *'some'* (27 per cent), but less were involved *'a great deal'* (11 per cent). This may suggest that there are fewer opportunities to be heavily involved in extra-curricular art activities at primary school, in contrast with music, where 19 per cent of pupils were involved *'a great deal'*, and dance, where 13 per cent responded *'a great deal'*.

Table 14.14 presents the frequencies of response for secondary age extra-curricular involvement, again by artform.

Table 14.14 Secondary age extra-curricular involvement in the arts, percentages of the whole sample

	'not at all'		'a little'		'some'		'a great deal'		No response		Total	
	%	N	%	N	%	N	%	N	%	N	%	N
Art	23	514	22	496	29	657	12	265	15	337	100	2269
Music	24	535	20	446	23	527	16	362	18	399	100	2269
Drama	29	651	20	444	20	460	14	314	18	400	100	2269
Dance	39	889	18	440	13	287	9	194	20	459	100	2269

Source: NFER 'The Effects and Effectiveness of Arts Education' Year 11 Survey student questionnaire
NB Due to rounding, percentages may not sum to 100.

Like the results for involvement at primary age, there were not large differences between artforms in extra-curricular participation at secondary age. The following points can be made:

- pupils were less likely to be involved in extra-curricular activities at secondary age (that is, for every artform, more pupils responded that they were *'not at all'* involved in extra-curricular activities at secondary age, than had at primary age) – this is explored further below;

- nearly two-fifths of pupils responded that they did not participate in extra-curricular dance activities, compared with a third who had no involvement at primary age; and

- whilst involvement in musical extra-curricular activities was lower than at primary age, music still had the highest percentage of pupils participating '*a great deal*' (16 per cent).

As noted above, participation rates were lower for secondary age. However, looking at each artform individually, it is possible to see how many pupils reported either an increase or a decrease in participation, moving, for example, from no involvement at primary to '*some*' at secondary, or from '*a great deal*' of primary age involvement to '*a little*' at secondary:

Art

⇑ 28 per cent of pupils reported an increase in involvement from primary to secondary age;

⇓ 28 per cent of pupils reported a decrease in involvement.

Music

⇑ 25 per cent of pupils reported an increase in involvement from primary to secondary age;

⇓ 32 per cent of pupils reported a decrease in involvement.

Drama

⇑ 25 per cent of pupils reported an increase in involvement from primary to secondary age;

⇓ 32 per cent of pupils reported a decrease in involvement.

Dance

⇑ 17 per cent of pupils reported an increase in involvement from primary to secondary age;

⇓ 27 per cent of pupils reported a decrease in involvement.

Music and drama had the highest levels of decreased involvement (32 per cent of pupils were involved less at secondary age than they had been at primary age), and art had the highest level of increased involvement (28 per cent). Dance had the lowest level of increased involvement (17 per cent of pupils were doing more extra-curricular dance activity at secondary age than at primary age).

When primary and secondary age extra-curricular involvement was broken down by pupil background variables including ethnicity, gender and social class, a variety of patterns emerged which are now discussed in detail.

Variation by ethnicity

Across the artforms, non-white pupils were slightly more likely to participate in extra-curricular activities than white pupils were. That is, for every artform, at both secondary and primary ages, a lower proportion of non-white pupils responded that they had not been involved at all, compared with white pupils.

The association between ethnicity and extra-curricular involvement appeared strongest for primary art, where 11 per cent of white, compared with 22 per cent of non-white pupils responded that they had participated '*a great deal*'.

Variation by gender

Girls were more likely than boys to be involved in any form of extra-curricular arts activity, at primary age. Gender differences in involvement were particularly noticeable when comparing proportions of pupils who responded that they had been involved '*a great deal*'. Some artform-specific examples were as follows:

* for extra-curricular primary art involvement, 17 per cent of girls responded that they were involved '*a great deal*', compared with only eight per cent of boys;

* 87 per cent of girls were involved to some degree in extra-curricular music activities at primary age, compared with 63 per cent of boys. In the category '*a great deal*', nearly a third of girls (31 per cent) responded, compared with a tenth of boys (11 per cent); and

* for dance, less than a quarter of girls were not involved at all in extra-curricular activity, compared with two-thirds of boys (67 per cent); 47 per cent of girls were involved '*some*' or '*a great deal*', compared with ten per cent of boys.

The same pattern was evident for extra-curricular involvement at secondary age, but differences were not as great. The greatest differences between boys and girls in secondary age extra-curricular involvement appeared in drama and dance. In drama, three-quarters of girls (75 per cent) responded that they were involved in the extra-curricular, compared with just over half of boys (51 per cent).

Variation by social class

The association between social class and extra-curricular involvement varied by artform, as described on the following page.

Art

Pupils' social class background did not appear to have any association with their extra-curricular involvement in art, at either primary or secondary age.

Music

Pupils from a professional and managerial background were more likely to have been involved in extra-curricular activities in music at both primary and secondary ages, and were also more likely to be involved 'a great deal'. For example, a quarter of pupils from a professional or managerial background were involved 'a great deal' at secondary age, compared with 15 per cent of those with parents in skilled occupations.

**3.
WHAT ARE
EFFECTIVE
PRACTICES
IN
ARTS
EDUCATION?**

Drama

At both primary and secondary ages, social class appeared to have more of an association with whether pupils were involved in any extra-curricular drama activities, rather than with level of involvement. That is, 68 per cent of pupils from a professional and managerial background were involved in extra-curricular drama at secondary age, compared with 63 per cent of those from social class III, and under half (48 per cent of those) from the lowest social class categories. Pupils from this group (social classes IV and V) were also more likely to be involved 'a little' rather than 'some', but the proportions of pupils involved 'a great deal' were similar across social class categories.

Dance

Pupils in social classes IV and V were least likely to be involved in extra-curricular dance activities at primary age (49 per cent were 'not at all' involved compared with 39 and 40 per cent for social classes I/II and III, respectively). However, a different trend was evident for the category 'a great deal': 18 per cent of pupils from the lowest and highest social class categories (IV/V and I/II) were involved 'a great deal', compared with 14 per cent of those in social class III.

Data on extra-curricular involvement at primary and secondary ages was also analysed against perceived parental interest, key stage 4 arts option choices, school provision of extra-curricular activities, and school catchment area.

Variation by level of parental interest in the arts

Two main points emerged in analyses of whether parental interest in the artform (as perceived by the pupil) was likely to relate to levels of involvement in extra-curricular activities:

- those pupils who perceived that their parents were interested in the artform were more likely to be involved (to any extent) in extra-curricular activities at both primary and secondary ages;

- parental interest also appeared to be associated with the extent to which pupils were involved in extra-curricular activities: pupils who did not perceive their parents to be interested in the artform were more likely to rate themselves as being involved '*a little*'; those whose parents were interested, however, were more likely to be involved '*some*' and '*a great deal*'.

Although this was evident for all artforms, it was particularly strong for dance. Only 19 per cent of pupils who indicated that their parents were interested in dance had no primary extra-curricular involvement, compared with 43 per cent of those whose parents were not interested. Thirty per cent of pupils who perceived their parents to be interested in dance were involved '*a great deal*' at secondary age, compared with just 14 per cent of those whose parents were not interested. Similarly, 36 per cent of those who perceived their parents to be interested in drama were involved '*a great deal*' at secondary age, compared with 13 per cent of those who did not perceive their parents to have an interest.

Variation by key stage 4 arts provision

Primary age extra-curricular involvement in any of the four artforms did not appear to be associated with whether pupils were taking an arts subject at GCSE. That is, similar proportions of those who were taking an arts subject for key stage 4 and those who were not taking any had been involved in extra-curricular activities at primary age.

However, such an association was clearly apparent at secondary age. Those pupils taking at least one artform were more likely to be involved in extra-curricular activities in all four artforms. The relationship appeared strongest for extra-curricular involvement in art and drama, for example:

- 43 per cent of those not taking any arts for GCSE were also '*not at all*' involved in extra-curricular drama activities, compared with 27 per cent of those who were taking at least one arts for GCSE; and

- 21 per cent of those taking at least one arts option for GCSE were involved '*a great deal*' in art extra-curricular activities, compared with just six per cent of those who were not taking any arts option for GCSE.

Variation by school provision of extra-curricular activities

Data on secondary age extra-curricular involvement was also cross-tabulated with data from the school questionnaire where schools indicated the extra-curricular activities they had available at key stages 3 and 4 for each artform. Some interesting findings emerged, with variation by artform, as described below.

Art

Whether the school was able to offer extra-curricular activities in art did not appear to have an association with levels of involvement in extra-curricular art. That is, there was no difference evident in levels of involvement from pupils in schools where key stage 4 art activities were offered or not.

Music

Interestingly, higher proportions of pupils were involved in extra-curricular music activities in schools where key stage 3 and 4 music groups were not available. That is, 20 per cent of pupils in schools without choir and instrumental groups at key stage 3 reported no involvement, compared with 29 per cent in schools where these groups were available. However, pupils in schools with extra-curricular groups available were more likely to be involved 'a great deal': 20 per cent of those in schools with extra-curricular music groups at key stage 4 were involved 'a great deal', compared with 14 per cent of those in schools not offering such activities.

Drama

Similar proportions of pupils from schools that did or did not offer extra-curricular activities in drama were involved to an extent in some form of extra-curricular drama. However, as with music, pupils in schools with drama groups or the opportunity to be involved in the production of plays or musicals were more likely to be involved 'a great deal': 17 per cent of those in schools with key stage 3 drama extra-curricular activities reported this highest level of involvement, compared with four per cent of those in schools without these activities.

Dance

A more straightforward relationship emerged for dance: pupils in schools where dance activities were offered at either key stage 3 or 4 were more likely to report all levels of extra-curricular involvement. For example, 58 per cent of those attending schools where key stage 4 dance groups were available were involved in dance extra-curricularly, compared with 41 per cent of those in schools where such groups were not available; 32 per cent of those in the schools offering activities were involved either 'some' or 'a great deal', compared with 20 per cent of those in schools not offering activities.

Variation by school catchment area

Pupils attending schools with an inner city catchment were more likely to be involved in secondary age extra-curricular activities – in every artform – than pupils living in other areas, for example:

- 84 per cent of pupils in inner city schools had been involved, to any extent, in extra-curricular art activities during their secondary schooling, compared with 72 per cent of those in towns, urban and rural areas, and 65 per cent of those in suburban areas; and

- similarly, 69 per cent of pupils in inner city schools had been involved in extra-curricular dance at secondary age, compared with 56 per cent of those in towns, 43 per cent in urban and rural areas, and 41 per cent of those in suburban areas.

Although not quite so marked, pupils in inner city schools were also involved to a greater extent in music extra-curricular activities. For example, 55 per cent reported 'some' or 'a great deal' of involvement in music extra-curricular activities, compared with half of those in towns, 44 per cent of those in rural and urban areas, and 42 per cent of suburban pupils.

14.8.2 Recent involvement in the arts (active participation)

Pupils were also asked more specific questions about their recent extra-curricular arts involvement, with an emphasis on distinguishing between 'active' participation and 'audience-' or 'consumer-oriented' participation, for each artform (although these terms were not used within the questionnaire). Literature was included in these questions, and high levels of both types of participation emerged for literature.

It should be noted that questions were closed; that is, respondents were only asked to circle 'yes' or 'no'. Specific forms of either participative or consumer-oriented activity in each artform were also given, for example *'During the last two years, have you participated in a dance performance or attended a dance club/lessons?'* and *'During the last two years, have you been to see a play/the theatre in your own time?'*. The possible effects of this form of questioning are twofold: (i) using closed, direct questions may have prompted positive responses which would not have been elicited from an open-ended question on participation in the arts; and (ii) whilst every attempt was made not to exclude particular forms of arts participation in the question, it may be that some pupils were involved in activities that they did not perceive were relevant to the question, for example textiles or photography.

Table 14.15 presents the basic frequencies for responses to questions about active participation. For each artform, pupils were asked a question with the stem *'During the last two years, have you ...'*. For music, two questions were asked, one specifically about learning an instrument, and the other about music-making with other people. This distinction was not made for other artforms.

Table 14.15 Recent (last two years) active participation in the arts as percentage of whole sample

During the last two years have you ...		Yes		No		No response	
		%	N	%	N	%	N
Art	... produced a piece of visual art for your own interest?'	40	910	46	1039	14	320
Music	... been learning to play a musical instrument?'	24	547	59	1328	17	393
	... been involved in music-making with other people?'	26	581	56	1280	18	408
Drama	... acted in a play or participated in a drama club/workshop?'	28	636	55	1243	17	390
Dance	... participated in a dance performance or attended a dance club/lessons?'	19	428	61	1388	20	453
Literature	... written any short stories or poetry (or similar) for your own interest?'	48	1078	40	914	12	277

Source: NFER 'The Effects and Effectiveness of Arts Education' Year 11 Survey student questionnaire
NB Due to rounding, percentages may not sum to 100.

The most noticeable points to emerge from Table 14.15 were:

- active participation was highest for literature, with nearly half (48 per cent) of pupils responding that they had written in their own time;

- art was also actively undertaken by a high proportion of pupils, with 40 per cent responding affirmatively to the question '... *have you produced a piece of visual art for your own interest?*'; and

- just under a quarter of pupils responded that they learnt a musical instrument, and just over a quarter were involved in music-making with other people. These figures were slightly lower than the percentage of pupils who responded that they had acted or participated in a drama club.

This data is consistent with that of the MORI study (O'Brien, 1996), which reported that although nearly half of 11- to 16-year-olds were learning to play a musical instrument, this proportion declined with age, with the majority of those learning aged under 15. Further analyses into which pupils were actively involved in the arts (including learning an instrument) are discussed below, and, later in this report. Chapter 9 explored the effect of extra-curricular involvement in music on general academic performance.

Data on pupil active participation in the arts was analysed further with the same variables identified earlier in this chapter: social class, gender, ethnicity, GCSE options, parental interest, school provision of extra-curricular activities, and school catchment area.

Variation by social class

Although overall, the data suggests that those pupils from a higher social class background were more likely to actively participate in the arts, the specifics of the relationship differed by artform. The proportion of those who responded that they had produced a piece of visual art for their own interest decreased from nearly half of those in social classes I and II (49 per cent), to 40 per cent of those in social classes IV and V. A similar pattern, and even more noticeable trend, emerged for learning to play a musical instrument. Thirty-six per cent of those in social classes I and II had been learning to play an instrument in the last two years, but this dropped to under a quarter (24 per cent) for other social class categories (indeed, only one pupil from an unskilled background responded positively).

The same correlation between social class and participation rates was evident for drama, but differences between social classes were much smaller (37 per cent of those from social classes I and II had acted in a play, compared with around 30 per cent from other social class categories). Social class did not appear to have an effect on participation in dance, as participation rates across class backgrounds differed by just three per cent.

It would seem, therefore, that parents of pupils from the higher social class groups were most likely to support extra-curricular participation in art and music activities over other artforms.

Variation by ethnicity

For all artforms, non-white pupils were more likely to respond that they had actively participated in the arts, than white pupils were. However, this difference was negligible for music and drama (a difference of between two and four per cent in participation rates, by ethnic group). The relationship was stronger for art and dance: 56 per cent of non-white pupils responded positively to the question '*During the last two years, have you produced a piece of visual art for your own interest?*', compared with under half (45 per cent) of white pupils; and for dance, a third (32 per cent) of non-white pupils had '*... participated in a dance performance or attended a dance club/lessons*', compared with 22 per cent of white pupils. The MORI survey (O'Brien, 1996) also found that dance participation was higher for children from ethnic minority groups.

Variation by gender

Artform differences were also evident in the relationship between gender and active participation. For art, no difference by gender was evident, with just under half of boys and girls responding that they had produced a piece of visual art for their own interest. More girls than boys reported learning a musical instrument, although the difference was not large: 31 per cent of girls, compared with 27 per cent of boys. This difference was slightly larger for the question '*During the last two years, have you been involved in music-making with other people?*'. Again, 27 per cent of boys responded positively, compared with 34 per cent of girls.

However, the greatest differences in participation by gender were for drama and dance: 40 per cent of girls had acted in a play or participated in a drama club or workshop, compared with a quarter of boys. For dance, consistent with earlier results, girls were much more likely to have participated in a dance performance, or attended a club or lessons (35 per cent of girls, compared with seven per cent of boys).

Variations by GCSE option choice

For all artforms, a very strong relationship emerged between taking a subject for GCSE, and active participation in the artform. This was strongest for music, drama and dance, with approximately 90 per cent of those taking the subject for GCSE also responding positively to the question on participation, compared with less than a quarter of those not taking the subject at GCSE. This equates with the high dependence on practical activities and performance identified as factors in effective arts education provision. Pupils also perceived that their own participation in their artform beyond the scope of arts lessons was important in developing their personal ability in these areas.

Variation by level of parental interest in the arts

Pupils who perceived their parents to be interested in the artform were more likely to have been actively involved in that artform. Although the relationship was clear for all artforms, it was most evident for dance and drama: 61 per cent of those who perceived their parents to be interested in drama had acted in a play in the last two years, compared with 29 per cent of those who did not perceive their parents to be interested in drama; and, over half (52 per cent) of those who perceived their parents to be interested in dance had participated in a dance performance themselves, compared with a fifth (20 per cent) of those who did not perceive their parents to be interested in dance. For learning a musical instrument, 41 per cent of those who perceived their parents to be interested in music were learning an instrument, compared with 17 per cent of those who did not perceive their parents to be interested. It is clear, then, that parental interest in the arts fosters young people's participation in the same artforms – a factor which, although expected, may not be adequately recognised or exploited by schools in their provision of arts education.

Variation by school provision of extra-curricular activities

A relationship between pupil active participation in the artform and school provision of extra-curricular activities was evident for music, dance and drama. That is, for these artforms, pupils in schools with activities available were more likely to have participated in the last two years, than those from schools where extra-curricular activities were not available:

- over a third (35 per cent) of pupils where extra-curricular activities were available in drama at key stage 3 had participated in drama in the last two years, compared with a quarter (25 per cent) of those in schools where such activities were not provided; and

- 27 per cent of those in schools where key stage 4 dance activities were available had participated in a dance club or performance, compared with 19 per cent of those in schools where dance was not available extra-curricularly.

Variation by school catchment area

The same pattern identified under general extra-curricular involvement emerged; that is, for all artforms, higher proportions of pupils attending inner city schools had actively participated in the arts, than those living in other locales. This relationship was strongest for art and literature.

14.8.3 Recent involvement in the arts (consumer-oriented)

Table 14.16 presents results from the complementary question, asking about consumer-oriented participation in each artform. Again, two questions were asked for music, distinguishing between attending a classical concert and a rock/pop concert.

Table 14.16   Recent (last two years) consumer oriented participation in the arts as percentage of the whole sample

During the last two years have you ...		Yes		No		No response	
		%	N	%	N	%	N
Art	... been to a gallery or an exhibition to look at art in your own time?'	29	648	57	1295	14	326
Music	... been to a musical performance /concert in your own time?' [Classical]	13	302	53	1191	34	776
	... been to a musical performance/ concert in your own time?' [Pop/Rock]	44	986	37	830	20	453
Drama	... been to see a play/the theatre in your own time?'	51	1145	33	743	17	381
Dance	... been to see a dance performance in your own time?'	26	593	54	1225	20	451
Literature	... read any novels, short stories or poetry for your own pleasure?'	70	1586	19	419	12	264

Source: NFER 'The Effects and Effectiveness of Arts Education' Year 11 Survey student questionnaire
NB Due to rounding, percentages may not sum to 100.

Literature again had the highest percentage of positive responses, with 70 per cent of pupils responding that they had read for their own pleasure in the last two years. However, this question about consumer-oriented activities elicited some different results for other artforms (when compared with results to the previous active participation question):

- although 40 per cent of pupils had responded positively to the question about producing art, only 29 per cent responded affirmatively to the question 'Have you been to a gallery or an exhibition to look at art in your own time?' (the same finding regarding art production and consumption was reported in the 1996 MORI survey);

- drama showed the opposite pattern, with half of the sample responding that they had been to see a play/the theatre in their own time, compared with just 28 per cent who said they had acted in a play or participated in a drama club/workshop;

- similarly, although active participation and consumer-oriented participation were both low for dance, a higher percentage of pupils indicated they had been to see a dance performance in their own time (26 per cent) than had participated (19 per cent); and

- attendance at a classical music performance was responded to positively by just 13 per cent of the sample, in contrast with 44 per cent who said they had attended a pop or rock concert.

Exploration of associations between recent consumer-oriented participation in the arts and other variables produced some interesting variations by artform.

Variation by social class

In analysis of consumer-oriented participation in art by social class, a 'U'-shaped relationship emerged. That is, whilst 42 per cent of those from a professional or managerial background (social classes I and II) responded that they had been to a gallery or an exhibition to look at art in their own time, this dipped to 26 per cent of those with parents in skilled occupations (social class III), and rose to 30 per cent of those in the semi- or unskilled categories (social classes IV and V). Indeed, 40 per cent of those in the lowest category (social class V) responded positively.

For the other artforms, a more straightforward positive correlation between class and consumer-oriented participation was evident:

- those from social classes I and II were much more likely to have attended a classical music concert in the last two years (27 per cent); only 15 per cent of pupils with parents in skilled or semi-skilled occupations had done so, and no respondents whose parents were unskilled responded positively;

- the difference was not as marked for attendance at a pop/rock concert, although those from a professional or managerial background were still more likely to have done so (61 per cent compared with just over half of those in other social class categories);

- pupils from a professional or managerial background were also more likely to have participated in consumer-oriented drama activity (70 per cent) – this decreased to 57 per cent of those with parents working in skilled occupations, and 54 per cent of those whose parents were semi- or unskilled; and

- similarly, for dance, 37 per cent of pupils in social classes I and II had been to see a dance performance, compared with under a quarter (23 per cent) of those from social classes IV and V.

Variation by ethnicity

Non-white pupils were marginally more likely to have visited an art gallery (three per cent difference in participation between white and non-white pupils) and attended a classical music concert (two per cent difference) or a dance performance (six per cent difference). However, white pupils were more likely to have been to a pop/rock concert in the last two years (56 per cent, compared with 45 per cent of non-white pupils) and to have been to see a play or to the theatre (62 per cent of white pupils, compared with 53 per cent non-white).

Variation by gender

For all artforms, consumer-oriented participation was higher for girls. This was most evident for dance and drama: 71 per cent of girls had been to the theatre in their own time, compared with under half (47 per cent) of boys. Corresponding figures for attending a dance performance were 46 per cent of girls and 12 per cent of boys. The same pattern was apparent for visiting art galleries and attendance at both classical and pop/rock concerts. This reiterates the finding of the MORI survey (O'Brien, 1996) that girls were more active in attendance at arts and cultural events, particularly those involving literature, drama and dance.

Variations by GCSE option choice

The trend outlined for active participation in the arts was repeated here for consumer-oriented participation. For all artforms, those taking the subject for GCSE were more likely to have visited a gallery, been to the theatre or a musical concert, or attended a dance performance in their own time. However, this relationship was slightly weaker; that is, the difference in consumer-oriented participation between those taking GCSE and those not was not as great. Under half (46 per cent) of those taking GCSE art had visited a gallery in their own time, compared with 27 per cent of those not taking GCSE art; and 87 per cent of those taking GCSE drama had been to the theatre, compared with 56 per cent of non-GCSE drama pupils.

The most interesting differences between the two groups was evident for music: 59 per cent of those taking GCSE music had been to a classical concert, compared with 16 per cent of those not taking GCSE music. However, although these pupils were still more likely to have been to a pop/rock concert (79 per cent of those taking GCSE had attended such a concert in the last two years), a larger proportion of non-GCSE music pupils had also done this (52 per cent).

Variations by level of parental interest

For all artforms, pupils who perceived their parents to be interested in an artform were more likely to be involved in consumer-oriented activity for that particular artform. Again, this relationship was strongest for dance (63 per cent of those who perceived their parents to be interested in dance had been to a dance performance, compared with just 30 per cent of those who did not perceive their parents to be interested in dance), and lowest for music (28 per cent of those who perceived their parents to be interested in music had attended a classical music concert, compared with 16 per cent of those who perceived no parental interest, and 63 per cent of those who perceived their parents to be interested in music had attended a pop/rock concert, compared with half of those who perceived no parental interest).

Variation by school catchment area

The relationship between consumer-oriented participation in the arts and school catchment area varied by artform. Consistent with earlier patterns, pupils in inner city schools were most likely to have attended an art gallery (49 per cent had, compared with between 27 and 33 per cent for other locales), a classical music concert (26 per cent, compared with between 15 and 22 per cent), and a dance performance (41 per cent, compared with between 28 and 36 per cent). However, pupils living in suburban areas were most likely to have attended a play or the theatre: nearly three-quarters (74 per cent) had, compared with 56 per cent of those in rural areas, 62 per cent of those in towns, 57 per cent in urban areas and 59 per cent those from the inner city. The proportion of pupils who had attended a pop/rock concert was similar across all locales, although highest was suburban (57 per cent), and lowest was inner city (51 per cent).

14.8.4 Summary of extra-curricular involvement activity: by artform

It would appear that there are clear and distinct differences in the patterns of pupil extra-curricular activity by artform – again emphasising the importance of examining the artforms independently, rather than as one homogenous body. A summary of extra-curricular involvement relating to each individual artform is therefore presented here.

Art

Art had the highest proportions of pupils involved in extra-curricular activities, at both primary and secondary ages. However, most reported either '*a little*' or '*some*' involvement, rather than '*a great deal*'.

Whilst, after literature, art had the highest proportion of pupils actively participating (40 per cent responded affirmatively to the question '*... have you produced a piece of visual art for your own interest?*'), fewer pupils had visited a gallery or exhibition in their own time.

Music

For both primary and secondary ages, music had the highest proportion of pupils participating '*a great deal*' in extra-curricular activities.

More girls than boys participated in extra-curricular activities, and girls were also more likely to report high levels of involvement. Social class also had the strongest association with music extra-curricular activities, with middle-class pupils the most likely to be involved.

Just under a quarter of pupils responded that they learnt a musical instrument, and just over a quarter were involved in music-making with other people. These figures are slightly lower than the percentage of pupils who responded that they had acted or participated in a drama club. The subsamples most likely to learn an instrument were girls and those from a professional background. There did not appear to be a relationship between ethnic background and learning an instrument.

Drama

There was a sizeable gap in participation rates in extra-curricular drama at secondary age, for boys and girls. Three-quarters of girls responded that they were involved extra-curricularly, compared with just over half of boys. Girls were also more likely to have acted in a play, or been to the theatre for their own interest.

Whilst over half of all pupils had been to see a play or been to the theatre in their own time, just over a quarter had actively participated, through acting or participating in a drama club.

White pupils were more likely than non-white pupils to have been to see a play or the theatre.

Dance

A third of pupils had no extra-curricular dance involvement at primary age, compared with about a fifth of pupils for other artforms. Non-participation rose to 39 per cent at secondary age.

Girls undertook all aspects of dance involvement (extra-curricular, active participation and consumer-oriented participation) more than boys did.

Those pupils who perceived that their parents were interested in dance were more likely to be involved (to any extent) in extra-curricular activities at both primary and secondary ages. This relationship, between perceived parental interest and extra-curricular activity, was stronger for dance than it was for other artforms.

Literature

Literature had the highest numbers of pupils involved either in active or consumer-oriented participation. Nearly half responded that they had written short stories or poetry for their own interest, and 70 per cent stated that they had read novels, short stories or poetry.

14.9 CONCLUSION

This chapter has presented the findings of the survey of 2,269 Year 11 pupils across 22 schools. It has dealt with some issues additional to those described in Chapter 12, relating to the provision of effective arts education, but has also examined statistically some of those already brought to light by interviewees' perceptions.

There are several key issues, illuminated by this chapter, which add further detail to the effectiveness typology developed within Chapter 12, and in some cases add supportive weight to the perceptions of pupils and school staff. The main themes that are drawn from this chapter are:

3.
WHAT ARE
EFFECTIVE
PRACTICES
IN
ARTS
EDUCATION?

- the importance of the numbers and characteristics of pupils opting to take arts subjects at key stage 4;

- pupils' rationale for choosing the arts at key stage 4;

- the importance of pupils' perceptions of their parents' attitudes towards, and participation in, the arts; and

- the substantial variations identified between schools

14.9.1 The numbers and characteristics of pupils opting to take arts subjects at key stage 4

Clearly, the number of pupils choosing to continue arts education to key stage 4 level, or a GCSE qualification, constitutes a valuable indicator of its recognition as a relevant and attractive curriculum subject, with appropriate and effective teaching within the school. Questions must be asked in terms of the extent to which pupils 'vote with their feet' when choosing options, and whether a school with low numbers opting to take the arts can deem themselves to be effective in this area.

The figures for all the arts subjects showed that recruitment numbers were considerably lower than for other GCSE core subjects such as technology, French and history. The numbers also included particularly low percentages of boys in music, drama and dance, and middle-class pupils were the most likely to be taking drama. In terms of ethnicity, music and art attracted the lowest percentages of non-white pupils – perhaps because of these subjects predominant dependence on the Western, classical tradition.

Pupils taking only one artform for GCSE were seen to have higher average key stage 3 scores than pupils taking either no arts or more than one artform. Music was particularly inclined to attract pupils from the higher-attaining group. In addition to this, it was seen that pupils taking more than one artform for GCSE had lower than average scores at key stage 3 – suggesting that, in some schools, it was a set of options which was considered acceptable for lower but not higher attainers. These two features suggest that music could benefit from attracting more lower-attaining pupils, and that a greater number of higher academic achievers could be permitted and encouraged by more flexible option structures to take more than one artform.

14.9.2 Pupils' rationale for choosing the arts at key stage 4

Increasing pupil participation in the arts, as suggested by the previous point, clearly relies on an understanding of the issues and criteria which pupils take into consideration when they make their option choices. The three most common reasons that pupils gave for opting to take an arts subject were personal interest and enjoyment, ability in the subject (*'because I'm good at it'*) and its relevance to a future career or employment. These reasons surely highlight potential barriers to pupil participation in the arts for GCSE – pupils not enjoying the subject, a talent or lack of aptitude barrier and a view that the arts are not suitably relevant to future employment. Pupils' reasons for their choices and their converse – barriers to participation – would seem to hold clear messages for the development of the arts in secondary schools.

Pupils who had chosen to take the arts frequently nominated an artform as one of their two favourite subjects, and as one of the two subjects they felt they were 'best at' – more frequently than students of other subjects. Again, this would suggest that the arts mainly attracted pupils with a perceived talent, or a particular interest in the artform. Conversely, however, it would imply that pupils chose some of their other subjects based on their currency and relevance to future life, rather than simply on the basis of their enjoyment or talent. Providing an arts education which could attract pupils on the basis of high levels of enjoyment, positive self-images of attainment in the arts, and a much greater attention to establishing their relevance amounts to a significant challenge, which the arts should clearly be aiming to meet.

Additionally, it would seem as though there was considerable unmet demand for arts GCSE courses and opportunities for arts participation at key stage 4. For dance and drama, the lack of suitable options to take these subjects at GCSE was a major problem and one that needs addressing by schools and curriculum policy makers. However, for art and music, in most schools the barriers to participation listed earlier were a more significant factor than the lack of suitable options. Clearly, then, for these subjects, especially music, the challenge in providing for the 55 per cent of the sample who wished to be taking more artforms than they were currently lies in increasing pupil enjoyment of the arts, increasing pupils' understanding of their own learning and abilities in the arts prior to their decision making at the end of key stage 3, and in making the arts more relevant to the lives of young people and their future employment.

14.9.3 The importance of pupils' perceptions of their parents' attitudes towards, and participation in, the arts

The perceptions which pupils expressed about their parents' participation in, and support of, the arts were a major factor in their own attitudes and involvement, which, as we saw in Chapter 12, were in turn key determinants of effective arts education at school. Bourdieu's theory of cultural capital – whereby parents with positive attitudes towards, and engagement in, the arts encourage their children to hold similar positive viewpoints – appears to hold here. All the evidence from this chapter suggests that pupils' perceptions of their parents' support, interest and participation in the arts exert great influence on their own attitudes and participation in different artforms. What strategies, therefore, might be available to foster greater parental support and participation in the arts?

3. WHAT ARE EFFECTIVE PRACTICES IN ARTS EDUCATION?

14.9.4 The substantial variations identified between schools

Throughout this chapter – and indeed throughout the report – a repeatedly emerging finding has been the considerable differences between the schools surveyed in the sample. Differences manifested themselves in almost all sections of this chapter – for example, in terms of the numbers of pupils choosing to take arts courses during key stage 4, pupils' attitudes towards the arts and their extra-curricular participation.

It is apparent that arts provision and take-up at key stage 4 are far from consistent across the board, and that useful lessons could be learnt from schools where the arts are flourishing. Some schools managed to attract high numbers of pupils on to GCSE arts courses – including some that attracted high numbers without the need for a formal requirement for all pupils to take at least one arts subject. These schools are obviously doing something which has broken down the barriers to participation which have been identified previously. If all pupils are to be given the same opportunities to benefit from the arts as those attending these schools, it is the practices in these schools, and those of the teachers that we have portrayed in Chapter 13, that need emulating and disseminating.

15. ARTS EFFECTIVENESS: OVERALL PERSPECTIVES

3.
WHAT ARE
EFFECTIVE
PRACTICES
IN
ARTS
EDUCATION?

CHAPTER OVERVIEW

This chapter draws together the main themes to emerge from the previous three chapters in Part Three. These offered:

- perceptions of the different groups of people interviewed on effective practices in the teaching and learning of arts (Chapter 12)

- analyses of the classroom observation of lessons at schools that generated high numbers of positive outcomes and effects (Chapter 13)

- analyses of responses to the Year 11 survey concerning the take-up of key stage 4 arts courses, pupil attitudes to the arts, extra-curricular involvement in the arts, and parental support (Chapter 14).

By way of summarising the results from the above, 11 key tenets of effective practices in arts education are identified.

The previous three chapters substantively forming Part Three of this report have examined the different factors and influences which were both *perceived* and *observed* to play a part in the effectiveness of arts education provision in secondary schools. As expected, isolating '*effectiveness*' and '*effective practice*' from the effects and outcomes of arts education has proven challenging. However, an attempt is made here to distil the key messages and factors contributing to the provision of effective arts education within secondary schools.

This chapter draws together the main themes emerging from the perceptions of the different groups of people consulted (Chapter 12), the classroom observation of lessons at schools deemed to provide high numbers of positive outcomes and effects (Chapter 13), and the statistical analysis of responses to the Year 11 survey (Chapter 14). Eleven key tenets of effective practice in arts teaching have thus been identified.

1. THE GENERAL STATUS AND PROFILE OF THE ARTS

Throughout this part of the report, the general status and relevance of the arts (i.e. beyond education) can be seen as a common undercurrent subtly influencing many other factors in the effectiveness of school-based arts education. For example, general perceptions of the value of the arts within society may influence their inclusion within the National

Curriculum, and the attitudes of school management, teachers, parents, pupils and employers. Hence, it would seem that raising the profile of the arts in general terms, and increasing public awareness of the positive outcomes of an effective arts education, are crucial activities in its maintenance and support.

2. THE STATUS OF THE ARTS IN THE NATIONAL CURRICULUM

The National Curriculum provides one formal indication of the emphasis and status attributed to the arts within the broad spectrum of secondary school education. Although art and music are established subjects within the National Curriculum (and clearly benefit from the credibility this provides), drama and dance were seen to face particular challenges based on their provision through other subjects – namely English and PE. The message implied by the decision not to include dance and drama as independent subjects could logically be interpreted as indicating that they are less important than art and music.

3.
WHAT ARE
EFFECTIVE
PRACTICES
IN
ARTS
EDUCATION?

However, in Chapter 13, the schools that were chosen as locations for drama lesson observations (on the basis of their high number and range of positive outcomes and effects) both provided it as a subject distinct from English. In addition, the observed dance lessons, whilst provided as part of PE, were taught by PE teachers specialising in dance, who had a strong personal interest and involvement in the subject, and who treated it as an artform, rather than a purely 'physical education' activity. The wide range of outcomes and effects reported as resulting from dance and drama, when taught as arts subjects in this way, provides a strong case for affording them a place in the National Curriculum in their own right. This would surely result in their extraction from any potentially restrictive relationships with PE and English – subjects with distinct characteristics and emphases not always in line with those of dance and drama artforms – and an increase in the wider range of outcomes observed in those schools that treat these subjects as an integral part of the arts curriculum.

3. PROVISION FOR THE ARTS IN SCHOOLS, AND KEY STAGE 4 PARTICIPATION

In terms of recruitment on to key stage 4 courses, the arts fared generally worse than other core subjects such as technology, French and history. Art was the most popular, followed by drama, music and then dance. Three main reasons were given by pupils for their choice of arts subjects at key stage 4: their personal interest and enjoyment of the subject, their current ability in it, and their perception of its relevance, status and value.

It is clear that pupils' choices at key stage 4 are based heavily on their previous experiences during key stage 3. In this sense, therefore, the provision of the arts during this phase of schooling provides the basis for participation at key stage 4. Pupils who do not experience adequate arts provision during the formative school years (particularly apparent in the cursory provision and experience of dance education observed during Chapter 13) would seem to be in a weak position in terms of choosing the arts at key stage 4.

The availability of the arts within key stage 4 option choices is also a significant issue – for example, the Year 11 survey revealed that only three per cent of the whole sample were taking dance, although it rose to 14 per cent of pupils at schools where it was an option. This would suggest that increasing the availability of different arts subjects may increase participation simply by increasing opportunities to take them. The other side of this issue is the way in which the arts are arranged within option structures. It seems to be the case that taking more than one artform was a route which only pupils of lower academic attainment were encouraged to take, and that some pupils would have chosen to take more than one artform at key stage 4 if this had been possible and was supported.

Therefore, five main barriers to participation in the arts at key stage 4 are apparent:

- pupils not experiencing adequate provision for the arts during key stage 3;

- pupils not finding arts experiences sufficiently engaging or enjoyable during key stage 3;

- a lack of provision of arts options at key stage 4, or a restrictive option structure;

- a talent barrier – pupils identifying participation in the arts at key stage 4 as being reserved for those with outstanding practical arts abilities; and

- pupils' perception of the arts as irrelevant, and lacking in status for both their current situation, and their future career paths.

Perhaps surprisingly, pupils did not often give '*school requirement*' as a reason for choosing the arts at key stage 4, even in schools where this was the case. It was clear, from the results of the Year 11 survey, that in schools where taking at least one arts option at key stage 4 was compulsory, participation in the arts was increased across the board. However, the results also suggested that this was achieved at the expense of pupil enjoyment of the artform during key stage 4 –

supported by the perceptions of pupils and teachers that pupils' commitment to taking the subject was an important factor in determining the levels of enjoyment and achievement which they experienced. Equally, it was apparent that some schools where such a requirement was not imposed had comparably high levels of participation. It would therefore seem a more appropriate priority for schools to focus on breaking down the identified barriers to participation, thus encouraging pupils to choose the arts for themselves, based on positive reasons, rather than simply imposing the arts as an obligatory key stage 4 requirement. Clearly, this relies on the provision of suitably stimulating and enjoyable learning experiences in the arts throughout key stage 3, and the availability and option structure of arts opportunities at key stage 4.

4. ENJOYMENT AND RELEVANCE OF THE ARTS IN SCHOOLS

As the previous point has suggested, pupils' enjoyment of the arts curriculum during the key stage 3 years plays an important role in shaping their perceptions of the arts, and determining their participation at key stage 4. In addition, however, pupil enjoyment was seen as an important outcome of arts lessons in its own right, and perceived to be a key factor in determining their effectiveness by teachers and pupils alike.

Although in some instances pupil enjoyment of arts lessons was based on their engagement with the subject matter, it was clear from the lesson observations that many different ways of making the arts curriculum relevant to the lives and futures of young people were possible. One tactic in music was the consideration of 'house' music, and the use of computers, although the observed drama lessons clearly demonstrated that considering contemporary material was not the only method in which relevance could be achieved. Lessons were observed which dealt with World War Two, and the fight for racial equality in America, and yet these two topics were mediated by the teacher so that the issues raised were related directly to pupils' own experiences and feelings. During one of the observed art lessons, both pupils and teacher referred to the opportunities that the subject matter – fruit and vegetables – provided in terms of exploration of colour and art media, and this was made relevant to pupils through the explanation of the skills and abilities they were developing through the project, and their application to future artwork, rather than simply engagement with the subject matter itself. Perhaps, the most important message to be gained from this evidence is that there are many alternative ways in which teachers can mediate the curriculum and present specific curriculum contents so that pupils will experience them as relevant and engaging.

5. INTERNAL AND EXTERNAL SUPPORT FOR THE ARTS AND ARTS TEACHERS

There were two key ways in which effective arts education could receive much-needed support: from internal sources including senior management, faculty and departmental structures, and other teachers; and from external sources such as LEA arts advisers, RABs, other arts organisations and local teacher networks.

In schools where arts lessons were observed, based on their perceived effectiveness, a commonly identified thread was the high level of support for the arts, as well as the high levels of encouragement and acclaim directed towards the individual teachers of the arts. This was seen to be a key factor in raising and maintaining the confidence levels of the staff, which in turn influenced their commitment to, and enjoyment of, teaching the arts in the school.

Another facet of senior management support for the arts involved the allocation of time within the timetable for the different arts subjects, and the allocation of teaching staff, resources and facilities. Again, there was a clear distinction between the different artforms. Art and music were often relatively well supported, with regular lessons within the timetable, dedicated rooms and equipment, and specialist teaching staff. Drama, and more particularly dance, were generally less well supported – often attracting only cursory amounts of time within the timetable, being taught by non-specialist staff from English and PE, and dependent on the use of inadequate facilities. Schools that provided adequate support for the arts in these terms were clearly seen to reap the benefits in terms of participation and outcomes.

In addition to the internal support described above, external teacher support mechanisms – whether provided by LEAs, RABs, formal or informal teacher networks, or artists and arts organisations – were also perceived by teachers and school management to be beneficial in terms of arts lesson effectiveness. The main source of external support described by staff from the case study schools originated from the LEA, and a wide variety of different mechanisms were described including: arts advisers, provision of resources and facilities and the organisation of artists-in-residence schemes. However, it was clear that the quality and extent of this type of provision varied widely between LEAs. Teacher perceptions of the support provided by other arts organisations were limited, and it is clear that these groups could usefully develop additional ways in which to support the work and professional development of arts educators in schools. Where these types of support were not forthcoming, teachers often referred to the benefits of meeting other teachers, and forming local support networks, although finding time for this type of activity was often a major constraint.

Clearly the arts, and individual arts teachers in secondary schools, could benefit from the support provided by both internal and external sources, and whilst some cases have illustrated the way in which external support can counter a lack of internal recognition, the ideal situation demands that support from all available channels be forthcoming.

6. TIMETABLING THE ARTS

Providing adequate time within the curriculum for the teaching of the arts was an issue clearly related to the status attributed to each individual artform by those planning the school timetable. As indicated earlier, dance fared particularly badly in this sense – with few schools providing any appreciable level of dance opportunities, although drama and music were also limited in some instances. The knock-on effects for perceptions of, and participation in, the arts at key stage 4 have already been described.

Arranging the school timetable, and the location of the arts within it, were also seen as an important senior management responsibility which affected arts provision. However, the perceptions of teachers relating to their ideal timetable arrangement differed between the artforms. In art (involving considerable time spent engaged in 'housekeeping' activities such as getting equipment out and tidying away), teachers described a preference for longer, or double, lessons. To a lesser extent this also affected music. However, some drama teachers perceived a benefit of having shorter, but more frequent lessons. This makes the case for treating each artform individually, rather than as a homogenous whole, and indicates where a supportive senior management and curriculum planning team could make sympathetic timetable arrangements.

7. SPECIALIST ARTS TEACHERS

Generally speaking, the research found that as far as the arts were concerned, individual teacher effectiveness was probably a more important factor than school effectiveness. The teachers of arts lessons were often perceived as the critical determinant of the effectiveness of those lessons and the outcomes and effects which could be achieved. Their influence within arts lessons was also unmistakably apparent during classroom observations. Clearly, they play a central role in mediating the arts curriculum and determining the quality of pupils' arts experiences and associated outcomes.

Teachers and school staff perceived a need for specialist arts teachers, and this was again supported by the lesson observations – all the lessons identified as demonstrating 'effective practice' were taught by specialist teachers, with high levels of personal involvement in the artform. Teachers' personal involvement in their artform was thought to be a direct influence on their level of passion and commitment to it, and the enthusiasm with which they approached arts lessons – a factor which was often perceived as crucial in fostering pupil enthusiasm for, and enjoyment, of the subject.

The observed specialist arts teachers approached lessons with an overwhelming enthusiasm which pupils often felt was infectious, and encouraged them to try hard in the lessons and enjoy the artform. This was also apparent in the culture of praise and encouragement which these specialist teachers provided – there was a clear sense that these teachers were communicating their own love of their artform to their pupils. Specialist drama and dance teachers particularly described their perceptions of the outcomes of lessons taught by English and PE teachers who did not have this personal attachment to the artform, and the subconscious negative messages which they could give out.

In addition to the clear enthusiasm for their artform, pupils perceived considerable benefit from, and described their additional respect for, teachers who were able to give practical demonstrations of the artform and participate in class activities. They described a negative attitude towards temporary and supply teachers on this basis – demonstrating their lack of respect for teachers who simply told them what to do rather than giving a demonstration. The advantages of specialist arts teachers were also apparent in this sense during the classroom observations. Teachers provided help and advice to individuals or small groups during the practical phases of the lessons, and in some cases (generally with pupils of lower arts ability), this involved them in modelling the desired outcome – providing practical demonstrations in music, drama and dance, and actually mixing colours, or making marks on the page in art. This clearly relies heavily on the teachers' own expertise in their artform.

8.   PRACTICAL ARTS ACTIVITIES

Arts lessons were traditionally recognised to rely heavily on practical *'doing'* activities, although increasingly this was tempered with performance and display which were used as opportunities for evaluation, arts discourse and the encouragement of critical *'arts consumption'*.

Pupils expressed considerable belief in the emphasis on practical activity within the arts, often insightfully recognising that they could produce something meaningful whatever their ability. They also described their enjoyment of *'doing their own thing'* and the personal satisfaction they gained from being creative, developing ideas and producing their own individual outcome. Pupils and teachers alike described their perception of the arts as providing a positive balance and alternative to the more structured, academic and desk-based subjects within the curriculum.

Within dance, drama and music, practical activities were seen to include considerable opportunities for group work, which was shown to contribute to the social and personal outcomes observed. However, art was identified more frequently with individual endeavour, although not to its detriment.

9. PERFORMANCE, DISPLAY AND EVALUATION

Displaying work and performing were activities deemed crucial to effective arts lessons, and which generally followed practical development. Two different functions were seen to be served by these activities:

3.
WHAT ARE
EFFECTIVE
PRACTICES
IN
ARTS
EDUCATION?

Firstly, they provided an opportunity for pupils to demonstrate what they had developed and learnt during practical arts activities. Pupils particularly described their perceptions of the irrelevance of developing dance and drama sequences if performance was not the intended outcome, and clearly the performance therefore acted as a motivating factor. There was also a sense that the performance formed the natural conclusion of the lesson or project – a sense of completion. These performances allowed pupils to experience a sense of satisfaction from their practical arts work – enhanced by the enthusiasm and praise with which teachers and peers celebrated positive outcomes.

Secondly, the performance or display of work developed within practical arts sessions provided subject matter for talking about the arts in general. This was perceived, and observed, to provide a vehicle for the evaluation of the arts (leading to enhanced self-evaluation within practical arts activities) and the development of a language of arts discourse and critical consumption. It also provided a vital opportunity for feedback and constructive criticism, which pupils and teachers recognised as essential for improvement.

10. A CULTURE OF PRAISE AND ENCOURAGEMENT

Throughout the observed arts lessons, a common mechanism employed by the teachers was the provision of a culture of praise and encouragement – a highly supportive and affirming environment in which pupils felt safe to explore the arts and take creative risks. This was an obvious manifestation of the teachers' enthusiasm for their artform and their desire to communicate this to the class – encouraging pupils to feel equally enthusiastic. Lesson observations indicated that a 'high-challenge/high-support' model was one feature of effective arts provision – echoed by the perceptions of pupils who indicated that, in their view, an effective lesson would provide them with a challenging activity, but one through which they could also develop some sense of achievement. Clearly, a culture of praise and affirmation allows pupils of all abilities to feel this sense of achievement.

In addition to the praise and affirmation which were lavished on pupils during arts lessons, teachers provided considerable help and advice during practical arts activities – generally to small groups or individuals. During the classroom observations, numerous instances were recorded of teachers providing encouragement, advice, help, constructive criticism or practical intervention (demonstrating or modelling the task to be achieved or the artwork to be produced). These were clearly a result of the teachers' knowledge of their pupils and the artform, and were specifically geared towards the needs of the individual – differentiated according to the pupils' ability and previous experiences. Both teachers and pupils felt that this approach – supporting small groups and individuals, and differentiating the help according to pupils' requirements – often based on the traditional workshop/ apprenticeship model of learning from an arts practitioner, was a significant strength of arts teaching which could be effectively applied to other school subjects.

11. PUPIL BACKGROUND AND PARENTAL SUPPORT

Finally, pupils and teachers alike recognised the impact that the pupils themselves had on the effectiveness of arts lessons. They particularly recognised their own behaviour, their motivation to work hard, their predisposition towards the arts, their prior involvement (at primary school and through extra-curricular participation) and their arts ability to be key factors, allowing them to develop the greatest number and quality of outcomes from arts lessons within school. This supports the view that a 'value-added' approach to gauging arts effectiveness would be appropriate – taking into account the different starting points of the pupils being taught. It also suggests that in order to improve the effectiveness of secondary arts education, pupils must be encouraged – through primary education, extra-curricular participation and parental support – to be involved in the arts from an earlier age. It is clear that effectiveness in secondary arts education cannot be achieved without adequate consideration of the backgrounds of the pupils that it is directed towards.

Parental support for, and participation in, the arts were key issues in the background of pupils which were shown during the Year 11 survey to have a specific effect on pupils' attitudes towards, and take-up of, arts options at key stage 4. Pupils from families where the parents supported the arts – as either participants or consumers – or provided adequate support for their children in terms of paying for private music lessons or arts club membership, were considerably more likely to take arts options at key stage 4 than their peers who were not from such 'arts-involved' families. Relating very closely to the status and relevance of the arts in society (the first issue raised in this chapter), this, then, presents another challenge to schools and arts organisations: to encourage whole families to become active participants, consumers and supporters of all forms of arts opportunity.

3.
WHAT ARE
EFFECTIVE
PRACTICES
IN
ARTS
EDUCATION?

PART FOUR: CONCLUSION

16. SUMMARY AND CONCLUSION

> **CHAPTER OVERVIEW**
> This final chapter concludes the report by:
> * outlining the study's aims and research methods (16.1)
> * summarising the main findings on the effects of arts education in secondary schools (16.2)
> * summarising the main findings on the effectiveness of teaching and learning in the arts (16.3)
> * highlighting some policy implications to emerge from the research (16.4).

4.
CONCLUSION

16.1 INTRODUCTION

This report has set out the findings of a three-year research project called *The Effects and Effectiveness of Arts Education*. As the title implies, the study set out to:

♦ investigate the range of outcomes attributable to arts education in English and Welsh secondary schools, in particular the hypothesis that engagement in the arts can boost general academic performance; and

♦ analyse the key factors and processes that may bring about these effects, including the identification and portrayal of particularly effective practices.

To pursue these aims, the research drew on evidence collected through:

● **case studies** of five secondary schools with good reputations in the arts – these included annual interviews with two cohorts of pupils (approximately 79 in total each year) who were performing well in the arts, interviews with school managers and arts teachers, and video observations of arts lessons;

● **analyses of wider-ranging information** compiled through NFER's QUASE project – data on a total of 27,607 pupils from 152 schools in three cohorts of Year 11 pupils taking GCSEs between 1994 and 1996 were analysed;

- **questionnaires** completed by 2,269 Year 11 pupils in 22 schools, with related information on their GCSE results, prior attainment scores and key stage 3 national test results, along with responses to a school questionnaire; and

- **interviews** with a cross-section of 20 employers and some of their employees.

16.2 WHAT ARE THE EFFECTS OF ARTS EDUCATION?

Findings from the case studies

The effects of arts education fell into ten broad categories – the first seven dealt with direct learning outcomes for pupils, while the remaining three covered other types of effect. The outcomes attributable to the arts comprised:

4.
CONCLUSION

- a heightened sense of enjoyment, excitement, fulfilment and therapeutic release of tensions;

- an increase in the knowledge and skills associated with particular artforms;

- enhanced knowledge of social and cultural issues;

- the development of creativity and thinking skills;

- the enrichment of communication and expressive skills;

- advances in personal and social development;

- effects that transfer to other contexts, such as learning in other subjects, the world of work and cultural activities outside of and beyond school;

- institutional effects on the culture of the school;

- effects on the local community (including parents and governors); and

- art itself as an outcome.

In schools with strong reputations in the arts, numerous and wide-ranging effects were reported by pupils who were performing well in at least one artform. Outcomes relating to advancements in the technical skills and knowledge associated with specific artforms were by far the most frequently mentioned type of effect. In addition, vivid testimonies to many other outcomes were recorded. These included a sense of fulfilment in their own achievements, social skills (especially those required for effective teamwork), self-confidence, expressive skills and creativity. Many of these effects (e.g. improved self-esteem, and personal and social development) are highly pertinent to the task of tackling disaffection and social exclusion amongst young people. The range of outcomes associated with strong arts provision was wider than that codified in the National Curriculum and broader than the current focus on 'creative and cultural education'.

Again, from arts-orientated pupils in schools strong in the arts, each of the main artforms generated distinctive effects. For example, dance offered increased awareness of the body and movement; art promoted expressive skills; drama nurtured empathy and the valuing of others; and music extended active listening skills. Thus, it was concluded that, to achieve the full canon of effects from the arts, pupils require exposure to each of the individual artforms. To this extent, the use of the term 'the arts' might be unhelpful if it leads to policies which wrongly assume that the learning gains associated with one artform are broadly the same as those of the others.

Even in those schools with good reputations for the arts, gaps in the outcomes identified by pupils were evident. The most noteworthy of these included:

4. CONCLUSION

- ♦ the development of critical discrimination and aesthetic judgement-making, especially the capacity to locate these in their social, artistic and cultural contexts;

- ♦ the furthering of thinking skills, or perhaps more accurately, a meta-awareness of the intellectual dimensions to artistic processes;

- ♦ preparation for cultural life as critical, reflective and active 'consumers' of the arts beyond school; and

- ♦ the development of techniques and skill-based processes in music at key stage 3.

Findings from the wider sample

From a larger and more representative sample of schools, there was no sound evidence to support the claim that the arts boost general academic performance at GCSE. From the case study schools, however, pupils volunteered accounts of arts-based learning that had transferred to other subjects. This was especially the case for art and drama, but less so for music. Overall, the findings add weight to the emerging literature that strikes a cautionary note on the alleged influence of the arts on general academic attainment. Certainly, on the basis of the evidence relating to 14–16-year-olds, such claims would not appear to be the most prudent form of arts advocacy at the moment – though more studies with larger samples and different age ranges are needed to test the claims further.

The contrasting patterns of effects exhibited in different schools indicated great variation in the ways that teachers approached the teaching of each of the artforms. Multiple interpretations of both the means and the ends of teaching art, dance, drama and music were apparent. Whether this is a problem or an advantage depends on the relative values placed on diversity in the curriculum and a common curriculum entitlement.

There were considerable inequalities in the provision of arts education available to pupils. The Year 11 survey found, for example, substantial variation in the range, frequency and quality of arts-related outcomes achieved by different schools. Only a small minority of schools registered high outcome scores in all the main artforms and succeeded in attracting higher than average numbers of pupils on to GCSE courses in the arts. The majority displayed weak outcomes in at least one artform. The evidence suggests that few schools make effective provision in all the major artforms, and that many are falling well short of the standards set by the best.

Another significant finding was the limited impact of arts education on the generality of pupils in many schools. Most pupils in the Year 11 survey signalled that the arts had made no impact on them. Too often, only the most committed of pupils registered any effects, especially in music. Certainly in terms of technical capabilities, some pupils in the case study schools saw music as 'special' and for the elite. To this extent, and with varying degrees of relevance to all artforms, the rhetoric of the 'arts as accessible to all' was not always borne out in reality.

4.
CONCLUSION

The evidence revealed marked differences in the overall health and buoyancy of the individual artforms.

Art achieved a wide variety of important effects on pupils, was the most likely to be perceived as having an impact, had the highest proportion of pupils taking it at key stage 4 and was afforded official status within the National Curriculum. Overall, art was the strongest and most robust of the artforms. For further development, though, consideration may be given to how art could give more emphasis to the general gaps in outcomes noted earlier in the chapter.

Dance and **drama** both registered an impressive array of outcomes for those pupils who took them, but both appeared to be lacking in status – in terms of curriculum coverage, the exposure that pupils received and their place within the National Curriculum.

Music, while benefiting from similar status to that of art, attracted the highest proportion of 'no impact' responses, registered a more limited range of outcomes compared with art and drama, had very low numbers enrolling for it at key stage 4 and, relative to other arts subjects, received lower levels of enjoyment in GCSE courses. Pupil enjoyment, relevance, skill development, creativity and expressive dimensions were often absent. Overall, music was the most problematic and vulnerable artform.

Finally, the arts were seen by many members of senior management in schools to impact on the whole school ethos, mainly by encouraging a positive cohesive atmosphere through enhancing pupils' enjoyment, self-esteem and achievement. While several senior teachers acknowledged that this made the arts particularly important in fostering a culture conducive to institutional change and development, they stressed that school improvement and effectiveness were dependent on many factors, including important contributions to the ethos of the school made by other areas of the curriculum.

16.3 WHAT ARE EFFECTIVE PRACTICES IN ARTS EDUCATION?

4. CONCLUSION

The report has examined the different factors and influences that were both perceived and observed to contribute to effective teaching and learning in the arts in secondary schools. The most influential factors are summarised below.

The status of arts subjects in the National Curriculum – the National Curriculum provides an indication of the importance attributed to different subjects, and thereby affects the nature and level of their provision. Although the arts are not deemed to be 'core' subjects, art and music are established foundation subjects; drama and dance have a more peripheral status, thus implying they are even less important than art and music.

Adequate provision of the arts at key stages 3 and 4 – the availability of the arts within key stage 4 options was a crucial issue. For example, the Year 11 survey revealed that only three per cent of the sample was taking dance, although it rose to 14 per cent at schools where it was an available option. Furthermore, flexible option structures that allowed all pupils – not just the lower attainers – to take more than one artform, were another key facilitating factor. However, the results also suggested that making at least one artform compulsory at key stage 4 was associated with reduced levels of pupil enjoyment – though, this is likely to be the case for all compulsory subjects. Some schools, however, achieved relatively high levels of participation and enjoyment without compulsion. It would, therefore, seem an important priority for schools to focus on breaking down the identified barriers to participation, thus encouraging pupils to choose the arts for themselves, based on positive reasons. Pupils gave three main reasons for their choice of arts subjects at key stage 4: their personal enjoyment of the subject, their ability in it, and their perception of its relevance, status and value. It was also clear that pupils' choices for key stage 4 were heavily influenced by their previous experiences during key stage 3.

Enjoyment and perceived relevance of the arts – as the previous point suggests, these two qualities were found to be key factors in determining the efficacy of learning in the arts. The observed lessons (e.g. one using the title song from a popular film as a stimulus for composition, in a school that had three times the national average enrolling for GCSE music) illustrated many ways in which teachers can mediate the curriculum so that pupils experience the arts as relevant and engaging.

Internal and external support for the arts and arts teachers – effective provision received support from internal sources including senior management, faculty and departmental structures, and other teachers, and from external sources such as LEA arts advisers, RABs, arts organisations and local teacher networks. In schools where arts lessons were observed, common threads were the high level of management support for the arts; high levels of encouragement and acclaim; appropriate teaching time; and specialist resources directed towards the arts. These were seen to be key factors in raising and maintaining the confidence levels of the staff, which in turn influenced their commitment. The main source of external support for the case study schools came from LEAs, and a wide variety of different mechanisms were described including: arts advisers, provision of resources and facilities and the organisation of artists-in-residence schemes. However, it was clear that the quality and extent of this type of provision varied widely between LEAs.

**4.
CONCLUSION**

Specialist arts teachers – generally speaking, the research found that as far as the arts were concerned, individual teacher factors were probably more important determinants of effectiveness than whole-school factors. School staff perceived a need for specialist arts teachers and all the lessons identified as demonstrating 'effective practice' were taught by specialist teachers with high levels of personal involvement, passion and commitment to the artform. Pupils described their respect for teachers who were able to give practical demonstrations of the artform, and participate in class activities. This was confirmed in many observations where teachers provided help and advice to individuals or small groups, and in some cases, this involved teachers in modelling the desired outcome. This clearly relied on the teachers' own expertise in the artform.

Practical task-based activities – the efficacy of arts lessons was often perceived to depend on the extent of practical '*doing*' activities. Pupils recounted their enjoyment of learning through '*doing their own thing*', and the personal satisfaction they gained from being creative, developing ideas and producing their own individual outcome. Pupils and teachers alike described their perception of the arts as providing a much-needed balance to the more structured, academic and desk-based subjects within the curriculum – though the practical emphasis might render it more difficult for arts teachers to achieve the more reflective, discursive and judgement-based outcomes noted earlier as gaps in the apparent effects.

Performance, display, evaluation and symbolic 'celebration' of what is produced – these were deemed to be crucial to effective arts lessons. They provided an opportunity for pupils to demonstrate what they had developed and learnt during practical tasks; they offered subject matter for discussing the arts in general; and they supplied a vehicle for the evaluation of the arts, and the development of an arts language to inform critical consumption. They also provided an opportunity for constructive criticism, which was recognised as essential for improvement.

A praise culture – effective teachers provided a highly supportive and affirming classroom environment in which pupils felt encouraged and safe to take creative risks. These teachers generated a climate for learning based on unconditional positive regard. Lesson observations indicated that a 'high-challenge/high-support' model was one feature of effective arts provision – echoed by the perceptions of many pupils, who indicated that an effective lesson offered a challenging activity, but one through which they could also develop some sense of achievement. During the classroom observations, numerous instances were recorded of teachers providing encouragement, advice, help, constructive criticism or practical intervention. These often demonstrated the professional judgements and skills to differentiate the type of interventions pupils of differing cultures, ability and confidence might need. Teachers and pupils felt that this approach – perhaps based on the traditional apprenticeship model of learning from an arts practitioner – was a significant and particular strength of arts teaching.

Pupils' own contribution, background and parental support – finally, a key finding was the substantial impact that the pupils themselves had on the effectiveness of arts teaching. They recognised their own behaviour, motivation to work hard, predisposition towards the arts, their prior involvement and their arts ability to be key determinants of the number and quality of outcomes they achieved. It also suggests that in order to improve the effectiveness of secondary

**4.
CONCLUSION**

arts education, pupils should be encouraged – through primary education, extra-curricular participation, and parental support – to be involved in the arts from an earlier age. Pupils with parents who supported the arts were also considerably more likely to take arts options than their peers who were not from such arts-orientated families.

16.4 POLICY IMPLICATIONS

At various points in the report, the research team has alluded to possible implications for policy. To conclude, we draw together some proposals for the consideration of policy-makers and practitioners. It is suggested that:

♦ for the full canon of effects from arts education to be available to pupils, all of the artforms need to be provided in the school curriculum;

♦ as a reflection of the most effective arts teaching and in recognition of their contribution beyond that of PE and English, dance and drama should be given comparable status in the National Curriculum to that of art and music;

4.
CONCLUSION

♦ in view of the critical problems facing music, there is an urgent need to tackle the quality of teaching in this subject – by mounting, for example, a programme of continuing professional development (CPD) for music teachers, in which those teachers achieving high outcomes should play a leading role as models of effective practice;

♦ the issues surrounding the lack of relevance perceived by pupils in some arts provision should be explicitly addressed in the programmes of study for arts subjects;

♦ there is a need to recruit and train teachers with specialist expertise in the arts and to encourage them to remain in the classroom by providing a career and CPD structure that offers regular opportunities for creative renewal;

♦ local consultation procedures between teachers of specific artforms and agencies such as LEA advisers, Regional Arts Boards and arts organisations should be set up to develop the external support systems available to teachers;

♦ ITT providers should ensure that student teachers are aware of the outcomes associated with different approaches to teaching arts subjects, that the factors characteristic of effective teaching are well covered in their courses and that sufficient time is available for student teachers to develop these practices; and

♦ strategies to encourage parents and families to participate in the arts and value their relevance would be helpful in laying the foundations for learning in the arts at school.

If the beneficial outcomes that the arts can stimulate are to be available to all pupils, there is a pressing case for reversing the trend towards selective policies that extend inequalities between schools and which result largely in the best schools for the arts becoming even better. The results establish that, in the context of the prevailing educational, political and financial climate, some schools can achieve high-quality provision in the four main artforms and that there are many substantial learning outcomes for those pupils fortunate enough to attend such schools. However, the study also indicates that the picture is less than satisfactory for the majority of schools and pupils. Policies are required that seek improvements across the board and might include strategies that encourage schools with demonstrable strengths in achieving high-quality outcomes in arts education to aid and support developments in schools without those strengths.

4.
CONCLUSION

REFERENCES

ARTS COUNCIL OF ENGLAND (1998). *Bringing New Art to New People. Arts Council of England Announces 'New Audiences' Projects* (Press Release, 21 September). London: Arts Council of England.

ARTS COUNCIL OF ENGLAND (1999). *Arias for All! Opera Companies Reach Out to New People as Part of the Arts Council's New Audiences' Programme* (Press Release, 10 February). London: Arts Council of England.

ASHWORTH, M., HARLAND, J., HAYNES, J. and KINDER, K. with BERGER, H. (1998). Creative Arts Partnerships in Education UK: Stage One Evaluation Report. Unpublished report.

BOURDIEU, P. and PASSERON, C. (1977). *Reproduction in Education, Society and Culture.* London: Sage.

COOPERS & LYBRAND (1994). *Review of Instrumental Music Services: a Report.* London: Incorporated Society of Musicians.

DOWNING, D. (1996). *Artists in Leeds Schools: a Review of Leeds City Council's Artists in Schools Programme.* Leeds: Leeds City Council, Department of Education.

DU PONT, S. (1992). 'The effectiveness of creative drama as an instructional strategy to enhance the reading skills of fifth graders', *Reading Research and Instruction,* **31**, 3, 41-52.

EISNER, E. (1998). 'Does experience in the arts boost academic achievement?' *Art Education,* **51**, 1, 7-15.

FEUERSTEIN, R. (1980). *Instrumental Enrichment: an Intervention Programme for Cognitive Modifiability.* Baltimore, MD: University Park Press.

FORSETH, S. (1980). 'Arts activities, attitudes and achievement in elementary mathematics', *Studies in Art Education,* **21**, 2, 22-7.

FOX, A. and GARDINER, M.L. (1997). 'The arts and raising achievement.' Paper presented at 'The Arts in the Curriculum Conference', organised by the Department of the National Heritage and the School Curriculum and Assessment Authority, 25 February.

FRYER, M. (1996). *Creative Teaching and Learning.* London: Paul Chapman.

GARDINER, M.F., FOX, A., KNOWLES, F. and JEFFRY, D. (1996). 'Learning improved by arts training', *Nature,* **381**, 23 May, 284.

GARDNER, H. (1993). *Frames of Mind: the Theory of Multiple Intelligences.* Second edn. New York, NY: Basic Books.

GOLEMAN, D. (1996). *Emotional Intelligence: Why It Can Matter More Than IQ.* London: Bloomsbury.

GREAT BRITAIN. DEPARTMENT FOR CULTURE, MEDIA AND SPORT (2000). *Government Response to All Our Futures: Creativity, Culture & Education* (14 January, 2000). London: DCMS.

GREAT BRITAIN. DEPARTMENT FOR CULTURE, MEDIA AND SPORT. POLICY ACTION TEAM 10 (1999). *Arts & Sport: a Report to the Social Exclusion Unit.* London: DCMS.

GREAT BRITAIN. DEPARTMENT FOR EDUCATION (1995). *The National Curriculum.* London: HMSO.

GREAT BRITAIN. DEPARTMENT FOR EDUCATION AND EMPLOYMENT (1998a). *Education Action Zones* [online]. Available: http://www.dfee.gov.uk/education/index.htm [8 August, 2000].

GREAT BRITAIN. DEPARTMENT FOR EDUCATION AND EMPLOYMENT (1998b). *GCSE/GNVQ and GCE A/AS Examination Results 1996/97 – England* (Statistical Bulletin 6/98). London: The Stationery Office.

GREAT BRITAIN. DEPARTMENT FOR EDUCATION AND EMPLOYMENT (1998c). *Study Support Projects Unlock New Learning Opportunities - Clarke.* (Press Notice 474/98). London: DfEE.

GREAT BRITAIN. DEPARTMENT FOR EDUCATION AND EMPLOYMENT (1999). *Fresh Start for Islington Arts and Media School – Blunkett* (Press Notice 462/99). London: DfEE.

GREAT BRITAIN. DEPARTMENT OF NATIONAL HERITAGE (1996). *Setting the Scene: the Arts and Young People.* London: DNH.

HARGREAVES, D.H. (1991). 'Coherence and manageability: reflections on the National Curriculum and cross-curricular provision', *The Curriculum Journal*, **2**, 1, 33-41.

HARLAND, J. (1990). 'An evaluation of a performing arts experiment in a special school', *Educational Research*, **32**, 2, 118-29.

HARLAND, J., ASHWORTH, M., BOWER, R., HOGARTH, S., MONTGOMERY, A. and MOOR, H. (1999). *Real Curriculum: at the Start of Key Stage 3. Report Two from the Northern Ireland Curriculum Cohort Study.* Slough: NFER.

HARLAND, J. and KINDER, K. (1995). 'Buzzes and barriers: young people's attitudes to participation in the arts', *Children & Society*, **9**, 4, 15-31.

HARLAND, J. and KINDER, K. (Eds) (1999). *Crossing the Line: Extending Young People's Access to Cultural Venues.* London: Calouste Gulbenkian Foundation.

HARLAND, J., KINDER, K. and HARTLEY, K. (1995). *Arts in their View: a Study of Youth Participation in the Arts.* Slough: NFER.

HARLAND, J., KINDER, K., HAYNES, J. and SCHAGEN, I. (1998). *The Effects and Effectiveness of Arts Education in Schools. Interim Report 1.* Slough: NFER.

HOGARTH, S., KINDER, K. and HARLAND, J. (1997). *Arts Organisations and their Education Programmes.* London: Arts Council of England.

JOYCE, B. and SHOWERS, B. (1982). 'The coaching of teachers', *Educational Leadership*, **40**, 1, 4-8.

KINDER, K., HARLAND, J., WILKIN, A. and WAKEFIELD, A. (1995). *Three to Remember: Strategies for Disaffected Pupils.* Slough: NFER.

KOKAS, K. (1969). 'Psychological testing in Hungarian music education', *Journal of Research in Music Education*, **17**, 1, 125-32.

LUFTIG, R.L. (1994). *The Schooled Mind: Do the Arts Make a Difference? An Empirical Evaluation of the Hamilton Fairfield SPECTRA+ Program, 1992-93.* Oxford, OH: Miami University, Center for Human Development, Learning and Teaching.

MAYER, J.D., CARUSO, D.R. and SALOVEY, P. (2000). 'Emotional intelligence meets traditional standards for an intelligence', *Intelligence*, **27**, 4, 267-98.

MUSIC EDUCATION COUNCIL. MUSIC INDUSTRIES ASSOCIATION and NATIONAL MUSIC COUNCIL (1998). *The Fourth 'R': the Case for Music in the School Curriculum.* West Horsley: Campaign for Music in the School Curriculum.

O'BRIEN, J. (1996). *Secondary School Pupils and the Arts: Report on a MORI Study* (ACE Research Report 5). London: Arts Council of England.

ODDIE, D. and ALLEN, G. (1998). 'Artists in school: a review.' Paper presented at the British Educational Research Association Annual Conference, University of Belfast, Belfast, 27-30 August.

QUALIFICATIONS AND CURRICULUM AUTHORITY (1999). *The Review of the National Curriculum in England: the Consultation Materials.* London: QCA.

QUALIFICATIONS AND CURRICULUM AUTHORITY (2000). *Personal, Social and Health Education at Key Stages 3 and 4: Initial Guidance for Schools.* London: QCA.

QUALIFICATIONS AND CURRICULUM AUTHORITY and ARTS COUNCIL OF ENGLAND (2000). *From Policy to Partnership. Developing the Arts in Schools*. London: QCA and the Arts Council of England.

RAUSCHER, F.H., SHAW, G.L., LEVINE, L.J., WRIGHT, E.L., DENNIS, W.R. and NEWCOMB, R.L. (1997). 'Music training causes long-term enhancement of preschool children's spatial-temporal reasoning', *Neurological Research*, **19**, 2-8.

ROBINSON, K. (Ed) (1982). *The Arts in Schools*. London: Calouste Gulbenkian Foundation.

ROBINSON REPORT. GREAT BRITAIN. DEPARTMENT FOR EDUCATION AND EMPLOYMENT and DEPARTMENT FOR CULTURE, MEDIA AND SPORT. NATIONAL ADVISORY COMMITTEE ON CREATIVE AND CULTURAL EDUCATION (1999). *All Our Futures: Creativity, Culture & Education*. London: DfEE.

ROGERS, R. (1995). *Guaranteeing an Entitlement to the Arts in Schools*. London: The Royal Society for the Encouragement of Arts, Manufactures and Commerce.

ROGERS, R. (1998). *The Disappearing Arts? The Current State of the Arts in Initial Teacher Training and Professional Development*. London: The Royal Society for the Encouragement of Arts, Manufactures and Commerce.

ROGERS, R. (1999). 'Current Influences on Arts Education in England.' Paper presented at the RSA and Getty Education Institute for the Arts Seminar, Dudley, 18 June.

ROSS, M. (1995). 'What's wrong with school music?' *British Journal of Music Education*, **12**, 3, 185-201.

ROSS, M. and KAMBA, M. (1997). *The State of The Arts in Five Secondary Schools*. Exeter: University of Exeter.

ROYAL SOCIETY FOR THE ENCOURAGEMENT OF ARTS, MANUFACTURES AND COMMERCE (1997). *The Arts Matter*. Aldershot: Gower.

SCHAGEN, I. (1995). *QUASE: Quantitative Analysis for Self-Evaluation. Technical Report of Analysis 1995*. Slough: NFER.

SCHOOL CURRICULUM AND ASSESSMENT AUTHORITY (1997). *The Arts in the Curriculum: a Joint Conference Held by the School Curriculum and Assessment Authority and the Department of National Heritage in February 1997*. London: SCAA.

SECONDARY HEADS ASSOCIATION (1995). *Whither the Arts? The State of the Expressive Arts in Secondary Schools*. Leicester: SHA.

SHARP, C. (1991). *When Every Note Counts: the Schools' Instrumental Music Service in the 1990s.* Slough: NFER.

SHARP, C. with BENEFIELD, P. and KENDALL, L. (1998). *The Effects of Teaching and Learning in the Arts: a Review of Research.* London: QCA.

SHARP, C. and DUST, K. (1997). *Artists in Schools: a Handbook for Teachers and Artists.* Revised edn. Slough: NFER.

SPYCHIGER, M., PATRY, J-L., LAUPER, G., ZIMMERMANN, E. and WEBER, E. (1995). 'Does more music teaching lead to a better social climate?' In: OLECHOWSKI, R. and KHAN-SVIK, G. (Eds) *Experimental Research on Teaching and Learning.* Frankfurt: Peter Lang.

TAMBLING, P. and HARLAND, J. (1998). *Orchestral Education Programmes: Intents and Purposes.* London: Arts Council of England.

TURNER, E. (1999). *Building Quality Links: Research on the Arts-Education Interface.* Stirling: University of Stirling, Institute of Education.

UNITED KINGDOM COUNCIL FOR MUSIC EDUCATION AND TRAINING and MUSIC ADVISERS' NATIONAL ASSOCIATION (1993). 'New research into instrumental music services', *United Kingdom Council for Music Education and Trainiing (UKCMET) Newsletter*, February, 5-11.

WINNER, E. and HETLAND, L. (forthcoming, 2000). 'The arts and academic improvement: what the evidence shows', *Journal of Aesthetic Education*, **34**, 3/4, (whole issue).

WOLFF, K. (1978). 'The non-musical outcomes of music education: a review of the literature', *Bulletin of the Council of Research in Music Education*, **55**, 1-27.

WYATT, T. (1996). 'School effectiveness research: Dead end, damp squib or smouldering fuse?' *Issues in Educational Research* **6**, 1, 79-112.

REFERENCES

APPENDIX I

THE ARTS AT SCHOOL

A questionnaire for Year 11 students

THE ARTS AT SCHOOL
A questionnaire for Year 11 students

1. Which of these subjects are you taking (or have you taken) for GCSE? *Please circle those which apply.*

English Literature	1	Geography	9	Art	17
English Language	2	History	10	Dance	18
Mathematics	3	French	11	Drama	19
Science - Single	4	German	12	Expressive Arts	20
- Double	5	Welsh	13	Music	21
Biology	6	Media Studies	14	Physical Education	22
Physics	7	Business Studies	15	*Other:*	23
Chemistry	8	Technology	16	*Other:*	24

2. Please list any subjects you are taking this year for **other** qualifications (e.g. GNVQ).

3. Please list any subjects you are taking this year, but not for any qualification (excluding RE, PE and PSE).

4. Of all the subjects you currently take, which are your favourite two? *Put your favourite one first.*

    i. _____ ii. _____

5. Of all the subjects you currently take, which two do you like the least? *Put the least liked first.*

    i. _____ ii. _____

6. Which two subjects do you think you are best at? *Put the subject you are best at first.*

    i. _____ ii. _____

If you are <u>NOT</u> currently taking art or dance, drama, the expressive arts or music, please go to Question 9.

7. If you <u>ARE</u> taking art, music, dance, drama or the expressive arts for GCSE, why did you choose this subject/these subjects? *Please circle as many reasons as apply for each of the subjects you take.*

	Art	Dance	Drama	Expressive Arts	Music
Advice from parents	1	1	1	1	1
Advice from the school	2	2	2	2	2
For personal interest and enjoyment	3	3	3	3	3
Because it may lead to a career	4	4	4	4	4
Because of the teacher taking it	5	5	5	5	5
Because I'm good at it	6	6	6	6	6
Because there wasn't much choice/limited options	7	7	7	7	7
Because there was no choice/school required me to take it	8	8	8	8	8
Because it's an easy option	9	9	9	9	9
Friends chose it	10	10	10	10	10
Other (please specify)	11	11	11	11	11

8. Do you enjoy your lessons in these subjects? *Please circle **one** number for each of the subjects you take.*

	Art	Dance	Drama	Expressive Arts	Music
Always	1	1	1	1	1
Most of the time	2	2	2	2	2
Sometimes	3	3	3	3	3
Hardly ever	4	4	4	4	4
Never	5	5	5	5	5

9. If you are not currently taking any of the subjects listed below, would you like to be taking any of them? *Please circle as many as apply.*

Art	1	Dance	2	Drama	3	Expressive Arts	4	Music	5

10. If you circled any subject(s) for question 9, what stopped you from being able to take it this year? *Please circle as many as apply.*

	Art	Dance	Drama	Expressive Arts	Music
Subject not available at my school	1	1	1	1	1
Advice from parents	2	2	2	2	2
I feel other subjects are more important	3	3	3	3	3
Advice from the school	4	4	4	4	4
Clashes with other subjects on the timetable/options	5	5	5	5	5
I'm not very good at it	6	6	6	6	6
Other (please specify)	7	7	7	7	7

11. What have **you** got out of studying these subjects during your time at secondary school (Years 7-11)? *Please circle as many as apply for each subject.*

I think that taking this subject at school ...	Art	Dance	Drama	Music	Literature, novels and poetry
teaches particular skills	1	1	1	1	1
gives you self-confidence socially/helps you to get on with people	2	2	2	2	2
helps you to feel good about yourself	3	3	3	3	3
helps you to learn in other subjects	4	4	4	4	4
helps you to think and clarifies your thinking	5	5	5	5	5
helps you to understand people's feelings and emotions	6	6	6	6	6
helps with a future job or career	7	7	7	7	7
gives you knowledge of the art form and appreciation of people's work in it	8	8	8	8	8
helps to express yourself better	9	9	9	9	9
gives you a sense of pleasure/enjoyment satisfaction	10	10	10	10	10
helps you learn more about social issues and problems	11	11	11	11	11
helps you to be more creative/ imaginative	12	12	12	12	12

12. How important would you say the arts (or any particular art form) are to you? *Please circle one number.*

Very important	1	Quite important	2	Not very important	3	Not important at all	4

13. In the questions below, please indicate **any extra-curricular involvement** (both at school but not in your main lessons OR in your own leisure time) you have had in the arts between the ages of 5 and 11 (primary age) and 12 and 16 (secondary age). *Please circle one number for each row.*

A) *ART (e.g. drawing, pottery, painting, sculpture making, printing etc)*

		not at all	a little	some	a great deal			
i.	Primary-age extra-curricular involvement in art	1	2	3	4			
ii.	Secondary-age extra-curricular involvement in art	1	2	3	4			
iii.	During the last two years, have you produced a piece of visual art for your own interest?				Yes	1	No	2
iv.	During the last two years, have you been to a gallery or an exhibition to look at art in your own time?				Yes	1	No	2

B) *MUSIC (playing an instrument, singing, playing in a band etc)*

		not at all	a little	some	a great deal			
i.	Primary-age extra-curricular involvement in music	1	2	3	4			
ii.	Secondary-age extra-curricular involvement in music	1	2	3	4			
iii.	During the last two years, have you been learning to play a musical instrument?				Yes	1	No	2
iv.	During the last two years, have you been involved in music-making with other people?				Yes	1	No	2
v.	During the last two years, have you been to a musical performance/concert in your own time?			Classical	Yes	1	No	2
				Pop/Rock	Yes	1	No	2

C) *DRAMA (taking part in improvisations, performances, plays etc.)*

		not at all	a little	some	a great deal			
i.	Primary-age extra-curricular involvement in drama	1	2	3	4			
ii.	Secondary-age extra-curricular involvement in drama	1	2	3	4			
iii.	During the last two years, have you acted in a play OR participated in a drama club/workshop?				Yes	1	No	2
iv.	During the last two years, have you been to see a play/the theatre in your own time?				Yes	1	No	2

D) *DANCE (learning and performing dance etc)*

		not at all	a little	some	a great deal			
i.	Primary-age extra-curricular involvement in dance	1	2	3	4			
ii.	Secondary-age extra-curricular involvement in dance	1	2	3	4			
iii.	During the last two years, have you participated in a dance performance or attended a dance club/lessons?				Yes	1	No	2
iv.	During the last two years, have you been to see a dance performance in your own time?				Yes	1	No	2

E) *LITERATURE (writing stores, poetry etc)*

i.	During the last two years, have you written any short stories or poetry (or similar) for your own interest?				Yes	1	No	2
ii.	During the last two years, have you read any novels, short stories or poetry for your own pleasure?				Yes	1	No	2

14. Are your parents **interested** in any of the following art forms? *Please circle as many as apply.*

    Art   1   Music   2   Drama   3   Dance   4   Literature   5

15. To what extent, if any, have either of your parents actively **taken part** in any of these art forms during the last two years? *Please circle one number.*

    Not at all   1   To some extent   2   A great deal   3

16. Do your parents support your involvement in the arts in any of the following ways? *Please circle as many as apply.*

Ask questions about what you do in the arts	1
Attend concerts, plays, exhibitions you are involved in	2
Pay for lessons, membership of a club	3
Provide equipment, e.g. musical instruments, art equipment, dance costumes	4
Encourage you to be involved	5
Provide transport	6
Other (please specify)	7
Don't provide any support for your involvement in the arts	8

Finally, some questions about yourself.

17. What is your name? _____

18. Are you: Male 1   Female   2

19. What is your date of birth?

Date	Month	Year

20. Which of the following do you consider to be your ethnic origin? *Please circle.*

White	1	Black-African	2	Black-Caribbean	3	Black-Other	4
Indian	5	Pakistani	6	Bangladeshi	7	Chinese	8

    Any other ethnic group   9   _____

21. Please tell us about your parents' (or guardians') jobs.
    *If either of them is not working at the moment, please tell us about the **last job** he or she had.*
    If you can't answer any of the following questions, write 'Don't know' in the appropriate space.

    Father   **Mother**

    a) What is the name of the job?

        _____   _____

    b) What kind of work do they do?

        _____   _____

        _____   _____

    c) What sort of place or organisation do they work for?

        _____   _____

        _____   _____

    THANK YOU VERY MUCH FOR YOUR HELP

APPENDICES

APPENDIX 2

THE ARTS AT SCHOOL

School questionnaire

THE ARTS AT SCHOOL
School questionnaire

This questionnaire is part of the research project 'The Effects and Effectiveness of Arts Education' and will help us analyse the questionnaires completed by Year 11 students at your school.

Your help in completing this questionnaire is greatly appreciated.

Your responses will be entirely confidential, and schools will be anonymous in any reports arising from the research.

*We would be grateful if you could return the questionnaire in the envelope provided, as soon as possible, and by **Friday 29th May** at the latest.*

School _____

Position of respondent _____

1.   Which of the following best describes your school's catchment area? *Please circle one number.*

Rural	1
Small/medium town	2
Suburban	3
Urban	4
Inner city	5

2.   a) How are arts subjects organised within the school? *Please circle one number.*

Departmental structure only	1
Faculty structure	2
Other	3

If other, please specify _____

b) Please provide details of the composition (including names and number) of arts-related faculties and departments.

_____

_____

_____

_____

3. Please provide details about specialist facilities and resources available in the school for the arts (e.g. dance studio, theatre facilities, music rooms).

_____

_____

_____

_____

4. Which of these subjects were available to the current Year 11 cohort, when they were in Key Stage 3 and Key Stage 4? *Please circle those which apply.*

	Key Stage 3	Key Stage 4
Visual Art	1	1
Music	2	2
Dance	3	3
Drama	4	4
Expressive Arts	5	5
Other arts: _____	6	6

5. a) Was it compulsory for current Year 11 students to take at least one arts subject for qualification at Key Stage 4? *Please circle one number.*

   Yes   1   No   2

   b) Was there any restriction on the number of arts subjects current Year 11 students could take at Key Stage 4? *Please circle one number.*

   Yes   1   No   2

6. Please provide details of the option choice system experienced by the current Year 11 students, including choices available, restrictions on choice, and banding of subjects.

_____

_____

_____

_____

_____

_____

_____

_____

_____

APPENDICES

583

7. **Please answer either a) or b)**

   a) If each of the GCSE arts subjects receive the **same** amount of teaching time at Key Stage 4, how much time per week is allocated to an arts subject?

   Year 10 [ ] minutes

   Year 11 [ ] minutes

   b) If each of the GCSE arts subjects receive **different** amounts of teaching time at Key Stage 4, please indicate the art form and time allocation, for Year 10 and Year 11.

   _____

   _____

   _____

   _____

   _____

8. What extra-curricular activities are available in the arts at Key Stage 3 and Key Stage 4? *Please circle as many as apply.*

	Key Stage 3	Key Stage 4
Choir or other singing groups	1	1
Instrumental groups	2	2
Art club or groups	3	3
Dance club or groups	4	4
Theatre or drama groups	5	5
Productions of plays or musicals	6	6
Creative writing groups	7	7
Other: _____	8	8
_____	9	9

9. Please provide details of any instrumental tuition available to current Year 11 students, including provider and time allocation.

   _____

   _____

   _____

   _____

   _____

   Thank you very much for your time.

APPENDIX III

NOTES ON THE DERIVED VARIABLES USED IN CHAPTER 9

School Questionnaire

CATCH   Catchment area (0 = rural to 4 = inner city)
Derived from Q1

TOTFAC   Total arts-related facilities listed in Q3 (codes in range 2 to 14)

ARTSCOMP   At least one arts subject compulsory at KS4 (from Q5a)

ACCESS   Index of access to arts subjects at KS4 (from Q5b, Q6)
= 0 if Q5b = 1 and 1 in Q6.1-4 (1 subject only);
= 1 if 2 in Q6.1-4 (2 subjects);
= 2 if 3 in Q6.1-4 (3 subjects);
& add 1 for each of 4, 5 or 6 in Q6.1-4 (arts in more than 1 option band).

HRSWK   Hours/week taught for each arts subject

ACTEXTRA   Count of extra-curricular activities available, based on Q8. It equals the number of codes 1 to 7, for either KS3 or KS4, plus the number of 'other' codes in the range 1 to 8.

Statistics for these variables for the 22 schools are given below.

Variable	Mean	Std Dev	Min	Max	Label
CATCH	2.05	1.50	0	4	Catchment area (0 = rural to 4 = inner c
TOTFAC	3.59	1.33	0	5	Total specialist arts facilities listed
ARTSCOMP	.14	.35	0	1	Arts subject compulsory at KS4
ACCESS	1.18	1.26	0	5	Index of access to arts subjects at KS4
HRSWK	2.41	.38	1.23	3	Hours/week per arts subject
ACTEXTRA	5.18	1.92	1	9	Total no. of arts extracurricular activ.

- - Correlation Coefficients - -

	CATCH	TOTFAC	ARTSCOMP	ACCESS	HRSWK	ACTEXTRA
CATCH	1.0000 (22) P= .	-.3963 (22) P= .068	-.2844 (22) P= .200	.1472 (22) P= .513	-.2730 (22) P= .219	-.2520 (22) P= .258
TOTFAC	-.3963 (22) P= .068	1.0000 (22) P= .	-.1803 (22) P= .422	.0464 (22) P= .837	.2288 (22) P= .306	.6636 (22) P= .001

ARTSCOMP	-.2844	-.1803	1.0000	.2644	.0969	.0321
	(22)	(22)	(22)	(22)	(22)	(22)
	P= .200	P= .422	P= .	P= .234	P= .668	P= .887
ACCESS	.1472	.0464	.2644	1.0000	-.0545	.1040
	(22)	(22)	(22)	(22)	(22)	(22)
	P= .513	P= .837	P= .234	P= .	P= .810	P= .645
HRSWK	-.2730	.2288	.0969	-.0545	1.0000	.2526
	(22)	(22)	(22)	(22)	(22)	(22)
	P= .219	P= .306	P= .668	P= .810	P= .	P= .257
ACTEXTRA	-.2520	.6636	.0321	.1040	.2526	1.0000
	(22)	(22)	(22)	(22)	(22)	(22)
	P= .258	P= .001	P= .887	P= .645	P= .257	P= .

Note that in the above correlation table (although with only 22 schools) the only significant correlations are between TOTFAC and ACTEXTRA, and between TOTFAC and CATCH (at the 10% level).

Pupil Questionnaire

Based on Q1, Q2 and Q3 to give indication of arts subjects studied at KS4 (GCSE or otherwise):

DUNART	= 1 if Art
DUNDAN	= 1 if Dance
DUNDRA	= 1 if Drama
DUNEA	= 1 if Expressive arts
DUNMUS	= 1 if Music
TOTARTS	= Total arts subjects studied
TOTSUB	= Total subjects studied
ARTSPC	= arts subjects as % of total
ARTSFAV	= Index with range 0 to 3 for arts subjects as favourites (+2 if first favourite, + 1 if second favourite) from Q4
ARTSHATE	= Index 0 to 3 for arts subjects most disliked (from Q5 as above)
ARTSBEST	= Index 0 to 3 for arts subjects best at (from Q6 as above)

APPENDICES

From Q7, indices of positive or negative reasons for studying arts subjects (codes 1 to 6 positive, codes 7 to 10 negative):

WHYART	Index for Art
WHYDAN	Index for Dance
WHYDRA	Index for Drama
WHYEA	Index for Expressive arts
WHYMUS	Index for Music
WHYARTS	Index for all arts subjects (sum of above)

From Q8, recoded on a range from –2 (Never) to 2 (Always) for enjoyment of lessons:

ENJOYART Enjoyment of Art lessons
ENJOYDAN Enjoyment of Dance lessons
ENJOYDRA Enjoyment of Drama lessons
ENJOYEA Enjoyment of Expressive Art lessons
ENJOYMUS Enjoyment of Music lessons
ENJOYALL Enjoyment of all arts lessons (sum of above)

ARTSCANT From Q9, the total number of arts subjects which the pupil would like to study, but cannot

From Q11, number of benefits stated from studying each arts subject:

BENART Benefits of Art
BENDAN Benefits of Dance
BENDRA Benefits of Drama
BENMUS Benefits of Music
BENLIT Benefits of Literature
BENARTS Benefits of all arts subjects (sum of above)

IMPARTS Importance of arts subjects (from Q12, recoded 0 to 3)

From Q13, indices of extra-curricular activities on a scale 0 to 17. Part i (primary) recoded 0 to 3, plus 2 times part ii (secondary) recoded 0 to 3, plus 4 if part iii equals 'Yes', plus 4 if part iv equals 'Yes'. For Music only, 2 points are added for 'Yes' answers to each section of part v.

ECART Index for Art
ECMUS Index for Music
ECDRA Index for Drama
ECDAN Index for Dance
ECLIT Index for Literature
ECALL Index for all arts subjects (sum of above)

PARSUP Index of parental support, from Q14 to Q16. Equal to sum of arts subjects in Q14, plus Q15 (recoded 0 to 3), plus number of codes 0 to 6 circled in Q16 (set to 0 if 8 circled in Q16).

SCLASS Social class from Q21 (highest of father's or mother's jobs)

Factor Analysis of Main Pupil Variables

Those pupil variables dealing with arts subjects overall have been put through a factor analysis, extracting three main factors. Basic statistics for the variables used are:

Variable	Mean	Std Dev	Min	Max	Label
TOTARTS	.58	.62	0	4	Total arts subjects taken
ARTSPC	5.85	6.40	0	50	Arts subjects as % of total
ARTSFAV	.58	.87	0	3	Index of arts subjects as favourite
ARTSHATE	.06	.30	0	3	Index of arts subjects as least favourit
ARTSBEST	.47	.82	0	3 I	ndex of arts subjects as best at
WHYARTS	1.07	1.69	-3	12 T	otal of +/- reasons for taking arts
ENJOYALL	.58	.88	-2	8	Lesson enjoyment: All arts
ARTSCANT	.77	.85	0	5	No. of arts subjects unable to take
BENARTS	9.07	8.74	0	60	Total benefits of arts subjects
IMPARTS	1.62	.98	0	3	Importance of arts subjects
ECALL	26.72	16.65	0	76	Index of extra-curricular activity: All
PARSUP	4.41	3.31	0	13	Parental support

Factor loading for the three factor solution are:

	Factor 1	Factor 2	Factor 3
TOTARTS	**.83915**	.07824	**.53628**
ARTSPC	**.80924**	.03593	**.49793**
ARTSFAV	**.84042**	.08071	-.15436
ARTSHATE	-.05278	-.02508	**.40440**
ARTSBEST	**.75844**	.06240	-.13069
WHYARTS	**.75030**	.26654	.01943
ENJOYALL	**.80262**	.17137	-.03648
ARTSCANT	-.16483	**.45694**	-.07728
BENARTS	.12829	**.51966**	-.04749
IMPARTS	**.47605**	**.48243**	-.00426
ECALL	.16857	**.81350**	.03953
PARSUP	.28706	**.67531**	.09208

(Factor loadings of 0.4 or above are shown in bold)

The three main factors identified above may tentatively be described as follows:

1. Doing lots of arts subjects in school, for practical reasons, good at them, but not especially involved outside school and no particular parental support: '*positive about arts in school*'.

2. High involvement outside school and parental support, but unable to do enough in school: '*positive about arts outside school*'.

3. Doing arts in school, but not enjoying them: '*negative about arts in school*'.

Each of the above characteristics describes individuals with high scores on each factor. They have each been rescaled to a mean of 100 and standard deviation of 15.

INDEX

Abbreviations (T) *and* (P) *following page numbers refer to teachers' and pupils' comments respectively.*

accommodation for arts faculties and departments, 329-31

activities, practical, 560-1, 570

age of pupil, factor in variation in effects, 275-8

appreciation of the arts, 54-66, 360-4

appreciation (praise of work done), 561-2, 570

art:

    appreciation, 58(T), 61-3(P)

    class behaviour, 428

    class social relationships, 425

    demonstrations, practical, 368

    effects on, of art education, 455-6, 463

    enjoyment, 29, 344

    as expressive tool, 129-30

    and extra-curricular activities, 549

        increase or decrease, primary to secondary, 536

        involvement as consumer, 546

        provision by school of, 540

        by social class, 538

    facilities, 331-2

    group work, 365

    increased knowledge and understanding, 40-1(T), 44-6(P)

    lessons:

        length, 322

        observed, 460-2, 467-9

        structure, 391

    marks and grades, 374

    peer review, 377

    practices, 455-72

    self-assessment, 380

    teacher/pupil relationship, 395

    teaching approaches, 456-9, 464-6

    development of technical skills and competence, 69-70(T), 75-6(P)

    transfer effects, 214-17

    variation in effects, 266

        by pupils' attributes, 282-3

        by school, 273-4, 286-9

art education, largely a success story, 567

artefacts and visual stimuli, 335-6

artforms:

    appreciation, 54-8, 54-6(T), 56(P)

        by artform, 58-66

    and extra-curricular involvement, 549-50

    knowledge, 39-51, 40-2(T), 43-50(P)

    skills, 51-4, 51-2(T), 53(P)

    variations in effects:

        by artform, 264-71

        by school, 272-4, 286-93

    see also the individual forms: art, dance, drama, English literature, music

arts:

    appreciation, 54-6, 360-4

    definition, 15-16

    effect on, of arts education, 245-6(T), 246-8(P)

    as empowerment to express, 131-2(P)

    enjoyment, 27(T), 28(P)

    importance to pupils, 527-8, 530

    support of, 558-9, 569

    status and profile, 554-5

        in National Curriculum, 555, 568

arts activities, practical, 560-1, 570

arts department, or faculty, 326-36

arts education:

    artefacts and visual stimuli in, 335-6

    effects, 455-6, 469, 565-8

    enjoyment and relevance, 569

    outcomes of, 22-5

        model, 23-5

    see also practices

arts effects, summary and conclusions, 294-7

arts faculty or department, 326-36

arts practice, 354-60

    see also arts activities

arts teachers, support for, 558-9, 569

arts theory and appreciation, 54-66, 360-4

assessment, 371-82

    constructive criticism, 378-9

    frequency, 381-2

    marks and grades, 372-6

    peer review, 377-8

    self-assessment and evaluation, 379-81

awareness of others, 164-5(T), 166-9(P)

awareness of surroundings, 89-90(T), 91((P)

behaviour management, 241-2, 397-8, 428-30

beyond-school factors, 300-12

case studies:
    arts effects in case study schools, 259-78
    findings from, 565-6
    and transfer effects, 208-13(T), 213-21(P)
    see also practices

catchment areas, *see* school catchment areas

class, *see* social class

classes:
    behaviour and discipline in, 428-30
    class action, 425-30
    class cooperation and support, 426-8
    classroom ambience, 392-4
    formation, 417-25
    membership, 420-5
    option choices, 424-5
    sets and streams, 420-4
    size, 418-20
    social relationships, 425-6

communication and expressive skills, 113-40

communication skills, interactive, 114-15(T), 115-17(P)

community:
    effect of arts education on, 244-5, 252
    factor in effectiveness, 301-7

community relationships, and effectiveness, 305-7

consumer involvement, extra-curricular activities, 545-9

contextual and historical studies, 362-4

creativity:
    development of, 102-9(T), 104-10(P)
    practical aspects, 358-9

critical listening, *see* listening and observation

cross-arts continuities and differences, 66-8(T), 68(P)

cultural domain, knowledge of, 85-9, 86(T), 87-9(P), 95-7

cultural factors, in effectiveness, 303-5

curriculum, arts, effectiveness, 433

curriculum factors, and effectiveness, 337-82

       assessment, 371-82

       challenging, 348-50

       content and planning, 343-54

       differentiation, 369-71

       National Curriculum, 337-43

       processes and activities, 354-60

       schemes of work, 350-2

       up-to-date and relevant, 347-8

       topic variety and length, 352-4

dance:

       appreciation, 58-9(T), 63(P)

       effects of dance education on, 441-2, 447

       enjoyment, 30-1, 345

       as expressive tool, 131(P)

       extra-curricular activities, 550

           increase or decrease, primary to secondary, 536

           involvement as consumer, 546

           provision by school of such, 540

           by social class, 538

       increase or decrease between primary and secondary, 536

       increased knowledge and understanding, 41(T), 46(P)

       lessons:

           observed, 444-7, 450-2

           structure, 391

       practices, 441-54

       teaching approaches, 442-3, 448-9

       development of technical skills and competence, 70(T), 77(P)

       variation in effects, 267

           by pupil attributes, 283-4

dance education, a fair success, 567

demonstrations, practical, 367-9

displays of work, 561, 570

drama:

       appreciation, 59(T), 64(P)

       class behaviour, 429

       class social relationships, 426

       demonstrations, practical, 369

       effects of drama education on, 493-4, 501

       enjoyment, 30, 344

       as expressive tool, 130-1(P)

       extra-curricular activities, 550

           involvement as consumer, 546

increase or decrease, primary to secondary, 536

provision by the school, 540

by social class, 538

facilities and equipment, 334-5

group work, 364-5

increased knowledge and understanding, 41-2(T), 47(P)

lessons:

length, 322

observed, 497-500, 505-9

speed/pace, 389

marks and grades, 374-5

peer review, 377

practical activities, 356

practices, 493-511

self-assessment, 380

teacher/pupil relationships, 395

teaching approaches, 494-7, 501-4

development of technical skills and competence, 70-1(T), 77-9(P)

transfer effects, 217-19

variation in effects, 268-9, 272-8

by pupil attributes, 284-5

by school, 272, 289-90

drama education, a fair success, 567

economic factors, in effectiveness, 301-3

effectiveness:

definition, 17-19

extra-curricular involvement, 534-50

GCSE, 514-18

key issues perceived by pupils, 434-6

key issues perceived by teachers, 431-4

key stage 4, 519-23

overall perspectives, 554-63

parental support for the arts, 532-3

pupils' attitudes to arts subjects, 523-8

pupils' views on parents' interest in arts, 529-31

pupils' views on parents' participation in arts, 531-2

wider picture, 513-53

effects 16-17

on the arts, 245-8

on community, 244-5

on school, 236-43

overall perspectives, 258-97
> by age, 275-8
> by artform, 264-71
> pupils' perceptions, 260-4
> by school, 272-4, 286-93
> summary and conclusions, 294-7
> in wider sample of schools, 278-93

emotions, *see* expression of feelings; self, sense of

empathy, *see* awareness of others

employers and employees, interviews with, 15

employment; transfer effects of arts education, 221-7, 222(T), 222-5(P)
> perspectives of employers on transfer, 225-7

encouragement of work, 561-2, 570

English literature:
> appreciation, 60(T)
> and extra-curricular activities, 550
>> as consumer, 546
> increased knowledge and understanding, 42(T)
> development of technical skills and competence, 71(T)
> variation of effects, by pupil attributes, 285-6

enjoyment of arts education, 26-33, 37-8
> by artform, 29-31
> of arts, 27-8, 557, 569
> of arts subjects, key stage 4, 525-7
> as 'buzz'/'excitement', 31
> as 'fun', 31-2
> as 'happiness', 32
> as 'satisfaction', 33
> for pupils, 344-6
> for teachers, 346-7

equipment, *see* facilities and equipment

ethnicity:
> and current involvement in arts, 543
> and current involvement as consumer, 547-8
> and extra-curricular activities, 537
> and importance of arts, 527-8
> parents' interest and, 530

evaluation, 561, 570

experiment, freedom to, 206-7(P), 359-60

expressing oneself, 132-6(P)

expression in groups, 138-9(P)

expression of feelings, 136-8(P)

expression of ideas/opinions, 138(P)

expressive skills, 125-39
    development of abilities, 132-9(P)
    tools for, 125-32, 125-8(T), 128-32(P)

extra-curricular involvement, 534-50
    current participation, 541-5
        by artform, 549-50
        as consumer, 545-9
    primary and secondary, 534-41
    school provision of facilities, 539-40

facilities and equipment, 331-6

family background, 407-10

freedom to do own thing, 206-7(P), 359-60

GCSE arts courses:
    and attainment, 516
    enrolment, 514-18
    and extra-curricular activities, 544
        as consumer, 548
    opting out of arts at GCSE, 518
    and parents' interest, 530-1
    performance, and arts education, 181-93
    variation between schools, 517-18
    Year 11 survey, 193-208

gender:
    and extra-curricular activities, 537
        as consumer, 548
        current involvement, 544
    in sample, 8

group work, 138-9(P), 364-5

headteachers, and effectiveness, 312-15

help, needed by pupils, 383-6

historical and contextual studies, 362-4

imagination, development of, 108-10
    see also creativity

initial teacher training, 310-11

institutional involvement, in arts and school, 248-55

interactive communication skills, *see* communication skills

interpretative skills, impact on, 51-4

jobs, *see* employment

key stage 4:
    choice of arts subjects, 519-29
        reasons for choosing arts, 519-21
        reasons for not choosing arts, 522-3
    unmet demand for, 521
    enjoyment of arts subjects, 525-7
    and extra-curricular activities, 539
    provision for the arts in, 555-7, 568-9
    pupils, numbers and characteristics, 551-2
    rationale for choosing arts subjects, 552-3
key terms (in the study), defined, 15-19

language development, 117-18(T), 118-22(P)
learning through doing, 355-8
leisure time, transfer effects, 227-8(T), 228-34(P)
lessons:
    activities in, 434-5
    length, 421-3, 433-4
    speed/pace, 389-90
    structure, 390-2
listening and observation, 122-4, 123(T), 123-4(P)
listening to the teacher, 366-7
literature, *see* English literature
local education authorities (LEAs), 307-9
    arts advisory support, 307-8
    facilities and resources, 308-9

marks and grades, *see* assessment
moods:
    of pupils, 416-17
    of teachers, 402-3
moral issues, *see* social and moral issues
music:
    appreciation, 60(T), 64-6(P)
    class behaviour, 429
    demonstrations, practical, 369
    effects of music education on, 473-4, 481-2
    enjoyment, 29-30, 344
    as expressive tool, 131(P)

extra-curricular activities, 549-50
> increase or decrease, primary to secondary, 536
> involvement as consumer, 546
> provision by school of such, 540
> by social class, 538

facilities and equipment, 332-4

group work, 365

increased knowledge and understanding, 42(T)

lessons:
> observed, 478-81, 486-9
> speed/pace of, 390

practical activities, 356

practices, 473-92

self-assessment, 380

teaching approaches, 474-7, 482-5

development of technical skills and competence 72(T), 79-81(P)

theory, 361-2

transfer effects, 220-1
> variation in, 269-71
> > by pupil attributes, 285
> > by school, 273, 291-3

music education, a difficult area, 567-8

National Curriculum, 337-43

advantages, 338-41

disadvantages, 341-3

status of the arts in, 555, 568

observation, *see* listening

organisation and effectiveness, 432

parents:
> and effect of arts education in the community, 244, 252
> and extra-curricular activities, 538-9
> > current, 544-5
> > as consumers, 548-9
> interest in the arts, 529-31
> participation in the arts, 531-2
> importance of pupils' perception of their interest, 553
> support for the arts, 532-3
> support of their children essential, 562-3

pastoral provision, in schools, 241-2

peer review, *see* assessment

performance, 561, 570

personal and social development, 141-78

personal skills, improved, 162-4, 163(T), 163-4(P)

personality of teachers, 401-2

personality, whole, development, 158-9(T), 159-62(P)

policy, 571-2

practical demonstrations, 367-9

practice, 570

practices (in arts education), 435-512
    art, 455-72
    dance, 441-54
    drama, 493-511
    music, 473-92

practices, effectiveness, 298-437
    arts faculty or department, 326-36
    beyond-school factors, 300-12
    curriculum factors, 337-82
    effective, 568-71
    model, 300-1
    pupil factors, 406-30
    teacher factors, 389-406
    whole-school factors, 312-26

praise (of work done), 561-2, 570

pride, in school, 239-40

problem-solving skills, development, 98-100(T), 100-2(P)

pupil-teacher relationships, improved, 176

pupils:
    achievement, 416
    arts, importance of, 527-8, 530
    attitudes to subject, 413-14
        attitudes to arts subjects, 523-8
    attributes, variation in effects, 282-6
    background, 562-3
    classes, 417-25
        action, 425-30
        formation, 417-25
    effectiveness, view of, 434-6
    enjoyment for, 344-6
    extra-curricular activities, 534-50

family background, 407-10

importance of contribution, 570-1

as individuals, 406-17

moods, 416-17

parents' attitudes, perception of, 553

parents' interest, pupils' view of , 529-31

parents' participation, 531-2

in sample, 14-15

as seen by themselves, 436

self-expression, 132-6

subject ability and extra-curricular participation, 410-13

subject enjoyment, 414-15

surroundings and their place 89-90(T), 91(P)

working hard, 415

quantitative analysis for self-evaluation (QUASE), 9, 181-208

report, structure, 19-21

research methods, in this study, 5-15

resources for arts faculties/departments, 329-36

schemes of work, 350-2

school arts organisation and resources, effectiveness, 432

school catchment areas

    and extra-curricular activities, 540-1

        as consumer, 549

        current, 545

    factor in effectiveness, 301-7

schools:

    involved in case studies, 6-8

    effectiveness of, 252-5

    effects on, of arts education, 236-43, 242-3(T), 243(P)

        variation in, 272-4

            by subject, 272-4

        wider sample, 278-93

    ethos/atmosphere, 237-41, 249-51, 316-18

    extra-curricular activities, 539-40

        provision by school, 555-6

            and current activities, 545

    image, 242-3, 251

    and institutions, 248-55

    questionnaire, Appendix 2, 581-3

sample, 11-14

variations between schools, 553

self, sense of, development, 142-8, 143-4(T), 145-8(P)

self-assessment, *see* assessment

self-confidence, 152-4(T), 154-8(P)

self-expression, 132-6(P)

self-worth and self-esteem, 148-9(T), 149-52(P)

senior management, and effectiveness, 312-16

sets and streams, in classes, 420-4

skills, *see* technical skills

social and moral issues, knowledge of, 91-5, 92(T), 92-5(P), 95-7

social class:

importance of arts by, 528

and extra-curricular activities, 537-8

as consumer, 547

current, 543

and parents' participation, 531

parents' interests by, 529

and parents' support of the arts, 533

social development, *see* personal and social development

social relationships, within classes, 425-6

social skills, improvement, 169-78, 169-71(T), 171-6(P)

specialist arts teachers, 559-60, 569

sponsors, 4-5

study (the present one):

aims, 5

background, 1-5

case studies, 6-9

research methods, 5-15

sponsors, 4-5

structure, 19-21

summary and conclusions, 564-72

surroundings, awareness of, 89-91

teacher communication, 386-9

teacher factors (in arts education), 383-406, 435

absence of usual teacher, 403-5

in effectiveness, 431-2

methods/pedagogy, 383-98

      personal qualities, 401-3

      special knowledge and skills, 398-400

teacher training, initial, 310-11

teacher networks, 309-10

teacher/pupil relationships, 395-7

teachers:

      of arts, support for, 558-9, 569

      effectiveness, view of, 431-4

      enjoyment for, 346-7

      listening to, 366-7

      and National Curriculum, 340-1

      as seen by pupils, 435

technical skills:

      acquisition, 73-5(P)

      development of, 68-72(T), 72-82(P)

therapeutic outcome of arts education, 33-4(T), 34-6(P)

thinking skills, development of, 98-100(T), 100-2(P)

timetable issues, 318-25

      frequency of lessons, 323-4

      length of lessons, 321-3

      time devoted to, 319-21

      timetabling, 559

      timing of, 324-5

transfer effects of arts education, 179-235

visual stimuli, 335-6

whole-school factors, 312-26

work, *see* employment

year 11 survey, 9-15

      evidence for involvement in arts and GCSE performance, 193-208

      questionnaire, 10, Appendix 1, 578-85

      sample, 11-15

          pupils, 14-15

          schools, 12-14

      questionnaire, 10, Appendix 1, 578-85